The Best in Children's Books

Edited by Zena Sutherland

The Best in Children's Books

The University of Chicago
Guide to Children's Literature
1966–1972

The University of Chicago Press
Chicago and London

ZENA SUTHERLAND, in addition to being editor of the *Bulletin of the Center for Children's Books,* is lecturer in the University of Chicago Graduate Library School and children's book editor of the *Chicago Tribune.* [1973]

The University of Chicago Press, Chicago 60637
The University of Chicago Press, Ltd., London
© 1973 by The University of Chicago
All rights reserved. Published 1973
Second Impression 1974
Printed in the United States of America
International Standard Book Number: 0–226–78057–0
Library of Congress Catalog Card Number: 73–77140

Book reviews were previously published in the *Bulletin of the Center for Children's Books,* © 1966, 1967, 1968, 1969, 1970, 1971, 1972 by The University of Chicago

Contents

Acknowledgments

The critical evaluations used in this book are based on the judgments of the members of the *Bulletin of the Center for Children's Books* advisory committee: Yolanda Federici, Sara I. Fenwick, Marjorie Hoke, Isabel McCaul, Hattie Lucas Power, and Charlemae Rollins. The compiler is also grateful to Frances Henne and Alice Brooks McGuire, who were instrumental in establishing the *Bulletin*, to the Graduate Library School which sponsors it, and to the many faculty members of the university and the laboratory schools who have given advice in specialized subject areas.

Introduction

When the Center for Children's Books was established at the University of Chicago in 1945 one of its goals in setting up a collection of trade books written for children was the evaluation and analysis of books in terms of uses, appeals, and literary quality. The *Bulletin of the Center for Children's Books,* which grew out of a memorandum that circulated within the Graduate School of Education, now is sponsored by the Graduate Library School and has international circulation.

Review copies of all children's trade books are sent to the center by publishers. Once each week, members of the advisory committee meet to examine the books and discuss the reviews prepared by the editor. The committee comprises teachers and librarians in public and private schools and libraries. When the editor or the committee feels that the subject matter of any book should be evaluated by an expert, the resources of the University of Chicago faculty are called upon, with teachers in the university's laboratory schools and in the college and divisions participating.

Books for children and young people of all ages are reviewed, and occasionally an adult book that may be of particular interest to adolescent readers is included. It is clear from the reading level index that some spans are heavily represented. There are many more citations listed for grades 4–6, for example, than for grades 4–7; however, material may also be found for the 7th grade reader in such groups as 5–7, 6–9, or 7–10. The book has not been planned as a balanced list in respect to an individual grade or age, or to subject or genre. The editor's selections have been made primarily on the basis of literary quality, with representation of subjects as a secondary consideration. The goal—a list of the best books published in the years 1966–72.

Why is it important to select children's books with discrimination? For one thing, the years in which such books are appropriate are fleeting, although some books can gratify readers of any age. There are so many activities and competing interests that fill children's time today that only the most inveterate readers read more than half a dozen books yearly beyond those required by their schools.

Second, studies of the adult reading population show how easy it is to fall into the pattern of reading only superficial material. Children exposed to flimsy mass market books, comics, and pedestrian series books will not necessarily proceed to good literature. It is possible for a child to acquire discrimination, but it isn't likely to happen unless some adult—a parent, a teacher, a librarian—suggests better books, encourages the ownership of books, and discusses good books with enthusiasm and understanding. It is incumbent on adults who are concerned with children's reading to select and counsel wisely, to appreciate the importance of both the content of books and the reading habit itself, and to comprehend what the elements of good children's books are.

In many ways, the literary criteria that apply to adult books and children's books are the same. The best books have that most elusive component, a distinctive literary style. A well-constructed plot; sound characterization with no stereotypes; dialogue that flows naturally and is appropriate to the speaker's age, education, and milieu; and a pervasive theme are equally important in children's and adults' fiction. Authoritative knowledge, logical organization of material, and accuracy are major considerations in informational books for any age.

In books for children, there are additional considerations based on limitations of comprehension and experience. Comparatively few children enjoy a story without action or conflict, however delicate the nuances of style, and most young readers abjure the tedious presentation of information in the guise of conversation. For very young children, it is important that a book not contain so much information as to confuse them. The vocabulary need not be rigidly controlled, but it should not include so many terms that the reader is discouraged. The concepts must be comprehensible—for example, a reader in the primary grades is not spatially sophisticated—and the subject appropriate. Format (type size, distribution of print, placement on page) and illustrations should be consistent with the level of the text, and maps or diagrams should be very carefully placed and labeled.

Because children are forming concepts of themselves and their society and are testing and acquiring ethical values, it is imperative that the books they read foster and nurture opinions and attitudes that are intelligent and flexible. Will the books they read serve to do this? The best ones will. Adults should be wary, however, of their own bias and should evaluate very carefully the author's values and assumptions lest agreement with their own ideas be confused with objectivity.

Each book must be judged on its own merits, and each book should be chosen—whether for an individual child, a library, or a classroom collection—with consideration for its strength even though it may have some weaknesses. This has been a precept in critical evaluation of books for the *Bulletin*. It is often illuminating to compare a book with other books by the same author or with similar books on a subject, but the judgment of each book is made on that book alone. With the spate of publication of children's books, selection is difficult. It is our hope that through this bibliography and its indexes, readers may more easily find the best in children's books.

Suggestions for using this book

The reviews included here have been selected by the editor from those already published in the *Bulletin of the Center for Children's Books*. Save for a few titles coded as "Additional" or "Special Reader," all of the books listed here had received a rating of "Recommended." The reviews are listed alphabetically by the author's name and are numbered in sequence to facilitate the use of the six indexes at the back of this book.

Of the indexes, only the *title index* does not refer the reader to the number assigned each book but gives the last name of the author.

The *developmental values index* is based on the analysis of each book for those elements that illustrate some aspect of achieving maturity, solving problems, or establishing relationships at any developmental stage in the life of a child or young reader. The developmental values covered range from the young child's acquisition of environmental concepts or adjustment to a new baby in the family, to the adolescent's attitudes toward his or her role in marriage.

The *curricular use index* suggests books for incorporation into the school curriculum, or for supplemental reading in relation to curricular units. Jeanne Bendick's *What Made You You?* (no. 110), for example, is included under "Sex Education" in the curricular use index, whereas it is cited under "Genetics" and "Reproduction" in the subject index.

The *reading level index* is arranged progressively by grades following the books for preschool children, which are listed by age. Books for independent reading begin with first grade, usually age six. The reading levels are given in a span that is intended to suggest probable use rather than to impose limits. A volume of poetry, for example, may be graded 4–6, indicating widest use in grades 4, 5, and 6; it may, however, be read aloud to younger children, used independently by proficient readers in grade 3 or even grade 2, or be read by older children or adults. The levels of reading difficulty have been determined by the *Bulletin* advisory committee after consideration of the vocabulary, the length and complexity of the writing, subject interest, latent content, organization of material, and the appropriateness of content, difficulty, and format to the maturity of the intended reader.

The *subject index* entries include both fiction and nonfiction; there is no division between the two, so that, for example, nonfiction books about Appalachia and fictional stories set in that region will be found under the single heading, "Appalachia."

The *type of literature index* makes it possible for the reader to find citations for all of the books of poetry, all of the mystery stories, and so on, that have been selected to be grouped together. The temptation to break this index down into fine categories has been sternly resisted, lest the book become inordinately massive. It is hoped that the separate indexes give ample access to the material in the volume.

Many of the books listed are from countries in the United Kingdom. The appended list of publishers includes British publishers of American books for children and of British titles available in the United States. It should be made clear that the inclusion of British publication information was determined through reference to the 1972 edition of *British Books in Print* and is not intended to be a comprehensive list of the best in British children's literature. It could be said that this bibliography reflects the best in American children's literature and, to the extent that information about British and American copublished books is available, some of the best in British children's literature.

Reviews of Books

1   **Aardema,** Verna. *Tales for the Third Ear;* From Equatorial Africa;
illus. by Ib Ohlsson. Dutton, 1969. 96p. Trade ed. $4.95;
Library ed. $4.90.

3–5   Nine folktales retold from original sources that gave verbatim versions of African storytelling. Several are about the familiar
character Ananse the spider, three about humans, and the rest
about other animals. All are concerned with trickery, the prankster
sometimes suffering retribution, sometimes emerging in triumph
from danger. The style is occasionally awkward, but the tales
are full of action and humor, and are an excellent source
for storytelling. The illustrations are in dull colors: mustard,
avocado, brown, and black, most of them busy with detail.
The print is large and clear; a brief section of notes gives
original sources and some explanations or definitions of words and
phrases.

2   **Abrahams,** Robert D. *The Bonus of Redonda;* illus. by Peter
Bramley. Macmillan, 1969. 136p. $4.50.

5–7   A first-person story set in the West Indies and told by a boy of
thirteen whose engaging naiveté permeates the book. Bonus lives
with his Gran'pa, a gentleman who objects to being told by a
government agent how to improve his fishing. Convinced that
his dealings with a local witch have resulted in the burning
of his village, Gran'pa goes into hiding; he and Bonus escape
to the island of Redonda, returning in triumph when they
learn that the village has not burned down and that they have
been mourned as drowned. There is no denigration of the
characters in the amusing depiction of local customs and dialect,
but a warm enjoyment of the flavorful people. A delightfully
different adventure.

3   **Adams,** Adrienne, illus. *The Twelve Dancing Princesses.* Holt,
1966. 42p. Trade ed. $3.95; Library ed. $3.59 net.

4–6   A retelling based on the French version used by Andrew Lang,
some passages being identical and some having deletions or
additions. The styles of both text and illustrations are romantic;
the painting is notable for the use of color. The handsome

1

young shepherd, Michael, goes to the castle to see the princesses and uses the cloak of invisibility to find the secret of the enchantment. Unlike the Grimm version, the youngest princess knows what Michael is doing; her love for him saves him and breaks the spell for all the princesses.

4

5–7

Adler, Irving. *Atomic Energy;* illus. by Ellen Viereck. Day, 1971. 47p. (Reason Why Series) $2.97.

A detailed discussion of the structure of atoms leads to an explanation of isotopes, thence to radioactivity, the obtaining of energy from fusion or from fission, and the operation of converter and breeder reactors. The organization is logical and lucid, the illustrations usually clear but occasionally inadequately labelled. The book closes with a brief history of the development of man's understanding and control of atomic reaction, and of the possibilities and advantages of obtaining energy from controlled nuclear fission rather than from dwindling fossil fuels. A glossary is appended. There is no index, but this is not a disadvantage since the text uses the same terms repeatedly.

5

K–2

Adler, Irving. *Sets and Numbers for the Very Young;* by Irving and Ruth Adler; illus. by Peggy Adler. Day, 1969. 47p. Trade ed. $2.50; Library ed. $3.96 net.

Big but crowded pages are filled with very simple, multiple examples—in words and drawings—to make clear to the very young child the cardinal and ordinal numbers (1 to 10) and the concept of sets, with counting introduced late in the text. With adult help, the child can learn to manipulate the objects used in the examples, such as toothpicks to be put down on lines, or pennies on circles.

6

8—

Adoff, Arnold, ed. *Black on Black;* Commentaries by Negro Americans. Macmillan, 1968. 236p. $5.95.

A collection of material from books, speeches, and correspondence, spanning the thinking of black Americans from Frederick Douglass to Dick Gregory. The writers are civil rights leaders, lawyers, novelists, journalists, playwrights, poets, and a few articulate voices from the area of mass entertainment (Bill Russell and Gregory). Their viewpoints or their topics may differ, but the contributors unite in speaking with candor and percipience of the dilemmas of a fragmented society. A section of biographical notes is appended.

7

6–9

Adoff, Arnold, ed. *Black Out Loud;* An Anthology of Modern Poems by Black Americans; ed. by Arnold Adoff; illus. by Alvin Hollingsworth. Macmillan, 1970. 86p. $4.95.

An excellent anthology and a handsome book. There are poems

by established writers like Gwendolyn Brooks, LeRoi Jones and Langston Hughes, but many are by gifted younger writers. Topically grouped in six sections, the selections are vigorous in their expression of black pride and a rejection of injustice. Most of them are serious, brief, and graceful; a minority have an intended and angular harshness. Biographical notes, and author, title, and first line indexes are appended.

8

Adoff, Arnold, ed. *It Is the Poem Singing into Your Eyes;* Anthology of New Young Poets. Harper, 1971. 121p. $4.50.

8–12

New and stirring, this anthology includes selections from thousands of manuscripts studied by Arnold Adoff. The young poets write about war, pollution, injustice, love, despair, beauty, and hate. They write, as poets do, about their world; if there is a quality common to their writing it is intensity. There is a concrete poem, some pregnant fragments that include haiku; most of the writing is free and much of it is angry. The whole is impressive.

9

Adoff, Arnold. *MA nDA LA;* pictures by Emily McCully. Harper, 1971. 22p. Trade ed. $3.95; Library ed. $4.43 net.

4–7 yrs.

Pictures that are suffused with sunshine and love echo the triumphant poem of the story, told in rhyming syllables. The jacket explains (the book does not) that MA is mother, DA father, HA laughing, RA cheering, LA is singing, NA sighing, and AH feeling good. A family goes out to sow, to see the seedlings come up, to gather the tall corn, grind it, cook it; and in each picture the ritual is celebrated "MA nDA LA, MA nDA HA, MA nDA LA LA LA. . ." It must be read aloud to get the full effect of a child's blithe crooning, it must be seen for the full effect of the dark figures (silhouette save for the brilliantly patterned clothing) against the colors of the tropical foliage. Not suitable for group use, but right for reading aloud to an individual child.

10

Agle, Nan Hayden. *Maple Street;* illus. by Leonora E. Prince. Seabury Press, 1970. 126p. $4.50.

3–5

Margaret is nine, black, and disconsolate because her best friend has just moved away from Maple Street. The neighborhood is black, but a poor white family from Virginia moves in next door and it is clear from the start that Ellie May, although she is Margaret's age, will have nothing to do with Negroes. But she is forced to. Her father is absent, her mother hospitalized, and Ellie May seethes while black neighbors generously care for the small children left alone. Margaret has been gathering signatures for a playground petition, her vision of green grass and flowering trees exploded by the reality: flat concrete. So Maple

Street does not become beautiful, and only a wary friendship is achieved between Margaret and Ellie May. What is beautiful are the people of Maple Street: so real, so honestly drawn. They are middle and lower class, many of those who help care for the white children aware of the Virginia family's bitter prejudice; if they can't love their neighbor, it never occurs to them not to help. The discussions about this in Margaret's home are candid and it is this mirroring of ordinary problems that distinguishes the book, also enjoyable for the vigorous dialogue.

11

3–5

Agle, Nan Hayden. *My Animals and Me;* photographs by Emily Hayden. Seabury, 1970. 119p. $4.95.

Nan Agle has done for the young reader what Gerald Durrell has for the adult: produced the reminiscences of an animal lover in a book that has warmth, humor, and a mingling of family anecdotes and memories of beloved pets. The background is rural, the period just before the first world war, and the snapshots charming in their ordinariness. The writing is blithe and informal, the episodes flowing along with easy spontaneity.

12

5–7

Aiken, Joan. *Nightbirds on Nantucket;* illus. by Robin Jacques. Doubleday, 1966. 215p. $3.50. (Cape, 1966. 188p. £1.00.)

A tongue-in-cheek, no-holds-barred adventure story, replete with a cheerful waif, an absent-minded sea captain and his fragile little daughter, a black-hearted villain-spy and his cruel spinster sister, a pink whale and a vaudeville stereotype comic German scientist. Dido, eleven, is picked up out of the sea and sleeps for ten months; she is asked by the captain to be a companion to his little daughter, Dutiful Penitence Casket. The girls come to Nantucket and are treated as slaves by Dutiful's dreadful aunt—who proves to be an imposter and none other than the villain's wicked sister; Dido is then instrumental in unmasking a plot to shoot Der Professor's transatlantic cannon in a Hanoverian scheme against King James. Naturally, the cannon is towed off by a friendly pink whale. Dripping with quaintnesses and brine and stereotypes and valor and all sorts of things that make the book a romping burlesque.

13

5–7

Aiken, Joan. *Smoke from Cromwell's Time;* And Other Stories. Doubleday, 1970. 163p. $3.95.

A collection of stories written in the last decade (there is no table of contents) all of which are on fanciful themes. Some of the tales have a gentle melancholy but most of them are robust and humorous, written with a practiced ease that permits a saucy variation of fairy tale formula without marring the story. Joan Aiken probably has, in her tales of magic, some of the most unusual fairy godmothers of the genre; the writing style is deft, the story lines imaginative even when they emerge from familiar patterns.

14   **Aiken,** Joan. *The Whispering Mountain;* illus. by Frank Bozzo. Doubleday, 1969. 237p. Trade ed. $3.95; Library ed. $4.70 net. (Penguin, 1970. £0.25.)

5–9   Broad burlesque of fantasy-adventure might be cloying, but Joan Aiken has a deft touch of the ridiculous that lightens a book that isn't to be taken seriously for one moment. A small Welsh boy, motherless and with a missing father, stays with a dour grandfather who rejects and suspects him. Grandfather is custodian of a magical harp which is stolen by the hired scalawags of the rich, cruel Marquess of Malyn. There are also a pair of good gypsies, a foreign potentate, a race of men who live inside the mountain, and—too broad Scots to be true—His Royal Highness, Davis James Charles Edward George Henry Richard Tudor-Stuart, Prince of Wales. The dialects are hilarious, especially the fractured Welsh, and the plot outlandish.

15   **Aitmatov,** Chingiz. *The White Ship;* tr. by Mirra Ginsburg. Crown, 1972. 160p. $4.95.

7—   Set in a remote Russian forest, a story of the Bugu clan of Kirghizia adeptly weaves the clan legend of the Horned Mother Deer into a contemporary story of stunning impact. The forester is a bullying lout who sells government property for his own benefit, who beats his wife, taunts his old father-in-law, and mistreats the small nephew who is the protagonist of the book. The boy receives all his love and protection from his grandfather, a man so placid and obliging that the forester is the more contemptuous. Deserted by his parents, the boy daydreams: he will be a fish and swim to his father's white ship, which he can see through binoculars, in the distant lake. From his grandfather the child has learned reverence for the clan traditions and the totem, and when his surly uncle forces the unhappy grandfather to kill a deer, the child is sickened with dismay, knows there is no hope for him, and goes to the water to be a fish, to swim to his father, to drown. The writing has a quiet and compelling surge, the material about the Horned Mother Deer and the Bugu beliefs beautifully integrated into a story that is distinguished for its perceptive characterization, for the stark and credible plot, and for the depiction of the locale.

16   **Alcott,** Louisa May. *Glimpses of Louisa;* A Centennial Sampling of the Best Short Stories by Louisa May Alcott; selected with an introduction and editor's notes by Cornelia Meigs. Little, 1968. 222p. $5.95.

6–9   A selection of ten stories, originally published in various collections between the years 1871 and 1884. The period background, the old-fashioned phrases, and the recurrent extolling of poor, virtuous protagonists give the collection that distinctive flavor so dear to confirmed Alcott fans; the sturdy vitality of the characters and lively style have a durable appeal that may well attract new ones.

17   **Aldridge,** Josephine Haskell. *Reasons and Raisins;* by Josephine and Richard Aldridge; illus. by John Larrecq. Parnassus, 1972. 31p. Trade ed. $3.75; Library ed. $3.78 net.

K–2   A nonsensical story with a bit of a bite here and there is illustrated with colorful pictures, beautifully detailed. A box of raisins looks tempting to Little Fox, but his mother says that too much of anything will make you sick; actually, she wants the fruit kept for a pudding. Little Fox takes the box, cadges a lift from Crow, is dumped (with the raisins) into the lap of a circus fat lady, escapes from her and her dog, is held up by a weasel, and gets home with the box of raisins. He gets a spanking but also gets his favorite dessert for dinner—raisin pudding. The "real reason" behind ostensible ones is used throughout the story, a device that may make the listening audience interested in motivation, but it is more than probable that they will enjoy the story for its circus setting, charming illustrations, lively action, and final note of reassurance.

18   **Alexander,** Lloyd. *The Castle of Llyr.* Holt, 1966. 201p. $3.95. (Heinemann, 1968. 192p. £1.25.)

5–8   A third delightful book about the land of Prydain. Here Taran escorts the Princess Eilonwy to the Isle of Mona, where Queen Teleria is expected to teach the obstreperous Eilonwy to behave like a princess. Eilonwy is kidnapped by the wicked Chief Steward, and the familiar heroes of *The Book of Three* and *The Black Cauldron* pursue and fight with might and magic. Good triumphs as it should, the villains suffer abasement, the story is enlivened by a faint trace of love interest (Taran and Eilonwy) and by a pervasive and sparkling humor. The author has conceived his legendary land in the whole: the characters fit the plot, the plot fits the style of writing, and the style of writing fits the genre.

19   **Alexander,** Lloyd. *The High King.* Holt, 1968. 285p. Trade ed. $4.50; Library ed. $3.97 net.

6–8   Although there is humor here, the grave and pressing matters of the story bring to a poignant finish the affairs of Taran and his circle; as the boy who wanted to be a hero has matured (indeed, has become a hero), so has his creator. Last of the cycle, this volume describes Taran's role in the final struggle of the good people of Prydain against the Death-Lord, and Taran's decision about his destiny when that struggle is over.

20   **Alexander,** Lloyd. *The Marvelous Misadventures of Sebastian.* Dutton, 1970. 204p. Trade ed. $5.95; Library ed. $5.89 net.

4–6   Steeped in an eighteenth century atmosphere, the fanciful story of a young musician who, having lost his position because of the harshness of the Royal Treasurer of Hamelin-Loring, goes off to seek his fortune. Sebastian meets a princess in disguise and devotes himself to saving her from a fate worse than death; he is aided by a mysteriously omniscient people's hero; he acquires a perceptive cat, becomes a clown, is given a violin with magical powers; he is imprisoned and saves his own life and the throne of the princess by playing the violin until the villainous Regent dances to his death. The intricacy of plot, the humor and allusiveness of the writing, the exaggerated characterization, and the derring-do of romantic adventures are knit into a lively and elaborate tale that can be enjoyed for its action and appreciated for its subtler significance.

21   **Alexander,** Lloyd. *Taran Wanderer.* Holt, 1967. 256p. Trade ed. $4.50; Library ed. $3.97 net.

6–8   A fourth book about the land of Prydain; here Taran, who has grown from a small Assistant Pig Keeper to a young man in love with a princess, goes off to find his identity. With no clue to his place of birth or parentage, Taran must ask for help where he can get it, and he is forced to meet an array of unsavory characters as well as some good, old friends. He doesn't learn who his parents were, but Taran learns something even more important: it doesn't matter who your parents are, but what sort of person you are. Ashamed because he has heretofore attached so much importance to position, Taran begins his journey home with a new pride in his ability and accomplishments rather than a vain longing for status. A bit more somber than the preceding books, this is also more significant; although the theme is serious, there is no paucity of daring forays, wicked enchanters, tiny people, desperate fights, et cetera; there is, in fact, all of the color and adventure one expects in the land of fantasy.

22   **Alexander,** Lloyd. *The Truthful Harp;* illus. by Evaline Ness. Holt, 1967. 26p. Trade ed. $3.50; Library ed. $3.27 net.

3–4   An engaging character familiar to older readers of Mr. Alexander's books about the land of Prydain, the amiable Fflewddur Flam here is presented at the beginning of his career as a wandering bard. At his examination before the High Council of Bards, Fflewddur failed miserably; in pity, the Chief Bard gave him a strange and wonderful harp. Every time the player told a lie a string snapped; since the would-be bard was prone to flamboyant exaggeration, he had a series of musical disasters until he realized what was happening. The illustrations are deft and humorous although sedate in color; the writing has humor, vitality, and a distinctive turn of phrase.

23   **Alexander,** Martha. *Blackboard Bear*; written and illus. by Martha Alexander. Dial, 1969. 26p. Trade ed. $3.50; Library ed. $3.39 net.

3–6   A charming book for the very young child who has felt the
yrs.   pangs of being left out of older children's games. A little boy asks if he can play with the others, and is told he is too small. Like Harold and his purple crayon, the child draws an enormous bear on his blackboard and pretends. All the big boys ask him to play and want to ride or pet the bear. Scornfully he says that only he can touch the bear. Small, bright pictures add appeal to a very simple and very satisfying story.

24   **Alexander,** Martha. *Nobody Asked Me If I Wanted a Baby Sister;* written and illus. by Martha Alexander. Dial, 1971. 28p. Trade ed. $3.50; Library ed. $3.39 net.

3–6   Pink and amiable, the new baby is getting all of the attention
yrs.   from visitors—so Oliver puts Bonnie in his wagon and goes off to see if he can get somebody to take her. Finally he finds a mother with five children of her own who beams at Bonnie. When she picks the baby up, there are screams from the hitherto smiling child, so she passes Bonnie to her oldest daughter. Screams. Oliver, disgusted, comes back from the next room, and is amazed to see his sister hold out her arms, instantly pacified. Well! She's a lot smarter than he thought, maybe when she gets bigger they can play together. Not a brand-new theme, but pictures and text together make a charming variation, the precise little drawings affectionate and humorous, the writing ingenuous and direct.

25   **Alexander,** Martha. *The Story Grandmother Told;* written and illus. by Martha Alexander. Dial, 1969. 27p. Trade ed. $2.95; Library ed. $2.96 net.

3–6   A little book, a pleasant tale, and tidy, precise drawings, with
yrs.   humor in both illustrations and story. Lisa begs Gramma for a story, and says she'd like the one about Ivan and Lisa and the green humming cat . . . the one in which Lisa buys a green cat-shaped balloon which unfortunately breaks (picture of Ivan, the real cat, smugly smiling at the clawed balloon which has been taking all attention away from him) . . . and, having told the whole story, Lisa sits in happy anticipation as Gramma obligingly

prepares to tell it. The routine is a familiar one, the story (and the story within it) are at just the right level for the very young read-aloud audience, and the illustrations add to the book's appeal with a bright-eyed brown child and a cat whose expressions range from malevolent to angelic.

26   **Alexander,** Rae Pace, comp. *Young and Black in America;* introductory notes by Julius Lester. Random House, 1970. 139p. $3.95.

7—   Episodes from the lives of eight black men and women (Frederick Douglass, Richard Wright, Daisy Bates, Malcolm X, Jimmy Brown, Anne Moody, Harry Edwards, and David Parks) describe the stark discrimination and despair of their youthful experiences. This is not new material, but the excerpts in toto have a bleak power that is impressive. Each selection is preceded by an editorial comment that gives biographical information and some background for the excerpt. An appended bibliography gives information about hardcover and paperback editions of the books from which the selections were made.

27   **Aliki,** ed. *Three Gold Pieces;* A Greek Folk Tale retold and illus. by Aliki. Pantheon Books, 1967. 27p. $3.50. (Bodley Head, 1968. 32p. £0.68.)

K–2   A simple retelling of a Greek folk tale, the pages illustrated alternately in black and white and in brilliant color. Yannis is a poor peasant who leaves home to serve a wealthy old man. His master keeps his pay, and at the end of ten years Yannis is given only three gold coins; then the master offers, three times, to give Yannis a piece of advice for a piece of gold. "Never ask about something that is not your concern" is the first piece of advice; Yannis is soon able to profit by it when he encounters a man grateful for one passerby that minds his own business. He returns to his family with a bundle of gold, having—by the third piece of advice—narrowly missed harming the grown son he has not recognized.

28   **Alkema,** Chester Jay. *The Complete Crayon Book.* Sterling, 1969. 156p. illus. $8.95. (Oak Tree P., 1970. 156p. £3.15.)

5—   The materials are comparatively inexpensive and the varieties of crayons and techniques in using them afford innumerable avenues to constructive and creative work. The author suggests simple projects that very young children can do, and more sophisticated and difficult exercises for the older reader. Information about the qualities of chalk pastel, fluorescent, water, oil pastel, and wax crayons, and of crayon pencils is followed by a discussion of techniques and by detailed discussions and profuse illustrations of the exploration of the media, backgrounds, and special effects. A relative index is appended.

29

7–10

Allen, Elizabeth. *You Can't Say What You Think;* And Other Stories. Dutton, 1968. 156p. Trade ed. $3.95; Library ed. $3.91 net.

Eight short stories that share a suburban high school as a setting, but do not overlap. The stories touch on many of the difficulties young people face as they grow up. One of them is, of course, not being able (or feeling able) to say what you think; in another tale, a boy who has been embarrassed by a salacious movie resorts to violence in protest; in a third, "The Label," a pair of loving but ambitious parents do all they can to discourage their only child's affection for a boy from the wrong part of town; when they learn he has just been accepted by Princeton, the tune changes: "Well! I just wouldn't be surprised if a certain young lady doesn't have a sort of understanding with a certain young man . . . I always did say he was a nice boy." Candid, varied, and nicely paced, the stories are concerned with problems that are familiar and ordinary; the characterization is good, and the solutions—if they are achieved—are logical.

30

4–6 yrs.

Allen, Robert. *Numbers;* A First Counting Book; photographed in color by Mottke Weissman. Platt and Munk, 1968. 60p. $2.50.

Big, clear photographs of familiar objects add to both the attractiveness and the usefulness of this book. First the reader is introduced to numbers one to ten; then there are other pages on which the child can see, again, nine blocks or ten cookies. The book introduces some simple addition (pictured: a photograph of two lemons, another photograph of two lemons, and—facing them—a photograph of four lemons) and the ideas that size and location do not affect the counting unit. The pattern is broken on one page, where the photograph showing the total number lacks a caption.

31

6—

Allen, Terry, ed. *The Whispering Wind;* Poetry by Young American Indians. Doubleday, 1972. 128p. Paper ed. $1.95; Library ed. $2.70 net.

The Institute of American Indian Arts is a combined high school and art institute attended by young people from Eskimo, Aleut, and American Indian tribes. The writings of each of the fourteen students included here are prefaced by a page of background information. Few of the poems have a note of bitterness, although many are grave; many have the fresh awareness that is universal to youth; many a fine lyric quality. If there is a pervasive emphasis, it is proud recognition of the poets' heritage.

32   **Almedingen,** E. M. *Anna (Anna Khlebnikova de Poltoratzky, 1770–1840).* Farrar, 1972. 180p. $4.50. (Oxf. U.P., 1971. £1.00.)

8–10   Another volume based on the author's family history, much of the material here gathered from the writings of Almedingen's great-grandmother, Anna Poltoratzky, and told in first person. Although at times the chronicle moves slowly, it is engrossing as a picture of a Moscow merchant's family of the late eighteenth century, and the book should especially appeal to readers who enjoy the myriad details that give historical writing verisimilitude. There is little that is dramatic in Anna's life, since she lives quietly at home, tutored in a fashion unusual for girls of that era, the only large events in her girlhood being a meeting with the Tsarina (Catherine the Great) and her only brother's decision to marry an Englishwoman and leave Russia forever. The story concludes with Anna's marriage, although an epilogue describes briefly the events of the remainder of her life. A glossary is appended.

33   **Almedingen,** E. M. *Fanny* (Frances Hermione de Poltoratzky— 1850–1916); illus. by Ian Ribbons. Farrar, 1970. 226p. $3.95. (Oxf. U.P., 1970. 176p. £0.90.)

8—   A lovely book of reminiscences, based on the sketches and family papers of the author, who presents the childhood of her Aunt Fanny as if written by Frances de Poltoratzky herself. Tenderly Fanny describes the golden days of her childhood on a huge Russian estate; her father was rich, scholarly, gentle, and loving, and her English mother was in complete argeement with her husband: the two little girls must be brought up as simply as possible. Naive and trusting, Serge Poltoratzky lost all his wealth due to the machinations of a crafty steward, and the suddenly-impoverished family fled to Paris. The style is graceful, the setting fascinating, and the book permeated with family affection and an abiding relish for the peace and beauty of country life.

34   **Almedingen,** E. M. *Katia;* illus. by Victor Ambrus. Farrar, 1967. 207p. $3.95. (Oxf. U.P., 1966. 204p. £0.80.)

6–9   A translation and adaptation of autobiographical material first published in Russia in 1874, the Katia of the title being the great-aunt of E. M. Almedingen. The story of a Russian childhood begins with the death of Katia's mother, when the five-year-old child was taken from her home in the city to become the ward of a spinster aunt in the Ukraine. Katia lived in the cheerful atmosphere of a big family of cousins for six years, then went back to her father's home and the welcoming arms of a loving— and soon loved—stepmother. The illustrations reflect the appeal of the period setting, but not the additional one of locale; the story has the appeal of universality in characterizations and relationships.

35   **Almedingen,** E. M. *The Story of Gudrun;* based on the third part
of the Epic of Gudrun; illus. by Enrico Arno. Norton, 1967.
123p. Trade ed. $3.75; Library ed. $3.48 net.

7–10   Based on the third part of an anonymous German epic of the
twelfth or thirteenth centuries, this is a romantic tale of stoicism
and valor, good overcoming evil, and of the court intrigue of feudal
life. Gudrun, a good and beautiful princess, is kidnapped just
before her wedding day; kept in bondage and cruelly treated by
the sadistic mother of the disappointed suitor who captured her,
Gudrun remains steadfast and gentle. When Gudrun is restored to
her lover and her throne, she wants peace, not revenge. The
story is retold in a most fitting style, dignified yet graceful,
with that larger-than-life portentousness that distinguishes the
epic from folk literature.

36   **Almedingen,** E. M. *Young Mark;* The Story of a Venture; illus.
by Victor G. Ambrus. Farrar, 1968. 178p. $3.75. (Oxf. U.P., 1967.
156p. £0.80.)

7–10   Based on the notes of his journey from the Ukraine to St.
Petersburg in the middle of the eighteenth century, this romantic
story describes Mark Poltoratzky's bid for fame and freedom.
The author, his great-great-grandchild, notes in her prefatory
remarks that Mark achieved his goal and became famous indeed
for his singing. His descriptions, however, were of the trip itself
and the events at home that prompted it. The book is a
reconstruction rather than a translation; the author's sparkling
style enhances the sense of theatre that provided dramatic
incidents. Explanatory notes and a glossary are appended.

37   **Ambrus,** Victor G. *Brave Soldier Janosh.* Harcourt, 1967. 23p. illus.
Trade ed. $3.75; Library ed. $3.54 net. (Oxf. U.P., 1967. 24p.
£0.80.)

K–3   Even the small child who is not a keen student of Napoleonic
history can get the point of this tall tale as Janosh, a traditional
figure in Hungarian folk literature, boasts of his martial prowess.
Singlehanded he defeated Napoleon and his men; magnanimously,
he spared the great Napoleon's life. In fact, they became very
good friends and, when Janosh visited Paris, the Emperor filled
his pockets with gold. The style of the retelling is ingenuously
simple and bland; the illustrations glow with color, humor, and
vitality.

38   *American Heritage* Magazine. *Franklin Delano Roosevelt;* by the
editors of *American Heritage* Magazine; narr. by Wilson Sullivan;
in consultation with Frank Freidel. American Heritage, 1970.
153p. illus. Trade ed. $5.95; Library ed. $5.49 net.

6–9   An excellent biography, broad in coverage and profusely illustrated with good photographs, the writing mature and straightforward, the attitude admiring but discerning. The author gives a vivid picture of the depression era, recovery measures, political campaigns and the "diplomatic minuet" that preceded World War II, concluding with a résumé of the war and a brief, poignant account of Roosevelt's death. An index is appended.

39   *American Heritage* Magazine. *The History of the Atomic Bomb;* by the editors of *American Heritage* Magazine; narr. by Michael Blow; in consultation with William W. Watson. American Heritage, 1968. 150p. illus. (American Heritage Junior Library Series) Trade ed. $4.95; Library ed. $4.79.

7—   A first chapter gives some background information about the scientific research that preceded the first successful nuclear chain reaction, and the book goes on to describe events at Stagg Field, Los Alamos, and other secret sites where the knowledge of American and European scientists and the resources of the United States made possible the development of the atom bomb. This sober look at a grim but important topic considers the conflict within the scientific ranks, and the continuing conflict about the weapons race versus the peaceful uses of applied nuclear energy. Profusely illustrated, competently written, and objective in approach, a very good piece of reporting. A glossary, a list of suggestions for further reading, and an index are appended.

40   **Andersen,** Hans Christian. *The Emperor's New Clothes;* with text ad. from Hans Christian Andersen and other sources by Jean Van Leeuwen; illus. by Jack and Irene Delano. Random House, 1971. 50p. Trade ed. $4.95; Library ed. $5.39 net. (Schlesinger, 1970. 16p. £0.69.)

3–5   One of the most popular of Andersen's stories in new dress— or perhaps it's new undress—is illustrated with fresh and imaginative pictures, beautifully detailed, lively, and humorous. The emperor is pudgy and pompous, the tailors crafty and leering, the faces of the crowd watching the regal procession a frieze of shock when the ingenuous child points out the truth. For the monarch is indeed naked here, with an ornate headdress, a string of bright beads, and a happy smirk on the royal face.

41   **Andersen,** Hans Christian. *The Fir Tree;* illus. by Nancy Ekholm Burkert. Harper, 1970. 36p. Trade ed. $3.95; Library ed. $4.11 net.

4–6   The story of the little tree that is admired at Christmas and cast aside is old and familiar and loved. The delicacy and meticulousness of the illustrative details of this edition, beautiful in soft colors or in black and white, should please old fans and the felicity of mood should attract new ones.

42   **Andersen,** Hans Christian. *The Little Match Girl;* illus. by Blair
Lent. Houghton, 1968. 43p. Trade ed. $3.95; Library ed. $3.57 net.

4–6   A new edition of the familiar and touching story of the lonely,
shivering child who sees visions in the flames of the matches she
cannot sell, and whose last vision is the loving grandmother who
is dead and who comes to take the child. The illustrations are
tremendously effective, the tiny figure lost and lorn against
towering grey buildings and driving snow; even the glorious
warmth and comfort of the hallucinations are pictured in muted
tones.

43   **Andersen,** Yvonne. *Make Your Own Animated Movies;* Yellow Ball
Workshop Film Techniques. Little, 1970. 101p. illus. $5.95.

5–8   A good survey of both the preparation techniques in making
animated film, and the intricacies of filming itself. Such media
as clay figures, cutouts, drawing (directly on the film), pixillation
(incorporating live actors), and tearouts are discussed, and the processes of positioning, filming, simulating motion, synchronizing
sound and motion, splicing film, et cetera are described. An index
would make the material in the book more accessible, but the
information it gives is clear, full, and adequately illustrated.

44   **Anderson,** Alan H. *The Drifting Continents.* Putnam, 1971.
192p. illus. $4.29.

8—   Long disparaged, the theory of continental drift has been
substantiated by the research techniques and equipment of today.
The text very smoothly incorporates into the history of the men
who contributed to the body of knowledge on the subject all
of the disputed theories and the errors that paved the way for
each advance. From this revolution in geological thinking will
come the possibility of predicting movement of the continental
plates, a probable fusion of separate areas of study, and a better
understanding of the nature of earthquakes. An index is appended.

45   **Anderson,** Lonzo. *Ponies of Mykillengi;* illus. by Adrienne Adams.
Scribner, 1966. 43p. Trade ed. $4.95; Library ed. $3.31 net.

3–5   A quiet story, set in Iceland, about two children who get caught
in, and fight their way through, a violent snowstorm that follows
an earthquake; during this ordeal one of their ponies has a foal.
The writing is simple, its quality perhaps due to the contrast
of short sentences and present tense with the drama of natural
events. The description of the foal's birth is dignified, tender
and touching. The illustrations are quite lovely, especially several
of the night scenes in which the cold blue-white expanses of
snow are contrasted with the small, bright touches of color

in the children's clothing or in the faraway lights of the farmhouse windows.

46   **Anderson,** Lonzo. *Two Hundred Rabbits;* by Lonzo Anderson and Adrienne Adams. Viking, 1968. 32p. illus. Trade ed. $3.95; Library ed. $3.77 net.

K–2   Based on a French folk tale, this is a humorous picture book in which the author proves, at the end of the story, to be a rabbit himself. A peasant lad, anxious to please his king, tries juggling (no good) and playing the violin (also no good) and singing (ditto). Finally the boy's kindness to an old woman gives him his desire: a magic whistle brings one hundred ninety-nine rabbits marching briskly in formation. The two-hundredth rabbit, who has been telling the story, joins the ranks when the monarch spots the uneven number. The writing style is brisk and unassuming; the illustrations are delightful in their depiction of the colorful scenes of the fifteenth-century castle or of the shadowed and dappled beauty of the forest.

47   **Anno,** Mitsumasa, illus. *Topsy-Turvies;* Pictures to Stretch the Imagination. Walker/Weatherhill, 1970. 27p. $3.50.

3–7
yrs.   First published in Japan, a picture book without words. On each double-page spread, there is an intriguing construction (a maze, crossed flights of stairs, a cutaway house) or an incongruity (a village of half-timbered houses along a stream that comes out of a giant faucet, a bottle floating in the sea with the water coming out of the bottle) peopled by tiny figures. The pictures are filled with oddly impossible actions: walking upside-down, casting shadows at right angles. Most of the little men are busy at definable tasks, and the book is the sort over which some children will pore and chuckle. Not, perhaps, for every child.

48   **Archer,** Jules. *The Extremists;* Gadflies of American Society. Hawthorn Books, 1969. 197p. illus. $6.95.

8—   Illustrated with old prints and cartoons, a detailed and objective history of extremists in this country; the author carefully defines the term as those "who pursued their goals by unlawful, unjust, or extravagant means—whether against the power structure, in defense of it, or against another group in the society." From the Puritans (in a chapter entitled "Ear-slicers, Witch-hunters and Rough-necks") through all of the political, racial, religious, and industrial aberrations of our society up to the demonstrations and assassinations of the sixties, the violent elements of American life are described. Covering a great deal of material and covering it well, the text has—of necessity—some fragmentation, but it is both useful as a source book and eminently readable. A bibliography and an index are appended.

49   **Ardizzone,** Edward. *Sarah and Simon and No Red Paint.* Delacorte,
             1966. 48p. illus. $3.25. (Longman Young Bks., 1965. 48p. £0.40.)

K–3   Although the setting is contemporary, this is a blandly Victorian
            story about a poor young artist and his loving family who are
            almost destitute when the young painter's wealthy uncle decides
            to forgive his nephew and offer his blessing and his purse. The
            illustrations are delightful, the writing is tongue-in-cheek, artfully
            artless. "Courage," the young painter says to his worried wife,
            "I have nearly finished my masterpiece and then we will be rich.
            In the meantime I will sell my gold cigarette case to tide things
            over." Sarah and Simon, the happy children of the young artist,
            are wont to spend their time in a neighborhood bookshop; one
            day the ferocious looking old gentleman who comes in daily
            hears the children say that all their money is gone, and that
            they cannot get credit at the paint store to buy red paint that
            is needed to complete the masterpiece. The old gentleman is, to
            no reader's surprise, the long-disdainful Uncle Robert.

50   **Ardizzone,** Edward. *Tim to the Lighthouse.* Walck, 1968. 46p.
             illus. $5. (Oxf. U.P., 1968. 48p. £0.90.)

2–3   Always heroic, Tim outwits some brawny criminals with the help
            of his friends in another delightfully understated story. Having
            been taken by their elderly friend Captain McFee to visit the
            lighthouse and its staff of two, Tim, Charlotte, and Ginger each
            separately notice and are alarmed by the absence, one stormy
            night, of the lighthouse beam. Captain McFee takes the children
            out and then goes off for the coastguards. Naturally, the brave
            youngsters save the day, a performance (as usual) just this side
            of credibility. The bland style and the fetching illustrations add
            appeal to a derring-do tale with a dramatic setting.

51   **Ardizzone,** Edward. *The Wrong Side of the Bed.* Doubleday, 1970.
             30p. illus. $3.95.

3–6   A story in pictures. A small, sullen figure appears at the breakfast
yrs.   table and is firmly led back to the bathroom and scrubbed. His
            manners at table are atrocious, he pulls his little sister's hair and
            is ordered out. Hammering away his hostility, he is scolded
            by his father for making too much noise. He goes outdoors;
            nobody will play with him. He falls down. Torn and filthy, he
            solaces himself with images (in balloons) of a wounded warrior
            and his weeping mother. He finds a coin, buys a nosegay, goes
            home and offers his mother the flowers. Last picture: tired
            child cuddled lovingly on mother's lap. The illustrations are
            engaging, the story one that should have the appeal of familiarity,
            the ending satisfying.

52   **Armer,** Alberta. *Troublemaker;* illus. by J. C. Kocsis. World, 1966. 192p. Trade ed. $4.50; Library ed. $4.76 net. (World Pub. Co., 1966. 191p. £1.60.)

6–9   The story of a delinquent child in a foster home, realistic and often touching. With a father in prison, Joe had had an unhappy life and had become a thief; his mother was in a state institution. Although there were some things he liked about living with the Murrays, Joe resented them, but he was unable to resist small Melvin, an adopted child of Jewish parentage. He invented for Melvin's benefit—and his own pride—a beautiful, magical, loving mother. Slowly the patience and kindness of the Murrays helped Joe to lose his hostility and to greet with love the subdued mother who came to visit him when she was released from the hospital. The characterization and motivation are excellent; the writing style is very good, although Melvin's conversation is occasionally a bit precocious.

53   **Armour,** Richard. *Odd Old Mammals;* Animals after the Dinosaurs; illus. by Paul Galdone. McGraw-Hill, 1968. 37p. $4.50. (World's Work, 1969. 40p. £0.90.)

4–6   Galdone's large-scale illustrations of ancient mammals have humorous touches that match very nicely the combination of humor and information of the text. The author makes no claim to being comprehensive; he has chosen a dozen beasts of Cenozoic times to describe in romping rhymes, mixing quips and puns with facts—but never confusing them. In re the sloth-like megatherium, for example, "The strangest thing was how he walked/ A queer, side-footed roll/ When asked, 'Why do you walk this way?'/ He said, 'To save my sole.' "

54   **Armstrong,** William H. *Sounder;* illus. by James Barkley. Harper, 1969. 116p. Trade ed. $3.95; Library ed. $3.79 net. (Gollancz, 1971. £1.10.)

7–10   The story of a black sharecropper's family, written with quiet strength and taut with tragedy. Having stolen to feed his family, the father is arrested at home; trying to protect his master, the dog—Sounder—is severely wounded. The oldest boy haunts the roads, seeking his father in chain gangs; he is taken in by a teacher and learns to read, his mother agreeing that he must have this chance. The boy bears with dignity the double burden of grief: the once-mighty animal crippled, and the shadow of a man who returns to die in silent desperation. Grim and honest, the book has a moving, elegiac quality that is reminiscent of the stark inevitability of Greek tragedy.

55   **Arnold,** Elliott. *A Kind of Secret Weapon.* Scribner, 1969. 191p.
Trade ed. $4.95; Library ed. $4.37 net. (Longman Young Bks.,
1970. 192p. £0.90.)

5–8   For almost as long as Peter can remember, the Germans have
occupied Denmark—men to be afraid of, to make fun of—but
he had been little then. Now that he was old enough to understand,
Peter helped his parents put out and distribute an underground
newspaper; at times it was necessary to take dangerous risks;
at all times, the boy found, he could count on the help and
sympathy of the ordinary people around him. Peter's father is
killed, and he and his mother escape to Sweden; there the book
ends. Although it has a great deal of drama and more action
than does *The House of the Four Winds* (by Colette Vivier) both
of these World War II stories demonstrate the courage of the
common man. This is written with adult humor and in a mature
style, but written so simply that it makes no demands on the
reader.

56   **Arnold,** Pauline. *How We Named Our States;* by Pauline Arnold
and Percival White. Criterion Books, 1966. 192p. $4.25.

5–9   A book that gives a great deal of information, some of it
ancillary but interesting and some basic to the topic as it is
indicated in the title. The material is grouped regionally, more
or less, under such divisions as "The Spanish Cavaliers," "The
French Explorers," "Moving Westward," and "The Oregon Trail."
Occasionally a statement about a name is based on conjecture
rather than fact, but the distinction is usually made clear. There
are interesting bits of historical information and, although the book
doesn't have reference use, it is useful for the information it
gives and enjoyable for browsing. An index is appended.

57   **Arora,** Shirley Lease. *The Left-Handed Chank.* Follett, 1966. 256p.
$3.95.

6–9   A story set in India today. Kumaran is the youngest son in a
family of fishermen; his father is leader of the men of their
village; father is the only man who believes that the Inspector
of Fisheries can help their impoverished village; to the others,
the Inspector is an enemy. Does he not advocate such ideas
as throwing some of the fish back? Kumaran is torn: he would
like to find the left-handed chank that brings luck and fortune,
but he also wants to learn from the Inspector. When the men go
out in a storm although warned by the Inspector, they are later
chastened and changed by the knowledge that his help has
saved them. Kumaran, who has carried the important telegraph
message, realizes that it is not a shell that will bring fortune,
but one's own efforts. The author creates most convincingly the

atmosphere of the small village and of the villagers' suspicious attitude toward the stranger whose ideas differ from their own. Characterization is good, with changes in relationships logically motivated; the details that reflect cultural patterns are unobtrusively incorporated into the story.

58   **Aruego,** Jose. *Look What I Can Do;* written and illus. by Jose Aruego. Scribner, 1971. 29p. $4.95.

K–2   There's very little text in this amusing story, and words are hardly needed. "Look what I can do," says one carabao to another, prancing about on its hind legs. The other animal immediately tries it. "I can do it too!" Off they go on a mad, exhausting follow-the-leader series of capers that end when they crawl, breathless, out of the river. Lying on the bank like two gaping fish, the animals are accosted by a third carabao. "Look what I can do," he boasts. Last page: the original pair sit, glaring, on the prostrate newcomer. The details of the illustrations are both handsome and amusing, especially the faces of other creatures watching the exhibition.

59   **Arundel,** Honor. *The Terrible Temptation.* Nelson, 1971. 173p. $4.95. (H. Hamilton, 1971. £1.25.)

7–10   Starting her student days at Edinburgh University, Jan is determined to make nice friends, to get into no close relationships, and certainly not to marry and become burdened with chores and children. Unable to find a room, she calls on her great-aunt Agnes and makes an arrangement to live in the house but to keep to herself. Jan resists falling in love, but eventually succumbs to the warmth and generosity of a man whose attention to other people—his landlord, children, anyone who needs help—irritates her. Given the chance of a Christmas visit with a wealthy girl, Jan leaves Edinburgh despite the fact that her aunt has just had a stroke and is completely alone. The book ends with her realization that Thomas is so appalled by her callousness that she has lost him too. Written in first person, the story is wonderfully convincing in establishing the character of a self-centered and selfish girl, and commendable in its consistency to the end.

60   **Ashe,** Geoffrey. *King Arthur;* In Fact and Legend. Nelson, 1971. 158p. $4.95.

7—   An intriguing exploration of the ways in which the legendary Arthur grew out of the known historical and archeological facts about the sixth-century war-leader who checked a Saxon invasion. Ashe discusses the legends and theories about Arthur and his court, carefully distinguishing between those facts substantiated by research and those that remain in the realm of theory.

Photographs of artifacts, reproductions of artistic depictions of
Arthurian legend, and aerial pictures of sites related to it, add
interest to an erudite text written in an informal style. An
annotated list of the most important characters, a bibliography,
and an index are appended.

61   **Asimov,** Isaac. *ABC's of the Earth.* Walker, 1971. 48p. illus. Trade
ed. $4.50; Library ed. $4.41 net.

3–5   Third in a series of alphabetically arranged overviews of our
environment, this is a useful collection of facts about phenomena
and forces that affect the surface of the earth. Two terms are
given for each letter of the alphabet, with photographs for each.
While the effects of the sun's heat, wind, and water action are
described, the most intriguing pictures are those of the dramatic
results: a natural rock bridge, an oxbow lake, stalactites and
stalagmites, an out-cropping of tilted bedrock. Although the book
doesn't cover all important terms in earth science, it includes
many and, with the clear definitions that are well-matched with
photographs, serves as a good introduction to the varied subjects
that are included in this field.

62   **Asimov,** Isaac. *ABC's of the Ocean.* Walker, 1970. 48p. illus. Trade
ed. $4.50; Library ed. $4.41 net.

3–5   From aquaculture to zooplankton, an introduction to aspects of
marine life and oceanography; the book is not comprehensive,
limited by the alphabetical format (two topics for each letter,
with a paragraph of information on each topic) but the facts
given are interesting and lucidly presented. The pages have an
imaginative and varied use of black, white, and blue-green in
illustrations, background, and print; on just a few pages this
results in print that is hard to read. The photographs are good,
the type large, the whole attractive.

63   **Asimov,** Isaac. *The Egyptians.* Houghton, 1967. 256p. illus. $4.75.

7—   A lively, intelligent, and eminently readable book that gives a
detailed and comprehensive picture of Egyptian history from
prehistoric times to today. As always, the author is as sensitive
to the ancillary external affairs that affect people as he is to the
small and fascinating intricacies of such indigenous events as a
power struggle within the dynastic structure. The book gives a
vivid picture of the Mediterranean world, including an analysis
of religions and their influences on Egypt and on each other.
Maps are included; a table of dates and an index are appended.

64   **Asimov,** Isaac. *Great Ideas of Science;* illus. by Lee Ames. Houghton,
1969. 140p. $4.

6–9   Some of the high moments in science history are described by

Asimov in his usual vigorous and lucid style, the focus of the book being on the contribution each theory or discovery has made to the body of knowledge. The book also shows clearly how such a body is built on the work of the past and how the scientific method is applied. From Thales, who thought that all things were water (wrong, but his great idea was that there was a natural order in the universe) to theories of cosmic evolution, men have had hypotheses about natural selection, atomic theory, conservation of matter, etc. Here, in brief chapters, are descriptions of some of the research projects that validated those hypotheses. An index is appended.

65   **Asimov,** Isaac. *The Land Of Canaan.* Houghton, 1971. 306p. $5.95.

7—   Crowded with detail, this covers over two thousand years of history, with a first section that gives historical background from Neolithic times. Although the scope of the book imposes a mass of names and dates, it is written clearly and sequentially, heavy with information but useful, particularly in the coverage of Judaism and the new religion, Christianity, and in the treatment of the legends and history incorporated into the Bible. Maps, a table of dates, genealogies, and an index are included.

66   **Asimov,** Isaac. *The Roman Empire.* Houghton, 1967. 277p. illus. $4.75.

8—   A sequel to *The Roman Republic,* which ended with Octavian's receiving the name of Augustus in 27 B.C. Now the power of Rome and her ideas began to spread through the known world, and much that was assimilated by Rome was affected by being sifted through the Roman culture. It is this appraisal of cultural diffusion that marks Asimov's writing; the easy style simply makes more palatable the familiar catalog of names and dates, but the importance of the book is in the discussion of such a topic as the place of Christianity in the spectrum of religions, the flexibility it offered to Jews, the natural incorporation of pagan customs in a religion spreading through regions of Greece and Asia Minor, and the natural reistance of Rome to this subversive sect. Somehow, the dauntless author manages to cover all the details of rulers, campaigns, battles, intrigues, sackings, burnings, and murders with enough vivacity and humor to make the crowded history interesting and pleasant to read. A long table of dates and an extensive index are appended.

67   **Asimov,** Isaac. *The Roman Republic.* Houghton, 1966. 257p. illus. $4.50.

8—   Long but not dull, erudite but not pedantic, a history that is well organized and written with flowing ease. The text gives an enormous amount of information, yet it has a conversational quality—a quality due in part to the entertaining digressions about such things as the cumbersome Roman calendar or the real estate speculations of Crassus. The book closes with Octavian's receiving the name of Augustus; the Republic had become an Empire. A table of dates (both the Christian year and the year from the founding of Rome) and an extensive index are appended.

68   **Asimov,** Isaac. *Words from History;* illus. by William Barss. Houghton, 1968. 265p. illus. $5.95.

6—   The indefatigable Mr. Asimov again delves into the derivations of words (two hundred fifty) whose roots are in the past. One page is devoted to each word, and this means that on some pages there is historical material that serves as background rather than as the origin of the actual words (for example, the fact that an ottoman is called that because the Ottoman Turks had an overstuffed backless seat; the paragraphs that precede this are pure history) but who cares? The material is made fascinating by the easy conversational style, is informative by virtue of the author's encyclopedic knowledge, and is amplified by an index.

69   **Aulaire,** Ingri (Mortenson) d'. *Norse Gods and Giants;* by Ingri and Edgar Parin d'Aulaire. Doubleday, 1967. 160p. illus. $5.95.

4–6   A collection of Norse myths, profusely illustrated with pictures in color and in black and white. The oversize pages are used to advantage in some of the bold full-page illustrations of the mighty warrior-gods. The writing is usually straightforward, moving occasionally into the ringing prose of legendry; the book is given reference use by a combined glossary and relative index.

70   **Aulaire,** Ingri (Mortenson) d'. *Trolls;* by Ingri and Edgar Parin d' Aulaire. Doubleday, 1972. 62p. illus. $5.95.

3–5   All you ever wanted to know about trolls but were afraid to ask: a big, delightfully illustrated book that describes the kinds of trolls that live in Norway, the deliciously awful ways they live, the horrid things they do to human beings when they catch them. The book includes several troll stories, one being the familiar tale of the wise lad who impressed a troll by squeezing a round of cheese, another the story of the huge trolls, the frost giants, who dared to look at the sun and turned to stone. There are several legends of the hulder-people, and one tale of the brave lad who rescued twelve princesses from the clutches of a twelve-headed troll.

71   **Avery,** Gillian, et al. *Authors' Choice;* illus. by Krystyna Turska. T. Y. Crowell, 1971. 216p. $5.95. (H. Hamilton, 1970. 224p. £1.50.)

6—   Seventeen of the most distinguished British writers for children
have each chosen their favorite stories for inclusion in an
anthology that ranges from Tove Jansson and Hans Christian
Andersen to Katherine Mansfield and Ray Bradbury. Most of
the selections are by children's authors and each is preceded
by a word of praise by its selector. Brief notes about contributors
and selectors of choice are appended.

72   **Avery,** Gillian. *A Likely Lad;* illus. by Faith Jaques. Holt, 1971.
223p. Trade ed. $4.95; Library ed. $4.59 net. (Collins, 1971.
224p. £1.25.)

6–8   First published in England, the story of a turn of the century
boyhood, set in an atmosphere of lower middle-class
snobbishness. Willy's parents are proud that they live on the
respectable side of the street and determined that Willy shall
not become a shopkeeper like his father. Shy and quiet, Willy
dreams of becoming a scholar, is crushed when his father decides
he cannot continue his schooling, and astonished when (due
to the intervention of a nobleman who has met and been impressed
by the boy) his father changes his mind. Woven through the
story are Willy's encounters with a complacent and bullying set of
relatives whose comeuppance, at the close, is delightfully in
accord with the Victoriana of the style and the setting. An
evocative book, *A Likely Lad* has a fidelity of language, of period
attitudes, and of Victorian mores that give it an impressive
consistency.

73   **Babbitt,** Natalie. *Dick Foote and the Shark;* story and pictures by
Natalie Babbitt. Farrar, 1967. 26p. $3.50.

4–6   A bouncy, silly, engaging story-poem with internal rhymes,
sustained metric quality, and the perennial appeal of a tall,
tall tale. A reluctant sailor, to the disappointment of his fisherman
father, young Dick Foote was finally beguiled into a boat.
Since young Dick was a poet, his reaction to the whale that terrified
his father was to spout poetry. (The illustrations, nautical and deft,
show the romantic youth of 1873, hand to heart and standing
". . . like a god, ankle-deep in dead cod.") Baffled by this
reaction, the shark paused in open-jawed stupefaction, enabling
the father and son to escape and the latter to become—for
the first time—appreciated by the former.

74   **Babbitt,** Natalie. *Goody Hall;* story and pictures by Natalie Babbitt.
Farrar, 1971. 176p. $4.50.

4–6   A mystery-adventure story, written with flair and humor and with
a vivid evocation of the Gothic setting, relieved by comic
moments. The characters are delightful: Hercules Feltwright,
wandering tutor; his sturdy charge, Willett Goody; the Widow

Goody who so strangely and regularly disappears; Mrs. Tidings the cook, a prototype of all gossiping busybodies; Mott Snave, the jewel thief. Then there are the jewels, long lost and found again. . . The plot is deftly handled, the suspense well paced, the denouement satisfyingly surprising but neat and credible.

75   **Babbitt**, Natalie. *Kneeknock Rise*; written and illus. by Natalie Babbitt. Farrar, 1970. 118p. $3.95.

4–6   The little town of Instep huddled against the foot of Kneeknock Rise, its occupants aware the terrible Megrimum lived on the summit. They could hear it—whatever it was—moaning on stormy nights. This is the story of a visitor who climbed Kneeknock Rise, not a rash boy but one goaded by a teasing cousin. What Egan found was a perfectly rational explanation for the moaning noises—but did they believe him? Did they even listen? No, the Insteppers refused to give up their mythical Megrimum, and Egan had learned a lesson about people: don't confuse them by presenting facts; they prefer their fancies. The pithy message, the moments of humor, and the freshness of the story are made more enjoyable by a smooth and lively writing style.

76   **Babbitt**, Natalie. *Phoebe's Revolt*. Farrar, 1968. 33p. illus. $3.95.

3–4   Delightful drawings brimming with Victoriana enhance the amusing story of a small rebel in Manhattan at the turn of the century. The sprightly verse describes the hatred Phoebe had for the elaborate, feminine clothes of her day; a sit-down strike in the bathtub, protesting frilly birthday garments, led to Phoebe's appearance in Father's clothes, his wayward daughter having chosen those garments. After a week of that, surrender by Phoebe—but Mother came to the rescue with a simple sailor dress. Peace reigned. Can be read aloud to a wider audience.

77   **Bacon**, Martha. *Sophia Scrooby Preserved*; illus. by David Omar White. Atlantic-Little, Brown, 1968. 227p. $4.95. (Gollancz, 1971. £1.20.)

7–9   In the mannered style of the early English novelists, a romantic story in which the heroine moves from one dramatic adventure to another. Born in 1768, the small daughter of an African chieftain is taken into slavery and lives with a Connecticut family that fosters her natural bent for education and musical training. Sophia and the Scroobys are separated, and she falls into the clutches of pirates, is the captive of a voodoo queen, the companion to an English lady of means, and a performer at Drury Lane before her reunion with the Scroobys in Canada. Sophia is an engaging heroine, and her story is written with flavor; the book tends, however, to have the indefatigable quality of *Anthony Adverse*.

78   **Baker,** Betty. *And One Was a Wooden Indian.* Macmillan, 1970. 170p. $4.95.

6–10   Set in the Southwest in the mid-nineteenth century, the story of a young Apache who has a first encounter with the white man. Hatilshay is unhappy about his weak eyesight, worried because his friend Turtlehead calls him a witch. He is cautious when a Papago brings him to the Yankee camp, but Turtlehead is terrified, sure that the stiffness in his body is due to the statue of the white-eyes, a statue that has taken away his health. Hatilshay is dubious but prepared to steal the image. In the course of the story, the cultural patterns of several tribes as well as the American-Indian relationship emerge as vividly as the patterns of Indian art. Hatilshay cannot see the omens that the conforming Turtlehead sees, but he finally realizes that it is his perception that has brought him to be called a witch; the wise old shaman of his tribe sees it too, and tells the younger man gently that this is the true vision of every shaman. The characters come alive, the story moves smoothly, the writing has humor and profundity.

79   **Baker,** Betty. *The Blood of the Brave.* Harper, 1966. 163p. Trade ed. $3.95; Library ed. $3.79 net.

7–10   A very good historical novel, based on accounts of the sixteenth century expedition of Hernan Cortez. Like most of the members of the Cuban colony who had come from Spain, young Juan had heard of the wealth of Mexico; he joined the expedition that sought Aztec conquest, and was used by Montezuma as an interpreter. The characters are vividly drawn, the cultural details and historical background convincing, and the plot developed with sustained pace.

80   **Baker,** Betty. *The Dunderhead War.* Harper, 1967. 216p. Trade ed. $3.95; Library ed. $3.79 net. (Harper & Row, 1968. 216p. £1.67½.)

6–9   Seventeen years old wasn't quite old enough to enlist, but Quincy, who wanted to go west, had a chance anyway. "An army of dunderheads" is what Uncle Fritz called the Grand Army fighting the Mexican War, but he and Quincy shared the adventures of the volunteers. A good story about the Mexican War, an even better one as a lively and perceptive tale of the reactions of an immigrant (Uncle Fritz) to the local scene and of the reactions of the Americans to the complacent superiority and the criticisms of Uncle Fritz.

81   **Baker,** Laura Nelson. *Go Away Ruthie.* Knopf, 1966. 178p. Trade ed. $3.95; Library ed. $3.39 net.

7–10   A good first-person story for girls: realistic, perceptive, and well written. Ruthie comes to live with her aunt after her mother dies; she is not a particularly attractive child, and Lynn—who lives next door and tells the story—is reluctant to befriend her. But Ruthie is starved for affection and insecure, and Lynn becomes used to her—almost fond of her. Lynn tells the story in retrospect, describing the way Ruthie gradually becomes part of an adolescent love-triangle. Eventually Lynn and her boyfriend drift apart, and Ruthie moves in—actually, in her desultory way, she sidles in. When the boy, for whom Lynn still cares, tells her that he and Ruthie are getting married because they are going to have a baby, Lynn feels more sympathetic pity than she does any other emotion. The shiftings of relationships are psychologically sensitive, and the story has a good balance of other interests and of family life. One of the most affective relationships is that between Lynn and the much-loved grandmother who lives with the family and who dies during the course of the story.

82   **Baker,** Margaret Joyce. *Porterhouse Major.* Prentice-Hall, 1967. 116p. $4.50. (Penguin, 1969. 112p. £0.20.)

4–6   Porterhouse Major is a cat, but a far from ordinary one; he is unusually large, unusually intelligent, and remarkably articulate when no adults are about. He has been created by a lonely boy who has been delving into his mother's books on magic and spells; Rory and his sisters dote on Porterhouse Major, and the cat accepts this homage as only his due. In fact, he feels capable of running the household, and tries to do so; eventually Rory's size is an embarrassment even to him, and something has to be done— so, again, something magical happens. The light humor and graceful style of writing combine nicely with the fanciful theme and its bland, realistic development.

83   **Baker,** Samm Sinclair. *The Indoor and Outdoor Grow-it Book;* illus. by Eric Carle. Random House, 1966. 66p. Trade ed. $2.95; Library ed. $4.29 net.

5–9   Mr. Baker has been giving gardening advice in print and on the air for many years, and this very clear, sensible, and useful book bears witness to his professional competence. The ideas are many and varied, and most of the suggestions are inexpensive and uncomplicated. The text is continuous, not precisely organized but precisely written and adequately indexed; the illustrations are not labeled, but they are helpful. The book covers such topics as starting plants from seeds or fruits, growing and curing herbs, caring for indoor plants and cut flowers, plant foods, and plants as gifts; a final section of random tips is included.

84   **Bales,** Carol Ann. *Kevin Cloud, Chippewa Boy in the City.* Reilly and Lee, 1972. 28p. illus. $4.50.

3–5   Excellent photographs, in color and in black and white, illustrate a documentary-style text in which ten-year-old Kevin describes his life in a depressed area of Chicago in which there is a large American Indian population. He is matter-of-fact about poverty and prejudice, and about the white father who has left the family; he discusses a visit to the Minnesota reservation, where he helps his relatives harvest wild rice. Throughout the book runs the thread of dignity and pride of heritage, as Kevin talks of Chippewa customs, especially when he describes his attractive grandmother. And what gives the book a bit more vitality than most photo-documentaries are the warmth of familial relationships and Kevin's good humor.

85   **Bamberger,** Richard. *My First Big Story-Book;* tr. by James Thin; illus. by Emanuela Wallenta. Harvey House, 1967. 220p. Trade ed. $4.95; Library ed. $4.79 net. (Penguin, 1969. 192p. £0.25.)

3–5   First published in Austria, an anthology in which the sprightly illustrations (some in black and white, some in color) add to the appeal of the tales. Some of the stories are as familiar as "Little Red Riding Hood," others less well known. Most of the seventy-three selections are from European sources. The print is not well spaced, but the material itself is good, and the book as useful for reading aloud or as a source for storytelling as it is for independent reading.

86   **Barne,** Kitty. *Barbie.* Little, 1969. 257p. $4.95.

6–9   First published in England in 1952. Barbie had spent all her life travelling with her parents, but her mother was in a rest home and her father touring as a ballet conductor. There was nowhere for her to go except to her English cousins. Laurel, who is Barbie's age, and Simon feel tremendous respect for Barbie's musicianship (violin) and are aware that she needs a worthy teacher. There is only one great teacher that Barbie wants to work with, and it takes the combined efforts of Barbie's cousins and friends to get an audience with Vascoletti. While this may have a special appeal for the musical reader, it is well enough written to appeal to others, and it has the combined attractions of a romantic mood, an unusual heroine, and a family situation that is lively and affectionate.

87   **Barnwell,** Robinson. *Shadow on the Water.* McKay, 1967. 214p. $4.25.

6–8   Set on a South Carolina farm in 1939, the story of a middle child in a family in which there is marital conflict. Cam is the only one of the children aware of this, since her older sister is away at college and small Tal too young to know. When her mother takes Cam and Tal to her mother's home, it is clear that divorce is being considered. Called home by the sudden illness of their paternal grandfather, they return to the farm; both parents have seen the need for compromise and, to Cam's deep relief, decide to try again. The story is low-keyed and realistic, with a skillful interweaving of small subplots: a sister's love affair, the relationship between grandparents on opposite sides of the family and between the children and each of those grandparents. A good and honest family story.

88   **Baron,** Virginia Olsen, ed. *Here I Am!* An Anthology of Poems Written by Young People of Some of America's Minority Groups; illus. by Emily Arnold McCully. Dutton, 1969. 159p. Trade ed. $4.95; Library ed. $4.90 net.

3–6   From schools all over the United States, the author solicited children's poems and chose approximately one hundred twenty for inclusion in a volume that has some moments of lightness but chiefly comprises candid observations on awareness, isolation, prejudice, and justice—or, more often, injustice. There are some poems about nature, family life, or the city, but most of the selections are intensely personal and infinitely moving.

89   **Barth,** Edna. *I'm Nobody! Who Are You?* The Story of Emily Dickinson; drawings by Richard Cuffari. Seabury, 1971. 128p. $4.95.

5–8   A very good biography that begins with the nine-year-old Emily, smoothly incorporates passages of her writing within the context of the text, and includes selected poems at the conclusion of the biographical material. The writing style is direct and informal, all of the dialogue based on research, and the tone is objective. A bibliography, a list of sources, an index of poems by first lines, and a general index are appended.

90   **Bartlett,** Susan. *Books;* illus. by Ellen Raskin. Holt, 1968. 42p. (A Book to Begin On) Trade ed. $3.50; Library ed. $3.27 net. (Chatto, Boyd & Oliver, 1970. 48p. £0.70.)

2–4   A handsome example of the art of which it speaks, this is a well-written and distinctively illustrated book that introduces the young reader to the essentials of the history of the book. It discusses the early forms of recorded communication and the first materials, the development of printing with movable type, and the forms of the book, both those of the past and the familiar form we know today.

91   **Bartos-Höppner,** B. *Hunters of Siberia;* tr. by Anthea Bell. Walck, 1969. 242p. $5.50.

7–10   Translated from the German, a novel set in the early part of the century that is both a plea for conservation of wild life and a remarkable picture of a way of life now ended. Ibrahim Karalkan is certainly the best hunter in the tiny village of Baltshara, but he is a Caucasian in exile, not one of the natives, and he is never quite accepted. When a government official comes from St. Petersburg with the power to regulate hunting, he chooses the reluctant Ibrahim as his guide. Slowly Ibrahim begins to see the senselessness of the depletion of species by wholesale shooting, to understand the benefits of a long-range conservation program for the very people who resist it. The obduracy and craftiness of the natives is rather harshly drawn, but the theme of the book is compelling, the hunting episodes are replete with danger and action, and the gradual development of the friendship between the two men who have, at the start, been enemies is wholly convincing.

92   **Batterberry,** Michael, ad. *Art of the Early Renaissance.* McGraw-Hill, 1970. 191p. illus. $9.95.

7—   Profusely illustrated with full color reproductions of the paintings, sculpture, and architecture, the elaborate beauty of small, jeweled art objects and the ornate interiors of the early Renaissance. The text discusses artists and techniques as well as individual works, most of the material organized by region or city. A list of illustrations, with locations, and an index are appended.

93   **Batterberry,** Michael. *Children's Homage to Picasso;* by Michael Batterberry and Ariane Ruskin; with 52 drawings by Picasso and 48 by the children of Vallauris. Abrams, 1972. 106p. $12.50.

5—   Pablo Picasso was so pleased by the gift he received on his 85th birthday from the children of Vallauris, a collection of their drawings of bullfights, that he added some of his own, selected the best of theirs, and suggested they be printed as a book. The text gives some facts about the artist and about bullfighting, and the illustrations are artfully arranged, the deft lines of a Picasso drawing coming always as a surprise after pages of the naive and vigorous pictures by the children.

94   **Baumann,** Hans. *In the Land of Ur;* The Discovery of Ancient Mesopotamia; tr. by Stella Humphries. Pantheon Books, 1969. 167p. illus. $4.95. (Oxf. U.P., 1969. 160p. £1.25.)

8—   A fine addition to the history of archeological research, documented in scholarly fashion and written with a communicable zest for the fascination of the unraveling of man's past. The author interpolates into the chronological record of early amateur and later professional excavators and interpreters enough source material to add historic relevance to the archeological interest. The illustrations are excellent: maps, drawings, and full-page photographs in color; a list of names (places, people, and words) with annotations is appended, as are lists of Mesopotamian explorers and major excavations, and a chronological table of kings.

95   **Baumann,** Hans. *Lion Gate and Labyrinth;* tr. by Stella Humphries. Pantheon Books, 1967. 183p. illus. $4.95. (Oxf. U.P., 1967. 176p. £1.25.)

7–12   Although there have been many other books about discoveries at the ruins of Troy, Crete, and Mycenae, this should be an interesting addition. The author not only describes the work of Schliemann and Evans (and some other archeologists) but incorporates into his accounts some of the myths and legends pertaining to those cultures. The photographs, maps, and diagrams are excellent; the writing style is lively and informed (although there are some minor errors, perhaps due to translation) and a chronology and glossary are appended.

96   **Bawden,** Nina. *A Handful of Thieves.* Lippincott, 1967. 189p. Trade ed. $3.50; Library ed. $3.59 net. (Penguin, 1970. £0.20.)

5–7   Determined to find the ex-lodger who had walked off with grandmother's savings, Fred McAlpine and his friends began a concerted effort to trace the thief. Unfortunately, the only way that they could think of—after some abortive sleuthing—was to sneak into his room. They did and they were promptly picked up by the police; and in a smash finish, the lodger was caught after a chase, and a handful of thieves were vindicated. The plot is just this side of credibility, with pace and suspense nicely maintained. The characters and their relationships are vivid and colorful: tough old Gran, with a soft spot for her grandson and his pal Sid; Fred's mother, who finds Sid common and her mother a troublesome old woman; friend Algy, overprotected but game for anything.

97   **Bawden,** Nina. *Squib.* Lippincott, 1971. 143p. Paper ed. $1.95; Library ed. $3.93 net. (Gollancz, 1971. 128p. £0.90.)

5–6   Seven years old, small, pale, always alone, the shy boy refused to answer to any name but "Squib" when the other children questioned him. Kate Pollack, who was eleven, was especially concerned about him—he was the same age her brother would have been if he were alive—but each of the other children worries too. Squib doesn't talk much about himself, but he lives in an old people's home, and one of the boys has seen Squib's pale face at a tower window. The children hear a woman threaten him: "Basket for you, that's what you're asking for. . ." The children's attempt to rescue Squib from a situation they don't quite understand but know is wrong, somehow, provides a dramatic and satisfying ending. The relationships among the children, and the family situation of each, are drawn with perception and warmth, and the story is written with just-bearable suspense.

98   **Baylor,** Byrd. *Before You Came This Way;* illus. by Tom Bahti. Dutton, 1969. 27p. Trade ed. $4.75; Library ed. $4.70 net.

2–4   A handsome book, thought-provoking and written with lyric simplicity; the illustrations, on handmade bark paper, are in the style of the prehistoric rock pictures on which the book is based. Walking in the quiet of a canyon in the Southwest, you wonder if you are the first to pass this way . . . then you see that some brother, long-dead, has made a record of his people and their lives: the animals they hunted, the battles and the feasts, the masks of the dancers. The writing style is sensitively attuned to the dignity and mystery of the subject.

99   **Baylor,** Byrd. *When Clay Sings;* illus. by Tom Bahti. Scribner, 1972. 29p. $4.95.

2–5   Every piece of clay, Indian parents tell children who find shards, should be treated with respect, since it was a part of somebody's life. "They even say it has its own small voice and sings in its own way." The pages, handsome in earth colors and black and white, show designs derived from prehistoric Indian pottery of the Southwest, and the text consists of what the children of today imagine about the four cultures (Anasazi, Mogollon, Hohokam, and Mimres) from which the clay pottery came. The book is dignified in format, the illustrations and text beautifully united, and the text both reveals the richness of the ancient cultures and hints, to the reader, the ways in which one learns about prehistory from artifacts.

100   **Beadle,** George. *The Language of Life;* An Introduction to the Science of Genetics; by George and Muriel Beadle. Doubleday, 1966. 242p. illus. $5.95. (Panther, 1969. 272p. £0.42½.)

9—   A lucid, comprehensive, and authoritative book on genetics; written with only the necessary minimum of scientific terminology and illustrated with diagrams that are carefully labelled and placed. The writing style is smooth, the use of clarifying analogies being particularly deft. The authors give enough background information and scientific history to place research and discovery in genetics in perspective in relation to the state of scientific knowledge, and give most vividly a picture of diffusion, the overlapping, the slow building of a body of knowledge. The meat of the book is, of course, in the examination of the accumulating information about genetics: the raveling of biochemical complexities of form and function from the early work of Mendel and Garrod to the ferment of research that resulted in the synthesizing of DNA and the cracking of the genetic code. A relative index is appended.

101   **Beatty,** Patricia. *A Long Way to Whiskey Creek.* Morrow, 1971.
           224p. Trade ed. $4.95; Library ed. $4.59 net.

5–7   From Cottonwood, it was four hundred miles to Whiskey Creek,
           but there wasn't anybody else who could go—so thirteen-year-old
           Parker set off on the grim errand of bringing back his brother's
           body. He'd suggested to Nate Graber, an orphan, that he go
           along for company even though Nate was a Yankee who liked,
           of all things, to read books. The story is set in Texas in 1879,
           and it shows both the lingering hostility between opposing factions
           and the easy violence of a frontier country. There are a few
           semi-stereotyped characters, but the two boys are convincingly
           drawn, their adventures have pace and excitement, and the
           moderating influence of Nate and Parker on each other is gradual
           and believable: Nate gains self-confidence and Parker some respect
           for education.

102   **Beaty,** Janice J. *Seeker of Seaways;* A Life of Matthew Fontaine
           Maury, Pioneer Oceanographer; illus. by Joseph Cellini. Pantheon
           Books, 1966. 162p. $4.50.

7—   An attractively illustrated and competently written biography of
           one of the great American scientists of the nineteenth century.
           Maury's accomplishments: textbooks on navigation and
           geography, pioneer work in oceanography, chartmaker, and
           college teacher among other things. Because of his work and his
           dedication, his life would be interesting in any case, but his
           biography is given added dramatic interest because of the jealous
           persecution he suffered from other scientists and their influential
           friends. A brief bibliography is appended.

103   **Behn,** Harry, tr. *More Cricket Songs;* Japanese Haiku; illus. with
           pictures by Japanese masters. Harcourt, 1971. 64p. Trade ed.
           $3.50; Library ed. $3.54 net.

5—   A companion volume to *Cricket Songs.* The haiku here are drawn
           from the work of twenty-nine poets, the selections varied in mood
           and subject, deceptively simple in their miniature perfection, and
           translated with that sensitivity and authority that indicate the
           poet's vision.

104   **Belting,** Natalia Maree. *Christmas Folk;* illus. by Barbara Cooney.
           Holt, 1969. 34p. Trade ed. $4.95; Library ed. $4.59 net.

3–6   A lovely book, the poetic text describing the festivities and
           customs of the Elizabethan Christmas from St. Andrew's Day
           to Twelfth Night. The illustration is exactly right, gay with
           bright costumes, fascinating in period details, and vigorous with
           movement; the page layout is particularly striking.

105   **Belting,** Natalia Maree. *The Stars Are Silver Reindeer;* illus. by

Esta Nesbitt. Holt, 1966. 42p. Trade ed. $3.50; Library ed. $3.27 net.

4–6   As in *The Sun Is a Golden Earring,* the author has compiled a series of legends from various sources; the illustrations have captions that are repeated with diagrams at the close of the book, a rather unwieldy way of showing patterns of constellations. The selections are imaginative, varied, and poetic; some are from lore as old as Babylonian, others from more modern, albeit often primitive, sources.

106   **Benchley,** Nathaniel. *Feldman Fieldmouse;* illus. by Hilary Knight. Harper, 1971. 96p. Trade ed. $3.95; Library ed. $3.79 net.

3–5   An engaging fanciful tale, spiced with brisk and sophisticated dialogue, about a mouse who aspires to one glorious night of beauty. Feldman is the uncle of a young fieldmouse, Fendall, who is a boy's pet and who has never learned to fend for himself. Since the boy can talk to Fendall and is entirely sympathetic with the viewpoint of mice, he is invited on several moonlight jaunts and is looking forward to Feldman's great evening: a dance by the light of the full moon. The boy's illness keeps him from attending and acting as guardian, with the result (sadly reported by Fendall) that Feldman is picked off by an owl. But beauty is not created in vain: Fendall plans to honor his uncle's memory with another gala night. It is worth it, he concludes, to take a risk for the sake of the creative experience. The style is delightful, the animal characters amusing, and the dialogue witty.

107   **Benchley,** Nathaniel. *Sam the Minuteman;* illus. by Arnold Lobel. Harper, 1969. 62p. (I Can Read Books) Trade ed. $2.50; Library ed. $2.57 net.

2–4   Mother said, "Go back to bed," but Sam's father thought the boy might as well get his gun, too; Sam could fight right along with the Minutemen if the British soldiers really showed up as Paul Revere had said they would. Massed, the colonials were an easy target; they soon learned to snipe from behind a tree or fence. Worn out, Sam fell asleep that night worrying about a wounded friend and unaware that the war had started, but he had lost his fear and felt ready to fight again. The story has plenty of action and historical authenticity; it is written with the deceptive ease that marks the series. It is most effective in creating a realistic mood of sober apprehension and in maintaining the child's viewpoint and reaction.

108   **Bendick,** Jeanne. *The Emergency Book;* written and illus. by Jeanne Bendick. Rand McNally, 1967. 144p. $3.95.

5–9   A book of advice and caution that is utterly sensible, quite comprehensive, and often entertaining; the material is neatly compartmentalized and cross-referenced for easy accessibility. Mrs. Bendick describes the dangers and problems in situations such as fire emergencies, sports accidents, emergencies on the road, and so on. General information on first aid precedes the discussion of specific situations; included are advice on animal emergencies and suggestions for the baby sitter. The illustrations are in cartoon style, some simply amusing and others in amplification of the text; a relative index is appended.

109   **Bendick,** Jeanne. *Living Things;* written and illus. by Jeanne Bendick. Watts, 1969. 71p. (Science Experiences) $3.95. (F. Watts, 1970. 67p. £0.80.)

2–4   A good introduction to biology, using the process approach and periodically interrupted by headings that say, "Look for yourself," or "What do you think?" The level of writing and the organization are admirably suited for the primary reader; the text discusses in simple terms the distinguishing features of living things, the balance of nature, the similarities and differences between types of animals and plants, and—very briefly—some facts about reproduction, habitat, adaptation, etc. The illustrations, cartoon-style and perky, are generally informative; a brief index is appended.

110   **Bendick,** Jeanne. *What Made You You?* written and illus. by Jeanne Bendick. McGraw-Hill, 1971. 48p. Trade ed. $4.50; Library ed. $4.33 net.

3–5   Jeanne Bendick adds tenderness to her usual breezy, informal style and blithe illustrations. Her text describes creation, gestation, and birth of a baby, the reference to copulation being "Part of your father fitted into your mother like a key in a lock, like a foot in a sock, like a hand in a glove, like a love in a love," not explaining which parts are referred to, although the next page shows a naked man and woman. The emphasis is on love, and this is carried throughout the text and the subsequent discussion of hereditary traits carried by genes. There is no mention of DNA or chromosomes, simply the fact that genes carry traits, stressing the continuity in generations. Nicely done.

111   **Bentley,** Phyllis. *Forgery!* Doubleday, 1968. 188p. Trade ed. $3.50; Library ed. $4.25 net.

6–9   A story set in Yorkshire in 1769, its fourteen-year-old protagonist, Dick Wade, being the son of a cottage weaver. The local authorities are upset because somebody in the area has been clipping and forging coins. Dick finds that his friend Jamie has been using him, contemptuously, to learn what the law is planning. Jamie and his family are the forgers, and they are caught—but not until one innocent man has died. The details of period and locale are excellent, the speech flavored but not overburdened with the vernacular. Good characterization and plenty of action in a smoothly written adventure story.

112   **Bergere,** Thea. *The Story of St. Peter's;* by Thea and Richard Bergere; illus. with photographs, prints, and with drawings by Richard Bergere. Dodd, 1966. 128p. $4.

8—   A detailed and competent account of the changes, developments, plans and their executions, and the contributing participants in the building of St. Peter's Basilica over thirteen centuries. The book is profusely illustrated with photographs, architectural diagrams, and details of art work. The Bergeres describe the many dramatic events connected with St. Peter's in a matter-of-fact style: the destruction during the Saracen's sack of Rome in 846, the massive plans of popes and kings, the Spanish looting in 1527, the disproved accusations against Michelangelo, the superb work of Bernini. The book is given reference use by the appended material, which includes a glossary, an index, a bibliography, a list of measurements, and a wonderfully extensive annotated list of descriptions that is numbered in correspondence with the architectural features of the entire building, as shown in a clear diagram.

113   **Berna,** Paul. *A Truckload of Rice;* tr. from the French by John Buchanan-Brown; illus. by Prudence Seward. Pantheon Books, 1970. 154p. $4.50. (Bodley Head, 1968. 152p. £0.80.)

5–7   First published in France under the title *Le Commissaire Sinet et le Mystère des Poissons Rouges.* Money is being collected in a Paris neighborhood to provide a truckload of rice for a famine-stricken Indian region, and two of the most assiduous and adept collectors are Lucien and Geoffrey Verdier. Geoffrey is robbed by a blind man, and this begins a long and lively chase in which the two boys help M. Sinet, the Police Commissioner, find the man, who isn't blind at all. The detective work is solid, the Parisian setting delightful, and the story written with vitality and color.

114   **Bernard,** Jacqueline. *Journey toward Freedom;* The Story of Sojourner Truth; illus. with photographs and engravings. Norton, 1967. 265p. Trade ed. $5.95; Library ed. $5.34 net.

10—   An impressive biography of the indomitable and dedicated woman whose courage in speaking out at religious and anti-slavery meetings all through the Northeast and Middle West made her one of the most famous Negroes of her time. Born a slave at the end of the 18th century, Sojourner took her new name (she had been named Isabelle) as a sign of freedom, and went forth to preach. When the Civil War broke out, she helped soldiers;

after the war, she worked for help for homeless and jobless
freedmen; always, she pleaded and fought for equality and reform.
During her long life, she knew and worked with most of the
leaders of the anti-slavery movement, men and women of both
races. The historical background is interesting, the subject
fascinating; the book, smoothly written, has vitality and
impressive evidence of thorough research. A selected
bibliography of sources and an index are appended.

115   **Bernheim,** Marc. *African Success Story;* The Ivory Coast; by
Marc and Evelyne Bernheim. Harcourt, 1970. 96p. illus. Trade ed.
$4.95; Library ed. $4.98 net. (Harcourt, Brace, 1970. 96p. £2.35.)

6–9   While some of its neighbors, eager for independence, broke with
France before they were economically ready to stand alone (and
have suffered since), the Ivory Coast, under the leadership of
President Houphouet-Boigny, has achieved remarkable prosperity
and growth. The first part of the crisp and lucid book gives
the historical background, dwelling in detail on the years between
the end of World War II and 1960, the year in which the Ivory
Coast gained independence; the second section describes several
citizens and their lives, giving a good cross section of
contemporary life and the assimilation of new ideas and practices
into an old and dignified culture. An index is appended.

116   **Bernheim,** Marc. *From Bush to City;* A Look at the New Africa;
by Marc and Evelyne Bernheim. Harcourt, 1966. 96p. illus. Trade
ed. $4.50; Library ed. $4.62 net.

6–10   Profusely illustrated with very good photographs, a most
interesting book on the ferment of progress in Africa today. The
text concentrates on the new nations south of the Sahara,
examining their political, religious, and educational patterns; it
discusses the role of women, the economic problems, and the
contributions of foreign countries; it describes the new directions
taken by African artists. The authors write in a lively style that
suits their crisp and intelligent objectivity. It is a drawback to
have a sequence of pages with no numbers. A one-page index is
appended.

117   **Bertol,** Roland, ad. *Sundiata;* The Epic of the Lion King; retold
by Roland Bertol; illus. by Gregorio Prestopino. T. Y. Crowell,
1970. 81p. $3.75.

4–7   The story of one of the early African empires; as are other great
legends, the story of Sundiata is that of good triumphing over
evil; here the tale is presented as though it were told by
a storyteller of today, so that the oral tradition in which the
legend grew is evident in the sweep and cadence of the writing

style. Mute and ugly, the crippled child whose coming had been prophesied did not speak or talk until he became a boy king. Not until he had come back from years of exile did Sundiata lead his people to victory over the tyrannical Sumanguru and found the great empire of Mali. The adaptation is based on material found during research being done for an African film.

118   **Bevans,** Michael H. *The Book of Reptiles and Amphibians;* written and illus. by Michael H. Bevans. Rev. ed. Doubleday, 1967. 87p. $4.95.

5–9   Although too large to be handy as a portable identification book, this does have that function, since the illustrations are full color and clearly detailed. The author makes no claim to be comprehensive; he gives descriptions of common varieties of poisonous and nonpoisonous snakes, of toads, salamanders, lizards, turtles, tortoises, and alligators. Each illustration is accompanied by a descriptive paragraph that gives habitat, common and proper names, characteristic behavior, and sometimes additional facts about the creature's appearance or about how dangerous it is (or isn't) to people. An index is appended—there was none in the original edition; the material is the same, but the arrangement has been changed somewhat.

119   **Bible.** *And It Came to Pass;* Bible Verses and Carols selected by Jean Slaughter; illus. by Leonard Weisgard. Macmillan, 1971. 32p. $4.95.

K–4   The story of the Nativity is told in verses from the Bible, each double-page spread (text and full-color illustration) alternating with an appropriate carol, the two pages of musical notation (simple arrangements) embellished by delicate drawings in black and white. The Biblical text and the music may be used separately or together, the illustrations are lovely, and the book is particularly suited to home use.

120   **Bible.** *Brian Wildsmith's Illustrated Bible Stories;* as told by Philip Turner. Watts, 1968. 135p. illus. $8.95. (Oxf. U.P., 1968. 142p. £1.75.)

K–7   A lovely book. Philip Turner, whose *The Grange at High Force* was awarded the 1968 Carnegie Medal, is an English minister. His Biblical adaptations, compact and dignified, give the Old and New Testament stories in a sweeping chronological continuum. The Wildsmith illustrations are stunning: vivid, colorful compositions that are both reverent and exciting. The book is as suitable for reading aloud to the very young as it is for the independent reader; it is beautiful enough to be enjoyed by the adult.

121   **Bible.** *The Christmas Story;* from the Gospels of Matthew and Luke; ed. by Marguerite Northrup. Metropolitan Museum of Art, 1966. 32p. $3.75.

5—   A very handsome book indeed, the text comprising selections from the King James Version of the Bible. The layout is spacious and dignified, each page that has print on it being faced by a full-page reproduction in color of a painting appropriate to that part of the Christmas story being told. The page of print has, in addition to the title of the painting, a small reproduction of a woodcut in black and white.

122   **Bible.** *The Creation;* illus. by Jo Spier. Doubleday, 1970. 23p. $3.95.

K–3   Not unlike Peter Spier's small-scaled illustrations, the pictures here emerge from the roiling darkness of the void as sunny landscapes filled with a profusion of creatures and plants. The poetic simplicity of the text, taken from the *Jerusalem Bible,* makes it an excellent choice for presenting Genesis to the young child, and the illustrations are in faithful accord with its spirit.

123   **Bible.** *Jonah and the Great Fish;* ad. by Clyde Robert Bulla; illus. by Helga Aichinger. T. Y. Crowell, 1970. 30p. $4.50.

K–2   A direct and simplified version of the Bible story in an edition particularly notable for the stunning use of color and the bold composition of the illustrations. The book does not have the humor of the Macbeth version (*Jonah and the Lord*) nor the flow of language, but it reads aloud well, and the illustrations are varied and subtle.

124   **Bible.** *Stories from the Bible;* retold by Alvin Tresselt; with lithographs by Lynd Ward. Coward, 1971. 61p. Trade ed. $5.95; Library ed. $5.39 net. (Ward Lock, 1971. 128p. £1.80.)

4–7   There have been many adaptations of Bible stories for children, but few have kept the spirit and the beauty of Biblical language as this does. The prose has been artfully simplified, retaining the sonorous and poetic quality of the Old Testament. The illustrations, reverent and handsome lithographs, are in harmony with the text, and the format does justice to both.

125   **Biegel,** Paul. *The King of the Copper Mountains;* English version by Gillian Hume and Paul Biegel; illus. by Babs Van Wely. Watts, 1969. 176p. $4.95. (Dent, 1968. 176p. £1.10.)

4–6   Highly original, and told in compelling style, a story that has within it a variety of tales, the whole nicely knit together. The old and fragile King of the Copper Castle, Mansolain, is close to death; to sustain his interest (and thereby his hold on life) a series of animals entertain him with tales, each bound to the other with a progress report on the whereabouts of the doctor who is hunting the magic herb that will save the monarch. The doctor's tale is the last, neatly rounding out a charming modern fairy tale that won the 1965 Dutch Children's Book Prize.

126   **Bierhorst,** John, ed. *In the Trail of the Wind;* American Indian Poems and Ritual Orations. Farrar, 1971. 201p. illus. $4.95.

5—   In this cross-cultural anthology there are songs, prayers, chants, dreams, and orations from forty languages representing tribes of North and South America. Some are brief, pithy fragments, some long and lyrical; the selections reflect all of the universal concerns of man as well as some of the anguish of defeat. A stirring book, this is given added value by the preface, a section of notes on individual selections, a reading list, and a glossary of tribes, cultures, and languages.

127   **Birmingham,** John, ed. *Our Time Is Now;* Notes from the High School Underground; ed. by John Birmingham. Praeger, 1970. 262p. $5.95.

9—   As editor of his high school's two papers ("Overground" and underground, the jacket puts it) John Birmingham became aware of the extent and intensity of high school students' growing concern with their own roles, the quality of their education, and the controls they feel are imposed upon them. Quite deftly tied together by his comments and explanations, the text consists of excerpts from underground papers all over the United. States. They range from satirical applause for the System and reasoned editorials to biting criticism and inflamed (possibly inflammatory) diatribes. In various ways they ask (or demand) student power, freedom from the dicta of authority, a voice in the shaping of curricula, less rigid attendance requirements, etc. The editorial comments are informative and astute, the book an eye-opener.

128   **Bishop,** Claire (Huchet). *The Truffle Pig;* illus. by Kurt Wiese. Coward-McCann, 1971. 47p. Trade ed. $3.95; Library ed. $3.64 net.

1–3   If they bought a piglet, Pierre's parents decided, they could fatten it up and have delicious sausages. So they saved their pennies and bought Marcel, of whom Pierre became so fond that he didn't want his pet killed. They ran away, and it was then that Pierre discovered that Marcel could detect truffles. Home they went to announce the glad news and to start a new way of life—and the story ends with Marcel receiving a medal in a nationwide Truffle-Pig Contest, fortune for the family, and for Marcel a blue-tiled pool in his sty. The illustrations have simplicity of style and verve in their economical lines and the print is large, but the writing, although direct and simple, has a flat quality that is awkward. Useful for beginning readers.

129   **Blackburn,** Joyce. *James Edward Oglethorpe.* Lippincott, 1970. 144p. $3.95.

7–10   An unusually good biography, objective in tone and balanced in treatment, written in serious vein but enlivened by the dramatic flow of events. Oglethorpe distinguished himself in Georgia as a colonial leader who abolished slavery, established several towns, had remarkable rapport with the local Indians, and outwitted the Spanish in a territorial dispute. The last section of the book describes Oglethorpe's years after returning to England, where his suspected sympathy with the Jacobite cause and his obvious sympathy for the American rebels put his career in eclipse.

130   **Blades,** Ann. *Mary of Mile 18;* written and illus. by Ann Blades. Tundra Books, 1971. 36p. $5.95.

2–4   Mile 18 is a real place, a little, remote Mennonite community in Canada, and Mary was a real child, one of the students in the Mile 18 school where the author taught. While the book has a fairly patterned plot (Father refuses to let Mary keep a half-wolf cub until it gives warning of a coyote) the story's major appeal is in the picture it gives of the hardworking, almost self-sufficient lives of the families of Mile 18 and of the frigid and beautiful country in which they live. The paintings have a primitive sturdiness and naive charm that is reminiscent of the work of Grandma Moses.

131   **Bleeker,** Sonia. *The Ibo of Biafra;* illus. by Edith G. Singer. Morrow, 1969. 160p. Trade ed. $3.95; Library ed. $3.78 net.

5–7   A fine addition to the author's series of studies of tribal cultures in Central and North America, and in Africa. Mrs. Bleeker's approach is anthropological, so that the descriptions of patterns, relationships, mores, and customs are both objective and adept; here the crisp, detailed examination of the Ibo society as it existed in the past is rounded out by a final chapter that describes recent history and the tragic attenuation of the Biafran people. An index is appended.

132   **Bleeker,** Sonia. *The Zulu of South Africa;* Cattlemen, Farmers, and Warriors. illus. by Kisa N. Sasaki. Morrow, 1970. 160p. Trade ed. $3.95; Library ed. $3.78 net.

4–7   Dependably comprehensive and authentic, another in the excellent series of books on African peoples by a noted anthropologist. The material is well organized, the writing straightforward and objective, particularly distinguished by the inclusion of mores and customs in addition to the more usual coverage of history, legends, and patterns of home and community life. The book closes with a chapter on relationships between the Zulu and

Europeans, pointing out in matter-of-fact style the poverty and oppression of the Zulu. An index is appended.

133   **Blegvad,** Lenore. *The Great Hamster Hunt;* by Lenore and Erik Blegvad. Harcourt, 1969. 32p. $3.25. (Harcourt, Brace, 1969. 32p. £1.25.)

2–4   Nicholas was delighted when his friend Tony, who was going away, asked if he'd take care of a hamster, Harvey. All week Nicholas took care of Harvey and played with him, wishing that his mother would change her mind and let him have a hamster, too. Then Harvey disappeared. Father made elaborate hamster traps, but no Harvey; Mother conceded that they had better buy Tony another hamster. What could she say when Harvey then appeared, except that Nicholas might keep hamster number two? The fetching humor that gently pervades the realistic drawings adds immeasurably to a story that is simply told, tightly constructed, and deft in the light handling of an appealing subject.

134   **Blishen,** Edward, ed. *Miscellany Three;* with line drawings and color plates. Watts, 1967. 204p. Trade ed. $7.95; Library ed. $5.96 net. (Oxf. U.P., 1966. 208p. £1.25.)

Blishen, Edward, ed. *Miscellany Four;* with line drawings and color plates. Watts, 1968. 208p. $7.95. (Oxf. U.P., 1967. 216p. £1.50.)

6–9   Like the two previous anthologies in this series, these are a happy combination of entertainment and information, with varied stories, poems, articles, and plays. The illustrations are as varied and as discriminatingly chosen as is the writing. First published in England, these are browsing (and browsing again) books of unusually high quality.

135   **Blume,** Judy. *It's Not the End of the World.* Bradbury, 1972. 169p. $4.95.

4–7   To Karen, it does seem like the end of her world. Surely, surely she can find some way of softening her adamant mother, of bringing her father back. She tries everything she can think of, including a desperate and unsuccessful effort to make herself ill; she discusses the problem with Val, whose parents have been divorced and who recommends a book: *The Boys and Girls Book about Divorce* by Richard Gardner. (This may be the most enthusiastic free plug in print.) Val *knows*, Karen feels, since she is so intelligent that she reads the *New York Times* every Sunday in its entirety. When Karen's brother disappears, her father comes over to help, and the acrimony between her parents makes her aware that separation is inevitable. Perceptive, funny, sad, and honest, Karen's story is convincingly told with all the volatile intensity of a twelve-year-old.

136   **Blume,** Judy. *Then Again, Maybe I Won't*. Bradbury, 1971.
        164p. $4.95.

5–7   Thirteen-year-old Tony is not as thrilled as his parents are
        when the family's finances improve and they move to affluent
        suburbia. The "nice" boy next door (of whom Tony's mother
        heartily approves) proves to be an inveterate shoplifter. Tony
        is, in fact, bothered by the eagerness of his parents to live up to
        their surroundings. He's also just discovered how he reacts to
        sexual provocation—and he worries about that, too; somebody
        may notice. So he decides he'll always carry a coat. Deftly
        handled, Tony's dilemma is really that he has become mature
        enough to see the conflicts and imperfections in his own life
        and in those around him, and he is sensitive enough to accept
        compromise. Although there are developments in the story, the
        book has no strong plot line. It is, however, impressive for its
        realistic and sympathetic identification with a boy's viewpoint.

137   **Boardman,** Fon Wyman. *America and the Gilded Age; 1876–1900*.
        Walck, 1972. 202p. $5.50.

7–10   A history that is divided into large areas of interest: political
        life, minority groups and immigration, the frontier, the literary
        world, American imperialism, et cetera. While the technique does
        not give a cohesive sequential picture, it does present a series
        of clear views, detailed and objective, occasionally analytical. It
        is particularly valuable for the inclusion of more material about
        cultural affairs than is commonly found in young people's
        books of American history. The style is direct and serious. A
        fairly lengthy and mature reading list and an index are appended.

138   **Boeckman,** Charles. *Cool, Hot and Blue;* A History of Jazz for
        Young People. Luce, 1968. 157p. illus. $4.95.

7—   An enthusiastic history of jazz by a former performer, written in a
        casual and conversational style; the table of contents indicates a
        few major figures, but much of the material about performers is
        buried and could be accessible were there an index. Nevertheless,
        the story of New Orleans and the Chicago school, the rise of
        swing and the emergence of bop and rock 'n' roll should be
        fascinating to anyone interested in popular music. One of the most
        informative aspects of the book is Boeckman's explanation of
        individual styles. A bibliography is appended.

139   **Bond,** Michael. *Paddington at Work;* with drawings by Peggy
        Fortnum. Houghton, 1967. 128p. $3.75. (Penguin, 1969. 124p.
        £ 0.20.)

4–6   Not often do sequels maintain the high level of the first story
        published, but this sixth story about an engaging bear is just as
        amusing as were the preceding ones. Paddington lives with an

English family, and one of the charms of the books is their bland acceptance of a bear that is all-but-human. In each chapter, Paddington gets into a jam of some kind; inevitably he emerges the victor over fate, enemies, or his own blunders. The style is breezy, the action nicely paced. Younger children are a good read-aloud audience for the episodic adventures, but the occasional word-play is a bonus for the independent reader.

140   **Bonham,** Frank. *Chief.* Dutton, 1971. 215p. $4.50.

7–10   Although he was hereditary chief of his tribe (Santa Rosa Indians) and was called "Chief," Henry Crowfoot was too young to be treated as a leader. Anxious to do something to improve the tribe's lot, Chief is excited when a lawyer tells him that old papers show that valuable city property actually belongs to the tribe. The lawyer is a has-been, sneered at by the wealthy businessmen who fight the case, but he is helped by the medicine man of the tribe when he is near collapse, and he goes on to outwit the legal battery of the establishment. The author writes, as always, with empathetic candor, the Indian characters neither glamorized nor disparaged. Dialogue and characterization have vitality, the story line has suspense and pace, and the background of Chief's home, a parolee house, is drawn with conviction.

141   **Bonham,** Frank. *The Ghost Front.* Dutton, 1968. 223p. $4.50.

8—   A story of the Second World War, with no glorification of war but with a recognition of the accrual of thousands of acts of individual bravery that surmount the bungling and compensate for ineptitude. Tom and Andy Croft are twins who enlist at the age of eighteen, are separated in training camp and sent, separately, to the Ardennes front. Tom had always been the leader, the strong one, but by the time Andy met him again, the first tremendous thrust of the Battle of the Bulge had toughened both of them, and Andy knew that never again would he lean on his brother. The episodes of the book are based on historical events; the writing is mature, realistic, and candid, and the book filled with action.

142   **Bonham,** Frank. *Mystery of the Fat Cat;* illus. by Alvin Smith. Dutton, 1968. 160p. $3.95.

5–9   For years the authorities had been threatening to tear down the Dogtown Boys Club; for years the club had been waiting for a large bequest. A wealthy woman had designated the club as recipient of her fortune when her pet cat died. Now the cat was twenty-eight years old—so its caretaker said, but the boys didn't believe it and decided to investigate, since they suspected that he had substituted another cat so that he could enjoy a permanent job. Their unraveling of the mystery is believable and exciting. The characters are lively, the dialogue natural, and the inclusion of a backward child as a sympathetic—and contributing—character adds to the book's appeal.

143   **Bonsall,** Crosby Newell. *The Case of the Dumb Bells.* Harper, 1966. 64p. illus. (I Can Read Books) Trade ed. $1.95; Library ed. $2.19 net. (World's Work, 1967. 64p. £0.75.)

1–2   Another amusing book about the four friends whose adventures in the bond of brotherhood and the pursuit of mysteries have been enjoyed by beginning independent readers. Skinny installs some telephone sets, purchased in a junk shop; the expectable occurs, and the crossed wires result in parents in anguish because of doorbells that ring repeatedly when nobody is at the door. The illustrations show the small detectives in various poses of despair or triumph; a particularly amusing picture is one in which Wizard is baby-sitting, having climbed into the playpen with small twins. The writing is a vast improvement over Dick and Jane; although the print is large, the sentences short, and the vocabulary repetitive, there is no sense of halting contrivance. Both text and illustrations use, just slightly, exaggeration to stress humorous aspects.

144   **Bonsall,** Crosby Newell. *The Case of the Scaredy Cats.* Harper, 1971. 64p. illus. (I Can Read Books) Trade ed. $2.50; Library ed. $2.92 net.

1–2   The indomitable heroes of earlier Bonsall books are horrified when they find a bevy of girls established in their own "Private Eye" clubhouse. Girls get scared, they reason, and they cry, so the boys try to intimidate the girls—who fight back. The littlest one disappears, however, and both sexes unite in an Annie-hunt. Annie admits she was afraid of the boys, but the boys deny that *they* were scared. Left in possession of their clubhouse, the boys are jubilant, but a sign in the snow reminds them that "Girls are still as good as boys." Embattled girlhood (preschool division) scores a point in a slight, pleasant story with an interracial cast.

145   *A Book for Eleanor Farjeon;* A Tribute to Her Life and Work 1881–1965; with an introduction by Naomi Lewis; illus. by Edward Ardizzone. Walck, 1966. 184p. $3.95.

4–7   First published in England, a collection of stories (plus two poems and Rumer Godden's "Tea with Eleanor Farjeon") dedicated to the memory of one of England's greatest writers for children. The Ardizzone illustrations are delightful; the list of other contributors is impressive and alluring: Ainsworth, Avery, Clewes, Dillon, Lynch, Mayne, Norton, Reeves, Serraillier, Sutcliff, and Willard.

146   **Boorstin,** Daniel J. *The Landmark History of the American People;*
From Plymouth to Appomattox; illus. with prints and photographs.
Random House, 1968. 185p. $4.95.

5–9   The first volume of a two-part history, in an oversize book that
is profusely illustrated, printed in double columns, and
unorthodox in approach. It eschews the traditional cataloging of
names and dates, but looks at the beginning and growth of this
nation as a record of the settlers and their contributions, of the
cultural patterns that were peculiarly American, and at the effects
and countereffects of diffusion of patterns, of natural resources,
of geography, and of the human beings whose actions were
instrumental in shaping our history. Like the Gerald Johnson
trilogy (*America Is Born, America Grows Up, America Moves
Forward:* Morrow) this gives the reader a sense of the times:
it is not as vigorous in style, but is more comprehensive albeit
uneven in treatment. An index is appended, as is a long
bibliography which consists, unfortunately, only of the publisher's
books.

147   **Boorstin,** Daniel J. *The Landmark History of the American People;*
From Appomattox to the Moon. Random House, 1970. 192p.
illus. $4.95.

5–9   Volume 2 of a two-part history that takes a broad view of the
development of this country and of the American way of life.
Oversize, printed in double columns, and profusely illustrated,
the book deviates from the usual compilations of facts and dates
and discusses the people who influenced patterns of change, the
American Go-Getters, Boorstin calls them. These were the
energetic, ambitious, and inventive people who had come from
many lands and who built the economy, made reforms, contributed
to progress by their inventions, organized the farmers, built ever
faster means of communication. The emphasis is on movements,
regional patterns, national policies, and changing labor conditions
rather than on political or military minutiae. Stimulating in its
approach, informally written, and acutely perceptive, a lively
history of the United States by a distinguished historian. An
index is appended.

148   **Booth,** Esma Rideout. *The Village, the City, and the World.*
McKay, 1966. 282p. $4.95.

8—   A long novel, written with a dignified simplicity of style, that
describes the tension and turmoil of the Congo at the time of
independence and of the ensuing conflict in Katanga. Masongo
is a teacher in a village school; when he decides to teach in
Elizabethville his wife and children are pleased; since Masongo
is a Luba and his wife a Lunda, their children have divided
tribal loyalties. The fighting and the fear sharpen all hostilities;

both Masongo and Sara realize that it is better that their older children study in Europe if they can—and better if they themselves stay in the city—until time has healed the breach between the tribes. Sympathetic but not sentimental, a book that gives a good picture of the conflict between old and new as well as between the tribes; the characterization is excellent and the dialogue good.

149   **Borack,** Barbara. *Grandpa;* pictures by Ben Shecter. Harper, 1967. 32p. Trade ed. $3.50; Library ed. $3.79 net.

3–7   A charming monologue by a small girl, the tender and humorous
yrs.   illustrations reflecting the mood of the text. Marilyn describes her grandfather (who is all grandfathers) and their relationship and it is lovely all the way. An example of the style and of the relationship: "But no Grandpa." (This is the morning ritual when Marilyn is visiting.) "He is hiding on me. I always find him though because he hides in the same place every time."

150   **Borack,** Barbara. *Someone Small;* illus. by Anita Lobel. Harper, 1969. 32p. Trade ed. $3.50; Library ed. $3.79 net.

K–2   A tender but matter-of-fact look at some growing years in the life of a small girl. Life is already full (of possessions, satisfactions, and love) when a baby sister comes along to disrupt the pattern. The girl asks for a pet bird, and enjoys Fluffy but finds, as time goes by, that a sister is more responsive; in fact, in time, she is fun. And in the fulness of his time Fluffy dies. The little sisters bury him lovingly, then go on to play. Life changes. The lesson isn't punched at all, but quietly insinuates itself; the story is realistic and low-keyed, touched faintly with humor. The illustrations have the same ingenuous quality.

151   **Boston,** Lucy Maria. *Nothing Said;* illus. by Peter Boston. Harcourt, 1971. 64p. Trade ed. $3.50; Library ed. $3.54 net.

4–6   Captivating from the start ("I don't want to go to Aunt Maud," said Libby desperately. "I don't like her."), a story that moves from realism to fantasy for a brief and cunningly wrought moment. Libby is spared the visit to Aunt Maud and sent instead to stay with her mother's friend Julia. The relationship between the two is a grave acceptance and respect, and Libby is content with Julia's isolated house in the English countryside. She is curious about the small dryad figurines on the mantelpiece and half-imagines there are such creatures; when a tree crashes into the river during a storm, she finds a small dryad weeping and tenderly promises to find her another tree. The next day it seems a dream—but caught in her hairbrush is a long green hair. The writing is mature and sensitive, the story line taut, the atmosphere evocative.

152   **Boston,** Lucy Maria. *The Sea Egg;* illus. by Peter Boston. Harcourt, 1967. 94p. $2.75. (Faber, 1970. 94p. £0.25.)

4–6   Two small brothers, vacationing in Cornwall, are smitten by an egg-shaped stone and buy it from a souvenir seller. The sea egg, they call it, and it proves indeed to be an egg, hatching into a merry water creature. The boy triton accepts the children's friendship and leads them into some magical adventures and an intimacy with the sea and its inhabitants. The adults never know the secret; all through the wonderful summer the children live a private life. This is a remarkable blend of fantasy and realism, and a remarkable evocation of the sounds and sights and smells of the ocean shore.

153   **Bova,** Benjamin. *The Amazing Laser.* Westminster, 1972. 122p. illus. Trade ed. $4.95; Paper ed. $2.95.

7—   An exciting scientific phenomenon that has already been found to have myriad uses in diverse fields, and will certaiñly have many more applications, is described with restrained enthusiasm and a clarity that takes into account the minimal scientific knowledge of the average reader. Bova explains the functioning of light, the theories and research that have contributed to the present state of knowledge, and the current and potential uses of the various kinds of lasers. Although Stambler's *Revolution in Light: Lasers and Holography* gives more information about holography, both books cover substantially the same material; both are written lucidly, Bova's book being somewhat better organized. An index is appended.

154   **Bova,** Benjamin. *The Uses of Space;* illus. by George Giusti. Holt, 1965. 144p. Trade ed. $3.50; Library ed. $3.27 net.

8—   A very good discussion of the probable and possible benefits that may come from space science. The author gives a brief— but adequate—description of the history of space flight and the results already achieved from knowledge gained, such as weather information and improved worldwide communications. He discusses the problems of building, maintaining, and repairing satellites, space stations, lunar bases, et cetera. He describes each of the planets and their possible contribution to man's resources or store of knowledge; he discusses, finally, the military uses of space. The chapter on the moon envisions the possibility of colonization, but does not mention the possibility of competition. The writing is lucid, straightforward, and knowledgeable but not formal. Several tables of facts and an index are appended.

155   **Bova,** Benjamin. *The Weathermakers.* Holt, 1967. 250p. Trade ed. $3.95; Library ed. $3.59 net. (Dobson, 1969. 250p. £1.25.)

7–10   A very good science fiction story, with a tight plot and good pace. Jerry Thornton and his friend Ted Marrett, a meteorologist, have been working on a method of drought alleviation based on Ted's long range forecasting. Ted's former boss, head of the Weather Bureau's Climatology Division, attempts to block and sabotage their work, using the machinery of government agencies to bring the matter into Congressional hearings. When the team stops a hurricane, the day is won; the book closes with a brief epilogue in which the President announces the establishment of a United Nations Commission for Planetary Weather Control.

156   **Bradbury,** Bianca. *Andy's Mountain;* illus. by Robert MacLean. Houghton, 1969. 150p. $3.50.

5–7   Andy and Ellen's grandfather had hoped that his son would live on the family farm; since his death, Gramps had become adamant about giving up the property to the state. Work on the new highway had almost reached the farm, but Gramps refused to accept the official papers and threatened to guard his property with a gun. Grandma packed. Andy tried several ways to reach a compromise, but not until he enlisted the help of a family friend who was a lawyer did they find the solution: move the house to a favorite spot on the mountain. Brisk and convincing, the story gives a warm and lively picture of a cantankerous and determined old man and his loving but exasperated wife, and of the love and loyalty between Gramps and Andy.

157   **Bradbury,** Bianca. *The Loner;* illus. by John Gretzer. Houghton, 1970. 140p. $3.50.

5–7   His older brother Mal got along with everybody, always was sure of himself, seemed to be a natural at any sport he tried. No wonder twelve-year-old Jay resented Mal. Jay didn't really need money, but he was delighted when he got a job as a dockboy at the summer resort. Nobody missed him, since he was always alone anyway, and Jay kept his work a secret. As he gained confidence and made new friends through his job at the marina, Jay began to realize that Mal wasn't so bad. In fact, Jay didn't even mind when his newly-made friend, Eddie, suggested Mal might make a good third for their crew. The achievement of self-respect and a broader perspective evolve quite naturally from the events of the summer; the scale of action is modest, but the easy writing style, realistic incidents, and economic structure give the book vitality and verisimilitude.

158   **Bradbury,** Ray. *S Is for Space.* Doubleday, 1966. 238p. $3.95. (Hart-Davis, 1968. 239p. £1.05.)

6—   A collection of sixteen science fiction stories, written by Mr. Bradbury over the past twenty years; many of the tales were published originally in magazines. The author's writing style is smooth; he has an excellent ear for dialogue, and his stories are varied and imaginative in plot and setting.

159   **Bramblett,** Ella, comp. *Shoots of Green; Poems for Young Gardeners*; illus. by Ingrid Fetz. T. Y. Crowell, 1968. 117p. $3.75.

4–8   A charming collection of poems about plants and gardens, the sections moving from "Spring Is Coming" to "To Pop into the Pot," "Fires in the Fall," and "A Song of Seasons." The black and white illustrations are gentle and realistic, the calibre of the selections far above the usual mediocre-to-good assortment. The poetry is almost all simple, some humorous, much of it written by poets whose forte is writing for children, but some from poets whose work is for all ages. Some of the writers whose work is included: Frost, Dickinson, Blake, Keats, Farjeon, Shakespeare, Behn, Zolotow, Hughes, etc. First line and title indexes are appended.

160   **Branley,** Franklyn Mansfield. *The Christmas Sky*; illus. by Blair Lent. T. Y. Crowell, 1966. 40p. $3.75.

4–6   The text of this attractive book, with dignified format and with woodcut illustrations in subdued colors, is based on the Christmas lecture at the Hayden Planetarium, where the author directs the educational program. Mr. Branley discusses the Biblical, astronomical, and historical clues to the true date of the birth of Jesus; he describes some of the theories that have been held about the nature of the star of Bethlehem. The tone is reverent; the approach is scientific; the book is quietly impressive.

161   **Branley,** Franklyn Mansfield. *Man in Space to the Moon*; illus. by Louis S. Glanzman. T. Y. Crowell, 1970. 38p. $3.75.

4–6   Clear, straightforward writing and labeled diagrams explain each step of the historic flight of Apollo 11. Prefaced by a brief recapitulation of the history of flight (controlled or manned) in outer space, the book describes each step in the maneuvering of the parts of the spacecraft, the problems of living in free fall (how the crew handled eating, sleeping, disposing of waste products, etc.), the stages of the landing, exploration, and return to earth. A chart giving data about space flights and an index are appended.

162   **Branley,** Franklyn Mansfield. *The Mystery of Stonehenge*; illus. by Victor G. Ambrus. T. Y. Crowell, 1969. 52p. $3.95.

4–6   How long did men toil to build the still-impressive ring of massive stones on the Salisbury plain? How did they do it, and what was it for? Scientists can only conjecture, save for the time of building, now determined by carbon-14 dating to have been approximately

1800 B.C. The author discusses the various theories about the
ways in which primitive men might have made the stone pillars,
brought them to the site, and erected them. He describes the
tentative answers as to the reason for its existence: the possibility
that it had religious significance or was used for astronomical
observation. Fascinating material in a lucid, measured book, the
handsome illustrations making vivid the massive effort that went
into the building of Stonehenge.

163   **Branley,** Franklyn Mansfield. *Oxygen Keeps You Alive;* illus. by
Don Madden. T. Y. Crowell, 1971. 32p. $3.75.

2–3   Another good book in a fine series, *Oxygen Keeps You Alive* is
perfectly clear, simply told, and accurate. The illustrations amplify
the text, which describes how oxygen in the air we breathe
is carried throughout the body, how people who are not able to
get oxygen (astronauts who leave their ships, divers, climbers of
high mountains) must carry a supply, and how other life forms
(fish, plants) use oxygen. A few home demonstrations are
suggested to show that there is air in water and that boiling
removes that air.

164   **Brelis,** Nancy. *The Mummy Market.* Pictures by Ben Shecter.
Harper, 1966. 145p. Trade ed. $3.95; Library ed. $3.79 net.

5–6   An engaging and sophisticated fanciful story in which three
orphaned children go shopping for a mother, have been under
the care of a rigid housekeeper. An elderly neighbor, magically
wise, tells the children about a market where they may find a
mother: a guitar player, an outdoor health fiend, a motherly
mother who fusses and coos. The children try a few; they just
don't work out. Then they find the right mother, and they begin,
all four, planning their memories of the past. The book has some
enjoyable tongue-in-cheek sketches of Standard Types available at
the market; the concept of the story is deftly developed, the writing
style pleasant.

165   **Brenner,** Barbara. *A Year in the Life of Rosie Bernard;* illus. by
Joan Sandin. Harper, 1971. 179p. $3.95.

4–6   A story of the Depression Era, set in Brooklyn, where Rosie
Bernard is sent to stay with her dead mother's family. Daddy is an
actor, and he has had to go away to get work. The story has
vivid and convincing period details, but it is primarily about
Rosie's ebullient acceptance of life in a big family and in a new
school. When Daddy appears with a fiancee, Rosie runs away, but
she is too sensible and pliant to maintain her resentment long, and
her year ends with acceptance of the new situation. The story has
an easy flow and humor, a delightful protagonist, and an

understanding portrayal of an only child learning to love and be loved by her grandparents.

166   **Briggs,** Raymond. *Jim and the Beanstalk;* written and illus. by Raymond Briggs. Coward-McCann, 1970. 38p. Trade ed. $4.95; Library ed. $4.39 net. (H. Hamilton, 1970. 40p. £1.05.)

4–7 yrs.   A sprightly sequel to the original tale, illustrated alternately in black and white and in melting color. Jim sees a tall plant outside his window, an invitation to climbing. He goes up, meets a sad and aging giant who complains that some boy once came up and robbed his father. Ruthfully, Jim arranges to improve the giant's lot by getting him false teeth and spectacles. The delighted giant, now able to read the poetry he had missed, pays the boy and suggests Jim cut down the beanstalk (now that he can chew again) lest he be tempted to indulge once more in fried boys on toast. Silly and engaging, the story is enhanced by the humorous details of the illustrations: Jim staggering under a set of huge false teeth, for example, or the giant poring over *The Baby Giant's Bumper Fun Book.*

167   **Briggs,** Raymond. *The Mother Goose Treasury.* Coward-McCann, 1966. 220p. illus. Trade ed. $8.95; Library ed. $6.87 net. (H. Hamilton, 1966. 220p. £2.10.)

3–6 yrs.   A big, handsome book first published in Great Britain. The rhymes used are those of the Opie version; the illustrations are a joy, the double-page spreads alternately color or black and white. Most of the pages have several small drawings or paintings; occasionally there is a bold splash of full page or double-page color. The illustrations are varied in mood and treatment: some are delicate, some bold; some are gentle, some grotesque; many are humorous and all have a sense of fun and a vitality that is utterly enjoyable.

168   **Brindze,** Ruth. *Investing Money;* The Facts about Stocks and Bonds. Harcourt, 1968. 128p. illus. $3.75.

8—   Practicing what she preaches, the author does *not* give any tips on investing; what she does give is a solid base for understanding of how the market operates, what the risks and safeguards are and what an amateur investor should know about the several ways he can invest his money. Some of the topics discussed in separate chapters are the New York Stock Exchange, over-the-counter stocks, bonds, group investment, reports to stockholders, and reading the financial news, especially the tabulations of stock market transactions. Clear, informative, and thorough. A relative index is appended.

169   **Brock,** Betty. *No Flying in the House;* illus. by Wallace
         Tripp. Harper, 1970. 139p. Trade ed. $3.95; Library ed. $3.79 net.

2–4   A convincing and lively fantasy is smoothly incorporated into a
         realistic background, has interesting characters (and not too
         many of them) and is attractively illustrated. Into the home of a
         rich, elderly woman comes a tiny dog, three inches high, who
         announces that her name is Gloria and that she is willing to
         stay and do tricks if her ward Annabel can live there too.
         Annabel is a precocious three, and she finds that Gloria's arch
         enemy, a cat, is actually a fairy. So is Gloria, whose
         mission it is to protect Annabel, child of a fairy and a mortal.
         The ending has a sentimental note: Annabel, who is perfectly
         happy save for the fact that she wants a real father and mother,
         has her wish granted when her parents appear and she
         discovers that her hostess is in fact her grandmother.

170   **Brooks,** Lester. *Great Civilizations of Ancient Africa.* Four Winds,
         1971. 340p. illus. Trade ed. $6.95; Library ed. $6.11 net.

8—   A magnificently detailed and authoritative book that includes
         evidence from recent archeological discoveries, this reviews the
         history and achievements of a series of African settings. A chapter
         that surveys the past and what has been known—or ignored—is
         followed by the first intensive examination, "Black Egypt,"
         and the last such, a chapter on Ethiopia, is followed by a resume
         of events in other African cultures than those discussed in detail
         and a chapter on North Africa. Scholarly and lively, an informative
         and enthralling book. A time chart, a bibliography, and an index
         are appended.

171   **Brooks,** Polly Schoyer. *When the World Was Rome;* 753 B.C.
         to A.D. 476; by Polly Schoyer Brooks and Nancy Zinsser Walworth.
         Lippincott, 1972. 235p. illus. $6.95.

7–12   A history of Rome is told in painstaking detail and in conservative
         style, with emphasis on leaders and battles, intrigue and
         succession. There is no broad canvas here, but a series of
         meticulously researched studies: a great deal of attention is, for
         example, given to Galen and his work, and to the architecture
         of Pliny's summer estate, but little that describes the life
         of the common people or the Roman colonies. The book is
         written carefully; the captions for illustrations are less careful—
         the text refers, for example, to the hut of Romulus thus: "The
         foundations of a primitive mid-eighth-century dwelling—which
         may have been his—have been found by modern archeologists."
         The picture of a thatched hut, two pages earlier, is labelled,
         "The hut of Romulus." Solid, accurate, and informative, a boon
         to the lover of history. An extensive bibliography and an index
         are appended.

172   **Brooks,** Polly Schoyer. *The World of Walls;* The Middle Ages
        in Western Europe; by Polly Schoyer Brooks and Nancy Zinsser
        Walworth. Lippincott, 1966. 256p. illus. $6.95.

6–10   A broad picture of the Middle Ages is given through a series
        of biographies in three sections: the early, middle, and late
        Middle Ages; each section begins with some background material.
        The subjects are Gregory the Great, Charlemagne, William the
        Conqueror, Eleanor of Aquitaine, Richard the Lion Heart,
        St. Francis, Simon de Montfort, and Chaucer. The authors have
        carefully selected material that illustrates and exemplifies the
        feudal system, royal intrigue, the common man's role, the role
        of the church, and the invasion and plunder that typified the
        times. The writing is serious in tone, balanced in treatment,
        and objective in attitude. An excellent bibliography and an index
        are appended.

173   **Brown,** Marcia Joan. *Backbone of the King;* The Story of Paka'a
        and His Son Ku. Scribner, 1966. 180p. illus. Trade ed. $4.50;
        Library ed. $4.79 net.

5–7   A version of an epic story in Hawaiian folk literature, stately
        in pace and retold in a style that is appropriate for the hero
        tale. Paka'a is a man of high station: the friend, the advisor,
        the "backbone of the king." Loving and loyal, Paka'a sails away
        when he is discredited by two jealous courtiers; the major part
        of the tale describes the long effort made by Ku-a-Paka'a, son
        of Paka'a, to reinstate his father in his once-high place and to
        prove to the king how loyal and how proud is his friend.
        Slow-moving, but that seems, somehow, fitting for the quiet
        grace of the legend. The linoleum block illustrations are handsome;
        an extensive glossary is appended.

174   **Brown,** Michael. *Shackleton's Epic Voyage;* illus. by Raymond
        Briggs. Coward-McCann, 1969. 36p. $3.29. (H. Hamilton, 1969.
        40p. £0.75.)

4–6   First published in England, the true and exciting story of
        Shackleton's trip to South Georgia Island after his ship had
        foundered in the Antarctic seas. With twenty-seven men marooned
        on desolate Elephant Island, it was a choice between certain
        death and possible rescue—if a boat could reach the whaling
        settlement on the island of South Georgia and bring help.
        This is a detailed account of the grim voyage, through icy seas and
        mountainous waves, in a small boat manned by Shackleton and
        five other members of the expedition. The writing is direct
        and sober, with a minimum of dialogue, all of the color coming
        from the drama of the facts. The illustrations are powerful,
        even the repetitious pictures of the wild seas contributing to the
        sense of endless space and ever-looming danger.

175   **Brown,** Pamela. *The Other Side of the Street.* Follett, 1967.
186p. Trade ed. $3.50; Library ed. $3.69 net. (Brockhampton P.,
1965. 192p. £0.75.)

6–8   First published in England in 1965, the lively and appealing
story of a youngster who, although not at the head of her class,
does very well indeed on a television quiz show. Linda's
motive is unselfish greed: she wants money desperately, but
she wants it to buy a house for her mother. Looking across
the crowded London street, Mum had once said, "If I ever
won the pools, what I'd like to do would be to live on the
other side. In a house." Widowed, with four children, Mrs.
Knight seemed to have little chance of achieving that goal.
She did, but—realistically—it was not through Linda's efforts
but through a second marriage. Thirteen-year-old Linda tells
the story and it bounces with vitality; it is funny and honest,
touched with that particular quality shared by so many British
books for children—an acceptance of the child's personality as
distinctive without a usurpation of the adult's role and status.

176   **Browning,** Robert. *The Pied Piper of Hamelin;* illus. by C. Walter
Hodges. Coward, 1971. 28p. Trade ed. $5.95; Library ed. $4.97
net. (Chatto & Windus, 1971. 32p. £1.10.)

4–6   The story of the piper whose revenge for a broken promise
resulted in the disappearance of the children of Hamelin is
delightfully illustrated by Walter Hodges. His full-color pictures
are rich and authentic in detail, the faces varied and the
composition dramatic; many of the illustrations bubble with
humor and most of them are scenes of action.

177   **Brownmiller,** Susan. *Shirley Chisholm.* Doubleday, 1970. 139p.
illus. $3.50.

5–9   "Ladies and gentlemen . . . this is fighting Shirley Chisholm
coming through," she would begin her talk from the sound truck,
and on November 5, 1968 the answer came. She was the first
black woman elected to Congress. While it gives some background
on Shirley Chisholm's childhood, the book focuses primarily on
her initiation into New York politics and her vigorous
participation in the House of Representatives. Courageous,
outspoken, articulate, "Unbought and Unbossed" (her campaign
slogan), Mrs. Chisholm is an exciting subject, and her story is
competently told. A list of "Facts You Might Like to Know"
about the House of Representatives is appended.

178   **Bryson,** Bernarda. *Gilgamesh;* Man's First Story; written and illus.
by Bernarda Bryson. Holt, 1967. 111p. Trade ed. $4.95; Library
ed. $4.27 net.

6–9   An oversize book in which the text of the classic legend of
Mesopotamia is retold in a version that is quite well written,

although there are occasional textual phrases that seem awkwardly modern, especially phrases in dialogue. The illustrations are outstandingly lovely: some are precise pictures of temple interiors, others mystical, brooding pictures of the gods, and some are small ornamental details. They are varied, sensitive, and quite in accord both with the Sumerian setting and with the melange of romance, legend, and history that is the story of Gilgamesh.

179   **Buck,** Pearl (Sydenstricker). *Matthew, Mark, Luke and John;* illus. by Mamoru Funai. Day, 1967. 80p. Trade ed. $3.95; Library ed. $3.69 net.

4–6   A book that treats with dignity and sympathy the problem of the illegitimate war baby, a problem here compounded by the fact that the four boys are spurned because their fathers were American soldiers. They can never be accepted as Korean. So the children drift together; Matthew is the oldest and names the others because he has heard the names in a quotation. He teaches Mark Korean and learns English from him; he teaches Luke not to steal, and he sees to it that the younger boys are fed and clothed. When an American soldier adopts Matthew, having seen him at a children's party, a new life in the United States begins for the boy. He accepts his new parents and his new country, but he cannot forget Mark, Luke and John. His parents decide that a community meeting may bring action, so they appeal to their friends and neighbors, and the first steps are taken to adopt Matthew's charges in homes nearby. The ending is a little sugary, with Matthew singing for the first time (and at Christmas) but it isn't at all unbelievable, because all of the story has emphasized the fact that Matthew is an unusually responsible child.

180   **Buell,** Hal. *The World of Red China;* illus. with photographs. Dodd, 1967. 79p. Trade ed. $3.95; Library ed. $3.23 net.

5–7   A discussion of China today is preceded by a rather hasty overview of earlier Chinese history and a brief discussion of the peoples and the geography of the country. The author's preface makes it clear that his material has been obtained from secondary sources, but the text is objective and fairly comprehensive in describing the struggle between the Communists and the Kuomintang, the relations between China and other powers, and the changes that have taken place in Chinese life under the Communist regime. The photographs are of good quality but not always of great relevance to the text. A one-page index is appended.

181   **Bulla,** Clyde Robert. *More Stories of Favorite Operas;* illus. by Joseph Low. T. Y. Crowell, 1965. 309p. $4.50.

6–9   A companion volume to *Stories of Favorite Operas* (Crowell,

1959) in which twenty-three libretti were given in simplified, present-tense narrative form. Here Mr. Bulla adds another twenty-two operas, a volume devoted to the Niebelungenlied having been published separately; the condensations here are in past tense, simply written, and certainly useful. Each story is preceded by a paragraph of background; the book closes with cast lists for the operas and with an index.

182   **Bulla,** Clyde Robert. *Pocahontas and the Strangers;* illus. by Peter Burchard. T. Y. Crowell, 1971. 180p. Trade ed. $3.95; Library ed. $4.70 net.

3–5   The familiar story of the Indian princess who married John Rolfe is told very simply here, with more detail than is usually provided for middle grades readers; for example, the incident in which Pocahontas saves John Smith's life is given background and added credibility by the descriptions of her secret watching of the white men and by her discussions with an older woman about the Indian law that permitted the claiming of a prisoner. The story gets off to a slow start with an episode perhaps intended as symbolic, in which Pocahontas sets free an eagle that has been caught in a snare, but it moves briskly enough thereafter and gives a balanced and objective picture of the motivations and actions of the Indians and the white men.

183   **Bulla,** Clyde Robert. *White Bird;* illus. by Leonard Weisgard. T. Y. Crowell, 1966. 79p. $3.75. (Macdonald, 1969. 85p. £0.70.)

4–7   An unusual story from a prolific author: here Mr. Bulla's simple writing style becomes almost stark, echoing the book's mood of isolation and the taciturn dialogue. A foundling child, John Thomas, has been brought up by Luke, the young man who found him. Luke will not let John Thomas leave the valley where they live, and he will not let the boy see any other people; he even resents the fact that the boy has made a pet of a white bird. When some passing travelers appear, a chain of events leads to the boy's running away. Thus John Thomas learns that Luke has been wrong when he said there was no kindness in people; he learns that there is brother love, and he comes back to the harsh man who has, in his own way, given John Thomas all his love and protection.

184   **Burch,** Robert. *Queenie Peavy;* illus. by Jerry Lazare. Viking, 1966. 159p. Trade ed. $3.50; Library ed. $3.37 net.

6–9   A story of the depression era in rural Georgia. Queenie is big and tough, a troublemaker in school and a scrapping, rock-throwing hoyden out of school; she has home responsibilities because her mother works in a canning plant. Her father is in jail. Every time Queenie is taunted about this, she fights back; finally she gets into real trouble when she causes a boy to break his leg. After some talks with the principal and with a friendly judge, Queenie decides she ought to curb her temper and to be more cooperative; the first reactions are so rewarding that she turns over a new leaf. The writing has just a little of the dated Penrod-and-Sam flavor, but the book gives a convincing picture of the impact of hard times on a rural community. Queenie's father is paroled; bitter, he violates his parole by carrying a gun and is sent back to jail. This realistically brings home to Queenie the acid fact that her father's leaving jail won't solve her problems, but that she must solve them by herself. One pleasant aspect of the story is in Queenie's relationship with the children next door. Dover Corry is eight and his little sister five; they are Negro neighbors who are better off than Queenie's family, and the two children depend on Queenie for the peculiar kind of affection that is partly shown in child-like imaginative play and partly the protection of a girl who can take an adult role.

185   **Burch,** Robert. *Renfroe's Christmas;* illus. by Rocco Negri. Viking, 1968. 59p. Trade ed. $3.50; Library ed. $3.37 net.

3–5   A gentle Christmas story, too merry to be sentimental but touched with sentiment. Renfroe's sister Clara thought he was becoming selfish, and that bothered him. He'd bought a better knife for himself than for his brother—that was selfish; he'd let another boy play with his Christmas yo-yo, but wondered if he should have given it to him. His very best present was a pocket watch, and he very kindly let another boy handle it at the community Christmas party. Then Renfroe stopped. He looked back. The other boy was a retarded adolescent who was about to go into an institution . . . and Renfroe gave the boy his watch, "feeling better than he could ever remember." The family scenes are natural and lively, the story giving a particularly pleasant picture of a rural community's close-knit relationships.

186   **Burch,** Robert. *Simon and the Game of Chance;* illus. by Fermin Rocker. Viking, 1970. 128p. Trade ed. $4.50; Library ed. $4.13 net.

5–7   Simon is one of six children in a family ruled by a stern, tyrannical father who is against any kind of fun, and who is given to long lectures punctuated with Biblical quotations. When the mother of the family becomes mentally ill after the death of a child, it is Clarissa, the only girl, who runs the family. Simon is resentful when Clarissa becomes engaged and is filled with guilt when his wish that something would happen to prevent the marriage coincides with the death of his sister's fiance. The story, written with depth and perception, ends on an encouraging note: mother is home, Clarissa has recovered to an extent from her bereavement and has assured Simon that she understands how he felt, and father has made a few conciliatory gestures. The characterization and style of writing are polished, and if there is little development, it is perhaps the more realistic in a story that focuses on relationships within a family with problems rather than on action.

187   **Burchard,** Peter. *Bimby*. Coward-McCann, 1968. 91p. illus. $4.50.

4–6   Set on the Georgia coast just prior to the Civil War, the story of a crucial day in the life of a young slave. Bimby had never faced the inexorable cruelty of a slave's life until the day his friend, old Jesse, was killed; when the boy talked to his mother, he discovered that his father had died of the punishment he had received when he tried to escape. Knowing that she would never see Bimby again, his mother gave the boy information to help him run away, both of them realizing that life without freedom was empty. The author writes with gentle calm, letting the poignancy inherent in the story reach the reader through events rather than statement, the characters in their brief appearance making the same impact that one finds in the compressed action of the theater.

188   **Burchard,** Peter. *Stranded;* A Story of New York in 1875. Coward-McCann, 1967. 255p. $4.95.

7–10   A novel that gives a vivid picture of the corruption and violence of New York's fourth ward in the 1870's. Gavin MacInnes, when his ship was in port for the night, got into a tavern brawl and woke the next morning on the pavement; his ship was gone and he was stranded in New York. Drawn into the efficient toils of a powerful gang, Gavin learned of the vicious methods used to keep gang members under control: the arranged arrests, the paternal protection that masked bribery, the street fighting, and the power politics. Grim and convincing, the story has pace and color.

189   **Burningham,** John. *John Burningham's ABC*. Bobbs-Merrill, 1967. 52p. illus. $4.95. (Cape, 1964. 64p. £1.05.)

4–6   An alphabet book that follows the traditional format and uses
yrs.   many of the traditional words; "A /a/ apple" it begins. The lettering is particularly satisfying in design, white (with an exception) against a colored background. The facing pages are stunning: big, bold pictures, marvelous in the use of color and often humorous; some pages are cartoon-like, some representational.

190   **Burningham,** John. *Mr. Gumpy's Outing;* written and illus. by John Burningham. Holt, 1971. 30p. Trade ed. $4.95; Library ed. $4.59 net. (Cape, 1970. 32p. £1.05.)

4–7   A modest story, simply told and very pleasant to read aloud,
yrs.   the large print making the book attractive also to young

independent readers. Mr. Gumpy is about to go off for a boat ride and is asked by two children, a rabbit, a cat, a dog, and other animals if they may come. To each Mr. Gumpy says yes, if—if the children don't squabble, if the rabbit won't hop, if the cat won't chase the rabbit or the dog tease the cat, and so on. Of course each does exactly what Mr. Gumpy forbade, the boat tips over, and they all slog home for tea in friendly fashion. The illustrations have a peaceful charm, the humor is bland, the whole completely engaging. The book was awarded the Greenaway Medal, a second time for the author-artist.

191   **Burton,** Hester. *Beyond the Weir Bridge;* illus. by Victor G. Ambrus. T. Y. Crowell, 1970. 221p. $4.95. (Oxf. U.P., 1969. 188p. £ 0.90.)

7–10   First published in England under the title *Thomas.* Richard and Richenda had both lost their fathers in 1644, both having died in battle under Cromwell's flag. Yet the dear member of their childhood trio was a Royalist child, the shy and studious Thomas. Both boys grew up to love Richenda, but she saw only Thomas. And when the other two became Quakers, Richard was completely alienated, for it was well known that these Friends were a disloyal and rabid lot. It is not until Richard, who as a doctor has stayed in London to cope with plague victims, sees the dedication and altruism of Thomas, who feels God's call to come to London from the safety of the countryside, that he understands the Quaker credo. Thoroughly steeped in period detail, consistent in language and viewpoint, this is both a dramatic story and a vivid piece of historical writing.

192   **Burton,** Hester. *The Henchmans at Home;* illus. by Victor G. Ambrus. T. Y. Crowell, 1972. 182p. $4.50. (Oxf. U.P., 1970. 144p. £0.90.)

6–10   Set in a small Suffolk town in the 1890's, this is a delightful period piece comprising six related episodes in the lives of the three Henchman children, with each episode focusing on one of the three. Obstreperous Rob, the youngest, runs away from home when he is sent to his room on his birthday and, on another occasion, poses as a visitor from India when the guest's illness prevents her participation in a charity bazaar. Ellen cannot understand why a servant has been dismissed and only later finds that Etty has had a baby. William, the oldest, appreciates his father's skill when he goes with him to visit patients, and understands for the first time why it has been expected that he, too, would become a doctor. The writing has vitality and an easy flow, and the convincing period details and historical background are buttressed by the pervasiveness of Victorian attitudes and mores.

193   **Burton,** Hester. *In Spite of All Terror;* illus. by Victor G. Ambrus.
World, 1969. 203p. Trade ed. $3.95; Library ed. $3.91 net.
(Oxf. U.P., 1970. 160p. £0.30.)

6–9   A good story of wartime England. Liz, who could hardly remember
her mother and had been happy as her father's companion, had
lived, for three unhappy years after his death, with relatives.
Sent to the country when the raids on London began, Liz was
at first uncomfortable in the aristocratic home of the Breretons
but soon began to feel that they were her own family. She
went to London on the eve of Dunkirk, hoping to help—and
she did, realizing for the first time the anguish and havoc of
the Battle of Britain. The writing has vitality and conviction, the
characterization is excellent, and the small events of one girl's
situation stand out vividly against the dramatic background of the
period.

194   **Burton,** Hester. *No Beat of Drum;* illus. by Victor G. Ambrus.
World, 1967. 190p. Trade ed. $4.95; Library ed. $4.91 net.
(Oxf. U.P., 1966. 194p. £1.00.)

7–10   A fast-paced and colorful adventure story that begins in England
in 1829, when sixteen-year-old Joe Hinton was stunned by the
fact that the girl he loved was sentenced to seven years of
servitude in exile. In the winter of starvation that followed, many
of the villagers were deported at the slightest sign of unrest,
and Joe among others was sent to the penal colony of Van
Diemen's Land. After being treated as a chattel, Joe was fortunate
in finding a new master; he also found Mary, now married
and with a child; he married her after her husband's death,
and slowly, carefully, Joe and Mary began to build a home and a
heritage in the new land. The print is uncomfortably small, but
captured readers will undoubtedly forge on to the satisfying
conclusion.

195   **Burton,** Hester. *The Rebel;* illus. by Victor G. Ambrus. T. Y.
Crowell, 1972. 154p. $4.50. (Oxf. U.P., 1971. 136p. £0.90.)

6–9   The oldest of three orphaned children, Stephen was severely
censured by his uncle and guardian for his radical views, and
told to stay at Oxford rather than to air his opinions at home.
With a college friend, Stephen went off to France to breathe the
liberated air of the Revolution that was in process, was mistaken
for an aristocrat and imprisoned. Rescued, he agreed to become a
French agent, but when he returned to England he could not
bring himself to spy. Ill, he sought refuge at the home of a
former teacher and decided to become a teacher of the poor
children whose plight had so long angered him. The historical
details are vivid, the writing style vigorous, the characterization
sound. The minor threads of the plot (the affairs of Stephen's

sister and brother, a thwarted romance, etc.) are not as firmly
meshed as they are in most of Burton's stories, but this is still
superior to most historical fiction written for young people.

196   **Byars,** Betsy C. *Go and Hush the Baby;* illus. by Emily A.
McCully. Viking, 1971. 28p. Trade ed. $3.50; Library ed. $3.37 net.

2–5
yrs.

Just as he is about to leave the house, bat in hand, Will is
asked by his mother to pacify the baby. He performs and the
baby smiles, but as soon as Will leaves the crying resumes.
Play a game, mother suggests. Finally Will launches on a story that
quiets the baby and so intrigues the storyteller that he is surprised
when he loses his audience to a nursing bottle. "Well, I have
to play this game of baseball anyway," he announces as he
goes off. The pictures, very simple, have vitality and humor;
the story has little plot but enough action—and more than
enough affection—to make it appealing.

197   **Byars,** Betsy C. *The House of Wings;* illus. by Daniel Schwartz.
Viking, 1972. 142p. $4.95.

4–6

Sammy and his parents had stopped to see his grandfather
en route to Detroit, and the boy was stricken with dismay
when he woke to find his mother and father gone. "It just
came about naturally that you would be better off staying with
me," the old man said, since Sammy's parents were worried about
getting settled in their new home. Sammy hated the dilapidated
old house, hated the old man he thought was crazy. Geese
in the kitchen! An owl flying around the house! Angry and
frightened, the boy ran away, shouting defiantly, when his
grandfather found him, that it was all a lie. But Sammy began
to be interested despite himself when grandfather found a
wounded crane, and impressed when he saw the tender care
the old man gave the bird, and by the time the crane was
well, the boy had learned to love and appreciate his grandfather.
Convincing and effective, a gentle story that makes the developing
relationship warm and believable, and that speaks more eloquently
than a homily about the wild creatures about us.

198   **Byars,** Betsy C. *The Midnight Fox;* illus. by Ann Grifalconi.
Viking, 1968. 159p. Trade ed. $4.50; Library ed. $4.13 net.
(Faber, 1970. 136p. £1.00.)

4–6

For a boy who was nervous about animals, there was nothing
enticing about the prospect of two months on a farm with his
aunt and uncle; Tom was sent there because his parents were
going on a European bicycle trip. The last thing Tom expected
was to have an animal become the focus of his life, but he
was so caught by the grace and beauty of a black fox that he
took every opportunity to watch her and her cub. When his

uncle caught and penned the cub as bait for the mother, Tom
set it free, and found, to his warm delight, that his uncle and
aunt (of whose sensitivity he had seen little evidence) wholly
understood. The story is written with quick, quiet humor and
some delightful daydreaming sequences, both as convincingly the
product of a nine-year-old's pen as are the more serious episodes of
the main theme.

199   **Byars,** Betsy C. *The Summer of the Swans;* illus. by Ted CoConis.
Viking, 1970. 142p. Trade ed. $3.95; Library ed. $3.77 net.

5–7   "Charlie, I'll tell you something," Sara confided, "This has been
the worst summer of my life." Sara was fourteen, newly aware of her
big feet and hands, happy one moment and miserable the next,
thinking for the first time of her beloved small brother, Charlie, as
retarded, conscious of her older sister's femininity. Her deepest
scorn is reserved for Joe Melby, the boy who had taken Charlie's
prized watch. Yet when Charlie is lost, a frantic Sara accepts
Joe's offer to help hunt and is therefore doubly embarrassed
when she learns that Joe had had nothing to do with it except
to intervene and get the watch back to Charlie. They find the
child, and Joe invites Sara to a party in a poignant scene that
marks for her the end of total self-doubt. Like the swans she
has seen, Sara will move from awkward flight to the confidence
of being in her own element. The book has a fine balance in
relationships, some sharp characterization and interaction, good
dialogue, and only enough action to be a foil for the perceptive
development of a situation.

200   **Byfield,** Barbara Ninde. *The Haunted Spy;* written and illus. by
Barbara Ninde Byfield. Doubleday, 1969. 35p. $4.95.

3–5   Although this can be read aloud to younger children, and despite
the fact that it looks like a picture book, it should intrigue the
middle-grades reader from the first page. Weary of his life as a
spy (having to wear a trench coat when it wasn't raining and pinch-
ing his finger in the false bottom of his attache case) the writer
retires to a crumbling and remote castle. His idyllic, solitary
life is disturbed by ghostly noises; wearily he dons his raincoat and
other paraphernalia and tracks down the intruder. The end (he
complies with the ghost's wish that the castle be completed
and they become chums) is a let-down, but the concept is amusing,
the style light, and the illustrations amusingly detailed.

201   **Cagle,** Malcolm W. *Flying Ships;* Hovercraft and Hydrofoils.
Dodd, 1970. 142p. illus. $3.95.

6—   A very good survey of the invention, operation, construction,
and uses of the two kinds of vehicles for which an increasing
number of uses are emerging, especially interesting because of

industrial or medical adaptations. The diagrams are excellent (although they are not numbered, the text frequently refers to them by number) and the material well organized and comprehensive. The writing style is brisk. Some of the information is covered in *Transportation of Tomorrow* by Ross, but this is more detailed, discussing uses of hovercraft and hydrofoils for war, industry, sport, and transportation. The book also considers such peripheral problems as legal distinctions in applicable laws, insurance, the use of such craft to solve traffic problems, and the future of flying ships. A list of manufacturers of sporting air cushion vehicles or kits for building them, a glossary of terms, and an index are appended.

202

9—

Cain, Arthur H. *Young People and Crime.* Day, 1968. 155p. $4.95.

A psychologist writes directly to the young person, analyzing the reasons people turn to crime and discussing the problems of the criminal. Dr. Cain does not opt for acceptance of the status quo, but for channeling constructively one's disagreement. With empathetic calm, he considers the frustrations and restlessness that beget drug addiction, prostitution, and the whole spectrum of criminal acts. His dispassionate logic is convincing; his attitude is realistic but not defeatist. A list of suggested readings is appended.

203

K–3

Calhoun, Mary (Huiskamp). *The Pixy and the Lazy Housewife;* illus. by Janet McCaffery. Morrow, 1969. 30p. Trade ed. $3.95; Library ed. $3.78 net.

Legend has it that the household pixies of Devon are hard workers but cunning in their teasing. So, at least, Old Bess found them when she trapped some to help her with her work, for Bess was the laziest woman there was, and the most slovenly. Outwitted by the pixies, Bess was tormented and punished until she changed her lazy ways. The tale is told in folk style, effective for reading aloud and good for storytelling. The writing has gusto and humor; the illustrations have an antic note.

204

5–8

Cameron, Eleanor. *A Room Made of Windows;* illus. by Trina Schart Hyman. Atlantic-Little, Brown, 1971. 271p. $5.95.

Julia's room was at the top of an old, rambling house in which there also lived an old man who loved, as she did, to write. His death came as a blow to her at a time when she was already upset by her mother's plans to remarry and by the mysterious unhappiness of the recluse next door. The book has several minor plots, but they are skillfully woven together in a solid and mature approach to the development of an adolescent's growing understanding. Julia, self-centered and sensitive, responds to the needs of others with increasing perception.

The characters are firmly delineated, the dialogue and interrelationships deftly conceived.

205   **Campbell,** Hope. *Why Not Join the Giraffes?* Norton, 1968. 223p. Trade ed. $3.75; Library ed. $3.48 net.

7–10   An entertaining novel for girls, not without a crisp comment on conformity. While other adolescents rebel against conservative parents, Suzie Henderson grieves because her mother and father are slightly beat, and her inclination toward conservatism is catapulted into action when she meets Ralph. Ralph's parents are not only conservative, they are stuffy; Suzie gets into trouble when one lie—made in an effort to impress Ralph—grows into a web of falsehood. In the end, Suzie finds that Ralph is more impressed with the honesty and candor of her parents than with the false values of his. The Giraffes are a combo, and to Suzie a symbol of the beatnik world she abjures. Good style, good dialogue, and good humor, despite the acid portrait of Ralph's parents.

206   **Campbell,** Peter. *Harry's Bee.* Bobbs-Merrill, 1971. 24p. illus. $4.95. (Methuen, 1969. 24p. £0.75.)

4–7 yrs.   Harry was delighted with the bee on his rosebush—it certainly was the biggest bee in England. The bee was delighted with the tastiness of the rosebush, and he returned for more. And that's how. Harry and the bee became friends and decided to travel together. Wherever they went, people gave them a wide berth, and on trains they usually had a compartment to themselves. Conscious of his status, the bee thought he should be seen by the chief bee-keeper of England; since there wasn't one, the friends tried the Prime Minister. No entry. Finally a museum director showed interest and measured the bee. Not the biggest bee in England, he said, the biggest bee in the world! Happy, the bee and Harry went home. The story is blandly and simply written, with a direct style and a quiet humor that are a good foil for the nonsensical situation.

207   **Carle,** Eric. *Do You Want to Be My Friend?* T. Y. Crowell, 1971. 29p. illus. $4.50. (H. Hamilton, 1971. 32p. £1.25.)

2–4 yrs.   A picture book with only a few words at the beginning, and a single word at the end. A small mouse asks the title question as he approaches the tail of a large creature; turn the page and there is a horse busily munching grass—but there, across the page, is a long green tail. Turn the page and there is an alligator. And so on . . . until another little mouse says, "Yes," and the two cuddle happily in a tree as the last long tail unwinds and proves to be a snake. The idea is not new, but it is nicely executed, and small children can enjoy the fun of guessing what's on the next page. The illustrations, bold against white space, are reminiscent of Munari's in composition and humor.

208   **Carlson,** Natalie Savage. *The Half Sisters;* illus. by Thomas de Grazia. Harper, 1970. 163p. Trade ed. $3.95; Library ed. $3.79 net.

4–6   Set on a Maryland farm in 1915, a delightful family story about six sisters. The three oldest, as eleven-year-old Luvvy impatiently explained to Little Maudie, were Papa's; she, Maudie, and baby Marylou were truly Mama's. What Luvvy wanted most in the world was to grow out of being one of "the children" and be accepted as one of "the girls." If only she could join them at the convent school in the autumn! Summer brings Luvvy's twelfth birthday and a chance to prove that she is old enough to go along with the girls when they return to school. The mood of the story is warm and quiet, although Luvvy is a forceful character. The book is permeated with family love, the writing is smooth, the pace sustained, and the dialogue natural.

209   **Carlson,** Natalie Savage. *Luvvy and the Girls;* illus. by Thomas di Grazia. Harper, 1971. 159p. Trade ed. $3.95; Library ed. $3.79 net.

3–6   A sequel to *The Half Sisters,* in which Luvvy Savage had, as so many middle children do, a goal of being accepted as one of the older group, "the Girls," by being allowed to go away to school with them. Now she is a pupil at Visitation Academy, and Luvvy goes through a period of adjustment to the propriety of boarding school life fifty years ago. As the Reverend Mother pointed out, Luvvy's grandmother would *never* have performed on a trapeze! By the end of the year, Luvvy had found her place in the group and had learned to tolerate even the most irritatingly saintly girl in class. Episodic, the story has warmth and humor, an easy style, and a vivid evocation of period and place.

210   **Cartey,** Wilfred. *The West Indies;* Islands in the Sun. Nelson, 1967. 224p. illus. Trade ed. $4.95; Library ed. $4.65 net.

6–10   Well-written and quite profusely illustrated with photographs, this is an interesting, informative, and astute book on the islands of the Caribbean. The author, a Jamaican, describes the lands, and peoples, and their histories; of even greater importance is his discussion of the economic history of the islands, and their present need for economic independence. A bibliography, a list of important dates, and an index are appended.

211   **Case,** Marshal T. *Look What I Found!* written and photographed by Marshal T. Case; illus. by Mary Lee Herbster. Chatham/ Viking, 1971. 95p. $4.95.

4–6   A discussion of all kinds of wild animal life that can be captured or bought and kept either as pets or for study purposes, with safety warnings to the reader and repeated adjurations about safety precautions on behalf of the animal forms. These include amphibians, reptiles, baby birds (recommended only when they are found out of the nest and after making sure that they have been abandoned or are injured), insects, small mammals, small marine life forms, and animals from pet shops. Instruction on feeding, housing, physical care, and precautions are given, with suggestions for duplication, insofar as is possible, of the natural habitat. There is little here that is not to be found in other pet books, but this is a good compendium and particularly careful in stressing respect for the creatures it discusses. A bibliography and an index are appended.

212   **Catherall,** Arthur. *Lapland Outlaw;* illus. by Simon Jeruchim. Lothrop, 1966. 160p. Trade ed. $3.95; Library ed. $3.78 net. (Dent, 1966. 160p. £0.50.)

7–9   A quite engrossing story set in Finnish Lapland, a tale with an unusual and tightly constructed plot, a fascinating picture of the reindeer-centered culture, and a vivid evocation of the bleak vastnesses of the far north. Sure that his hospitalized father is being deceived by a reindeer trader, sixteen-year-old Johani Sarris runs away with the cattle. With his young sister and an old herdsman, Johani escapes the police more than once. Caught, the outlaw is relieved to find his sins forgiven, since his family had indeed been cheated; the bill of sale had been altered from thirty to three hundred reindeer.

213   **Caudill,** Rebecca. *Come Along!* illus. by Ellen Raskin. Holt, 1969. 31p. Trade ed. $3.95; Library ed. $3.59 net.

2–4   Haiku through the year: direct and simple, the poems capture the brief and compact moments of delight in the natural beauty of the seasons, of flora and fauna, and the moods of weather. The illustrations, strong but never harsh, show a small girl and a still smaller boy gazing at golden forsythia, a leaping gleam of scarlet fish, the pristine iciness of winter boughs. Although there are some words and concepts that impose a challenge, most of the poems can be read to children even younger than the independent reader.

214   **Caudill,** Rebecca. *Contrary Jenkins;* by Rebecca Caudill and James Ayars; illus. by Glen Rounds. Holt, 1969. 34p. Trade ed. $3.50; Library ed. $3.27 net.

K–3   Vigorous, comic illustrations capture the obdurate bravado of Ebenezer Jenkins, called Contrary, in a charming tall tale for the read-aloud audience. "Too bad you're in such a big hurry," called Dan'l, as Contrary set off to see his brother in Kentucky. So, of course, Contrary stopped off for dinner and stayed almost three years. His various adventures are hilarious, and the writing style has the true storyteller's cadence and rhythm.

215   **Caudill,** Rebecca. *Did You Carry the Flag Today, Charley?* illus. by Nancy Grossman. Holt, 1966. 95p. Trade ed. $3.50; Library ed. $3.27 net.

K–2   A read-aloud story about a small and lively boy, just turned five, who has his first encounter with the necessary strictures of the classroom at a summer school in Appalachia. Charley, obstreperous youngest in a family of ten, is given a full picture of the joys and the responsibilities he will encounter; his brothers and sisters tell him that one child "who has been specially good that day" has the honor of carrying the flag at the head of the line to the bus. They ask everyday, but they hardly expect Charley to carry the flag, since he has an affinity for trouble, usually emanating from curiosity. He does, of course, carry the flag in the last episode. This is a realistic and low-keyed story with good dialogue, although Charley seems precocious, and excellent classroom scenes. Indeed, the teaching staff is almost too good to be true; they are patient, understanding, firm, tactful, and wise. It may paint a too-rosy picture for the child who is about to start school, but it's an encouraging picture. The one slightly contrived note in the story is in the family reception for Charley each day; the most appealing aspect is in the perfectly believable way in which a free spirit like Charley learns to adapt to a new pattern. He is neither pushed nor coerced into obedience; he is not asked to conform beyond the need to avoid classroom disruption; he is simply led to a desire to learn, guided by a teacher who is wise enough to channel his energy and who has taken the time to learn his interests.

216   **Caufield,** Don. *The Incredible Detectives;* by Don and Joan Caufield; pictures by Kiyo Komoda. Harper, 1966. 76p. Trade ed. $2.95; Library ed. $3.27 net.

4–6   A good middle-grades mystery story, larded with humor, that deftly mingles fanciful and realistic elements. When young Davy is kidnapped while visiting a museum, his parents receive a threatening letter. The family's three animals decide that the police are bungling the job and that they must take matters into their own hands. The three track down the kidnappers and—after creating a mild commotion at the museum—rescue Davy. The animals talk to each other, but not to humans; they have personalities but they are drawn as caricatures, not as people. Perhaps the aspect of the story that most contributes to its success as a fantasy is the consistency with which the animals' deeds (as opposed to their words) are kept within the bounds of credibility.

217   **Chaffin,** Lillie D. *John Henry McCoy;* illus. by Emanuel Schongut. Macmillan, 1971. 169p. $4.95.

4–6   A sensitive story of Appalachia, with a vivid evocation of locale and speech-patterns. John Henry's father had moved his family back and forth from city to country as he was hired and fired; now Daddy is working in Columbus, trying to find a place for them to live. John Henry loves the Kentucky countryside and wants to stay—indeed his greatest yearning is to stay in one place, to make and keep friends, to go to one school, to "put down roots," as Granny says. It is these two, John Henry and Granny, who take the initiative in changing the family pattern and who find a home that holds them all and that perhaps Daddy will come to—and stay. The pace of the story is sedate, but it suits the resigned, day-to-day existence of the McCoys; the characters ring true, and the book gives a good picture of the plight of the Southern Appalachian worker without being a treatise in disguise. Not a story filled with excitement, this has a depth and tenderness that are appealing.

218   **Chalmers,** Mary. *Be Good, Harry;* story and pictures by Mary Chalmers. Harper, 1967. 32p. Trade ed. $1.95; Library ed. $2.57 net.

3–6   The appealing kitten of *Throw a Kiss, Harry* and *Take a Nap,*
yrs.   *Harry* has a new experience. Mother is going to visit a sick friend, and Harry is taken over to stay with Mrs. Brewster, an elderly cat. Fortified by a wagon full of toys, Harry sobs briefly and accepts the status quo; the status quo consists of being fed cookies, being cuddled and read to, and having Mrs. Brewster soothe her visitor with praise and appreciative laughter. Mother returns, Harry packs up his belongings, and they go back home. The illustrations have a gentle affection; the story and the pictures are beautifully matched in their understatement.

219   **Chambers,** Bradford. *Chronicles of Negro Protest;* A Background Book for Young People Documenting the History of Black Power; comp. and ed. with a commentary by Bradford Chambers. Parents' Magazine, 1968. 317p. illus. Trade ed. $4.50; Library ed. $3.75 net.

7—   A compilation of forty-two documents in the history of black power, chronologically arranged and each preceded by informative notes about the document's background or that of its author or authors; some of the selections are followed by a post-script that describes contemporary reaction to the document. The editor's thesis is that prejudice developed not as a result of the Afri-can's helplessness in the face of white exploitation as a thing apart, but that white men have always hated black men because of their color. Somber and significant, this places the black man's protest in a sociological framework that may make the intricacies of today's problems more comprehensible. A list of documentary sources and an index are appended.

220 **Charosh,** Mannis. *Straight Lines, Parallel Lines, Perpendicular Lines;* illus. by Enrico Arno. T. Y. Crowell, 1970. 33p. $3.75.

3–4 One of a new series of mathematics books for the young, each volume examining basic ideas and demonstrating patterns and relationships. Using string, a checker set and board, pencil, and paper, the reader can follow suggestions for investigating straight, parallel, and perpendicular lines. The text, brisk and straightforward, also points out some of the familiar objects that illustrate these phenomena: the edge of the table, the corner of a rug, the opposite sides of a blackboard. The illustrations, like the print, are large and clear, with good correlation between pictures and text.

221 **Chase,** Alice Elizabeth. *Looking at Art.* T. Y. Crowell, 1966. 119p. illus. $4.50.

7— An excellent book for the novice. The author, an art historian, describes the ways in which artists have seen and interpreted such broad areas of their work as people and space, the human figure, or landscape. Perhaps the most valuable aspect of the book is the discussion, in the first chapter, of what art is; the author's views are explicit, lucidly presented, and widely expanded in succeeding chapters. The reproductions of works of art are of good quality (chiefly in black and white) and they are placed well in relation to the text. An index, with italics denoting entries of illustrations, is appended.

222 **Chase,** Mary. *The Wicked Pigeon Ladies in the Garden;* illus. by Don Bolognese. Knopf, 1968. 115p. $3.95.

4–6 A highly original fanciful story, the macabre characters of the pigeon ladies nicely balanced by the light touch of a leprechaun and by the realistic character of Maureen, the protagonist. Maureen is an enfante terrible, and she disobeys her father by going into an old, empty house; there she finds (and unfortunately makes enemies of) the seven unpleasant sisters who can turn themselves into pigeons and can either trap Maureen in their past or move into her present. These are the most delightfully malignant ghosts to appear in many a book, and their chastening effect on the termagant Maureen is deftly convincing.

223 **Chase,** Stuart. *Danger—Men Talking!* A Background Book on Semantics and Communication. Parents' Magazine, 1969. 215p. Trade ed. $4.50; Library ed. $4.12 net.

7–12 As he has before, the author writes with profound perspective about the tyranny of words. Much of what he says will be

familiar to readers of his adult books, and the comments
here have a patchwork effect, but what is said is topical, lucid,
and of tremendous importance for the young reader. The reasoned
arguments are spiced with humor and flavored with quite
subjective and impassioned opinions about the wasteland of
television, the madness of war, et cetera. The author discusses
human speech and semantics, techniques of improving
communication in human dialogue, communication in the learning
process, facts and opinions, group therapy, and many ancillary
topics. An excellent annotated bibliography and an index are
appended.

224   **Chekhov,** Anton. *Shadows and Light;* selected and tr. by Miriam
Morton; illus. by Ann Grifalconi. Doubleday, 1968. 122p. $2.95.

6—   Nine stories, skilfully translated, varied in subject and mood,
unvaried in excellence. "Van'ka" is a most touching story about
a nine-year-old boy, newly apprenticed and away from home,
writing a letter on Christmas Eve; "The Evildoer" is the hilarious
dialogue between a magistrate and a peasant so stupid and
stubborn that he carries the day by his very obtuseness. Several
tales are about animals, several about children.

225   **Chenery,** Janet. *Wolfie;* illus. by Marc Simont. Harper, 1969.
64p. (I Can Read Books) Trade ed. $2.50; Library ed. $2.57 net.
(World's Work, 1970. 64p. £0.75.)

1–3   Engagingly illustrated, a good first science book in which the
story and the information about spiders are smoothly integrated
save for some rather obtrusively informational dialogue with an
adult. The style is light and humorous, the facts accurate, the
illustrations perky. Harry and George zealously guard their pet
from the interfering advances of a little sister; Harry tells Polly
that she can see Wolfie (a wolf spider) if she brings him a
hundred flies. The boys learn about spiders and about how to
take care of Wolfie from a worker at the Nature Center; going
out one dark night to give Wolfie some water, Harry finds
Polly, also visiting Wolfie, a consolation. Next morning Polly is
thrilled by permission, at last, to feed Wolfie.

226   **Cheney,** Cora. *The Incredible Deborah;* a story based on the life of
Deborah Sampson. Scribner, 1967. 203p. illus. Trade ed. $3.95;
Library ed. $3.63 net.

6–9   A lively biography of the Massachusetts girl who became a soldier
during the Revolutionary War. Deborah was twenty-one,
intelligent, restless, and curious about life; she also was an ardent
patriot. Not until she fell ill was Deborah's sex discovered; she
had even managed to escape medical attention when wounded
while a member of a raiding party. Deborah left her husband

and children, in later years, to lecture on her experiences and, in 1805, was granted a pension as an invalid soldier. The story is exciting, the writing crisp and straightforward. A bibliography is appended.

227   **Child Study Association of America.** *Brothers and Sisters Are Like That!* illus. by Michael Hampshire. T. Y. Crowell, 1971. 131p. Trade ed. $3.95; Library ed. $4.70 net.

2–4   Ten stories are included in this pleasant anthology, each the entire text of a short book for the beginning reader. Some of the stories included are Elizabeth Hill's *Evan's Corner*, Charlotte Zolotow's *Big Sister and Little Sister*, and Grace Berquist's *The Boy Who Couldn't Roar.* As the title indicates, the binding theme is sibling relationship; the children are Indian, Japanese, black and white; each tale ends on a note of acceptance if not affection. A useful compilation of easy-to-read stories that can also be read aloud to younger children.

228   **Child Study Association of America,** comp. *Round about the City; Stories You Can Read to Yourself;* illus. by Harper Johnson. T. Y. Crowell, 1966. 117p. $2.95.

2–4   A compilation of stories set in an urban environment; two are printed for the first time, and the other selections are books or excerpts from books already published. The illustrations are realistic but humorless; the print is large; the selections excellent fare for the independent reader in primary grades. The ten stories are: "Wake Up, City, " "Hurray for Bobo," "Saturday Surprise," "Nobody Listens to Andrew," "Olaf Reads," "How to Find a Friend," "Show and Tell," "Betsy and Ellen Go to Market," "A Tulip for Tony," and "Meet Miki Takino."

229   **Christopher,** John. *Beyond the Burning Lands.* Macmillan, 1971. 170p. $4.95. (H. Hamilton, 1972. £1.25.)

6–9   Second in a trilogy that began with *The Prince in Waiting,* this continues the story of Luke, who is destined to become ruler of a city-state in an England returned to feudalism and abjuring all technology. Luke has learned that there is a nucleus of men, the Seers, who have access to all the knowledge and machines of the past and now they send him from their sanctuary, back to his home. Luke goes on a quest to the land beyond the still-smouldering volcanic plains that divide the country, and there wins a beautiful princess and becomes a hero when he slays a monster; he returns home to fulfill the prophecy and become a Prince. The setting is wholly conceived, the story well paced and full of action, and the book is given depth by the subtle— and at times not so subtle—ways in which Christopher mocks the frailties of our own society.

230   **Christopher,** John. *The City of Gold and Lead.* Macmillan, 1967.
185p. $4.95. (Brockhampton P., 1970. £0.25.)

6–9   The second book in this science fiction trilogy is just as effective
as was the first, *The White Mountains.* Here Will, who had
taken refuge in the mountains where the few still-free people in
the world dwelt, has been trained to compete in an athletic
contest. If he wins, he will be chosen to serve the Masters of
the world, the mysterious beings who control humans by capping
their heads with steel mesh. Will does win, and he goes with
the other victors to serve as slaves to the Masters; the others
go in a spirit of sacrifice, Will as a spy. He serves, he learns,
and he escapes as the story ends. The concept of the world of
the Masters is beautifully developed, a whole alien culture grafted
onto the submissive remnants of mankind in the world of the
future; the story is kept within a tight framework, and the suspense
is masterfully maintained.

231   **Christopher,** John. *The Prince in Waiting.* Macmillan, 1970. 182p.
$4.95. (H. Hamilton, 1970. 160p. £1.25.)

6–9   Like the taut and suspenseful science fiction story, *The White
Mountains,* this is the first of a trilogy, a book that stands alone
but whets the reader's appetite for volume two. It has a familiar
theme in science fiction, man's destruction of his own civilization.
Here the setting is England after the debacle, and Luke, who is
destined to become a ruler of a city-state in a society in which
machines and technology are anathema, learns that there is a secret
society of Seers, a superbody with headquarters in an underground
sanctuary. Here Luke finds a cache of all the marvelous inventions
of the old days, and he is told that the Seers will strike—when the
time comes. Style, dialogue, and characterization are good although
not outstanding; the strongest qualities of the book are the
wholly conceived setting and the well-paced and well-constructed
plot.

232   **Christopher,** John. *The Sword of the Spirits.* Macmillan, 1972.
162p. $4.95. (H. Hamilton, 1972. £1.40.)

6–9   Third in a science fiction trilogy (*The Prince in Waiting* and *Beyond
the Burning Lands* were the first two) this is the continuing
story of Luke, Prince of Three Cities in an England reverted to a
feudal, anti-technological society. Exiled after a mutiny among his
captains, Luke marshals an army and becomes a hero and a stiff,
proud and lonely man; he brings some of the long-hidden
machines back into acceptance and use, and he reinstitutes
general education, but he knows that there are still other wars
ahead. So the book ends on a note that is hopeful for the society
and resigned for Luke, who tells the story. Vividly conceived,
occasionally heavy in style, but dramatic in concept and
development.

233   **Christopher,** John. *The White Mountains*. Macmillan, 1967. 184p.
            $4.95. (Brockhampton P., 1970. £0.25.)

6–9   A science fantasy based on the familiar theme of a world
            controlled by robots, a world in which the young protagonists find
            traces of our present culture; planned as a first story about the
            Tripods, the book is slightly weak in having an inconclusive
            ending, but the writing is imaginative enough to more than
            compensate for this. The plot develops with sustained pace, as
            three boys of the future world make their hazardous way to the
            White Mountains—Switzerland—wherein exists the only colony of
            men who are free of the dreaded Tripods, the machines that rule
            the world by implanting steel controls on men's brains.

234   **Chubb,** Thomas Caldecot. *The Venetians;* Merchant Princes.
            Viking, 1968. 162p. illus. Trade ed. $6.95; Library ed. $6.43 net.

7—   A detailed history of the founding and the intricately eventful
            development of the small colony of muddy islands that became
            one of the great city-states of the western world, a commercial
            power, and a stronghold of wealth and the cultural amenities
            wealth provides. The career of a fourteenth-century merchant is
            followed to exemplify and dramatize the potency of the Venetian
            Empire. Inevitably the discovery of new trade routes sapped that
            potency and the city, weakened, was buffeted about in the turmoil
            of the European power struggle. A few paintings and maps are
            included; a bibliography is appended, as is a list of suggestions for
            further reading.

235   **Chute,** Marchette Gaylord. *The Green Tree of Democracy*. Dutton,
            1971. 197p. $4.95.

7–10   An excellent history of the franchise in America, from the first
            democratic representation in colonial times, with the
            establishment of representative governments empowered to make
            laws and levy taxes, to the extension, in 1970, of the franchise
            that gave eighteen-year-olds the right to vote. The major portion
            of the book is devoted to developments before 1850. Smoothly
            written and fully documented, with sources cited for all quoted
            material, objective in tone, this is a book interesting in itself
            and most useful as supplementary curricular material. An index
            is appended.

236   **Chwast,** Seymour. *Still Another Number Book;* by Seymour Chwast
            and Martin Stephen Moskof. McGraw-Hill, 1971. 59p. illus. Trade
            ed. $4.95; Library ed. $4.72 net.

4–6   Gay, silly illustrations add appeal to an imaginative introduction
yrs.   to numbers one to ten. There is no cumulation of objects on
            each page, save for a recapitulation at the back of the book.
            Instead, there is one page used for the number one, two for two,
            et cetera. A child and another child: $1 + 1 = 2$. Five dogs:

$1 + 1 + 1 + 1 + 1 = 5$, and on the five pages, dogs of varied and peculiar mien appear. The new number is introduced each time almost as an appendage to its predecessor: the first of eight birds is sitting on a branch of the tree that holds the seventh of seven houses. Inventive, attractive, and amusing.

237   **Clapp,** Patricia. *Constance;* A Story of Early Plymouth. Lothrop, 1968. 255p. Trade ed. $4.95; Library ed. $4.59 net.

7–10   Probably the best colonial story for girls since *The Witch of Blackbird Pond,* this journal of a young girl is based on the life of an ancestress of the author. Constance describes the grim first winter at Plymouth with its many deaths, the colonists' relations with the Indians, the struggles with the English backers of the colony, and her own family life. The story ends with her marriage in 1626. The characters come alive, the writing style is excellent, and the historical background is smoothly integrated.

238   **Clark,** Ann (Nolan). *Circle of Seasons;* illus. by W. T. Mars. Farrar, 1970. 113p. $3.95.

5–9   In dignified and reverent style, a description of the rites and observances of the Pueblo year begins with the transfer of authority from the Sun Chief, who guards the days of the summer for his people, to the Winter Chief. The People isolate themselves for the Day of the Dead, and soon thereafter celebrate the Fiesta Mass before the advent of the long winter months. Christmas is celebrated with dances that were old before Christ's birth; so through the year the Pueblo Indians merge old and new customs. Solemn as the writing is, it has a poetic quality, and the book portrays evocatively the gentle, harmonious life of the Pueblos, encroached on by the pressures of the white man's civilization yet maintaining its deferential rapport with the phenomena of nature.

239   **Clark,** Electa. *Cherokee Chief;* The Life of John Ross; illus. by John Wagner. Crowell-Collier, 1970. 118p. $3.95.

5–9   John Ross, who fought in the War of 1812, was a man whose Scottish ancestors had married into the Cherokee Nation and whose probity and integrity earned him the respect of many white statesmen as well as the leadership of the people of his tribe. This is a long record of the duplicity and persecution of the Cherokee people, of the schism within the tribe, of the harrowing eviction and forced march during which four thousand of the eighteen thousand who were sent to the Indian Territory died. A dramatic and tragic story, this is bluntly written; although John Ross is depicted as a strong character he is not vividly portrayed as a personality. The book is, nevertheless, a stirring documentary of historical value. A bibliography and an index are appended.

240   **Clarke,** Clorinda. *The American Revolution 1775–83;* A British View; contemporary drawings and engravings illus. by H. Toothill and H. S. Whithorne. McGraw-Hill, 1967. 64p. $3.50. (Longman, 100p. £ 0.25.)

5–9   First published in England in 1964, this non-partisan history has a judicious, long-range view and a lively, straightforward style. The author covers the major figures, British and Colonial, Patriot and Tory, and the important campaigns and decisive battles. In addition to having the value of an objective history, the book has the merit of being historically thoughtful, pointing out that the outcome of a battle often may have depended on a personality, or a relationship between people, or the secondary effect of some political manoeuvre. The maps and endmaps are useful, as are the illustrations; the index is incomplete.

241   **Cleary,** Beverly. *Mitch and Amy;* illus. by George Porter. Morrow, 1967. 222p. Trade ed. $4.25; Library ed. $3.94 net.

4–6   Mitch and Amy are twins; they are in fourth grade, and they are almost always in a state of rivalry—except when they present a united front. Against the determined bullying of Alan Hibbler, Mitch and Amy are united: no adults need interfere. Academically, the competitive relationship between the twins is that of a cold war, with occasional flaring of active hostility. Mitch is a slow reader, Amy proficient; Amy gets great satisfaction out of her superior status, yet it is she who finds a book that starts Mitch on the road to self-motivated reading. The writing style and dialogue, the familial and peer group relationships, the motivations and characterizations all have the ring of truth. Written with ease and vitality, lightened with humor, the story is perhaps most appealing because it is clear that the author respects children.

242   **Cleary,** Beverly. *Ramona the Pest;* illus. by Louis Darling. Morrow, 1968. 192p. Trade ed. $3.95; Library ed. $3.78 net.

3–5   Ramona Quimby comes into her own. Beezus keeps telling her to stop acting like a pest, but Ramona is five now, and she is convinced that she is *not* a pest; she feels very mature, having entered kindergarten, and she immediately becomes enamoured of her teacher. Ramona's insistence on having just the right kind of boots, her matter-of fact interest in how Mike Mulligan got to a bathroom, her determination to kiss one of the boys in her class, and her refusal to go back to kindergarten because Miss Binney didn't love her any more—all of these incidents or situations are completely believable and are told in a light, humorous, zesty style.

243   **Cleary,** Beverly. *Runaway Ralph;* illus. by Louis Darling. Morrow, 1970. 175p. Trade ed. $3.95; Library ed. $3.78 net.

3–5   A sequel to *The Mouse and the Motorcycle,* in which Ralph, the intrepid mouse who learned to ride a toy motorcycle, communicated with a boy. Here Ralph wishes desperately to repeat the intercourse, when he is trapped in a serious predicament at a children's camp. Ralph has run away and been taken prisoner; the boy is an unhappy camper suspected of theft. Each has the power to help the other if only they can talk . . . and Ralph knows there is one way to achieve communication. The camp scenes are amusing, the message about runaways given with the lightest possible touch, and the style and humor have sturdy vitality.

244   **Cleaver,** Vera. *Delpha Green & Company;* by Vera and Bill Cleaver. Lippincott, 1972. 141p. $3.95; paper, $1.95.

5–7   Readers who enjoyed the irrepressible loquacity and precocity of Ellen Grae will warm immediately to Delpha, who is the lively oldest of a family that has just been separated for a year (Daddy was in jail) and is happily reunited. Daddy has a glossy new diploma to prove that he is a minister of the Church of Blessed Hope; Delpha has acquired, while at a foster home, a vigorous acquaintance with astrology, and between the two of them and the procession of odd characters whose lives cross theirs, the story crackles and fizzes with humor and action. Each chapter is named for a sign of the zodiac; father wins converts to an unorthodox church and holds his own by petitioning against the Establishment that wants to tear the rented building down.

245   **Cleaver,** Vera. *Ellen Grae;* by Vera and Bill Cleaver; illus. by Ellen Raskin. Lippincott, 1967. 89p. $2.95.

4–6   Ellen Grae's divorced parents had sent her to stay with Mrs. McGruder, who was fascinated by the child's tenacious mendacity. Not that Ellen Grae had any purpose, she just enjoyed Instant Tall Tales; when she suddenly drooped into days of silence, her parents were called. Together, gently, they pried out of Ellen Grae the fact that she was worried about an adult friend, Ira; solitary and odd, but harmless, Ira had told Ellen Grae a tale of patricide and she had been torn between loyalty to him and her obligation to tell the police. When she did tell the story, it was dismissed as just Ira's peculiar rambling; immediately Ellen Grae reverted to her normal role as an imaginative gamine, to the great relief of the adults. The intelligent affection of Mrs. McGruder and the relationship between Ellen Grae and Ira are touching; the relationship between Ellen Grae's parents is handled with dignity.

246   **Cleaver,** Vera. *Grover;* by Vera and Bill Cleaver; illus. by Frederic Marvin. Lippincott, 1970. 125p. $3.50. (H. Hamilton, 1971. 128p. £1.10.)

4–6   More serious than are the two books about Ellen Grae (to which this is a sequel) but with passages of very funny dialogue, *Grover* gives a touching picture of a boy's staunch acceptance of death. Grover knows that his mother has cancer, but she has told him that he is like her side of the family—they don't howl. Unable to bear the pain, she kills herself, and Grover's father is so wrapped in grief that he can neither comfort his son nor accept comfort from him. What the child learns is that he must accept his father's pattern; sustained by the understanding of his friends and some wise advice from sympathetic adults, Grover is able to show his unhappiness and know that there are times when one can howl. A wise and honest book with superb characterization and dialogue.

247   **Cleaver,** Vera. *I Would Rather Be a Turnip;* by Vera and Bill Cleaver. Lippincott, 1971. 159p. Trade ed. $4.25; Library ed. $4.19 net.

5–7   It wasn't a very big town, and everybody in it knew about her nephew Calvin, Annie realized. Eight years old, he was her sister's illegitimate child, a small genius, and he was coming to live with them. Annie didn't see how she could stand the shame; prepared to hate Calvin, she resisted the sensible advice of their housekeeper and resented her father's obvious love for his grandson. Only as she sees the corrosive effect of the prejudiced behavior of others does Annie gain perspective. She's a wonderfully belligerent character, and the gentle, amiable Calvin a striking contrast. Their relationship is perceptively developed, and the loving, no-nonsense black housekeeper's relationship with both children is warm and sensitive. It is surprising that the term "bastard" is several times referred to tangentially as the "name" that some girls have called Calvin, but neither the housekeeper nor the father uses it when Annie remarks on it. A very small flaw in a well-constructed book that is written with verve, humor, and compassion.

248   **Cleaver,** Vera. *Lady Ellen Grae;* by Vera and Bill Cleaver; illus. by Ellen Raskin. Lippincott, 1968. 124p. $2.95.

4–6   That highly original character Ellen Grae Derryberry in a second and equally enjoyable book. In *Ellen Grae,* the articulate and imaginative heroine learned that her parents, who were divorced, still were her refuge in time of trouble. Here they agree that

Ellen Grae needs to become more feminine via a visit to Aunt
Eleanor in Seattle; against all Ellen Grae's blandishments they
stand firm and united. While she is visiting Aunt Eleanor,
Ellen Grae not only picks up a few feminine habits but passes
on to her cousin Laura (the shining example of a nice, feminine
girl) some of her careless, hoydenish ways. The plot is adequate
but of minor interest compared to people and dialogue; the
Cleavers are gifted in their ability to draw salty, individual
characters without making them caricatures.

249   **Cleaver,** Vera. *Where the Lilies Bloom;* by Vera and Bill Cleaver;
illus. by Jim Spanfeller. Lippincott, 1969. 174p. $3.95. (H.
Hamilton, 1970. 160p. £1.25.)

6–9   An old hymn calls it the land "where the lilies bloom so fair,"
the Appalachian hills abounding in roots, herbs, and flowers that
have medicinal use. It is to this that Mary Call Luther turns
after her father's death; wildcrafting provides the money to keep
together the small family of which she is head: a younger
brother and sister and an older sister, gentle Devola, "womanly
in form but with a child's heart and a child's mind." Mary
Call, the fourteen-year-old child of a sharecropper, hides the fact
of her father's death (and buries him herself) so that the authorities
will not send them all to a home, and with grim determination
fights to keep Devola from marrying—even to offering herself as a
substitute to the neighbor in love with the older sister. Mary
Call inveigles him into signing over the ramshackle home in
which the family lives, she sternly organizes the wildcrafting
expeditions, and she is in every way an unforgettable character,
tough and courageous, tenacious as a bittersweet vine. The setting
is fascinating, the characterization good, and the style of the
first-person story distinctive.

250   **Clifford,** Mary Louise. *The Land and People of Malaysia.*
Lippincott, 1968. 160p. illus. Trade ed. $3.95; Library ed. $3.79 net.

7–12   A well-written and particularly well-organized book that ravels the
complicated history of the states, islands, tribes, immigrant
peoples, ethnic and racial strains, and colonial conquerors of the
areas that are now East and West Malaysia. The author
immediately makes clear the distinction between Malayan and
Malaysian, and she maintains this awareness of the reader's need
for clear definition throughout the book. The geography and
history of the Malaysian Federation and the origins of its
diverse peoples are the principal topics of the book, but there
is also discussion of agriculture, industry, cultural patterns, and
the place of Malaysia in the larger sphere of Southeast Asia. The
photographs are often poorly placed, but the book is otherwise
an excellent addition to the series. An index is appended.

251   **Clifton,** Lucille. *Some of the Days of Everett Anderson;* illus. by
        Evaline Ness. Holt, 1970. 25p. Trade ed. $3.95; Library ed.
        $3.59 net.

K–2   A week of days, a poem for each day, and a charming picture
        of a six-year-old black child whose fears and pleasures have a
        universal quality. Monday, for example: "Being six/ is full of
        tricks/ And Everett Anderson knows it./ Being a boy/ is full
        of joy/ and Everett Anderson shows it." Or Friday (Mom is Home,
        Payday): "Swishing one finger/ in the foam/ of Mama's glass/
        when she gets home/ is a very/ favorite thing to do./ Mama says/
        foam is a comfort/ Everett Anderson/ says so too."

252   **Clymer,** Eleanor (Lowenton). *My Brother Stevie.* Holt, 1967. 76p.
        Trade ed. $3.50; Library ed. $3.27 net.

4–6   After Pa died, Mama went away again—this time for good. She
        told Annie to take care of her little brother, and Annie felt the
        responsibility keenly; even though they lived with Grandma,
        Annie had to instruct Stevie as much as she had to protect
        him. Grandma was very strict and very suspicious of the gang
        that Stevie trailed around with; Annie worried because she
        recognized the pattern of delinquency. There came a change in
        Stevie when he found a teacher whose loving kindness made him
        feel accepted; although he moved back to his old pattern to some
        extent, he never again had the same hostility. Annie tells the
        story, and very convincingly; the characterization and dialogue are
        good, and the ending is realistically moderate.

253   **Clymer,** Eleanor (Lowenton). *The Spider, the Cave and the Pottery
        Bowl;* illus. by Ingrid Fetz. Atheneum, 1971. 66p. $3.95.

3–5   Each summer Kate and her mother had gone back to the Indian
        village where her grandmother lived, to help with the work and
        enjoy life on the mesa. But this summer Kate and her brother
        had come alone, and Kate—who tells the story—was disturbed
        because Grandmother was so listless. Not until Kate and Johnny
        found a source of good clay for pottery did Grandmother bestir
        herself. The story line is simple, but woven around it are the
        traditions of the mesa people; simply told, the story is particularly
        effective because it takes for granted the advantages of Kate's
        two cultures: she is irritated when a white tourist is patronizing,
        but her pride of heritage is not shaken.

254   **Clymer,** Eleanor (Lowenton). *We Lived in the Almont;* illus. by
        David K. Stone. Dutton, 1970. 102p. Trade ed. $3.95; Library
        ed. $3.91 net.

4–6   Linda tells the story herself, remembering with what joy her
        family moved from a dilapidated old building to the Almont.
        Once it had been elegant, now it was neglected, but her

father felt it would be much easier to superintend and the whole family enjoyed the space of their apartment. In this milieu lives a small group of varied and perceptively delineated tenants, one of whom is the Plant Lady, from whose basement overflow Linda steals a guitar. When the announcement comes that the Almont has been sold, Linda frantically tells her mother—who has found the instrument—that the Plant Lady lent it to her. Marched to the woman's apartment, Linda gulps out her thanks for the "loan." And the eccentric old woman at whom Linda has giggled teaches a lesson in charity. "Why, Linda," she says, "You misunderstood me. I didn't lend it to you. I gave it to you." And then, with no other place to live, she goes to a Home. Thus endeth the Almont. There is no strong story line but this is a strong book, picturing with fidelity the concerns of a young adolescent and the small world of an urban apartment house.

255   **Coatsworth,** Elizabeth Jane. *Bess and the Sphinx;* illus. by Bernice Loewenstein. Macmillan, 1967. 88p. $4.50.

3–5   When Papa decided that the family ought to take a trip to Egypt before the milestone year of 1900, small Bess was both delighted and apprehensive. Looking back to her own childhood, Elizabeth Coatsworth describes that trip with rueful sympathy for the shy and awkward child she once was. Bess had one mortifying experience after another; once, for example, she fell into the Nile and ruined a beautiful red jacket of which she had been proud. But when the family went to see the Sphinx, timid Bess felt she had a friend. "She hadn't had this feeling anywhere else in Egypt, as though a great something was aware of her, and felt kindly, too." Then Bess found a clay figure of Osiris in the sand, and felt it was a gift of the Sphinx, a protective charm she had discovered alone. A gentle, touching story in itself, the book is doubly interesting because it is Miss Coatsworth's first narrative of her own childhood.

256   **Coatsworth,** Elizabeth Jane. *The Place;* illus. by Marjorie Auerbach. Holt, 1966. 72p. Trade ed. $3.50; Library ed. $3.27 net.

4–6   Ellen, who has come to Mexico with her father, an archeologist, learns from little Jorge that there is a wonderful and secret Place. Jorge's older sister, Natividad, is shocked to hear that Ellen knows the Place exists; understanding that Ellen is most curious, Natividad decides to take Ellen to the Place after Ellen has saved her life. Ellen finds that the secret site is a beautiful limestone cavern in which there are priceless artifacts and wall paintings that have accumulated in the long years in which the Place has been used secretly by worshippers. Although she could win an award for

revealing the place as a new site of archeological interest, Ellen
is moved both by loyalty to her friends and by the unspoiled
beauty of the Place to promise silence. The story is constructed
deftly, a natural series of incidents leading to the denouement with
a gradual heightening of tension. The children are believable and
the relationships among them sympathetic; the setting is presented
as interesting rather than quaint.

257   **Coatsworth,** Elizabeth Jane. *The Sparrow Bush;* wood engravings by
Stefan Martin. Norton, 1966. 63p. Trade ed. $3.95; Library ed.
$3.69 net.

4–7   A charming book of poetry, most of the poems being about
some aspect of nature: birds or beasts, the weather, the seasons,
the stars; a few are about an emotion or a mood. The writing
is lucid, springy, gay, and affectionate. Nice to read alone, nice
to read aloud. The wood engravings in black and white are
attractive in themselves and are used with discrimination in the
page layout.

258   **Coatsworth,** Elizabeth Jane. *Under the Green Willow;* illus. by
Janina Domanska. Macmillan, 1971. 21p. $3.95.

K–3   In tones of green and yellow, stylized and handsomely composed,
Domanska's illustrations show the water creatures of the crowded,
busy spot beneath the willow tree. The text, brief and lyric,
describes the darting life in the clear, sunny waters: the wily
trout that snatches a crumb before the others can get near, the
catfish nipping at the ducks' toes, the confident ducks kicking
at the turtles in their way. Not a story, but a small, incisive
picture of water life.

259   **Cohen,** Barbara. *The Carp in the Bathtub;* illus. by Joan Halpern
Lothrop, 1972. 48p. Trade ed. $3.95; Library ed. $3.78 net.

3–4   When she was a little girl, Leah tells us, she and her brother
knew that their mother had the reputation of making the best
gefilte fish in New York—but they never ate it, for by the time
the carp was to be killed, it had become their friend, their pet.
This is the story of one Passover week, when Leah and Harry
decide that the carp (the nicest one they ever had) keeping
fresh in the bathtub should be rescued. They take it to a neighbor's
tub, but Papa finds out, scolds them, and retrieves the fish.
He later brings home a cat, and they like it—but they never
eat gefilte fish. Lightweight but amusing, the tender solicitude of
the children balanced by the no-nonsense realism of their parents,
this is an amiable story of a Jewish family two generations ago.
The illustrations are awkward, the figures out of proportion but
designed well and with some touches of humor.

260   **Cohen,** Miriam. *Best Friends;* pictures by Lillian Hoban. Macmillan, 1971. 29p. $3.95.

3–5
yrs.   Engaging illustrations show the setting of a busy kindergarten room for a story of boy-meets-boy, boy-loses-boy, boy-gets-boy, the simple text enlivened by a quiet humor. When life is at its lowest ebb, and Paul and Jim are on the outs: "And the cookies were the plain kind." When Jim and Paul are sent into the room on an errand during recess, and they notice the incubator light is out, Paul goes for the janitor and Jim, hovering anxiously, tries "to be as warm as he could." The rupture is caused by just a bit of bickering and jealousy, and the coolness between the two best friends is mended as easily as it started; the light touch, good style, and realistic treatment make a pleasant tale out of an experience with which most children can identify.

261   **Cohen,** Miriam. *Will I Have a Friend?* pictures by Lillian Hoban. Macmillan, 1967. 26p. $4.50. (Collier-Mac., 1969. 32p. £1.12½.)

4–6
yrs.   A very nice book for the child who is ready for nursery school or kindergarten, and an especially nice one for the child who is *not* ready, and needs support. Jim, escorted to his first day of school by his father, is worried about making a friend. He rather wistfully stands around watching the other youngsters play and finally makes contact at rest time, so called—most of the children are resting by waving their legs in the air, quietly. The drawings of schoolroom activities are very funny and quite beguiling, and the locale is a city neighborhood that seems architecturally, economically, and racially mixed.

262   **Cohen,** Robert. *The Color of Man;* illus. by Ken Heyman. Random House, 1968. 114p. Trade ed. $3.95; Library ed. $3.99 net.

5–9   The jacket adds, "What it's all about. Why we are confused and concerned about it. How it will affect our future." The emphasis is on what it's all about: what causes differences in skin color and how those differences probably came about is discussed; the process of natural selection as it affects eye and hair colors is described; the social as well as the physiological aspects are considered. The author discusses the nature of prejudice, and its dangers. A lucid book, the writing straightforward and the material rather loosely organized. The photographs are truly impressive, pictures of people from many parts of the world, pictures that amplify the text's message of brotherhood.

263   **Cohen,** Tom. *Three Who Dared.* Doubleday, 1969. 144p. $3.50.

7–10   Henry Aronson went south for two weeks to do legal work for the Mississippi Summer Project—and gave up his job in Hartford to stay on. John O'Neal sacrificed his personal ambition in order to bring the Free Southern Theater to black people. Eric Weinberger withstood maltreatment and jail to keep viable a work project that brought dignity as well as a livelihood to a black community in Tennessee. Their contributions to the civil rights movement are impressive as individual efforts and inspiring as examples of the persistence and devotion of so many. The writing style is not outstanding; the book, nevertheless, is.

264   **Cole,** William, comp. *Oh, What Nonsense!* poems selected by William Cole; drawings by Tomi Ungerer. Viking, 1966. 80p. $2.95. (Methuen, 1968. 80p. £0.80.)

4–6   An engaging compilation of nonsense verse and rhymes from children's games, appropriately illustrated by Ungerer's daft drawings. Mr. Cole announces, in the preface, that he has tried to use only new or unfamiliar material; there is no Nash or Belloc, and the compiler has omitted Lear and Carroll because they are easily found elsewhere.

265   **Cole,** William. *The Poet's Tales;* A New Book of Story Poems; illus. by Charles Keeping. World, 1971. 320p. Trade ed. $6.95; Library ed. $6.87 net.

5–9   Handsomely illustrated in black and white, this excellent anthology is a revised edition of *Story Poems Old and New,* with many more poems included, and with a particularly nice preface that actually seems addressed to young readers rather than their parents and teachers. The poems are grouped in sections under such rubrics as "Strange and Mysterious," "Love Stories," "Fighting Men," and "At Sea." Separate author, title, and first line indexes are appended.

266   **Cole,** William, comp. *The Sea, Ships and Sailors;* Poems, Songs and Shanties selected by William Cole; with drawings by Robin Jacques. Viking, 1967. 236p. $4.95. (Hart-Davis, 1968. 240p. £2.10.)

6—   A book that is dignified in format and handsomely illustrated with drawings in black and white, delicate in detail but with a great deal of vitality. The anthology has been compiled with a discriminating eye and ear; the selections range from familiar narrative poetry to delightful nonsense, of which not the least is Mr. Cole's own contribution, "Undersea Fever." Title and first line indexes are appended.

267   **Coles,** Robert. *Dead End School;* illus. by Norman Rockwell. Atlantic-Little, Brown, 1968. 100p. $3.95.

4–6   The author of *Children of Crisis* tells it like it is for the young reader. Jim had just moved to the Saunders school district, and he found the sixth grade there was noisy and crowded; on the second day of school the principal came in and announced that

the class would have to be moved to another school. Jim's mother
was among the many parents whose protest was effective: a
move to a good school, yes, but a move to another crowded
ghetto school, no. Jim was one of the children who went by
bus to an uncrowded school in an all-white neighborhood. The
story ends with Jim's description of that first day at school and his
report on it at home that evening; realistically, nothing startling
happens. Some children are friendly, some uncomfortable, and
almost everybody is self-conscious. But it's a start. Simple, direct,
quiet, and effective.

268   **Colman,** Hila. *Claudia, Where Are You?* Morrow, 1969. 191p.
Trade ed. $4.25; Library ed. $3.94 net.

7–10   Claudia is an unhappy sixteen-year-old who cannot communicate
with her mother. In alternate chapters, they speak; Claudia in
first person, her mother in third. A successful woman who deludes
herself constantly, Claudia's mother refuses to believe that her
daughter doesn't care about clothes and parties; she even talks
about sexual relations in a way that makes the girl enraged.
Claudia runs off to Greenwich Village, finally finding a job, an
apartment, and a boy friend, calling on her parents only when she
needs money. Her distraught mother doesn't understand at all;
her father does. Unhappily, the parents go back to their lovely
suburban home while their daughter rejoices in her freedom.
Although the story is patterned in the sense that it is so
typical of the suburban rebel, it rings true; the book offers no
easy answer. Mother cannot understand, and Claudia rejects all
that her mother holds dear. Claudia's experiences in the Village
are believable, the writing style is competent, and the portrait of
mother is devastating.

269   **Colman,** Hila. *End of the Game;* photographs by Milton Charles.
World, 1971. 92p. Trade ed. $4.95; Library ed. $4.89 net.

4–6   In her first book for younger children, Hila Colman describes with
sensitivity the variation of attitudes in the members of a white
family who are visited by a black child. Donny had been invited
to come from a ghetto home for a few weeks in the country.
Mrs. Stevens, proud of her liberality, warns her children that
Donny is a guest, and that he must have whatever he wants.
No squabbling. The twelve-year-old twin girls are not particularly
interested, but Timmy is Donny's age and excited about the
prospect of a companion. The boys dive into friendship, but they
are both aware that Timmy's mother doesn't see Donny as a person
but as a symbol, the symbol of her own gesture to a black
child. She is so polite, so permissive, so cautious that her
own children quickly learn that any small mishap can be
attributed to Donny and go unpunished. Donny wishes she would

scold, at least enough to show him that he is accepted. She doesn't. What she does do, finally, is accuse Donny of a serious misdemeanor that has been committed by the girls. The boys run off together, and Donny's mother is called; she is angry at Donny, "acting the scapegoat for these white kids," and Mrs. Stevens is shocked by her realization of her own bias beneath the veneer of acceptance—but the damage is done. Only the youngest, Timmy, has thought of Donny as a person, not a black person. The photographs add little to the book, introducing a case-history note to a story with depth and candor.

270   **Colman,** Hila. *Making Movies;* Student Films to Features; illus. by George Guzzi. World, 1969. 191p. Trade ed. $4.95; Library ed. $4.61 net.

7–10   Explicit and varied, this book is written in a direct style that is both easy and dignified. It includes long quotations from interviews, but the advice or experience given here is usually more pertinent to career guidance than personal. The author discusses the opportunities in all areas of film making, describing succinctly the duties and perquisites (if any) of each job, and mentioning the increasing participation of Negro and Puerto Rican men and women in the industry. Appendices include a list of colleges and universities that grant a degree in film (including a full listing of specific courses), a list of unions, the duties of a script supervisor, apprenticeship programs, a sample of such a program in detail, outlines of training course work processes for several positions, and an index.

271   **Colum,** Padraic. *The Stone of Victory;* and Other Tales of Padraic Colum; illus. by Judith Gwyn Brown. McGraw-Hill, 1966. 119p. $3.95.

4–6   Illustrated with softly executed drawings in black and white, thirteen tales are included in this volume, the selections having been made from seven of Colum's previously published books. The stories are delightful in writing style and humor, pleasant to read silently or aloud.

272   **Columbia Broadcasting System, Inc.** *Pope Paul VI;* by The Staff of CBS News; based on the CBS News Television Series "The Twentieth Century"; illus. with photographs. Watts, 1967. 66p. $2.95.

6–9   A sickly child, Giovanni Montini was an excellent scholar and was chosen, as a young priest, to attend the Vatican school for diplomacy. He ran an information bureau during World War II and became an advisor to the Pope at the close of the war, then became Archbishop of Milan, later serving as a diplomat of the Church during the reign of Pope John. His visits to the

Holy Land, to India, and to the United States have given Pope Paul the sobriquet of the Apostle on the Move; there is little doubt that his concern for world peace has made this Pope a figure of world importance. The text, based on a television program, is straightforward but not dry, its tone admiring but not adulatory. An index is appended.

273   **Cone,** Molly. *Annie Annie;* illus. by Marvin Friedman. Houghton, 1969. 112p. $3.95.

6–9   Annie is in despair because of the carefree way in which her parents live: no schedule, no rules for the children, just an assumption that intelligence means you can take care of yourself. Her friend Migs is always being forbidden to do things or told she must do things, and that's what Annie wants. She takes a job in the home of a couple who always do the same things the same way, whose thinking echoes this rigidity, who discourage initiative. Annie learns, living with the Sigbys, to appreciate her own home and her parents. An honest book, refreshingly different, wise in understanding and delightful in the humor and percipience with which the characters are depicted.

274   **Cone,** Molly. *The Other Side of the Fence;* illus. by John Gretzer. Houghton, 1967. 117p. $3.75.

3–5   Joey visited his aunt every summer, enjoying the familiarity of Pearl Street, even enjoying Aunt Liz, who was stubborn and strict—but fair. That was why Joey was surprised when Aunt Liz said a house was empty—when Joey could see that somebody had just moved in. It soon became clear to Joey that the neighbors had decided to ignore the existence of the newcomers because they were Negro; uncomfortably, Joey made a few feeble attempts to defend the newcomers—even more uncomfortably, he kept quiet when he found nobody to agree with him. Torn between his desire to be accepted by his own circle of friends and the inner conviction that they were wrong, Joey rebelled when a spiteful neighbor painted his own side of the fence white and the Foster's side black. The small victory he achieves is that Aunt Liz invites Mrs. Foster in for a cup of coffee; a straw in the wind is the fact that the child of a prejudiced woman comes over to play in the Foster's yard. The amount of change is modest, and there is no implication that all problems are solved, but change has begun. The problem of conflict is presented with just the right amount of depth for the younger reader, and the message of individual responsibility is given with conviction.

275   **Coolidge,** Olivia E. *Gandhi.* Houghton, 1971. 265p. illus. $5.95.

7—   This is certainly one of the most astute and objective biographies of Gandhi that have been published for young people, giving an unusually balanced picture of his strengths and weaknesses. In an excellent preface, the author discusses Gandhi's inconsistencies, his mistakes in judgment, his proclivity for giving advice on subjects (like medical treatment) on which he was uninformed. The book substantiates and illustrates these failings, but it is equally forthright about Gandhi's dedication, his integrity, his charismatic personality—and it gives a coherent picture of Gandhi's role in India's struggle for independence, and of his place in the movement for peaceful reistance. A glossary of Indian terms and an index are appended.

276   **Coolidge,** Olivia E. *George Bernard Shaw.* Houghton, 1968. 226p. illus. $3.95.

7–12   Objective, thoughtful and astute, this biography of Shaw is written in a style that has vigor and literary grace. Shaw's personal relationships, his political role, and his idiosyncrasies of dress and diet are described in a book that is balanced and entertaining, with analyses of his work smoothly incorporated into the biographical material.

277   **Coolidge,** Olivia E. *The Golden Days of Greece;* illus. by Enrico Arno. T. Y. Crowell, 1968. 211p. $4.50.

4–6   Written for a younger audience than most of the recent Coolidge books, this series of highlights or samples of Grecian history give as smooth a historical picture as does any chronological survey. The story of Schliemann's discovery is followed by a chapter in which the ideologies of Greece and Asia are exemplified by the standards of Croesus and Cyrus; a description of the Olympic games, an account of a Spartan upbringing, chapters on Socrates and Plato, and a discussion of the great dramatists bring ancient Greece to life. The illustrations, which use black and white very effectively, are related to the text but are primarily decorative. A list of Greek words and proper names, divided by chapters, gives both pronunciation and identification; an index is appended.

278   **Coolidge,** Olivia E. *The King of Men;* illus. by Ellen Raskin. Houghton, 1966. 230p. $3.50.

7—   Beautifully written, a novel based on the Agamemnon legend, incorporating into the matrix of the story the Greek Gods, the round, flat world of the Bronze Age, and the traditional stories of mythology. The reign of Agamemnon begins with the tragic multiple deaths of father, brother, and uncle; the young, new King of Men does not feel himself truly a king until he joins Odysseus in a fight against marauding pirates. In all of Agamemnon's adventures, the Gods intervene; in fact, they are frequently in conflict and the fates of men thereby may suddenly shift and change. The story ends with the king's marriage to a jealous Clytemnestra, and the pitying comment of the Goddess Athene, "It is not in your nature to understand, but kings have many cares in heaven or on earth."

279   **Coolidge,** Olivia E. *Marathon Looks on the Sea;* pictures by Erwin Schachner. Houghton, 1967. 248p. $3.50.

7–10   Legend and fact are smoothly and vividly interwoven in an excellent historical novel that culminates in a tense and vigorous account of the Battle of Marathon. Son of a Greek general, Metiochos became, as he grew to manhood, a favorite of the Persian king, Darius. When Persia and Athens met at Marathon, Metiochos was torn by his conflicting loyalties, feeling that he was not only deciding his own fate, but that he also might be a decisive factor in the outcome of the battle. The pictures of court intrigues and martial campaigns are brilliantly real.

280   **Coolidge,** Olivia. *Tales of the Crusades;* illus. Adapted from prints by Gustave Dore. Houghton, 1970. 225p. $3.95.

8—   Although each of the stories that chronicle some facet of the long years of the Crusades is a splendid entity, wonderfully evocative and vividly written, the book does not give a cohesive picture of the centuries of credulity, idealism, chicanery, heroism, opportunism, and blind faith. It does, however, illustrate them vividly; it does create unforgettable moments and memorable men; it is impressive both as a literary and as a historical work.

281   **Coolidge,** Olivia E. *Tom Paine, Revolutionary.* Scribner, 1969. 213p. Trade ed. $3.95; Library ed. $3.63 net.

7—   With her usual—or perhaps one should say unusual—skill at depicting a period, Mrs. Coolidge gives an infinitely detailed and vivid picture of the turbulent political affairs of France, England, and the colonies that became a country as a background for the storm-tossed career of Paine. At times a hero, at times despised for his ideas or his behavior, the obdurate champion of reason and man's rights was cast into a French prison, reviled by the British, and later rejected or ignored by some of the most ardent of friends made earlier in America. Although this is not imperfect (the author says on one page, "Truth was, Paine had become a party man . . ." and two pages later, in apparent contradiction, "If he had been a party man . . .") it is sophisticated biographical writing, giving the young reader an objective picture of Paine, an intelligent assessment of the effect of the man on the times, and of the times and other men on the fortunes of Thomas Paine. A reading list and an index are appended.

282   **Coolidge,** Olivia E. *Women's Rights;* The Suffrage Movement in
America, 1848–1920; illus. with photographs. Dutton, 1966.
189p. Trade ed. $4.95; Library ed. $4.90 net.

8—   A comprehensive, detailed, and quite fascinating history of the
women's suffrage movement. Particularly good in incorporating
biographical background into the text with smooth brevity, the
book is objective in assessing the personalities and peculiarities
of some of the famous leaders of the movement. The long struggle
for suffrage is marked by the dedication, courage, and persistence
shown by the men and women who worked and suffered censure
over the years. The book is illustrated with photographs and with
reproductions of cartoons; a list of important dates, a list of
suggested readings, and a relative index are appended.

283   **Coombs,** Charles Ira. *Cleared for Takeoff;* Behind the Scenes at an
Airport. Morrow, 1969. 190p. illus. Trade ed. $4.50; Library ed.
$4.14 net.

6–10   Passengers at an airport see a good deal of the activity there, and
are all too familiar with the problems of ground transportation,
crowding, flight delays, and stacking; these aspects of air travel
are covered, but this very useful book also discusses the
processing of international traffic, the adaptation of passenger
planes for carrying large cargoes, the layout and improvement of
present facilities, the details of maintenance and briefing of crews,
and the equipment and procedures in the flight control tower.
The writing is straightforward and the material well organized;
the step-by-step procedures of a takeoff are included. Photographs
and diagrams are helpful; an index is appended.

284   **Cooper,** Margaret. *The Great Bone Hunt;* illus. by Harold Goodwin.
Macmillan, 1967. 58p. Trade ed. $2.95; Library ed. $2.94 net.

4–6   As was the author's *The Ice Palace* (Macmillan, 1966) this is an
amusing story based—as an afterword explains—on real events.
The tale is told in a blithe, exaggerated style that is echoed
by the attractive black and white illustrations. Once upon a time
in an unspecified country, some enormous bones were discovered
and they created a great stir; the bone finders went to a famous
sleuth and he organized a hunt that resulted in the discovery
of so many bones that the sleuth was able to construct a skeleton
for his home museum. The tale is based on the true story of
Peale's construction of a mastodon skeleton in his home-and-
museum in Philadelphia at the end of the eighteenth century.

285   **Cooper,** Susan. *Dawn of Fear;* illus. by Margery Gill. Harcourt,
1970. 157p. $5.75. (Harcourt, Brace, 1970. 157p. £2.15.)

5–6   An English story, written with sensitivity and with a rare

understanding of the way in which children can be impervious
to danger until it touches them. The small group of boys who
are engrossed in their own games and little touched by the war
(World War II) are shocked into fear when one of their number is
killed in an air raid. The story line is tenuous: the boys build a
camp, it is demolished by a rival gang, there is a pitched battle,
etc. The book is strong in other ways, however, the characterization
deft and the dialogue natural, the relationship between the boys
and a young man who is about to enter the Merchant Navy
particularly perceptive.

286   **Coopersmith,** Jerome. *A Chanukah Fable for Christmas;* illus. by
Syd Hoff. Putnam, 1969. 47p. $3.95.

K–3   Fun to read, an adaptation of Moore's poem that blithely
incorporates Moshe Dayan, flying saucers, and brotherhood.
" 'Twas the night before Christmas," little Murray begins, and
explains that it isn't the colored lights and presents that he
envies, but the fact that Jewish children have no fat man in
red—even if, deep down, one knows he isn't real. Along comes
a humming machine in the sky, and therein sits a fat man in
red, with a patch over his eye and a soldier's kepi. Murray
hops out of bed and goes along for a ride on a flying version
of a Chanukah draydle; in his dream, they fly over the world
and see the wonderful variety of peoples and their ways of
celebrating. The illustrations are lively, the parody salty and sweet.

287   **Copeland,** Paul W. *The Land and People of Libya.* Lippincott,
1967. 158p. illus. (Portraits of the Nations Series) Trade ed.
$3.95; Library ed. $2.93 net.

7–10   One of those rarities, an enjoyable informational book, this survey
of Libya is well organized and competently written. The author
refers to the Romans as the first organization men of history;
in speaking of the elaborate ritual of the Islamic hajj, or pilgrimage,
he says, "Processions and prayers include the trial of running
from hill to hill in the hot sun. Some of the more aged worshippers
achieve their wish for paradise." Mr. Copeland gives historical
and geographical facts; he describes the peoples of Libya, religious
and educational patterns (school is free from kindergarten through
college), and the problems and benefits of modern life. An index
is appended.

288   **Corbett,** Scott. *The Baseball Bargain;* illus. by Wallace Tripp. Little,
1970. 140p. $3.95.

4–6   Woody had never been able to play as much baseball as he
wanted, so when he heard that Leo was organizing a team,
he was willing to do anything to belong. But what Leo wanted

him to do wasn't easy: to be on the team, Woody had to steal a mitt from Stoneham's sporting goods shop. He almost did it—and Mr. Stoneham knew it. So Woody struck his second bargain, terms dictated by Mr. Stoneham: if he could do three good deeds in one day, he could work in the store and earn a mitt. The ensuing olio of humorous events, baseball action, and the acquisition of insight makes a pleasant story, realistic and lightly written but with serious overtones.

289   **Corbett,** Scott. *Ever Ride a Dinosaur?* illus. by Mircea Vasiliu. Holt, 1969. 113p. Trade ed. $3.95; Library ed. $3.59 net.

4–6   A fanciful story, told in first person and imaginatively illustrated. A middle-aged man, meek and quiet, Charlie runs into Bronson (a brontosaurus) in Rhode Island. Terrified at first, Charlie soon realizes that Bronson is friendly. In fact, Bronson—talking a mile a minute and not too modestly—tells him so. What Bronson really wants out of life, and he's been living a long time, is to see the dinosaur exhibit at the New York Museum of Natural History, but he has a poor sense of direction. So Charlie and Bronson become a team, and their adventures make delightfully zany reading—because Bronson can make himself invisible when he chooses, and the possibilities for ploys are infinite.

290   **Corbett,** Scott. *What Makes a Light Go On?* pictures by Len Darwin. Atlantic-Little, Brown, 1966. 56p. $3.50. (Muller, 1968. 48p. £0.55.)

4–6   An excellent introductory book on electricity; the illustrations are very clear, well placed, and adequately captioned. Mr. Corbett uses lucid analogies and familiar phenomena in explaining the movement within an atom, magnetic attraction and repulsion, and the nature of electricity. He describes the functioning of a generator, and explains the workings of flashlights and of electric bulbs. The terminology is accurate but is never more complex than is necessary; the text includes a discussion of the necessity for caution and precaution. A combined index and glossary is appended.

291   **Corbett,** Scott. *What Makes a Plane Fly?* pictures by Len Darwin. Atlantic-Little, Brown, 1967. 58p. $3.50.

4–6   A very good book about the principles of flight; the author discusses the shape of an airplane and of its wings as they add to—or diminish—drag, lift, and speed, and the functioning of air pressure in relation to wing shape. He describes the various methods used to obtain thrust, the aberrations of flight (what causes them and what corrects them) and the balancing forces of lift, thrust, weight, and drag. The illustrative diagrams are very

helpful, as are the clear examples used in the text. A glossary
of terms is appended, with page references within it serving
as an index.

292   **Corcoran,** Barbara. *Sam;* drawings by Barbara McGee. Atheneum,
1967. 219p. Trade ed. $4.25; Library ed. $4.08 net.

6–9   Sam and her brother were used to the isolation of the island
on which they lived; their father had always felt that being
involved with other people only brought trouble. But Sam was
fifteen; she wanted to be with her peers. When she did have
a chance to test her father's theories, it looked as though he
were right: the boys at school were tough, the girls snobbish;
her uncle was a weak man and a gambler, his wife a foolish
and helpless woman. Yet Sam found, after her uncle's death,
that she never regretted the protective affection she'd given him,
that even if her father were right about people she was one
of them and couldn't avoid her commitment as a human being.
With good characterization and writing style, and with a balanced
treatment of facets of Sam's life, the book will appeal especially
to those readers who are interested in dogs, since a good portion
of the story is devoted to Sam's dog, their participation in a dog
show, and plans for attending future shows.

293   **Corcoran,** Barbara. *A Star to the North;* by Barbara Corcoran and
Bradford Angier. Nelson, 1970. 156p. $3.95.

6–9   The Canadian wilderness is the setting for a vigorous tale of
two young people coping with unexpected problems on a runaway
journey. Kimberly, fourteen, had followed her older brother when
she learned that he was going off to the woods to visit a
young uncle he'd helped the summer before. So there she was—
and what could Nathaniel do but take her along on his planned
canoe trip to Uncle Seth's remote cabin? Staunch and determined,
the two learn to accept each other's inadequacies in amiable fashion,
arriving at the cabin to find their polarization fixed. (Uncle Seth,
it appears, has shacked up with a woman and is not at all
enchanted to see them.) Kimberly has learned that roughing it
is not for her, and departs. Nathaniel is just as sure that the
simple life is for him; although disappointed in Seth, he arranges
for a cabin of his own. The wilderness journey has a felicity
of detail that is appealing, the plot is sound and nicely developed,
there is action and excitement in the young people's adventures,
and the brother-sister relationship is drawn with perception.

294   **Cosgrove,** Margaret. *Bone for Bone;* written and illus. by Margaret
Cosgrove. Dodd, 1968. 128p. $3.95.

6–10   A most interesting introduction to comparative vertebrate
anatomy, the author using paleontology, ontological

recapitulation, and morphology to establish the likenesses and differences between animal forms. The writing style is informal, the infrequent diversion more than compensated for by the appeal of the conversational approach and by the author's sense of relish. The illustrations are at times not placed to best advantage in relation to the text, but they often are ingenious in clarifying or supplementing a description. A brief glossary and an index are appended.

295   **Cottrell,** Leonard. *The Mystery of Minoan Civilization.* World, 1971. 128p. illus. Trade ed. $4.95; Library ed. $5.22 net.

8—   Through the work of archeologists, primarily that of Sir Arthur Evans, the palace at Knossos has emerged to enthrall and puzzle later scientists. There is little in this account that cannot be found in other surveys of Cretan exploration and comparisons of Crete and Mycenae, but this is one of the more smoothly written of the many books on the subject. Details of finds and of facts that substantiated theories or raised new questions are incorporated with skill into a text that goes into considerable detail about the work of Ventris and about the possible causes for the destruction of Cretan palaces and cities. A final chapter describes recent (the 1960s) discoveries. An index is appended.

296   **Coy,** Harold. *The Mexicans;* illus. by Francisco Mora. Little, 1970. 326p. $5.95.

8—   A successful use of a literary device gives this history of Mexico an aura of involvement and affection: it is purportedly written by a young Mexican, educated and alert. The illustrations are attractive, but less informative than are the photographs in *Here Is Mexico* by Elizabeth Trevino and *Hello, Mexico* by Morris Weeks. The style is vigorous, the research obvious; there is less information about contemporary cultural patterns here than in the other two books, but this is better written, the treatment of the war with the United States particularly good. A divided bibliography, a guide to pronunciation, and a relative index are appended.

297   **Crane,** Caroline. *A Girl Like Tracy.* McKay, 1966. 186p. $4.25.

7–9   A junior novel about seventeen-year-old Kathy Allen whose older sister is retarded. A girl like Tracy has to be protected when she is beautiful, and the Allen family's life is built around Tracy; in order to take care of Tracy when her mother is at work, Kathy has to rush home from school every day. Sure that Tracy can be taught some things, Kathy tries to teach her to shop and cook—it doesn't work. Knowing that Tracy needs recreation, Kathy takes her to a movie—they have a fight because Tracy wants to join some tough boys. Eventually her parents agree with Kathy that Tracy needs professional help; Kathy instigates this after she realizes that her mother is ashamed of Tracy as well as feeling overprotective in her love. Kathy acquires a boy friend in the course of the story, a boy whose Ukrainian family is drawn with affection; realistically, Alex simply goes off to military service, with no dramatic ending. Realistically, Tracy begins to enjoy her school, with no miraculous changes; realistically, Mrs. Allen accepts the fact that Kathy was right about Tracy, with no more than a grudging acceptance.

298   **Crawford,** Deborah. *Somebody Will Miss Me*. Crown, 1971. 215p. $4.95.

6–10   In a story of the Depression Era, twelve-year-old Abby van Eyk and her grandparents are forced to accept the grudging hospitality of relatives in a resort town on the New Jersey coast. While the book is pervaded by the bleak despair of the period, it is balanced by a vigorous and convincing picture of a young adolescent's problems, as Abby makes new friends, resists Grandma's efforts at interference in those friendships, adjusts to the death of her grandfather and to the ignominy of going on relief. There is no strong story line, but the book has strength in its felicity of period details, its vivid characterization, convincing dialogue, and—unusual in a book of episodic structure—in the fact that every episode has relevance to Abby's growth.

299   **Cresswell,** Helen. *The Night Watchmen;* illus. by Gareth Floyd. Macmillan, 1970. 122p. $4.50. (Faber, 1969. 148p. £0.90.)

4–6   At first it seemed wonderful to Henry that he should have three weeks of freedom from school, three weeks in which to recuperate from illness. Then he was bored—until he met Josh and Caleb, who are perhaps the most distinctive pair of tramps in contemporary fiction. Intrigued by their observations on the "ticking" of the town (Its pulse? Its aura?) and their secrecy about their hidey-hole, enchanted by Caleb's gourmet meals, by the cumulating manuscript that Josh is and has been writing, Henry spends all his time with these supreme do-as-you-pleasers, listening enthralled to their talk of the Night Train that will take them from Here to There. And when they go off, he is not quite sure that it really happened. Not deep characterization, but marvelously vivid characters; not a strong plot but a strongly constructed story; the people, the dialogue, and the atmosphere have a theatrical quality, as though seen and heard from a distance but caught in a battery of spotlights.

300   **Cresswell,** Helen. *Up the Pier;* illus. by Gareth Floyd. Macmillan, 1972. 144p. $4.95. (Faber, 1971. 144p. £1.30.)

5–6   A seaside resort can be a dreary place when the season is over,

and Carrie hasn't expected much fun when she comes to stay
with Aunt Ester at her rooming house in a little Welsh town.
Then she meets the boy on the pier, a strange boy whose
family lives on the pier and seems apprehensive about her. And
their clothes are so odd, like some she had seen in old
photographs . . . and then Carrie finds out that the family on
the pier have been trapped in time and are longing to get
back to 1921. In the end, she knows that only her own wishing
can set her new friends free. Written with grace, the realistic
and the fanciful adroitly blended in a convincing story that has
suspense and freshness, the book also captures with remarkable
fidelity the briny, lonely chill of October in a boarded-up seaside
amusement area.

301   **Cretan,** Gladys Yessayan. *All except Sammy;* illus. by Symeon
Shimin. Atlantic-Little, Brown, 1966. 42p. $3.50.

3–5   A story that is far from run-of-the-mill, charmingly illustrated,
and very deftly constructed. Sammy is the only member of the
Agabashian family who doesn't play a musical instrument; attracted
by the idea of being in a family publicity picture, Sammy takes
lessons. He is awful. In fact, he decides to stick to playing baseball.
On a school assignment, however, Sammy goes to an art museum
and becomes fascinated; he enrolls in a Saturday morning class
and has to defend himself against taunts and teasing when he is late
for a ball game. After a small scuffle, Sammy (sitting firmly on
his opponent) explains that painting is just as tough to do as
playing first base. He goes on learning, and the next concert
publicity picture includes Sammy—holding up his concert poster.
The dialogue and the relationships could hardly be better done.

302   **Crossley-Holland,** Kevin. *The Callow Pit Coffer;* illus. by
Margaret Gordon. Seabury, 1969. 48p. $4.50. (Macmillan, 1968.
32p. £0.75.)

4–6   First published in England, a retelling of an old folk tale of feudal
times. The three sons of the old cottar, Thor, have been told to
keep away from a dark, brooding pool in the gloomy hollow.
Mysterious and haunted, people said, and concealing in its
dangerous depths a coffer filled with treasure. The two older
brothers bravely go to the pit and bring up the coffer, but a
huge hand rises up from the water and pulls it down, leaving
in their possession only the huge iron ring with which they had
hooked the chest. Nailed to the church door, the ring becomes
an attraction that brings visitors and wealth to the town, so
the courage of the brothers has not been wasted. Notes on the
origin of the tale and on its historical background are given in a
brief epilogue; an eight-entry glossary is appended. The
illustrations are spare and stylized; the story is told with

considerable artistry, with a storyteller's flow and cadence and a restrained blending of natural and supernatural.

303   **Crossley-Holland,** Kevin. *The Pedlar of Swaffham;* illus. by Margaret Gordon. Seabury, 1971. 44p. $5.95.

4–6   A retelling of the English folk tale is illustrated by pictures, strong in color and design, that have a medieval quality. The pedlar of Swaffham, John Chapman, had a recurrent and persuasive dream: he must go to London Bridge. "Good will come of it," said the man in the dream. So John Chapman went to London Bridge, and there he met a man who had had a dream, a dream that in a place called Swaffham a pot of gold lay buried under a hawthorn tree. Home John went, and he dug under his own hawthorn tree, and there it was—a pot of gold, and still another beneath that. There is a basis for the ending of the story; the money given by the pedlar to help rebuild the church is corroborated by old records. The story is told in a vigorous and fluent style, and the details give a colorful picture of the period background.

304   **Cullen,** Countee. *The Lost Zoo;* illus. by Joseph Low. Follett, 1969. 95p. Trade ed. $4.95; Library ed. $4.98 net.

5—   First published in 1940 by Harper & Row, and long out of print, *The Lost Zoo* is the unauthenticated and amusing story of the response to Noah's invitations to join the cruising party on his ship. The acceptances are entertaining, especially the explanations of why some animals (the squilililigee, the ha-ha-ha) never made it in time. These are poems; they are preceded and followed by some rather acrimonious dialogue between the author and his know-it-all cat, Christopher. The vocabulary is not simple, but the book is well-suited to reading aloud to younger children.

305   **Curry,** Jane Louise. *Mindy's Mysterious Miniature;* illus. by Charles Robinson. Harcourt, 1970. 157p. $4.50.

4–6   There was something odd about Mr. Putt. Why was he snooping around her mother's antique shop? Mindy was sure he had a particular interest in the old dollhouse she had found at an auction sale, a toy marvelously fitted with authentic miniature furniture in perfect scale. The story moves from realism to fantasy when Mindy and her neighbor, Mrs. Bright, are captured by Mr. Putt, who has inherited a magical contraption that miniaturizes houses and the people in them. Mindy finds that her dollhouse, once a real house, is now part of a collection in a miniature community. What Mr. Putt doesn't know is that there are tiny captive people living in his museum, "Lilliput, U.S.A." There's a suggestion of caricature in some of the inhabitants, but the concept is entertaining, the solution is convincing within the fanciful framework, and the writing has suspense and pace.

306   Curtis, Richard. *The Life of Malcolm X.* Macrae, 1971. 160p. illus. $4.95.

6–10   A competent biography of the black leader whose conversion to Islam while in prison changed the pattern of his life. Malcolm Little had been a thief and a pusher, involved in prostitution and gambling. When he became a disciple of Elijah Muhammad, changing his name to Malcolm X, he lived a life of utter propriety and preached total separation from the white community. Spurned and threatened later by the very cadre he had helped train, Malcolm X changed both his role and his views. He became a voice of national, then international, importance and his experiences in Asia and Africa convinced him that it was possible for the races to work together against racism. The epilogue points out that Malcolm X, after his assassination by members of the Black Muslim movement, has been recognized even more than he was during his lifetime as one of the major voices in the struggle for black equality. Although the author's attitude is objective, there is an occasional comment that has an adulatory tone, and the writing style is far from distinguished, but on the whole the book gives a comprehensive and accurate account of Malcolm X.

307   Cutler, Ivor. *Meal One;* illus. by Helen Oxenbury. Watts, 1971. 29p. $4.95. (Heinemann, 1971. 29p. £1.10.)

K–3   A gay read-aloud story, first published in England, is permeated with affection and humor, and is illustrated with deft and engaging pictures. Helbert McHerbert and his Mum are pals: together they wrestle, play football, eat fish and chips with their fingers, and joke. One morning Helbert wakes to find a plum in his mouth; he and Mum plant it, and an enormous plum tree sprouts up and extends its roots down to forage in the kitchen. Breakfast time and no food! Wise Mum sets the clock back, the tree vanishes, and Helbert tucks in to breakfast. The story is crisp and gay, with a pleasant choice for the reader: was Helbert dreaming, or did he and Mum share a fantasy as they share everything else?

308   D'Amelio, Dan. *Taller Than Bandai Mountain;* The Story of Hideyo Noguchi; illus. by Fred Banbery. Viking, 1968. 185p. Trade ed. $4.50; Library ed. $4.13 net.

5–7   A biography of the Japanese doctor whose bacteriological research in several areas was arduous and devoted. The writing is fluid, highly and skillfully fictionalized; the book concentrates on Noguchi's childhood and his medical training, which are in truth material for romantic fiction. Severely burned as an infant, Noguchi had to overcome the obstacle of having little use of one hand, as well as the obstacle of abject poverty, in his determined pursuit of his profession.

309   **Danaher,** Kevin. *Folktales of the Irish Countryside;* illus. by Harold Berson. White, 1970. 103p. Trade ed. $4.95; Library ed. $4.76 net. (Mercier P., 1968. 144p. £0.37½.)

5–7   Fourteen tales heard by the author (a staff member of the Irish Folklore Commission) from six storytellers. The illustrations capture the waggish humor and earthiness of the stories, which have just enough of the lilt of the Irish tongue to flavor them without being burdensome. Most of the tales poke affectionate fun at country people, but some have magical elements and some familiar themes, such as "The Proud Girl" who, counting her chicks, comes to disaster. Delightful to read alone or aloud, and a good source for storytellers.

310   **Dangerfield,** Stanley, ed. *The International Encyclopedia of Dogs;* ed. by Stanley Dangerfield and Elsworth Howell. Howell Book House, 1971. 480p. illus. $19.95.

6—   An oversize book, profusely illustrated with diagrams and photographs, with several sections of color photographs to which there is an alphabetical index. The entries are written by professional people: breeders, trainers, judges, kennel club directors, and veterinarians, and are full and informative. Each breed is shown in a picture, the entries give cross-references, and words that are used as entries are capitalized when referred to elsewhere. Most of the entries give descriptions (and desirable attributes) of breeds, but there are many entries that give facts about dog care, training, disease, feeding, physiology, etc. The entry for "Rare Breeds" includes four pages of photographs that show some breeds not specifically cited in the entry and for which there is no separate entry—but this is a minor flaw in a very handsome and useful book.

311   **Daniels,** Guy, comp. *The Falcon under the Hat;* Russian Merry Tales and Fairy Tales; selected and tr. by Guy Daniels; illus. by Feodor Rojankovsky. Funk and Wagnalls, 1969. 111p. $5.95.

3–6   Dramatic, often busy, illustrations have both the folk humor and the sentiment of the tales in an attractive collection. The themes are typical of the genre; the style is vigorous yet smooth, good for reading aloud or storytelling as well as for independent reading. An interesting foreword discusses some of the idiosyncrasies of Russian folk literature.

312   **Daniels,** Guy, tr. *Foma the Terrible;* A Russian Folktale; illus. by Imero Gobbato. Delacorte, 1970. 36p. $4.50.

K–3   A Russian merry tale adapted from the collection of the folklorist

Afanasiev, and illustrated with prankish vigor. Foma (squinty eyes, bulbous nose, and a thatch of hair like a haystack) goes on a fly-killing binge and decides that he is too great a hero to plow like a peasant. Off he goes to perform feats of valor. Sent by the King of Prussia to battle against the Emperor of China, Foma the Terrible so befuddles the enemy that he triumphs, winning the hand of the lovely Princess. Epilogue: "It is not only real heroes who triumph: the louder a man blows his own horn, the better he fares in this world." A funnier Slavonic noodlehead there never was, his deeds and misdeeds told in lively style.

313   **Daniels,** Guy, ed. *The Tsar's Riddles;* or The Wise Little Girl; retold from the Russian by Guy Daniels; Paul Galdone drew the pictures. McGraw-Hill, 1967. 32p. $3.75.

K–2   A retelling of a Russian folktale with engaging illustrations that reflect both the humor and the setting of the story. Baffled by a difficult legal decision, the courts finally presented a knotty problem to the Tsar. To whom did the colt belong, the owner of the mare or the owner of the cart under which it was first found? Had the cart really had a colt? Understandably stumped by this, the Tsar set a series of riddles; neither man could solve them, but all the answers came easily to the seven-year-old daughter of the mare's owner. And so the case was decided. The nonsensical nature of the basic problem is appealing, and the common sense of the child, faced with the necessity of outwitting the Tsar, should evoke gratification in young readers.

314   **Davidson,** Margaret. *The Story of Eleanor Roosevelt.* Four Winds, 1969. 152p. illus. $3.75.

4–6   One of the better biographies of Mrs. Roosevelt, with a balanced treatment of her childhood, her life as a bride dominated by the matriarchal Sara Roosevelt, her years in the White House, and the active role she played after her husband's death. The tone is candid, admiring but not adulatory, and the author gives a vivid impression of the shy and lonely ugly duckling, for whom the first years of public life were a constant effort and whose old age was spent in vigorous enjoyment of that same life. Photographs are included; an index is appended.

315   **Day,** Beth. *The Secret World of the Baby;* by Beth Day and Margaret Liley; illus. with photographs by Lennart Nilsson, Suzanne Szasz, and others. Random House, 1968. 113p. $3.95.

7—   In this successful collaboration by a pediatrician and a layman, a simply written, authoritative text is given added usefulness by photographs of the infant in utero and added charm by photographs of newborn and very young babies. The authors describe the baby's behavior before birth, the processes of labor and birth, and the ways in which an infant learns and expresses himself. The final chapters—on the infant's ways of communicating and on the evidences of mental and physical growth—are particularly interesting. An index is appended.

316   **Dayrell,** Elphinstone. *Why the Sun and the Moon Live in the Sky*; an African folktale; illus. by Blair Lent. Houghton, 1968. 26p. Trade ed. $3.25; Library ed. $3.07 net.

K–2   Originally told by Mr. Dayrell in *Folk Stories from Southern Nigeria, West Africa* (Longmans, 1910), a story about the beginnings of time from the Efik-Ibibio peoples. Urged to visit the sun, who lived on earth and was his great friend, the water demurred, saying that his people would take up a lot of room. The hospitable sun insisted, and so the water came with all his people and in the sun's house the water rose. Thus were the sun and his wife, the moon, floated up to heaven. The beautifully detailed and stylized art work is based on African sources; the artist uses cool colors for the water, a pale blue-grey for the moon, and shades of gold and white for the sun.

317   **DeForest,** Charlotte B. *The Prancing Pony*; Nursery Rhymes from Japan; ad. into English verse for children by Charlotte B. DeForest; with "kusa-e" illus. by Keiko Hida. Walker, 1968. 63p. $3.95.

3–7   First published in Japan in 1967, a compilation of fifty-three
yrs.   favorite nursery songs. The translation occasionally forces metrical flaws, but the subjects are of universal appeal: snow or springtime, butterflies and elves, and many about animals of all kinds. The illustrations are very handsome paper collage pictures, with sophisticated and effective use of color.

318   **de Gerez,** Toni. *2-Rabbit, 7-Wind;* Poems from Ancient Mexico; retold from Nahuatl texts. Viking, 1971. 56p. illus. Trade ed. $4.75; Library ed. $4.31 net.

5—   Handsomely designed and illustrated, a book of poems that are retold from ancient Nahuatl texts. Fragmentary, untitled, poignant and lyrical, the selections reflect both the attributes of the culture and the universality of emotion that speaks to all people. Some of the selections are in other collections, but this volume is outstanding for the quality of the telling, the dignity of the format, and the informative preface.

319   **DeJong,** Meindert. *The Easter Cat*; illus. by Lillian Hoban Macmillan, 1971. 110p. $4.95.

3–5   Since her mother was allergic to cats, Millicent knew that she couldn't have one, but she kept hoping something would change. Therefore, when she found a kitten in the house on Easter morning, she was thrilled—until she realized that it was a stray. Disappointed, Millicent took refuge under the front porch and hid until her family called the police. The situation is resolved when a sister-in-law offers to take the cat for Millicent. The plot is not strong, but the situation is appealing, the style deft, and the family relationships both realistic and warm.

320   **DeJong,** Meindert. *Journey from Peppermint Street;* pictures by Emily Arnold McCully. Harper, 1968. 242p. Trade ed. $4.95; Library ed. $4.79 net. (Lutt P., 1969. 242p. £1.05.)

4–6   Set in Holland in the early 1900's, the story of a small boy who goes with his grandfather to visit an "inland aunt." On their long walk through the night, Siebren is torn between homesickness and the delight of being a traveler; he is immediately enchanted with the brisk little aunt, so loving and understanding, but only slowly loses his fear of her huge, deaf-mute husband. Siebren is enthralled by the fact that he sleeps in a room with a well, and he sturdily copes with both his nervousness about being alone in a strange place and the more drastic trouble of being caught in a tornado. Beautifully written, with vivid characterization and a compelling evocation of the excitement, the atmosphere of the dark night and the strange surroundings, and the warm comfort of achieving new horizons. The relationships between Siebren and the members of his family are particularly good; they have a universality that is compelling.

321   **DeJong,** Meindert. *Puppy Summer;* pictures by Anita Lobel. Harper, 1966. 100p. Trade ed. $3.95; Library ed. $3.79 net. (Lutt P., 1966. 112p. £0.80.)

4–6   The theme of children who must part from pets is not unusual, but Mr. DeJong's handling of the theme makes this an unusual book. A small brother and sister are spending the summer at their grandparents' farm; they are told they may have a puppy, and they find it difficult to decide which of three pups to choose. Grandma, who hasn't been enthusiastic at all, is captivated, too, and she agrees to take all three. The rest of the story describes the children's caring for their pets—or shirking the job—and their acceptance of the fact that things won't be quite the same next summer. Quietly written, with a gentle affection that permeates the story, both an affection for the puppies and a sympathetic and quite charming relationship between the children and their grandparents.

322   **Dennis,** J. Richard. *Fractions Are Parts of Things;* illus. by Donald Crews. T. Y. Crowell, 1971. 33p. $3.75.

2–4   Clear, simple pictures show, in various ways, the segments of shapes (using color to differentiate) or portions of a set of figures to illustrate some of the most common fractions: a half, a third and two-thirds, a fourth and three-fourths. The ideas are repeated, but they are given variety by using, for example, a half-full glass, a half-drawn window shade, half of a candy bar, half of a group of six children, and halves of squares, circles, rectangles, etc. broken in different ways to reinforce the idea of "half."

323   **Denny,** Norman. *The Bayeux Tapestry;* The Story of the Norman Conquest: 1066; by Norman Denny and Josephine Filmer-Sankey. Atheneum, 1966. 72p. illus. $7.95. (Collins, 1966. 72p. £1.25.)

6–10   A most handsome presentation of the story told in the tapestry, the color reproductions of the panels of the tapestry being of excellent quality. The panels tell the story of the Norman Conquest and the events that preceded it. The text uses two kinds of type; one paragraph in large type describes the scene of the panel strip; a second, and longer, section in small type gives more details and some background information. The writing style is brisk, competent, and often amusing.

324   **De Rossi,** Claude J. *Computers;* Tools for Today. Childrens Press, 1972. 95p. illus. Trade ed. $4.75; Library ed. $3.56 net.

4–6   An excellent explanation of how computers work, the binary system, programming, and the flow chart is prefaced by a history of mechanical calculating machines. Each aspect is lucidly described, with illustrations placed to best advantage for integration with the text, and the author is very careful to make both the limitations and the spectrum of uses of computers clear. An index is appended.

325   **Dickinson,** Alice. *Carl Linnaeus;* Pioneer of Modern Botany; illus. with photographs and drawings. Watts, 1967. 209p. (Immortals of Science) $4.50.

7–10   An excellent biography of the great botanist whose major contribution to science was his development of a system of taxonomy and classification of plants. The book is well written and well researched, with a good balance of interest in the subject's personal life and his professional achievements, and with the additional asset of giving historical perspective that underlines the importance of the work of Linnaeus far better than could an author's encomium. An index, a list of important dates, and a list of source materials are included.

326   **Dickinson,** Peter. *The Devil's Children.* Little, 1970. 188p. $4.95. (Gollancz, 1970. 192p. £1.00.)

6–9   Mysteriously, England had changed; its people detested machines and demolished them in a mass fury of controlled minds. Thousands fled to France, and Nicky thought perhaps her parents had gone there. They had not meant to desert her, she knew, but there she was: one of the few people left in London. A group of Sikhs, unaffected by the changes, take Nicky on so that she can warn them lest they offend the villagers near whom they live. Nicky joins them for security but quickly learns to respect them all and to love many of the "Devil's children," as the townspeople nearby call the Indians. The good will and the skill of the Sikhs save the local inhabitants from a band of robbers, and an entente cordiale is established. The story is original in concept, deftly written, and sharply characterized, with pace and suspense in the action.

327   **Dickinson,** Peter. *Emma Tupper's Diary;* illus. by David Omar White. Atlantic-Little, Brown, 1971. 212p. $5.95. (Gollancz, 1971. 192p. £1.00.)

7–10   Only a small portion of the story is told as excerpts from Emma's diary, most of it being narrated in lively and sophisticated style. Emma comes to visit her Scottish cousins and plans a record of a quiet vacation in the Highlands. Instead, she finds that the family has inherited an old submarine that was used for hunting sea monsters. When one of the cousins conceives the idea of changing the appearance of the submarine and perpetrating a hoax on the news media, the others go along in the elaborate plans. Although the semi-feud between two brothers becomes a little tedious, the book is for the most part written with verve, the characters merry and the plot inventive. And the ending is a real surprise.

328   **Dickinson,** Peter. *The Weathermonger.* Little, 1969. 216p. $4.95. (Penguin, 1970. 176p. £0.20.)

5–9   An unusual science fiction book, written in a lively, spontaneous style. The characterization is vivid, the fantasy deft, and the plot inventive; the compelling story is lightly brushed with sophisticated humor. Five years into the future, the British Isles have been mysteriously pushed back to a feudal superstition and a fear of all mechanical objects. Even the weather is controlled by magical spells. One young weathermonger, Geoffrey, escapes from the bewitched island and gets to France; he and his younger sister are sent back to find the cause of the enchantment. They do find it, and both the cause and the ending are wonderfully conceived.

329   **Dihoff,** Gretchen. *Katsina; Profile of a Nigerian City.* Praeger, 1970. 166p. illus. $5.95.

7–10   During the fifteenth and sixteenth centuries, Katsina was one of the flourishing cities of northern Nigeria, a trading center and a stronghold of Islam. This survey of Katsina today, by an anthropologist who lived there for two years, is sharply observant and objective, giving a detailed picture of the peoples and their complicated history of relationships, cultural patterns and the impact of the western world, the changing economic and educational situations. Written in a direct, easy prose and permeated with respect and affection, this is a rounded view of an ancient and intricate segment of African life.

330   **Dillon,** Eilis. *The Cruise of the Santa Maria;* illus. by Richard Kennedy. Funk and Wagnalls, 1967. 190p. $3.50. (Faber, 1967. 191p. £0.90.)

7–10   John, at sixteen, feels that he is old enough to sail the boat his grandfather had built and had named, just before he died, the *Santa Maria.* He and his friend are carried to a lonely island, and the solitary inhabitant there convinces the boys that they ought to sail from Ireland to Spain to visit his daughter, married to a Spaniard. So, with the old man's grandson as the third member of the crew, they set off. The story of their small adventures at sea and their experiences in Spain are colorful but not unbelievable, and the story line is sturdy; as in other Dillon books, the plot is outshone by the vigor of the characterization and the pithy, flavorful dialogue.

331   **Dillon,** Eilis. *A Herd of Deer;* illus. by Richard Kennedy. Funk and Wagnalls, 1970. 189p. $4.95. (Faber, 1969. 188p. £1.00.)

7–10   Michael Joyce had come from Argentina to Ireland to enjoy his wealth in the country of his ancestors. Aware that his neighbors were hostile, and suspecting that they had had something to do with the theft of some of his deer, Joyce hired a lad who was on a summer hike to act as his spy. This is the story, as told by the boy, Peter Regan, of his adventures in getting to know Joyce's neighbors and tracking down the deer. The book has some suspense and very good pace, excellent characterization and dialogue, and a convincing plot. The humor is in the characters themselves, and the writing is evocative and cadenced.

332   **Dillon,** Eilis. *The Seals;* illus. by Richard Kennedy. Funk and Wagnalls, 1969. 127p. $4.50. (Faber, 1968. 112p. £0.75.)

6–9   A novel set on a small island off the coast of County Clare in the time of the troubles. Two adolescent boys volunteer to cross over to the mainland to pick up a relative, and they decide to ask a third boy even though his family has a reputation for being informers in the far past. The dangers of the crossing and of the boys' encounter with the Black and Tans add excitement to a story with a colorful setting; the book has historic interest, the impeccably authentic Dillon dialogue, and the satisfactions of a mission accomplished and a family reputation vindicated.

333   **Divine,** David. *The Stolen Seasons.* T. Y. Crowell, 1970. 185p. $4.50. (Macdonald, 1967. 160p. £0.75.)

6–9   "You will get excessively wet," father prophesied, "you will all three of you catch preposterous colds, you will return sneezing, and your mother will take it out on me." But Peter and Mig and their American friend Clint were determined to prove their point: it was possible to get over Hadrian's Wall without being spotted. The ploy is organized and executed with finesse, the triumphant trio happily accosting friends at an archeological dig with their presence. The second—and separate—plot is in the more exciting night adventure the children have when they flee the men who have stolen a valuable artifact and know that the children have witnessed their act. The first part of the book is entertaining, the second tense with suspense; the whole is attractive, markedly British in the erudite badinage of the younger characters and in the quality of the relationships between adults and children.

334   **Dobrin,** Arnold. *The New Life—La Vida Nueva;* The Mexican Americans Today; illus. with photographs. Dodd, 1971. 109p. $3.95.

5–7   An overview of the Chicanos: their history, their problems as a minority group, and their goals. Using examples of individual citizens, the author brings into focus such elements in the life of Mexican-Americans as family solidarity, the role of the Catholic church, the appreciation of education, and the discriminatory treatment they have received. Most of the people described are ordinary citizens; a few (Ricardo Montalban, Cesar Chavez) are famous. The text moves abruptly from one topic to another at times, but the writing style is clear and direct, the subject of urgent importance, and the use of the interview technique gives a sense of immediacy and personal involvement. A chronology, a bibliography, and an index are appended.

335   **Dodge,** Bertha Sanford. *Big Is So Big;* illus. by Ben F. Stahl. Coward, 1972. 47p. $3.49.

2–4   Although the text begins here with a discussion of "big" as a relative term, this is really a book about measurement rather than size. Tom, eager to see how big he has to be before he is as tall as his father, measures himself against a wall and calls that unit a "tom." His father explains why a standard unit is preferable to one conceived independently, and shows Tom how to estimate area and volume. The clear illustrations and the lucid writing make this one of the best books on measurement for the primary grades reader.

336   **Domanska,** Janina, illus. *I Saw a Ship A-Sailing.* Macmillan, 1972.
            28p. $4.95.

3–5   A well-known rhyme is illustrated by pictures that are composed
yrs.   with a high sense of design and a deft use of color. The
            patterns are often geometric, the details intricate, and the bold
            colors of the ship, her crew, and the cargo effectively set off
            by the cool pastel shades of water or a patterned background.
            The illustrations are not primarily humorous, but there are
            amusing conceits like the clouds that emanate from a giant pipe
            smoked by the man in the moon.

337   **Domanska,** Janina, illus. *If All the Seas Were One Sea;* etchings
            by Janina Domanska. Macmillan, 1971. 29p. $4.95.

3–5   The familiar nursery rhyme about a tree made of all the trees in
yrs.   the world falling into a sea made of all the seas in the world
            (". . . what a splish splash that would be!") is illustrated with the
            intricate but not too-busy geometric figures that are distinctively
            Domanska's style. The designs are stunning and sophisticated,
            and color is used with enough restraint so that the two do not
            compete.

338   **Domjan,** Joseph. *The Little Cock;* retold by Jeanne B. Hardendorff.
            Lippincott, 1969. 30p. illus. $4.95.

3–5   An old Hungarian folktale, good for storytelling (although it is
            not as flowing as the version in Seredy's *The Good Master*) and
            reading aloud as well as for independent reading, is illustrated
            with brilliant color woodcuts that alternate with black and white
            designs; the interpretation is not literal, although within the highly
            stylized convolutions of the pages are figures from the story.
            The little cock who tries to regain his rightful possession from
            the greedy Turkish Emperor, and is successful, may have particular
            meaning to children whose Hungarian forbears were for long
            decades under Turkish dominion, but the theme of the small,
            doughty fighter triumphant over an oppressor is universal.

339   **Donovan,** John. *I'll Get There. It Better Be Worth the Trip.* Harper,
            1969. 189p. Trade ed. $4.95; Library ed. $4.11 net. (Macdonald, 1970.
            196p. £1.00.)

6–9   Davy is thirteen when his grandmother dies and he comes from a
            small town to live with his divorced mother in New York. Bereft,
            he clings to his dog, Fred, aware that his mother is irritated
            by Fred and aware, finally, that she is irritated by him, too. Davy
            makes one new friend when he goes to school; he finds that
            Altschuler, too, is painfully adjusting to bereavement. In this con-
            text it is not surprising that the two boys are catapulted
            temporarily into a homosexual relationship. It is one of the
            scarring things that happen to Davy on the way to growing up;

it is not the crux of the story, and it is handled with dignity.
The story comes from Davy in a candid, touching document of
childhood's end.

340   **Donovan,** John. *Wild in the World.* Harper, 1971. 94p. Trade ed.
$3.50; Library ed. $3.27 net.

6–9   There were no other homesteads on the New Hampshire mountain
where the Gridleys lived in isolation. One by one his four sisters
and six brothers had died, and John was alone. He seldom saw the
neighbors, never told them that he had buried the last of his family
himself. Living in solitude and silence, John welcomed the wolf
that hung about the farm, and when it became friendly, decided it
must be a stray dog. So begins the touching story of a love that
releases a lonely human being; happy with his dog, whom he calls
"Son," John becomes loquacious, content, even merry. Then in a
stark and poignant ending, John dies of pneumonia, and the
neighbors are sure that the animal they find with the body is a
wolf that has killed him. They run Son off, but when they are gone,
he comes back to sleep where John had lain. The writing is direct
and deceptively simple, with depth and perception in subtle overtones, and with a remarkably high sustention of movement in a
story with one human being (two brothers appear briefly, and
an occasional meeting with a neighbor takes place) on a bleak,
unchanging stage.

341   **Dorman,** Michael. *Under 21; A Young People's Guide to Legal
Rights.* Delacorte, 1970. 210p. $4.50.

7–12   A discussion of the legal and social difficulties and of court rul-
ings that pertain to the rights of young people in social, military,
business, parental, academic, cultural, and legal areas. Serious
and straightforward, the book has an objective tone although the
author's sympathies are clearly with the young. A few fictional cases
are used as illustrative examples, but most of the anecdotes and
examples are from cases on record. State requirements
pertaining to marriageable age, driving, and drinking, and an
index are appended. The summaries that conclude each section
add to the book's usefulness.

342   **Douglass,** Frederick. *Life and Times of Frederick Douglass;* ad.
by Barbara Ritchie. T. Y. Crowell, 1966. 210p. $4.50.

6–10   First published in 1842 and last revised by the author in 1892, a
book that was and is an exciting and remarkable record. This is a
very good adaptation of the final revision, with no deletion of important material and with consistent adherence to Douglass' style.
The life of a man who was born a slave and who died a national
figure of deserved esteem is described with modesty and candor;
Mr. Douglass speaks with objectivity about personal matters and
with articulate passion about public affairs.

343   **Douty,** Esther M. *Forten the Sailmaker;* Pioneer Champion of Negro Rights; illus. with photographs. Rand McNally, 1968. 208p. $4.95.

7–10   Ten years before the American Revolution, a son was born to Thomas and Sarah Forten, free-born Negroes of Philadelphia; James served as powder boy on a privateer, was imprisoned by the British, and came home to become one of the pioneers for the rights of Negroes, a wealthy man and a respected citizen, and an individual who gave generously of his wealth and his time to help others, buying the freedom of many slaves. Although the book is written with a sustained note of admiration, it has no aura of being adulatory or uncritical; carefully researched and written, it is useful as a contribution to the history of our country and it is particularly interesting as a biography of a Negro whose fame rests on no dramatic accomplishment but on the record of a continuing service to the cause of justice. A bibliography and an index are appended.

344   **Downer,** Marion. *Roofs over America.* Lothrop, 1967. 75p. illus. Trade ed. $3.95; Library ed. $3.70 net.

6–10   A handsome book with full-page photographs faced by a spacious page with a few paragraphs of comment or explanation. The book is divided into four sections: the seventeenth century, the eighteenth, city roofs, and modern country roofs. The examples are interesting, the text crisply informative and occasionally subjective. The author discusses the simple lines of the early roofs, the increasing diversity and decoration of eighteenth-century architecture, the conglomeration of city roofs and the sterility of many housing projects, and the inventiveness and beauty in the work of some contemporary architects. A brief list of suggestions for further reading is appended.

345   **Downie,** Mary Alice, comp. *The Wind Has Wings;* Poems from Canada; comp. by Mary Alice Downie and Barbara Robertson; illus. by Elizabeth Cleaver. Walck, 1968. 95p. $6.75. (Oxf. U.P., 1969. 96p. £1.75.)

4–7   An absolutely delightful anthology, some of the selections about things peculiarly Canadian, some on topics of a serious nature, and some of deft absurdity. There are folk-like poems translated from the French, some particularly nice animal poems, and some very conventional selections. The illustrations have a great deal of vitality and are as varied as is the poetry.

346   **Drury,** Roger W. *The Finches' Fabulous Furnace;* illus. by Erik Blegvad. Little, 1971. 149p. $4.95.

4–6   There wasn't a house in town available for rent except the one about which the agent seemed so doubtful, and even when Mr.

Finch found out what the trouble was, he decided that he could cope. Maybe he could even keep his wife from finding out that the reason the house was so hot was that there was a little volcano in the cellar. His son Peter discovered it, too, and rigged an alarm system (it was sort of a thermostat, he told his mother) just in case the volcano ever erupted. When the dreaded event takes place, it is not in the house, but in another vent in an old quarry, and the ensuing publicity delights the officials who had discovered the secret and been apprehensive about the town's reputation. The book gives a perceptive picture of the relationships in a small town, with good characterization and natural dialogue; the writing is light, humorous, and deft in merging the fanciful element and its realistic matrix, and the illustrations have a tidy precision and wit.

347   **Du Bois,** William Pène. *Bear Circus.* Viking, 1971. 48p. illus. $4.95.
4–7
yrs.   When an army of grasshoppers stripped the leaves on which koalas live, the bears of Koala Park were convoyed to a new spot by their friends, the kangaroos. Since an airplane hurtled to earth carrying the equipment for a circus (just the right size equipment, since the midgets on the flight had jumped to safety) it seemed only logical that the bears put on a circus to show their gratitude. It takes twelve years, and the act originally called "Baby Parade" has to be changed to "A Child's Garden of Bears" but the show is magnificent. The clown act, the acrobats, the magician—each set of pictures is charming, gay with color and humor, beautifully composed. Bear Power!

348   **Du Bois,** William Pène. *Call Me Bandicoot;* written and illus. by William Pène du Bois. Harper, 1970. 63p. Trade ed. $3.95; Library ed. $4.43 net.
5–9   Ermine Bandicoot stalks his prey on the Staten Island ferry. A natural con man, a born storyteller, the sharp-nosed lad spins any tale that will engross a listener to the point of handing over food and money. Here he captures a victim with a tale of Bandicoot's campaign to end smoking and pollution by creating an enormous cigarette with tobacco collected from hoarded butts, an enterprise that ends with the clogging of the harbor waters . . . a fantastic story marvelously told. A note of contrast is effectively introduced at the end, when his listener follows Bandicoot and discovers that the lad is rebelling against his tycoon father. "It's tough to be a kid and have principles," he muses, after Ermine (Hermann Vanden Kroote, Jr. is his real and rejected name) refuses a meal, saying that he does not accept charity. Fourth in the author's series of books on the seven deadly sins, this has stinginess as a leitmotif, but the imaginative embroidery of the storyteller's art almost eclipses the theme. Written with wit and sophistication and illustrated with elegance.

349   **Du Bois,** William Pène. *The Horse in the Camel Suit.* Harper,
        1967. 80p. illus. Trade ed. $3.95; Library ed. $4.43 net.

4-6   To be read, as it is written, with tongue firmly in cheek. Again the
        ingenious lad who solved the problem of *The Alligator Case* is faced
        with an entangling—possibly dangerous—alliance. Partly to pro-
        tect a small town policeman from causing himself trouble, and
        partly to solve a crime, our hero works (with success) to outwit a
        gang of horse-stealing desperadoes under a theatrical cover. The
        illustrations are charming and very funny; the story is very funny,
        rather complicated, and sophisticated in both vocabulary and
        humor.

350   **Du Bois,** William Pène. *Lazy Tommy Pumpkinhead;* story and
        pictures by William Pène Du Bois. Harper, 1966. 32p. Trade
        ed. $3.95; Library ed. $3.79 net.

2-4   A nonsense story with delightful, daft illustrations; in the terrible
        tale of Tommy there is a not-so-subtle message about sloth, or the
        mechanized age, or physical fitness, or Something. It isn't likely
        that the reader will care, since the spectacle of Tommy Pumpkin-
        head sliding from his electric bed to his automatic bath and down to
        automatic dressing and feeding is capped by the spectacle of all
        this happening with an upside-down Tommy after the electricity
        fails.

351   **Dugdale,** Vera. *Album of North American Birds;* illus. by Clark
        Bronson. Rand McNally, 1967. 112p. Trade ed. $4.95; Library ed.
        $4.79 net.

5-9   An oversize book that describes over fifty birds, devoting a page or
        two to each; some of the birds are pictured in full-page, full-color
        illustrations, and there are smaller drawings in black and white,
        precise and delicate, of all the birds. The text is written with a note of
        dry humor added to a sprightly style; the author gives information
        about appearance, habitat, habits, migratory patterns, mating,
        appearance of eggs and of fledglings, patterns of flight, and calls
        and songs, although not all of this information is given for each
        bird. The scientific name for each bird is given. The book has
        reference use for younger children.

352   **Duggan,** Alfred. *The Falcon and the Dove;* A Life of Thomas Becket
        of Canterbury; decorations by Anne Marie Jauss. Pantheon
        Books, 1966. 217p. $3.95. (Faber, 1967. 288p. £1.05.)

8—   Again, a superb work of history by the late author. Here the
        biography is impressive both as a picture of Becket and as a
        twelfth-century tapestry. It was a rare combination of scholarly
        background and wit that enabled Mr. Duggan to write historical
        material that has the appeal of an adventure story. A brief
        bibliography is appended.

353   **Duggan,** Alfred. *Growing Up with the Norman Conquest;* illus.
by C. Walter Hodges. Pantheon Books, 1966. 217p. $3.95.
(Faber, 1965. 185p. £1.05.)

7—   A delight. Mr. Duggan's writing has style, vivacity, delightful wit,
and the easy familiarity with detail that is born only of deep
knowledge. As in *Growing Up in 13th Century England,* the book
views a series of households and the communities and socio-
economic strata of which they are a part. Here the time is July
in the year 1087, and the households are those of a Norman Baron, a
socman, a Londoner, a peasant, and a cloister in which live the
children whose parents have dedicated them to a monastic life. A
most enjoyable and informative book.

354   **Dunning,** Stephen, comp. *Reflections on a Gift of Watermelon Pickle
. . . And Other Modern Verse;* by Stephen Dunning, Edward
Lueders, and Hugh Smith; design: Donald Marvine. Lothrop,
1967. 139p. $4.50.

6—   An adaptation of a 1966 Scott, Foresman textbook, and an attractive
book in every way, with stunning photographic illustrations,
carefully composed page layout, and a particularly impressive
selection of poetry. The theme that binds the poems together is
contemporary life, but the variations on the theme give the book a
many-faceted appeal; the topics range from wild geese and base-
stealing to skyscrapers and sonic boom, the moods from hilarity
to sombre reflection.

355   **Dunning,** Stephen, comp. *Some Haystacks Don't Even Have Any
Needle;* And Other Complete Modern Poems; comp. by Stephen
Dunning, Edward Lueders, and Hugh Smith. Lothrop, 1969. 192p.
illus. $5.95.

7—   Illustrated with reproductions of works of modern art in full color,
a second anthology from the compilers of *Reflections on a Gift of
Watermelon Pickle.* Some of the poets are famous, some little
known although they have had work published. The poems are
grouped by theme, they have been chosen with discrimination,
they reflect almost every aspect of modern life, and they are
written in varied moods and styles. Separate author and title
indexes are appended.

356   **Dunsheath,** Percy. *Giants of Electricity.* T. Y. Crowell, 1967. 200p.
illus. $4.50.

7—   An exceedingly well-written collective biography of some of the
greatest of those pioneers in electrical advances whose work was
the basis for the sophisticated state of electrical theories and
appliances today. Most of those discussed are inventors and
researchers of the eighteenth and nineteenth centuries. The
writing is crisp and straightforward, the emphasis being on the

scientist's work rather than on his personal life; the author describes major contributions, but he also considers some lesser-known research. A bibliography and a quite extensive relative index are appended.

357   **Dupuy,** Trevor Nevitt. The Military History of World War I; twelve volumes: *1914: The Battles in the West.* Watts, 1967. 90p. illus. $3.75.
1914: The Battles in the East. Watts, 1967. 85p. illus. $3.75.
Stalemate in the Trenches: November, 1914–March, 1918; by Trevor Nevitt Dupuy and Gay M. Hammerman. Watts, 1967. 111p. illus. $3.75.
Triumphs and Tragedies in the East, 1915–1917; by Trevor Nevitt Dupuy and Wlodzimierz Onacewicz. Watts, 1967. 89p. illus. $3.75.
The Campaigns on the Turkish Fronts; by Trevor Nevitt Dupuy and Grace Person Hayes. Watts, 1967. 109p. illus. $3.75.
Campaigns in Southern Europe; by Trevor Nevitt Dupuy and Molly R. Mayo. Watts, 1967. 100p. illus. $3.75.
1918: The German Offensives; by Trevor Nevitt Dupuy and Julia Crick. Watts, 1967. 100p. illus. $3.75.
1918: Decision in West; by Trevor Nevitt Dupuy and Julia Crick. Watts, 1967. 115p. illus. $3.75.
Naval and Overseas War, 1914–1915. Watts, 1967. 110p. illus. $3.75.
Naval and Overseas War, 1916–1918; by Trevor Nevitt Dupuy and Grace Person Hayes. Watts, 1967. 118p. illus. $3.75.
The War in the Air. Watts, 1967. 98p. illus. $3.75.
Summation: Strategic and Combat Leadership. Watts, 1967. 94p. illus. $3.75. (F. Watts, 1970. 96p. £1.05.)

6–9   Like the excellent series on the Second World War, this gives well-organized and well-rounded accounts of segments of action or theatres of operation. The maps, photographs, and diagrams are excellent; each volume has an index. The matter-of-fact, crisp writing and objective attitude in this series are especially valuable because of the dramatic and emotional nature of the contents; a good military historian, Dupuy discusses motives and pressures as dispassionately (and as clearly) as he does strategy and tactics. The final volume gives separate comments on political and military leaders or major combatants, and an extensive section of charts, with parallel action on the several fronts being shown. Lucid and informative, the series is clear and simple enough for the young reader, analytical and comprehensive enough for the adult reader.

358   **Durham,** Mae, ed. *Tit for Tat and Other Latvian Folk Tales;* retold by Mae Durham; from the tr. of Skaidrite Rubene-Koo; notes by Alan Dundes; illus. by Harriet Pincus. Harcourt, 1967. 126p. $3.25.

4–6   A good source for storytelling as well as for reading aloud or independently, this compilation of twenty-two folk tales is enhanced by the distinctive, humorous illustrations in black and white. The style of the retelling is right for the genre: direct, colloquial, and clearly relishing the mischief and humor of the dunces and wits of Latvian folklore. A section of notes written by Alan Dundes, Associate Professor of Anthropology and Folklore at Berkeley, is appended and it includes several suggestions for background reading.

359   **Duvoisin,** Roger. *Veronica and the Birthday Present;* written and illus. by Roger Duvoisin. Knopf, 1971. 28p. $3.95. (Bodley Head, 1971. £1.05.)

K–2   Farmer Applegreen, bringing a white kitten he called "Dancy" to his wife for a birthday present, found that it was gone when he got home. The kitten had slipped away while he was changing a tire and wandered to the Pumpkin's farm, where she instantly made friends with Veronica the hippopotamus. The rest of this engagingly silly story is like a ping-pong match, as Veronica and Candy follow each other back and forth from farm to farm, refusing to be separated. The only solution: another white kitten for the Applegreens and a new member of the Pumpkin menage. Lively black and white pictures alternate with gay full-color pages.

360   **Eckert,** Allan W. *Incident at Hawk's Hill;* illus. by John Schoenherr. Little, 1971. 173p. $5.95.

7—   An adult novel that should appeal to many young readers, written with sensitivity and a convincing familiarity with wild life. Six-year-old Ben had always shown a kinship with animals that made them trust him, and the description of his parents' worry about this strange affinity sets the stage for the events that follow: Ben wanders away from home and is given up after two days and nights. He is alive, however, adopted by a badger and living underground as a feral creature. When, weeks later, his older brother finds Ben, he must fight off the badger to get the boy. A touching story, adeptly written and economically constructed, is based on a real incident.

361   **Edwards,** Sally. *The Man Who Said No.* Coward-McCann, 1970. 191p. $4.95.

7–10   James Petigru's father had been a thoughtful man who was determined that his son should have the education that he deserved. So, in 1804, the farm family scraped together the money to send the boy to an academy. From teacher to lawyer, from a poor country home to an established position in Charleston society, James Petigru was a staunch Unionist despite the loss of friends and the disagreement of his wife. At the age of 48, he bought a plantation and over a hundred slaves that came with it, but he had no real interest in farming (it was simply the thing for a retired gentleman to do) and lost the property. As the talk of secession grew, Petigru spoke more openly and with bitter eloquence of the folly of disrupting the Union. As he had grown older, he had become more and more convinced that slavery must not spread, and with the state's vote to secede he had broken all ties with the leaders of South Carolina who had for years been his friends and colleagues. "The Old Lion," they called him, but when James Petigru died in 1863, the quarrel was forgotten and the whole city took a day to mourn the death of an upright man. A good biography with well-integrated historical background, written in a forthright style with restrained fictionalization. An index is appended.

362   **Elgin,** Kathleen. *The Quakers;* The Religious Society of Friends; written and illus. by Kathleen Elgin. McKay, 1968. 96p. $4.50.

5–9   A useful, handsome, and tastefully designed book, the black and white pictures adding distinction to a clear and informative text. The beginnings of Quakerism and its history in this country are described; the author uses the participation of one man, Levi Coffin, to illustrate the work of Quakers before and during the Civil War. A question-and-answer section gives specific information about beliefs and ceremonies, and the concluding pages discuss the work of Quakers today. A bibliography and an index are appended.

363   **Ellis,** Harry B. *Ideals and Ideologies;* Communism, Socialism, and Capitalism. World, 1968. 256p. illus. Trade ed. $5.95; Library ed. $5.88 net.

7–10   A most intriguing book, especially for those interested in the relationships between politics and industry. The approach is comparative, the tone objective, and the observations candid and thoughtful. The author gives the historical background of each of the three ideologies and points out the repeated evidences that, in practice, the lines of demarcation are fading: private profit as an incentive in a factory in communist East Germany, the growth of social welfare in the United States. He discusses at some length the cumulative cause-and-effect relationships between different factions within an ideological community; for example, the Social Democrats in Germany after World War I, affected by the fact that other parties absorbed some of their doctrines, were forced to shift their program. A bibliography and a lengthy index are appended.

364   **Ellis,** Harry B. *Israel;* One Land, Two Peoples. T. Y. Crowell, 1972. 183p. illus. $4.95.

7–10   One of the most detailed and comprehensive books on Israel that has been written for young people, this is distinguished for its impartiality and its clear perception of the complexities of relationships, needs, obligations, and loyalties of the two groups that share an ancestry, each having a firm conviction that the land must be their own. Harry Ellis gives excellent historical background for the problem that seems insoluble yet has, in some small areas, already seen some amelioration. A thoughtful and informative book, with a list for further reading and an extensive index to add to its usefulness.

365   **Elting,** Mary. *The Mysterious Grain;* by Mary Elting and Michael Folsom; illus. by Frank Cieciorka. Evans, 1967. 118p. $4.50.

6–9   There's an element of suspense in this well-written report on investigations into the origin of that mysterious grain, corn. For many years scientists had been puzzled by the ancestry of a plant that could not reproduce itself; corn depends on man for propagation. Darwin puzzled about this and Burbank conducted experiments; the painstaking research and the discarded theories of many botanists were the base for the discovery of three contemporary scientists (Galinat, MacNeish, and Mangelsdorf) of the wild plant from which corn evolved. The book gives a clear picture of the slow accrual of a body of scientific knowledge as well as of the cautious testing of theories. A bibliography and an index are appended.

366   **Emberley,** Barbara, ad. *Drummer Hoff;* illus. by Ed Emberley. Prentice-Hall, 1967. 28p. $4.95. (Bodley Head, 1970. 32p. £0.90.)

5–7   An adaptation of a folk verse, with bouncy rhythm and the twin
yrs.   appeals of rhyme and repetition for the very young. The tale begins with Private Parriage who brought the carriage and Drummer Hoff who fired it off, then—part by part—the cumulative verse brings in other military men of increasing rank and convenient surnames. The illustrations are delightful; bright colors over woodcut lines give an ornate leaded-glass effect; the amusing details are, as in the text, repeated; the lurid, dramatic double-page spread in which the cannon is finally fired is followed by a single page in which the passing of time has clothed the weapon with sweet signs of bucolic peace—a lovely surprise.

367   **Emberley,** Barbara, ad. *One Wide River to Cross;* adapted by Barbara Emberley. Illus. by Ed Emberley. Prentice-Hall, 1966. 28p. $4.50. (Chatto, 1969. 32p. £0.80.)

K–5   A delightful romp, a visual delight. The familiar old song that begins, "Old Noah built himself an ark . . ." is illustrated with charm and inventive humor in black woodcuts silhouetted against pages of luscious colors. The door of the ark gets smaller and smaller as the pages go by, and the book concludes with page of prose (a little anticlimactic) followed by the words and music.

368   **Emrich,** Duncan, comp. *The Nonsense Book of Riddles, Rhymes, Tongue Twisters, Puzzles and Jokes from American Folklore;* illus. by Ib Ohlsson. Four Winds, 1970. 266p. $6.50.

2–6   Illustrated with jaunty little drawings, a fine collection of riddles, games, autograph album rhymes, tongue twisters, game rhymes, and jingles that are pure nonsense. A section of notes and a bibliography are appended, adding to the value of a collection of Americana (much of it having traveled with immigrants) by an eminent folklorist.

369   **Englebardt,** Stanley L. *Careers in Data Processing.* Lothrop, 1969. 127p. illus. Trade ed. $4.50; Library ed. $4.14 net.

7–10   Following a brief but adequate résumé of the simpler machines that preceded the electronic digital computer (the need for which had become established by the growing inadequacy of the punched card system) this briefly describes the binary system and operation of computers. The author discusses the range of career opportunities from technicians and machine operators to programmers and systems specialists. There is also information about middlemen and designers, about women in data processing, and about some of the areas (medical diagnosis, primary grades education, the social sciences) in which computers are serving. There is advice given on education and on getting a job, but not in any great detail. The text is clear, well organized, and capably written; many of the photographic illustrations are of little use. An index is appended.

370   **Epstein,** Beryl (Williams). *Who Says You Can't;* by Beryl and Samuel Epstein. Coward-McCann, 1969. 254p. $4.50.

7—   "You can't beat the system?" the jacket copy asks. "You can't fight City Hall? WHO SAYS YOU CAN'T?" There have been instances of causes won that seemed lost, and the determined people who campaigned for those diverse causes are described in a lively and provocative book. The writing is informal but dignified, the tone enthusiastic. The causes and their proponents: Ralph Nader's fight for safer cars, Gene Wirge's battle against an Arkansas political machine, the massive efforts of New Jersey conservationists to save the Great Swamp, Leon Sullivan's program to help the Negro poor in Philadelphia, Daniel Fader's method of stimulating reading in young non-readers, the efforts of Frances Kelsey and Helen Taussig to demonstrate the dangers of thalidomide, and the persistent struggle of Joseph Papp for a program of free theater in New York City.

371   **Erdoes,** Richard. *A Picture History of Ancient Rome.* Macmillan, 1967. 60p. illus. Trade ed. $4.95; Library ed. $4.94 net (Collier-Mac., 1967. 64p. £1.05.)

5–9   Over a thousand years of Roman history are covered in this oversize book; the text is topical and continuous, and it does a quite good job of skimming over salient facts in the years from the time of Rome's establishment in A.D. 476. The illustrations are a profitable delight, beautiful in design and color, meticulous in period and architectural detail, and often wonderfully funny.

372   **Erdoes,** Richard. *The Sun Dance People;* written and photographed by Richard Erdoes. Knopf, 1972. 218p. Trade ed. $4.95; Library ed. $5.49 net.

7—   A comprehensive and thoughtful survey of the Plains Indians also includes much additional material on other American Indians and their cultures, and on the relationships between white men and Indians. The treatment is wholly sympathetic to the red man, the author permitting the drama and tragedy of history to speak forcefully, only occasionally adding a personal indictment. The material is topically arranged, with chapters on such subjects as "Life in a Tepee," "The Give-away Party," and "The Spirit World." The reproductions of old prints are interesting, the contemporary photographs informative. An index is appended.

373   **Erwin,** John. *Mrs. Fox;* illus. by Wallace Tripp. Simon and Schuster, 1969. 127p. $3.95.

5–6   Although there were bigger animals living in the forest there were none more wily or more self-confident than Mrs. Fox. She had a glib and boastful tongue that might have got most animals in trouble—but she would go to any length to maintain her aura. Having boasted that she had diving medals, for example, Mrs. Fox practiced in secrecy until she could stun the crowd with her prowess. Although basically episodic, the plot hinges on Mrs. Fox's stealing a baby monkey (she needed someone to open a hoard of canned food) and bringing him up. Thumb goes back to the circus but he is used to Mrs. Fox's standards and he thinks the other monkeys smell. (Besides, they fed him peanuts and bananas—ugh.) Very brittle, very pointed, very funny, a book that demands a certain level of sophistication on the part of the reader.

374   **Estes,** Eleanor. *The Tunnel of Hugsy Goode;* illus. by Edward Ardizzone. Harcourt, 1972. 244p. $5.25.

4–6   A sequel to *The Alley,* the story of that delightful community of faculty houses in which Connie Ives and her friends lived. Connie is in college now, and a new group of children has taken over the Alley; indeed, two enterprising boys have been pursuing the theory, evolved by Connie's old pal Hugsy, that there is a duplicate underground alley tunneling beneath the visible one. Although the elaborate superstructure of boy-girl hostilities threatens to swamp the action, there is enough humor and warmth in the story of the investigations of the tunnel to compensate more than amply. The characters are vivid, and the Alley community retains its distinctive charm.

375   **Ets,** Marie Hall. *Bad Boy, Good Boy.* T. Y. Crowell, 1967. 50p. illus. $3.95.

K–3   Any child has some obstacles to overcome in learning socially acceptable behavior patterns, but Roberto's were enough to make him seem obdurate. He spoke only Spanish, and the neighbors and shopkeepers scolded him often when his behavior was based on lack of comprehension. His parents quarreled. He was too old for the babies and not old enough for school. Bored, fractious, bewildered, worried, the small boy was taken to a Children's Center when his mother left (temporarily) after an argument. As he learned skills and acquired confidence, Roberto's behavior changed. The story is told with too much candor and simplicity to be grim, but it is bluntly realistic. Five children sleep in one room—a teacher does lose her temper sometimes—parents do quarrel, and some people do, like Roberto's mother, find it hard to discipline or be disciplined.

376   **Eyerly,** Jeannette. *The Phaedra Complex.* Lippincott, 1971. 159p. Paper ed. $1.95; Library ed. $3.93 net.

7–9   Laura tells the story of her mother's remarriage and the subtle shifting of emotions that caused trouble. Michael is a glamorous figure, a foreign correspondent whose efforts to act like a father are misinterpreted. Jealous, Laura's mother has a nervous breakdown; Laura herself realizes that her feeling for Michael includes hero worship and that her own boy friend is jealous. The story is written in retrospect, after a year of family counseling and the establishment of better relationships have made Laura and her parents see their roles more clearly. The book is written with no sensationalism, both the problem and its solution handled with understanding and dignity. Good characterization, and a convincing first-person style of writing.

377   **Fairfax-Lucy,** Brian. *The Children of the House;* by Brian Fairfax-Lucy and Philippa Pearce; illus. by John Sergeant. Lippincott, 1968. 190p. $3.95. (Longman Young Books, 1968. 160p. £1.10.)

6–8   In the comfortable years before the First World War, many an English household was run as was the Hatton's: father was at best the total authority, at worst a despot. Here the lives of the four Hatton children are made almost miserable by their tyrannical father; it is not quite so because the children have made, in self-defense, a life of their own. United in their plans and abetted by sympathetic servants, the children manage to

enjoy life despite parental strictures, although in one wistful
moment one of them says of a kind manservant, "I wish we
were his children." The story has been adapted successfully by
Philippa Pearce from a book intended for adults. There is enough
humor and action for children, yet there remains a nostalgic
note and an evocation of period that adults can best enjoy.

378   **Fall,** Thomas. *Dandy's Mountain;* illus. by Juan Carlos Barberis.
Dial, 1967. 200p. $3.95.

5–7   Bruce's mother was hospitalized, so his relatives invited him to
spend the summer with them in the Adirondack country; his
cousin Dandy (Amanda) was particularly delighted, since they
were about the same age. A fringe delinquent, Bruce was sullen
and hostile; he caused Dandy to have an accident; he irritated
his aunt and uncle. It was Dandy who insisted that Bruce not
be sent home, Dandy who insisted that he needed only time, and
Dandy who effected a change in Bruce. Knowing that he was
running away and heading for the mountain where he would
surely get lost, Dandy followed; both children were finally located
by an airplane pilot, and by the time that happened, Bruce had
indeed shown his real mettle, just as Dandy had hoped. The
children's experiences are exciting but quite believable; both of
their patterns of actions and attitudes are in character, and the
relationships within the larger family circle are convincingly
drawn.

379   **Farb,** Peter. *The Land, Wildlife, and Peoples of the Bible;* illus.
by Harry McNaught. Harper, 1967. 171p. Trade ed. $3.95;
Library ed. $3.79 net.

7—   Illustrated with beautifully detailed drawings of plants, animals,
or artifacts of the Holy Land, a fascinating book that describes
some of the events of the Old Testament and the New Testament
as they can be interpreted today by a scientist. The locust, for
example, eaten by John the Baptist is now thought to be the
pod of the carob (or locust tree) and the behemoth described
by Job is now assumed to be a hippopotamus. The final chapter
briefly discusses some of the changes of the past two thousand
years. A bibliography (divided into general and advanced
readings), an index of Biblical references, and a subject index
are appended. The writing style is polished, the information
interesting.

380   **Farley,** Carol. *Mystery of the Fog Man;* illus. by Joseph Escourido.
Watts, 1966. 116p. $3.95.

6–8   A very good mystery story, tightly constructed and written in a
style that is believable as a story told by a thirteen-year-old boy.
Kipper is visiting his cousin Larry for the first time in the

Lake Michigan town where Larry's father is chief of police. When some money is stolen from a lake ship's safe, the boys do some investigating on their own. Kipper is sure the culprit is the "fog man" who shambles about the beach; the fog man, it develops, has nothing whatsoever to do with the story except to provide false clues. The money is recovered by Larry in a believable way; his zeal is caused by the fact that he feels his father could have a more interesting life alone (Larry is motherless) and that helping his father will ease his own feeling that he limits his father's opportunities.

381   **Farmer,** Penelope. *Charlotte Sometimes;* illus. by Chris Connor. Harcourt, 1969. 192p. $4.95. (Chatto, 1969. 192p. £0.90.)

5–7   Another fantasy-adventure from the deft pen that produced *Emma in Winter* and *The Summer Birds.* Here a newcomer to boarding school finds that she has somehow been shifted back to the days of World War I; not always, but sometimes she becomes Clare instead of Charlotte, living with a younger sister at the same school. Slowly Charlotte realizes that she and Clare are changing places and that her life as Charlotte is being lived by Clare on the days she herself is in the past. Trapped by a mishap in Clare's time, Charlotte must scheme to get back to the present. The concept has been used in science fiction, but seldom has it been used to such dramatic effect in books for the young. The boarding school setting and the period details are quite convincing, and the suspense is maintained even when the mechanics of the mystery are explained.

382   **Fatio,** Louise. *The Happy Lion's Treasure;* illus. by Roger Duvoisin. McGraw-Hill, 1970. 28p. Trade ed. $4.95; Library ed. $4.72 net.

K–2   The pigeon started it by telling the Happy Lion that she had heard a zoo visitor comment on what a rich life the lion had. It seemed perfectly clear that he should make a will, but as the raven (knowledgeable because his ancestors were lawyers) pointed out—he owned nothing. Not true, said the lion's friend François, the Happy Lion had a great treasure. The animals, excited, began quarreling; the lion calmed them. And so they guessed: the Happy Lion's treasure was his loving heart. Although the tale ends in a veritable frenzy of kissing among the beasts, the light style and tone keep the whole from being saccharine. The message is love, the tale amiable, the illustrations engaging.

383   **Fatio,** Louise. *The Happy Lion's Vacation;* illus. by Roger Duvoisin. McGraw-Hill, 1967. 32p. $3.95.

K–2   Another pleasant tallish tale about the Happy Lion, told in bland, direct style and illustrated with busy, lively drawings. Here the zoo-keeper's son takes the Happy Lion along when starting out for a day at the seashore, and finds he has a problem. Nobody

wants a lion as a traveler. With one thing and another, the
Happy Lion is in and out of jail, a passenger on a runaway
balloon flight, a refugee in an Eskimo community, and an honored
guest on an ocean liner. This fanfaronade of nonsense has the
same blithe appeal as other Happy Lion escapades.

384   **Feagles,** Anita MacRae. *Me, Cassie.* Dial, 1968. 158p. $4.50.

7–10   Although the action verges occasionally on slapstick, this is a
merry and sophisticated story, convincingly told by eighteen-year-
old Cassie. A suburbanite whose mother is a frustrated liberal
(frustrated because there isn't enough to reform) and an
indefatigable organization woman, Cassie is almost crowded out of
her home by Mother's causes: two African exchange students and
some orphaned cousins. She is having her own troubles with
Jonah, a reluctant suitor; and the longer she waits for Jonah to
commit himself, the more Cassie lets herself become involved in a
modeling career. She doesn't really enjoy it, however, and is
delighted when Jonah finally capitulates and admits he is in love.
The dialogue is breezy and intelligent, and the characters piercingly
real.

385   **Fecher,** Constance. *Bright Star;* A Portrait of Ellen Terry. Farrar,
1970. 236p. $4.95.

7—   For more than fifty years Ellen Terry was a great star of the
theatrical world. Daughter, sister, and mother of actors, she
managed, amazingly, to flout Victorian mores and yet be loved
and respected—even entertained by the Queen. Impetuous and
tender, she was without enemies, although not always without
critics, and her biography is sown with anecdotes about many of
the great figures of the period: Tennyson, Carroll, Bernhardt,
Duse, Disraeli—and, of course, Shaw and Irving. The details of
her relationship with Irving are given in an account that balances
nicely their personal and professional ties. The author makes her
subject move with reality and warmth, and the biography is
excellent both as a personal portrait and as a large, plummy slice
of theatrical history. The photographs are enticing; a section of
author's notes, a bibliography, and an index are appended.

386   **Feelings,** Muriel L. *Moja Means One;* Swahili Counting Book;
pictures by Tom Feelings. Dial, 1971. 20p. $4.50.

4–7   Swahili for numbers one to ten is given in a counting book
yrs.   illustrated with softly drawn pictures, strong in composition, that
show aspects of East African life. The digits are followed by the
Swahili word, its phonetic pronunciation, and a sentence in which
the names of objects that are to be counted are printed in the
same dark red as the Swahili word, the rest of the print in
black. "Snowy Kilimanjaro is the highest *mountain* in Africa . . .
Many kinds of *animals* roam the grassy savannah lands . . . The

Nile River, which flows between Uganda and Egypt, is filled with *fish . . ."* (one mountain, five animals, seven fish). Although such references to river boundaries or to mountains may mean little to children young enough to be learning to count, the setting, the use of Swahili words, and the serenity and dignity of the pictures make this an impressive addition to the genre.

387   **Feelings,** Tom. *Black Pilgrimage;* written and illus. by Tom Feelings. Lothrop, 1972. 72p. Trade ed. $5.95; Library ed. $5.11 net.

5—   An eminent illustrator of children's books describes his life experiences as an interpreter of black people here and in Africa, discusses the biased treatment he received as a black artist, and explains the reasons for his decision to move his family to Africa. His statement is honest, often bitter, and always sensitive, particularly interesting for the insight his own work gave Tom Feelings into the attitudes of black Americans after he had been in Africa and returned. The illustrations, some in color and some in black and white, are stunning.

388   **Fehrenbach,** T. R. *The United Nations in War and Peace;* illus. with photographs, cartoons, and maps. Random House, 1968. 179p. $2.95.

7–10   An excellent history of the United Nations by the author of an adult book on the subject, *This Kind of Peace* (McKay, 1966). Although the book gives a brief and adequate description of the other aspects of the organization, and of the powers in other decision-making areas, it focuses on the role of the United Nations in the maintenance of world peace since 1945. The writing style and organization of material are very good, and the author is objective and thorough in discussing the problems of conflicting powers, financial limitations, those limitations on the United Nations' powers that arise out of the compromises necessary to make at inception, and the realities of the international situation.

389   **Felton,** Harold W. *Mumbet; The Story of Elizabeth Freeman;* illus. by Donn Albright. Dodd, 1970. 63p. $3.95.

4–6   Elizabeth Freeman has a unique position in black history. Uneducated, intelligent, and firm in her purpose, she insisted on trying in the Massachusetts courts the principle she had heard was embodied in the new constitution of the commonwealth. Thus, in 1781, a black slave won her freedom by due process of law. The appeal of the dramatic event is enhanced by the suspense of the barriers erected by Mumbet's owner and by the tenacity and shrewdness of the protagonist.

390   **Fenten,** D. X. *Plants for Pots; Projects for Indoor Gardeners;* illus. by Penelope Naylor. Lippincott, 1969. 125p. Trade ed. $4.95; Library ed. $4.82 net.

5–9   A good book for the beginner, but not oversimplified; there is enough detail about plant feeding, propagation, and potting to make the book useful to the practiced amateur as well. The drawings are precise and attractive, showing methods (leaf cuttings, starting flats, forcing bulbs) but not illustrating every kind of plant mentioned. The writing is brisk and businesslike, but rather informal; a glossary, pronunciation list, and index are appended.

391   **Feuerlicht,** Roberta Strauss. *America's Reign of Terror;* World War I, the Red Scare, and the Palmer Raids; illus. with photographs. Random House, 1971. 122p. $4.95.

6–10   A sober and sobering review of the years 1917–20, in which the persecution of those who were "different" and therefore suspect: aliens, radicals, blacks, pacifists, labor leaders, etc. reached new heights in the United States. From President Wilson's espousal of the war and the propaganda machine of the Committee on Public Information to the hysteria of the Palmer Raids, the book speaks not only in condemnation of the particular excesses it describes but also speaks to the danger in any period of the abridgement or negation of the democratic process, and of the civil liberties to which aliens as well as citizens are entitled. A bibliography and an index are appended.

392   **Feuerlicht,** Roberta Strauss. *Zhivko of Yugoslavia;* photographs by Herbert A. Feuerlicht. Messner, 1971. 64p. Trade ed. $3.95; Library ed. $3.79 net.

3–6   Like the Gidal books and the many comparable books that describe a culture by focusing on the life of one child's family, this text is concerned both with the family and with the town and the country in which they live. The writing is direct and matter-of-fact, the description of Zhivko's activities interspersed with information about the earthquake that almost demolished the town (Skopje, capital of Macedonia) and the holiday ceremonies in memory of that day. There is some material about Tito and about Yugoslavian history and government, a bit about education, and so on, but most of the text discusses such homely things as Zhivko's chores and Baba's cooking. Pleasantly low-keyed. A pronunciation guide is appended.

393   **Finkel,** George. *Watch Fires to the North.* Viking, 1968. 311p. Trade ed. $3.95; Library ed. $3.77 net. (Angus & R., 1967. 224p. £1.05.)

7–9   First published in England under the title *Twilight Province,* an absorbing story set in Britain after the withdrawal of the Roman troops. Lucius Bedwyr Marcianus, who tells the story, is thirteen and the descendant of a centurion. His friend Artyr is a natural leader; his cousin Gwenyfer a harum-scarum girl at the start of the book; as Bedwyr describes the raids and rivalries of the countryside, the battles and pilgrimages, there emerges a brilliant version of the Arthurian legend—the names slightly different, the personalities far more convincing than they usually are. The writing is sedate in style, occasionally ponderous, but that is easily compensated for by the historical fidelity, the vivid characterization, and the flow of action.

394   **Fisher,** Aileen Lucia. *But Ostriches . . .*; illus. by Peter Parnall. T. Y. Crowell, 1970. 43p. $3.95.

3–5   Good for nature study, delightfully illustrated, and a pleasure to read aloud, this book of flowing poetry contrasts with humorous wit the ostrich and other birds. Pattern: "Most birds surely/ Walk quite poorly/ Most birds merely/ hop around/ They're securest/ swiftest, surest/ on their wings/ *above* the ground," and at the turn of a page, "But OSTRICHES . . ." So, in most palatable fashion, the habits of the ostrich are explored and explained. The spare precision of the Parnall pictures resembles the anatomical exactness of Ravielli's work.

395   **Fisher,** Aileen Lucia. *Feathered Ones and Furry*; illus. by Eric Carle. T. Y. Crowell, 1971. 37p. $4.50.

6–8   Simply written poems about animals, in a book illustrated with handsome linoleum cuts in black on white or beige pages. The tidiness of meter and rhyme are exemplified by "A Robin." "I wonder how a robin hears?/ I never yet have seen his ears/ But I have seen him cock his head/ And pull a worm right out of bed." The appeal of the subjects and the level of writing make this a good book for reading aloud to younger children as well as for independent reading.

396   **Fisher,** Aileen Lucia. *Jeanne D'Arc*; illus. by Ati Forberg. T. Y. Crowell, 1970. 52p. $4.50.

3–5   At last, a fine book about the Maid of Orleans for younger readers, handsomely illustrated with pictures (some black and white, some in color) that have a grave beauty. The writing is simple and dignified, and the story is well suited to the middle grades reader also because of the clean, large print, the amount of historical information, and the fact that the retelling begins in Jeanne's eleventh year.

397   **Fisher,** Aileen Lucia. *Valley of the Smallest*; The Life Story of a Shrew; illus. by Jean Zallinger. T. Y. Crowell, 1966. 161p. $3.75.

6–9   An exceptionally good book on the life cycle of an animal, written in a smooth narrative style, yet never popularized or sentimental. The tiny shrew is an animal, not a winning personality; in describing her life, fraught with danger, the author gives a fine picture of the whole ecology. The illustrations, handsome and realistic in black and white, have both softness and strength. A list of suggested readings and an index are appended.

398   **Fisher,** Aileen Lucia. *We Alcotts;* by Aileen Lucia Fisher and Olive Rabe; decorations by Ellen Raskin. Atheneum, 1968. 278p. Trade ed. $4.95; Library ed. $5.25 net.

6–9   This is the story of the Alcott family told from Mrs. Alcott's point of view and written in an appropriately old-fashioned style. "My brother had prepared me for Mr. Alcott's advanced ideas, but he had not prepared me for the striking figure and charming manners of the young educator, just a year older than I." And so Abba May and Bronson met and wed, to begin a long financial struggle alleviated by family love, lofty ideals, and the friendship of such men as Emerson and Thoreau. There is an emphasis on Louisa, but the real interest of the book is in the family's participation in the intellectual ferment of the day, in Bronson's theories about the teaching of children, in the Brook Farm venture, and in the abolitionist movement. A bibliography is appended.

399   **Fisher,** Leonard Everett. *The Potters;* written and illus. by Leonard Everett Fisher. Watts, 1969. 47p. (Colonial Americans) $3.75.

5–7   Another in a series (originally called Colonial American Craftsmen) that is as handsome as it is useful. This volume is, like the others, divided into a first section that gives a brief history of the development of potteries in the colonies and a second that describes the processes and the raw materials used, the machinery, the variations in the craft, and the role of the craftsman.

400   **Fisher,** Leonard Everett. *The Schoolmasters;* written and illus. by Leonard Everett Fisher. Watts, 1967. 47p. (Colonial American Craftsmen) $3.75.

5–7   A very good book in the series, this gives ample background for discussing the role of the colonial schoolmaster, since it describes the change of attitude about education and the changes in society's attitudes toward learning and the common man. Mr. Fisher describes the training of the schoolmaster, his status in the community, and his problems in coping with the deficiencies of buildings and equipment. As the colonies became more self-reliant and sophisticated, better-trained teachers were demanded and a growing number of academies and even colleges fed the demand. The illustrations are starkly handsome, the writing style straightforward. An index is appended.

401   **Fisher,** Leonard Everett. *Two If by Sea;* written and illus. by
             Leonard Everett Fisher. Random House, 1970. 64p. $3.95.

5–6   The strong lines and dramatic contrast of dark blue and white
             illustrations are an attractive complement to the tension of the
             minutely described events of the evening of April 18, 1775.
             The book is in four sections, each giving an exact account,
             historically based and with some background information, of the
             actions of four men during two eventful hours of that night:
             Joseph Warren, who sent the message to Revere; Paul Revere;
             the young man who lit the signal lanterns, Robert Newman; and
             the commanding general of the British forces, Thomas Gage. The
             shift of viewpoint adds to the suspense, the writing style is
             adequate, and the book is an attractive variant on the many
             books about aspects of the American Revolution. Its weakness is
             minor: there is, in some sections of the book, a noticeable
             drawing-out of material when the immediate action of the hours
             between nine and eleven is slight.

402   **Fitzgerald,** John D. *Me and My Little Brain;* illus. by Mercer
             Mayer. Dial, 1971. 137p. Trade ed. $4.95; Library ed. $4.58 net.

4–6   In the two earlier books to which this is a sequel, John described
             the usually mercenary exploits of his older brother T.D., the
             Great Brain. Now T.D. has gone away to school, and John tries
             to live up to his brother's standards for wheeling and dealing—
             but he just doesn't have the knack. That John has a brain and
             can use it is shown beyond question when he outwits a dangerous
             criminal who has taken a small child (orphaned, and adopted
             by John's family) as hostage. Lively, funny, and at times tender,
             the story of a boyhood in a small Mormon town at the turn of
             the century is full of action.

403   **Flanagan,** Geraldine Lux. *Window into an Egg;* Seeing Life Begin.
             Scott, 1969. 72p. illus. $5.95.

4–6   The title is literal: through a glass window sealed into an eggshell
             one sees the growth of a chick from single cell to embryo to fetus
             to newly hatched, bedraggled, wide-eyed chick. Although the text
             moves with slow, infinite detail, it holds interest because it is
             illustrated with many excellent enlarged photographs. An index is
             appended.

404   **Fleischman,** Sid. *Chancy and the Grand Rascal;* illus. by Eric von
             Schmidt. Atlantic-Little, Brown, 1966. 179p. $4.95. (H. Hamilton,
             1967. 179p. £0.90.)

5–7   An entirely diverting story by a master of the tall tale. Orphaned
             Chancy, separated from his siblings, leaves the family he'd been
             living with and goes off to Paducah to find his long-lost little
             sister, Indiana. He meets a wonderful rogue and shyster, Colonel

Plugg (invented, too late, to be played by W. C. Fields) and is
outwitted by him; he meets his own uncle, the tallest teller of
them all. The fact that Chancy and Uncle Will eventually rescue
Indiana from a curmudgeon and take her to Abilene, to be
reunited with the two younger children, is of less importance
than the fact that Uncle Will and Chancy have a series of
wonderfully improbable adventures.

405   **Fleischman,** Sid. *McBroom and the Big Wind;* illus. by Kurt Werth.
Norton, 1967. 42p. Trade ed. $4.25; Library ed. $3.99 net.

4–6   In *McBroom Tells the Truth,* Sid Fleischman introduced one of the
most amusing and extravagant liars of our time; here is another
hilarious tall tale about the amazing events on the one-acre
McBroom farm; no ordinary wind attacked it, but a powerful gale
that blew the eleven childen into the sky, trapped a bear into
skipping rope with the laundry line, and bent McBroom's gun
at right angles so that it brought down a brace of ducks
over Mexico.

406   **Fleischman,** Sid. *McBroom's Ear;* illus. by Kurt Werth. Norton,
1969. 44p. Trade ed. $4.25; Library ed. $3.93 net.

3–6   Another blithe tall tale about the marvelous McBroom farm, where
instantaneous growth from superfertile soil and blazing Iowa sun
provide magnificent crops of food and stories. Plagued by
grasshoppers who would eat anything green, including McBroom's
socks, the harvest disappeared; only one seed was left and from it
grew a cornstalk that had only one ear. But what an ear! Adults
should enjoy reading the book aloud or using it for storytelling,
and independent readers are already a captive audience.

407   **Fleischman,** Sid. *McBroom Tells the Truth;* illus. by Kurt Werth.
Norton, 1966. 48p. Trade ed. $4.25; Library ed. $3.99 net.

3–6   A romping and delightful tall tale, written in a blandly ingenuous
style, and illustrated with lively and humorous drawings. McBroom,
a farmer, describes his marvelous farm: the rich soil produced
four crops a day; the eleven McBroom children had to stand
weed-guard; the just-planted beans grew so fast the vines caught
at McBroom's ankles. The story ends, "That's the entire truth of
the matter. Anything else you hear about McBroom's wonderful
one-acre farm is an outright fib." Entertaining to read aloud,
a tale that should be enjoyed by young listeners and by readers
from middle grades through middle age.

408   **Fleming,** Alice. *Ida Tarbell;* First of the Muckrakers; illus. with
photographs. T. Y. Crowell, 1971. 170p. $4.50.

6–9   Ida Tarbell spent her childhood in the oil region of Pennsylvania,
and so had a long-standing interest that spurred her investigation

of the monopolistic tactics of the Standard Oil Company. She was already an established journalist when her exposé made her famous as the first of the muckrakers. Most of the book is devoted to a detailed account of her work on *The History of the Standard Oil Company*, but the treatment of the rest of her life is balanced, the text written in a lively style and in an informal tone. A bibliography and an index are appended.

409

7—

Forman, James. *Ceremony of Innocence*. Hawthorn Books, 1970. 249p. $4.95.

Based on actual events, with only a few fictional characters, this is a story of heroism and high principle during World War II. Hans and Sophie Scholl, brother and sister, are young Germans who love their country and are appalled by Nazism. When they are picked up by the Gestapo for printing and distributing treasonous leaflets, both accept the death penalty rather than traducing their beliefs. In a flashback technique, Hans remembers, while he awaits the guillotine, the events of his childhood and his days as a student at Munich University, the risks he and his sister took, the friends who worked with them, the fears of their family, and the adamant cruelty of the Hitler regime. Strong, evocative, and convincing, another book in which James Forman pleads effectively for peace and sanity.

410

9—

Forman, James. *Horses of Anger*. Farrar, 1967. 249p. $3.95.

A mature and powerful novel about a young German soldier in World War II. Hans, like many of his friends, had idolized Hitler and only slowly begun to question the Nazi philosophy. A soldier at fifteen, Hans had once believed all of the propaganda; as he saw the discrepancies between facts he knew and official statements, he began to doubt. Even after defeat, he believed some of the myths perpetrated against American soldiers, particularly Negro soldiers, until he met them. Understanding that his own prejudice had been without basis, Hans looks forward to a future in which there is truly brotherhood of men. Written with depth and conviction, this is a deep indictment of racism and war.

411

7–12

Forman, James. *My Enemy, My Brother*. Meredith, 1969. 250p. $5.95.

Dan was sixteen when he got out of the concentration camp, an emaciated young Jew who hated war even more than he hated the Germans, a boy who wanted to be the enemy of no man. A long and hazardous trek from Poland to the coast, a trip during which one companion dies and Dan himself is captured by the British (as an illegal Israel-bound infiltree) and escapes, and a voyage across the Mediterranean finally bring Dan to the kibbutz where his two friends live. He becomes a shepherd and, despite increasing

Arab-Israeli tension, makes friends with Said, an Arab shepherd. They lose each other when hostility erupts into war, and Dan—sickened by the killing—looks forward to the future with painful ambivalence. The book closes with a brief episode in which Said, now in the Arab army, looks at the bleak prospects ahead and wonders if his people, displaced and distrait, will ever again see their homeland. The author shows both viewpoints with understanding; he makes no judgments; he pleads only for peace. The story, although at times moving with ponderous detail, gives a vivid if depressing picture of the bitter plight of the young in wartime and a grim one of their struggle to escape. Thoughtful and impressive, the book has a taut mood of suspense that is never quite dissipated.

412

8—

Forman, James. *The Traitors*. Farrar, 1968. 238p. $3.95.

A powerful story of World War II, set in a small Bavarian town in the years 1938 to 1945. With dismay, Pastor Eichhorn sees his congregation adopting the Nazi cause; with anguish, he knows that his only child, Kurt, is a confirmed Nazi. He turns to his foundling son, Paul, for understanding, but Paul wavers, insecure and frightened. Unfit for military service, Paul sees the war machine crumbling; he hides a Jewish friend; he joins a small group of traitors who conspire to save the town when the Nazis plan to destroy it as a deterrent to the advancing enemy. Distinctive characterization and a dramatic situation add impact to Forman's sweeping style and fine narrative sense.

413

8—

Forsee, Aylesa. *Men of Modern Architecture*; Giants in Glass, Steel and Stone. Macrae, 1966. 222p. illus. $4.50.

A collective biography, the subjects being Louis Sullivan, Frank Lloyd Wright, Walter Gropius, Mies van der Rohe, Eric Mendelsohn, Richard Neutra, Edward Durrell Stone, and Eero Saarinen. The biographical sketches are focused on each architect's work, although there is an adequate amount of information about personal life. The author writes competently about the training and career of each man, and describes their philosophies and their places in architectural history as well as describing the things they built. The photographs are good, but there are many buildings described that might well be illustrated; the one slight weakness of the book is that so much is described that, toward the end of each biography (when the architect received many commissions) there is a crowded catalog of buildings. A glossary and a selected bibliography are appended.

414

7—

Foster, G. Allen. *Sunday in Centerville*; The Battle of Bull Run, 1861; illus. by Harold Berson. White, 1971. 166p. $4.95.

A long, detailed, and well-researched description of the first Battle of Bull Run, the battle that created Confederate heroes and that made it clear to the North that it might be a long, long war. The account is preceded by a discussion of the complex causes of the war, Northern and Southern attitudes and misconceptions, the response to secession, and the military preparations of the Union and Confederate Armies. The writing is straightforward, serious but vigorous and occasionally leavened by humor, as are the illustrations. A bibliography and an index are appended.

415   **Foster,** Laura Louise. *Keeping the Plants You Pick;* written and illus. by Laura Louise Foster. T. Y. Crowell, 1970. 149p. $4.95.

5–9   Meticulously detailed and delicately drawn, black and white pictures of plants and diagrams for preserving them are as attractive as they are informative. In a direct, competent text, the author gives instructions on methods of pressing or drying flowers, arranging them for collections or for ornamental use, and caring for them. The instructions for all procedures are full and explicit, with frequent suggestions for alternate materials or for artistic results. A list of field guides, a list of sources for seed catalogs, and an index are appended.

416   **Fowke,** Edith, comp. *Sally Go Round the Sun;* Three Hundred Children's Songs, Rhymes and Games; comp. and ed. by Edith Fowke; musical arrangements by Keith MacMillan; illus. by Carlos Marchiori. Doubleday, 1970. 160p. $6.95.

4–5   Younger children, too, will appreciate the material in this collection, since the book is ideally suited for adult use with small children in groups. The musical arrangements are simple, and there are instructions for forty of the games. The illustrations are lively, the songs and games come directly from children, having been taped by the compiler, an expert on Canadian folklore. The book has been awarded the 1970 medal as the best Canadian book of the year for children in English. A bibliography, notes on sources, and an index are appended.

417   **Fox,** Paula. *Blowfish Live in the Sea.* Bradbury Press, 1970. 116p. $4.50.

6–9   Twelve-year-old Carrie had never understood why Ben wrote that sentence about blowfish everywhere but accepted it, as she accepted anything about her half-brother. When he was invited to meet his long-absent father in Boston, Ben asked Carrie to go along. In the story of that visit, as Carrie tells it, is a piercingly sweet and tender picture of a young girl's love for her brother. The book also is unusual in its sensitive characterization of Ben's father: the failure, the drifter embarrassed at meeting his son, but so clearly lonely that he touches the heart. He touches Ben's heart enough to make the young man decide to live with him, forsaking the convention and stability of his mother's and stepfather's home. Only after she returns alone does Carrie discover that Ben's father had once sent him a dried blowfish that he had found, he said, in the Amazon. It was after Ben discovered that the blowfish lives in salt water only that he began to write "Blowfish live in the sea," his testimony of resentment at his father's lies. And his leaving home is testimony of maturity: a realization that there are other values and softer judgments. A fine book.

418   **Fox,** Paula. *How Many Miles to Babylon?* illus. by Paul Giovanopoulos. White, 1967. 117p. Trade ed. $4.50; Library ed. $4.27 net. (Macmillan, 1968. 128p. £0.67½.)

4–5   James has been staying with three aunts since both of his parents have gone; where his father went, nobody knows and where his mother is, James doesn't want to believe. The hospital, say the aunts; but James daydreams about his mother being in Africa. Sent on a school errand, James runs off to a deserted house where he is found and menaced by a gang of boys who steal dogs; they take James to Coney Island and keep him prisoner; he finally escapes and gets home; when he does, there is his mother. The ending is inconclusively handled, the plot heavy, the characters not well differentiated; nevertheless, the book has several appealing aspects, the major one being the fine creation of mood and atmosphere. The illustrations show a sensitive, dreamy Negro child of ten; the story makes James a sympathetic character even before he performs his one act of courage, but few readers of ten will appreciate the subtleties of the writing.

419   **Fox,** Paula. *A Likely Place;* illus. by Edward Ardizzone. Macmillan, 1967. 57p. $3.50. (Macmillan, 1968. 64p. £0.67½.)

4–6   Lewis is tired of people who want to help him, especially those who want to help him improve. When his loving parents go off for a brief trip, Lewis is taken over by the delightfully peculiar Miss Fitchlow, whose ideas of supervising a nine-year-old boy are entirely casual and man-to-man. Lewis befriends an elderly man who frequents the same park; directed by Mr. Madruga, Lewis writes a letter of protest, the old gentleman's problem being that he resents the life of ease forced on him by his children—he wants to work. The writing has distinctive style, the characterization is smooth, the humor is sophisticated: "Lewis shrugged. He knew his mother was smiling only because she wanted him to do something different from what he was going to do."

420   **Fox,** Paula. *Maurice's Room;* pictures by Ingrid Fetz. Macmillan, 1966. 64p. Trade ed. $3.95; Library ed. $3.24 net.

3–5   An absolutely enchanting book, written in low key, with deadpan humor, and with marvelously real people. Maurice is an only child and his room is a collector's joy and a mother's despair. Maurice collects anything that looks interesting; his friend the janitor and his chum Jacob extend aid and comfort. His parents try to distract him with a pet; Maurice quietly collects. He is scheduled for music lessons. He adds a few more things to his collection. The family moves to the country, and Maurice is bored—until he sees the barn; it is very big, and it is full of Things. The writing style is deft, the illustrations engaging.

421   **Fox,** Paula. *Portrait of Ivan;* illus. by Saul Lambert. Bradbury Press, 1969. 131p. $4.50. (Macmillan, 1970. 144p. £1.05.)

5–7   The special gift of Paula Fox is that of seeing from the child's viewpoint and maintaining that viewpoint while feeling the sympathy of an adult and the detachment of an artist. Her children move our hearts because they are so true, yet there is neither sentimentality nor pity in her writing. Ivan's mother is dead, his father a rich and busy man, the housekeeper kind but preoccupied with her own family. Sitting for his portrait, Ivan finds in Matt, the artist, and in the elderly Miss Manderby who sits and reads aloud a warm comfort he has never known. This curious but completely believable trio goes off to Florida, and there Ivan meets a girl his own age who becomes a dear companion—the first person who has ever wept to see Ivan leave. But when he leaves, he has a new confidence in people; in part this is due to his friend, in part to the fact that he has been able to talk to Matt about his mother; he is indeed ready to bridge the gap between himself and his father. Skilled writing, and an engrossing story.

422   **Fox,** Paula. *The Stone-Faced Boy;* illus. by Donald A. Mackay. Bradbury, 1968. 106p. $4.25. (Macmillan, 1969. 96p. £0.90.)

4–6   One of the ways to erect a defense against the world is to keep an impassive face, and this Gus had mastered to the extent that his brothers and sisters called him "stone face." Only Great-aunt Hattie, when she came to visit, seemed to see that there was something behind the mask; the geode she gave Gus became the symbol of his inner self, a shining thing cased in rock. The symbolism is the more meaningful because, in this short book, the author gives a vivid and poignant picture of a small and rather frightened boy surrounded by family members who are boisterous, secure, or complacent. The plot is believable but of minor interest, serving principally to round out the characterizations and relationships.

423   **Franchere,** Ruth. *Cesar Chavez;* illus. by Earl Thollander. T. Y. Crowell, 1970. 42p. $3.75.

2–4   A simply written biography of the Mexican-American labor leader.

In direct, matter-of-fact style the author describes the plight of the Chavez family when they had to give up their farm during the depression and turn to migrant labor, learning the bitter facts about the poor housing, low pay, and inadequate schooling. Cesar Chavez, after serving in the Navy, joined the Community Service Organization to help improve the lot of the farm worker, and went on to found the National Farm Workers Association, the labor group that instituted the massive strike and boycott of the Delano vineyards.

424   **Franzen,** Greta. *The Great Ship VASA;* written and designed by Greta Franzen. Hastings House, 1971. 96p. $5.95.

6–9   In 1628, the warship *Vasa,* grandest of the King's fleet, sailed out of Stockholm on her maiden voyage and sank before she had gotten out of the harbor. This is the enthralling story of her salvage, told in meticulous detail and superbly illustrated with photographs and diagrams of the ship and the salvage operation, and concluding with a discussion of what has been learned about the *Vasa* and a description of the museum in which she is housed. The story has the allure of detective fiction, and the writing style is smooth and straightforward. A bibliography and an index are appended.

425   **Freedgood,** Lillian. *An Enduring Image;* American Painting from 1665. T. Y. Crowell, 1970. 387p. illus. $7.95.

7—   A good survey of American painting, the emphasis on individual artists but the background filled in solidly with discussion of trends here and influences from abroad. The writing is direct, the tone moderate, the information authoritative. The illustrations are all in black and white, with some artists being discussed (O'Keeffe, for example) but with no examples of their work included. The last section is a lucid discussion of contemporary art; a long, divided bibliography and an index are appended.

426   **Freeman,** Mae (Blacker). *Finding Out about Shapes;* illus. by Bill Morrison. McGraw-Hill, 1969. 47p. Trade ed. $3.95; Library ed. $3.83 net.

K–3   A good introduction to spatial conceptualization, with simple definitions of shapes, lines, and forms. The examples given are often ramified by repetition or by the illustrations, and the text is limited to the most familiar shapes, using what has already been described in defining the more complex shape. (In describing a pyramid, for example, the ideas of flatness and of the straight line are combined with the already-explained triangle.) The final double-page spread incorporates all of the material in the text in a busy picture in which the child can hunt for examples of what he has just learned.

427   **Freeman,** Mae (Blacker). *Finding Out about the Past;* illus. with
photographs. Random House, 1967. 79p. (Gateway Books) $1.95.

3–5   Archeology is introduced in a well-organized book illustrated with
good photographs, the text written in a crisp but casual style.
The author discusses the difficulty man has had in knowing
the cultures of prehistory, and the growing techniques that
emerged with the growth of the science of archeology that have
helped solve those difficulties. She describes some of the major
finds, procedures at a dig, methods of investigation and dating,
and the complicated planning of an archeological expedition. A
brief index is appended.

428   **Freshet,** Berniece. *The Flight of the Snow Goose;* illus. by Jo
Polseno. Crown, 1970. 42p. Trade ed. $3.50; Library ed. $3.35 net.

2–4   A description of a year in the life of the wild snow goose begins
with the spring migration from California to an Alaskan bay.
The gander and his mate produce a family of five, teach them
to care for themselves and to be wary of the predators of the
region, and join the fall migration. Hampered by a fire, threatened
by hunters, trapped by an oil slick (and rescued by students
from the University of Washington) the geese make their way to
California, stopping at a wildlife refuge. The writing is direct
and clear, the living pattern broadened to include ecological
aspects, and the illustrations dramatic in black and white.

429   **Friis-Baastad,** Babbis. *Don't Take Teddy;* tr. from the Norwegian
by Lise Sømme McKinnon. Scribner, 1967. 218p. Trade ed. $4.50;
Library ed. $4.05 net.

5–8   Not sentimental, but a moving story about a retarded boy of
fifteen; Teddy is loved and protected by his younger brother, who
tells the story of their trip. Mikkel runs away with Teddy because
he fears that the police have heard that another child has been
hurt when Teddy threw a stone. They arrive at a mountain
cottage in a state of exhaustion, and both boys are ill by the
time their parents arrive. Mikkel has a met a woman who, working
with retarded children, seems to understand Teddy; he realizes
that Teddy can learn more with professional help and is happy
that Teddy will go on living with the family. Because the story
is so straightforward in style and so tender in its implications, it
is a most effective book for the young reader who doesn't
understand—or is embarrassed by—the mentally defective person.
It is interesting to compare this book with Crane's *A Girl Like
Tracy* (McKay, 1966) in which, again, a younger sibling tells the
story; again there are only the two children and a heavy burden
falls on the normal child. Tracy is educable and is sent to a
training school at her sister's insistence, but in both books the

solution avoids both the isolation of home care and the separation of full-time institutional care.

430   **Friis,** Babbis. *Wanted! A Horse!* tr. from the Norwegian by Lise Sømme McKinnon; illus. by Charles Robinson. Harcourt, 1972. 188p. $4.75.

4–6   Svein had tried to act grateful for his birthday presents, but he had told his parents repeatedly that all he wanted when he was twelve was a horse. Nothing but a horse. The best they can do is pay for riding lessons, the price to be reduced because Svein does stable work. While the book doesn't have the strong story line or the dramatic impact of the author's *Don't Take Teddy!* it has the same sympathetic, no-nonsense understanding of children and a smooth writing style, and it is particularly sensitive to the relationships within a family and the effect that home situations and external relationships have upon each other.

431   **Fritz,** Jean. *Early Thunder;* illus. by Lynd Ward. Coward-McCann, 1967. 255p. $4.50. (Gollancz, 1969. 256p. £1.05.)

6–9   There was dissension in the air in Salem, Massachusetts in 1775; as were the adults, the youngsters were hotly partial. Fourteen-year-old Daniel knew that most of his schoolfellows were patriots, but he proudly followed his father's path of loyalty to the king. Bit by bit, reluctantly, Daniel began to have creeping doubts about the British attitude and intentions, to see the patriot viewpoint, and to join—when a clash was incipient—with the townspeople against the British troops. The period details and the historical background are excellent, both in themselves and in the easy way they are incorporated into the story. The characters are believable, but are less interesting as people than as examples of people's attitudes. The plot, based on some facts, is adequate; here again, the plot is less interesting in itself than it is as a means of showing the general pattern and movement of events and morale.

432   **Fritz,** Jean. *George Washington's Breakfast;* illus. by Paul Galdone. Coward-McCann, 1969. 41p. Trade ed. $3.75; Library ed. $3.86 net.

3–5   It is perfectly natural that a boy born on February 22 and named in honor of George Washington should want to know everything he can about Washington's life. George W. Allen knew a great deal, but it struck him one morning at breakfast that he did not know what the Father of His Country might have had for *his* breakfast. He enlisted the librarian's help and tried every Washington book in the library; he went to visit Mount Vernon, and he finally emerged from the attic at home with exactly the information he needed. The fictional framework is deft, the illustrations echoing its light humor, and the story gives both a believable picture of a small, determined boy and a good introduction to the vicissitudes of historical research.

433 **Frolov,** Vadim. *What It's All About;* tr. by Joseph Barnes. Doubleday, 1968. 254p. $3.95. (Macmillan, 1970. 224p. £1.25.)

8–10   Translated from the Russian, a contemporary novel that has both the universality of adolescent problems and the specific interest in one young person's crucial affairs to give it interest. Written in first person, Sasha's story is convincingly that of a teenager; the style is vigorous, the translation unobtrusive, the plot and characters excellent. It takes a long time for Sasha to find out what it's all about: his mother has gone to join her lover, and this bitter fact, gleaned from a schoolmate, explains the way his father has behaved. Sasha's budding love affairs, his friendships with other boys, his academic career, and his doubts about himself balance and complement the moving story of the breaking-up of his home.

434 **Froman,** Robert. *Bigger and Smaller;* illus. by Gioia Fiammenghi. T. Y. Crowell, 1971. 33p. $3.75.

2–4   The concepts of relative size, including the possibility of interpretations of "size" (does one mean taller or heavier when one says a football player is bigger than another player?) are introduced in a simply written book with lively illustrations. After showing the fact that size is relative, the author elaborates: some adults are smaller than some children; some animals are bigger than people, some are smaller; some animals are smaller than the smallest human being, etc. Some of the ideas are iterated, but the repetition is varied in form and the text is both clear and provocative.

435 **Froman,** Robert. *The Many Human Senses;* illus. by Feodor Rimsky. Little, 1966. 161p. $4.95. (G. Bell, 1969. 145p. £1.00.)

7—   A most interesting book about sensory powers: how they function—or malfunction—and how scientific research has exposed the range of individual differences in response (of kind or degree) to identical stimuli. Some of the text discusses the familiar mysteries of ESP and internal "clocks"; the final chapter describes man-made senses and sense extensions. The writing is crisp and straightforward, the illustrative diagrams clear and well-labeled. A divided bibliography and an index are appended.

436 **Froman,** Robert. *Racism.* Delacorte, 1972. 156p. $4.95.

7—   *Racism* is an important book, written in a moderate and dignified style and pulling together aspects of the subject to give it breadth and illumination. First describing the scientist's viewpoint on races and the misuses of the term, Froman discusses genetic inheritance, the achievements and potentials of human beings of all races, and the infrequency of "pure" racial strains. A history of racism and intolerance in the United States includes prejudice against all minorities, although the emphasis is on the history of black Americans. A final section, which discusses the struggle against underground racism, touches on racial pride and bigotry in many parts of the world and strikes a note of cautious hope. A bibliography and an index are appended.

437   **Fry,** Rosalie Kingsmill. *The Castle Family;* with drawings by Margery Gill. Dutton, 1966. 128p. $3.95. (Dent, 1970. 128p. £0.40.)

6–8   A family-mystery-countryside story for girls, set in England in an old castle. What could be more satisfying than an only child—Richenda—and a motherless one, finding an advertisement that provides her beloved father with an experienced and pretty assistant for his nursery, a widow, and with a daughter just Richenda's age. Instant rapport all around leads to a satisfying marriage; the mystery is solved (believably) with the help of experts, and the advent of baby brother adds a last happy note. Fortunately, the author's style is good enough to keep the story from being too sweet; dialogue is natural, and it is quite refreshing to have a deviant from the adjustment-to-stepmother formula. Mrs. Browning is an intelligent woman who is sensitive to Richenda's feelings and who obviously enjoys the prospect of another daughter.

438   **Frye,** Burton C., comp. *A St. Nicholas Anthology;* The Early Years; comp. and ed. by Burton C. Frye. Meredith, 1969. 439p. $8.95.

5—   An intriguing selection of stories, poems, articles, and letters from the best-known children's magazine ever published, the material grouped by seasons and the authors including some of the most famous writers for children: Alcott, Kipling, Pyle, Wiggin, and the editor of the magazine, Mary Mapes Dodge. There is also a selection of the work of child contributors in the St. Nicholas League, including such Honor Members as Bennett Cerf, Rachel Field, and Edna St. Vincent Millay. Although the book's primary audience is the young reader, it has both nostalgic appeal and professional interest for adults. Appended are author and artist, title and artwork, and subject indexes.

439   **Fuja,** Abayomi, comp. *Fourteen Hundred Cowries;* And Other African Tales; illus. by Ademola Olugebefola. Lothrop, 1971, 256p. Trade ed. $4.95; Library ed. $4.59 net. (Oxf. U.P., 1962. 172p. £0.80.)

4–7   An anthology of Yoruba tales collected in the 1930's and 40's by the late Abayomi Fuja. Many of the tales are about clever animals, many are "why" stories of fables with a pointed moral. There are chants within the stories that have a flowing, free quality, but most of the writing is sedate. An excellent source for storytellers and for the student of folklore.

440   **Fyson,** J. G. *The Journey of the Eldest Son;* illus. by Victor G. Ambrus. Coward-McCann, 1967. 214p. $4.95. (Oxf. U.P., 1965. 224p. £0.80.)

7–9   Published in England in 1965, this is a sequel to *The Three Brothers of Ur*. Here the oldest brother, Shamashazir, is deemed capable enough to travel with one of his father's caravans from the Sumerian city of Ur to the faraway mountains. Injured, the boy is taken in by the tribe of Enoch, wandering shepherds; he becomes intrigued by the likenesses and differences in their religions: Enoch's tribe also has a story of a Great Flood, for example, but they have no pantheon of gods. Shamashazir, by the time he returns to Ur, has found convincing the idea of One Lord of All the Earth; he removes from his family's temple the household image. An epilogue notes that some of the events in the story have historical basis and some are invented; and that one might find, in another interpretation, that Shamashazir is called Abraham. The setting and period are most convincingly created, the pace of the story is good, and the dialogue is used to develop plot in the same way it does in a play. The black and white illustrations are dramatic and handsome: small pictures deftly set on the page with—sometimes—a frame of printed lines.

441   **Fyson,** J. G. *The Three Brothers of Ur;* illus. by Victor G. Ambrus. Coward-McCann, 1967. 254p. $4.95. (Oxf. U.P., 1964. 248p. £0.75.)

7–9   Published in England in 1964, this was a runner-up for the Carnegie Medal. Set in the ancient world, the story makes vividly real the cultural patterns of Sumerian society, particularly the structure of urban life. Although the story line focuses on the ploys and mishaps of the mischievous youngest son, Haran, and in particular on his concern with replacing a religious image he has damaged, the most significant event in the book is the change in fortune of the oldest son, Shamashazir. Handsomely illustrated, the book has historical interest and significance; better still, it has excellent pace, characterization, and writing style.

442   **Gage,** Wilson. *The Ghost of Five Owl Farm;* illus. by Paul Galdone. World, 1966. 127p. Trade ed. $4.95; Library ed. $4.51 net.

5–7   Ted, a sixth grader, was delighted by the family move to a house in the country; he liked the outdoors, he liked the idea that their old house was haunted, and he was delighted to hear that his sisters were both going away for a visit. Gloom set in when he heard that he was not going to have the place to himself, because his odd twin cousins were coming. Winkie and Bobbin: thin, pale, and not quite with it, Ted felt. As the twins and Ted explored the mysterious evidence of Something going on in the barn (ghosts? spies?) it became clear to Ted that his cousins might be odd but they were both courageous and intelligent. The mystery has a logical explanation; the characterization is good, the twins being odd but not exaggerated; the country background is evocatively described; and the story has pace and an economy of construction.

443   **Gage,** Wilson. *Mike's Toads;* illus. by Glen Rounds. World, 1970. 93p. Trade ed. $4.50; Library ed. $4.28 net.

3–5   Mike knew from experience that it wasn't wise to proffer other people's help without consulting them, but he had thoughtlessly done it again. A friend of his brother's had asked if David would care for his pet toads while he was away. Of course he would, Mike said—but he'd forgotten that David was going to camp, and he himself was saddled with the responsibility. His small catastrophes are entertaining, and the story—written in an easy, natural style—incorporates information unobtrusively. The outcome is satisfying, the relationships and dialogue felicitous.

444   **Gard,** Joyce. *The Mermaid's Daughter.* Holt, 1969. 319p. Trade ed. $4.50; Library ed. $3.97 net. (Gollancz, 1969. 288p. £1.25.)

6–9   Set in Britain at the time of the Roman occupation, an intricate novel that has good historical background, a romantic and adventurous plot, and a mature style of writing. It is based on the mermaid-goddess cult of the Scilly Isles, where each maiden chosen as the daughter-on-earth of the goddess must promise never to leave the isles. But Astria, mourning a young husband who has gone off to war and been reported dead, marries again and follows Justinian, her husband, to Britain, where she aligns herself with the natives in their struggle against the occupying Roman rule. The book creates vividly both the period and the mystic mood of the religious cult. Notes on sources of information about the Sea Goddess cult and a bibliography are appended.

445   **Gard,** Joyce. *The Snow Firing.* Holt, 1968. 196p. Trade ed. $3.95; Library ed. $3.79 net. (Gollancz, 1967. 160p. £0.80.)

7–9   A deftly written story set in the Cotswold Hills just after World War II, when handmade pottery appealed to the many people tired of the utility-ware of wartime. Young Philip Ruddock knows that his widowed mother has some burdensome secret to do with pottery; she is fiercely opposed to his learning the craft. Philip, aware that his grandfather had been a master potter, learns to make pottery when a young couple buys the old kiln that had been his grandfather's. Only when Philip is stranded by a blizzard and must keep the kiln fire going does his mother capitulate and help him, and thus he learns about the secret. His grandfather had died a slow, cruel death because of lead poisoning, an industrial hazard in potteries in the past. This rather anticlimactic revelation is the only weak point of the book; there seems no reason why Mrs. Ruddock couldn't have told Philip long before, especially since she was concerned for his safety. This single inconsistency is, however, more than compensated for by the book's many charms: the style is silky-smooth, the characters colorful without being quaint, the details of locale interesting and those of the potter's art quite fascinating.

446   **Gardam,** Jane. *A Long Way from Verona.* Macmillan, 1972. 190p. $4.95. (H. Hamilton, 1971. £1.40.)

6–8   Set in England during World War II, a story told by thirteen-year-old Jessica Vye is lively, funny, and wholly engrossing. The dialogue and narration are deft, the characterization vivid and perceptive. Smitten by an elderly author, Jessica is thrilled when he responds—after reading something she has written—JESSICA VYE YOU ARE A WRITER BEYOND ALL POSSIBLE DOUBT! There are hilarious school episodes, a bittersweet visit to a wealthy household where Jessica feels she is being patronized, the excitement of love's first pangs, some experiences of wartime danger. The story line is almost nonexistent, but the book has a high sense of story.

447   **Gardner,** Martin. *Perplexing Puzzles and Tantalizing Teasers;* illus. by Laszlo Kubinyi. Simon and Schuster, 1969. 95p. $3.95.

3–6   A good book of puzzles, including scrambled words, palindromes, mazes, problems of logic, tricks with matches or money, riddles, etc. The problems are simple but few have too-obvious answers; there are enough sticklers to tempt the quick child but not so many as to discourage the slow thinker. Illustrations are clear, and answers are given at the back of the book. There are a few answers for which no logical clues have been given, but very few.

448   **Gárdonyi,** Géza. *Slave of the Huns;* tr. by Andrew Feldmar; illus. and with a foreword by Victor C. Ambrus. Bobbs-Merrill, 1969. 358p. $5. (Dent, 1969. 358p. £1.50.)

8–10   First published in Hungary in 1901 under the title *Láthatatlan,* a historical adventure story that has become a classic. The tale is told by Zeta, whose Thracian father had sold him, at the age of twelve, into slavery. Educated and freed by his master, Zeta goes along on a diplomatic mission to the camp of Attila; he falls in love with the lady Emmo, to whose hand he can hardly aspire, and decides to stay with the Huns. As one of their entourage, he becomes involved in the last bitter battle in which Attila is killed. The writing is almost somber, but it fits the dark magnificence of the Hunnish life, the contrast between opulent wealth and savage vigor. Historically interesting and full of color and drama.

449

6–9

Garfield, Leon. *Black Jack;* illus. by Antony Maitland. Pantheon Books, 1968. 243p. $3.95. (Longman, 1968. 192p. £1.10.)

A hanged man comes back to life, captures an orphaned boy, and together they hold up a coach from which an insane girl escapes; the boy and girl join a caravan, she regains her sanity and they fall in love. Her father is murdered, she goes to an asylum, the repentant highwayman rescues her, and the boy and girl sail off together in his uncle's ship, in which they have stowed away. Sounds wildly implausible? Yes, but Leon Garfield makes it wholly convincing, rich with the color and the speech of England in the mid-eighteenth century, full of pathos and suspense.

450

8—

Garfield, Leon. *The God beneath the Sea;* by Leon Garfield and Edward Blishen; illus. by Zevi Blum. Pantheon Books, 1971. 212p. Trade ed. $4.95; Library ed. $5.39 net. (Longman Young Books, 1970. 168p. £1.75.)

A stunning book, dramatically illustrated and told in a fluent, imaginative style that has the perception of the poet and the sense of effect of the gifted storyteller. The legends of the gods of Greece and of the human creatures they brought to life are told as a continuous story that begins with the infant Hephaestus, flung into the sea by his mother Hera because of his monstrous ugliness. Awarded the 1970 Carnegie Medal, the book is distinguished both for the lucid manner in which it presents the intricacies of the Olympian pantheon and for the marvelous sonority of its style, a style that makes it particularly appropriate for reading aloud.

451

5–7

Garfield, Leon. *Mister Corbett's Ghost;* illus. by Alan E. Cober. Pantheon Books, 1968. 87p. $3.50. (Longman, 1969. 160p. £1.00.)

Through the bitterly cold and wind-tossed night of long-ago London a miserable boy is sent on an errand. The boy, Benjamin Partridge, resenting the fact that it is New Year's Eve and his family awaits him, wishes his master dead. And so Mr. Corbett dies, Benjamin having made a pact with a strange old man who promises Corbett's death for a lifetime share in Ben's earnings. Mr. Corbett's ghost, however, persists in accompanying Benjamin, and the boy is terrified and guilty. In a Dickensian twist, it comes back to life and the grateful Benjamin never forgets "that obliging, anxious and oddly touching ghost. . . ." Garfield's writing is always evocative, his dialogue period-perfect, and his characters vivid; his previous books have been vastly enjoyable but crowded with minor characters and incidents, while this is a starkly designed and possibly more memorable story.

452   **Garfield,** Leon. *The Restless Ghost;* Three Stories, illus. by Saul Lambert. Pantheon Books, 1969. 132p. $3.95. (Collins, 1971. £1.50.)

7–10   Three short stories, each different and each splendid in its own way; all are set in the past and have in common a felicitous fidelity to the genre. The ghost story could have been written by Wilkie Collins, the two sea stories have the authentic detail and vigorous language of the period. In the title story a boy's place is usurped by a ghost; in "Vaarlem and Tripp" a Dutch lad finds that Tripp, whom he despises for fleeing a sea battle, has his merits; in "The Simpleton" a young criminal being transported to Virginia is inspired, through love, to heroism. All of it has an authentic ring, but Garfield's masterpiece is always his villain, and the dastardly villain of "The Simpleton" will stand with any of the past.

453   **Garfield,** Leon. *The Strange Affair of Adelaide Harris;* illus. by Fritz Wegner. Pantheon Books, 1971. 223p. $4.95. (Longman Young Books, 1971. 176p. £1.25.)

7–10   Garfield's picaresque tales of high adventure are usually concerned with unscrupulous villains; here, using the same exaggeration and humor, he writes a rollicking story of pompous braggarts and churlish gentry that is every bit as lively and funny. The characters center about a small and notably undistinguished school: Dr. Bunnion's Academy; handsome young Ralph Bunnion is offended by the treatment he has received from Tizzy, the sweet daughter of one of the teachers, and finds that Tizzy's father thinks his daughter's honor impugned and demands satisfaction. All the errors in communication stem from the mysterious appearance of an apparently abandoned infant (Adelaide) who is taken to the poorhouse kept by a gin-sodden woman, and they are abetted by the appearance (in Adelaide's cradle) of a gypsy babe. Well, add to all that two rascally schoolboys, a brooding sleuth who guesses wrong about absolutely everything, the machinations of two doting mothers, a duel, a renegade brother . . . all tied into Gordian knots by a master storyteller, and the reader is in for one of the prime romps of the year.

454   **Garner,** Alan, ed. *A Cavalcade of Goblins;* illus. by Krystyna Turska. Walck, 1969. 227p. $6.50. (H. Hamilton, 1969. 230p. £1.50.)

4–7   First published in Great Britain under the title *The Hamish Hamilton Book of Goblins,* an excellent anthology of excerpts, poems, and stories from world-wide sources. The styles and subjects are as varied as the origins, and the illustrations, black and white, are attractive. A treasure for storytellers, the book lists sources in an appendix, and there are brief notes preceding many of the selections.

455   **Garner,** Alan. *The Owl Service.* Walck, 1968. 202p. $5. (Penguin, 1969. 176p. £0.22½.)

5–8   A marvelous combination of realism and fantasy, in a story that brings into the lives of contemporary children the powerful forces of Celtic myth. The "owl service" refers to a set of dishes on which the floral decorations look like owls, and when Alison and Gwyn find the service, they open the door for an inexorable re-enactment of the tragedy of the flower-maiden, Blodeuwedd, who became an owl when her unfaithfulness brought death to her husband and her lover. The characterization is magnificent, with sharp contrast between the mystic and mysterious Welsh Huw, who knows the dark secret all along, and the crass, jovial English visitor, Alison's stepfather. Beautifully written, with sparing use of the Welsh cadence; beautifully plotted, with the contrapuntal quality of a musical composition.

456   **Garnett,** Emmeline. *Madame Prime Minister;* The Story of Indira Gandhi. Farrar, 1967. 144p. illus. $3.95.

7–10   Although there have been many biographies of Nehru and Gandhi that give a vivid picture of the emergence of an independent India, this biography of Nehru's daughter (much of it devoted to Nehru and to Gandhi) adds another facet to the rounded view. Brought up in the politically conscious Nehru household, Indira shared in the penalties for political activity: jail sentences and separation from her family. Not until she was forty did she become a member of the Congress Working Committee: ten years later she became Prime Minister. The story of Indira Gandhi has poignancy, drama, bitterness, and romance; it is of considerable historical interest; it is told in a style that is dignified but not dull. A brief bibliography and an index are appended.

457   **Garson,** Eugenia, comp. *The Laura Ingalls Wilder Songbook;* favorite songs from the "Little House" books comp. and ed. by Eugenia Garson, arr. for piano and guitar by Herbert Haufrecht; illus. by Garth Williams. Harper, 1968. 160p. Trade ed. $5.95; Library ed. $5.11 net.

4—   The softly-executed illustrations add to the appeal of a book that will give especial delight to Wilder fans, old and young. Mrs.

Garson has collected the words and music for sixty-two of the songs mentioned in the "Little House" books; each is prefaced by a note on the selection (usually on the composer and lyricist) and a reminder about the mention of that song in Mrs. Wilder's writing. The arrangements are simple and sturdy, the songs grouped under such titles as "Home and Memories," "Hymns and Sacred Songs," and "Patriotic Songs."

458   **Gates,** Doris. *The Elderberry Bush;* illus. by Lilian Obligado. Viking, 1967. 160p. Trade ed. $3.50; Library ed. $3.37 net.

4–6   A warm and lively look back at family life in a small town early in the twentieth century. The pattern of events is episodic and the overall effect nostalgic, although the writing has no sentimentality. Julie is nine, her sister Elizabeth eight; they enjoy a vacation trip to the shore despite a case of mumps, they occasionally find good deeds do not always bring rewards or mischief punishment; they are reasonably convinced that there is a Santa Claus . . . but they wonder.

459   **Gault,** William Campbell. *Stubborn Sam.* Dutton, 1969. 158p. $4.50.

6–9   "I suppose being stubborn is what kept me out of the grocery business," Sam Bogosian explains. Sam wanted to play baseball; his father wanted him to go to college. Sam went to college— but he knew that he still wanted to play baseball when he came out, and he did. Sam has trouble when he goes into a hitting slump, but he sticks it out. The plot is routine; the writing style is far better than that of most sports fiction, and the characters are warm, believable human beings.

460   **Gemming,** Elizabeth. *Blow Ye Winds Westerly;* The Seaports and Sailing Ships of Old New England. T. Y. Crowell, 1972. 183p. illus. $4.95.

6–9   Mrs. Gemming has managed to capture the romance and adventure of the days of sailing and whaling while achieving a scholarly investigation of the life of that time. The text describes the towns from which the ships sailed with infinite detail and broad coverage, and goes on to vivid pictures of fishing and whaling. Informative, exciting, well-written, and packed with facts about the industries, the ships and the people who sailed them, the builders, and the communities from which the ships sailed. A treasure trove. A glossary, a list of books suggested for further reading (fiction and nonfiction) and a relative index are appended.

461   **George,** Jean (Craighead). *All Upon a Stone;* illus. by Don Bolognese. T. Y. Crowell, 1971. 42p. $3.95.

2–3   A fine nature study book introduces the concept of the small scale community by following a mole cricket through his day. Under the big gray stone that looks so placid, the mole cricket tunnels, hearing other tiny creatures, looking for one of his own kind. Not until he has come to the surface, swum in the rock pool, and emerged does he meet other mole crickets. It is the one night that each member of the species, usually solitary, meets the others in a frenetic round of contact (not mating) before retreating again to its subterranean tunneling. The soft, detailed pictures are each a magnified part of the whole rock community that is shown in the final illustration.

462   **George,** Jean (Craighead). *Spring Comes to the Ocean;* illus. by John Wilson. T. Y. Crowell, 1965. 109p. $3.50.

6—   This is a tremendously impressive book written with quiet authority, imbued with a sense of wonder and pleasure in the marvelous intricacies of marine creatures. The author writes with great simplicity and dignity, her prose only just verging on the lyric; this is fine writing and a fine contribution to literature in the biological sciences. Each chapter describes one form of animal life, beginning with the stirring of the reproductive instinct in the spring; the book discusses the courting—if there is any— and the start of a new life form. In the course of this description, the author gives an excellent picture of each creature: the structure, habitat, enemies and protective devices, et cetera. The illustrations are attractive, but are not clear in details of the smaller creatures. A bibliography and a relative index are appended.

463   **Gidal,** Sonia. *My Village in Ghana;* by Sonia and Tim Gidal. Pantheon Books, 1970. 74p. illus. $4.50.

4–7   Another in the excellent series of cultural portraits illustrated by good photographs, the story told by a child who describes his family and friends, village crafts and agriculture, mores and patterns of living. Kodjo is destined to be the chief of his village some day, succeeding the uncle with whom he lives; he describes the meeting of chiefs, the tribal relationships, daily pursuits, and the manifold indications of a happy assimilation of contemporary devices and knowledge into the traditional ways of the Ashanti. The continuous text has the informal cadence of conversation, and the book gives a genuine feeling for the depth and dignity of the people as well as information about them.

464   **Gidal,** Sonia. *My Village in Japan;* by Sonia and Tim Gidal. Pantheon Books, 1966. 74p. illus. $3.95.

4–7   In this seventeenth of the My Village series, young Masao Kitamura describes a mountain village an hour from Kyoto; as in other books in the series, a trip to a city (in this case, Kyoto) gives opportunity for additional information about the nation and the people. Masao rambles on conversationally about his family, friends, school, baseball, village industries, art, legends, farm life, foods, et cetera. The photographs are very good; a glossary and a map are appended.

465   **Gidal,** Sonia. *My Village in Korea;* by Sonia and Tim Gidal. Pantheon Books, 1968. 74p. $3.95.

4-6   Sung-je describes the South Korean village in which he lives, talks about his family, rambles on blithely about some of the things he does in school, visits Seoul with his class. As are the other books in this series, this is illustrated with uncaptioned photographs and is written in informal style. Sunj-je is a tease, and his sense of fun permeates the book; through his comments and his discussions with others, the reader gets a broad and intimate picture of rural life and of urban life, of the close-knit family patterns, and of the indelible effects of living in a divided land. Painlessly informative, pleasantly brisk.

466   **Ginsburg,** Mirra, tr. *The Kaha Bird;* Tales from the Steppes of Central Asia; illus. by Richard Cuffari. Crown, 1971. 159p. $4.95.

4-6   Endpaper maps show the areas from which the nineteen stories, non-Russian tales from Russia, in this collection came; their sources are a dozen cultures with mixed heritage. Some of the tales are heroic, some earthy, some explanatory ("Living Water," for example, is a "why" story) and many have a robust, sly peasant humor. The style of the retelling is smooth and flavorful, so that the book is as useful and enjoyable for reading aloud as it is for storytelling.

467   **Glass,** Paul. *Singing Soldiers;* A History of the Civil War in Song; selections and historical commentary by Paul Glass; musical arrangements for piano and guitar by Louis C. Singer. Rev. ed. Grosset, 1968. 300p. illus. $6.95.

6—   First published under the title *The Spirit of the Sixties* (Educational Publishers, 1965), a quite impressive collection of Civil War Songs. In addition to a long and informative introduction, the authors explain their modernization of the piano settings (all fairly simple) and provide some background information for each song. Topically grouped, the songs—with the compilers' notes—do indeed have historical as well as musical value. The book is oversize, the pages lie flat for group use or piano rack, and illustrations are reproductions of old prints; a selected bibliography is appended.

468   **Glubok,** Shirley. *The Art of Ancient Mexico;* designed by Gerard Nook; special photography by Alfred H. Tamarin. Harper, 1968. 41p. Trade ed. $4.50; Library ed. $4.11 net.

4–6   A handsome book, as are the others in this series. The photographs of art objects of several ancient civilizations are presented in spacious format; the writing is very simple and the organization haphazard. The book gives a good picture of the highly distinctive achievements of ancient Mexican cultures, with some background information included.

469   **Glubok,** Shirley. *The Art of Ancient Peru;* designed by Gerard Nook; special photography by Alfred H. Tamarin. Harper, 1966. 41p. Trade ed. $4.50; Library ed. $4.11 net.

4–9   As are Miss Glubok's previous books, this is a handsome, informative volume. The writing is simple and lucid, with professional authoritativeness but without technical terminology. The illustrations of art objects are stunning, and they are carefully placed in relation to the textual references to them. The text concentrates on the objects pictured, but in describing their uses or the ways in which they were made, also gives facts about their cultural matrix.

470   **Glubok,** Shirley. *The Art of India;* designed by Gerard Nook; photographs by Alfred H. Tamarin and Carol Guyer. Macmillan, 1969. 48p. $5.95.

5–9   Since almost all Indian art is religious art, most of the text here is either descriptive of the object or structure shown in a photograph or it is an explanation of the religious background. There is, therefore, a little less historical material here than in the author's previous books; it is handsome in design, clearly written, and extremely useful, since there is comparatively little material available on Indian art for the elementary level. The illustrations are preponderantly sculpture and the lack of color is no limitation, but the miniatures lose effectiveness in black and white. There is no discussion of the Mogul period, although some miniatures are pictured, or of the ceramics or textiles in which it excelled.

471   **Glubok,** Shirley. *The Art of Japan;* designed by Gerard Nook; with special photography by Alfred Tamarin. Macmillan, 1970. 48p. $5.95.

4–7   A brief chronological survey of Japanese art forms, the pictures primarily in black and white, none being in full color. The writing is very simple, almost abrupt in places, giving both some historical background for, and some description of, the art object pictured. Much of the subject matter is religious or expresses appreciation of nature; only recently have Japanese artists reflected to any great extent the common people and the events of ordinary life. Perhaps the most impressive aspect of the book is in the reflection of the consistency of stylized elegance and economy in painting as opposed to the ornamentation in architecture and sculpture.

472   **Glubok,** Shirley. *The Art of the Etruscans;* designed by Gerard Nook; special photography by Alfred H. Tamarin. Harper, 1967. 43p. Trade ed. $4.50; Library ed. $4.11 net.

4–9   Another book in the author's series of descriptions of the art forms of an ancient civilization. Dignified in format and beautifully illustrated with photographs of art objects, the text is written with great simplicity. The textual descriptions of objects illustrated give information about the Etruscan culture as well as specific facts about a statue or a painting.

473   **Glubok,** Shirley. *The Art of the Southwest Indians;* photographs by Alfred Tamarin. Macmillan, 1971. 48p. $5.95.

4–6   Information about some aspects of tribal cultures is woven into discussions of the works of art of the Apache, Navajo, and Pueblo peoples. The photographs of rock carvings and paintings, pottery and basketwork, weaving, carving, jewelry, sand paintings, ceremonial robes and masks, and kachina dolls are accompanied by an informative, rather staccato, text. The large print and dignified design of the pages add to the attractiveness of a useful book.

474   **Glubok,** Shirley. *Knights in Armor;* designed by Gerard Nook. Harper, 1969. 48p. Trade ed. $5.50; Library ed. $4.79 net.

4–9   An oversize book with a simply written text, some reproductions of paintings, and many photographs of armor. The labeled diagrams, the clear descriptions, and the many examples of armor for jousting or for fighting give the book minor reference use in addition to its historical and artistic relevance. Almost all of the examples shown are from the Metropolitan Museum of Art, where the author lectures to children on knights and armor.

475   **Gobhai,** Mehlli. *Lakshmi;* The Water Buffalo Who Wouldn't; written and illus. by Mehlli Gobhai. Hawthorn Books, 1969. 27p. $5.25.

2–4   A simply written story about a family in India today, the illustrations just right for story hour, since they have a soft brilliance that is particularly effective in bold, simple composition. The tale has humor as well as an interesting setting, and the theme (mother and son amused at the come-down of father) a broad applicability. Small Gokul and his parents are aware of Lakshmi's importance; from her they get food and fuel. It is necessary to honor her idiosyncrasies, therefore, and when Gokul's mother is ill and cannot milk the water buffalo, there is a problem. Lakshmi will allow nobody else to milk her. There is one way, says mother. . . . "Never!" says father. But Lakshmi must be milked and so, to the delight of his family, its dignified head sheepishly puts on his wife's red head scarf and her many golden bangles and milks Lakshmi.

476   **Goble,** Paul. *Red Hawk's Account of Custer's Last Battle;* written and illus. by Paul and Dorothy Goble. Pantheon Books, 1970. 59p. $4.50. (Macmillan, 1970. 64p. £1.05.)

5–7   Poster-bright, small figures against clean white are sharply delineated and effective, complementing the stark straightforward reporting of Red Hawk, a fifteen-year-old Sioux who fought against Custer at Little Big Horn. The Indian victory was definitive, but the Indian's fight was hopeless: "Once all the earth was ours; now there is only a small piece left which the White Men did not want." The historical details and most of the combatants are authentic; Red Hawk is a fictional character. The style is excellent, the text precise and dramatic. A list of sources and a list of suggested further readings are appended.

477   **Godden,** Rumer. *The Old Woman Who Lived in a Vinegar Bottle;* illus. by Mairi Hedderwick. Viking, 1972. 44p. $4.95.

K–3   Softly colored illustrations with intricate details are set off by ample white space, echoing the gentle quality of a folktale retold in a style that has an elegant simplicity. The vinegar bottle is actually an old oast house built in the shape of the stone bottles once used to hold vinegar, and the old woman lives there with her cat, poor but cheerful. One day she finds a sixpence, buys a wee fish, and—seeing it gasp—tosses it back in the sea. The fish tells her he is a prince and will grant anything she desires. First it is just a hot meal, but then she asks for one thing after another: a house, a maid, a car—until the fish is irritated and she herself unhappy with the demands made by possessions. The fish sends the old woman back to her vinegar bottle; in some versions of the story, this is the moralistic ending, but here the old woman reverts to her old plump, pleasant self and apologizes to her benefactor, announcing that she prefers her vinegar bottle and the simple life.

478   **Goffstein,** M .B. *Goldie the Dollmaker.* Farrar, 1969. 55p. illus. $3.50.

3–5   A gentle story, simply written and illustrated with clean-lined, almost naïve drawings. Goldie Rozensweig carves her dolls so that each one has in her face something of the sweetness of the dollmaker. Goldie lives alone, shy and industrious, happy in her work. One day she buys a costly lamp; her friend chides her for this and says, "You know, Goldie, I think you must be a real artist . . . Because you're crazy." Dejected, Goldie goes home and broods about her extravagance—until she dreams that the maker of the lamp, an unknown artisan in far-off China, tells her that he made the lamp for her; she wakes, and goes to her beautifully painted lamp and feels a deep contentment. This is how Goldie herself feels about her dolls: with infinite love, she has created something for a person who will receive joy.

479   **Goffstein,** M. B. *Two Piano Tuners;* written and illus. by M. B. Goffstein. Farrar, 1970. 65p. $3.50.

3–4   The subject is fresh, the theme universal, and the style of writing delightful, in a story simple enough to be read to younger children but most likely to be appreciated by the middle-grades reader. Orphaned Debbie lives with her grandfather, an expert piano tuner. His ambition for Debbie is that she become a concert pianist; Debbie's ambition is to be a piano tuner as good as Grandpa. Matters come to a head when an old friend of Grandpa's, a distinguished concert pianist, listens to Debbie's playing . . . and when Grandpa Reuben listens to the job that Debbie has begun (on her own initiative) in tuning a piano. The story has humor, affection, and charm; without deep characterization the characters are somehow vivid and real.

480   **Goldston,** Robert C. *The Civil War in Spain.* Bobbs-Merrill, 1966. 224p. illus. $5. (Dent, 1971. 224p. £0.40.)

8—   A long, detailed, and fairly objective analysis of the struggle between the Republican government of Spain and the Fascist rebels. With the support of the International Brigade to the Loyalists and the support of Hitler and Mussolini to the Franco forces, the Civil War in Spain aroused the passion of the thinking world. The text is heavy, not in approach but in writing style; the level of objectivity achieved is rather remarkable in view of the author's candor in identifying with the Republicans. Some of the illustrations are merely decorative, but there are some interesting photographs and good battle maps. A long bibliography and a good index are appended.

481   **Goldston,** Robert C. *The Great Depression;* The United States in the Thirties; illus. with photographs and drawings by Donald Carrick. Bobbs-Merrill, 1968. 218p. $5.

8—   A long, hard look at the grim years that followed the crash of 1929, prefaced by a description of the United States in the optimistic decade that preceded the disaster. The author examines in authoritative detail the political and financial intricacies of the depression: the role of the farmers and of organized labor, the futile efforts of the Hoover administration and the turbulent activity of the New Deal, the actions of the Congress and of big business. Carefully written, objective and analytical, this is an absorbing and important book from both financial and historical viewpoints. An extensive bibliography and index are appended.

482   **Goldston,** Robert C. *The Life and Death of Nazi Germany;* illus. with photographs and drawings by Donald Carrick. Bobbs-Merrill, 1967. 224p. $5. (Dent, 1968. 224p. £0.40.)

8—   A third title in Mr. Goldston's series of books dealing with contemporary international issues, and a fine piece of writing, both as a literary product and as a historical treatise. The history of Germany is covered in enough detail to give the reader an understanding of the forces and factors that made possible the emergence of a Hitler and the subservience of a people whose cultural achievements and heritage should have made them impervious to demagoguery. The author's contempt for Hitler and his followers makes this a much less objective book than the first two. The rise of the Nazi party and the course of events that led to the war are described in great detail; as he has done before, the author gives a broad picture of the roles of other nations and of the forces and important figures within the country. Intelligent, lucid, and dramatic—an absorbing and important book. A bibliography and an index are appended.

483   **Goldston,** Robert C. *The Negro Revolution.* Macmillan, 1968. 247p. illus. $5.95.

8—   There have been several other good histories of the American Negro people and their fight for recognition; this is a welcome addition because it is well written, thoroughly researched, and comprehensive. The author covers the material included in most such histories, and adds to it a continuing and perceptive examination of underlying motives and ancillary factors. A bibliography, reading list, and relative index are appended.

484   **Goldston,** Robert C. *The Rise of Red China;* illus. with photographs and drawings by Donald Carrick. Bobbs-Merrill, 1967. 256p. $5.

8—   Another excellent book in the author's series of examinations of events in the life of a nation that are of far-reaching international importance in the one world of today. Here the historical background of the emergence of communism in China begins with her ancient history and the book examines in particular the exploitation of China by imperialist Occidental tactics in the nineteenth century. Mr. Goldston describes in great detail the power struggle between Mao Tse-tung and Chiang Kai-shek, aspects affected by foreign intervention, and the relationship between the United States and Formosa. Objective, lucid, and intelligent. A list of readings, a bibliography, and an index are appended.

485   **Goldston,** Robert C. *The Russian Revolution;* with drawings by Donald Carrick and photographs. Bobbs-Merrill, 1966. 224p. $5. (Dent, 1971. 224p. £0.40.)

8—   A beautifully balanced book in its coverage, well organized and written in a straightforward style that has vitality but never verges on journalese. The author gives an excellent capsule history as background to an understanding of recent events and of the political developments that contributed to the emergence of Bolshevik power. The author's explanation of Marxism is particularly lucid, and his exposition of the shifting and tumultuous power struggle is clear and incisive. A lengthy bibliography and an index are appended.

486   **Goodall,** John S. *Jacko.* Harcourt, 1972. 59p. illus. $3.50.

2–5   A story in pictures uses the familiar Goodall technique: full
yrs.   pages alternate with half pages, so that half of each scene changes with the turn of the mini-page. The setting is England in the eighteenth century, and Jacko is a monkey who escapes from his owner and stows away on a sailing ship inadvertently. He has hidden himself in a sea chest, and emerges in the captain's cabin, where he frees a caged parrot. When pirates board the ship, Jacko and his friend scamper over to man the pirate vessel, eventually landing on a tropical beach—and there he is met by the outstretched arms of what is indubitably a fond mother monkey. The color and action of the pictures, the appeal of the animal hero, and the humorous treatment combine to good effect in a lively tale for pre-readers.

487   **Goodall,** John S., illus. *Shrewbettina's Birthday;* illus. by John S. Goodall. Harcourt, 1971. 58p. $3.50. (Macmillan, 1970. 60p. £0.75.)

3–5   As in his earlier books, John Goodall has used half-page insertions
yrs.   between the pages to add an extra bit of action to a story without text. The Victorian dress and the English village setting give a quaint and pastoral flavor to the story of the shrew's gala day. It gets off to a bad start with a purse-snatching, but the masked thief is caught, and Shrewbettina is able to shop for the feast she has prepared for her guests. The animals dance, their best clothes flying about with the vigor of their performance; the hostess leaves the confetti-strewn chamber after the guests depart, yawning over her candle. She sleeps. Soft, sentimental drawings have a pastel charm, telling the tale very clearly.

488   **Gorodetzky,** Charles W. *What You Should Know about Drugs;* by Charles W. Gorodetzky and Samuel T. Christian. Harcourt, 1970. 121p. illus. $4.95. (Harcourt, Brace, 1970. 122p. £2.15.)

5— Although this gives enough coverage to be useful to adults, it is so simply written that it serves as an excellent source of information for the young reader. Separate chapters describe the origins, effects, uses, and abuses of narcotics, marijuana, hallucinogens, sedatives, stimulants, alcohol, and organic solvents such as those found in glue. The tone is dispassionate, the style straightforward. Tables give the generic, trade, and slang names for stimulants and sedatives; a glossary of terms and a relative index are appended.

489 **Gosfield,** Frank. *Korea:* Land of the 38th Parallel; by Frank Gosfield and Bernhardt J. Hurwood. Parents' Magazine, 1969. 254p. Trade ed. $4.50; Library ed. $4.12 net.

9— A thoughtful book, comprehensive and informative, that is well written for the serious reader, and that has a good balance between material that is historical and material about contemporary problems and relationships. Particular attention is given to the USS PUEBLO affair and to the Korean War and its aftermath. A series of documents (the report of a Dutch sailor shipwrecked in Korea in the 17th century, some official correspondence, papers on the PUEBLO and on U.N. truce violations), a bibliography, and an index are appended.

490 **Goudey,** Alice E. *Red Legs;* illus. by Marie Nonnast. Scribner, 1966. 59p. Trade ed. $2.95; Library ed. $3.63 net.

2–4 A very nice book about an insect familiar to most children. In a very simply written text, the author describes the life cycle of the red-legged grasshopper; the writing is never coy or supercilious, and the information is given succinctly. The soft, realistic illustrations are attractive, and the visual appeal and readability of the book are increased by the large print, liberal use of space, and good placement of illustrative material.

491 **Graham,** Lorenz. *David He No Fear;* pictures by Ann Grifalconi. T. Y. Crowell, 1971. 33p. $3.75.

K–3 Another tale in the series of single-story editions from Graham's retellings of Bible stories in *How God Fix Jonah,* his version based on the story of David and Goliath as told by an African storyteller. All the drama, humor, and colloquial cadence of the oral tradition are in the fluid and poetic prose. The illustrations effectively match the strength and simplicity of the story.

492 **Graham,** Lorenz. *Every Man Heart Lay Down;* illus. by Colleen Browning. T. Y. Crowell, 1970. $3.75.

K–3 A lovely story that first appeared in *How God Fix Jonah,* a retelling of Bible stories in the style of an African who knows little English. The poetic simplicity of the writing and the ingenuous interpretation of the events of the first Christmas are quite beguiling; the stylized illustrations are attractive. The familiar story of the Nativity is preceded by an explanation of God's anger at his people and by the intercession of God's son on their behalf. "And the pican go down softly/ And hold God's foot/ And God look on Him small boy/ And Him heart be soft again."

493   **Graham,** Lorenz. *A Road Down in the Sea;* illus. by Gregorio Prestopino. T. Y. Crowell, 1970. 37p. $3.95.

4–6   Taken from the author's *How God Fix Jonah,* a collection of Bible stories retold in Liberian dialect, the story of the exodus from Egypt. Cadenced and colorful, the prose has an ingenuous simplicity. The illustrations (double page spreads alternately in color and in black and white) have an echoing simplicity and strength, some of the pages in appropriate flat frieze composition; the pages in color are particularly effective because of the contrast of black faces (both Hebrews and Egyptians) and bright hues.

494   **Greaves,** Griselda, comp. *The Burning Thorn.* Macmillan, 1971. 184p. $5.95. (H. Hamilton, 1971. £1.50.)

8—   An eclectic compilation of poems that have been chosen for their depth of emotion and their relevance to the human condition. Most of the poets are English or American; some are the compiler's students; the contributors range in time from the fourth century to today. This is a book with unusual choices representing often-anthologized contributors, choices made with discrimination.

495   **Greenaway,** Kate. *The Kate Greenaway Treasury;* an anthology of the illus. and writings of Kate Greenaway, ed. and selected by Edward Ernest, assisted by Patricia Tracy Lowe. World, 1967. 319p. $9.95. (Collins, 1968. 320p. £2.25.)

all   An anthology that should find an eager audience of adults (who are
ages   either professionally interested or nostalgically smitten) as well as of the children for whom Miss Greenaway's work was designed. Much of the material included has been out of print; in addition to the charming illustrations (facsimile reproductions from published books) there are sketches included with the biographical and literary comments by Ruth Hill Viguers, Anne Carroll Moore, and others. There are many excerpts from letters, and several photographs of Kate Greenaway. A bibliography is appended.

496   **Greene,** Constance C. *A Girl Called Al;* illus. by Byron Barton. Viking, 1969. 127p. Trade ed. $3.95; Library ed. $3.77 net.

4–6   "There's a new girl moved down the hall from us," and we meet Al, who does not wish to be addressed as Alexandra.

Al is plump, intelligent, caustic, and—she says it herself—a nonconformist. Living alone with her divorced mother, Al is slow to relax her guard. Taken by the old resident (the author, who is another seventh-grade girl and never named) to visit the building superintendent, Mr. Richards, Al finds a friend. The book ends on a poignant note with Mr. Richards' death, and the two girls beginning to move into adolescence—part of the relationship missing with Mr. Richards gone, part of the change due to the inevitability of time. The first person telling is most convincing, the characterization and dialogue sharply observant, and style permeated not with humor but with the awareness of a sense of humor.

497   **Greene,** Constance C. *Leo the Lioness.* Viking, 1970. 118p. $3.95.

5–7   There is a point in every young person's life at which he discovers, as Tibb does in her thirteenth summer, that "people and things are not always what they seem. I know that people you think are strong sometimes turn out to be weak . . . when the chips are down, I turned out to be mean and small and almost didn't go to Carla's wedding." Carla was the girl who had been Tibb's adored baby-sitter, and it had come as a real blow to learn that she was pregnant. It had been a traumatic summer. When your older sister and your best friend can think of nothing but boys, it is hard to be flat-chested and have big feet. Tibb's only consolation is that she was born under the sign of Leo, and is therefore strong, forceful, steadfast "and practically everything good." Not an unusual theme, the adolescent girl who grows into a more mature person, but it is handled unusually well here. The writing is convincingly that of a teen-ager, the problems are universal and imbued with a humor that does not lessen their importance, the dialogue is excellent and the relationships are drawn with sympathetic understanding.

498   **Greenfeld,** Howard. *Pablo Picasso;* An Introduction; illus. with reproductions of the artist's work. Follett, 1971. 192p. $5.95.

7–10   An excellent biography of Picasso is profusely illustrated by reproductions of his work. The book has a good balance both in the attention paid to periods of the artist's life and in the discussion of the man and his work. Much of the text is devoted to analyses of individual drawings and paintings, with a final chapter that investigates other media used by Picasso. The information is interesting and the writing style competent, but what makes the book distinctive is the constant awareness of Picasso's role in art history and his relationships with other artists, and the relationship between Picasso the artist and Picasso the political and sentient human being.

499   **Greenfeld,** Howard. *The Waters of November.* Follett, 1969. 159p. illus. $7.95.

8—   As impressive as it is dramatic, a detailed account of the Florentine tragedy of 1966, when the rain-swollen Arno inundated the city, leaving in its wake irreparable damage and destruction. The photographs record the grim scenes of swirling streets and mud-soaked art treasures, and the text—written with infinite passion and compassion—creates vividly both the terror and the courage of the Florentines and of the visitors from all over the world who shared in the rescue work with spontaneous heroism. The latter sections of the book describe, separately, the intricate and sophisticated techniques being used to repair paintings, books, and statuary; the book ends on a note of sobriety, as the author comments on the later cavalier treatment of those students who gave so generously of their time and energy, and on the fact that the Italian government has done little or nothing about prevention of a recurrence of the event. Endpaper maps show the major sites mentioned in the book.

500   **Greenleaf,** Barbara Kaye. *America Fever;* The Story of American Immigration. Four Winds, 1970. 288p. illus. Trade ed. $5.95; Library ed. $5.38 net.

7—   An excellent study of immigration, sharply examining the causes of immigration and pointing out that many of the first settlers were redemptioners, slaves, deported convicts, and indentured servants, that whatever the motives or mores of the immigrants they had to accept the English language and customs of the first colonists. Lucidly written, the book is both profound and comprehensive. A bibliography and an index are appended.

501   **Greet,** W. Cabell. *Junior Thesaurus;* In Other Words II; by W. Cabell Greet, William A. Jenkins and Andrew Schiller. Lothrop, 1970. 448p. illus. Trade ed. $5.95; Library ed. $5.49 net.

5–9   There are so many visual devices to help the reader that this book is a bit hard on the eyes—but—each device is useful. Color underlining, blue, for antonyms; various types of print used for different, specific purposes; wide margins in which there are listed the synonyms explained on that page, or in which a symbol in color is used to indicate formal words, weak words, strong words, etc. The explanations are quite simple; the only weak aspect of the book is that many of the marginal illustrations are meaningless without the text; for example, "effect" is the word and the picture shows two out of three pupils in a classroom with their hands before their open mouths. In the column, "Effect also means result. The effect of smog on your eyes could be to make them smart. One effect of a stuffy room may be a sleepy class. What effect does too much ice cream have on you?" The first part of the book explains the codes, type face use, arrangement of material, et cetera; the second part is the thesaurus; the third part is the index.

502 **Greet,** W. Cabell. *My First Picture Dictionary;* by W. Cabell Greet, William A. Jenkins, and Andrew Schiller. Lothrop, 1970. 192p. Trade ed. $5.50; Library ed. $4.81 net.

1–3 Color-coded, words are arranged in subject areas: people, animals, storybook characters, what we do, things, and places; they are alphabetized within each group, and each word is followed by its plural form and a simple sentence or two, and is illustrated. Cross-references are included; for example: "niece/nieces/Penny is Uncle Al and Aunt Ruth's niece. See the picture for *family* on page 12." A final section is headed "Words That Help" and includes words that help tell when, how, how much, where, which one, what kind, what color, etc. An index is appended. The arrangement is logical, the format and print size clear, the pictures usually helpful.

503 **Greet,** W. Cabell. *My Pictionary;* by W. Cabell Greet, Marion Monroe, and Andrew Schiller. Lothrop, 1970. 95p. illus. Trade ed. $3.95; Library ed. $3.78 net.

3–6 yrs. A compilation of labeled actions or objects in broad categories: people, animals, storybook characters, what we do, things, places, colors, numbers, and "words that help" (prepositions). Although the pages are crowded and objects are not always in scale, the clear pictures and the categorization provide good orientation for reading readiness. In some cases, both the singular and plural are given ("goose" and "geese") or the names for both young and adult animals ("cat" and "kitten"). In "Things" there is clear grouping: food, play equipment, household paraphernalia, etc.

504 **Gregory,** Horace. *The Silver Swan;* Poems of Romance and Mystery; by Horace Gregory and Marya Zaturenska; wood engravings by Diana Bloomfield. Holt, 1966. 221p. Trade ed. $3.95; Library ed. $3.59 net.

7— A fine anthology, compiled by two poets, husband and wife; small black and white wood engravings are used to illustrate with distinction the selections of poetry. The poems reflect moods of mystery, mirth, longing, nostalgia, gloom, joy—the gamut of emotions one feels when in awe or in love. The poems are printed on separate pages with the writer's name cited; for each page the compilers give, in an appended section, a note on the author and, in some cases, some comment on the poem. Author, first line, and title indexes are included, the latter using italics to indicate references to notes.

505   **Grey,** Elizabeth. *Behind the Scenes in a Film Studio.* Roy, 1968.
            102p. illus. $3.50. (Dent, 1967. 96p. £1.00.)

7—   Like Theodore Taylor's *People Who Make Movies* (Doubleday,
            1967) this is organized on the basis of function, i.e., chapters
            on the stuntmen, the film editor, the producer, etc. but does
            not cleave closely to that organization. Music, for example, has
            no separate chapter as in the Taylor book, but there are half
            a dozen scattered index entries. First published in England in
            1966, the book has a British flavor that is no obstacle and is
            occasionally amusing. The humor in Taylor tends to be anecdotal
            or quippish, while Grey sees humor in the idiosyncrasies of
            the industry. Informal and informative, the book has eye-taxing
            small, close print. An index is appended, as is a glossary of
            terms which differ from those in Taylor—not an Anglo-American
            split, but a difference of emphasis.

506   **Griffin,** Judith Berry. *Nat Turner;* illus. by Leo Carty. Coward-
            McCann, 1970. 62p. $3.69.

3–5   Written in a simple, dignified fashion, a brief biography of the
            slave whose unsuccessful rebellion was one of the events that
            paved the way for the abolition of slavery. The author describes
            Turner's childhood, his learning to read and to dream of freedom,
            his growing conviction that he must lead a rebellion, and the
            details of the revolt and his death by hanging. Objective for the
            most part, the text has an occasional florid phrase, but it is,
            on the whole, straightforward. The illustrations are adequate.

507   **Grimm,** Jakob Ludwig Karl. *About Wise Men and Simpletons;*
            Twelve Tales from Grimm; tr. by Elizabeth Shub; illus. by Nonny
            Hogrogian. Macmillan, 1971. 115p. $4.95.

4–6   Newly translated from the first edition of the Grimms' stories,
            this collection includes such favorites as "Hansel and Gretel,"
            "The Bremen Town Musicians," and "Rumpelstiltskin." The
            versions are brief, less ornamented than they are in familiar
            versions, and chosen because, Elizabeth Shub says in her preface,
            "Here, even more than in later editions, the storyteller's voice is
            omnipresent." The directness of the style is matched and
            complemented by the simplicity and grace of the illustrations,
            black and white. A brief note on the Grimm brothers is appended.

508   **Grimm,** Jakob Ludwig Karl. *The Four Clever Brothers;* a story by
            the Brothers Grimm; with pictures by Felix Hoffmann. Harcourt,
            1967. 30p. $4.95.

K–3   First published in Switzerland in 1966, a distinguished picture
            book version of the tale also known as "The Four Accomplished
            (or, Skillful) Brothers." The style is brisk but not brusque,
            the illustrations pure delight. The colors are soft and rich, the

composition distinctive, and the pictures remarkable for their evocation of mood and movement. Four brothers, sent into the world by a poor father, learn four separate trades; to rescue the King's daughter, they pool their skills (stargazer, thief, hunter, and tailor) and outwit the dragon. Unable to agree on the traditional award, the hand of the princess, the four brothers gallantly agree to accept a fourth of the kingdom each.

509   **Grimm,** Jakob Ludwig Karl. *Grimm's Fairy Tales;* based on the Frances Jenkins Olcott ed. of the English tr. by Margaret Hunt; paintings in full color by children of fifteen nations. Follett, 1968. 412p. $6.95.

4–6   For many long months children of sixty countries created illustrations that were submitted to a group of editors and artists. The fifty illustrations that were chosen (out of 8,000) are remarkable for their vitality, color, sensitivity, and sense of design; they are diversified, sharing particularly the quality of being imaginative and lacking almost as completely the quality of humor. The three prize winning pictures are noted in the table of contents, which gives the name, age, and nationality of each young artist. The versions of the stories are based on the Hunt translation; a title index is appended.

510   **Grimm,** Jacob Ludwig Karl. *Jorinda and Joringel;* by the Brothers Grimm; tr. by Elizabeth Shub; illus. by Adrienne Adams. Scribner, 1968. 34p. Trade ed. $4.95; Library ed. $4.37 net.

3–5   A handsome edition of the story of a maiden bewitched and of her rescue by her lover. Joringel dreams of a magic flower that will enable him to pass the enchanted barrier and find the room where the wicked witch has turned seven thousand maidens into caged birds; he finds it, enters the castle, and sets his Jorinda and the other maidens free. The Adams illustrations are, as always, delicate and lovely.

511   **Gripari,** Pierre. *Tales of the Rue Broca;* by Doriane Grutman; illus. by Emily McCully. Bobbs-Merrill, 1969. 111p. $4.95.

5–7   First published in France in 1967, a half-dozen tales prefaced by the author's explanation of their purported origin; in the Parisian neighborhood in which he lived he told so many stories to the local children that he used all his material, so M. Pierre called for collaboration on new stories. The tales have a fresh and fertile imaginative quality that is truly childlike, but they are mature in style and interpretation, the humorous quality somewhat reminiscent of Twain's in moments of acerbity. One story is about the little devil who, a great disappointment to his parents, wants to be good; another is concerned with the highly improbable origin of the first piggy bank; two are about inanimate objects that love in romantic style (a pair of shoes in one case, a potato and a guitar in the other). The weakest of the lot is a rather long-drawn fairy tale, and it has enough barbs and nonsense to be enjoyable; one of the best is the sad tale of an immortal hero who never received posterity's plaudits because nobody could bear to record his ridiculous name.

512   **Gripe,** Maria. *The Night Daddy;* tr. from the Swedish by Gerry Bothmer; illus. by Harald Gripe. Delacorte, 1971. 151p. Trade ed. $4.50; Library ed. $4.17 net.

4–6   First published in Swedish under the title *Nattpappan,* this gentle story has a quality of universality and mild humor that add to the appeal of an unusual situation. Julia's mother is a nurse who is on night duty; she employs a young writer to stay with her daughter through the night. Fatherless, Julia is intrigued by the night daddy. Not only does he teach her fascinating things about his subject, stones, but he brings with him a little tame owl. These are the things that are the first attraction, but it is the sensitivity and kindness of the night daddy that awaken the child's love. The young writer and the small girl write alternate chapters—convincingly—and their small adventures add variety to a story that is basically an exploration of the relationship between child and adult.

513   **Grissom,** Virgil. *Gemini;* A Personal Account of Man's Venture into Space. Macmillan, 1968. 212p. $5.95. (Collier-Mac., 1968. 212p. £1.75.)

7—   Articulate and knowledgeable, Gus Grissom gives a detailed account of his participation in the manned space flight program; the book is informally written, and as pleasant to read as it is informative. Often humorous and always lucid, the author has both the advantage of immediate observation and ability to take nothing for granted, so that there are no gaps in background information to baffle the layman. He discusses the three basic types of flights (long duration, development, and rendezvous-and-docking) in the Gemini program. A brief epilogue describes the author's death. A glossary of space terms and an index are appended; many photographs are included, and the endpapers provide a useful chart of facts about all Russian and American manned space flights through 1967.

514   **Grossbart,** Francine. *A Big City*. Harper, 1966. 30p. illus. Trade ed. $3.50; Library ed. $3.48 net.

3–6   A delightful alphabet book, wonderful in the way it uses space
yrs.   and color, although one or two of the pages seem crowded. The book lacks the humor of Munari's *ABC* (World, 1960) but has some of the same appeal in its large, clear pictures; it has,

like Matthiesen's *ABC* (Platt and Munk, 1966), the appeal of familiar objects. Familiar, that is, to the urban child and not too unfamiliar for the child of suburb or country. Most of the pages show solidly drawn silhouettes in simple poster style; against the colored backgrounds of the pages there is a word or phrase printed in black or in white, in each case the initial letter of the first word being large and clear. In a few cases, the operative word seems a weak choice, since it is an adjective— for example, "O" is "Outdoor art show."

515   **Gruenberg,** Sidonie Matsner. *The Wonderful Story of How You Were Born;* illus. by Symeon Shimin. rev. ed. Doubleday, 1970. 38p. Trade ed. $3.50; Library ed. $4.25. (World's Work, 1962. 48p. £0.62.)

3–5   Good when it first appeared in 1952, improved by revision and by the lovely, tender pictures, a very good sex education book for the young. The combination of straightforward writing and no-nonsense information, and the recurrent note of marvel at the miracle of human birth is effective, and the book is eminently suitable for reading aloud to younger children.

516   **Guilcher,** J. M. *A Fern Is Born;* J. M. Guilcher and R. H. Noailles. Sterling, 1971. 96p. illus. Trade ed. $3.95; Library ed. $3.69 net.

5–7   Photographs, some highly magnified, show the different species of the graceful plant that reproduces without fruits or seeds. The text, first published in France, describes lucidly the sporangia that disburse the tiny spores that take root to germinate into a new and separate organism from which the familiar plant later grows. The text also describes how one can grow either form from the other. An index is appended.

517   **Guirma,** Frederic. *Princess of the Full Moon;* written and illus. by Frederic Guirma; tr. by John Garrett. Macmillan, 1970. 30p. $4.95.

4–6   Like other beautiful princesses of folk literature, Kiugu Peulgo sets a high standard for her husband, disdaining the love of her humble shepherd and accepting the dazzling stranger from a remote kingdom. But the princess soon finds that her husband is a monster, the Devil Prince of Midnight, and her life is saved only after a titanic struggle between him and the poor, ugly shepherd. So familiar are the components of this African tale in western literature that readers of the genre will expect (and get) a happy ending in which the shepherd bests the monster and is revealed as a handsome prince in disguise, and the repentant princess learns love and humility. The illustrations have awkward details but are interesting in the use of design and color.

518   **Gurko,** Leo. *Ernest Hemingway and the Pursuit of Heroism.*
T. Y. Crowell, 1968. 248p. (Twentieth-Century American Writers)
$4.75.

9—   A very long biographical chapter is followed by a series of
detailed critical analyses of Hemingway's writings in a serious and
absorbing book that should be stimulating to anyone interested
in Hemingway or in American literature. The biography is compact
and objective; the essays are discerning and critical, scholarly
but not arid, the author exploring with consistent percipience
the theme of heroism in Hemingway's books. A list of books
by Hemingway, a selected bibliography of books about him,
and an index are appended.

519   **Haber,** Louis. *Black Pioneers of Science and Invention.* Harcourt,
1970. 181p. $4.50. (Harcourt, Brace, 1970. 182p. £1.95.)

5–9   A good collective biography, one of a publisher's series of
curriculum-related books. Some of the subjects are men about
whom many books have been written, but most are little known.
The fourteen are Benjamin Banneker, Norbert Rillieux, Jan
Matzeliger, Elijah McCoy, Lewis Latimer, Granville Woods, Garrett
Morgan, G. W. Carver, Percy Julian, Lloyd Hall, Ernest Just,
Daniel Williams, Louis Wright, and Charles Drew. Personal
information is minimal, the focus being on the subject's
professional contribution; a wide variety of fields is covered, so
that the appeal of the book is broad. The writing is serious but not
heavy. A long divided bibliography and an index are appended.

520   **Hagon,** Priscilla. *Cruising to Danger;* illus. by William Plummer.
World, 1966. 192p. Trade ed. $3.75; Library ed. $3.61 net.
(Harrap, 1968. 186p. £0.75.)

7–10   A good mystery and adventure story, told in first person by
Joanna, who has just finished attending a London high school.
When she answers an ad that asks for an "ordinary" girl to help
care for two children on a cruise, Joanna hears a conversation
that makes her realize that she must hide the fact that she has a
scholarship to Oxford and pretend to be stupid. She becomes
increasingly suspicious of the children's father: suspicious that
he is an enemy agent, that he is the cause of his wife's
illness, and that he is using his little daughter's dolls as a front
for an operation concerning stolen information. The story has
pace, suspense, love interest, and the colorful setting of a
Mediterranean cruise ship. The author deviates from the patterned
mystery for the young reader in having the criminal be the father
of two children; it adheres, happily, to a logical development and
conclusion based on the premise that Joanna's intelligent
apprehensions are correct: no hidden facts, no sudden
contrivances.

521   **Halacy,** Daniel S. *Experiments with Solar Energy*. Norton, 1969.
147p. illus. Trade ed. $4.50; Library ed. $4.14 net.

6–9   "Experiments" is not precisely what the projects described here
consist of; rather, they are step-by-step directions for assembling
various devices for putting solar energy to practical use: a stove,
a radio, a water heater, a still for extracting potable water from
salt water. The author discusses solar energy in general, pointing
out some of the present and future installations that use it, but
most of the book is devoted to the projects. None is expensive,
and none is really difficult to build, although it would be hard
for a beginner to cope unless he had already acquired some
basic skills. There are few pictures of diagrams to guide the reader,
but no single step in construction should be'incomprehensible to
anyone with experience in carpentry. A list of firms engaged
in solar energy applications, a brief bibliography, and an index are
appended.

522   **Haley,** Gail E., ad. *A Story A Story; An African Tale*; ad. and
illus. by Gail E. Haley. Atheneum, 1970. 32p. Trade ed. $5.95;
Library ed. $5.73 net.

K–2   Although this gets off to a slow start with an explanation—and a
generalization about the genre—it soon moves to cadenced prose,
the author adeptly using repetition at points of emphasis. The
woodcut illustrations, busy with detail, are sometimes
overcrowded and almost garish, but they have vitality, humor,
and a good sense of design. The story explains the origin of
that favorite African folk material, the spider tale. Here Ananse,
the old spider man, wanting to buy the Sky God's stories,
completes by his cleverness three seemingly impossible tasks set
as the price for the golden box of stories which he takes back
to earth.

523   **Hall,** Lynn. *Sticks and Stones*. Follett, 1972. 220p. Trade ed.
$4.95; Library ed. $4.98 net.

7–10   There weren't many adolescents of Tom's age in Buck Creek,
Iowa, and Floyd Schleffe, fat and awkward, wasn't one he desired
as a friend. When Ward Alexander, just out of the Air Force,
appeared, Tom was delighted: a friend who liked good music
and books, a sensible guy to whom you could really talk. But
Buck Creek was a small town; Floyd was jealous, so was a girl
who had hoped to interest Tom. And so the snickering began,
the snickering and rebuffs and the gossip. When Tom is forbidden
to go to the state music finals because parents don't want him
on a two-day bus trip with their sons, he learns from the
school principal what is being said. Stunned, he withdraws from
his classmates—then he begins to wonder about himself. Is he a
homosexual? Ward's the only one he can talk to—and Ward

tells Tom he had been discharged from the service because of a homosexual incident. Tom, shocked, retreats, but in his utter loneliness he misses his friend. Not until he is in the hospital after an automobile accident does he gain enough perspective to see what gossip has done to his life and his emotional stability; he realizes that he has had feelings of guilt and shame imposed on him by the community, that he has no real reason to doubt his own heterosexuality—and that he can now accept Ward as a valued friend. Both the accident and the instant insight of the ending are weak compared to the strength and realism of the story; characterization is good, the picture of a small community candid and perceptive, the treatment of attitudes toward homosexuality understanding.

524   **Halliday,** F. E. *Chaucer and His World.* Viking, 1968. 144p. illus. $6.95. (Thames & H., 1968. 144p. £1.75.)

9—   A book for the mature reader, and probably only for those interested in literature or history, for the writing is detailed and scholarly, only its elegance saving it from being tedious. Chaucer's life is so much a part and an example of the intrigue and romanticism of medieval times that the author's infrequent historical digressions are more than justified. The description and analysis of Chaucer's writing are more explanatory than critical. Profusely illustrated with photographs of cathedrals, tapestries, manuscripts, and effigies, the book has artistic distinction. A divided bibliography, a chronology, a section of notes on the illustrations, and an index are appended.

525   **Hamblin,** Dora Jane. *Pots and Robbers.* Simon and Schuster, 1970. 258p. Trade ed. $4.95; Library ed. $4.73 net.

7—   A most interesting series of true stories about some of the dramatic aspects of archeology. With wit and zest, the author describes the excitement of finding some of the treasured sites of the past, the organized despoliation of tombs, the marauding of tourists, the perpetration of expert forgeries, and the embattled police, archeologists, and art experts who ferret out the tomb robbers and the peddlers of stolen goods. The material is fresh, the writing style lively. An index is appended.

526   **Hamilton,** Virginia. *The House of Dies Drear;* illus. by Eros Keith. Macmillan, 1968. 246p. $4.95.

6–9   A hundred years ago, Dies Drear and two slaves he was hiding in his house, an Underground Railroad station in Ohio, had been murdered. The house, huge and isolated, was fascinating, Thomas thought, but he wasn't sure he was glad Papa had bought it— funny things kept happening, frightening things. The caretaker was forbidding, the neighbors unfriendly. The secret of the house

is revealed in an exciting final sequence that maintains
beautifully the mysterious and dramatic story of a Negro family
caught in an atmosphere of fear and danger. Written with
distinction, an imaginative and imposing book.

527   **Hamilton,** Virginia. *The Planet of Junior Brown.* Macmillan, 1971.
           210p. $4.95.

7–9   A memorable book despite the intricacies of the plot, the book
           hovering between grim realism and improbability in scope. Junior
           and Buddy are eighth-graders who never go to class, their absence
           abetted by the school janitor, who has made a mock-up of the
           solar system in a basement hideaway. Junior, who weighs
           three hundred pounds, is a musical prodigy whose overprotective
           mother has made him as neurotic as she is. Buddy, who lives in an
           underground hideout as the protector of a group of smaller,
           homeless boys, is also Junior's protector. When Junior loses his
           grip on reality after visiting his piano teacher (an insane but
           harmless creature who gives "lessons" without letting Junior
           touch her piano) and being convinced by her that there is a dead
           body in her apartment, Buddy rescues him. With the help of
           the janitor, he installs his friend in his "planet"—the name for the
           hideout—and adjures the other boys to take care of Junior.
           "Everybody is to see that Junior doesn't hurt himself," he says,
           "We are together because we have to learn to live for each other."

528   **Hamilton,** Virginia. *The Time-Ago Tales of Jahdu;* illus. by Nonny
           Hogrogian. Macmillan, 1969. 63p. $4.50.

3–5   After school each day, Lee Edward stayed with Mama Luka until
           his mother came home from work. Each day, she told a story of
           Jahdu, sitting "in a fine, good place called Harlem . . . telling
           Jahdu stories to Lee Edward. She told them slow and she told
           them easy . . ." Breathless, Lee Edward listens to the stories
           of long ago, stories of the crafty boy who grew wiser and more
           powerful, and he knows that when he grows up he will be, like
           Jahdu, strong and proud. Both the Jahdu tales and the Harlem
           setting have a potent charm; the quiet black and white illustrations
           echo the dignity and affection of an enchanting book.

529   **Hamilton,** Virginia. *W. E. B. DuBois;* A Biography; illus. with
           photographs. T. Y. Crowell, 1972. 218p. $4.50.

7–10   Carefully researched and documented, sympathetic toward the
           subject yet candid about his failings, this is a sober record of
           the long career of William Du Bois. The biography concentrates
           on his adult life, giving a detailed account of the teacher, writer,
           and political activist and very little about his personal life.
           This lacks the warmth that characterizes Virginia Hamilton's
           fiction, but it makes a particular contribution in placing the events

of Du Bois' life not just in the stream of black history but against the background of what was happening in the United States and how it inevitably affected what was happening to William Du Bois. A section of chapter notes, a selective bibliography of writings by and about DuBois, and an extensive relative index are appended.

530   **Hanff,** Helene. *The Movers and Shakers;* The Young Activists of the Sixties. S. G. Phillips, 1970. 190p. $6.95.

8—   Helene Hanff confesses in the foreword that she had planned quite a different sort of approach when she first began to do research for a book about the youthful movements of the 60's. The more facts she discovered, the more her viewpoint shifted toward sympathy with the young movers and shakers who, she came to feel, had been challenging the corruption of the establishment with high goals and moral courage. The four sections of the book cover the rebellions against the military, political, academic, and segregationist powers, although not with full coverage. Often passionate, always candid, carefully researched, and only occasionally given to generalized statements, this is exciting to read and a useful document of our times. A divided, selected bibliography and an index are appended.

531   **Hannum,** Sara, comp. *The Wind Is Round;* comp. by Sara Hannum and John Terry Chase; illus. by Ron Bowen. Atheneum, 1970. 100p. $4.75.

5—   In this anthology of nature poems, the compilers say in their preface, are words that "may yet prompt us to discover our Eden before we destroy it" and it is with this in mind, as well as the intention of showing what modern poets feel about nature, that the compilation was made. The selections are arranged through the cycle of the year—although many pertain to no special season—and have been chosen with discrimination. Sources are cited; an author-title index is appended.

532   **Hardendorff,** Jeanne B., comp. *Just One More;* illus. by Don Bolognese. Lippincott, 1969. 169p. Trade ed. $3.50; Library ed. $3.39 net.

4–6   A retelling of forty stories, chosen for their brevity, for the occasion when an additional tale is begged for or a sample needed of the story-hour to come. This is a widely varied collection, good for independent reading or reading aloud as well as for telling; an appendage gives the source for each tale, the audience level, and the time each takes in the telling—half of the forty taking three minutes or less.

533   **Harman,** Humphrey. *Tales Told near a Crocodile;* Stories from

Nyanza; illus. by George Ford. Viking, 1967. 185p. Trade ed.
$3.95; Library ed. $3.77 net. (Hutchinson, 1961. 144p. £0.75.)

5–6   A collection of ten stories from six tribes that live near the
African Lake Nyanza—Lake Victoria. One romantic tale describes
the lovers who were able to escape because he had the magical
power to call up crocodiles, another is about a quarrel between
brothers, another in the familiar pattern of the curious young
wife who learns the secret of her husband's wealth and is
punished. Almost all of the stories have both people and animals
as characters; there is little humor, save in side remarks; there
is much sagacity and drama.

534   **Harrington,** Lyn. *The Grand Canal of China;* illus. with photographs
and maps. Rand McNally, 1967. 110p. $3.95.

6–9   Neither a complete history nor a geography of China, this
interesting book approaches China's past—and to some extent its
present—by focusing on the canal in relationship to the five
great river systems it serves and links. Inevitably, in the repeated
pattern of historical background followed by recent events in
areas affected by the 1100-mile waterway, there is some repetition,
but the technique of shifting from one region to another is
quite effective, and the writing style is informal and easy. The
careful statements of the text are not always echoed by the
captions to illustrations, but the illustrations themselves are
interesting, and the several maps very helpful. A glossary and
an index are appended.

535   **Harris,** Christie. *Confessions of a Toe-Hanger;* drawings by Moira
Johnston. Atheneum, 1967. 209p. Trade ed. $4.50; Library ed.
$4.13 net.

7–10   A companion volume to *You Have to Draw the Line Somewhere*
in which the story of a fashion artist's career was based on the
experiences of the author's daughter. Here the younger sister
of that artist tells the story of her childhood and youth, her
marriage, and her experiences as a young wife and mother.
Having felt always eclipsed by her brother and sister, Feeny
discovers comparatively late in life she need make no comparisons,
need imitate no patterns—that she has a freedom of choice about
her hobbies and her work. This is an excellent story of a
Canadian family, a good story of a girl's growing up, and an
amusing book in general, written with humor and with good
dialogue in an easy, colloquial style.

536   **Harris,** Christie. *Raven's Cry;* illus. by Bill Reid. Atheneum, 1966.
193p. Trade ed. $3.95; Library ed. $3.81 net.

5–10   A most impressive book, both because of its cultural authenticity
and because it tells a story that has dramatic and historic impact.

Mrs. Harris describes most movingly the terrible effects on the Haida people of the white men who came in 1775; the white men came for sea otter, and in their greed and ignorance they cheated and destroyed the Haida. The story is told from the viewpoint of the Indian, told with vigor and sympathy and illustrated with bold black and white drawings by an artist whose ancestors were Haidas.

537   **Harris,** Janet. *The Long Freedom Road;* The Civil Rights Story; illus. with photographs. McGraw-Hill, 1967. 150p. $4.95. (Longman Young Books, 1968. 144p. £0.75.)

6–10   A well-balanced history of the American Negro's fight for civil rights, quite objective and written in a direct and simple style that is marred slightly by the author's proclivity to put between quotation marks words or phrases that seem quite ordinary. "The churches that served as 'freedom schools' were bombed." or, "The 'long hot summer of 1963' began with two rifle shots . . ." The author is sympathetic to the civil rights movement (she has worked with CORE and the NAACP) but the tone of her writing is restrained and quiet. A bibliography of adult and juvenile books and an index are appended.

538   **Harris,** Marilyn. *The Runaway's Diary.* Four Winds, 1971. 222p. Trade ed. $4.95; Library ed. $5.12 net.

7–10   The author's preface explains that the diary was one she found after an accident victim had been taken to the hospital; a final note explains that Catherine Toven died of injuries sustained in the accident, and that parental permission has been given for publication. Cat, who is sixteen and unhappy about the rift between her parents and whose hostility toward her mother is evidenced by the fact that the latter is referred to as "she" in the book, runs away. The incidents of her journey and the people she meets give vitality and flavor to her story, but the meat of the book is in the revealing of her character and her philosophy. Cat is gentle, introspective, idealistic, and sensitive, a human being with a great and unfulfilled potential for love.

539   **Harris,** Rosemary. *The Bright and Morning Star.* Macmillan, 1972. 254p. $4.95. (Faber. 239p. £1.60.)

5–8   First published in England, the third of a trilogy of which the first was *The Moon in the Cloud* (winner of the Carnegie Medal) and the second, *The Shadow on the Sun.* The appeal of familiar characters and the deft mixture of period details and fanciful humor in the Egyptian setting (the land is called Kemi) and the vigor of the writing style add to the attraction of a fast-moving plot. Reuben and Thamar have come from Canaan with their son, hoping to find a cure for the sick boy, and they become involved in the power struggle that is going on in Kemi, the evil No-Hotep, advisor to the Prince, pitted aginst the wise advisor to the Princess Ta-Thata, the half-sister who is to rule jointly over the land.

540 Harris, Rosemary. *The Moon in the Cloud.* Macmillan, 1970. 182p. $4.95. (Faber, 1968. 176p. £0.90.)

5–8 Winner of the 1969 Carnegie Medal, a fanciful story with a Biblical setting and a sophisticated humor that permeates even those scenes that are more dramatic or expository than humorous. Reuben and Thamar are a young couple who live in a tent near Noah and his family, and it is Reuben who goes to Egypt to hunt for the animals needed to make up Noah's quota. Ham is supposed to go, but he is lazy and besides, he has his eye on pretty Thamar, so he promises Reuben passage on the Ark if he returns with a cat and two lions. Most of the story is concerned with Reuben's adventures: his captivity, his friendship with the Lord of Two Lands, and his escape into the desert. The cat Cefalu, which Reuben has brought from home, has some adventures of his own, events on which Cefalu makes caustic and frequent comments. Written with skill, a tale that has suspense, action, wit, and wisdom.

541 Harris, Rosemary. *The Seal-Singing.* Macmillan, 1971. 245p. $4.95. (Faber, 1971. 224p. £1.25.)

7–10 This is a memorable novel for young readers, the Scottish island setting flavorful, the characters blazingly real, the style, dialogue, and plot masterful. Seventeen-year-old Toby and his younger cousin Catriona are joined by another cousin, Miranda, whose uncanny resemblance to an infamous and beautiful ancestress strikes a boding note. And Miranda does, indeed, find herself possessed of strange powers: like the ancestress, she can call the seals. The isle of Carrigona is a seal nursery, and Toby adores the baby seal he is raising as a pet. It is through Miranda that the seals are driven away and court disaster. The supernatural aspect of the story is astutely blended with the realistic, and the reality is remarkably vivid.

542 Harris, Rosemary. *The Shadow on the Sun.* Macmillan, 1970. 198p. $4.95. (Faber, 1970. 189p. £1.00.)

5–8 A sequel to *The Moon in the Cloud* in which the young couple Reuben and Thamar have Egyptian adventures while hunting animal species for Noah's Ark. The scene is again Egypt, but Reuben plays a secondary role; this is primarily a love story in which the young king wins the love of Meri-Mekhmet, the Court Chamberlain's daughter, who doesn't know his identity. Her capricious behavior when she learns the truth leads to a series of adventures, with Reuben sent to rescue Meri-Mekhmet when she is kidnapped. The plot has flamboyant embroidery, but the sophistication of humor and writing style, the half-invented background of the land of Punt and the colorful Egyptian setting, the vigorous characterization and dialogue make this as diverting as its predecessor.

543   **Harshaw,** Ruth Hetzel. *In What Book?* by Ruth Hetzel Harshaw and Hope Harshaw Evans. Macmillan, 1970. 130p. $4.50.

K–8   After many years, a volume that supplements *What Book Is That?* Here there are no sketches, only the kind of questions (grouped by age level) that were the first part of the earlier book. The preface, which gives the sources from which recommended books were chosen, explains that the questions are so phrased that they are as explicit as possible, to encourage the child who has read the book and to lure the one who has not. Each set of questions ("In what tale did a boastful father tell the king his daughter could spin gold out of straw?") is followed by answers. Mrs. Harshaw and her daughter have performed a service, again, for children and books.

544   **Haugaard,** Erik Christian. *The Little Fishes;* illus. by Milton Johnson. Houghton, 1967. 214p. $3.75. (Gollancz, 1968. 224p. £0.90.)

7—   An absorbing story of wartime Italy, told by Guido, the twelve-year-old waif who lives by begging and stealing, as do so many other derelicts of Naples. With two smaller children he sets off for Cassino; occasionally they meet a kind adult, but most of the adults are also starving and desperate, and must compete to survive. A terrible, true, and touching story; beautifully written, it is an assertion of the tenacity of love and hope.

545   **Haugaard,** Erik Christian. *The Rider and His Horse;* illus. by Leo and Diane Dillon. Houghton, 1968. 243p. $3.95. (Gollancz, 1969. 256p. £1.05.)

7–12   A story of the Masada, where Eleasar ben Ya'ir and the Zealots died rather than submit to the Roman attackers, in a grim but heroic mass suicide. The story is told by David ben Joseph, who is irritated by the criticism of the historian Joseph ben Matthias, a Jew who has gone over to the Romans. The young, idealistic David walks the long way from Tyre to Jerusalem, a ruined city, and lives with the gentle Rabbi Simon ben Judas, who tells him, "In the wilderness, David, the Zealots are masters and I fear their ignorance has made them arrogant." But David goes to the Masada; he learns love and pity; he acquires the strength to keep his promise to Eleasar that he will not kill himself but will escape so that he can tell mankind of the courage of the Zealots. The book ends with David's visit to Rome to tell the turncoat, now called Josephus, of the last days of the Masada so that the records may tell the story. Serious and dramatic, a moving story that is given immediacy by David's telling and verisimilitude by the philosophical gravity of its tone.

546   **Hautzig,** Esther. *The Endless Steppe;* Growing Up in Siberia. T. Y. Crowell, 1968. 243p. $4.50. (Penguin, 1971. £0.25.)

6–10   Esther was ten when her comfortable and happy life in Vilna was completely disrupted. An only child, she had lived with a big and loving family of grandparents, aunts and uncles, and numerous cousins. Sent to Siberia, she lived in cramped and desolate quarters with her parents and one grandmother, all of them forced to labor in field or mine, and forced to live in cramped and dismal quarters. They managed. Esther went to school, worked at home, did odd jobs for—literally—a crust of bread. This true and harrowing story of five arduous years is all the more effective because it is told with direct simplicity and no bitterness.

547   **Hautzig,** Esther. *In the Park;* an Excursion in Four Languages; pictures by Ezra Jack Keats. Macmillan, 1968. 27p. $4.95. (Collier-Mac., 1969. 32p. £1.05.)

3–4   Very simple, very functional, very attractive. Parks are fun to visit, the text states, in New York—or Paris—or Moscow—or Madrid. Following this pattern, the names of familiar things are given in each of the four appropriate languages, with pronunciation below each word. The pictures are gay, the word-comparison can be fun, and the universality of children's interests is an implicit additional message. This book does not attempt to tell a story, so that it need not bear the label of a picture-book to discourage independent readers. A list of additional words and pronunciation guide to the Russian alphabet are appended.

548   **Haviland,** Virginia. *Favorite Fairy Tales Told in Czechoslovakia:* retold by Virginia Haviland; illus. by Trina Schart Hyman. Little, 1966. 90p. $3.95. (Bodley Head, 1970. 96p. £0.80.)

3–6   Five stories, told in a pleasant, direct style: "The Twelve Months," "Kuratko the Terrible," "The Wood Fairy," "The Shepherd's Nosegay," and "The Three Golden Hairs of Grandfather Know All." Sources are cited, both secondary and primary. The format is handsome; the illustrations are most attractive, appropriate for the genre as well as for the Czechoslovakian setting.

549   **Haviland,** Virginia, ad. *Favorite Fairy Tales Told in Denmark;* illus. by Margot Zemach. Little, 1971. 90p. $3.95.

4–6   Six tales are retold with directness and simplicity, and are

illustrated with pictures in soft details touched with humor. The
tales are "The Wonderful Pot," "Ee-aw! Ee-aw!," "The
Knapsack," "Grayfoot," "The Tree of Health," and "A Legend
of Christmas Eve." Useful as a source for storytelling as well as
for independent reading.

550   **Haviland,** Virginia. *Favorite Fairy Tales Told in Sweden;* retold by
Virginia Haviland; illus. by Ronni Solbert. Little, 1966. 92p.
$3.95. (Bodley Head, 1969. 96p. £0.80.)

4–6   Six tales, retold in a straightforward and modest style, illustrated
with pictures in black, white and orange—lively and attractive.
The text is printed in large, clear type; the tales are all typical
of the genre: the magic castle that is envied by a king, the
boy who outwits a water sprite, the daydreamer whose inflated
fancies lead to his own downfall, et cetera. A pleasant addition
to the author's excellent series of fairy tales from different
countries.

551   **Havrevold,** Finn. *Undertow;* tr. and illus. by Cathy Babcock
Curry. Atheneum, 1968. 186p. Trade ed. $4.50; Library ed. $4.08
net.

6–9   Translated from the Norwegian, a very good novel about two
teenage boys. Jørn, who tells the story, is rebelling against his
pleasant middle-class family who disapprove of his new friend,
Ulf. Choosing to visit Ulf rather than share his own family's
vacation, Jørn discovers that Ulf's parents are away and that a
sailing trip is planned. Almost every day Jørn learns something
new about Ulf: he lies, he boasts, he steals (he has, indeed,
stolen the boat they are using) and he is reckless and vain.
Ulf dies when the boat capsizes, but the sobering realization
of his own share in the escapade has already come to Jørn,
as has the acceptance of the need, still, for parental guidance.
A novel full of action, with a perceptive understanding of
adolescent striving for independence.

552   **Hawkinson,** John. *Our Wonderful Wayside.* Whitman, 1966. 40p.
illus. Trade ed. $3.50; Library ed. $2.63 net.

4–6   It's a pity that this charmingly casual book looks like a book for
quite young children, since many of the projects it suggests—
and much of the information it gives—should interest older
children as well. Mr. Hawkinson describes in three sections
(spring, summer, autumn) some of the beauties one can see
on a country walk, the foods one can find—and how to identify
them, store them, or prepare them—and the collections to be
made, and some few crafts and games using objects picked up
on the wayside. The small, bright paintings are both informative
and attractive; the writing has an easy conversational flow.

553   **Hayden,** Robert, ed. *Kaleidoscope;* Poems by American Negro
            Poets. Harcourt, 1967. 231p. $3.95.

8—   An unusual anthology because of the scope it offers; some forty
            poets are represented, with just a poem or two from some and
            with perhaps half a dozen selections from such established
            artists as Brooks and Dunbar. The poems are varied in subject
            and mood, the editor's introduction pointing out that his choices
            were made on a literary basis rather than on the basis of racial
            statement. Mr. Hayden, whose work is also represented, is a
            professor of English. Notes on the authors precede their poems;
            the notes are literary in emphasis, with a minimal amount of
            biographical information.

554   **Hays,** Wilma Pitchford. *May Day for Samoset;* illus. by Marilyn
            Miller. Coward-McCann, 1968. 62p. Library ed. $3.49 net.

3–5   A story of colonial times, set on the island of Monhegan, Maine.
            Susan has been trying to think of a May Day present for her
            good friend Samoset; reluctantly she decides that one should
            give the best one has, and she gives the Indian her beloved
            kitten. The story line is tenuous, but the book is simply written
            and gives a picture of a little-known segment of colonial history.

555   **Haywood,** Carolyn. *Eddie the Dog Holder;* written and illus. by
            Carolyn Haywood. Morrow, 1966 187p. Trade ed. $4.75;
            Library ed. $4.32 net.

2–4   Eddie and Annie Pat strike again. In another pleasantly rambling,
            slightly repetitive, and quite realistic story the two friends who
            are so familiar to Miss Haywood's readers spend a busy summer.
            Annie Pat has taken up painting and Eddie offers to hold dogs
            for her, since Annie Pat paints only dogs. The children bumble
            along, with little profit to show for a great deal of activity.
            Fall comes, Eddie enter fourth grade, and he is delighted when
            his pal's dogs win plaudits at a school art exhibit. The writing
            style is simple and natural; the episodic plot, lightly threaded
            together, is just right for the primary grades reader; and the light
            humor of the problem situations is just the sort that small children
            relish.

556   **Headington,** Christopher. *The Orchestra and Its Instruments;* with
            drawings by Roy Spencer. World, 1967. 95p. Trade ed. $5.95
            Library ed. $6.21 net. (Bodley Head, 1965. 96p. £1.05.)

7–12   An excellent book on this subject, first published in England
            and profusely illustrated with meticulous drawings and diagrams,
            and with photographs of young orchestral musicians. The author
            describes the instruments of each section, explaining the
            differences between related instruments and, in many cases,
            explaining very lucidly how changes of pitch are produced

in a particular instrument. The text includes a discussion
of the vocalist and the conductor, gives a brief survey of the
history of the orchestra, and concludes with a chart of seating, a
list of orchestral examples of instrumental use, some suggested
readings, a list of instrumental ranges, and an index.

557   **Heady,** Eleanor B. *High Meadow;* The Ecology of a Mountain
Meadow; written by Eleanor B. Heady and Harold F. Heady;
illus. by Harold F. Heady. Norton/Grosset, 1970. 120p. Trade ed.
$4.50; Library ed. $4.59 net.

6–9   Large print, clear illustrations, good organization of material, and
an easy style of writing add value to a book that gives a lucid
picture of the intricacies of an ecological situation as it responds
to seasonal change. First describing the geological background of
the meadow, formed by successive plants filling in a glacial
lake, the authors discuss the changes, internal and external, of
the flora and fauna of the meadow through the cycle of the year.
A bibliography and an index are appended.

558   **Heady,** Eleanor B. *When the Stones Were Soft;* East African Fireside
Tales; illus. by Tom Feelings. Funk and Wagnalls, 1968. 94p. $4.95.

4–6   Sixteen East African folktales are illustrated with softly executed
pictures in black and white; the stories are retold from familiar
versions of traditional material from Kenya, Tanzania, and Uganda,
and each is prefaced by a repeated pattern, in which Mama
Semamingi—the storyteller—gathers the village children around
the fire. Many of the tales are about animals, some are about
nature, others about human behavior. Good style, and a nice
source for storytelling as well as for reading aloud.

559   **Heaps,** Willard A. *Riots, U.S.A. 1765–1965.* Seabury, 1966. 186p.
$3.95.

8—   A book that gives the stories of thirteen major riots in our country,
from the Stamp Act Riots in 1765 to the Southern Michigan
Prison riot of 1952; the two closing chapters of the book describe
the many struggles within the civil rights movement: the sitdowns,
the marches, the protests, and the riots. Objective, detailed, and
well organized, the text gives an interesting picture of the spectrum
of causes that have moved men to violence in our history, and
now in our time. A long and impressive list of sources and
readings, divided by chapters, is appended, as is a relative index.

560   **Heaps,** Willard A. *Wandering Workers;* The Story of American
Migrant Farm Workers and Their Problems. Crown, 1968. 192p.
$4.95.

7—   A piercing look at a grim picture. The author's extensive research is obvious in the carefully documented text, and the use of transcriptions of taped interviews with migrant workers gives the book an immediacy that is tremendously effective. The spelling in these interviews (attempting to replicate dialect) is the only weak point of the book: "specials" is spelled "speshuls," and "auto," "otto." A clear picture of the variety of migrants and their patterns emerges; the chapters on legislation and inspection of housing and sanitary conditions, on health hazards and wages are as shocking as they are informative. A long list of suggested readings and an index are appended.

561   **Heide,** Florence Parry. *Maximilian;* by Florence Heide and Sylvia Van Clief; illus. by Ed Renfro. Funk and Wagnalls, 1967. 28p. $3.95.

4–6   The idea of an animal wanting to be something other than
yrs.   what he is is not a new idea in picture books, but it has seldom been more amusingly handled. Maximilian's mother takes it calmly when he announces that he wants to be a bird instead of a mouse. He doesn't like squeaking or scampering or crouching; Maximilian wants to fly. He stows away in a nest and pretends to be one of the nestlings; Mother Bird (who has been offended when one of her friends said that one of the children looked like a mouse) reluctantly admits that this one can't fly. Indeed, that it's a mouse. Thankfully, Maximilian gives up the whole project. The style is light and humorous, the scratchy illustrations full of vitality.

562   **Hellman,** Hal. *Biology in the World of the Future.* Evans, 1971. 188p. illus. $4.95.

7—   A knowledgeable and witty foray into the frontiers of biological research, well organized and provocative. The author discusses genetic, eugenic, and nutrition research, the uses of machines in diagnosing and treating physical and mental illness, control of waste products, and the possibility of creating androids or delaying old age. A lengthy bibliography and an index are appended.

563   **Hellman,** Hal. *Defense Mechanisms;* From Virus to Man. Holt, 1969. 150p. illus. Trade ed. $3.95; Library ed. $3.59 net.

5–8   A most interesting book about the amazing variety of ways in which members of the animal kingdom defend themselves from aggression, competition, disease, and extinction. The material is loosely organized, although chapters are focused on aspects of defense mechanisms such as protective coloration, the role of the senses, defensive behavior, and adaptation. Despite a rather coy first page the text is solid with facts but not dull, straightforward, and briskly competent. A list of suggested readings and an index are appended.

564   **Hellman,** Hal. *Transportation in the World of the Future.* Evans,
1968. 187p. illus. $4.95.

7–12   Any discussion of the modes of transportation of the future must
be prefaced by an analysis of those in use today: their
inadequacies, their susceptibility to improvement, and their
interrelationship with other factors such as roads, cooperating
systems, and the pattern of business and residential districts in
urban areas. Considering all these factors, the author describes
some of the projected or already designed systems and vehicles
for travel by sea and air, on the ground, and underground. The
Hovercraft, the electric car, the monorail and the super-express
train are in existence; the drawing boards of engineers have
produced the air-cushion vehicle system, hypersonic transport,
all-weather highways, automatic control of automobiles, road-rail
systems, and a dozen other ideas. Some are impractical but
all are possible. An intriguing subject is handled with authority;
the writing style is brisk, informal, and only occasionally smacks
of journalese. A bibliography and an index are appended.

565   **Henry,** James P. *Biomedical Aspects of Space Flight.* Holt, 1966.
184p. illus. $2.95.

8—   A comprehensive and clearly written book by a physician who
has for twenty years been doing research in space flight. Dr.
Henry discusses such problems as temperature toleration, oxygen
tension, weightlessness, cosmic radiation, elimination of waste
materials, isolation, design of controls, and the selection and
training of astronauts. A divided bibliography and an index are
appended. The text uses comparatively few technical or scientific
terms; the illustrative diagrams are clear, although the captions
are not always adequate.

566   **Henry,** Marguerite. *Mustang, Wild Spirit of the West;* illus. by
Robert Lougheed. Rand McNally, 1966. 224p. Trade ed. $3.95;
Library ed. $3.97 net. (Collins, 1968. 224p. £1.25.)

6–9   This is the story of "Wild Horse Annie," a real person (Mrs.
Charles Johnston) and a most courageous and determined one.
The fact that the story is written in first person gives it both
conviction and urgency. Annie has already proved her inner
strength in her adjustment to the crippling effects of polio; when
she espouses the cause of the wild mustangs, she needs again
and again to call on that inner strength. First in Nevada, then
in Washington she fought and argued against the killing of the
wild horses she loved; in 1959 the federal legislation against
running down mustangs from a vehicle was passed. Although
the last pages of Annie's story strike a lyric note, the book is
the best this author has written for many years, engrossing as a

story of the preservation of wild animals and truly moving as a story of a dauntless woman.

567   **Hentoff,** Nat. *I'm Really Dragged but Nothing Gets Me Down.* Simon and Schuster, 1968. 127p. $3.95.

9–12   Jeremy Wolf is a high school senior. His father doesn't understand him and Jeremy doesn't understand his father; the only girl he likes isn't interested; above all, he is in conflict about the draft—he doesn't want to kill, and he doesn't have the courage to take action. Endlessly, painfully, Jeremy and his friends talk about their responsibilities and goals, and just as painfully Jeremy and his father argue about their differences. The vitality of Hentoff's style and the scope of his perception and understanding give the book an impact that comes from the importance of its concepts rather than the drama of its action.

568   **Herrmann,** Frank. *The Giant Alexander in America;* illus. by George Him. McGraw-Hill, 1968. 32p. $3.50. (Methuen, 1968. 32p. £0.90.)

K–2   After a wire from the President, "Need your help. Will you come?" the giant Alexander, always ready to help friend or stranger, sails for the United States. He learns that he is being asked to help with the program intended to land a man on the moon (by tests for physical reactions) and he manages, with a young English friend tucked into his breast pocket, to sightsee quite a bit. Alexander comes to the rescue when something goes wrong with the pickup of a rocket crew, saving the astronauts and becoming a hero. The oversize pages are used to advantage in scenes that show the giant towering over New York Harbor or gently moving cattle (three in each hand) when there is a landslide at the Grand Canyon. The style is light, the character engaging, the space flight theme amusingly set off (in both the story and the pictures) by the amicable relationship and dialogue between Alexander and some whales.

569   **Hess,** Lilo. *Sea Horses;* story and photographs by Lilo Hess. Scribner, 1966. 47p. Trade ed. $4.95; Library ed. $3.12 net.

3–6   A captivating book because of the many photographs of the small, engaging sea horse, a fish that has an external skeleton, a prehensile tail, and eyes that move independently. The author describes the habits and the reproductive process of the sea horse, the latter unusual because the eggs of the female are deposited in the male's pouch for gestation. The book closes with instructions for raising sea horses in a home aquarium. The photographs are intriguing, the text straightforward and crisp, the print large and clear.

570   **Hieatt,** Constance, ad. *The Joy of the Court;* illus. by Pauline
Baynes. T. Y. Crowell, 1971. 71p. $3.95.

4–6   A retelling of a portion of the Arthurian cycle, with distinguished
illustrations, in black and white, of the medieval setting. While
hunting a white stag, the young knight Erec rides off to avenge
the cruel treatment of a court maiden and returns with the
beautiful Enid, who had been a captive of the same Yder who
had mistreated the queen's attendant. Erec, who refused to leave
his bride to join the knights in a quest, was dubbed a coward;
in his wrath he then sought adventure and, in a series of dangerous
encounters, proved his courage. There is a sameness about the
episodes of the journey, but the book should appeal to lovers of
romantic adventure, and the style of the retelling is wonderfully
appropriate for the story.

571   **Hieatt,** Constance, ad. *The Knight of the Cart;* illus. by John
Gretzer. T. Y. Crowell, 1969. 85p. $3.95.

5–7   In a companion to *Sir Gawain and the Green Knight* and *The
Knight of the Lion,* the author (a medieval scholar and university
professor) confesses to adding her own interpretations to the
versions of Chrétien de Troyes and Malory, thus giving a fresh
and vivid cast to the familiar Arthurian legends. The king, already
troubled by the disappearance of many good men of Camelot,
is struck with dismay when a messenger comes to report that
the queen and her ladies have been taken captive by the evil
Sir Malagant and transported to the Land of Gorre. Sir Lancelot,
hot in pursuit, submits to the indignity of riding in a cart
(a disgrace usually meted out to criminals) to save his queen,
an episode that is only the first of his adventures. The writing
style is wonderfully fluent and appropriately romantic.

572   **Hieatt,** Constance, ed. *Sir Gawain and the Green Knight;* retold
by Constance Hieatt; illus. by Walter Lorraine. T. Y. Crowell,
1967. 41p. $3.50.

5–7   The centuries-old story of gallant Sir Gawain is nicely adapted
from the poetry of the unknown author. To spare King Arthur,
Sir Gawain offers in his stead to exchange blows with the green
giant who offers his head; he asks only that a year later he have
the chance to behead Sir Gawain. The giant knight proves to have
been enchanted by Morgan le Fay; and when Sir Gawain has
passed his tests and offered his life, he learns the truth and is
ashamed, since to spare his own life he has failed to keep one
part of the agreement. For love of Gawain, all Arthur's court wear
the green sash that is Gawain's badge of shame. Although this
retelling lacks the elegance of the Serraillier version, the simpler
language and the prose form are more suitable for the somewhat

younger reader, and the book is both competently written and usable for storytelling.

573   **Hieatt,** Constance, ad. *The Sword and the Grail;* illus. by David Palladini. T. Y. Crowell, 1972. 82p. $4.50.

5–7   Written with direct simplicity, the story of the raw youth who became a great part of the Arthurian legend is based on very early versions in which the Grail was a magic, rather than a religious, object. Raised in bucolic seclusion by his unhappy mother, a youth sees some knights and thinks them so beautiful he decides to become a knight; he rides to Arthur's court and announces this decision. An engaging character who is brash and literal, the youth who becomes the Red Knight is shaped and polished by his experiences and led by his destiny to save the King of the Grail after he learns that he himself is Percival, son of King Pellinore, who had grievously wounded the King of the Grail, or the "Fisher King." The anecdotes are filled with action and magic, romantic in essence but told in forth-right fashion; *The Sword and the Grail* is an excellent choice for reading aloud or as a source for storytelling.

574   **Higdon,** Hal. *The Electronic Olympics.* Holt, 1971. 105p. Trade ed. $3.50; Library ed. $3.27 net.

6–9   One of the publisher's "Pacesetter" books, a series intended for the older reluctant reader, this should capture that audience and sports fans as well. The characters have no depth, but in such a light-hearted tale it seems hardly necessary. The marvelous new computer that instantly judges contestants and gives results is the predominant factor in a blithe tale about a conceited track star and the pleasant young reporter who is delighted to see him lose the Olympic race to an affable African track star. A bit of chicanery, a bit of nonsense, a dollop of love interest, a soupçon of suspense.

575   **Hightower,** Florence C. *Fayerweather Forecast;* illus. by Joshua Tolford. Houghton, 1967. 219p. $3.25. (Macdonald, 1968. 144p. £0.80.)

5–8   The Fayerweathers are an entirely delightful family, each distinctively drawn and all a cohesive unit; they understand each other's idiosyncrasies, tolerating them nicely and occasionally using them to flagrant advantage. Father is a writer, and broke; they all go to live with his sister and somewhat backward brother in a small town and promptly become involved in community life. Bob Fayerweather, an alert and suspicious boy, is determined to find the solution to the strange disappearance of his aunt's fiance—and he does; the man had been murdered. Any suspicion of grimness is alleviated by the highly carbonated

Hightower style and the bland ploys of the family; for example, the youngest child is used quite deliberately by her Machiavellian mother (lovely and innocent looking) when a petition for a new school is being circulated. Bitsy, young and crafty, mendaciously puts on a wonderfully piteous monologue about the horrors of the decrepit school.

576

5–8

Hildick, E. W. *Louie's Lot.* White, 1968. 146p. Trade ed. $3.95; Library ed. $3.76 net. (Macmillan & Pan Bks., 1968. 160p. £0.17½.)

First published in Great Britain in 1965, an amusing story about a group of boys in an English village. All of them want to become part of Louie's lot, since Louie—the local milkman—is much admired. Honest, sharp, and uncompromising, Louie expects his helpers to be dependable, imaginative, and intelligent; he has set up a complicated battery of tests in which the boys are selected by a process of elimination. This is a situation story rather than a story with plot, but it lacks neither humor nor action. The writing has flair, the setting is intriguing, and the episodes of the trials are diverting.

577

5–7

Hildick, E. W. *Manhattan Is Missing;* illus. by Jan Palmer. Doubleday, 1969. 239p. $3.95.

"You'll be sure to look after Manhattan properly, won't you?" Oh yes, the Clarkes promised, they would look after the cat and take good care of the New York City apartment they were subleasing complete with a Siamese. When Manhattan disappeared and they received a ransom note, the Clarkes were really upset, and Peter enlisted the help of a new American friend to track down the culprit. The friend enlisted his friends, and the chase was on. The writing style is sprightly, the characters distinctive, and the dialogue has a low-keyed humor that is especially enjoyable in the amiable bickering of the family scenes.

578

6–9

Hildick, E. W. *Top Boy at Twisters Creek;* illus. by Oscar Liebman. White, 1969. 151p. Trade ed. $4.95; Library ed. $4.76 net.

Mr. Hildick is one of the most dependable producers of humorous fiction for young people; here he focuses on a popularity contest (tied to grocery purchases) in a small academic community in Ohio. Andy, fourteen, is determined that the prize will be won by one of his gang, and he uses all the statistical lore absorbed from his father to manipulate the voters' support. The book is a deft jibe at the politics of college faculty as well as an amusing story about some lively boys; it occasionally inclines toward stereotype of adult semi-comic characters, and there is little expansion beyond the contest theme, but the yeasty writing compensates.

579   **Hill,** Elizabeth Starr. *Evan's Corner;* illus. by Nancy Grossman.
            Holt, 1967. 42p. Trade ed. $3.95; Library ed. $3.59 net.

K–2   Eight people in a two-room apartment doesn't afford much
        privacy, so Evan's mother suggests that he might like to choose a
        corner of his own. Joy! Evan gets some orange crates, a turtle,
        and a plant, carefully dug up from a dusty playground. He
        enjoys the privacy, scorning the wistful advance of his younger
        brother; then he realizes that he is both lonely and unfriendly,
        so he offers to help small Adam beautify a corner for himself.
        The setting is Harlem, the family Negro, the atmosphere
        cheerful and affectionate.

580   **Hill,** Kay. *And Tomorrow the Stars;* The Story of John Cabot; illus.
            by Laszlo Kubinyi. Dodd, 1968. 363p. $5. (Dent, 1970. 363p.
            £1.60.)

7—   An excellent biography, giving vivid pictures of Venice at the
        zenith of her power and of the ferment of exploration in the
        fifteenth century as well as of the dream-driven mariner John
        Cabot. Born Giovanni Caboto in Genoa, the boy had been sent
        to Venice to live with a wealthy uncle; well-educated, he became
        a Venetian citizen. Always lured by the prospect of finding a
        quick route to the Spice Islands, always in competition with
        Columbus and Vespucci, Cabot's belief that his English-sponsored
        expedition had reached Asia was rudely shattered by his rivals.
        The book closes on a note of hope and vision, as Cabot alone
        realizes that two new continents have been discovered. Written
        with brio, convincingly fictionalized, and carefully researched, the
        book has pace, suspense, action, and historical value. A
        bibliography is appended.

581   **Hill,** Margaret. *Time to Quit Running.* Messner, 1970. 191p. Trade
            ed. $3.50; Library ed. $3.64 net.

6–9   Definitely not a formula high school romance. Val has just moved
        to town and hopes that she will fade into anonymity at school,
        because she doesn't want anyone to see her home or meet her
        family. Her father is shiftless and her mother a whining
        hypochondriac, both of them speak ungrammatically, and their
        squalid home is in the worst part of town. The book has a good
        balance of school and social life, and both of these affect and are
        affected by Val's home situation, but it is primarily her shame in,
        and later acceptance of, her milieu that give body to the story.
        Characterization and dialogue are good, and the plot develops
        with natural evolution: Val lies about her situation to evade
        discovery and is trapped by her lies; the awkwardness she creates
        leads to misunderstanding. She is ready to marry an older man,
        partly to get away, but circumstances force her to return home

and to accept her family, an acceptance made easier by the
clear evidence that her friends will not spurn her because of
them; thus she is able to drop the burden of deceit and the
pressure of constant dissimulation.

582   **Hinton,** S. E. *The Outsiders*. Viking, 1967. 188p. $3.95.

9—   The outsiders are the tough, lower class boys who have a running
feud with a middle class gang; Ponyboy, who tells the story, is an
outsider. Orphaned and living with two older brothers, Ponyboy
is witness to a murder by one of his pals; the two boys go to a
hideaway, decide to give themselves up, and stop to help rescue
some small children from a fire. Ponyboy's partner dies in the
hospital, and out of his grief and despair come some insight:
he knows that the advantages will always be with the insiders,
yet he appreciates the folly of perpetual hostility and realizes
that if he cannot have help, he can help himself. The story has a
powerful impact; the writing is honest and skilful, with excellent
dialogue and characterization.

583   **Hinton,** S. E. *That Was Then, This Is Now*. Viking, 1971. 159p.
Trade ed. $3.95; Library ed. $3.77 net.

8–10   Mark had lived with Bryon's family since he was nine (his
parents had shot each other) and the two boys were like brothers.
Now they are adolescent, skirmishing on the edge of delinquency.
Bryon, who tells the story, is in love with a girl whose younger
brother is a gentle, candid thirteen-year-old; when he and Cathy
find that the boy has taken drugs and is on a bad trip, Bryon
is deeply upset. Then he finds a cache of pills in Mark's room
and realizes that Mark is a pusher. Shall be betray his brother?
He does, and he knows that Mark will never again have
anything to do with him. Heartsick, he rejects Cathy, "worn
out with caring about people." The book has a bitter realism,
and far more shock value than a treatise on addiction; it is
distinguished by percipience in characterization, natural dialogue,
and a sensitivity toward the complexity of human relationships.

584   **Hirsch,** S. Carl. *On Course!* Navigating in Sea, Air, and Space;
illus. by William Steinel. Viking, 1967. 156p. Trade ed. $4.50;
Library ed. $4.31 net.

7–10   One of those writers who have the ability to discuss highly
complex scientific matters in terms comprehensible to the layman,
Mr. Hirsch has here done a splendid job on the history of
navigation. The words flow along with apparently effortless ease,
brightened by an occasional phrase of notable color; the material
is logically organized but the book has no rigidity of structure.
Moving from the earliest seamen and scientists of the

Mediterranean world to the great sea explorers, inventors, and astronomers, physicists and mathematicians, the text describes the intricate problems of astrogation in deep space flight. Theories and discoveries of major figures in navigational history are introduced unobtrusively, and the principles that underlie the laws, the techniques, and the operation of machines are explained with crisp competence. A list of suggestions for further reading and an index are appended.

585   **Hirsch,** S. Carl. *Printing from a Stone;* The Story of Lithography. Viking, 1967. 111p. illus. Trade ed. $3.75; Library ed. $3.56 net.

7—   A most interesting book that describes the history of lithography, giving first the background of earlier methods of duplicating print and—after describing Senefelder's discovery in 1798— surveying all of the developments and the modern improvements. Mr. Hirsch gives particular attention to lithography in art and in book illustration, although most of his text is devoted to an examination of lithographic printing. The writing style is a bit dry, straightforward, and lucid; a brief reading list and an index are appended.

586   **Hitchcock,** Patricia. *The King Who Rides a Tiger and Other Folk Tales from Nepal;* with illus. by Lillian Sader. Parnassus, 1966. 133p. Trade ed. $3.95; Library ed. $3.87 net.

4–6   A dozen stories are included here, many with familiar basic plots or standard genre characters. The tales are colorful and varied; Mrs. Hitchcock, who collected them during a two-year stay in Nepal, retells them in a light and graceful style. The illustrations are attractive; a section of notes is appended.

587   **Hitte,** Kathryn. *Mexicali Soup;* written by Kathryn Hitte and William D. Hayes; illus. by Anne Rockwell. Parents' Magazine, 1970. 36p. Trade ed. $3.95; Library ed. $3.78 net.

K–3   Now that they had moved to the city, Mama looked forward to her shopping. The grocery stores had the best of everything— the potatoes, celery, peppers, tomatoes, garlic, and onions for the Mexicali soup that her family all said was the best soup in in the world. But—as she shops, Mama meets one after another of her children, and each has learned that in the city one doesn't eat this or that for some reason. They persuade her to leave out various ingredients. Mama comes to a slow boil, and teaches them a lesson. Gathered at the table, anticipating the best soup in the world, they are served "soup" with no onions, garlic, tomatoes, etc. A subtle lesson in over-adapting to the Joneses, and a good picture of a cheery Chicano family, not often placed in an urban setting.

588   **Hoban,** Russell C. *A Bargain for Frances;* illus. by Lillian Hoban. Harper, 1970. 63p. (I Can Read Books) Trade ed. $2.50; Library ed. $2.57 net. (World's Work, 1971. £0.80.)

1–3   "Be careful," Mother warns as Frances (the endearing small badger of *Bedtime for Frances*) goes off to play with her friend Thelma. Frances remembers the times that she somehow got the worst of it, and she agrees to be careful. But it happens again: Frances has been yearning for a new tea set and is duped into buying an old one from Thelma, who uses the money to buy the very set Frances had wanted. But Frances uses her head, and by the end of the story she has the new tea set as well as Thelma's agreement that it is better to be friends than to have to be careful. The writing is blithe and natural, the situation familiar, the development satisfying. The book can be used for reading aloud as well as for independent readers, and the humor of the story obviates any hint of preaching.

589   **Hoban,** Russell C. *Best Friends for Frances;* illus. by Lillian Hoban. Harper, 1969. 31p. Trade ed. $3.50; Library ed. $3.27 net.

K–2   A sequel to several popular picture books about the small badger who has gone, book by book, through the problems so familiar to small children. Having adjusted to the threat of a younger sister, Frances now has to cope with Gloria's wanting to play. Frances, above such things, turns to her friend Albert. Rebuffed by being refused a turn at bat ("This is a no-girls game") Frances plans an elaborate picnic ("Best friends outing— no boys") with a delighted Gloria, and Albert falls into the trap. He trades best-friendship for a good meal after Frances has played hard-to-get for a while. The Hobans see through all the camouflage of small children to the calculations beneath; what makes the stories endearing is that both the writing and illustration show very clearly that the camouflaging procedures evoke a fond delight in the Hobans. The style is light and ingenuous, capturing with fidelity the cadence of childlike speech.

590   **Hoban,** Russell C. *A Birthday for Frances;* pictures by Lillian Hoban. Harper, 1968. 31p. Trade ed. $3.50; Library ed. $3.27 net. (Faber, 1970. 32p. £0.75.)

K–2   Little sister Gloria is having a birthday party and Frances, a classic dethronement case, announces that she is NOT going to give Gloria a present. "That is all right," says Mother; so Frances cries because she is the only person not giving Gloria a present. The manner and extent of altruism that finally emerge are hardly magnificent, but Frances, thawing under gentle parental handling and festive bonhomie, gives Gloria a present. The illustrations are a charming accompaniment to a story that has humor, affection, and the appeal of a familiar situation.

591 **Hoban,** Russell C. *The Mole Family's Christmas;* illus. by Lillian Hoban. Parents' Magazine, 1969. 34p. Trade ed. $3.95; Library ed. $3.78 net.

K–2 Delver Mole didn't even know what Christmas was until one of the house mice told him about it, including the odd fact that a fat man in a red suit came down the chimney. "It's quite an odd thing, really, but he does it only once a year, and nobody seems to mind." Delver, who is too near-sighted to see the stars, wants a telescope and enlists his parents in Christmas preparations for the first time. The spirit even spreads to old Ephraim Owl, who, under the season's spell of amicability, kindly refrains from eating the Moles when they fall asleep out in the open. Verging on the sentimental, the story is saved from that by the brisk and often funny dialogue; the plot is original and the book is not too Christmas-oriented for year-round use.

592 **Hoban,** Russell C. *The Mouse and His Child;* pictures by Lillian Hoban. Harper, 1967. 182p. Trade ed. $4.95; Library ed. $4.11 net. (Faber, 1969. 200p. £1.05.)

4–6 Hands clasped together, the mouse and his child are never parted in all their search for love and security; they are a single unit, a wind-up tin toy. Broken and discarded, the toy is repaired by a tramp, and then the father and child have a series of adventures—many of them in an effort to escape the vengeance of Manny the Rat, vicious head of a gang of foraging rats. In the end, the mouse and his child achieve the serenity of being part of a household, a queerly assorted but compatible world of toys and animals. The book has some marvelously tender scenes, some that are humorous, some that are pointed and sophisticated. The unusual reader who sees the subtle comment on society will enjoy the book, but it will probably be limited in appeal to the general reader because of the long drawn chase, and because of the odd blend of a cast of characters best suited to the rather young child and a plot in which the nuances and the complications—as well as the vocabulary—demand an older reader.

593 **Hoban,** Tana. *Count and See;* written and photographed by Tana Hoban. Macmillan, 1972. 40p. $4.95.

2–5 yrs. A counting book that moves from 1 to 15, then—in tens—to 50, and then to 100. The left hand pages are black, with large numerals and the number-word in white, and with large white dots to corroborate the counting. The right hand pages are clear photographs in black and white, all objects that are easy to recognize: 4 children, 8 windows, 12 eggs in a carton, 15 cookies on a baking sheet, 40 peanuts, 100 peas in their pods, ten per pod. A familiar device, but very nicely done.

594   **Hoban,** Tana. *Look Again!* Macmillan, 1971. 36p. illus. $4.95. (H. Hamilton, 1971. £1.10.)

2–4
yrs.   A book of photographs that can be used to pique the curiosity of the young child, to discuss with him the objects shown or the whole process of observation. Blank pages with a square cut out of the center of each are spaced between a series of pictures, the exposed portion a challenge to the eye. For example, a series of parallel curves proves to be part of a shell; a pattern that looks like an ink-blot is the underside of a turtle. A provocative book, and a handsome one.

595   **Hoban,** Tana. *Push-Pull Empty-Full.* Macmillan, 1972. 30p. illus. $4.95.

2–4
yrs.   Clear and uncluttered, black and white photographs show pictures that illustrate opposites; the terms are used on facing pages, sometimes shown by separate pictures, sometimes by two parts of the same picture. Two boys rush "up" a flight of stairs, and they rush "down"; elephants are shown for "thick," and facing them are stilt-legged birds for "thin"; a hand holds a brick, another a feather, "heavy" and "light". Very simple, perfectly clear, and most attractive, this is a book that may well stimulate small children to think about other terms of comparison.

596   **Hoban,** Tana. *Shapes and Things.* Macmillan, 1970. 29p. illus. $4.95.

2–5
yrs.   Silhouette pictures, white on black pages, show clearly the shapes of familiar household objects, plus a few less familiar shapes such as a fish skeleton. On some pages the small child can see, large and page-filling, an outline of a telephone or a pail and shovel; on other pages the grouping of objects (materials for desk use, sewing equipment, or kitchen utensils) may inculcate principles of classification. The book, which has no text, is handsome as well as useful for encouraging observation.

597   **Hodges,** Cyril Walter. *Magna Carta;* written and illus. by C. Walter Hodges. Coward-McCann, 1966. 32p. $4.29. Oxf. U.P., 1966. 32p. £0.75.)

5–9   A companion volume that is a chronological sequel to *The Norman Conquest*, reviewed below. After a description of the hierarchy of power in Norman England, the author traces briefly the state of affairs during the reigns of Stephen, Matilda, Henry, Richard, and then John—whose mercenary oppression led to a revolt of the barons and to the signing of the Magna Carta at Runnymede. The illustrations are superb in their conveyance of action, as well as in the use of color and space.

598   **Hodges,** Cyril Walter. *The Marsh King;* written and illus. by C. Walter Hodges. Coward-McCann, 1967. 253p. $4.95. (Penguin, 1970. 240p. £0.25.)

7–10   A sequel to *The Namesake,* this historical novel continues the story of King Alfred's struggle against the Danish invaders of England. Having spared the Danish King Guthorm, Alfred is reproached by his advisers when Guthorm seeks revenge. "Surely it is a better thing to be merciful than to be cruel in cold blood," the king answers, and prepares for the long siege that will rise out of his encampment in the Somerset Marshes. He has been saved by a hasty retreat from an ambush, a journey into which the author incorporates the familiar anecdote of the burned cakes. This is a story full of action, of fascinating historical detail, and of dramatic characterization; it is written with sweep and vigor and is handsomely illustrated.

599   **Hodges,** Cyril Walter. *The Norman Conquest;* written and illus. by C. Walter Hodges. Coward-McCann, 1966. 32p. $4.29. (Oxf. U.P., 1966. 32p. £0.75.)

5–9   A stunningly illustrated book that describes the events of the Norman Conquest, first giving some general background and an account of the state of affairs immediately preceding William's victory. The text is crisply informational; the pictures are unusual in being both beautiful and highly informative.

600   **Hodges,** Cyril Walter. *The Overland Launch;* written and illus. by C. Walter Hodges. Coward-McCann, 1970. 119p. $3.95. (G. Bell, 1969. 192p. £1.00.)

7–10   Based on an actual event, with invented dialogue, a few fictional characters, and—as the author explains in a preface—only slight changes in the names of the characters who were the heroic men of the overland launch. On the night of a historic storm in 1899, the lifeboat crew of an English village was called to rescue a ship—but the storm made it impossible to launch the lifeboat. Thirteen miles away, over steep hills and narrow paths, there was another village with a calmer harbor. . . . This is the dramatic and vivid story of the long night's struggle over land, through lashing rain and wind, with every kind of ingenious makeshift, with courage and good humor, to get the boat into water and rescue the crew of the foundering three-master in the Bristol Channel. The illustrations are superb.

601   **Hodges,** Cyril Walter. *The Spanish Armada;* The Story of Britain;
written and illus. by C. Walter Hodges. Coward-McCann, 1968.
32p. $4.29. (Oxf. U.P., 1967. 32p. £0.80.)

5–7   It is unfortunate that the crowded print of this well-written
book makes it so difficult to read. The author is both informed
and objective; he writes with ease and clarity and with an
occasional note of dry humor. The illustrations are quite lovely,
full of color and movement, and as fascinating in mass effects as
they are in the small nautical details. This is one of the few
books written for young people on the topic that deals effectively
with the Spanish viewpoint and with their problems of personnel
and naval operations.

602   **Hodges,** Margaret. *The Hatching of Joshua Cobb;* illus. by W. T.
Mars. Farrar, 1967. 135p. $3.25.

4–6   A good camp story for boys. Josh has never before been away
from his widowed mother, and he's apprehensive about camp.
Will they find out that he keeps one foot on the bottom while
pretending to swim? (They will.) The tough and unpleasant
counselor of Josh's cabin is fired when he disappears for long
periods to telephone his girl, and everything improves when the
new man takes over. Nothing remarkable happens, except that
the boys of Cabin 13 begin to enjoy camp life, and that Josh,
who has been a diffident participant, learns to swim, makes
friends, and writes a skit for the camp show. Pleasantly low-keyed
and smoothly written.

603   **Hodges,** Margaret. *The Making of Joshua Cobb;* illus. by W. T. Mars.
Farrar, 1971. 170p. $4.50.

4–6   A sequel to *The Hatching of Joshua Cobb* in which Joshua, only
child of a widowed mother, was away from home for the first
time and adjusted to camp life. Here Joshua has to adjust again,
this time to a preparatory school. The pattern of school life,
the relationships between teachers and pupils, the pranks and
ploys of the boys, all have a touch of Mr. Chips-milieu-American-
style, and the episodic structure is firmly based on good
characterization and on Joshua's growing acceptance of—and being
accepted by—the school community. This has good humor, in both
meanings of the term.

604   **Hoff,** Syd. *Irving and Me.* Harper, 1967. 226p. Trade ed. $3.95;
Library ed. $3.79 net.

5–8   Poor Artie, he wanted to live in Brooklyn forever, but a thirteen-
year-old has little choice. His parents wanted to move to Florida,
and that was how Artie met Irving. He had a few problems:
girls, bullies, the youth director of the Community Center, and
no dog; and his life was not eased by the determined

companionship of Irving, a boy with a real flair for doing the wrong thing. Once Artie resigned himself to the fact that his girl had given her heart to another, and decided to keep a stray dog, he was willing to admit that Florida wasn't so bad. The story has a zestful, zany, sometimes sophisticated humor; told by Artie, it is spontaneous and colloquial; and it is refreshingly casual about being Jewish and about being an only child. Because of the style and humor, the book should be enjoyed by many high school readers despite the fact that the protagonist is only thirteen.

605   **Hoffmann,** Felix. *A Boy Went Out to Gather Pears;* an old verse with new pictures by Felix Hoffmann. Harcourt, 1966. 30p. $2.75. (Oxf. U.P., 1966. 32p. £0.40.)

K–2   Twice as wide as it is high, this book is of a shape that has some nuisance value, but the size and shape of the pages are admirably suited to the artist's illustrations of an old rhyme. The drawings are small, but sturdy rather than delicate; they have the compartmentalized brightness of good poster art, and the figures march across the pages; gradually the empty space is filled with the cumulated characters of the rhyme.

606   **Hofmann,** Charles. *American Indians Sing;* drawings by Nicholas Amorosi. Day, 1967. 96p. $6.27.

5–8   Although the writing style is dry, the rich variety and vivid details of information about music, song-poems, dances, and ceremonial rites make this a fascinating book. The text incorporates many melodic notations and even some dance notations, and gives explanations of the significance of ceremonies and of the importance of song and dance in the Indian tribal cultures. One chapter describes instruments; reading lists, a list of recordings, and a record are included.

607   **Hofsinde,** Robert. *Indian Arts;* written and illus. by Robert Hofsinde. Morrow, 1971. 95p. Trade ed. $3.75; Library ed. $3.56 net.

4–7   One of the most interesting, and probably the most decorative, of Hofsinde's many books on aspects of North American Indian cultures. The first chapter describes some of the earliest rock paintings and petroglyphs, the last one discusses Indian arts today, and the major portion of the book is divided by the kinds of materials used in arts and crafts. The chapter on wood and stone, for example, describes the utensils and masks carved from wood by the Iroquois, Cherokee masks, the totems, masks, and personal and ceremonial objects carved by the Northwest Coast Indians, the hats of the Haida and Chilkat, the kachina dolls of tribes in the Southwest, and the pipestems that were made, with great variation, by widely scattered tribes. In some instances, the step-by-step method of making objects is described. The book is intriguing both for its information about Indian culture and for the facts about art forms per se.

608   **Hofsinde,** Robert. *The Indian Medicine Man;* written and illus. by Robert Hofsinde. Morrow, 1966. 96p. Trade ed. $3.75; Library ed. $3.56 net.

4–7   Another concise and interesting book in the author's series of brief texts on single aspects of the lives of North American Indians. Here the first chapter discusses the role of the medicine man in Indian cultures, the last chapter describes the medicine man today, and the six intervening chapters examine the medicine man in each of six tribes: Sioux, Iroquois, Apache, Navajo, Ojibwa, and the Totem People. The black and white drawings are excellent in giving details of costumes, buildings, and artifacts but are awkward in depicting people.

609   **Hofsinde,** Robert. *Indian Music Makers;* written and illus. by Robert Hofsinde. Morrow, 1967. 96p. $3.75.

4–7   A great deal of detailed information about Indian instruments is provided in straightforward, dry style. Illustrations amplify the descriptions of how drums, tom-toms, rattles, and flutes were made, several variations of each kind being discussed. The last two chapters are devoted to Indian songs, past and present; some musical notation is included, but most of the text describes the ceremonial uses of songs. A brief index is appended.

610   **Hofsinde,** Robert. *Indians on the Move;* written and illus. by Robert Hofsinde. Morrow, 1970. 95p. Trade ed. $3.50; Library ed. $3.36 net.

4–6   After a general discussion about Indian migration, planned or forced, and ordinary travel patterns, the author discusses techniques and equipment for different methods of moving about. He also describes some of the environmental and cultural factors that were operative. The illustrations are clear and detailed, and in some cases the descriptions of equipment are couched so that the reader can follow, step-by-step, and make the article. The final chapter discusses briefly Indian modes of travel today; an index is appended.

611   **Hogben,** Lancelot Thomas. *Beginnings and Blunders;* Or Before Science Began. Norton/Grosset, 1971. 110p. illus. Trade ed. $4.95; Library ed. $4.99 net. (Heinemann, 1970. 128p. £1.50.)

7–10   A good survey of the development of early civilization from the first tool-making activities of prehistoric man. The first of four volumes on science, history, and understanding, this is written in straightforward, quite staid, style but is well organized in a sequential and comprehensive text which unfortunately lacks an index. The author stresses man's ability to communicate, and the living patterns that changed as tools improved, animals were domesticated, and diversification led to trade and cultural exchange. The book ends with the building of the first cities.

612   **Hogrogian,** Nonny. *One Fine Day*. Macmillan, 1971. 27p. illus. $4.95.

K–3   A picture story book based on an Armenian folk tale is illustrated with bold, simple compositions in soft colors, the pictures echoing the humor of the story. Nicely told, the tale uses a familiar cumulative pattern: when a fox drinks all the milk from an old woman's pail, she cuts off his tail; he begs her to sew it on so that his friends won't laugh at him. She agrees—if he will return her milk. So the fox goes from one creature to another, each asking for a reciprocal favor, until a kind man takes pity, and gives him grain to take to the hen to get the egg to pay the peddler, etc. A charming picture book that is just right for reading aloud to small children, the scale of the pictures also appropriate for group use.

613   **Holland,** Isabelle. *Amanda's Choice*. Lippincott, 1970. 152p. $4.50.

7–9   Like the author's *Cecily*, this is a book with a young protagonist (Amanda is twelve) but sensitive and sophisticated enough to appeal to older readers. Amanda is an enfante terrible whose hostility, temper tantrums, and bitter obduracy have antagonized all those she meets. Her mother is dead, her father seldom home and all too clearly, it seems to Amanda, glad to be rid of her. She is at the family's summer home in the care of a bewildered governess when Manuel appears. A nineteen-year-old musical prodigy from a New York slum, he has been given the use of a guest cottage. Manuel is just as tough and just as hostile as Amanda, and she feels that he is the first person who can understand her. He does; and he will take no nonsense from her. The child is distraught when he leaves, having begun to feel a deep affection; she trails him to New York with only the slightest of clues as to his whereabouts. The ending is not as sharply etched as the rest of the book, but the whole is impressive. Memorable characterization, good style, and a note of poignancy in the harsh reality of the situation that is reminiscent of the tender loyalty of *Tiger Bay*.

614   **Holland,** Isabelle. *The Man without a Face*. Lippincott, 1972. 159p. Trade ed. $4.95; Paper ed. $1.95.

6–9   One side of Justin McLeod's face was scarred completely, and he had been dubbed *"The Man without a Face"* by his neighbors, whom he shunned. But fourteen-year-old Charles had heard that the man might tutor him, and Charles wanted desperately to be admitted to a private school in the fall, so he went to McLeod. The story is told by Charles, a boy who is fatherless, whose mother is going to remarry, who has been an academic failure, who has no close friend. Through the course of the summer and the tutoring program, the man and the boy draw closer; in a moment of crisis, Charles turns to his friend, and there is one night in which the two sleep together. The boy is stunned, the man compassionately explains that it could have happened with anyone, given the tension of the background situation. And that is the end of their relationship—McLeod disappears. Only later does Charles realize that he himself had made every overture, and (when he learns that McLeod is dead) how much the man had helped him, how he had given in friendship. The homosexual aspect is handled with dignity and is kept in perspective both in the relationships between Charles and McLeod and in the whole pattern of the story, which is written with a sensitive understanding of the complexity of the human personality and its needs.

615   **Holland,** Ruth. *Mill Child;* The Story of Child Labor in America. Crowell-Collier, 1970. 138p. illus. $4.50.

6–10   In the mills and mines and sweatshops of America, the children of the poor—particularly those of immigrant families—worked long hours for little pay under the most deplorable conditions. The facts were glossed over, hidden, or minimized by those who profited from cheap child labor, but some of the journalists and social reformers persisted, finally achieving legislation that ended the shocking status of the child worker. Background information about cottage industry and the industrial revolution makes the evolution of this evil understandable; the text concludes with a discussion of the still-deplorable plight of the children of migrant workers. No sources are given, but the evidence of research is clear; photographs are informative; the writing style is direct and serious; an index is appended.

616   **Holman,** Felice. *At the Top of My Voice;* And Other Poems; illus. by Edward Gorey. Norton, 1970. 55p. Trade ed. $3.75; Library ed. $3.54 net.

3–5   Edward Gorey's beak-faced people have a Victorian elegance that is often seasoned with a touch of the grotesque or humorous, and they contrast effectively and harmoniously with the more placid style and more significant content of the writing. Most of the poems in this sturdy collection are short and direct, some funny but the majority a flash of childlike reaction to people, or natural beauty, or the vicissitudes and delights of being a child.

617   **Holman,** Felice. *The Cricket Winter;* illus. by Ralph Pinto.
Norton, 1967. 111p. Trade ed. $3.95; Library ed. $3.73 net.

4–6   A most charming fanciful story, the below-stairs world of the
cricket and his friends being skillfully touched at points by the
realistic life of the boy who lived upstairs. The boy was nine,
an articulate and inventive child whose parents failed to
appreciate his ideas, one of which was to build his own telegraph
key; thus began the communication between the boy and the
cricket, a dialogue of clicks that broadened into understandable
conversations, a dialogue in which the boy's intelligence solved
the tender-hearted cricket's ethical dilemma. The style is delightful,
the message about relationships subtle, the humor gentle; the
illustrations are in black and white, strong in execution yet
delicate in detail.

618   **Holman,** Felice. *Elisabeth and the Marsh Mystery;* illus. by Erik
Blegvad. Macmillan, 1966. 49p. $3.95.

2–4   A sequel to *Elisabeth, the Bird Watcher* and *Elisabeth, the Treasure
Hunter.* Again, a charming book that combines surprisingly an
assortment of delights. The illustrations are exactly right; the style
is ebullient and lightly humorous; the story has unity, good
relationships, and a smooth incorporation of scientific attitude
and a positive approach to conservation. Elisabeth and her father
become curious about the mysterious bird in a nearby marsh,
especially when Papa can't find any local bird to fit the description
in the bird-book. They quietly stalk the bird with a friend who
is on a museum staff and a friend of Elisabeth's whose zeal
exceeds his caution; Stewart, hoping to lure the strange bird,
gets trapped in the bird-trap. The trapped bird, a sandhill
crane, is rescued and shipped carefully back to his proper
habitat. Good science, good nature study, utterly satisfying story—
also nice to read aloud to younger children.

619   **Holman,** Felice. *The Future of Hooper Toote;* illus. by Gahan
Wilson. Scribner, 1972. 138p. $4.95.

4–7   Locked out of their new apartment in New York, Hooper's
parents were worried about their problem until they realized
that the solution was simple: their son Hooper could simply skim
up to the third floor window. Unfortunately, he was seen—
and that was how it became known that Hooper Toote was a
skimmer, a fact that had been taken for granted in their home
town, but caused quite a stir in the city. The devices that
were used to keep Hooper's feet on the ground, the disguises
he assumed to hide from reporters, and the scrapes he got
into are combined in a lively and very funny story. Hooper's
problem was solved when an ingenious inventor tested him

and realized what it was that caused Hooper's skimming, and
enabled Hooper Toote, age eleven, to walk for the first time.
The characters are engaging, the dialogue delightful, and the story
deftly combines realism and fantasy in plot that is filled with
action and palatable nonsense.

620   **Holman,** Felice. *Professor Diggins' Dragons;* illus. by Ib Ohlsson.
        Macmillan, 1966. 135p. Trade ed. $4.50; Library ed. $3.64 net.

5–6   An unusual story for the middle grades, unusual in setting and
        in its characters. Professor Diggins is an elderly biology teacher
        who is about to lose his position at the University because he
        has expressed a belief in dragons. During the course of a field
        trip-cum-vacation, he makes clear to his companions what he
        means by dragons; his companions are five children who have
        come with him in a converted bus for a stay at the beach.
        Each child is different; with each one Professor Diggins points
        out the way to conquer his own dragon: a fear, a bad habit,
        et cetera. This is so well done that it is charming rather than
        minatory; the pat ending would weaken the story were it not
        just ever so slightly, but ever so clearly, tongue in cheek.

621   **Holme,** Bryan. *Drawings to Live With.* Viking, 1966. 159p. illus.
        $4.50.

5–10   A pleasant ramble through the world of art, with occasional
        humorous comments and with a considerable amount of
        information about techniques; the writing is coy here and there,
        and some of the captions seem redundant (a picture of a cat
        notes, "Obviously after a very satisfactory meal—fat, proud,
        happy, and serene.") Mr. Holme explains the differences between
        representational, impressionistic, and abstract art; interspersed
        through the text are interesting comments about interpretation
        or facts about media. For the most part, however, the book
        consists of reproductions of works of art grouped about some theme
        (the universality of drawings of animals) or by medium ("Pen,
        Pencil, and Chalk") or by function: the chapter entitled "The
        Open Book" comments on illustrations.

622   **Honig,** Donald. *Johnny Lee.* McCall, 1971. 115p. $4.50.

5–9   A good baseball story that has a realistic level of success, is
        written convincingly in first person, and gives the reader more
        than the sequence of game descriptions that is the bulk of the
        story in much baseball fiction. Johnny Lee is black, and when
        he comes from Harlem to a small mountain town in Virginia
        to play minor league ball, he has to cope with prejudice in a
        form that is different from the kind he's known. He copes—
        with mixed success. There's some discrimination on the field
        and in the town, although Johnny finds friends on the ball

club and a measure of acceptance in the town when his ability as a player has been demonstrated. Honest, low-keyed, and competently written.

623   **Hopf,** Alice L. *Biography of an Octopus;* illus. by Mamoru Funai. Putnam, 1971. 63p. $3.49.

2–4   Lightly fictionalized, this is an excellent description of the octopus, giving information about its structure, the way eggs are laid and guarded (there is no mention of mating) and the ways in which an octopus feeds and protects itself from predators. The octopus here is given a name—Ollie—and his life is followed from birth to maturity, with one long episode in which he is caught, used for research purposes (his learning a conditioned response indicating that he has a brain capable of memory) and released by a scientist. Informative and smoothly written.

624   *Horizon* Magazine. *Beethoven;* by the editors of *Horizon* Magazine; narr. by David Jacobs; in consultation with Elliot Forbes. American Heritage, 1970. 152p. illus. Trade ed. $5.95; Library ed. $5.49 net.

7—   A vivacious text is almost over-illustrated, many of the pictures being of such scenes as the market square in Bonn or a theater in Vienna, of many contemporaries of Beethoven as well as of him and his homes. The book gives a broad historical background, pointing out the relationships between the composer and both the aristocratic and republican factions, owing his living and (in large part) his reputation to the former and dedicating his allegiance to the latter. The surly genius Ludwig van Beethoven is vividly evoked, and his place in music history made all the clearer because it is carefully analyzed; the integration of historical, musical, and personal material is remarkably smooth. A basic Beethoven record library, a bibliography, and an index are appended.

625   *Horizon* Magazine. *The Holy Land in the Time of Jesus;* by the editors of *Horizon* Magazine; narr. by Norman Kotker; in consultation with Frederick C. Grant. American Heritage, 1967. 153p. illus. (Horizon Caravel Books) Trade ed. $4.95; Library ed. $4.79 net.

7—   Beautifully and profusely illustrated, this is one of the most vividly written books in an excellent series. The story of Jesus and his followers, and of Rome's domination over the Jewish people, is told with discernment and vigor, giving a broad yet detailed picture of the political, religious, and historical intricacies of events. A list of suggestions for further reading and an index are appended.

626   *Horizon* Magazine. *Lorenzo De' Medici and the Renaissance;* by the Editors of *Horizon* Magazine; narr. by Charles L. Mee; in consultation with John Walker. American Heritage, 1969. 153p. illus. (Horizon Caravel Books) Trade ed. $5.95; Library ed. $5.19 net.

7—   A remarkably fresh and vivid treatment of a familiar figure and of one of the best-known periods in the history of the western world. The captions to illustrations, set in a wide margin bordering a single column of type, are in italics, but they are visually distracting enough to interrupt reading of the text. Both are interesting, the correlation between the two more important than in many of the books in the series because of the emphasis on Lorenzo's encouragement of art for art's sake and because of the attention devoted to Renaissance artists. The author's detailed examination of the power struggle between the major powers on the peninsula and within Florence gives the reader an excellent background for understanding the devious and bold machinations and achievements of the Medici. A bibliography and an index are appended.

627   *Horizon* Magazine. *The Search for King Arthur;* by the editors of *Horizon* Magazine; narr. by Christopher Hibbert; in consultation with Charles Thomas. American Heritage, 1969. 153p. illus. Trade ed. $5.95; Library ed. $5.49 net.

7—   Detailed and intricate, the story of the growth of the Arthurian legend is intriguing both as a literary and a historical puzzle. This is an exploration of the earliest references, direct and indirect, to the historical figure—a task made more difficult by some of the dubious evidence of early invention of added fiction that became the basis for the legend that has been, for centuries, the epitome of romance and chivalry. The authors describe the growth and change in the legend, and the investigations that have gone on for so many hundreds of years in a search for the truth about the once and future king. The book is profusely illustrated; unfortunately there are several instances where a turn of the page brings a double-spread illustration with a caption that may seem confusingly like a continuation of the text. The writing is competent, the material so organized that there is some overlapping; in toto, however, the text has not only historical and literary interest, but an element of detective-story appeal. A bibliography and an index are appended.

628   **Horne,** Richard Henry. *Memoirs of a London Doll;* with an introduction and notes by Margery Fisher; with four illustrations by Miss Margaret Gillies and additional decorations by Richard

Shirley Smith. Macmillan, 1968. 173p. $4.50. (Deutsch, 1967. 176p. £1.05.)

4–6   Although a lengthy and very interesting essay on the author and on children's literature in England in the 1840's is clearly directed to adults, as are the appended notes, the story of Maria Poppet is a direct doll-to-girl message. The period details and the old-fashioned turns of phrase have their own appeal, while the harrowing adventures of the London doll as she survives the vicissitudes of fortune and passes from one beloved girl to another provide drama in a sprightly, sometimes ingenuous, story. A new edition of an 1846 publication.

629   **Horvath,** Betty. *Be Nice to Josephine;* illus. by Pat Grant Porter. Watts, 1970. 43p. $3.95.

2–4   Charley was perfectly willing to be late to the Saturday baseball game to help his mother. But to spend the whole day with a *girl?* Yes, his mother said firmly, little Josephine and her mother were coming for the day, they were cousins, and blood was thicker than water. Disgruntled, Charley planned a day that a girl would hate, fishing. But Josephine volunteered as worm digger (actually, she preferred snakes) and knew about fishing, and was so pleasant that Charley found himself having a halcyon day. All cousins aren't as compatible as Josephine and Charley, but this puts in a good word for family obligation and for boy-girl relations while telling a pleasant and believable story in a simple, natural style.

630   **Hotton,** Nicholas. *The Evidence of Evolution.* American Heritage, 1968. 160p. illus. $4.95.

8—   Written by a distinguished paleontologist and curator of the United States National Museum, a solid discussion of evolution that begins with a review of theories of biological differentiation and classification that preceded the Darwinian revolution. The material included is not unusual: fossil evidence, adaptation, species survival, affective factors, etc. Although not as well-written or as comprehensive as *Evolution* (Ruth Moore and the staff of Life Magazine; Time, 1962) which has a better section on genetics, this is accurate and detailed; the appended material adds to the usefulness of the book. It includes an evolutionary timetable, a series of brief biographical sketches of major theorists, highlights from the *Voyage of the Beagle,* a bibliography, and an index.

631   **Houston,** James. *Akavak;* An Eskimo Journey; written and illus. by James Houston. Harcourt, 1968. 80p. $3.75.

4–6   Stark and dramatic, Houston's black and white pictures reflect remarkably the elemental and violent quality of the setting, the frozen isolation of the Far North. Young Akavak sets out on a dangerous journey; alone with his grandfather, he crosses the treacherous high mountains that are on the way to his great-uncle's home, for grandfather has a great yearning to see one of his own generation before he dies. Their dogs, sled, and food lost, the old man and the boy seem destined for death; they are able to reach their goal because of the acumen of the old man and the determination of the young one, and the courage of both. The style has rugged simplicity and a cadence that are eminently suitable for the setting and theme.

632   **Houston,** James. *Eagle Mask;* A West Coast Indian Tale; written and illus. by James Houston. Harcourt, 1966. 63p. Trade ed. $3.25; Library ed. $3.30 net.

5–7   Illustrated with bold drawings in black and white, this story of the Northwest Indians is starkly simple, quietly forceful in picturing the tribal patterns of living. A young prince of the Eagle Clan hunts and fishes with his companion, goes salmon fishing with the men of the tribe, and goes on a whale hunt; Skemshan comes of age and assumes adult responsibilities when he is honored by a five-day potlatch.

633   **Houston,** James. *Ghost Paddle;* A Northwest Coast Indian Tale; written and illus. by James Houston. Harcourt, 1972. 63p. $4.25.

4–6   Houston's writing, like his illustrations, has a stark and dramatic simplicity that is eminently right for the dignity of the Indian peoples he describes. The protagonist who wields the ghost paddle is Hooits, an adolescent prince who has never known peace in his lifetime, and yearns for it. He is delighted when his father decides to take a small band of young people to the mainland, to prove to the Inland River people that they come as peacemakers and that the hostility between them had been craftily engendered by a third tribe. The story is so deftly imbued with the spirit and the cultural details of Hooits's people that the incorporation seems effortless, and the theme has a pertinence for today.

634   **Houston,** James. *Tikta'liktak.* Written and illus. by James Houston. Harcourt, 1965. 63p. Trade ed. $3.25; Library ed. $3.30 net.

4–6   An Eskimo legend is told as straight fiction in a book that has all the appeal of the Crusoe situation plus the embellishment of the exotic setting. The illustrations, strong and stark in black and white, enhance the mood of solitude and isolation. A young Eskimo, Tikta'liktak is out hunting when he is caught on a moving ice floe; he is carried to a remote island where his battle for survival begins. He resourcefully acquires food, fuel, shelter, and—eventually—the improvised craft that will take him back to his home. Winner of the 1966 Canadian Library Association Award for the best children's book published in the English language in Canada.

635   **Houston,** James. *The White Archer;* An Eskimo Legend; written and illus. by James Houston. Harcourt, 1967. 95p. Trade ed. $3.50; Library ed. $3.54 net.

5–7   Kungo is a young Eskimo whose parents are killed and whose sister is taken captive by a band of Indians; determined to get revenge, the boy seeks out the remote island where there lives the one man who can teach him to become a great hunter. Old Ittok, still a great hunter himself, takes the boy as his son and trains him superbly. When Kungo is grown, he takes Ittok's great white bow and the new white clothes that Ittok's wife has made and goes forth to find the Indians. A white wraith against the snow, Kungo terrorizes the Indians; then he finds his sister, now married to an Indian, and he must choose between revenge and charity. The writing is in low key, helping convey the atmosphere of quiet and Kungo's own years of cold, patient planning; the illustrations are sometimes awkward, but they have vigor and a starkly dramatic quality.

636   **Houston,** James. *Wolf Run;* A Caribou Eskimo Tale; written and illus. by James Houston. Harcourt, 1971. 63p. Trade ed. $3.50; Library ed. $3.54 net.

4–6   Stark and primitive in mood, black and white drawings echo with fidelity the somber isolation of the far northern setting. The caribou herd had not come that year, and all the members of Punik's small community were dying of starvation. Thirteen, the only male in his family still capable of exertion, the boy sets out alone on a trek to find food. Maybe the fish cache of the next community could save his life? But it is empty, ravaged by starving animals. Driven to chewing pieces of his clothing, Punik is near death when two wolves appear. He expects attack, but they kill a caribou and trot off, waiting nearby for the boy to see that it is for him. Simple yet forceful, a dramatic and moving tale.

637   **Howard,** Vanessa. *A Screaming Whisper;* photographs by J. Pinderhughes. Holt, 1972. 59p. Trade ed. $4.95; Library ed. $4.59 net.

7—   Vanessa Howard's poems were first published in the anthology *Voice of the Children* compiled by June Jordan and Terri Bush, who had worked with Vanessa and other children in a creative writing workshop. Now seventeen, the author has proved to be one of the outstanding younger black poets. Her writing has a depth and insight that give substance to yearning, or anger, or compassion. Some of the selections have appeared in *Voice of the Children* or in Nancy Larrick's collection *I Heard a Scream in the Street* which is also a collection of poems written by young urbanites.

638   **Hsiao,** Ellen. *A Chinese Year;* written and illus. by Ellen Hsiao. Evans, 1970. 64p. $3.95.

4–6   Born in China, the author describes her year in a small town; she and her family had come for grandmother's funeral, and it had been decided that two children should be left there for a time to comfort grandfather. The text is simply written, its continuity broken by topical headings; despite the episodic structure, the book has an easy, conversational flow. The details of family rites and funeral observances, of New Year festivity and school games, of learning to use an abacus and sing her first English song are told by Ai-lan (Ellen) with unpretentious directness. The illustrations include decorative cut paper designs (a Chinese folk art) and drawings in black and white.

639   **Hudlow,** Jean. *Eric Plants a Garden;* story and photographs by Jean Hudlow. Whitman, 1971. 34p. Trade ed. $3.95; Library ed. $2.96 net.

2–4   Written with direct simplicity, with short sentences in goodsized, easily legible type and illustrated with photographs that make some of the steps in gardening very clear, a fine first book for the beginning gardener. Eric draws a plan for his garden, carefully measures the plot, buys seeds, weeds and cultivates his plot, waters it, and has the pleasure of eating the vegetables he has grown. The text includes some helpful hints and strikes a nice balance in presenting information in a lightly fictionalized framework.

640   **Huggins,** Edward, ad. *Blue and Green Wonders and Other Latvian Tales;* illus. by Owen Wood. Simon and Schuster, 1971. 128p. $5.95.

4–6   An unusual collection, published in English for the first time. Although the stories often reflect familiar themes (a set of impossible tasks, the good brother and the evil one, the child who is given three magical objects) they are rich and varied in detail, highly moral, only occasionally humorous, and told with the cadence of oral tradition. A few of the stories, like the title story and "The Golden Bird" seem long and complicated, but most of the tales are excellent for storytelling; several of the selections include some poetry. An afterword discusses the traditions of the Latvian folktale.

641   **Hughes,** Langston. *Don't You Turn Back;* Poems by Langston

Hughes; comp. by Lee Bennett Hopkins; woodcuts by Ann Grifalconi. Knopf, 1969. 79p. $3.95.

5— Handsomely illustrated with woodcuts in black, red, and white, a good collection of poems by Hughes, many of them written early in his career. The poems are grouped in four sections: "My People," "Prayers and Dreams," "Out to Sea," and "I Am a Negro." Direct and succinct, the poems have a sensitive and elemental simplicity that have made them particularly popular with the black children with whom Lee Hopkins has worked.

642 **Hughes,** Ted. *Poetry Is.* Doubleday, 1970. 101p. $3.95.

6— Based on a series of BBC talks, a discussion of poetry intended for young writers. The advice is sage, the style graceful, the tone of address dignified. Although the chapters are subject-oriented ("Writing about People," "Writing about Landscape") the elements of imagery and technique discussed in any section have wide application. The examples, poems by the author and other poets, are discriminatingly chosen and lucidly illustrative of the principles described. Particularly useful for writers, but interesting for readers of poetry as well.

643 **Humphrey,** Henry. *What Is It For?* Simon and Schuster, 1969. 48p. illus. $4.50.

3–4 Although the oversize pages and the iteration of the title question make the book seem more appropriate for very young children than for independent readers, the subjects and the way they are treated are eminently suited to primary grades readers. The large photographs show a series of objects (not necessarily but commonly urban) that may be familiar but unexplained sights: a ventilator, a manhole cover, a watchman's key station, et cetera. Interesting and unusual material is presented in a text with brisk, not-too-long descriptions. Can be read aloud to younger children.

644 **Hunt,** Irene. *Trail of Apple Blossoms;* illus. by Don Bolognese. Follett, 1968. 64p. Trade ed. $4.95; Library ed. $4.98 net. (Blackie, 1970. 64p. £1.00.)

5–7 A story about John Chapman that emphasizes his philosophy and his personality rather than the role that won him the nickname of Johnny Appleseed. The Bryant family, traveling by Conestoga wagon, are taken in and helped by Chapman, and they do not forget him. Some years later, Chapman finds the family in the Ohio valley and helps save the community in which they live from Indians. The writing has an almost lyric quality in parts of the book, a note echoed in the illustrations; the story moves slowly and has curiously little impact despite the drama of some events and the appealing figure of Chapman himself, a humanitarian in the rough world of the frontier.

645 **Hunt,** Irene. *Up a Road Slowly.* Follett, 1966. 192p. $4.95. (Penguin, 1971. £0.25.)

6–9 Julie Trelling describes her life from the time her mother dies until her high school graduation: ten years. Aunt Cordelia's ramrod soul seems hard to live with, but Julie finds, to her surprise, when her father remarries and wants his daughter at home again, that she has become used to Aunt Cordelia and loves her dearly. The problems of jealousy, first love, parental relations, and snobbishness are handled with ease and honesty; the more serious problems of alcoholism and of emotional disturbance in adult characters are handled with dignity. A moving and beautifully written book.

646 **Hunter,** Deirdre, ed. *We the Chinese; Voices from China;* ed. by Deirdre and Neal Hunter. Praeger, 1971. 292p. illus. $8.

8— Australian teachers who specialize in Chinese studies, the Hunters have assembled a range of material from the Chinese, from an ancient cautionary tale and selections from a favorite contemporary play to speeches, transcriptions of broadcasts, and official statement. The selections are imbued, of course, with the fervor of communist ideology and adoration of Mao; they also give a very vivid picture of China today (there is only a little historical material) and of the tenacious zeal of its citizens. Each selection is prefaced by editorial comment that gives background. A chronology of Chinese history, a list of suggestions for further reading, and an index are appended.

647 **Hunter,** Kristin. *The Soul Brothers and Sister Lou.* Scribner, 1968. 248p. Trade ed. $4.50; Library ed. $3.63 net. (Macdonald, 1971. 256p. £1.10.)

7–10 Lou was no fighter, but she trusted no white policeman, so she warned the gang that one was around trying to stir up trouble. Thus began the association that was to teach a fourteen-year-old girl where she really stood. The boys were tough, but Lou enjoyed singing with them; she knew that the gang carried weapons, but she also saw a weaponless boy shot by police. She knew her beloved older brother was respectable, yet white authorities seemed to give no recognition to this. Angry and frustrated, Lou found it hard to accept any overture from white people—but as she gained pride in her own cultural heritage, as she began truly to feel that black was beautiful, Lou realized that her position was that of moderation rather than militancy. The author has given a picture of one segment of black society with great fidelity and sympathetic percipience, the ending (sudden success as a vocal group) the only note of contrivance.

648   **Hunter,** Mollie. *The Ghosts of Glencoe.* Funk and Wagnalls, 1969. 191p. $4.50. (Evans Bros., 1966. 160p. £0.37½.)

6–9   First published in England in 1966, a story of the Massacre of Glencoe in the seventeenth century, based on historical events and illustrated by maps and by reproductions of portraits of some of the participants. The fictional approach gives poignancy and strength to the facts, the story of young Ensign Stewart only one incident in the struggle between the English and the Scots, but an illuminating one. Loyalties were divided in the army, some of the Scottish-born officers sympathetic to the rebel clans and others vindictively vengeful. Ensign Stewart, torn, finally chooses to warn the rebels when an attack is planned. The story has pace and momentum, the use of first person giving both a period flavor and an authenticity.

649   **Hunter,** Mollie. *The Haunted Mountain;* illus. by Laszlo Kubinyi. Harper, 1972. 126p. Trade ed. $3.95; Library ed. $4.11 net.

5–7   A consummate storyteller, Mollie Hunter has used the stuff of Scottish legendry in an exciting tale of man's conquest of supernatural creatures. Deft in structure and taut with suspense, *The Haunted Mountain* is the story of brave MacAllister's defiance of the magical creatures of the mountain, of his long years of captivity, and of his rescue by a doughty son and an old dog. The dog, indeed, gives its life to save MacAllister in his final confrontation with the blind ghost, the huge grey stone man who haunts the mountain and guards its treasure.

650   **Hunter,** Mollie. *A Pistol in Greenyards.* Funk and Wagnalls, 1968. 191p. $3.95. (Evans Bros., 1965. 191p. £0.37½.)

6–9   A story of the Scottish Highlands in 1854 is told by fifteen-year-old Connal; writing his account on the ship that is sailing to America, Connal describes the brutal evictions of small farms and the resistance of the tenant-farmers. He himself is wanted by the authorities for his part in the resistance and as the ship is ready to sail he escapes capture for a last time. The story has pace, suspense, and danger to add spice to the historical interest.

651   **Hunter,** Mollie. *A Sound of Chariots.* Harper, 1972. 242p. Trade ed. $4.95; Library ed. $4.79 net.

7–10   Set in Scotland, the story of Bridie McShane is quite unlike the ghostly tales or adventure stories which Mollie Hunter writes with such skill. This is no less skilled, but it is a quiet book, thoughtful and mature, its deliberate pace and nuance likely to be most appreciated by the sensitive reader. Bridie was her father's favorite, and when word came from the hospital that he was dead, she was flayed with grief, unable to accept the loss, terribly and suddenly aware of the fragile quality of life. Although there are dramatic moments in the story, there is little action; the book ends with Bridie, away from home for the first time as a young adult (she is nine at the beginning of the story) accepting the fact that she will be a writer although she cannot afford college, that she can live to express all that she had learned from her father and all the fears that his death had aroused, and that she can use her emotions in creative ways rather than burrow in them.

652   **Hunter,** Mollie. *The 13th Member.* Harper, 1971. 214p. Trade ed. $4.50; Library ed. $4.11 net.

6–9   An excellent suspense story is set in Scotland in the sixteenth century, and is based on records of a plot to murder James I. Young Adam Lawrie follows the timid little kitchen maid, Gilly, one night when she steals away from the house, and becomes aware that she is attending a witches' coven. It becomes increasingly clear that the followers of the Devil are gullible people who are being used to further the murder plot, and the story ends in a dramatic confrontation at court. The characters are vivid, the pace swift, the setting convincing, the period details effortlessly incorporated in dialogue, costume, and historical background.

653   **Hunter,** Mollie. *Thomas and the Warlock;* illus. by Joseph Cellini. Funk and Wagnalls, 1967. 128p. $3.95. (Blackie, 1967. 108p. £0.80.)

6–8   A tale of witchcraft, a tall tale, and a very funny book. Deftly written, this is the story of a good-hearted rascal. Thomas is a blacksmith in a village in the Scottish Lowlands; his wife is a good woman and most unhappy about his poaching—but Janet is also a good cook, and she cannot resist the game he brings home. Thomas incurs the wrath of a warlock by poaching on his land, and the wicked wizard steals Janet, whereupon the dauntless smith organizes the very people who have tried to reform him (the minister, the sheriff, and the laird) and with their help not only rescues his wife, but drives all the witches out of the Lowlands.

654   **Hunter,** Mollie. *The Walking Stones;* illus. by Trina Schart Hyman. Harper, 1970. 143p. Trade ed. $3.95; Library ed. $3.79 net.

5–7   In a smooth blending of realism and fantasy, a story that reflects

Celtic folklore. In the Highland glen where Donald Campbell lived, a dam was to be built so that the residents would have electricity and those who lived there would be moved to the village, which stood on higher ground. The majestic old man, the Bodach, who was the Campbell's neighbor, wanted to stave off the flooding so that the towering stones that walked every hundred years could have their chance, and he passed on to the boy his magical powers. In a wonderfully graceful and convincing fanciful episode, Donald sends his double flickering through the glen and halts the flooding. The story has pace and suspense, and the writing has an authentic cadence that adds to the flavor of the Scottish setting.

655   **Huntsberry,** William Emery. *The Big Wheels.* Lothrop, 1967. 158p. Trade ed. $3.50; Library ed. $3.35 net.

8–10   If they planned it carefully enough, campaigned the right way, and exchanged favor for favor, they could be the big wheels of the senior class, six boys decided. One of the six tells the story, growing more uncomfortable as it progresses; Doc realizes that what had begun as just a small plan has grown into collusion, and he begins to suspect that some of his friends are not only calculating, but dishonest. Faced with his questions, the leaders admit they have rigged some of the elections and appointments; Doc and one other boy drop out of the gang, having learned that there is no such thing as partial involvement in deceit. The story is fast-paced, with good characterization and dialogue; its message is the more powerful because it emerges vividly out of Doc's own reactions and his disillusionment.

656   **Hurd,** Edith Thacher. *Johnny Lion's Bad Day;* illus. by Clement Hurd. Harper, 1970. 64p. (I Can Read Books) Trade ed. $2.50; Library ed. $2.57 net.

K–2   Intended as a book for independent reading, the story seems more appropriate for reading aloud, both because of the subject and because of the occasional difficult polysyllabic word. The illustrations have movement and humor but are repetitive, the story is gay and charming. Little Johnny Lion, in bed because of a cold, keeps urging his mother not to give him medicine, and mother's calm handling of this is exemplary. He has a series of bad dreams (attributed by mother to illness and by Johnny to the medicine) and then—finally—one in which he is triumphant. Happily he bounces into his parents' bedroom to have a cuddle, falls asleep, and has a dreamless night to end the bad day. A light touch, a familiar situation, and a balanced combination of real events and the dozing dreams of illness.

657   **Hurd,** Edith Thacher. *Johnny Lion's Rubber Boots;* illus. by Clement Hurd. Harper, 1972. 63p. (I Can Read Books). Trade ed. $2.50; Library ed. $2.92 net.

1–2   Light, amusing, and affectionate, another story about Johnny Lion (a cub who might almost be a small boy) and the small activities that make a child's life interesting. Like rain, staying out of— or rain, playing in. Johnny's efforts at amusing himself on a rainy day are described in a simple, moderately repetitive text that is intended for the beginning independent reader but can also be used for reading aloud to preschool children. Johnny's indoor cavortings have just about run dry when Father Lion appears with a pair of red rubber boots and our hero goes off to face the elements with great joy.

658   **Hurd,** Edith Thacher. *The White Horse;* illus. by Tony Chen. Harper, 1970. 27p. Trade ed. $3.50; Library ed. $3.27 net.

K–3   After a rather slow start, this gentle story crystallizes into an imaginative and wistful mood piece. As small Jimmie Lee describes himself, it becomes clear that he keeps to himself, dreaming alone but not a lonely child. On a visit to the zoo with his class, Jimmie Lee intently empathizes with the animals he sees, then he finds a white horse . . . and off they ride into the sky. The other children come . . . but the boy goes off, again alone, remembering the splendor of the wild ride through wind and sky. The illustrations complement the mood of the writing, and the simple directness of the style somehow encompasses the effective portrayal of an introspective child—again, echoed by the last picture: Jimmie Lee is walking away, and the reader sees the backs of five other children, standing silently as he goes off.

659   **Hurd,** Michael. *Young Person's Guide to Opera.* Roy, 1966. 119p. $3.25. (Routledge, 1963. 127p. £0.62½.)

8—   First published in Great Britain in 1963, an utterly delightful book; delightful in style, dreadful in its use of very small print, and incorporating a remarkable amount of information in a text so smoothly flowing and witty. Mr. Hurd discusses first the ingredients of opera: composer, performer, production, the house, the audience, and operatic conventions. The second part of the book is an outline (but not a superficial one) of operatic history; after reviewing four centuries of opera, the author concludes with a brief chapter on English opera. It begins, "The history of English opera is short and singularly depressing." An index is appended.

660   **Hutchins,** Pat, illus. *Changes, Changes.* Macmillan, 1971. 27p. $4.95. (Bodley Head, 1971. 32p. £1.00.)

2–5
yrs.

Another book for the very young child who delights in "reading" by himself, the lack of text amply compensated for by the bright, bold pictures and the imaginative use of blocks and two stiff little dolls. The clocks are used to build a house, the house catches fire (How? It just does.) and the copious use of water puts out the fire and floats the house away. It then becomes a boat, the boat is beached and the blocks used to make a truck, then a train, and at last—a house again.

661   **Hutchins,** Pat. *Clocks and More Clocks;* written and illus. by Pat Hutchins. Macmillan, 1970. 29p. $4.95. (Bodley Head, 1970. 32p. £0.90.)

4–6
yrs.

A quaint old gentleman, Mr. Higgins, in a neat little cutaway house, is shown in simple drawings with elaborate detail. To check his grandfather clock, he buys another; there is a discrepancy, so he buys a third and a fourth. Still they disagree. He calls in a specialist, who goes from clock to clock, watch in hand, and pronounces them all correct. Mr. Higgins promptly buys a watch . . . "And since he bought his watch all his clocks have been right," the story ends. Children who are ready— or just beginning—to tell time will enjoy the fact that Mr. Higgins never sees the very obvious answer. Simply told, nicely conceived.

662   **Hutchins,** Pat. *Rosie's Walk.* Macmillan, 1968. 27p. illus. $4.95. (Penguin, 1970. 32p. £0.20.)

3–6
yrs.

"Rosie the hen went for a walk across the yard, around the pond, over the haystack, past the mill, through the fence, under the beehives, and got back in time for dinner." That is the whole text of this very funny picture book, its big, bold, stylized illustrations just right for showing to a group of children so that they can enjoy the joke. The joke is that Rosie, with a high, waddling step and a blandly impervious air, does not notice the predatory fox who is trailing her and who suffers every possible disaster en route, from stepping on a rake to being pursued into the far distance by a swarm of bees.

663   **Hutchins,** Ross E. *Scaly Wings;* A Book about Moths and Their Caterpillars. Parents' Magazine, 1971. 64p. illus. $3.47.

2–4

Clear photographs, some magnified, are helpful in identification of moths and their caterpillars and in showing the differences between moths and butterflies. The author describes the stages of a moth's life cycle, then discusses some of the common and easily identifiable moths, describing them and giving their habitats. The final chapters discuss moths that are dangerous, those that help plants by pollination, some varieties that are destructive to plants or clothing, and some that are unusual, such as the

caterpillar in a seed pod that is known as the Mexican jumping
bean. Succinct, to-the-point, and authoritative. A relative index is
appended.

664   **Hutchins,** Ross E. *The Travels of Monarch X;* illus. by
Jerome P. Connolly. Rand McNally, 1966. 64p. Trade ed. $3.95;
Library ed. $3.79 net.

3–5   The description of a southward migration of a Monarch butterfly,
based on the recorded arrival in Mexico. The Monarch, tagged
near Toronto, Canada, was released by the youngster who found
it; many of the incidents on its flight are, the author explains,
imaginary but probable. Mr. Hutchins is an excellent observer,
but his writing is at its best when it is strictly factual. The
illustrations are very attractive, particularly some pages done in
silhouette.

665   **Hyde,** Margaret Oldroyd. *Mind Drugs.* McGraw-Hill, 1968. 150p.
$4.50.

7—   Nine lengthy articles give a broad and comprehensive picture
of the patterns of drug use and addiction, and discuss the
motivation of users and the effects upon them. Four of the
articles are written by the editor; the others are contributed by
medical experts whose professional records are included in an
appendix. The authors describe health hazards, and discuss the
addictive properties of alcohol, heroin, LSD, methamphetamine,
barbiturates, and marijuana, indicating that long-term research
is needed to estimate properly the permanent effects of the latter.
The tone is consistently objective, neither adjuring the reader
nor indulging in man-to-man-let's-lick-this-thing-together
heartiness. A glossary, reading list, and index are appended, as is a
list of places to get help in New York City.

666   **Ipcar,** Dahlov (Zorach), ad. *The Cat Came Back;* ad. and illus.
by Dahlov Ipcar. Knopf, 1971. 36p. $4.50.

K–3   A simple arrangement of an old folksong precedes the rollicking
text, which almost sings itself when read aloud. The illustrations
have vitality and humor, with the indestructible cat beaming
complacently as she emerges unscathed from every peril that
man and nature have put in her path.

667   **Irwin,** Keith Gordon. *The Romance of Physics;* illus. by Anthony
Ravielli. Scribner, 1966. 240p. Trade ed. $4.95; Library ed. $4.37
net.

7—   Impressive in every way, a history of physics that emphasizes the
work of major contributors to the science; the book concentrates on
major research before the nineteenth century, but a final section
discusses the work of Einstein, Rutherford, and Fermi. There is a

modicum of biographical material given; most of the text is devoted to basic research and experiments. The writing is well organized and clear, firmly supported by Ravielli's illustrations which are both lucid and handsome. A glossary, a chronology, a list of suggested readings, and an index are appended.

668   **Ishii,** Momoko, ad. *Issun Boshi, the Inchling;* An Old Tale of Japan; retold by Momoko Ishii; tr. by Yone Mizuta; illus. by Fuko Akino. Walker, 1967. 38p. $3.50.

K–2   Beautifully illustrated with vigorous and colorful paintings that capitalize on the magical size of the hero, this old Japanese folktale is told in direct, crisp style. The tiny, thumb-sized boy who had come so miraculously in answer to the prayers of an old, childless couple goes forth into the world to seek his fortune; his bravery is rewarded when he is granted one wish and becomes normal size, winning the hand of the princess who had already loved the inchling.

669   **Ish-Kishor,** Sulamith. *Our Eddie.* Pantheon Books, 1969. 183p. $4.50.

6–9   "The children of the poor and troubled," writes the author in her dedication, "rarely do come to full growth." Eddie is the older son in a large family of English Jews, the Raphels; they are poor, and they are poor primarily because Papa, headmaster of a Hebrew school, is more interested in serving the needy than in improving his own situation. The family follows Papa to the United States after he has a nervous breakdown; although the other Raphels adjust to the change, they find little change in Papa. Intransigent and tyrannical, Papa refuses to see that Eddie, with whom he has an increasingly abrasive relationship, is really fatally ill. Only when Eddie dies does Papa begin to show consideration for those nearest him. Although there are some awkward shifts of viewpoint (the story is written by a friend, a sister, and—again—the friend) the book has a strength and vigor that outweigh this minor flaw. The characterization is excellent, particularly that of Papa; any change in him is due to the pressure of his burdens, not to an atypical change of heart. A candid and moving story.

670   **Issa.** *A Few Flies and I;* Haiku by Issa; comp. by Jean Merrill and Ronni Solbert; from tr. by R. H. Blyth and Nobuyuki Yuasa; illus. by Ronni Solbert. Pantheon Books, 1969. 96p. $3.95.

3–6   One of the four great haiku poets of Japan, Issa was a man who revered life in all its forms; many of his poems have an ingenuous sweetness and simplicity that make them particularly appropriate for children. The editors have chosen such poems and have couched the introduction in direct language that indicates the book is for young readers (although all poetry is for all ages if it is good) unlike the collection assembled by Lewis, *Of This World,* which includes more sophisticated and serious poems. The illustrations, as befits the genre, are small, precise drawings; the pages have, therefore, a balance of brief poem and brief picture against plenty of space.

671   **Jablow,** Alta, tr. *Gassire's Lute;* A West African Epic; tr. and ad. by Alta Jablow; illus. by Leo and Diane Dillon. Dutton, 1971. 47p. $4.50.

5—   A fragment of a longer epic, the *Dausi,* this legend of the Soninke people of West Africa has been put in poetic form by the author, an anthropologist and folklorist. The sonorous style has dignity, the story drama. Gassire longs to rule the city-state of Wagadu, but a wise man tells him that he will never do so, that he shall carry a lute rather than a sword, and that his lute will cause the loss of Wagadu. In his vanity, Gassire fights until all but one of his sons is killed and the people are weary of war— then he is sent into the desert and his lute sounds for the first time. Gassire's rage melts, and he weeps, and Wagadu is lost.

672   **Jacker,** Corinne. *The Biological Revolution;* A Background Book on Making a New World. Parents' Magazine, 1971. 266p. Trade ed. $4.95; Library ed. $4.59 net.

8—   Early chapters in this exciting survey of biological frontiers supply the background for an understanding of the progress and research in the field. The author writes for the mature reader, her discussions going beyond the presentation of facts to include the legal and ethical complications and implications of such subjects as transplants and transduction, prolongation of human life, genetic control, reproduction by cloning, and the use of host mothers for embryonic transplants. The text includes objective discussions of chemical and biological warfare, of man-machine units, of intelligent life in space. Comprehensive, well researched, and smoothly written, the book is given added value by an extensive glossary, a relative index, and a selected bibliography, with books for readers who do not have an extensive scientific background marked by an asterisk.

673   **Jacker,** Corinne. *Window on the Unknown;* A History of the Microscope; illus. with drawings by Mary Linn and photographs. Scribner, 1966. 188p. Trade ed. $3.95; Library ed. $3.63 net.

8—   A serious but not a stolid book, describing the physical theories that led to the invention of the microscope as well as giving the history of its invention and improvement. Miss Jacker gives ample background for an understanding of the operation of a microscope, explaining the kinds of lenses used, the problems of optical aberration, and the development of methods of scientific investigation. She describes microscopic technology and the use of the instrument in specialized areas of study. Notes on sources, a glossary, a chronology, a list of suggested readings, and an index are appended.

674   **Jackson,** Jacqueline. *Chicken Ten Thousand;* illus. by Barbara Morrow. Little, 1968. 31p. $3.95.

K–2   A most engaging picture book that traces the life of a chicken in the mechanized world of big-business egg-packing. One of ten thousand chickens to move from hatcher to brooder, Little Ten Thousand had the frustrating experience of laying eggs that disappeared (dropping through the wire floor of the cage) onto a moving belt that carried them on to washing and packaging. Depleted, our heroine was destined for destruction—but a fallen crate enabled her to escape—and in a new environment of sunshine and flowers and delicious worms she began a new life that culminated in seeing her own chicks hatch. The combination of information about the egg business and a somehow touching— but not quite sentimental—story is achieved very smoothly and with just a touch of humor.

675   **Jackson,** Jacqueline. *The Orchestra Mice;* illus. by Robert Morrow. Reilly and Lee, 1970. 27p. $3.50.

K–3   Once upon a time there were a father and mother mouse who so doted on music that they lived with a symphony orchestra, unbeknownst to the musicians. Their twelve offspring were carefully trained as musicians, and it was this virtuosity that saved their lives, for one night the little mice were unfortunately trapped in some instruments just as a concert began, and the orchestra members (who were making strange musical noises) attacked. But the mouse parents, cool-headed, called for an impromptu performance of the Goldberg Variations, and the human beings were so enthralled that the mice were promptly taken on as permanent advisers and esteemed house-guests. The writing is in gay rhyme, which only occasionally falters metrically, and the pace is andantino; the illustrations are scribbly but not too busy, and they have some charming touches—such as the adult mice taking a bow, each mounted on a lens of an upturned pair of opera glasses. The musical references may add to the pleasure of the knowledgeable, but they are all comprehensible within the context.

676   **Jackson,** Jacqueline. *The Taste of Spruce Gum;* illus. by Lilian Obligado. Little, 1966. 212p. $4.50.

5–7   A story for girls, set in Vermont in 1903. Libby Fletcher had lived all her eleven years in Illinois, and she didn't want to live in a lumber camp. She didn't want her widowed mother to be marrying the man who had proposed by mail, Libby's uncle. Libby found the lumber mill community rough, tough, lonely and fascinating; she was slower to feel affection for Uncle Charles. The author describes vividly the brawling, bustling mountain camp and the beautiful countryside; the story line has pace, and the characterization is very good. Libby's changing feelings toward her new stepfather are gradual and believable.

677   **Jackson,** Robert B. *The Gasoline Buggy of the Duryea Brothers.* Walck, 1968. 67p. illus. $4.25.

5–9   Few inventions have so quickly affected the lives of so many as did the gasoline-powered automobile; the story should be interesting to anybody and quite irresistible to old car buffs. Stately, bearded gentlemen sit stolidly in the high-wheeled and literally horseless buggy, in old photographs of cars with forgotten names or names that are still selling: Benz, Renault, Daimler. The searing details of the first race in the United States are fascinating; the race was won by the Duryea brothers (Chicago to Waukegan and back; ten hours, twenty-three minutes) who, one year later, began the American automobile industry by building motorcars that were "Noiseless, Odorless, No Vibration, Starts Automatically from Seat . . ." Ralph Nader, where were you when we needed you?

678   **Jackson,** Robert B. *The Remarkable Ride of the Abernathy Boys.* Walck, 1967. 69p. illus. $4.25.

3–5   Illustrated with reproductions of fading photographs, the true story of a trip taken by two small brothers who, in 1910, rode from Oklahoma to New York on horseback; they were alone, and they were ten and six. Bud and Temple Abernathy's father had agreed to let the boys ride to New York City to join him in welcoming Teddy Roosevelt back from abroad. The boys did a great deal of sightseeing and were themselves an object of curious sight-seers in the East. Their father bought an automobile for the ride homeward; Bud and Temple also bought an automobile and drove back to Oklahoma, with their old Brush being followed along the roads by father's chauffeur-driven Maxwell. The writing style is informal but rather dry, the book's appeal being in the interest of the unusual facts themselves.

679   **Jacobs,** Joseph, ad. *Hudden and Dudden and Donald O'Neary;* illus. by Doris Burn. Coward-McCann, 1968. 40p. $3.29.

K–3   A Celtic folk tale, illustrated with vigorous, attractive black and white drawings. All that Donald O'Neary owned was a bony cow and a poor strip of land, but that didn't keep his wealthy and avaricious neighbors from envying him his wee bit of property. So they schemed and planned, killing the one cow so that Donald would lose heart and leave. Each time Hudden and Dudden grasp for gain, they are outwitted by Donald in a story that has humor, style, and the great satisfaction of seeing the greedy get their comeuppance.

680   **Jacobs,** Joseph. *Munachar and Manachar; An Irish Story;* illus. by Anne Rockwell. T. Y. Crowell, 1970. 28p. $4.50.

K–2   Droll illustrations with clean lines and light, clear colors add zest to a Celtic tale. "There once lived a Munachar and a Manachar a long time ago, and it is a long time since it was, and if they were alive now, they would not be alive then," the story begins. As many raspberries as Munachar picked, Manachar would eat. So off Munachar went to look for a rod to make a gad to hang his companion. The tale cumulates, as each person or animal asked for help asks a favor in return, so that finally the would-be hangman has to fill a sieve to get flour to give the threshers to get the straw to feed the cow to get the milk to give the cat, etc. etc. And when at last he comes back—Manachar has burst. Both the cumulation and the nonsense humor are appealing, and the style of the telling is flavorful. Good for storytelling or reading aloud.

681   **Jagendorf,** Moritz Adolf. *The Ghost of Peg-Leg Peter;* And Other Stories of Old New York; with illus. by Lino S. Lipinsky and songs of old New York selected by June Lazare. Vanguard, 1966. 125p. $3.50.

5–7   A delightful addition to the author's collections of American folklore, these tales are invariably well told and varied in type— ranging from ghost and hoax stories set in the earliest days of the city's history to tales about the first Macy's store or about Fiorello LaGuardia. One story, indeed, is about the Indians who lived in what is now Westchester. The style and humor are highly enjoyable either for silent reading or reading aloud; the book is a good source for storytelling, particularly because a section of notes is appended. The words and music for some songs about New York are included.

682   **Janson,** Horst Woldemar. *History of Art for Young People;* with Samuel Cauman. Abrams, 1972. 413p. illus. $15.

7—   A revision of the college text, *History of Art,* "for the general reader and readers of high-school age," according to the jacket copy, this uses some of the material—in revised form—of Janson's *The Story of Painting for Young People.* This volume does not go into as great detail in discussing individual painters; it includes sculpture and architecture, and it provides more informational captions for many of the pictures. Solid and authoritative, it gives a comprehensive picture of artists and styles in art from the time of the cavemen to today's pop art. Maps, a glossary of terms, synoptic tables, a list of books for further reading, and an extensive index are appended.

683   **Jansson,** Tove. *Comet in Moominland;* written and illus. by Tove Jansson; tr. by Elizabeth Portch. Walck, 1967. 192p. $4.50. (Penguin, 1970. £0.20.)

3–5   Love comes to Moomintroll as he rambles across the land in an effort to learn the awful truth about the ominous comet that seems to be on a collision course with the world. The comet veers off, and all are safe. The pending danger adds a bit of impetus, but the real appeal of the story, as in previous Moomintales, is in the motley collection of engaging and silly characters, among whom is the beguiling Snork Maiden who wins Moomintroll's heart.

684   **Jansson,** Tove. *The Exploits of Moominpappa;* Described by Himself; set down and illus. by Tove Jansson; tr. by Thomas Warburton. Walck, 1966. 160p. $4.50. (Benn, 1952. 160p. £0.42½.)

5–6   The Moomin world has, in its characters, the same sort of set of individualists that are in the Milne books; the plot is more complicated and the writing—especially the dialogue—far more sophisticated. Although older readers may enjoy subtler references that the younger ones miss, there is enough humor even at the simplest level to amuse any age. Indeed, the book can be used for reading aloud to children of eight and nine. Moominpappa, writing the Memoirs that are obviously going to make him famous, reads them aloud to Moomintroll, Snufkin, and Sniff; they are enthralled at hearing about the deeds of their three fathers and the ridiculous adventures of the oddly assorted crew of the "Oshun Oxtra." (The Muddler had been asked to paint the boat's name, "The Ocean Orchestra" in marine blue.)

685   **Jeffries,** Roderic. *Patrol Car.* Harper, 1967. 180p. Trade ed. $3.50; Library ed. $3.27 net. (Brockhampton P., 1967. 124p. £0.80.)

6–9   Harry Cole is a young English constable who becomes involved in an exciting chase while he is taking the final test that concludes an advanced driving course. Six men have escaped after staging a payroll robbery, and Harry becomes convinced that they have used an ambulance in getting away. His superiors are first doubtful, then amused, and finally irritated when he persists in following up this theory. By the time Harry proves his point and the criminals are captured, there have been a series of chases and dodges filled with action and suspense. The story has the same logical construction and authority of detail that distinguish the author's adult titles, written under the name of Jeffrey Ashford.

686   **Jenkins,** Alan C. *The Golden Band;* Holland's Fight against the
              Sea; illus. with photographs, maps and reproductions of old
              prints. Coward-McCann, 1968. 159p. $3.86. (Methuen, 1967. 169p.
              £ 1.05.)

6–10   An excellent survey of the long struggle of the Dutch to protect
              and extend their land. The material is well organized, the photo-
              graphs informative, and the book strikes a good balance between
              historical background and the details of engineering and
              reclamation projects. Although the writing style is sober and
              straightforward, there is a piquant undercurrent of drama in the
              building of the "golden band" of bulwarks against the ever-
              encroaching sea.

687   **Jenness,** Aylette. *Dwellers of the Tundra;* Life in an Alaskan
              Eskimo Village; with photographs by Jonathan Jenness.
              Crowell-Collier, 1970. 117p. $5.95.

6–10   Writing in an easy, straightforward and serious style, the
              author describes the impact of white culture on the residents,
              pointing out that there is dissatisfaction and a feeling of personal
              demotion among the young. The vivid and objective picture of
              living patterns is given immediacy and strength by a number of
              brief accounts of individual households as well as by the careful
              descriptions of food-hunting, recreation, tundra ecology, and the
              village school. The approach is candid and mature, the material
              fascinating.

688   **Jenness,** Aylette. *Gussuk Boy;* body illus. by the author. Follett,
              1967. 159p. Trade ed. $2.95; Library ed. $3.30 net.

4–6   A story based on the author's experience of living (with her
              anthropologist husband, son, and baby daughter) in an Alaskan
              village on the Bering coast. The protagonist here is the son, Aaron,
              who is fascinated by the pattern of small events that his
              Eskimo friends take for granted. Nicely fictionalized, the story
              incorporates unobtrusively details about the Eskimo culture; there
              is enough action to sustain interest, and there isn't the slightest
              hint of patronage. The Eskimos have a different way of life, but
              Aaron and his family are interested in them as individuals;
              indeed, when there are some small misunderstandings about
              behavior patterns, Aaron's father points out that it is they who are
              the strangers and it is therefore incumbent on them to adopt the
              indigenous mores.

689   **Jennings,** Gary. *The Shrinking Outdoors.* Lippincott, 1972. 191p.
              $5.50.

6–10   Of the many books about pollution that have appeared in
              recent years, this is one of the most specific in pointing out the
              causes, both primary and secondary; it is especially detailed in

indictment of automobiles, with their accompanying byproducts of car dumps, deaths, concrete wastelands, and air pollutants. Although the author is occasionally careless in his statements ("The study of the whole problem—of environmental decay, pollution, erosion, extinction, and depletion of natural resources—has been given the name of 'ecology.' ") the total effect of the book is stirring, a call for action perhaps the more effective because it is addressed specifically to the young reader, and in a tone of respect. A reading list and an index are appended.

690   **Johnson,** James Weldon. *Lift Every Voice and Sing:* Words and Music; by James Weldon Johnson and J. Rosamond Johnson; illus. by Mozelle Thompson. Hawthorn Books, 1970. 27p. $4.95.

4–6   Written in 1900 for school children to sing during a celebration of Lincoln's birthday, this is a song that has endured, a hymn of black hope. The illustrations are strong without harshness, vigorous in movement although simply composed. Although the song is for all ages, the format imposes limitations of appeal. The music, simply arranged for piano with chords for guitar, is included at the back of the book.

691   **Johnson,** Virginia Weisel. *The Cedars of Charlo;* illus. by Lydia Rosier. Morrow, 1969. 192p. $4.50.

6–9   Above Becky's happy home in Montana loomed the beauty of the cedars in the forest wilderness, and her distress was almost that of her neighbor, old Spike, when the logging industry threatened to move in. Becky's life had been gladdened by the pleasure of owning her first horse, and she had looked forward to riding Hobby in a show; when she didn't get a ribbon, she lost interest in the horse, to Spike's dismay. But it was Hobby she turned to in a crisis, riding into Charlo to get help when the old cowboy threatened to shoot surveyors. The dual themes of conservation and of Becky's maturing are deftly interwoven, the treatment is realistic, and the characterization good. In Becky's defeated father and the other men who work for the loggers, accepting despoliation because it provides a livelihood, the author shows an aspect of the conflict rarely touched in books for young people.

692   **Jones,** Adrienne. *Sail, Calypso!* illus. by Adolph LeMoult. Little, 1968. 210p. $4.95.

5–7   Poor as Clay's family was, they had made it possible for him to have a summer of rest and sunshine after a winter in which he had been critically ill; they had left the city to work in a migrant camp near the seashore, and Clay had endless days of solitude ahead. He was, therefore, ecstatic when he found a derelict sailboat—and proportionately dismayed when another boy showed up to claim her. Adamant at first, each boy reluctantly admitted, as the days went by, that it needed two people working together to salvage the *Calypso*. Through the long, slow summer days the boys became close friends, a development as inevitable as the ripening of fruit. The story is unusual in the evocation of summer and salt and solitude, the atmosphere a fitting setting for the sparse cast. Although there is no large action until the end of the book, the writing is deft enough to hold the reader firmly, as the boys work patiently toward their goal and as the tentative overtures of an interracial acquaintanceship change into the clear evidence of a solid friendship.

693   **Jones,** Hettie, comp. *The Trees Stand Shining;* Poetry of the North American Indians; illus. by Robert Andrew Parker. Dial, 1971. 26p. Trade ed. $4.95; Library ed. $4.58 net.

3–6   Full color paintings by a distinguished artist face each page of text, with one poem—or a few brief poems—printed in a dignified format with ample space to set each off. The poems are grouped by subject, with sources given, most of them reflecting the love and respect for natural things that are part of the great heritage of the Indian cultures of North America; they were originally songs, many of them brief fragments that seem almost chants or lamentations.

694   **Jones,** Weyman. *Edge of Two Worlds;* illus. by J. C. Kocsis. Dial, 1968. 143p. $3.95.

5–8   Stumbling alone in the scorching prairie heat, the sole survivor of a Comanche massacre, Calvin is terrified when he encounters Sequoyah, an old Cherokee. Half-white, the man who had invented the "talking leaf" (a written language for the Cherokee) wants Calvin for protection against hostile men from his white world. Calvin travels with Sequoyah, hoping he will be rescued, but he finds—when that day comes—that Sequoyah has become a trusted friend, and he goes back to say goodby. The book is beautifully written, economically constructed, and so far removed from sentimentality or triteness that it takes on a dimension of grandeur of spirit.

695   **Jordan,** June. *His Own Where.* T. Y. Crowell, 1971. 90p. $3.95.

7–9   A touching black love story, a tell-it-like-it-is book in black talk, a poem in prose—but this is probably for the special reader who can appreciate the flow of "She brokenhearted in the brokenland of Brooklyn small-scale brokenland." Buddy's love is for his father, dying in a hospital, and for Angela, whom he has met there. Angela's parents think she is wild, and when her father beats her she comes to Buddy for help. By court order she is sent to a shelter, and when she gets a weekend pass, Angela goes home with Buddy and they go, then, to an empty house near a cemetery and there they take refuge, there where "love is all the land they need." Buddy is sixteen; Angela, fourteen, and their love is a beautiful and poignant thing, a hope that can save them.

696   **Jordan,** June. *Who Look at Me.* T. Y. Crowell, 1969. 97p. illus. $5.95.

5—   Twenty-seven paintings of black people are accompanied by poems that vary in strength and passion but that speak, on the whole, with piercing clarity of the pathos, beauty, pride, and anger in Negro lives. The format is dignified, and notes on the artists (some of whose work is reproduced in full color) are appended. The author, young and black, has interpreted some of the paintings rather narrowly, so that the poems cannot quite stand alone, but these are in the minority, and the quality of the writing is consistently compelling.

697   **Jordan,** Mildred. *Proud to Be Amish;* illus. by W. T. Mars. Crown, 1968. 144p. $3.95.

5–6   "Ach, I feel so for old Mrs. Keffer," said Mom, "even if she's Lutheran and Gay." But Katie didn't feel sorry for Mrs. Keffer's grandchild Gloria, who had a red dress. Amish girls didn't have red dresses, nor were they supposed to listen to radios; Katie shared with her twin brother Jake the little radio that belonged to their older brother, and they prayed that Pop and Mom wouldn't find out. Katie, troubled by her worldly desires, is much relieved to discover that even Mom and Pop occasionally fail to resist the temptations of progress—and that even Grossdawdi has capitulated! A pleasant story of the Pennsylvania farming country, the flavor of Amish life and speech much stronger than it is in *The Little Fox* by Edith Brecht. A glossary is appended.

698   **Joslin,** Sesyle. *There Is a Bull on My Balcony;* Hay un Toro en Mi Balcon, and other useful phrases in Spanish and English for young ladies and gentlemen going abroad or staying at home; illus. by Katharina Barry. Harcourt, 1966. 58p. Trade ed. $2.95; Library ed. $2.97 net.

3–5   Another delightful bilingual phrasebook with phonetic spelling and irrepressible nonsense on every page. Here the reader is instructed in the appropriate Spanish conversation for a trip to Mexico; most of the phrases are actually ordinary ones that might be used on any trip. Occasionally there is a nonsensical sentence, such as the title sentence, but for the most part the humor is dependent on the contrast between the innocuous text and the daft picture. For example, "What's going on?" . . . "And this is when to say it." is illustrated by a picture of the young visitor (female) being hoisted up a long flight of sacrificial stairs by four Toltec-type gents. She looks blank but undismayed; the questioner looks puzzled but undaunted.

699   **Justus,** May. *A New Home for Billy;* illus. by Joan Balfour Payne. Hastings House, 1966. 56p. Trade ed. $3.25; Library ed. $3.03 net.

3–4   The story of a Negro family's move from a crowded tenement to a small house in the country, written in a bland style and sedate pace but pleasant because of the honest treatment and realistically happy ending. Billy's parents are disturbed when one of his friends is hit by a truck; they go house hunting, but are told by the first man they see that he won't rent or sell property to colored people. Billy has had white friends and is baffled by this; his father's explanation is a simple statement of fact. Prejudice exists. When the family moves to the new house, Billy finds that the neighborhood is already integrated; when father hurts his foot, a group of neighbors come to help work on the house and have an impromptu picnic.

700   **Kadesch,** Robert R. *Math Menagerie;* illus. with photographs; drawings by Mark A. Binn. Harper, 1970. 112p. Trade ed. $4.50; Library ed. $4.11 net.

7–10   Twenty-five projects, puzzles, and demonstrations are described, with not all questions answered: a provocative book for the math lover. The material is grouped under the headings of probability, binary numerals, unusual numbers, menagerie of shapes, mappings and transformations, soap-film mathematics, and mathematical machines. Some of the experiments referred to in the text are not experiments at all (as in the construction of a pantograph or a nothing-grinder) but the ideas are intriguing, the writing enthusiastic, and the diagrams and photographs helpful.

701   **Kahn,** Ely Jacques. *A Building Goes Up;* illus. by Cal Sacks. Simon and Schuster, 1969. 63p. $3.95.

5–9   An architect describes the step-by-step planning of an office building, with a clear explanation of the attendant complications of zoning laws, varieties of sub-soil, available utility lines, etc. There is less emphasis on the actual building of the structure than there is in Iger's *Building a Skyscraper* (Scott, 1967) and more on the roles of planners and consultants. Although the introduction talks down to the reader, the text does not. A glossary is appended.

702   **Kahn,** Joan. *Some Things Fierce and Fatal.* Harper, 1971. 241p. Trade ed. $4.95; Library ed. $4.79 net. (Bodley Head. 256p. £1.25.)

7—   Fourteen suspense stories, chosen with discrimination by the Harper & Row editor of adult mysteries, are included in an unusually good anthology for young readers. Some of the tales are factual, some fictional; the selections are varied in style, mood, and setting. Biographical notes on the contributors are appended.

703   **Kalnay,** Francis. *It Happened in Chichipica;* illus. by Charles Robinson. Harcourt, 1971. 127p. $4.95.

4–6   Chichipica is a little Mexican village where Chucho goes to school, works for the baker Don Rodolfo and lives with his uncle Don Pepe, both of whom he considers great men. And they are indeed great when Chucho's coveted chance at a scholarship for further schooling is almost lost when he is falsely accused of criminal activities and threatened with a stay at a reformatory. The book has a blithe tone and humor, the characters are delightful, and the warm, affectionate tone is reminiscent of engaging stories of Don Camillo.

704   **Kantrowitz,** Mildred. *I Wonder If Herbie's Home Yet;* illus. by Tony De Luna. Parents' Magazine, 1971. 34p. Trade ed. $3.95; Library ed. $3.47 net.

K–2   Good drawings in cartoon-strip style illustrate the woeful thoughts of a small boy whose friend has gone off to play with somebody else. Smokey is solacing himself with remembering his own loyalty and is planning revenge when he runs into Herbie's mother. "Home from the dentist so soon," she says. Smokey realizes in a flash that not only has he forgotten his appointment but that Herbie knew he was busy. And he can't wait to find out if Herbie's home yet.

705   **Kassil,** Lev. *Once in a Lifetime;* tr. from the Russian by Anne Terry White. Doubleday, 1970. 187p. $3.95.

6–9   The first-person story of a thirteen-year-old Russian girl's experience as a movie find. Sima is spotted for her resemblance to a portrait and asked to try out for the part of Oostya, a serf girl who masqueraded as a soldier to help in the defeat of Napoleon. She is enthralled by her new world, worships the director, and is a success—but the next role offered is in a mediocre movie, and Sima decides to take the advice of her mentor and go back to school. The story has a Moscow setting, with good balance of school and family life; the writing style is occasionally heavy but fairly smooth, and the characterization is excellent. The skillful interweaving of film-shooting sequences with the historical material concerned gives the book an added dimension of interest.

706   **Kästner,** Erich. *The Little Man;* tr. from the German by James Kirkup; pictures by Rick Schreiter. Knopf, 1966. 184p. $3.95. (Cape, 1966. 160p. £ 0.90.)

5–6   Translated from the German, a charming fanciful story, original in conception and written in a most diverting style. Maxie, who is two inches tall, has been left an orphan by the tiny parents who came from a Bohemian village of tiny people. A protégé of the famous conjuror, Professor Hokus von Pokus, Maxie becomes a famous circus and television star; among his ancillary activities, he rescues himself from his own kidnapping. Nicest of all: the style of writing, which is lively, intelligent, and entertaining.

707   **Kastner,** Jonathan. *Sleep; The Mysterious Third of Your Life*; by Jonathan and Marianna Kastner; illus. by Don Madden. Harcourt, 1968. 116p. $3.25.

6–9   A most interesting book about the research that has been done on sleeping patterns, dreaming, the lack of sleep, and the activation of sleep or wakefulness in the brain. The writing is lucid, the material well organized, and the subject should be of universal interest, particularly the discussions of experiments on restriction of dreaming time and its effects, and on those about experiments that test the control centers of the hypothalamus. The illustrations have a cartoon quality, but there is no levity in the text.

708   **Kaufman,** Mervyn D. *Fiorello La Guardia*; illus. by Gene Szafran. T. Y. Crowell, 1972. 33p. $3.75.

2–4   Although sedately written, this biography of La Guardia does give a warm, sympathetic picture of the lively and beloved former mayor of New York City. A fighter for the oppressed, a man of honesty and courage, La Guardia is a fascinating person, and his story is interesting also because of the picture it gives of the political scene in New York. The book gives balanced treatment to his personal life and his career, emphasizing his years in office but giving adequate attention to his childhood and youth.

709   **Kaula,** Edna Mason. *Leaders of the New Africa*; illus. by the author. World, 1966. 192p. Trade ed. $3.75; Library ed. $3.61 net. (World Pub. Co., 1966. 192p. £1.50.)

7—   Although the ferment in Africa makes it impossible for a book such as this to be completely up-to-date, it is a tremendously useful book, written with objectivity, intelligence, and the sort of vivid details that are the product of discriminating observation. The black and white drawings of African leaders are of excellent quality; they are indicated by asterisks in index entries, although this is not stated. The text is prefaced by a map and a list of countries in the order in which they will be mentioned; although the focus is on biographical sketches, there is a more than adequate amount of information about each country given as background. An appendix lists the heads of states at the time each country achieved independence, and a pronunciation key and index are included. This is an unusual combination: a book with ready reference use and a book that gives a broad and colorful picture of a continent in the process of complex change.

710   **Kavaler,** Lucy. *Dangerous Air;* illus. by Carl Smith. Day, 1967. 143p. $4.95.

7—   "Will we end pollution before it kills us?" That question precedes the title on the book's cover, and the author proceeds to expound convincingly and in detail how and why this looms as a possibility. Buildings are corroded, gases from cars and industrial plants foul the air, animal life is destroyed by sprays, plants become diseased, humans suffer increasingly from respiratory reactions. There are, Mrs. Kavaler points out, municipal and federal anti-pollution programs, but the support for such programs— although growing in strength—has not yet effected measures stern enough to clear the dangerous air. The book is serious, matter-of-fact, and alarmingly precise. An index is appended.

711   **Keats,** Ezra Jack. *Goggles!* Macmillan, 1969. 32p. illus. $4.50. (Bodley Head, 1970. 40p. £1.05.)

5–7
yrs.   Peter, the charming small child of *Snowy Day,* is now old enough to encounter the power structure that exists in every urban neighborhood. Having found a pair of rimless motorcycle goggles, Peter is showing them off to Archie when some big boys come along and demand them; Peter is knocked down and his dog runs off with the fallen goggles. By clever maneuvering, Peter gets rid of the bullies and has a session of quiet exultation with Archie. The illustrations are lovely: big, clear, colorful pictures with a city background, excellent for using with a group. The story is slight but realistic; a situation encountered by most small boys should evoke the pleasure of recognition and the added pleasure of vicarious triumph.

712   **Keats,** Ezra Jack. *Hi, Cat!* written and illus. by Ezra Jack Keats. Macmillan, 1970. 32p. $4.50. (Bodley Head, 1971. 36p. £1.05.)

K–2   Peter's back again, but Archie holds the stage, his Afro moderate, his glasses gleaming over a pert nose, and his sense of fun in firm control. Horsing around for the benefit of a peer audience, Archie is startled when a cat he has just greeted climbs inside a paper bag being used as a costume. Violent activity ends in a broken bag and the friendly cat being chased by Peter's dog; the day ends with Archie giving a progress report to his mother while the cat sits, hopefully, on the mat in front of the door. The pages are gay with color and movement, the children of the city neighborhood are engaging, and the story has a natural ease and humor that compensate for the slight story line.

713   **Keats,** Ezra Jack. *Peter's Chair*. Harper, 1967. 28p. illus. Trade ed.
$4.95; Library ed. $4.43 net. (Bodley Head, 1968. 32p. £0.80.)

3–6
yrs.
Here, again, is the family so endearingly shown in *Snowy Day*
and *Whistle for Willie;* Peter is now bigger and is no longer the
only child. What does his father mean, anyway, "Would you like to
paint sister's high chair?" It's Peter's high chair, and it is his
crib, too, being painted pink. Dispirited and jealous, Peter
rescues his little chair and other belongings—like his own baby
picture—and plans to run away (but not very far). When he finds
that he is too big to fit into the chair, Peter realizes that he has
superior status and is able to make the magnanimous gesture of
offering to paint the chair pink. The illustrations combine
painting and collage, and they are quite charming.

714   **Keeping,** Charles. *Alfie Finds "The Other Side of the World"* written
and illus. by Charles Keeping. Watts, 1968. 31p. $4.95. (Oxf.
U.P., 1968. 32p. £0.90.)

K–2
To a small Cockney boy, the varicolored bright lights of an
amusement park ("The Other Side of the World") loom through
the fog like an enchanted palace. Alfie has come across the Thames
by ferry, looking for a news vendor who is his friend; he finds
him, and the two go home—Alfie transported with delight by his
adventure. The plot is slight and the writing style adequate; the
book is lifted to beauty by the illustrations: with shimmering lights
and vigorous colors, the strongly patterned London street scenes
are made fairylike by the artist's interpretation.

715   **Keith,** Eros. *Rrra-ah;* written and illus. by Eros Keith. Bradbury
Press, 1969. 27p. $4.95.

K–3
Bad enough to go from a life of freedom, sunshine, and the indolent
joys of clover-sniffing to captivity and inedible food, but to be
called a frog when you are a toad . . . poor Rrra-ah. Caught by
some children and taken to their home, he was dumped into a
match box and given—ugh—turtle food. After several chase
scenes, the children's mother ordered the "frog" out. Sadly they
took Rrra-ah back to the watermeadow, and the story ends with a
blissful little toad listening to the lovely twilight chorus of toad
voices. The illustrations are soft in color, moving from a peaceful
beginning to the excitement and action of capture and escape
attempts, and back to the first theme. The style is light and
polished, the humor subtle.

716   **Keith,** Eros. *A Small Lot;* story and pictures by Eros Keith.
Bradbury Press, 1968. 26p. $4.50.

K–2
Bob lived in a house on one side of the small lot, Jay on the
other; the space between was their playground, big enough for
magic voyages or medieval castles. When they heard an adult

talking about using the space for a business venture, the boys put in a bench and flowers; the man thought it must be a park, and he walked off, leaving the small but precious lot to the children. The story has some weaknesses, but the setting is appealing and the illustrations lovely: reality in black and white, and imaginative scenes of play in color—until the page shows the park. Almost all of the action takes place in the little lot's one tree, with snarled kite strings or hand puppets emerging from the foliage.

717   **Kellogg,** Steven. *Can I Keep Him?* written and illus. by Steven Kellogg. Dial, 1971. 29p. Trade ed. $4.50; Library ed. $4.17 net.

4–6
yrs.   Amusing illustrations capture the light humor of a story that successfully blends realism and a child's fanciful imaginings. Arnold's mother is quite used to the fact that her wandering boy is going to return home with any stray animal that crosses his path. "I found this dog sitting all by himself. Can I keep him?" No, she explains, dogs are too noisy. Arnold tries a kitten. A fawn he just happened to see at the edge of the forest? A bear cub? Each time, mother explains why not; bears, for example, have a disagreeable odor. The illustrations show mother's wildest fears coming true: the fawn, grown, shredding the furniture with his antlers; the bear, enormous, lying amid garbage and bones; mother being chewed by the tiger that had been a charming cub, etc. Finally Arnold produces a boy. Well, mother says, he may stay for the afternoon but Arnold can't keep him. Last page, no words, Arnold's little friend shoving a large turtle at mother's face when she looks up from floor-scrubbing. A merry story, and one that has every possibility of raising dissension among proponents of feminine liberation because the illustrations show mother (with a ruffled apron, too) engaged in menial household tasks while the one picture of father shows him reading.

718   **Kempadoo,** Manghanita. *Letters of Thanks;* illus. by Helen Oxenbury. Simon and Schuster, 1969. 28p. $2.95. (Collins, 1969. 32p. £0.52½.)

5—   A sophisticated little spoof, delightfully illustrated with period-piece drawings, in the form of letters from a Lady Katherine Huntington to an admirer. The receipt of a partridge is welcomed with joy, as is the pear tree; Lady Katherine grows effusive as other gifts arrive, and she positively dotes on the lovely golden rings. However, as milking maids and laying geese and drumming drummers amass, the flirtatious tone of the letters drops to coolness and then to hostility. The handwriting becomes shaky. The final note, typewritten by Lady Katherine's secretary, states frigidly that Lady K. has had a nervous breakdown, and that all gifts are being returned, save for the partridge and rings. Great fun, nice Victorian pictures.

719   **Kerr,** Judith. *When Hitler Stole Pink Rabbit;* written and illus. by
Judith Kerr. Coward, 1972. 191p. $4.95. (Collins, 1971. 192p.
£1.25.)

4–7   The story of a Jewish German refugee family is based on the
author's life, and it has the illuminating verisimilitude of detail
and the acuteness of observation that come from personal
experience. Although the jacket states that "one day her father was
unaccountably, frighteningly missing," the book describes Anna's
father's departure as deliberate, for he realized what would happen
when Hitler came to power. Joined by his wife and children in
Switzerland, Anna's father decided to take his family to France.
Interesting both as a family story and a wartime story, the book
is particularly appealing for its reflection of a range of attitudes
and as a picture of the adaptability and courage of displaced
persons.

720   **Kerr,** M. E. *Dinky Hocker Shoots Smack.* Harper, 1972. 198p.
Trade ed. $4.95; Library ed. $4.79 net.

7–10   Dinky Hocker spent all her money on food, she looked it, and
who would want to date her? But Tucker, who was smitten
by Dinky's visiting cousin, had to get her a date or Natalia
wouldn't go to the dance with him. So he found P. John, the
plump school square—and there was instant rapport, with
Weight Watchers an added bond. The young romance is blighted
by Dinky's parents, who cannot take P. John's open espousal
of reactionary ideas, and who are too busy running home encounter
groups for drug addicts to see that their child is miserable.
The title phrase is one that Dinky paints on walls and sidewalks
in angry protest—she doesn't use drugs. This is both hilariously
funny, with sparkling dialogue, and sharply observant. The
characterization, the relationships (particularly those between
parents and children) and the writing style are excellent.

721   **Kessler,** Leonard P. *Kick, Pass, and Run.* Harper, 1966. 64p. illus.
(I Can Read Books) Trade ed. $1.95; Library ed. $2.19 net.

1–2   Well, it isn't exactly a sports classic, but it is an amusing book
about football and animals, even though the real and the fanciful
don't quite mesh. A group of animals wonder what kind of an
egg the big brown thing is; then a boy calls out "Here's
our football." The animals watch the game, immediately becoming
totally engaged fans; they then go off to try a game of their own.
Slight plot, but enjoyable dialogue for the beginning independent
reader.

722   **Kettelkamp,** Larry. *Dreams;* written and illus. by Larry Kettelkamp.
Morrow, 1968. 94p. Trade ed. $3.95; Library ed. $3.78 net.
(World's Work, 1969. 96p. £0.90.)

5–7   A good first book on the subject, giving some background information about theories of the ancients and some about recent scientific research on sleep patterns and dreams. In discussing both the psychological aspects of dreaming and the studies of physiological processes, the author goes into the subjects only enough to make them comprehensible, so that the amount of information given is not too heavy for the understanding of the intended audience.

723   **Kettelkamp,** Larry. *Sixth Sense;* written and illus. by Larry Kettelkamp. Morrow, 1970. 95p. Trade ed. $3.75; Library ed. $3.56 net.

5–9   A discussion of psychic phenomena and some of the supportive research, of which a small amount is anecdotal, most of the evidence being documented. Phenomena described are psychometry, precognition, telepathy, clairvoyance, retrocognition, astral projection, psychokinesis, and mediums. Psychic healing and psychic photography, sham and genuine "magic", and influence on plants are also discussed. All of these topics are treated seriously and briefly, and the final pages define levels of consciousness and suggest ways in which the reader can increase the possibility of having psychic experiences. Simply written, a good introduction to a fascinating topic.

724   **Kidder,** Harvey. *Illustrated Chess for Children;* written and illus. by Harvey Kidder. Doubleday, 1970. 127p. $4.95.

5–8   A really fine book for the beginning chess player; although there seems an undue stress on the relationship of each piece to its real-life equivalent (the pawns were pikemen who fought side by side, the knight's move can be remembered as the charge of a leaping horse, etc.) the concept gives the book an added dimension. Each piece and its moves are explained separately, and a blitzkrieg game is illustrated. There are illustrations of games-in-process, with questions and answers about possible moves and why some are preferred. The clear diagrams are very helpful, as is the proceeding from basic moves to more and more complicated problems.

725   **Kilian,** Crawford. *Wonders, Inc.;* illus. by John Larrecq. Parnassus, 1968. 37p. $4.50.

3–5   Handsome illustrations with lively and inventive details enhance a fantasy in which the humor consists of some diverting play with words. Christopher is the first person to tour the new firm of Wonders, Inc. and to learn the proud catalog of their products. In the Space Mill department outer space is popular, but the biggest demand is still closet space; they also make related products such as elbow-room, loopholes, and stop-gaps. In the Clockwork room where time is made, some of the special items are bedtime, pastime, split seconds and fleeting moments. Christopher becomes a distributor, selling the wares of Wonders, Inc. to local tradesmen and, every now and then, selling a dream to the Board of Education. Even for the younger readers who can't get the full measure of the jokes and references, this should be a refreshingly different and attractive book.

726   **King,** Mary Louise. *A History of Western Architecture;* illus. with photographs and diagrams. Walck, 1967. 224p. $8.50.

7–12   A survey of western architectural history that is both useful and interesting, explaining functional factors, social or artistic influences, and the limitations (or advantages) of material, climate, or technical proficiency. The photographs and diagrams are good, although some of the diagrams lack, in their labeling, terms used in the text. The author focuses on the new developments of each architectural period or school, usually pointing out some modern building that incorporates features typical of, for example, Gothic or classical Greek style. The chapter on modern architecture is not extensive, but is adequate. An excellent index distinguishes between textual and illustrative entries; sources for illustrations are cited, and a glossary is included.

727   **Kingman,** Lee. *The Peter Pan Bag.* Houghton, 1970. 219p. $3.95.

8–11   At seventeen, Wendy feels that she needs freedom; when her parents refuse permission for her to live in New York with a friend, she slips off secretly—only to find that her friend Miggle is gone. Nobody home but older brother Peter, who takes Wendy in tow on a trip to Boston, having convinced her that it is the Big Scene. And it is. The floating population of young people who live on Beacon Hill and meet on the Common are serious about establishing their independence, but Wendy finds many of them pathetic or irritating, a few impressive. Her experiences with communal living are told in a dramatic, effective, and convincing novel with distinctive (if not always sympathetic) characters vividly depicted.

728   **Kingman,** Lee. *The Year of the Raccoon.* Houghton, 1966. 246p. $4.25.

6–9   Joey is the middle child; an ordinary boy (and he knows it). Joey admires his two gifted brothers and adores the forceful and handsome father whose work keeps him too much away from home. Feeling inferior and rather inadequate because he has no goals ahead, Joey becomes easily attached to a baby raccoon; Bertie proves to be an increasingly destructive pet. In the year that Bertie is with him, there are many changes in Joey's life; his older brother—who has seemed so sure of his goal—almost has a breakdown, the raccoon, who had been let free, returns home to die, and Joey begins to understand his parents and himself.

729   **Kirk,** Ruth. *The Oldest Man in America;* An Adventure in Archaeology; photographs by Ruth and Louis Kirk. Harcourt, 1970. 96p. Trade ed. $4.75; Library ed. $4.83 net.

5–9   In a small cave in a wall of Palouse Canyon, in southeast Washington, a geologist and an archeologist, hunting for traces of prehistoric man, discovered a skull fragment. Judging by the artifacts and shells already found, the piece of bone was about 10,000 years old—the oldest known man on our continent. The details of the dig and of further finds are fascinating, particularly because the archeological volunteers who quickly rallied to search for other traces (which were, indeed, found) were fighting against time. The site was threatened by a projected reservoir for which a dam was being constructed. The combination of suspense in the outcome and of the detailed description of meticulous scientific work is dramatic, the matter-of-fact writing style leaving the stage clear for the exciting facts. An index is appended.

730   **Klein,** Aaron E. *Threads of Life;* Genetics from Aristotle to DNA. Natural History Press, 1970. 158p. illus. $3.95.

7—   An excellent account of the scientists whose work contributed to the body of knowledge that, accumulating over centuries, led to the discovery of DNA. Some of the earlier theorists were incorrect, yet their investigations led to further inquiry that advanced scientific knowledge about inherited characteristics and the mutability of species. Darwin's work and Mendel's research, to which the second and third chapters are devoted, are discussed in detail against the background of accepted fact and disputed theories; with the discovery of the microscope new avenues opened. The electron microscope contributed immeasurably to the genetic studies of contemporary scientists, and the identification of DNA as the hereditary substance was a catalyst for the structural breakthrough of Watson and Crick. Lucidly written, with material chronologically organized and handled with judicious balance between accomplished research and explanations of comparative or sequential theories. An index is appended.

731   **Klein,** H. Arthur. *Peter Bruegel the Elder;* Artist of Abundance; by H. Arthur Klein and Mina C. Klein. Macmillan, 1968. 188p. illus. $8.95.

8—   An impeccable book. The authors not only do justice to Bruegel's work in their analyses of his techniques and his interpretations, but they are lucid in their explanations of the artist's importance in art history and his expressions of the turbulent period reflected in his work. The social, political, and religious upheaval of the Low Countries and the mercantilism of Antwerp are reflected in the ebullient, satirical, and perceptive details so abundantly present in Bruegel's work, and the textual explanations are carefully matched by illustrative details. The authors are explicit in distinguishing between fact and conjecture about the artist's life. Reproductions of Bruegel's work are of excellent quality; the index is preceded by a list of works in the United States.

732   **Klein,** Mina C. *Käthe Kollwitz;* Life in Art; by Mina C. Klein and H. Arthur Klein. Holt, 1972. 182p. illus. $10.95.

8—   Lavishly illustrated, a biography that shows the power and diversity of the artist, with reproductions of sculpture, lithographs, woodcuts, posters, pen and ink drawings, charcoal . . . many on such universal themes as death or motherhood, most on the somber aspects of social injustice and war. Born in 1867, the young Käthe was brought up in a family strongly conscious of religious persecution and communal idealism; her devotion to her career was steady despite the additional hardship of gaining recognition because of her sex. (At that time, art dealers requested women artists to use only their initials, lest the picture be recognized as a woman's work.) The first woman to become a member of the Prussian Academy of the Arts, Kollwitz resigned in protest against the Hitler regime, and she was subsequently forbidden to exhibit her work. Visually stunning, her biography is written with a grave candor; while the events of her personal life are included, the emphasis is on her philosophy and the strong, dramatic art in which that philosophy is so eloquently articulate. A selected bibliography and an index are appended.

733   **Knight,** Damon, ed. *Toward Infinity;* 9 Science Fiction Tales. Simon and Schuster, 1968. 319p. $4.95. (Gollancz, 1970. 320p. £1.25.)

6—   A splendid collection of stories, with not a mediocrity in the lot. Asimov, Bradbury, Campbell, McCormack, MacLean, Schmitz, Shiras, Sturgeon, and van Vogt are the contributors to a book that has variety in subject and style, with most of the stories in patterns familiar to science fiction fans but chosen with a discriminating awareness of literary quality.

734   **Knight,** Damon, ed. *Worlds to Come;* Nine Science Fiction Adventures. Harper, 1967. 337p. Trade ed. $4.95; Library ed. $4.43 net. (Gollancz, 1969. 352p. £1.05.)

7—   The stories in this volume are by some of the best of writers of science fiction: Asimov, Blish, Bradbury, Budrys, Clarke, Fyfe, Heinlein, Kornbluth, and MacDonald. All of the selections have to do with man's exploration of outer space, and the editor points out (in a brief, provocative introduction) that these are the kinds of stories that may well have influenced the very sort of achievements they described. A list of other titles by the authors included and by the editor in science fiction is appended.

735   **Kohn,** Bernice. *The Beachcomber's Book;* illus. by Arabelle Wheatley. Viking, 1970. 96p. Trade ed. $3.75; Library ed. $3.56 net.

4–7   Profusely illustrated with precise drawings, useful for identification or for understanding directions given in the text, this is a how-to-do-it book with charm. The writing is light and competent, the projects varied, and the instructions clear. The book includes advice on shell collecting, a home aquarium, collecting and cooking food, drying flowers, and making objects out of sand, driftwood, pebbles, shells, animal skeletons, et cetera. There are several projects for which adult assistance is suggested, but most of them are fairly simple; some supplies are needed, but these tend to be easily obtainable and not expensive. An index and a short bibliography follow several pages of pictures of shells.

736   **Kohn,** Bernice. *Chipmunks;* illus. by John Hamberger. Prentice-Hall, 1970. 29p. $4.50.

3–4   Blest be the author who, having a limited amount of information to give, gives it without padding. Here, in a good introduction to the topic, the author describes the three kinds of chipmunks and discusses their habits and habitat, with brief mention of mating and reproduction. The illustrations are adequate, the text simple enough for independent readers or for reading aloud to younger children.

737   **Kohn,** Bernice. *The Organic Living Book* illus. by Betty Fraser. Viking, 1972. 91p. $4.50.

6–10   Delicate line drawings illustrate the text of a book that speaks with fervor on the topics of organic gardening, unadulterated foods, conservation and recycling of waste materials, and living closer to nature. The author gives advice on shopping, gardening, cooking (including recipes for some gourmet dishes and separate chapters on baking bread and making your own yogurt), and making compost. The final chapter lists ways of conserving materials and avoiding pollution. The tone is moderate, the style of writing direct, the author's viewpoint enthusiastic. A list of books recommended for futher reading and an index are appended.

738   **Kondo,** Herbert. *Adventures in Space and Time; The Story of Relativity;* illus. by George Solonevich. Holiday House, 1966. 93p. $3.95.

7–10   A good introduction to the subject, illustrated with black and white drawings of which only a few add to the value of the book. Mr. Kondo skims briefly through Einstein's life and some statements on the importance of his theories; the major part of the book is devoted to a quite lucid explanation of the special and general theories of relativity. The text is particularly clear in the use of analogies and in the avoidance of terminology too technical for the young reader. Since the author never talks down to his audience, his book should also be useful for older readers with language problems. A bibliography and an index are appended.

739   **Konigsburg,** E. L. *Altogether, One at a Time;* illus. by Gail E. Haley et al. Atheneum, 1971. 79p. $4.50.

4–6   Four short stories that are varied in plot, alike in excellence, and united by the theme of compromise, are each illustrated by a different artist. The compromise is not in action, but in the acceptance of the fact that life consists of good things and bad. In "Inviting Jason," a boy gets a new perspective on a handicapped child who comes to his birthday party and in "The Night of the Leonids" another child comes to a new understanding of his grandmother. "Camp Fat" is the only story with a fanciful twist; "Mamma at the Pearly Gates" has a wry humor in the story of an interracial friendship that develops from enmity, due to the acumen of the black child. The writing is deft and polished, the development of relationships subtly percipient.

740   **Konigsburg,** E. L. *From the Mixed-up Files of Mrs. Basil E. Frankweiler;* written and illus. by E. L. Konigsburg. Atheneum, 1967. 162p. Trade ed. $4.95; Library ed. $3.81 net.

5–7   Claudia, when she decided to run away, planned very carefully: she would stay away long enough to have her parents appreciate her, and she would (with the help of her brother, who had not yet been informed of his role) live in dignified seclusion at the Metropolitan Museum of Art. With great skill, Claudia and Jamie evaded the guards, sleeping and even bathing in comfort. Their ploy ended when an interest in a new museum acquisition brought them into the home of the donor, Mrs. Frankweiler. This is an engaging romp of a story, trembling on the brink of unbelievability—but not quite getting there, since the setting is real and the children seem no less so—a sturdy, rational, thoughtful pair.

741   **Konigsburg,** E. L. (*George*); written and illus. by E. L. Konigsburg. Atheneum, 1970. 152p. $4.95.

6–9   George is Benjamin's alter ego, living inside him. Ben is a brilliant boy, fully aware that his mother doesn't want to hear about the imaginary George—but to Ben he is real, a constant companion and dear friend. Ben's younger brother believes, because George talks to him, too. Ben is upset by the fact that one of his teachers is courting his divorced mother, irritated because George is jealous of a school friendship, troubled by fears that he will be sent to live with his father and stepmother. As his schizophrenic symptoms become clear, he is sent to a psychiatrist—and the book ends on a cheerful note of recovery. Although the book deals with a serious problem, it is not somber. There is tenderness in Ben's relationships with his mother and brother, humor in the description of the sedate courtship, and contrast and action in a dramatic school problem in which Ben becomes involved. The characters are vividly portrayed, the writing style vigorous.

742   **Konigsburg,** E. L. *Jennifer, Hecate, Macbeth, William McKinley, and Me, Elizabeth;* written and illus. by E. L. Konigsburg. Atheneum, 1967. 117p. Trade ed. $3.50; Library ed. $3.41 net. (Macmillan, 1968. 128p. £0.90.)

4–6   An unusual and engrossing story about sustained imaginative play. Jennifer convinces Elizabeth, who tells the story, that she is an accomplished witch. She permits Elizabeth to study with her as an apprentice, and the two children solemnly observe the complicated rigmarole Jennifer has invented through most of a school year. Elizabeth's acceptance of the fantasy finally disappears, but it is convincingly described; her descriptions of the events at school are amusing, especially her acid comments on another classmate: "Every grown-up in the whole U.S. of A. thinks that Cynthia is perfect." Jennifer contributes zealously to the demolition of that myth. The author treats with commendable irrelevance the fact that Jennifer is Negro and Elizabeth white: they are simply two little girls.

743   **Koren,** Edward. *Behind the Wheel.* Holt, 1972. 28p. illus. Trade ed $4.95; Library ed. $3.59 net; Paperback ed. $1.25.

2–4   Something new under the sun: pictures of what you see from the driver's seat. Each drawing (steamshovel, ship, crane, helicopter, racing car, tractor) with a beaming saw-toothed creature at the helm is followed by a picture of the driver's view and accompanied by a diagram of all the handles, gauges, levers, switches, pedals, meters, and other delightful impedimenta of control panels. The adult who is bored by this had best brace for repeated readings to the vehicle-loving preschool child—until memorization sets in. A glossary is appended.

744

Kosterina, Nina. *The Diary of Nina Kosterina;* tr. from the Russian with an introduction by Mirra Ginsburg. Crown, 1968. 192p. $3.95.

7–12

Nina began her diary when she was fifteen, bubbling with vitality, intrigued by boys, diligent in her duty as a member of the Komsomol, fiercely devoted to her friends, rapturously impressed by books. The entries record her growing maturity and her increasing involvement in political life. When her father is exiled and she herself refused entrance at the school she'd expected to attend, Nina is in bewildered despair. She finally gets her degree, she falls in love . . . and then the raids begin. Her last entry is in November of 1941; the book closes with an official letter to Nina's mother: killed in action. The book gives a good picture of Moscow in the years before the war and a vivid record of a young girl growing into womanhood.

745

Kraus, Robert. *How Spider Saved Christmas;* written and illus. by Robert Kraus. Windmill/Simon and Schuster, 1970. 38p. Trade ed. $3.95; Library ed. $3.79 net.

3–5
yrs.

Invited by his friends, Fly and Ladybug, to Christmas dinner, Spider relates, he hesitated. Spiders don't usually celebrate Christmas. But he decided to go and knew that he should bring gifts. What could be more Christmasy than snow and icicles? Of course (as small listeners can gleefully predict) the presents were water by the time they were opened—but then, when Ladybug's house was on fire (her cupcakes were burning) whose presents doused the fire and saved the day? A slight tale, but merry; the drawings are almost childlike in their simplicity and the thin plot is compensated for by the ingenuous style and the humor that is appropriate for the young child's understanding.

746

Kraus, Robert. *Leo the Late Bloomer;* illus. by Jose Aruego. Windmill, 1971. 28p. Trade ed. $4.95; Library ed. $4.89 net.

3–5
yrs.

A charming picture book that should warm the heart of other late bloomers. All the other animals can read and write, draw, eat neatly. Not Leo—he can't even talk. His mother is confident, his father worried. And, with the passing of time, Leo suddenly blossoms on all fronts: he can do everything! The illustrations are riotously vernal as Leo blooms, and they are a delightful contrast to an earlier view of a disconsolate cub draped limply along a tree-limb while his anxious father peers from a hiding place at his retarded offspring. Nonsense with a sympathetic message is enhanced by the blithe cavortings of assorted beasts.

747   **Kraus,** Robert. *Whose Mouse Are You?* illus. by Jose Aruego. Macmillan, 1970. 28p. $4.95.

2–5
yrs.

Very simply written, a question-and-answer book that moves from a wistful mood ("Whose mouse are you? Nobody's mouse. Where is your mother? Inside the cat.") to a happy affirmation of family love ("What will you do? Shake my mother out of the cat! . . . Now whose mouse are you? My mother's mouse, she loves me so.") The pattern includes mother, father, sister, new brother; the text has rhyme and rhythm, and can easily be memorized for "reading" alone. The pictures are big, so that the book can be used nicely for showing to a group of children.

748   **Krauss,** Ruth. *I Write It;* illus. by Mary Chalmers. Harper, 1970. 22p. Trade ed. $2.50; Library ed. $2.57 net.

5–6
yrs.

A small book, a single thought, a charming interpretation. The text is continuous, happily cataloging the many ways and places that "I write it," and the precise, beguiling figures of children show that it is a universal activity. On the last pages are scribbled and printed all the names of the children who have so enjoyed the thrill of achievement, the satisfaction of having learned to write their own names. The writing is breezy and blithe, the theme appealing.

749   **Kredenser,** Gail. *1 One Dancing Drum;* pictures by Stanley Mack. Phillips, 1971. 23p. $4.95.

3–6
yrs.

The illustrations are all that matter in this gay counting book, as a frenzied bandmaster collects musicians and instruments in an old-fashioned circular bandstand. The players of one dancing drum, two tinkling triangles, and so on—march up and are piled—literally—in the limited space of the platform. Each group is allotted a different color, so the child can easily pick out all nine of the 9 tooting trombonists as they perch on the roof or on top of other players.

750   **Krementz,** Jill. *Sweet Pea;* A Black Girl Growing Up in the Rural South. Harcourt, 1969. 95p. illus. $4.50.

3–5

Good photographs of Sweet Pea's family, friends, neighbors, classmates, and church acquaintances make vivid the milieu in which she lives. Just turned ten and in fourth grade, Sweet Pea (teacher and the minister, she says, persist in calling her Barbara) lives with a working mother and four little brothers in a rented house in Alabama; father, separated from his wife, lives nearby and visits the children, and several older sisters live away from home. Sweet Pea (a charmer) prattles on about school, chores at home, the weekly climax of churchgoing, her dreams for the future, the happy Christmas when each child received (among other things) the bicycle for which mother had saved all year. This is, of course, the way of life for only some black people in the rural south, but it is a clear picture of that way of life: hard but not intolerable, busy and hard-working, the warmth of family love and the fellowship of religion looming large.

751   **Krumgold,** Joseph. *Henry 3;* drawings by Alvin Smith. Atheneum, 1967. 268p. Trade ed. $4.75; Library ed. $4.37 net.

6–9   When the Lovering family moved to Crestview, Henry hoped that nobody would find out how smart he was; he made it clear that he was Henry 3—not Henry the Third—and he hoped, with the rest of his family, that Dad would finally become a vice-president. All the Loverings agreed that they must be very careful and make all the right gestures toward the right people, but they made one wrong move: they installed (company orders) a bomb shelter. The resultant animosity didn't abate until the stress of a hurricane brought people closer—and Henry 3 had learned something very important about the superficiality of material goals. Beautifully written, but the middle of the book sags somewhat, the affair of the bomb shelter being drawn out and not quite convincing.

752   **Krumgold,** Joseph. *The Most Terrible Turk;* A Story of Turkey; illus. by Michael Hampshire. T. Y. Crowell, 1969. 41p. $3.75.

3–5   Soft and precise, the attractive illustrations for a wry and tender story show a vigorous, ebullient middle-aged man and a serious small boy: Uncle Mustafa and Ali, all that are left of a once-large family. Ali discovers that his uncle has been shooting at the tires of the noisy trucks that interfere with his hunting. He pretends to read in the paper that the police are after such a man, taking advantage of the fact that Mustafa cannot read the new Turkish alphabet. Mustafa decides to decamp, Ali follows him, the truth comes out. There is no hunt for a "Truck murderer." So Mustafa finds out that the boy was deeply enough concerned to lie, and he realizes how much Ali needs him. The setting, Turkey today, is interesting; the characters and their relationship are warm and appealing, and the story is written with humor and an earthy simplicity.

753   **Kurtis,** Arlene Harris. *Puerto Ricans;* From Island to Mainland; illus. with photographs. Messner, 1969. 96p. Trade ed. $3.95; Library ed. $3.64 net.

4–7   A simply written, comprehensive survey of Puerto Ricans, dry but informative, and firmly confident about the gradual improvement of difficulties in Puerto Rico and in the United States. The historical background is ample and interesting, and the analyses of present-day problems briskly competent. The author is candid about inadequacies and hopeful about the future. The Puerto Rican, she says, ''can cement understanding between the black and white community because he embraces them both.'' Puerto Ricans can read this with pride. A glossary and an index are appended.

754   **Kyle,** Elisabeth. *Duet;* The Story of Clara and Robert Schumann. Holt, 1968. 213p. Trade ed. $4.50; Library ed. $3.97 net. (Evans Bros., 1968. 192p. £1.05.)

6–9   When young Robert Schumann came as a pupil to her father's house, little Clara Wieck was a child prodigy already becoming known in Leipzig's musical circles. Quiet and precocious, Clara recognized Robert's genius and realized, when she became older, that she loved the young composer of whom her father so disapproved. For four long years, the docile Clara followed a concert career and lived without her beloved before she rebelled and married him; in one of the most romantic marriages in the world of the performing arts, they lived happily until Robert became insane. Well written, this is a tender story that never becomes saccharine in the telling; it has, in addition to the dramatic appeal of a thwarted love between two famous people, a special interest for music lovers and it gives a most interesting picture of paternal dominance in the early nineteenth century.

755   **Kyle,** Elisabeth. *Princess of Orange.* Holt, 1966. 255p. Trade ed. $3.95; Library ed. $3.59 net.

7–10   A good biographical novel based on the life of Mary Stuart, who returned from Holland to become Mary II of England. Mary was bitterly unhappy at her arranged marriage to the stiff-mannered stranger, William of Orange, but she learned to love and respect her husband, later insisting that he share her throne. The book has good historical background, convincing characterization, and lively and natural style of writing.

756   **Lacy,** Leslie Alexander. *Cheer the Lonesome Traveler;* The Life of W. E. B. Du Bois; illus. by James Barkley and with photographs. Dial, 1970. 183p. $4.95.

7–10   An excellent biography for young people, long overdue, of one of the most eminent of black American leaders, a man whose ideas were prophetic, whose career was distinguished, whose death in Ghana at the age of ninety-five was the occasion for a world-wide acknowledgment of William Du Bois as an outstanding political and literary figure. His conversion to communism at the age of ninety-three is discussed objectively; indeed, the critical dispassion of the author is such that he can occasionally voice— as he does—his love and reverence for Du Bois without sacrificing perspective. The writing style is brisk and competent; separate bibliographies of works by and about Du Bois precede the index.

757   **Ladd,** Elizabeth Crosgrove. *The Indians on the Bonnet;* illus. by Richard Cuffari. Morrow, 1971. 190p. Trade ed. $4.50; Library ed. $4.14 net.

4–6   The Bonnet is a point of high land on the Maine coast where Jess and his grandmother live, and when Cory and her father come to live there as caretakers for a man who has bought the house on the Bonnet, they are pleased to have them as neighbors. Jess is not quite as pleased after he has known the owner for a while; it seems odd that the always-affable Mr. Barnes is so unpleasant to Cory's father, a quiet and hardworking man, yet so tolerant of the shoddy work of two disreputable local characters he has hired to work on his boat. Is it because Cory's father is Indian? It is in part, but Jess—with Cory's help—ferrets out the real reason: Mr. Barnes is involved in an insurance fraud and plans to scuttle the boat. The ending is dramatic, the pace well maintained, the structure of the mystery workmanlike, with a convincing setting and a forthright treatment of bias added to the appeal of suspense.

758   **La Fontaine,** Jean de. *The Hare and the Tortoise;* pictures by Brian Wildsmith. Watts, 1967. 29p. $4.95. (Oxf. U.P., 1966. 32p. £0.90.)

K–2   The familiar fable is adequately told and beautifully illustrated in an oversize picture book version. The pages glow with color, some of the pictures rather heavy with detail and others—more impressive—in a page layout in which the ample use of space makes all the more effective the humorous details and spectrum of hues in the drawings of plants and animals.

759   **Lampman,** Evelyn (Sibley). *The Tilted Sombrero;* illus. by Ray Cruz. Doubleday, 1966. 264p. $3.95.

6–9   A story of the beginnings of the Mexican War of Independence in 1810. Nando, motherless, is thirteen when his father dies; he learns from his older brother a family secret: they had an Indian grandmother. As a proud creole (a Mexican with only Spanish forebears) Nando has always looked down upon the mestizos, the Spanish-Indians. Sent off to be out of the way, Nando rides alone and is stripped by bandits; he then has many adventures—due in part to the war and in part to the zealous machinations of a young girl who loves intrigue and who is more inventive than truthful. Both Nando and his oldest brother, who had been a soldier loyal to Spain, are won over to the popular cause, and Nando learns to be proud of his heritage. A colorful book about an interesting period in Mexican history; the writing style is good, the characterization variable in quality. The story gives a vivid picture of the stratified society that united to fight the oppressive rule of Spain. Some real characters are prominent in the story, primarily Father Miguel Hidalgo Y Costilla, the priest who led the first Indian revolt.

760   **Land,** Barbara. *The Telescope Makers;* From Galileo to the Space Age. T. Y. Crowell, 1968. 245p. illus. $4.50.

8—   Although many of the astronomers whose investigations and discoveries are described here are familiar to readers of science biographies, there are some less known names in this most interesting book. The subjects whose research is described are Lippershey, Galileo, Kepler, Newton, Herschel, von Fraunhofer, Rosse, Hale, Schmidt, Reber, and Friedman. The writing has vigor and clarity, the author bringing in enough about other astronomers to make the book useful as historical material. The explanations of recent developments (the radio telescope and the rocket telescope) are clear, as are the diagrams. A bibliography and an index are appended.

761   **Langstaff,** Nancy. *Jim Along, Josie;* A Collection of Folk Songs and Singing Games for Young Children; comp. by Nancy and John Langstaff; illus. by Jan Pienkowski. Harcourt, 1970. 127p. $5.50.

K–3   Amusing silhouette pictures add to the appeal of a good collection of songs, varied and—with a few exceptions—lively and gay. The material is divided into folk songs, action songs, and singing games, and a preface discusses the use of songs with children. Sources are cited; many of the songs are accompanied by instructions for children's participation.

762   **Langton,** Jane. *The Swing in the Summerhouse;* pictures by Erik J   Blegvad. Harper, 1967. 185p. Trade ed. $3.95; Library ed. $3.79 net. (H. Hamilton, 1970. 192p. £1.05.)

5–7   Charming illustrations echo the graceful fantasy of the writing in a sequel to *The Diamond in the Window.* Here too there is a successful blending of the real and the fanciful, natural dialogue that is often humorous, and a spectrum of pleasant family relationships. The summerhouse has six sides, and swinging out through each one the children are transported to magical adventures, each of which has some relevance to the children's real life. Written with a light, sure touch.

763   **Larrick,** Nancy, comp. *I Heard a Scream in the Street;* Poems by Young People in the City; illus. with photographs by students. Evans, 1970. 141p. $4.95.

5—   From class magazines, workshops and community centers, student newspapers and college poetry projects, from young people in twenty-three cities, Nancy Larrick has chosen almost eighty poems that testify to the perception, vision, and candor of the young. There is little humor or gentleness: the poems are fierce in statement of condemnation or pride, sometimes rough in structure but often impressive. The author's names are given but not their ages (the range was fourth grade through high school at the time of writing) and the material is divided into five sections: "People Pushing and Rushing," "Walk Down My Street and See," "I Walk Through Crowded Streets and Ask, 'Who Am I?'," "I Dream of Blackness," and "I Am Frightened That the Flame of Hate Will Burn Me." Author-title and first line indexes are appended.

764   **Larrick,** Nancy, ed. *Piping Down the Valleys Wild;* Poetry for Young of All Ages; illus. by Ellen Raskin. Delacorte, 1968. 247p. $4.95.

3–6   A pleasant, quite comprehensive collection that includes little unfamiliar material; the selections range widely in source, somewhat less widely in mood. The poems are grouped in subject areas, with an index of first lines and an author-title index appended. The compiler's introduction is addressed to adults and discusses reading aloud to the young; this plus the fact that so much of the poetry is for quite young children suggests that the book may be best suited to a home collection, although it should be useful in any collection of books for children.

765   **Larson,** Jean Russell. *The Silkspinners;* illus. by Uri Shulevitz. Scribner, 1967. 93p. Trade ed. $3.95; Library ed. $3.63 net.

3–6   Illustrated with stunningly economical pictures in black and white, the gently humorous fanciful story of the wanderings of a young hero. Li Po had set out to find an isolated colony of silk spinners, since the art had been lost in China, save for the rumored colony; his immediate reason was that his sister had started a public weeping session because she wanted a new silk garment. Li Po's adventures—before he finds the silk spinners and convinces them to return to society—are told in a graceful, bland style.

766   **Latham,** Jean Lee. *Far Voyager;* The Story of James Cook; maps by Karl W. Stuecklen. Harper, 1970. 242p. Trade ed. $4.50; Library ed. $4.11 net.

5–9   A very good biography, deftly fictionalized, with natural dialogue and good characterization. The text concentrates on Cook's years of service and voyages of exploration, culminating in his attainment of rank and his membership in the Royal Society (both unusual for a self-educated man who had come up through

the ranks) and ending with his death at the hands of some
Hawaiian natives in 1779.

767   **Lauber,** Patricia. *Bats;* Wings in the Night; illus. with
photographs. Random House, 1968. 77p. $1.95.

4–6   A crisply written introduction to the subject, with good
photographs, some diagrams, and an index. The author discusses
the classification of bats, and those habits or abilities that
distinguish them from other mammals or, within the order of
Chiroptera, from each other. The extraordinary hunting and
feeding patterns of bats, their mysterious migrations, and their
almost death-like hibernation are fascinating aspects of the topic
that have been and are being studied.

768   **Lauber,** Patricia. *Who Discovered America?* Settlers and Explorers
of the New World Before the Time of Columbus. Random House,
1970. 128p. illus. $4.95.

4–6   A good survey of the settlers and explorers of the new world,
giving both facts and theories and distinguished by careful
organization of material, a lively style, and interesting illustrations
judiciously placed. The account begins with the Columbian
expedition, then goes back to describe the Ice Age migrants,
the spreading and varied Indian civilizations, the Viking
settlements, the disputed evidence of other explorations, and the
indisputable evidence of cultural diffusion. Throughout the book
there is a vigorous sense of the challenge of archeological mysteries,
and the study concludes with a summary statement. A selected
bibliography and an index are appended.

769   **Laurence,** Margaret. *Jason's Quest;* illus. by Staffan Torell. Knopf,
1970. 211p. $4.95. (Macmillan, 1970. 160p. £1.05.)

4–6   A fanciful story about an oddly matched band of small animals
on a quest—episodic and humorous—is fairly common, but this
is an uncommonly good book. The major characters (a mole,
an owl, and two cats) are strong, the minor ones acceptably
satirized types; the dialogue is entertaining, the London setting
(with an underground copy of almost every scene above ground)
intriguing. The illustrations are appropriately engaging.

770   **Lawson,** John. *The Spring Rider.* T. Y. Crowell, 1968. 147p. $3.95.

6–8   "When Jacob had been young he thought the whole Civil
War had been fought in his meadow . . ." and the lad, dreaming,
had always known that some day he would see the soldiers
that peopled his dreams. In this deftly written fantasy, he does
see them; he follows a southern general and meets a northern
soldier, and he sees the familiar apparition of the Spring Rider—
Abraham Lincoln. The gaunt and gentle man knows that Jacob
and his sister have befriended ghosts, and he realizes that the

bridging of time has brought near-tragedy to the living young, that the romantic ghosts must be exorcised. The fanciful plot, the wistful and dolorous mood, and the homely charm of the Spring Rider will have most appeal to the mature reader who can appreciate the nuance of style and symbol.

771   **Lawson,** John. *You Better Come Home with Me;* illus. by Arnold Spilka. T. Y. Crowell, 1966. 125p. $3.50.

6–7   An unusual fantasy in which a boy comes home to stay with the Scarecrow; Boy had been orphaned in a flood and raised by foster parents, and he told people he was wandering about looking for his brother because one cannot tell people that one is looking for "warmth or strength or love or whatever." The caustic fox warned the Scarecrow against the Boy, but they had become friends; the three together made a Snowman who came alive and talked to the Boy of important things. In the end, the Boy is carried down from the mountain by an old man; perhaps he has died and perhaps, asleep, the Boy is being carried home at last to "love or whatever." The writing is often lyric, often ironic, and always subtle; the story is always fanciful, even when the people meet such characters as the Witch, the Snowman, or Mr. Fox. The book is absorbing to read because of the writing style, the permeation of aching love, and the intriguing, imaginative incidents. Occasionally the dialogue seems fragmented and the plot lost in mist, but the book will probably attract chiefly that audience that will read it for style and nuance.

772   **Lazarus,** Keo Felker. *The Shark in the Window;* illus. by Laurel Schindelman. Morrow, 1972. 159p. Trade ed. $4.75; Library ed. $4.32 net.

3–5   Shelly's older brother had told him that the odd object found on the beach was a shark's egg, but who would have expected it to hatch? And who would have known it would grow so big so fast? And who would have believed that it could live out of water? What begins as a pleasant, science-oriented pet story romps merrily off into fantasy, as Shelly's tame shark swims happily through the air of a home in which the children are enthralled and the parents dismayed. Trying nervously to keep a large shark hidden proves impossible, and after a few nerve-wracking incidents, the shark is finally sold to a delighted aquarium owner. The fantasy and realism are nicely combined, with believable family scenes and good dialogue as background for the story of the big one that didn't want to get away.

773   **Lea,** Alec. *To Sunset and Beyond.* Walck, 1971. 157p. $4.75. (H. Hamilton, 1970. 160p. £1.25.)

5–9   Set in the English countryside at the close of the last century, a story that is distinguished for its sharp characterization, its evocation of locale and period, and above all its creation of mood and suspense. Nine-year-old Peter, sent to bring the cows home on a day when each member of the family is working frantically to bring the hay in before an impending rain, finds that a gate has been left open and the cows have wandered into another field. By the time he realizes that the Devonshire fog has become impenetrable, Peter is lost. The night alone on the moor, filled with courage and terror, while the village hunts for the boy, is the focus of the story, but it is beautifully balanced by the preceding scenes that make the reactions of the villagers and of each member of the family more meaningful.

774   **Leach,** Maria, ed. *How the People Sang the Mountains Up;* How and Why Stories; illus. by Glen Rounds. Viking, 1967. 159p. $3.75.

4–6   A collection of myths and legends about the origins of natural phenomena, primarily of distinctive patterns of behavior or appearance in flora and fauna. The tales are grouped (plants, constellations, animals, et cetera) and a bibliography and list of notes on sources are appended. The selections come from around the world; many are of American Indian origin, very few are European. The style of the retelling is crisp, humorous, and usually brief: good storytelling material.

775   **Leach,** Maria. *Riddle Me, Riddle Me, Ree;* illus. by William Wiesner. Viking, 1970. 142p. Trade ed. $3.95; Library ed. $3.77 net.

3–6   A collection of over 200 riddles drawn from folk materials the world over. They are grouped by kind: riddles about the universe, or animals, or—reflecting a contemporary type—elephants. The last section is a selection of jokes and tricks. The source for each riddle is given, and a section of notes makes the book particularly useful for adults interested in folklore.

776   **Lear,** Edward. *The Scroobious Pip;* completed by Ogden Nash; illus. by Nancy Ekholm Burkert. Harper, 1968. 18p. Trade ed. $3.95; Library ed. $3.79 net.

4–   A beautiful book, its large pages filled with pictures of birds, beasts, fish, and insects; handsome in format and design, the book is distinguished by the delicate charm of the illustrations. The Lear verses, left incomplete at his death, have been filled in by Nash; his additions are in brackets. The nonsense poetry bears a subtle message of acceptance, as all the creatures challenge the Pip (a bit of every species, class, genus, etc. in one appealing package) to explain what he is; his firm and only response is that he is himself, the Scroobious Pip.

777
7–10

Lee, Mildred. *Fog.* Seabury, 1972. 250p. $5.95.

Lucky Luke: nice parents, the friendship of the guys in the
clubhouse gang, and best of all—Milo. Pretty, popular Milo,
who had turned to him after she broke up with Forrest, who
could have had any guy she wanted. True, Milo didn't seem to
be deeply in love with him, but that would change. But growing
up isn't easy, and Luke had a series of blows: a clubhouse
fire in which Luke and all the others were hurt, and then the
death of his wise and gentle father. When Forrest came back
to town, Luke was apprehensive—and his fear was justified.
Milo had not forgotten him, still loved him, and told Luke so,
weeping. Stunned, Luke went home and in the quiet, sober way
that was so like his father's put Milo's picture away. End of a
story. Written with consummate skill and understanding
compassion, the story is remarkable for its balanced treatment,
for the realistic way in which the plot develops, for the
perceptive characterization, and for the wholly convincing and
moving picture of the painful process of growing up.

778

6–9

Lee, Mildred. *Honor Sands.* Lothrop, 1966. 255p. Trade ed. $4.50;
Library ed. $4.14 net.

This is a book as honest as was the author's *The Rock and the
Willow,* but it hasn't the same strength—or the same harshness.
Honor is a freshman in high school, a pleasant girl with a pleasant,
ordinary family; but even girls with sense and stability have problems when they're thirteen. Honor has a crush on one of her
teachers; she is impatient with her mother; she is really most
troubled by the evidence of a burgeoning affection between her
father and her aunt. Her suspicions are not justified, since all of the
remarks (misinterpreted by Honor) have been advice about Aunt
Catherine's love affair with a man she subsequently marries.
The writing has ease and vitality; the characters and relationships
are drawn with conviction and in some depth.

779

6–8

Lee, Mildred. *The Skating Rink.* Seabury, 1969. 126p. $3.95.

"Looks like you just can't stand it to act like ever'body else.
Got to be different—like you was tetched!" That was how Tuck's
father felt. Girls teased him, and at school he was either tongue-
tied or he stammered—as shy and lacking in confidence as a
fifteen-year-old could be. Tuck's life is changed when Pete Degley
builds a skating rink and secretly teaches the boy to become so
expert that he does an exhibition number with Mrs. Degley on
opening night. The ending is no dream-of-glory; Tuck has worked,
despaired, worked on, and hoped for this one night that would
show his family and his peers his true mettle. The setting is
rural Georgia, the family situation bitterly realistic, and the

relationship between Tuck and his mentor a bright note; the dialogue is good, the characterization splendid.

780   **Lee,** Virginia. *The Magic Moth;* drawings by Richard Cuffari. Seabury, 1972. 64p. $4.50.

4–6   Most children's stories about adjustment to death concern a pet, a grandparent, occasionally a parent; few describe, as this does, the death of a sibling. Although it is a six-year-old boy who is the protagonist, this is really a family story, for Maryanne's death affects each of the others. The third of five children, Maryanne has been an invalid for some time due to a heart condition, and her parents have tried to prepare the others for the end they know is imminent. Although a somber book, *The Magic Moth* is not morbid: it approaches its sad subject very gently, and the "magic" moth that emerges from a caterpillar is impressive to small Mark, but is not used as a symbol. The children are all aware that their sister cannot live, are stricken by her death, and are resilient enough to cope with a house filled with visitors and with the funeral service.

781   **Legum,** Colin. *The Bitter Choice;* Eight South Africans' Resistance to Tyranny; by Colin and Margaret Legum. World, 1968. 207p. illus. Trade ed. $5.95; Library ed. $4.28 net. (World Pub Co., 1969. 208p. £3.00.)

7–10   Eight chapters are devoted to Alan Paton, Nelson Mandela, Albert Lutuli, Robert Sobukwe, Beyers Naudé, Nana Sita, Dennis Brutus, and Michael Scott, black men and white, Asians and Africans, white men of English stock and Dutch. The authors give two chapters of background information that make clearer the courage and tenacity of those who fight against apartheid, and the final chapter discusses the bitter choice of weapons that lies ahead: violence, guerilla warfare, partition, international intervention. Informative, timely, sober, and stirring, a well-written book by South African exiles who were forbidden to return home after the publication of an adult book on South Africa's crisis. A chronology, a list of books by the eight subjects, and an index are appended.

782   **Leighton,** Margaret (Carver). *Cleopatra;* Sister of the Moon. Farrar, 1969. 215p. $3.95.

7–10   A very good biography in which Cleopatra is seen as an intelligent woman rather than a siren, an important figure but only one figure in the complicated pattern of Mediterranean politics. Even as a child, Cleopatra was aware that her greatest enemies were within the palace and that she could rely on nobody as she could on herself; even while she was at the height of her influence with Caesar and with Mark Antony she knew that

that influence was transitory. Written in a serious but not heavy style, with strong characterization and a broad view of historical patterns. A bibliography is appended.

783   **Lenski,** Lois. *Lois Lenski's Christmas Stories;* written and illus. by Lois Lenski. Lippincott, 1968. 152p. Trade ed. $4.50; Library ed. $4.29 net.

3–5   A collection of Christmas stories, most of which have been excerpted from the author's books, with some poems and a play not previously published. Some of the excerpts were originally published as short stories, then incorporated into books, and the Christmas passages now included here with prefatory notes that give enough background for continuity. The separation of tale and commentary gives the book a utilitarian air, but the variety (in time, locale, and ethnic or economic focus) of backgrounds makes the book indeed useful and interesting. The first three stories are grouped under the heading "Early Christmases"; in the second section, "Regional Christmases 1940–1967," there are two new stories, one urban and one set in the backwoods, and a Nativity play; poems are scattered throughout the volume.

784   **Lent,** Blair. *John Tabor's Ride;* story and pictures by Blair Lent. Atlantic-Little, Brown, 1966. 48p. $3.75.

K–3   A tall tale based on a New England legend about a shipwrecked sailor from Nantucket. Picked up by a strange old man, John Tabor was taken on a long, wild ride on the back of a whale; past Samoa they sped, past the Bay of Bengal. John played cribbage with King Neptune and came to a lighthouse manned by a walrus and an albatross. Eventually he was delivered by the whale to the very heart of town; grateful, John Tabor had his whale towed back to the sea and freedom. The style of the telling is adequate, the appeal of the story being in the exaggeration, the fantastic situations, and the abundance of salty marine terms. The illustrations are stylized and handsome, subdued in color but bursting with movement, vigor, and fun.

785   **Lester,** Julius, ad. *The Knee-High Man, and Other Tales;* illus. by Ralph Pinto. Dial, 1972. 29p. Trade ed. $5.95; Library ed. $5.47 net.

K–2   Rural scenes in quiet colors are a background for nicely detailed creatures in an appealing collection of six animal stories from black folklore. The clever Mr. Rabbit outwits Mr. Bear and a farmer in two of the tales; two are "Why" stories, another proves that you should never trust a snake, and the sixth is on the familiar theme of the person (sometimes it's an animal) who is dissatisfied with himself, tries to change, and gratefully accepts what he can't do anything about—in this case, the knee-high man resigns himself after consultation with a wise owl. The style of telling is direct and simple, and the book should be useful for storytelling as well as for reading aloud. Sources are cited.

786   **Lester,** Julius. *Long Journey Home; Stories from Black History.* Dial, 1972. 147p. $4.95.

7—   Six stories about slaves and freedmen in black history are based on such sources as interviews and footnotes. In a foreword, Julius Lester explains that he has chosen minor figures because the mass of people were the "movers of history" while the great figures are their symbols. Although one monologue, the title story, is slow-moving, the others are dramatic, some poignant and some bitter; the selections are diversified in their settings and alike in their sharply etched effectiveness.

787   **Lester,** Julius. *To Be a Slave;* illus. by Tom Feelings. Dial, 1968. 160p. $4.95. (Longman Young Bks., 1970. 160p. £1.10.)

6—   Excerpts from original material (usually signed) are arranged chronologically in a moving and explicit documentary record that is given continuity by the author's comments and explanations that link the quoted remarks. Much of the material was obtained from the Federal Writers' Project, stored at the Library of Congress; some of it is in the words and the language of the slaves, other segments had been edited for propaganda purposes by abolitionists. From capture to action, from servitude to freedom, the black man speaks eloquently of his history and his bondage. Not better than the Meltzer compilations, but more immediate a picture of slavery. A bibliography is appended.

788   **Levin,** Jane Whitbread. *Star of Danger.* Harcourt, 1966. 160p. $3.50.

7–10   A very good World War II story. Peter and Karl were German refugees in Denmark when, in 1943, the Nazi policy toward Danish Jews changed and the boys had to flee to Sweden. The flight for many others and for the two young men was dangerous; for both the Jews and the Resistance workers, the execution of the escape plans required patience and courage. The writing is a bit stodgy, but the plot, based on actual war experiences, is constructed well; the most appealing aspect of the book, however, is in the picture it gives of the Danish people: their kindness, their efficiency, and their courage in putting into practice their belief that all men truly are brothers.

789   **Levitin,** Sonia. *Journey to America;* illus. by Charles Robinson. Atheneum, 1970. 150p. Trade ed. $4.25; Library ed. $4.08 net.

5–7   Lisa Platt tells the story of a momentous year in her family's life. It had become dangerous for Jews in Germany, so Papa left his wife and daughters in Berlin in 1938 and went to America. When he could send for them, they were to leave everything behind and pretend to be going on a vacation. To keep little Annie quiet about their plans, Lisa sacrificed her favorite doll, and off they went on "vacation" to Zurich, where the long wait for passports was made more worrisome by Mama's illness, constant apprehension, and the tragic news of the Berlin massacre. Lisa's experiences at a refugee camp for children and her happier time staying with a Catholic family are vivid and poignant. This reads more like a documentary script than a novel, but it is a dramatic script, well written and perceptive in describing the tensions and reactions of people in a situation of stress.

790   **Lewis,** Richard W., ed. *I Breathe a New Song;* Poems of the Eskimo; illus. by Oonark. Simon and Schuster, 1971. 128p. Trade ed. $5.95; Library ed. $5.70 net.

4—   Illustrations that resemble the stick figures of cave paintings complement the directness and simplicity of the lovely poems chosen from the writings (chiefly anonymous) of many Eskimo groups. The introduction by Edmund Carpenter explains that poems, to the Eskimo, are transitory—not because poetry is unimportant, but because it is accepted as a spontaneous expression of idea or mood: the Eskimo word for "to make poetry" is the word also used for "to breathe." The poems reflect a closeness to nature, and a concern with the aspects of life that loom large in a primitive culture, and the love poems are enchanting. A bibliography is appended.

791   **Lewis,** Richard W., comp. *Journeys;* Prose by Children of the English-speaking World. Simon and Schuster, 1969. 215p. $4.95.

3–7   A companion volume to *Miracles,* an anthology of children's poetry. The children, four to fourteen, live in the United States, Canada, New Zealand, Australia, India, Ghana, Liberia, Great Britain, and Ireland. The selections range from a single line to a page or two, varying in style, mood, subject and tempo. A delightful book for browsing, for coming back to, for discussion.

792   **Lewis,** Richard W., ed. *Miracles;* Poems by Children of the English-speaking World. Simon and Schuster, 1966. 214p. illus. $5.95. (A. Lane, 1967. 128p. £1.50.)

all
ages   Pure joy. Mr. Lewis has collected almost two hundred poems written by children between the ages of five and thirteen. He intends the volume to be considered a poetry anthology rather than an exercise in precocity; form and punctuation have been followed, the only errors corrected having been spelling errors. The book is divided into approximately a dozen sections in which

the poems are loosely grouped by theme. Each selection is printed
on a separate page, with the author's name, age, and place of
residence at the foot of the page. Very dignified, the format; not
a "cute" poem in the lot, and the compiler's respect for his
contributors is evidenced by the small fact that there is no
title cited if the author had given none. The poems vary in
mood, subject, length, subtlety, and form, and they constitute a
remarkable and charming book.

793   **Lewis,** Richard W., comp. *Of This World;* A Poet's Life in Poetry;
photographs by Helen Buttfield. Dial, 1968. 96p. Trade ed. $4.95;
Library ed. $4.58 net.

5—   Each of the four sections of this collection of poetry is preceded
by a biographical sketch of a part of the life of Issa, the eminent
Japanese haiku poet. Although based on the same translations
(Blyth and Yuasa) as is the Issa collection reviewed above, some
slight differences obtain: "Come and play with me, Fatherless,
motherless Sparrow" and "Come, Motherless sparrows, And play
with me." The poetry is not chosen in chronological order but
selected by Richard Lewis to reflect the mood of each segment
of Issa's life. The two-page introduction discusses haiku as a form
and Issa's genius as a haiku poet; the biographical material
comprises five pages.

794   **Lewis,** Richard W., ed. *Out of the Earth I Sing;* Poetry and
Songs of Primitive Peoples of the World. Norton, 1968. 144p.
illus. Trade ed. $3.95; Library ed. $3.73 net.

3—   A delightful anthology, the dignified layout of pages and the
handsome photographs adding to its value; the latter are identified
at the close of the book; the songs and poetry are identified
on the pages on which they appear. The illustrations are not
matched by source but by mood or subject; the poems and
songs are simple and moving, collected from sources the world
over.

795   **Lexau,** Joan M. *Archimedes Takes a Bath;* illus. by Salvatore
Murdocca. T. Y. Crowell, 1969. 56p. $3.50.

4–6   A sprightly story that very deftly weaves into the fictional
matrix some scientific facts. Xanthius is a boy slave who has
been detailed by King Hiero to see that the absent-minded
Archimedes gets to his meals and baths. " 'I do not need you,'
Archimedes said. 'Long ago you saved my life,' Xanthius said.
'When I was a baby you fell over me and brought me to the
king.' " Archimedes keeps stumbling over things . . . and he
keeps thinking, and he keeps resisting the boy's efforts to get
things done on schedule. Meanwhile he explains some of his

inventions and he comes up with the most famous in-the-tub-discovery of all time. The almost-cartoon style illustrations are admirably suitable for the sophisticated nonsense of the tale. A brief epilogue gives some facts about the life and work of Archimedes, pointing out which characters in the story are fictional.

796   Lexau, Joan M. *Benjie on His Own;* illus. by Don Bolognese. Dial, 1970. 34p. Trade ed. $3.95; Library ed. $3.69 net.

K–3   After many years, a sequel to *Benjie,* in which a small Harlem boy, living alone with his grandmother, gets over being painfully shy. Benjie is in school now, and convinced that Granny doesn't need to pick him up—but he's quite worried when she doesn't appear. He finds his way home, but he also finds that the streets are not quite a safe place. Granny is not well, just as Benjie has feared, and he manages to call an ambulance and get the help of some of the neighbors. The story gives a good picture of the isolation of many urban neighborhoods, and of the poverty of the Harlem ghetto. Written with colloquial flow, the text and the illustrations have a sympathetic acceptance of the toughness and the kindness that can exist side by side in a community.

797   Lexau, Joan M. *Me Day;* illus. by Robert Weaver. Dial, 1971. 27p. Trade ed. $4.95; Library ed. $4.58 net.

K–3   When Daddy lost his job, Mamma went out to work, and then the quarrels started. Now they are divorced, and Rafer especially misses Daddy on his birthday. Otherwise, it's a good day, a "me" day: no chores, and Rafer can choose the television programs. Sent on an errand, Rafer grumbles until he sees a familiar figure and realizes that the "errand" is a prearranged surprise meeting with Daddy. Are they undivorced, he asks . . . and Daddy explains that nothing will ever separate him from his boys. Poignant, candid, and simply written, a story written with perceptive sympathy.

798   Lexau, Joan M. *The Rooftop Mystery;* pictures by Syd Hoff. Harper, 1968. 64p. (I Can Read Books) Trade ed. $2.50; Library ed. $2.57 net. (World's Work, 1969. 64p. £0.75.)

1–3   One of the nicest things about a book like this, designed for the beginning independent reader, is that the somewhat older child with reading difficulties can accept it because of the format and humor rather than labeling it as a "baby-book." Sam and Albert are helping Sam's family move to another home within walking distance; unfortunately Sam finds any distance too long in which he can be seen in public carrying his sister's large, conspicuous doll. The situation is realistic, the problem and solution simply handled, and the book is as appealing as it is useful.

799   **Lexau,** Joan M. *Striped Ice Cream;* illus. by John Wilson. Lippincott, 1968. 95p. Trade ed. $3.25; Library ed. $3.11 net.

2–4   Last year for her birthday, Becky had had chicken-spaghetti and striped ice cream; now, for her eighth birthday, Becky feared they were too poor to have even that. But love and industry work wonders: not only did she get the ice cream, but a brand new dress! Only the youngest of four girls in a family of modest means could so rejoice at something that wasn't a hand-me-down; Becky, who had been coaxed out of the way while the dress was being made, was especially happy because she had wondered if her family really cared for her. This is a simple, realistic story of a working-class family; it is not a problem book nor does it have a message. The illustrations show a buxom, amiable, tired mother and five lively children.

800   **Lezra,** Giggy. *The Cat, the Horse, and the Miracle;* drawings by Zena Bernstein. Atheneum, 1967. 114p. Trade ed. $3.75; Library ed. $3.59 net. (Macdonald, 1969. 114p. £0.70.)

3–5   The horse and cat, who lived alone on an abandoned farm, were quarrelsome and lazy until they had a mission; some great thing would happen, the tiny woman told them, if they would follow the golden thread. So they did, and as they met one obstacle after another the cat and the horse became more and more brave and resourceful in guarding their growing ball of thread. At the end of the story, they roll it to a mountain-top, where it glows like a huge sun and causes the people of a gloomy, silent village to erupt into new activity and into praise of the horse and the cat. The deeper meaning is clear, but the story can be enjoyed even without it, since the verbal sparring between the animals is crisp and humorous.

801   **Lidstone,** John. *Building with Cardboard;* photography by Roger Kerkham. Van Nostrand, 1968. 95p. $4.95. (VanNost. Reinhold, 1968. 96p. £2.55.)

4–7   A particularly attractive and explicit how-to-make-it book, with lucid instructions and good, sharp photographs that illustrate some of the many things that can be made of an inexpensive material. All of the pictures show objects made by children, or in the making. The techniques of working in the medium are clearly explained, and the reader is encouraged to experiment.

802   **Lifton,** Betty Jean. *A Dog's Guide to Tokyo;* photographs by Eikoh Hosoe. Norton, 1970. 60p. Trade ed. $3.95; Library ed. $3.69 net.

K–3   Female dogs (the canine "author" says) will be interested in the doll exhibits on Girl's Day, and all dogs in the fact that Japanese children are like children everywhere. Jumblie, the poodle who makes the comments, is shown in many of the very good photographs, but the text is happily free of cuteness. It has, instead, a rather tart humor that makes the captions enjoyable as well as informative; the book gives a good picture of contemporary Tokyo life.

803   **Lifton,** Betty Jean. *Kap and the Wicked Monkey;* illus. by Eiichi Mitsui. Norton, 1968. 59p. Trade ed. $3.75; Library ed. $3.54 net.

K–2   The legendary kappas (water elves of Japan) must keep water in the shallow depression in the top of their heads—or they will die. Here a wicked monkey tricks a kappa prince, Kap, when the elf is hunting a way to save his sick father. A white crane, whose life Kap has saved, rescues the elf prince and enables him to outwit his enemy and revive his father. The story has action and humor; the illustrations combine vigorous movement and the inimitably furry softness of brush and ink.

804   **Lifton,** Betty Jean. *The One-Legged Ghost;* illus. by Fuku Akino. Atheneum, 1968. 34p. Trade ed. $4.50; Library ed. $4.29 net.

K–3   Was it a ghost? It had wings and bones, and it was silent; it landed near a small Japanese boy of long ago, Yoshi, who went running· to his mother. She was sure it was not a bird; the village elders, when consulted, weren't sure what it was. Until the day Yoshi picked the thing up while it was raining, there seemed no purpose to the one-legged creature—but that day, it kept Yoshi from getting wet. So the people made copies of the one-legged ghost and each one then could have his own umbrella. Based on a legend, the sprightly tale is told with verve and humor; the illustrations are handsome.

805   **Lifton,** Betty Jean. *Return to Hiroshima;* photographs by Eikoh Hosoe. Atheneum, 1970. 91p. Trade ed. $5.95; Library ed. $5.69 net.

5–12   "Ask of the city—What of the old, have they forgotten? What of the young, do they remember? What of the wounded, have they healed?" These somber questions are answered in a text that is matter-of-fact in approach, serious in tone, objective in assessing the enduring ramifications of the bombing of Hiroshima. The photographs are excellent, showing the crowded streets of a flourishing metropolis in contrast to scenes of ruins; most of the pictures are of survivors as they look and live today, or of ceremonies and memorials that show that the younger generation has not forgotten.

806   **Lindgren,** Astrid (Ericsson). *Springtime in Noisy Village;* pictures by Ilon Wikland. Viking, 1966. 31p. Trade ed. $3.50; Library ed. $3.37 net.

K–3   First published in Denmark in 1965 under the title *Vår i Bullerbyn,* an attractive sequel to the preceding books about Noisy Village; the illustrations are charming scenes of children, flowers, and animals—scenes with vitality, humor, and a touch of sweetness. Again the description of seasonal ploys is given by Lisa, one of the six compatible children of Noisy Village; here a slightly larger role is given to a seventh child, the very small and beguiling sister of one of the boys.

807   **Lindquist,** Jennie Dorothea. *The Crystal Tree;* pictures by Mary Chalmers. Harper, 1966. 297p. Trade ed. $3.95; Library ed. $3.79 net.

3–6   A sequel to *The Golden Name Day* and *The Little Silver House,* with charming illustrations that are just right for the gentle, old-fashioned tone of the story. Here Nancy and her friends become fascinated by the family who had once owned the silver house; nobody seems to know anything about them or about the little tree made of crystal that one woman remembers. As they talk to residents and write letters to former residents, the children learn more and more about the Crane family. In the course of their investigations, Nancy and her friends give a lovely picture of the friendliness and decorum of a small town early in the century and of the Swedish-American customs preserved in the Benson home.

808   **Lionni,** Leo. *Alexander and the Wind-up Mouse;* written and illus. by Leo Lionni. Pantheon Books, 1969. 29p. $3.95. (Abelard-Schuman, 1971. 32p. £1.40.)

4–6 yrs.   Friendship triumphs over self-interest in a slight but engaging fanciful story about a real mouse, Alexander, and a toy mouse, Willy. Sadly Alexander comes to realize that all the people who shriek at him and chase him dote on Willy, whom they cuddle and take to bed. A wise lizard promises to change Alexander into a wind-up mouse if he can find a purple pebble—but when the big chance comes, Alexander uses his one wish to turn Willy (who has just been tossed away) into a real mouse. The oversize pages are used to full advantage for the handsomely designed collage illustrations; the story is very simply told.

809   **Lionni,** Leo. *The Biggest House in the World.* Pantheon Books, 1968. 29p. illus. Trade ed. $3.95; Library ed. $3.99 net.

3–7 yrs.   Lionni is one of the illustrators who uses to best advantage the oversize book; space and design are adapted to achieve a striking effect. Here the colorful pictures support and complement the text in the best picture book tradition. The biggest house in the world is the huge shell, encrusted with dazzling superstructures, that belongs to a proud snail; hampered by the burden he has achieved by his own vain wishes, the snail dies— at least, that's the way a father snail tells it to his offspring when *he* expresses a wish for the biggest house in the world.

810
5–7
yrs.

Lionni, Leo. *Frederick*. Pantheon Books, 1967. 27p. illus. $3.95.

All through the summertime, the other field mice worked diligently, storing food for the long winter. Frederick sat; he expained that he *was* working, he was "gathering sun rays for the cold dark winter day." He gathered words, he gathered colors; and at the close of the long, cold, grey days Frederick shared with the other mice his colors and words and sun-warmth when he described the joys of the verdant season. The gentle, busy mice are charmingly pictured in handsome collage illustrations touched with brightly painted colors; the writing is direct and simple, and the book closes with Frederick's charming poem ". . . Who grows the four-leaf clovers in June? Who dims the daylight? Who lights the moon? Four little field mice who live in the sky. Four little field mice . . . like you and like I. One is the Spring-mouse who turns on the showers. Then comes the Summer who paints in the flowers. . . ."

811

6–10

Lipsyte, Robert. *Assignment: Sports*. Harper, 1970. 157p. Trade ed. $3.95; Library ed. $3.79 net.

A compilation of articles, several of which have been previously published in *The New York Times,* for which the author is a sports columnist. It is expectable that he would write with competence and authority; what gives the book impact is its dramatic flair and a facility for quick and vivid character portrayals. The articles cover many sports, some little-known athletes and some as well known as Casey Stengel and Cassius Clay, vignettes from the 1968 Olympics, even a brief and poignant piece about a dog show.

812

7–10

Lipsyte, Robert. *The Contender*. Harper, 1967. 182p. Trade ed. $3.50; Library ed. $3.95 net.

Running from a Harlem gang, seventeen-year-old Alfred takes refuge in a boxing club. Thus begins his training for the ring, a desperate effort to break away from the dreary life he knows— living with a prying aunt, working in a grocery store, worrying about the fact that his best friend has become a dope addict. Alfred wins some bouts, but he learns that boxing isn't enough of a life; he decides to finish his education and to work for more substantial goals. The book has a vitality and honesty that are impressive; there is drama without melodrama, and a realistic treatment of the burdens and problems of Harlem life.

813   **Liston,** Robert A. *Downtown;* Our Challenging Urban Problems. Delacorte, 1968. 173p. $3.95.

8—   A serious study of the complicated problems of the metropolis: pollution, congestion, crime, deterioration, taxation, and governments that are at best unwieldy and at worst corrupted by entrenchment. The efforts made (with varying success) by some cities are described, not as total solutions but as efficacious methods of coping with the massive problems cited and with the concomitant spectrum of human problems to which they give rise. The writing style is not heavy, although the pages look solid with print; the material is vitally important and as dramatic as the author's tone is calm and objective. A reading list and an index are appended.

814   **Little,** Jean. *Kate.* Harper, 1971. 162p. Trade ed. $3.50; Library ed. $3.27 net.

5–8   A sequel to *Look through My Window* in which Kate Bloomfield became Emily's best friend. Now Kate, who had often talked to Emily about the problems of being a child with one Jewish parent, becomes even more perturbed when a new neighbor, Mrs. Rosenthal, makes it clear that she once knew Kate's father and that she feels he ought to heal the breach with his family. He takes Kate along for a visit, but their welcome is spoiled when Kate speaks of her mother, since it was the marriage to a non-Jew that caused the breach. In her search for identity and understanding, Kate persuades her father to take her to a synagogue, and the story closes with the two entering together, each nervous, each hopeful. The story is balanced by a continuation of the friendship with Emily, and by Kate's delighted appreciation of a younger child she finds endearing. Stimulating and smoothly written, the book has fine characterization and relationships and a realistic development of a modest but significant plot.

815   **Little,** Jean. *Look through My Window;* illus. by Joan Sandin. Harper, 1970. 258p. Trade ed. $3.95; Library ed. $3.79 net.

4–6   Because Aunt Deborah has tuberculosis, her four lively children are coming to stay with Emily and her parents. Emily, an only child, braces herself for the turmoil of the children, but she finds it both exciting and rewarding to have them. She also finds her horizons broadened by knowing Kate. Kate has one Jewish parent and deep feelings of confusion about herself, feelings that are explored in sensible and tender discussions with her parents and Emily's. Both girls love to read and to write poetry, so the story is studded with references that devoted readers should enjoy. The book is episodic, very well written and perceptively characterized, the theme (suggested by the title) sturdily but not obtrusively pervasive.

816   **Little,** Jean. *One to Grow On;* illus. by Jerry Lazare. Little, 1969. 140p. $4.95.

4–6   Janie was so in the habit of telling lies that she often did so for no reason; she almost believed them herself. It didn't seem so bad to her until she realized that one of her friends was lying to her, and that she felt betrayed by Lisa. The one person to whom Janie never lied was her godmother and friend, Tilly; it was while she was on vacation with Tilly that Janie was faced with a surprise visitor: Lisa. Looking at Lisa, Janie was able to understand and control her own bad habit, but even more indicative of the maturity she was gaining was her ability to feel understanding and compassion for Lisa. Although the vacation sequence moves slowly, it offers a contrast to the vigorous scenes of family life that precede it; the book approaches a common problem with discernment, and the characters are wholly conceived—especially Jane and Lisa, and their roles in their circle of friends.

817   **Little,** Jean. *Take Wing;* illus. by Jerry Lazare. Little, 1968. 176p. $4.95.

5–7   Laurel had always had a special love for her brother James, had always tried to hide her fear that he was not quite normal, and had always protected him. He shouldn't have been wetting the bed at the age of seven, or needing help with his clothes. Not until a series of small crises, during mother's absence, did shy Laurel dare to talk to her father about a medical examination, and only after it proved that James was mentally retarded but educable did Laurel acknowledge that she had coddled her brother. There are several other themes to give the story balance: Laurel's shyness causes her trouble in making friends and also in accepting, with composure, a role in a school play. The ending is satisfying, with some problems solved but no occurrence of miracles; the book's only contrived aspect is that the girl with whom Laurel has been hoping to become friends also has a retarded sibling, an older sister.

818   **Livingston,** Myra Cohn. *Speak Roughly to Your Little Boy;* a collection of parodies and burlesques, together with the original poems, chosen and annotated for young people; illus. by Joseph Low. Harcourt, 1971. 180p. $6.75.

6—   An amusing collection of parodies of English and American poetry, some serious in intent and satirical in approach but most of the selections simply—or not so simply—funny. Some

parodies by Lewis Carroll (his "How doth the little crocodile. . ."
and its original, "How doth the little busy bee. . ." by Watts)
are included, and there are other poems that imitate Carroll's
original peoms. "Rhyme for a Botanical Baby" begins, "Little
bo-peepals/ Has lost her sepals. . . ," there is a Swinburne
parody of his own work, E. B. White takes a poke at Walt
Whitman and at book clubs in the same poem. A section of
notes is appended, unfortunately neither numbered nor with
page references; separate title, author, and first line indexes are
included.

819   **Livingston,** Myra Cohn, ed. *A Tune beyond Us;* A Collection of
Poetry; illus. by James J. Spanfeller. Harcourt, 1968. 280p. $5.75.

7—   An anthology that includes many of the lesser-known works of
well-known poets (an exception is Dylan Thomas, with four
excerpts from "Conversation about Christmas") and many poems
of other countries, both the original and the translation. The
selections are discriminatingly chosen and varied. The compilation
of indexes is meticulous: an index of titles, with asterisks
noting foreign-language poems; an index of first lines; an author
index that includes nationality and life dates; and an index of
translators.

820   **Lobel,** Arnold. *Frog and Toad Are Friends;* written and illus. by
Arnold Lobel. Harper, 1970. 64p. (I Can Read Books) Trade ed.
$2.50; Library ed. $2.57 net.

1–2   Five very short stories in a direct and ingenuous style, appealing
because of their ease and the familiarity of the situations, translated
into animal terms. The mild humor that permeates the tales
(a swimming expedition, a lost button, a slight malaise) adds
to the value of some of the concepts obliquely presented
(differences in shape and size in "A Lost Button"; time concepts
in "Spring") and the give-and-take of a fast friendship is gently
affectionate.

821   **Lobel,** Arnold. *Frog and Toad Together;* written and illus. by
Arnold Lobel. Harper, 1972. 64p. (I Can Read Books) Trade ed.
$2.50; Library ed. $2.92 net.

1–2   A sequel to *Frog and Toad Are Friends* that is even more appealing,
if that is possible, than that first hymn in praise of friendship.
All compulsive adult listmakers will enjoy reading aloud the story
of Toad's preoccupation with his list of what-to-do-all-day, for
these stories, designed for the beginning reader, are excellent
also for the preschool child. They combine familiar elements and
a fresh approach, the humor of the illustrations complementing
the simplicity of the writing style.

822   **Lobel,** Arnold. *On the Day Peter Stuyvesant Sailed into Town.*

Harper, 1971. 35p. illus. Trade ed. $4.95; Library ed. $4.79 net.

K–3   "On the day Peter Stuyvesant sailed into town/ All the people came running to greet him/ They shot off a cannon and waited in line/ So that every last Dutchman could meet him," begins the story of how the new Governor cleaned up the deterioration and filth of the colony by putting its citizens to work. Children should enjoy the fun of seeing pictured (in Stuyvesant's dream) the New York of today, a punctuation mark to an ingenious presentation of a bit of colonial history, told in blithe verse and illustrated with pictures that are humorous and handsome.

823   **Longsworth,** Polly. *I, Charlotte Forten, Black and Free.* T. Y. Crowell, 1970. 248p. $4.50.

6–9   Charlotte's father and grandfather had been free men; the Forten name and fortunes had been made in Philadelphia and now Charlotte, age sixteen, had come to Salem to go on with her studies, since the Philadelphia schools were segregated. This is her account of the years from that time—1854—through the Civil War and the period thereafter, the book closing with Charlotte's marriage to Francis Grimké, nephew of the celebrated Grimké sisters. The style of writing is heavy and ornate, much of the material based on Charlotte Forten's journal and on contemporary sources. The book has appeal despite the style, since it reads like a roll call of all the distinguished people, black and white, who fought against slavery and for black equality. A bibliography, a list of contemporary publications, and an index are appended.

824   **Lopshire,** Robert. *A Beginner's Guide to Building and Flying Model Airplanes.* Harper, 1967. 128p. illus. Trade ed. $5.95; Library ed. $4.43 net. (Harper & Row, 1968. 128p. £2.75.)

5–7   This may well prevent many cases of Acute Pathetic Frustration on the part of young builders, since it most clearly describes, step-by-step, the putting together of a model plane. The illustrations are clear and are fully labelled; the author describes the types of planes, then discusses the details of parts and assembly. He gives tips on soldering, sanding, and the use of wire; he supplies charts in which are shown (actual size) the thicknesses of plywood, the size of dowels, the measurements of strip and sheet balsa. The text concludes with more complicated procedures of assembling an engine or flying a control line model. Sources of additional information and an index are appended to this very useful and carefully compiled book.

825   **Lopshire,** Robert. *It's Magic?* written and illus. by Robert Lopshire. Macmillan, 1969. 30p. illus. $3.95. (World's Work, 1970. 32p. £1.00.)

2–4   A compilation of tricks (no magic) some of which are jokes and some very simple demonstrations of physical principles. The perpetrator is a bear, Tad the Great, and the stooge is another bear, Boris. The author-illustrator has infused the simply written text with a gaiety shared by the illustrations. Tad really seems deflating as he calmly points out or demonstrates the solutions to the ever-credulous Boris. All the tricks are simple to do and require only such ubiquitous articles as toothpicks, handkerchiefs, paper clips, a glass of water, etc.

826   **Lord,** Beman. *Shrimp's Soccer Goal;* illus. by Harold Berson. Walck, 1970. 63p. $4.25.

2–4   Straightforward writing style and a simple plot line combine with a modicum of facts, pleasant illustrations, and large print to make a very good sports story for the primary grades reader. There's a good balance of action in and out of school as Shrimp and his friends adjust to the fact that the new teacher is a soccer fan. Shrimp, who had been looking forward to playing football with Mr. Allen, the teacher who left, was not enchanted, but Miss Taylor was enthusiastic and knowledgeable, and her fervor sparked not only the team of boys and girls but also their cheering classmates.

827   **Low,** Alice. *Kallie's Corner;* drawings by David Stone Martin. Pantheon Books, 1966. 246p. $5.19.

5–9   Jane is in seventh grade at a private school on the upper east side of New York; she is overprotected, carefully nurtured, and completely conventional. Jane's clique is hostile to Kallie, an odd new girl whose father is an archeologist and lives in Greenwich Village. At first Jane's overtures to Kallie are calculated and wary, but she becomes more and more drawn to the freedom and creativity in Kallie's life, and more and more aware that she herself has been a sheep. As Jane struggles for a balance of power with her old group and establishes an independence she has never had at home, she finds new powers of perception and a clearer perspective about herself. Jane's heavy concentration of time and energy in planning an elaborate party for Kallie seems a bit out of proportion, but not unbelievable. The characters really come alive; the writing style is smooth and lively.

828   **Lowenfels,** Walter, ed. *The Writing on the Wall;* 108 American Poems of Protest; ed. by Walter Lowenfels. Doubleday, 1969. 189p. $4.95.

9—   An excellent anthology, diverse in style and form, echoing the tempo of our times; some of the poets are of past generations but of contemporary vision, but most are the poets of today. The selections reflect the restlessness of youth and its rejection of ephemeral values, the protest against war and racial injustice, the isolation of man from fellow man.

829   **Lubell,** Winifred. *In a Running Brook;* by Winifred and Cecil Lubell. Rand McNally, 1968. 64p. illus. Trade ed. $3.95; Library ed. $3.79 net.

4–6   A description of the flora and fauna (chiefly the latter) of a mountain brook, the material arranged in short sections ranging from one to four pages. The tone is conversational, with an occasional lyric note; the information is accurate and interesting. The relative index adds to the book's usefulness, and the cool colors and precise drawing of the illustrations add to its appeal.

830   **Macarthur-Onslow,** Annette. *Uhu;* written and illus. by Annette Macarthur-Onslow. Knopf, 1970. 55p. $4.50. (Rapp & W., 1969. 64p. £1.05.)

3–5   An oversize book with charming illustrations of the small Tawny Owl that became the author's pet. Uhu (German for an Eagle Owl, but appropriated for the occasion) had fallen out of his nest and quickly became acclimated to home life, following his humans about the house, making friends with a pet monkey, passively going along for shopping trips via bicycle basket. The writing is anecdotal, with some diffusion in background description; for example, the author refers frequently to "Buddi"· with whom she lives, but does not introduce him. Nevertheless, the beguiling pictures and the loving, amused tone of the writing combine to appealing effect.

831   **MacBeth,** George. *Jonah and the Lord;* illus. by Margaret Gordon. Holt, 1970. 28p. Trade ed. $3.95; Library ed. $3.59 net. (Macmillan, 1969. 32p. £0.90.)

K–2   A version that follows the Bible story fairly closely, but is couched in today's language (with a few words invented by the author) and has minor variations on the theme. The stylized illustrations, in gay full color, have a stern Assyrian note in the figures and a wild freedom in design; the cresting waves, for example, curl almost in a circle and the big fish (it isn't called a whale) is resplendent with scales of green, orange, and yellow. The writing has zest and humor, yet it makes clear that Jonah was spared only because he learned humility and became wise in the ways of the Lord.

832   **McCarthy,** Agnes. *Room 10;* illus. by Ib Ohlsson. Doubleday, 1966. 71p. $2.50.

3–5   A book that really captures the classroom atmosphere as it touches on various episodes through the year with Miss

Lavender's third grade class. The anecdotes have a modicum of continuity; told by one of the children, they reflect the compartmentalized world of school realistically. The writing is direct, lightly humorous, and never cute; Miss Lavender is nicely depicted as a young, competent, and sympathetic teacher who is occasionally exasperated but never unkind, and who occasionally makes a mistake but who has the respect and affection of the children of room 10.

833   **McClung,** Robert M. *Bees, Wasps, and Hornets;* And How they Live; written and illus. by Robert M. McClung. Morrow, 1971. 64p. Trade ed. $3.95; Library ed. $3.78 net.

3–5   Written with lucid simplicity, this is a discussion of the order Hymenoptera that is authoritative in both the writing and in the carefully detailed drawings. A description of general characteristics such as the four life stages, the membranous wings, and the characteristic wasp waist is followed by brief discussions of individual members of the order, giving facts about nest building, the evolution and use of the sting, eating habits, behavior patterns, et cetera. All of the material is interesting, but the communications system of the bee and the fact that bees are more useful to men than are other members of the order make the section on bees particularly valuable. An index is appended.

834   **McClung,** Robert M. *Thor;* Last of the Sperm Whales; illus. by Bob Hines. Morrow, 1971. 64p. Trade ed. $3.95; Library ed. $3.78 net.

3–5   The life cycle, not quite completed, of a sperm whale is described in narrative form; although given a name, *Thor* is not fictionalized. McClung uses the story to describe modern hunting techniques in the whaling industry and to discuss the disappearance of some species because of wholesale slaughter. Primarily, however, the book is devoted to giving details of mating and birth, feeding habits, behavior, and travel patterns of the sperm whale. Direct and informative, the book is yet another example of the competence and ability that make McClung one of the most dependable science writers for children.

835   **McCord,** David Thompson Watson. *All Day Long;* Fifty Rhymes of the Never Was and Always Is; drawings by Henry B. Kane. Little, 1966. 104p. $4.50.

4–6   A book of rather light, entertaining poems of which several have been previously published in magazines. The poems are well suited to reading aloud, although a few that play with words will lose in the translation, such as the poem about ptarmigan, playing on the prefixing of the silent "p" to other words: "ptolerate" or "pterritory." Or, for example, "Supposing though's

not tho, but more like thoff, and sough's sow's not a pig
that sows, but soff?" The topics are simple but intriguing, the
writing has rhythm, humor, and imaginative zest; the black and
white illustrations are attractive, many of them also humorous.

836   **McCord,** David Thompson Watson. *Every Time I Climb a Tree;*
illus. by Marc Simont. Little, 1967. 43p. $4.95.

2-4   Culled from previously published collections, two dozen of Mr.
McCord's poems best suited for younger children, many of them
nice to read aloud to the very youngest. The writing has both
emotional appeal and literary distinction; it comments on the
familiar with loving zest and on the unfamiliar with a childlike
wonder. Both kinds of poems are echoed and enhanced by the
illustrations, as often comic as they are beautiful; some are
almost cartoons, some are lovely and delicate scenes of nature.

837   **McCord,** David Thompson Watson. *For Me to Say;* Rhymes of the
Never Was and Always Is; illus. by Henry B. Kane. Little, 1970.
100p. $4.50.

4-6   A new collection that is, with few exceptions, light in topic
and tone, with breezy humor and relish of word play, and with
small neat illustrations that often implement the poems. Some of
the selections are, indeed, word games as well as poetry.
Continuing the teaching-by-example of the "Write Me a Verse"
section of an earlier book, the author shows, in a final section
entitled "Write Me Another Verse," examples of verse forms.
Included here are the ballade, the tercet, the villanelle, the
clerihew, the cinquain, and haiku.

838   **McCord,** Jean. *Bitter Is the Hawk's Path.* Atheneum, 1971. 149p.
$4.95.

7—   Ten short stories, each a sharp vignette, about people who are
loners, each a victim of a circumstance beyond his control. In
one, a boy meets an old man on his way to an old people's
home, in another a crippled child is set apart by the taboos
of a cave men's tribe, and in the title story an Indian boy is
betrayed by his best friend. Poignant and evocative, perhaps the
outstanding story in the collection is "Images of Loss," in which
a seventeen-year-old orphan, working as a maid for a family
she loves, is thrilled when she overhears plans to move to
Alaska and is stunned with dismay when she realizes that they
have never had any intention of taking her along.

839   **McCoy,** J. J. *The Hunt for the Whooping Cranes;* A Natural History
Detective Story; maps and drawings by Rey Abruzzi. Lothrop,
1966. 223p. $4.95.

8—   It had long been known that the whooping crane was faced with extinction when, in 1945, the National Audubon Society and the United States Fish and Wildlife Service announced jointly that a project had been established. The purposes of the Whooping Crane Project were several, but the primary one was the location of the nesting grounds of the species. The account of the search is detailed and fascinating; the material is well organized and is written in a straightforward style that is not pedantic. Although there are now only forty-odd whooping cranes returning each year to the refuge in Texas, scientists hope that the species will increase. A list of suggestions for additional reading, a glossary, and an index are appended.

840   **McCullough,** Frances Monson, ed. *Earth, Air, Fire and Water;* a collection of over 125 poems selected and ed. by Frances Monson McCullough. Coward-McCann, 1971. 190p. $5.95.

7—   Although some of the poets whose work is included in this very good anthology were born in the previous century, the book is a commentary on contemporary life: war, discrimination, death, love, hate, politics, baseball, or simply reactions to a scene. Many of the poets and their contributions are well known, but there are many new voices included. A section of notes on contributors and an author-title index are appended.

841   **McDermott,** Gerald, ed. *Anansi the Spider;* A Tale from the Ashanti; ad. and illus. by Gerald McDermott. Holt, 1972. 40p. $5.95.

K–2   The story of Anansi, the spider-hero of many African folk tales, here combines two plots. The six sons of Anansi each has a special talent, and together they are able to rescue their adventuresome father when he wanders a long way from home and gets into trouble twice over; then the question of award comes up, and Anansi has so much trouble deciding which son should get the beautiful silver globe in the sky that The God of All Things leaves it there—and the story ends, "It is still there. It will always be there. It is there tonight." The simplicity of the writing style makes this a good adaptation for reading aloud to young children or as a source for storytelling.

842   **MacDonald,** George. *The Light Princess;* illus. by Maurice Sendak. Farrar, 1969. 110p. $4.50. (Gollancz, 1966. 288p. £0.90.)

3–6   A charming story that has stood the test of time, in an edition that follows the full text of the original. The problems of the princess who had been deprived, as an infant, of her gravity and whose life hung in the balance when she grew up are amusing as ever and the sweet capitulation to love that brings her (literally) to her feet, just as touching. All of the best of MacDonald is reflected in the Sendak illustrations: the humor and wit, the sweetness and tenderness, and the sophistication—and they are beautiful.

843   **McFarlane,** Brian. *The Stanley Cup.* Scribner, 1972. 192p. illus. $6.95.

7—   A veteran Canadian sportscaster with a wry sense of humor and an authoritative fund of knowledge about the game of hockey and its history manages, in this book about hockey's top trophy, to get in some wonderful yarns about the colorful and chaotic early days of organized (or, often, disorganized) competition. Several sections of photographic inserts and an appended section of statistical records add to the book's usefulness and its appeal to hockey fans.

844   **McGinley,** Phyllis Louise, comp. *Wonders and Surprises;* A Collection of Poems; chosen by Phyllis McGinley. Lippincott, 1968. 188p. $4.95.

6—   A very pleasant anthology, this, with a preponderance of good, light writing and some pointed or poignant selections. There is traditional material but not the usual accumulation of anthologized pieces, for the most part; the greater number of contributors are modern. A combined author-title index is appended.

845   **McGinley,** Phyllis Louise. *A Wreath of Christmas Legends;* illus. by Leonard Weisgard. Macmillan, 1967. 62p. $4.95.

5–8   A very pleasant gathering of fourteen previously published poems to which has been added one new selection, "The Stars' Story"; all are based on medieval legends about Christmas. The black and white illustrations of birds and beasts have a precise grace, and the page layout is dignified. The poems have the felicitous phrasing, the polished simplicity, and the quick shafts of humor that distinguish Miss McGinley's work.

846   **McGovern,** Ann. . . . *If You Grew Up with Abraham Lincoln;* pictures by Brinton Turkle. Four Winds, 1966. 79p. Trade ed. $2.95; Library ed. $3.27 net.

2–4   Like the author's . . . *If You Lived in Colonial Times,* a simply written and delightfully illustrated book that describes the day-to-day aspects of frontier living; here the book adds some information and some anecdotes about Lincoln. Where would you live? What kind of house would you live in? What was the furniture like? Incorporated into the answers to these and other questions are some facts about how Abe Lincoln (and other boys) dressed, what his chores were, what his frontier cabin was like. The text moves from the Kentucky frontier to New Salem, then to Springfield; thus the author has an excellent opportunity to describe country life, the small town, and the larger town.

847   **McGovern,** Ann. . . . *If You Lived in Colonial Times;* pictures by
Brinton Turkle. Four Winds, 1966. 79p. Trade ed. $2.95; Library
ed. $3.27 net.

2–4   A book that gives a great deal of information and is nicely
appropriate to the capability of the beginning reader: short
topics, simple style, large print; the illustrations are plentiful,
attractive, and often humorous. The running text is divided into
short topics, each headed by a question; for example, "Did
children have to worry about table manners?" or "How did
people get the news?" Through the answers to such questions,
the young reader can get a good picture of daily life in the
colonial period; much of the text is directly concerned with the
activities or living habits of colonial children, but some of the
book gives basic information about colonial industry, or
administration, or communication.

848   **McGovern,** Ann. *Robin Hood of Sherwood Forest;* illus. by Arnold
Spilka. T. Y. Crowell, 1968. 164p. $3.95.

4–6   A simplified version of the Robin Hood legend, with the story
line being stripped of material that is either complicated or
ancillary, and the writing stripped of ornate phrases and obsolete
words. There is still, in the dialogue, enough medieval language
to give color and verisimilitude to the tale.

849   **McGowen,** Tom. *The Apple Strudel Soldier;* pictures by John E.
Johnson. Follett, 1968. 48p. Trade ed. $3.95; Library ed. $3.99 net.

K–3   Maxl was indisputably the best baker in Glutenstern; in fact, the
best in the kingdom of Tuffleburg. His delectable apple strudel had
even caused one dotard to turn back at death's door rather than
give up Maxl's products. Our hero reaches his greatest hour when
a mass baking of strudel by the entire army of Tuffleburg
results in a new kind of ammunition. Unable to resist the smell
of apple strudel, the other army eats to a point of satiety,
surrenders, and adds a medal to the one Maxl receives from
his king. A pleasant bit of nonsense, the exaggeration of the
story and illustrations, and the cozy quality of the war adding to
the appeal of the little man who saves the day.

850   **McGowen,** Tom. *Dragon Stew;* illus. by Trina Schart Hyman.
Follett, 1969. 32p. Trade ed. $1.95; Library ed. $2.49 net.

K–3   As every cook knows, it's how you handle the ingredients that
makes the dish; here the author makes a light-hearted and palatable
story by using familiar components in a new combination. The
king, a man who enjoyed his food, was always losing his
royal cooks because he kept giving culinary advice. When he held a
contest to find a new cook, the winner was a young man who

promised dragon stew—but let the king do all the cooking while waiting for a dragon to appear. The king was happy; he was even happier when he was served dragon stew one day. Turned out that the clever young man (who couldn't cook at all) had asked the dragon for *his* advice, and the result was a delicious dragon stew—that is, stew prepared by a dragon. The illustrations are gay and humorous, matching nicely the slight burlesque of the writing.

851   **McHargue,** Georgess, comp. *The Best of Both Worlds;* An Anthology for All Ages; with designs by Paul Bacon. Doubleday, 1968. 773p. $6.95.

6—   An anthology packed with short stories and excerpts from books for adults and children, the editor's theory being that "if there are many teens who will enjoy reading Hemingway, there are many adults who will enjoy *Stuart Little* with equal zest." Much of the adult material is light fiction of the best grade; many of the children's stories from which material has been used are contemporary. Several old favorites (*Tobermory, The Secret Life of Walter Mitty*) are included, but the range of sources gives the book a niche of its own.

852   **Mackay,** David, comp. *A Flock of Words;* An Anthology of Poetry for Children and Others; compiled, introduced, and annotated by David Mackay; illus. by Margery Gill. Harcourt, 1970. 328p. $5.95. (Bodley Head, 1969. 352p. £1.75.)

6—   A splendid anthology, not representative but highly personal in choice, and based on children's reactions in an English school classroom. The poems are loosely arranged in semi-chronological order, with some suggestion of subject clustering; the general effect, however, is of a flow of poems—as though Mr. Mackay had said, "Oh yes, that reminds me of another. . . ." The poems cover a range of time and sources; a section of notes is followed by author, title, and first-line indexes.

853   **McKay,** Robert. *Dave's Song.* Meredith, 1969. 181p. $4.95.

7–10   A junior novel that is far removed from the formula high school love story, some of the chapters by Kate (who considers Dave a loner, an oddball) and some by Dave (who considers Kate, but secretly). They live in a small Ohio town, which Kate detests, while Dave is devoted to animals and particularly interested in breeding birds. Both are aroused by the injustice of the treatment of a completely rehabilitated ex-convict; Dave is able to see that Kate is more than just a pretty girl, and Kate that Dave is secure in his own philosophy as few young men are. His song is a solo, but it is from strength. Well written, the book is both realistic and romantic. One of the best of the many good relationships is that between Dave and his mother: theirs is a respectful friendship, warmed but not choked by love.

854   **Macken**, Walter. *The Flight of the Doves*. Macmillan, 1968. 200p. $4.50. (Pan Bks., 1971. 160p. £0.20.)

5–7   Orphaned, the two Dove children live in England with their sadistic stepfather, and Finn—who is twelve—decides that he and his seven-year-old sister Derval must run away to their grandmother in Ireland. Since their stepfather learns, just after the children have gone, that they have inherited money, he enlists the help of the police. Tracked by a young detective, Michael, the Doves travel westward; their adventures are varied and believable, and so sympathetic is the author's treatment that it is quite credible that Michael helps them avoid and—in the end—escape permanently from their stepfather. Characterization, style, and dialogue are equally good; the plot is tight-knit and suspense maintained to the very end of the story.

855   **Macken**, Walter. *Island of the Great Yellow Ox*. Macmillan, 1966. 206p. Trade ed. $4.95; Library ed. $3.76 net. (Macmillan, 1966. 196p. £1.05.)

5–9   Set on an Irish island, an adventure story that has a tightly constructed plot, adequate characterization and very good dialogue, a smattering of archeology, and a background that has been beautifully created to give convincingly the atmosphere of the isolated island and its mysterious buried treasure, the Great Yellow Ox. Quite accidentally Conor sees two people— Lady Agnes and her husband, the Captain—looking at an odd map. Conor's next meeting with the elderly couple is on the island, where he and two other lads (plus Conor's baby brother, a delightful and not-too-cute boy of five) have been stranded by a storm. From then on, it is shivers all the way, as malevolent Lady Agnes grimly persecutes the boys who stand between her and the Great Yellow Ox, a long-lost archeological treasure that had been the Golden God of the Druids.

856   **McKown**, Robin. *Lumumba; A Biography*. Doubleday, 1969. 202p. illus. Trade ed. $3.95; Library ed. $4.70 net.

7–10   Although the sympathetic tone verges on the adulatory in some passages, this is an excellent biography of Patrice Lumumba, whose early political life was devoted to moderation and included (to the disapprobation of some of his followers and opponents) a recognition of Belgian accomplishment in the Congo. As the African atmosphere changed and as Lumumba's political experience led to sophistication, he became both more militant and more forthspoken. The history of Congolese independence is complicated; this is as clear as it is possible to be about the factions, successes, reversals, compromises, and betrayals. After Mobutu's coup, Patrice Lumumba's days were numbered; murdered by arrangement at the age of thirty-five, he has been as much venerated as maligned. A bibliography and an index are appended.

857   **McLean,** Allan Campbell. *A Sound of Trumpets.* Harcourt, 1966. 192p. $3.50. (Collins, 1967. 192p. £0.75.)

6–10   A stirring sequel to *Ribbon of Fire,* this novel continues the story of Alasdair Stewart and the struggle of the Skye crofters to hold their land against the depredations of the Factor. Set in 1885, the book gives a forceful and vivid picture of an oppressed people. Alasdair's partisan activities, in the group led by Lachlann Ban, result in his departure for America.

858   **McNeill,** Janet. *The Battle of St. George Without;* illus. by Mary Russon. Little, 1968. 188p. $4.50.

5–7   First published in England, an appealing story of a group of children in a heterogeneous urban neighborhood; first one boy, Matt, then his friends, discover the small fenced area of greenery in which stands an abandoned church. The children realize that some thieves are destroying church property, and they marshall their forces to save the church and to get help from the authorities. In the end, the children learn from the Bishop that the whole area is condemned, but they also realize that—both for him and for themselves—their effort has brought satisfaction and pleasure. The writing style has resilience and humor, and the author gives a lively and varied picture of the urban neighborhood in which, amongst the transient people, live those who remember the old days.

859   **McNeill,** Janet. *Goodbye, Dove Square;* illus. by Mary Russon. Little, 1969. 196p. $4.50. (Faber, 1969. 156p. £1.10.)

5–8   A sequel to *The Battle of St. George Without* is set two years later, when the Dove Square residents have all left the area, cleared for renewal. Matt Mudge discovers that an old man still lives there, hiding in the basement of a deserted house. Matt, determined to protect old Mr. Frick, tries to fend off an inquisitive and unpleasant salesman whose motives he suspects. He discovers that the man had once hidden some money in the old house and is sure that Mr. Frick knows where it is. The story has suspense and pace, but its chief appeal is the same as that of the first book: it is a deftly written and realistic picture of urban life and the characters (Londoners) have both individuality and universality.

860   **McNeill,** Janet. *The Other People*. Little, 1970. 185p. $4.50.
              (Chatto B. & O., 1971. £1.30.)

6–8   Already sad because they were moving to a new house, Kate
              (whose mother had married and was on her honeymoon) was
              even more dejected when she came to Sea View. She had
              envisioned her aunt's guest house as a glamorous resort; it was
              old, shabby, and filled with unexciting people; Aunt Poppy
              was a tired and defeated woman. But Kate became involved
              with the sullen boy whose father bullied him, with the odd young
              man she called the Mad Hatter, with the beautiful girl whose
              boy friend seemed to have forgotten her, and above all with
              the elderly recluse who lived in the house next door. Kate's
              sympathy and initiative are the fulcrum for events that change, to
              some extent, the lives of most of the others, and she finds that
              the experience has created in her an acceptance both of her new
              stepfather and of the move to a new house. The writing has
              vitality and flow, the characters are sharply drawn, and the plot—
              if one can accept Kate's assumption of command in the situation—
              is sturdy. The milieu of the seedy guest house, in which a
              random group of people make the best of a rather dreary holiday,
              has an acrid fidelity.

861   **McNeill,** Janet. *The Prisoner in the Park*. Little, 1972. 184p. $5.95.

5–6   Ned is the first of a group of children to discover the boy
              who is hiding in the Wild End, a neglected part of the park
              that was supposed to be turned into a cycle track. The children
              had been protesting the "improvement" but now their attention
              is turned toward the mysterious newcomer whom they believe
              to be James Morton. James, they've heard on the news, has
              run away from a children's home. The boy not only seems
              ungrateful for the food they bring, but also threatens them. They
              are accomplices, he claims. Then Ned hears that the missing
              James Morton has turned up—so who is the boy they have all
              been helping? Ned's Gran says he's the boy who once tried to
              snatch her purse. The mystery comes to a logical conclusion and
              is woven deftly into the group-life of the children, the effort to
              save the park, the scenes of Ned's family, and the sub-plot: Gran
              has been secretly working as a char. The characterization and
              dialogue are sound, the writing deft enough to bring suspense to a
              story in which there is little dramatic movement.

862   **MacPherson,** Margaret L. *The Rough Road;* illus. by Douglas Hall.
              Harcourt, 1966. 223p. $3.95.

7–10   Rough it was for everyone on the Isle of Skye during the
              depression of the 1930's; rougher still for Jim, whose foster
              parents were unkind as well as poor—as ready with their tongues
              as their hands. Then Jim found a hero, the debonair Alasdair

MacAskill who became a friend—and had the boy help him in his work. When he was goaded beyond endurance, Jim turned on his foster mother, and was later taken to court, where it was ruled that he be sent to a new and more amicable family. The atmosphere, the characterization, and the dialogue are all vivid and convincing.

863   **Madison,** Arnold. *Drugs and You.* Messner, 1971. 80p. illus. Trade ed. $3.95; Library ed. $3.64 net.

4–7   An excellent book on this subject, direct in approach, comprehensive, and well organized. The text covers the legal and illegal use of drugs; types of drugs, their effect, and their abuse; illegal drug traffic and drug control; and the problems of the young person who faces the temptation to try drugs. There is no preaching, but the facts given are so clear and so somber that they may well be more effective than a sermon. The author makes one remark in passing that is succinct and effective, when speaking of the fact that many people have lived to regret their addiction: "But many other people have not lived to regret it, because the misuse of drugs has killed them." The photographs are informative; a glossary and an index are appended.

864   **Mahy,** Margaret. *A Lion in the Meadow;* illus. by Jenny Williams. Watts, 1969. 26p. $4.95. (Dent, 1969. 26p. £1.05.)

5–7   An oversize picture book with strong, bright, page-filling
yrs.   illustrations. The writing style is almost staccato but is an effective foil for a story about imaginative play, and it is strengthened by the lavishness of the pictures. The story begins, "The little boy said, 'Mother, there is a lion in the meadow.' The mother said, 'Nonsense, little boy.' " Mother says firmly that this is a made-up story; she gives the child a match box, telling him that there is a tiny dragon there that will grow huge when it is let free in the meadow, and that it will chase the lion away. Naturally, the boy makes capital of this, coming in to report that the terrible dragon had frightened him and the lion (who turned out to be friendly) away. Protesting that she had just made up a story, mother is firmly told that it had come true. "The mother never made up a story again." The idea of a parent coping with an imaginary situation isn't wholly new in picture books, but the theme is nicely handled and the ending should please and amuse young listeners.

865   **Manchel,** Frank. *When Movies Began to Speak;* illus. with photographs and line drawings by James Caraway. Prentice-Hall, 1969. 76p. $4.25.

7–10   A history of the industry from the time of *The Jazz Singer* to the advent of the large screen, the impact of television, and the competition of foreign films. A sequel to *When Pictures Began to Move,* this describes the outstanding directors and the days of the great stars, the formula pictures, the spectaculars, the wartime films, the international film festivals and their influence on Hollywood, unions and censorship, and technical progress. The writing is informal and straightforward, the photographs interesting. A quite lengthy bibliography and an index are appended.

866 **Manchel,** Frank. *When Pictures Began to Move;* illus. by James Caraway. Prentice-Hall, 1969. 76p. $4.25.

6–9 One of the best of the relatively few books about the history of the motion picture industry for young people. The author describes the first struggling efforts to invent a way to make pictures move, the patent fights and the cut-throat competition, the problems of distribution and the pirating of films as well as the many problems of artistic improvement in the popular new entertainment medium. The photographs illustrating the chapters on the evolution of the star system and the popularity of spectaculars are from classic old films; the names of great inventors, romantic stars, and directorial geniuses stud the pages. The writing is matter-of-fact, the comments pithy; the book ends with the death of the silent film. A good bibliography and an index are appended.

867 **Mann,** Peggy. *When Carlos Closed the Street;* illus. by Peter Burchard. Coward-McCann, 1969. 71p. $3.86.

3–5 Another story about the heterogeneous urban neighborhood of *The Street of the Flower Boxes.* Here the enterprising young hero, Carlos, solves the problem of no play space by closing off the street for a ball game between two rival gangs. He finds that the police take a dim view of tied-up traffic, and learns both that one must go through channels and that the heretofore-feared police can be friendly and helpful. The all-neighborhood turnout and integrated jamboree at the close of the story seems a large dose of sunshine, but the setting and the people are real and sympathetically depicted, and the story should be, because of the background, useful as well as enjoyable.

868 **Manning-Sanders,** Ruth. *A Book of Mermaids;* illus. by Robin Jacques. Dutton, 1968. 128p. $3.95. (Methuen, 1967. 128p. £1.10.)

4–6 Sixteen tales of mermaids and mermen are retold here in sprightly style; they are varied and eminently suitable for reading aloud or storytelling as well as for independent reading; they are from a dozen countries, and they are illustrated with effective black and white pictures. Many are tales of mortals who loved or were loved by the merpeople; one very amusing story is about a young mermaid who fell in love with a whale who was exceedingly irritated by her unwelcome attentions; another is on the familiar theme of the beautiful girl mistreated by her stepmother.

869   **Manning-Sanders,** Ruth. *A Book of Witches.* Drawings by Robin Jacques. Dutton, 1966. 127p. Trade ed. $3.50; Library ed. $3.46 net. (Methuen, 1965. 128p. £1.05.)

4–6   A nicely illustrated compilation of a dozen stories from many countries; some of the tales are as familiar as "Hansel and Gretel" while others are less well known. The writing style is smooth and colloquial, with just enough of that turn of phrase appropriate to the genre to give the stories color without burdening them with either quaintness or floridity. Useful for reading aloud or for storytelling.

870   **Manning-Sanders,** Ruth. *A Choice of Magic;* illus. by Robin Jacques. Dutton, 1971. 319p. $4.95. (Methuen, 1971. 320p. £2.00.)

4–6   Four additional tales have been combined with twenty-eight folk and fairy tales chosen by the compiler as favorites in her own previously published anthologies. Each story has a delicately drawn picture in black and white; a few full-page illustrations in color are included. Most of the sources are European, but some tales come from Africa, India, and Arabia. Since all of Ruth Manning-Sanders's anthologies have been notable for the discrimination of selection and the graceful retelling, this creme-de-la-creme is, as one might expect, a book to treasure, to read alone or aloud, and to use for storytelling.

871   **Manning-Sanders,** Ruth. *Gianni and the Ogre;* illus. by William Stobbs. Dutton, 1971. 192p. $4.95. (Methuen, 1970. 192p. £1.50.)

4–6   Eighteen tales from Mediterranean sources are included in an anthology that maintains the high standard of earlier ones by Manning-Sanders, and that is illustrated with vigorous, dramatic pictures in black and white. Many of the story patterns are familiar: the spurned ragamuffin who returns a wealthy suitor and wins the sultan's daughter; an ogre outwitted by the lad he sought to trap; the stepmother who sends her own daughter off to gain the same wealth that her stepdaughter brought home. The style of the retelling is delightful, the conversational tone livened by dry wit and felicitous phrasing. A good book to read alone or aloud, and a fine source for storytelling.

872   **Mari,** Iela, illus. *The Apple and the Moth;* illus. by Iela and Enzo Mari. Pantheon Books, 1970. 37p. $3.95.

       Mari, Iela, illus. *The Chicken and the Egg;* illus. by Iela and Enzo Mari. Pantheon Books, 1970. 30p. $3.95. (Black, 1970. 36p. £0.75.)

3–5 yrs.   First published in Italy under the titles *La Mela e La Farfalla* and *L'Uovo e La Gallina,* two charming books for the youngest biologists. They have no text, but tell their stories clearly: in the first a moth larva is feeding within an apple, emerges, and spins a cocoon; time passes (indicated by the budding of the branch to which the cocoon is attached). The adult moth flies off, lays an egg on an apple blossom, and the new fruit grows with the tiny egg inside. A clear pictorial presentation of a reproductive cycle. The pictures are dramatically simple, with lots of white space and sharp, clear colors. The *Chicken and the Egg* shows the egg being laid; the growth of the embryo; the brooding hen; the hatching, bedraggled chick becoming fluffy; finally, the chick, imitating its mother, learning to peck for grain and snap at insects.

873   **Marks,** Mickey Klar. *Op-Tricks;* Creating Kinetic Art; kinetics by Edith Alberts; photographed by David Rosenfeld. Lippincott, 1972. 38p. $3.93; Paper ed. $1.95.

5–9   A series of fascinating projects is prefaced by a brief introduction that explains how "the interplay of shapes, the placement of lines, the vibrations of color upon color, reflected light, all create changing optical effects." Although the art projects shown present only an opportunity for copying, the techniques used can be adapted for other, original work by the reader. Most of the projects require only materials that are easily available, but a few may necessitate purchase of supplies of plexiglass, fishing line, compass, etc. The explanations are clear, the projects not too complicated, the results—as shown in photographs—intriguing.

874   **Martin,** Patricia Miles. *Rolling the Cheese;* illus. by Alton Raible. Atheneum, 1966. 44p. Trade ed. $3.95; Library ed. $3.79 net.

K–3   A charming read-aloud story set in San Francisco early in the century; the focus is unusual, the story tightly-constructed, the style simple and lightly humorous. Maria, visiting her uncle Pasquale, is most anxious to join in the weekly contest of Pasquale and his friends; she is sure that she has a chance to roll a wheel of cheese farther than the others. Then she will get the other four cheeses and give them as gifts. Cleverly, Maria gets the other market men to agree that they would like to see her; Pasquale is forced to consent. Maria's small cheese doesn't go farthest, realistically, but it is pushed along by the cheese of the next contestant and a happy little girl wins on a technicality.

875   **Matterson,** Elizabeth, comp. *Games for the Very Young;* Finger Plays and Nursery Games. American Heritage, 1971. 206p. illus. Trade ed. $3.95; Library ed. $3.83 net.

2–5 yrs.   First published in England, an excellent selection of rhymes, with diagrams for the finger plays. The material is divided into categories that are related to the interests and activities of very young children: rhymes and songs about toys, about animals, about things seen in town or on the farm; games to play with feet, number songs, singing and dancing games, etc. Directions for playing games are given in italics, and the musical notation gives the melodic line for songs. A first-line index is appended.

876 **Matthiesen,** Thomas. *ABC; An Alphabet Book;* photographed in color by Thomas Matthiesen. Platt and Munk, 1966. 52p. $2.50.

3–6 yrs. An alphabet book in which each page of text has a facing page that is a full-page, full-color photograph; the quality is excellent, the objects in the photographs familiar ones. The letters are very clear: big, bold upper and lower case with plenty of space to set them, and the word for the facing object, clearly apart from the read-aloud sentence or two at the bottom of the page. This part of the text is a wee, wee bit coy here and there, but it is simple, apposite, and occasionally humorous; for example, eggs: "Eggs have a white shell that protects the food inside them. It is not good to drop an egg unless you like to mop the floor."

877 **May,** Julian. *The Land beneath the Sea;* illus. by Leonard Everett Fisher. Holiday House, 1971. 36p. $4.25.

3–5 As simply written as is consistent with the use of correct terminology and sometimes complex phenomena, this is a good introduction to a subject of growing interest. The sharp lines of the scratchboard drawings show vividly the formations of underwater mountains and trenches, the deep abysses and the guyots. Pictures in series make clearer the textual explanations of volcanic action and erosion. There is brief mention of marine creatures and of the research vehicles used to explore the deep sea, but most of the book is devoted to the terrain of the ocean deeps.

878 **May,** Julian. *Why People Are Different Colors;* illus. by Symeon Shimin. Holiday House, 1971. 31p. $4.50.

2–4 Softly drawn portraits and facial details illustrate a book on racial differences that is written with succinct simplicity. Despite the narrow implications of the title, the text covers a much wider area than color differences; in fact, the substances that cause this are not mentioned, although the relationship between exposure to the sun and skin color is discussed. The book describes many kinds of differentiation: noses, eyes, lips, hair, and size of heads and bodies. The text does not stress the point obtrusively, but makes it clear that all of these adaptations are only superficial distinctions.

879 **Mayer,** Mercer. *Frog, Where Are You?* Dial, 1969. 29p. illus. $2.50.

3–5 yrs. A small book, its story told in pictures (one or two here really are worth a thousand words) and the plot easily comprehensible to the very young pre-reader. A small boy and his amiable dog, who have been gazing dotingly at bedtime at a pet frog in a jar, wake the next morning to find the pet gone. The search is on, and the illustrations show one silly situation after another with just the sort of humor small children love (boy clinging to branches discovers he is draped between the prongs of a deer's antlers). The ending is satisfying, and a general air of cheerful nonsense pervades all.

880

6–9

fantasy

Mayne, William. *Earthfasts.* Dutton, 1967. 154p. Trade ed. $3.95; Library ed. $3.91 net. (Penguin, 1969. 190p. £0.22½.)

Keith and David, dawdling about in the English countryside late one summer evening, encounter an odd lad who seems to appear from nowhere. He is a drummer boy wearing a uniform centuries old, and hard as it is for Keith and David to absorb the fact that Nellie Jack John comes from the 18th century, it is harder for the time traveler. After a series of odd events, David disappears and is presumed dead, but he is found by Keith in still another time slot—the days of King Arthur. The writing style is distinctive, the story line is strong, and the characters vividly drawn, with an occasional affectionate poke at rural community life.

881

5–8

fantasy

Mayne, William. *A Game of Dark.* Dutton, 1971. 143p. $4.50.

Donald Jackson is an English schoolboy, an only child whose mother is stern and puritanical; his father is an invalid, and Donald's only comfort is the vicar—and Mrs. Jackson discourages their friendship. Lonely and unhappy, Donald takes refuge in a fantasy world, a medieval setting in which a huge and predatory worm destroys everything it is path. The story moves back and forth between the two worlds, each superbly drawn, and Donald's victory over the worm comes just as, in real life, his father dies. The psychological implications of Donald's struggle against being beaten down and of his feelings of guilt and resentment may not be obvious to all readers, but his story can be read and enjoyed at surface level, since it has strong development, astute characterization, and a compelling style of writing.

882

6–10

Mayne, William. *The Incline.* Dutton, 1972. 192p. $4.95. (H. Hamilton. 191p. £1.40.)

Set in England early in this century, this is both a moving story of an adolescent boy's difficult introduction into problems of adult life and an engrossing picture of the intricate relationships within a small community. Mason's father is manager of a quarry owned by an old friend, Jedediah, and is incredulous when he learns that Jedediah has turned against him along with the quarrymen who blame the financial failure of the business on him—indeed, they question his probity. Mason, who has just begun his first job as a bank clerk, is doubly troubled because he adores Jedediah's daughter. The owner's actions, in the solution of the problem, are consistent with the wonderfully vigorous character Mayne has drawn, and the ending is dramatic, satisfying, and convincing. Mayne's writing has always been distinguished for its evocation of mood and place, and for the flavor and vitality of its dialogue. Here it is, in addition, especially effective in characterization.

883   **Mayne,** William. *The Old Zion;* illus. by Margery Gill. Dutton, 1967. 64p. $4.50 (H. Hamilton, 1966. 63p. £0.75.)

5–7   First published in England, a new and distinguished Mayne story, with a setting unlike his others. The setting is a small island in the South Seas; the Old Zion is a church, and the plot concerns the shifting of the church to a new location. George, father of two small boys, is the protagonist; naturally lazy, but too much of an opportunist not to work when there might be some glory involved, George is the driving force in organizing the move. Small Beni rides on the roof of the Zion, ringing the church bell in coded directions that tell those carrying the building which way to walk. The characterization and the dialogue are a joy; the picture of the cultural patterns of the islands not seeming colored by an attitude, but seeming only to mirror reality.

884   **Mayne,** William. *Pig in the Middle;* illus. by Mary Russon. Dutton, 1966. 160p. Trade ed. $3.50; Library ed. $3.91 net. (Penguin, 1968. 176p. £0.17½.)

6–9   First published in England in 1965, the story of a group of boys who potter about, working on the rehabilitation of an old barge, The Pig, in an English coastal town. The Pig, hidden away in an old wheat mill, was being readied for a trip to Holland by a small group of adolescent entrepreneurs. No goal save adventure in mind, the boys work in great secrecy, their ploy ending when the old barge catches fire. That's the plot, and it is far overshadowed by the vivid characterization, the good dialogue, and the perceptive portrayal of relationships, both among the boys and within their families.

885   **Mayne,** William. *Ravensgill.* Dutton, 1970. 174p. Trade ed. $4.25; Library ed. $4.21 net. (H. Hamilton, 1970. 174p. £1.25.)

7–10   It was old Wig who started Judith wondering what the family mystery was, when he had a letter from his brother. "That policeman's dead," he said, "the one that was after your Lizzie that time. That was a bit since." Who was Lizzie, and why did Mother refuse to talk about it? If Judith was curious, Bob White—a school acquaintance who lived over the hill at

Ravensgill—was even more so, because he had stumbled onto the mystery as well. And Lizzie was his grandmother. Thus begins the unfolding of an old family feud, with high drama, suspense, taut action, and a vivid set of characters. The dialogue and writing style are excellent, the Yorkshire setting colorful.

886   **Mayne,** William. *Royal Harry.* Dutton, 1972. 160p. $4.95.

5–7   Harriet, when she heard from a lawyer that she had inherited a house and a mountain, was definitely not enthralled by the idea of moving to an isolated place in the country, but her parents were firm. They moved. What twelve-year-old could resist the appeal of the mysterious mountain inhabitants, the lure of finding an old ship, the thrill of being a hereditary Queen? In his deft and graceful style, William Mayne unravels the history of Hartacre House and Royal Harry, the characters and the setting intriguing, the plot somewhat weakened by lack of focus.

887   **Means,** Florence (Crannell). *Us Maltbys.* Houghton, 1966. 250p. $3.25.

6–9   Mary Jane Maltby and her younger sister, Sylvia, are stunned by the news that their parents have decided to take in foster children. Not only that, but five teenage girls with problems! First Bobbi, tough and cynical, then two sisters whose mother is in a mental hospital and whose father is an alcoholic; the last two are Spanish-American sisters. The family adjusts to their new members slowly; the newcomers adjust even more slowly. One of the problems is the town's prejudice against Prudencia and Letitia. There is a town rule that no Negro may stay over night, and Mrs. Maltby decides to test this rule, too; she has become enamored of a deserted baby boy who is Negro. With family agreement, tiny Jamie is taken in; the Maltbys give a party, hoping that Jamie will charm people into acceptance, and that's just what happens. The ending is a wee bit pat, but the characterizations, the relationships of the characters, and the shifts in those relationships, are excellent. Mrs. Maltby, an effusive woman given to cute speech ("a mell of a hess" or "One sell fwoop") is particularly well-conceived, since her gay, childish, affectionate, and energetic personality is one that provides good motivation for her actions.

888   **Mehta,** Rama. *The Life of Keshav; A Family Story from India.* McGraw-Hill, 1969. 223p. $5.95. (Angus & R., 1971. 160p. £1.05.)

6–9   A very good story of contemporary India, the young protagonist caught between the impositions of traditional patterns of living and the desire for an education that will inevitably change those patterns. Helped by a wealthy family, Keshav enters a private school—but there are always pressures in his poverty-stricken and ritual-bound home life that make it difficult to study. The story line is firm, but it is not as important in itself as it is in the role of a sort of rope on which are strung the adornments of the book: the sharply drawn characters, the dramatic or tragicomic scenes of village and family life.

889   **Meigs,** Cornelia Lynde. *Jane Addams;* Pioneer for Social Justice. Little, 1970. 274p. $5.95.

6–10   An excellent biography of the founder of Hull House, whose work inspired hundreds of followers and whose integrity won her international fame. Jane Addams had consistency and conviction, espousing unpopular causes if she deemed them just and accepting with equanimity the public censure expressed in the press. Her role as an instigator of social reform and corrective legislation, her participation in the battles for women's suffrage and world peace, her books, and her political acumen were no more impressive than was her gift for friendship. The writing has warmth and cohesion; it gives a vivid picture of an era. An index is appended.

890   **Meilach,** Dona Z. *Creating with Plaster.* Reilly and Lee, 1966. 73p. illus. $6.95. (Blandford P., 1968. 80p. £1.25.)

7—   An oversize how-to book, profusely illustrated with photographs— some informative, some decorative. The text is straightforward, lucid in its step-by-step explanations, and most explicit about the small techniques that give a professional touch. The author, an artist and art educator, describes several kinds of work with plaster and gives good information about supplies and about the special attributes of different materials. The book should be as useful as guidance for adults working with children as it is for the adult or young adult reader.

891   **Meltzer,** Milton. *Bread—And Roses;* The Struggle of American Labor 1865–1915; Illus. with contemporary prints and photographs. Knopf, 1967. 231p. $3.95.

7–12   A vivid document, profusely illustrated with reproductions of old prints and photographs, and written with compelling force and directness. Using a considerable amount of commentary from contemporary sources, the author describes the horrors of child labor, the misery and poverty of immigrant piece workers and mill hands, the sweat shops and the company towns. Battling against the privileged and wealthy, against hired strike-breakers, and depressions that brought starvation, the laboring class in the United States fought and lost, and fought again; organized and were overthrown, organized and were imprisoned—and organized again. The history ends with the long and bitter struggle of the miners at Ludlow in 1913–1914. A glossary of labor terms, a bibliography, and an index are appended.

892   **Meltzer,** Milton, ed. *In Their Own Words;* A History of the American Negro, 1916–1966. T. Y. Crowell, 1967. 213p. illus. $4.95.

7–10   A third volume in the author's trilogy of American Negro history drawn from primary sources: letters, autobiographical material, excerpts from magazine articles and books, testimony from hearings. Explanatory notes and comments by Mr. Meltzer give background for the excerpts. Like its predecessors, this is an important and stirring book; the three volumes provide a historical study that is uniquely moving and an indictment more powerful than any polemic harangue. Because of the stir and protest of the Negro people, of the legislation of the recent past, of the growing strength of the civil rights movement, this third volume has even more stark and bitter voices than did the other two.

893   **Meltzer,** Milton. *Langston Hughes;* A Biography. T. Y. Crowell, 1968. 281p. $4.50.

7—   An excellent biography, written with vigor and clarity, about the gifted and prolific writer whose life and writing were a testament to his belief that it was a proud thing to be black. Any book about Hughes would be fascinating because of his travels, his friends in the literary world, his involvement in causes; Milton Meltzer has added to that by making vivid the poet's passion for justice and truth. An extensive bibliography of Hughes' writings and an index are appended.

894   **Meltzer,** Milton. *Thaddeus Stevens and the Fight for Negro Rights.* T. Y. Crowell, 1967. 231p. $4.50.

8—   A mature and thoughtful biography of the Pennsylvania lawyer whose years in the United States Congress were marked by bitter opposition from the southern states, since he not only opposed the fugitive slave laws but favored legislation beneficial to northern businessmen. Stevens was the leader of those who moved to impeach President Johnson, was an advocate of public education, and was particularly effective in working for the cause of Negro rights in the years after the Civil War. The writing style is straightforward and the author's viewpoint objective: one of the most useful qualities of the book is that it gives information about the reconstruction period. A bibliography and an index are appended.

895   **Meredith,** Robert, ed. *Exploring the Great River;* Early Voyagers on the Mississippi from De Soto to La Salle; ad. and ed. by

Robert Meredith and E. Brooks Smith; illus. by Leonard Everett Fisher. Little, 1969. 161p. $4.50.

6–9   A vivid account of the journeys of De Soto, Marquette and Jolliet, Hennepin, and La Salle between the years 1541–1682, when La Salle reached the delta and claimed the Mississippi Valley for France. The material is from three original sources, all eyewitness accounts. Save for the illustrations that make many of the Indians seem almost comic characters, this is a valuable book, with fresh, excellent treatment of familiar material. An index is appended.

896   **Meredith,** Robert, ed. *The Quest of Columbus;* ed. and ad. by Robert Meredith and E. Brooks Smith from *The History of the Life and Actions of Admiral Christopher Colon* by Ferdinand Colon; illus. by Leonard Everett Fisher. Little, 1966. 125p. $4.50.

7–10   An adaptation, with no fictionalization or extraneous material, of the history written by Ferdinand Columbus, incorporating material from the correspondence and journals of Christopher Columbus. The adaptors sustain an attitude of simple gravity, presumably inherent in the original; at any rate, the respectful and occasionally ingenuous tone (combined with recurrent notes of filial pride and of piety) lends authenticity and flavor. The format is attractive, with many stark Fisher illustrations in black and white, and with two maps; an index is appended.

897   **Meriwether,** Louise. *The Freedom Ship of Robert Smalls;* illus. by Lee Jack Morton. Prentice-Hall, 1971. 29p. $4.25.

3–5   The story of the black slave who sailed a Confederate ship past the forts guarding Charleston Harbor, and turned *The Planter* over to the Union forces is simply told in an understated partial biography. The book covers Smalls's childhood and ends with the fact that he became captain of the ship he had captured. The illustrations are pleasant, but in several of them the clothing has a modern look. Nevertheless, the drama of the story and the importance of Smalls's contribution make the book valuable for children too young to read Sterling's *Captain of the Planter.*

898   **Merrill,** Jean. *The Black Sheep;* illus. by Ronni Solbert. Pantheon Books, 1969. 74p. $3.95.

4–6   An entertaining fable about our organized and conforming society, written with sharp wit. Into a rigidly structured community of white sheep there is born a black lamb who grows up to be a pacific rebel. He will not wear a sweater, when the whole focus of the group is the perpetual knitting of sweaters, with accompanying rituals of shearing, carding, et cetera. The black sheep wears his own shaggy coat and is perfectly comfortable, and he wastes all his time growing gardens, enjoying the color and scent. In fact, being useless. As the society becomes increasingly compulsive, some of its members wonder about the black sheep, now a pariah; the story ends with a mass realization of the futility of the established pattern, and a new order based on the simple, gentle way of life of the black sheep. Sly but not acid, pointed but not minatory.

899   **Merrill,** Jean. *Mary, Come Running;* illus. by Ronni Solbert. McCall, 1970. 26p. $4.95.

3–5   An unusual Christmas story based on an old Spanish carol and illustrated with small, brilliantly colored pictures of the Nativity, the stiff little figures suggesting the grouping in a crèche. An old gypsy tells a small boy how the gypsies came, too, to Bethlehem. They stole from everybody, old Rom explains, but only so much as each good man would have given gladly; from the tax collectors they stole as much as they could. Joseph was worried. "Mary, come running," he called, when he saw the gypsies taking some chocolate. But Mary serenely made hot chocolate and just as calmly let the gypsy women hold the Babe. Like a queen, the gypsies felt, she welcomed them with grace; with the same dignity she accepted the gifts of the Magi. The vitality and humor of the story have no note of irreverence. A good choice for reading aloud to younger children.

900   **Meshover,** Leonard. *The Guinea Pigs That Went to School;* story by Leonard Meshover and Sally Feistel; photographs by Eve Hoffmann. Follett, 1968. 64p. Trade ed. $3.95; Library ed. $2.99 net. (Blackie, 1970. 64p. £0.80.)

K–2   A description of a first grade class project, with a lightly fictionalized framework and with large, clear photographs that have little of the contrived air that most such books do. A child brings her pet to school, and the teacher grasps the opportunity to teach the children; they get another guinea pig and learn about caring for the animals and later about gestation, the children taking turns measuring and weighing the expectant mother. The amount of information is not too burdensome for the young child, and the style of writing is simple and direct.

901   **Meyer,** Edith Patterson. *That Remarkable Man;* Justice Oliver Wendell Holmes. Little, 1967. 189p. illus. $4.75.

6–9   Although the writing style of this biography is rather quiet and sedate, the subject was a man so lively—as well as remarkable—that the book is not dull. Overshadowed by his loquacious and famous parent, young Wendell was determined to achieve status; after serving in the Civil War and being wounded three times, he entered Harvard Law School and thus began his long career as one of the great thinkers of our legal history. Revered and admired for his professional eminence, Holmes was also a man of great charm and humor; all of these qualities are made vivid by the author, who gives a balanced attention to the personal and professional aspects of the life of Mr. Justice Holmes. A list of books by and about Holmes, and an index are appended.

902   **Meyer,** Howard N. *Colonel of the Black Regiment;* The Life of Thomas Wentworth Higginson; illus. with photographs and engravings. Norton, 1967. 346p. Trade ed. $5.50; Library ed. $4.98 net.

8—   A biography of the young minister whose active participation in abolitionist affairs led to his being appointed commander of a newly formed regiment of black volunteers. Thomas Higginson never lost confidence in the expectation of making soldiers out of slaves, fought for equal pay for his troops, and considered part of his job to be their total education. An important figure in the literary world, Higginson was the confidant of many major authors as well as an author of repute himself. His whole long life was devoted to intellectual and social concerns, so that his biography is inspiring as well as instructive, giving a vivid picture of historical and literary events of almost a century. A divided bibliography and an index are appended.

903   **Michailovskaya,** Kira. *My Name Is Asya.* McGraw-Hill, 1966. 254p. $3.50.

7–10   A junior novel set in Leningrad, where Asya Maikina, just out of school, has her first job; she is a guide and interpreter for Intourist, speaking English and Finnish. Some of the people she escorts are such strong characters that they add to the value of the story rather than making it diffuse. The setting is interesting, the characterization good, and the style mature and distinctive. Asya's love affair with an architectural student comes to an unhappy end when she realizes that he is self-preoccupied and feels no concern for other people. A fine story.

904   **Millard,** Reed. *Clean Air—Clean Water for Tomorrow's World;* by Reed Millard and the editors of Science Book Associates. Messner, 1971. 190p. illus. Trade ed. $4.50; Library ed. $4.29 net.

6–9   One of the most detailed of the many recent books about pollution, this serious approach to the causes and effects of pollutants in our atmosphere includes the discussion of past disasters, present ominous facts, and the research that has brought some solutions and promises others. Well organized, well written; the bibliography and index are preceded by a list of U. S. government agencies concerned with air pollution, water pollution, and water resources.

905   **Miller,** Katherine. *Saint George;* A Christmas Mummers' Play;
illus. by Wallace Tripp. Houghton, 1967. 48p. $3.95.

5–8   A special pleasure for those who enjoy keeping traditional folk
and art forms alive, this is a version of the old English Christmas
play performed in people's homes by enthusiastic amateurs.
The costumes and much of the dialogue are set by custom,
but there is room for improvisation, especially in stage business.
The script and stage directions are given together, with production
notes at the end of the book. The atmosphere of slapstick
humor is echoed in the illustrations.

906   **Milne,** Lorus J. *Gift from the Sky;* by Lorus and Margery Milne.
Atheneum, 1967. 141p. illus. Trade ed. $3.95; Library ed. $3.81 net.

6–10   Telling the true story of a mute swan that came to the author's
home town and settled into living in a pond, the Milnes very
deftly introduce background information about swans. For
example, the "naturalist" of the book writes to Great Britain for
information, and the correspondence provides facts about the
protection and marking of swans. The writing is easy, warmed
by a note of affection and lacking sentimentality. The swan,
later named Alice, aroused so much interest that the town decided
to send for a mate; before that happy day, there had been
exciting months of getting acquainted with Alice—and
occasionally, hoping that *this* disappearance of Alice wasn't a final
one.

907   **Milne,** Lorus. *The Phoenix Forest;* by Lorus and Margery Milne;
drawings by Elinor Van Ingen. Atheneum, 1968. 114p. Trade ed.
$3.95; Library ed. $3.81 net.

5–7   Explaining the legend of the phoenix, the authors go on to
describe the flora and fauna of a hardwood forest in which a
fire starts after a bolt of lightning strikes. Animals flee, and
men fight the raging fire for hours, but the forest is doomed.
Slowly, like the phoenix, the forest is born again, the pioneer
plants paving the way for a gradual return to ecological balance.
The illustrations have a fragile appeal, and the writing is vivid
when it describes the natural environment directly; the book
loses impact when human dialogue is introduced as a method of
giving information. Very informative, this should be hailed by
nature lovers and conservationists. A list of suggestions for further
reading is appended.

908   **Minarik,** Else Holmelund. *A Kiss for Little Bear;* pictures by
Maurice Sendak. Harper, 1968. 32p. (I Can Read Books) Trade
ed. $2.50; Library ed. $2.92 net. (World's Work, 1969. 32p. £0.75.)

1–2   There's always an appeal in a familiar character, and the author and illustrator again prove an irresistible combination in making that character as endearing and amusing as before. Here Grandmother sends Little Bear a kiss in return for a picture he has drawn; the ambassador of good will is Hen, who cocks a leery eye at all the kissing, especially when she has to retrieve the kiss from Skunk, who has been in the communications chain. The chain has broken down because Skunk found it so delightful to pass a kiss to a girl skunk, and the story ends with a skunk wedding attended by the full cast and a somewhat disgruntled Little Bear. The writing is simple, direct, and sunny, and the pictures echo and ornament the story's charm.

909   **Mitchell,** Donald, comp. *Every Child's Book of Nursery Songs;* arranged by Carey Blyton; illus. by Alan Howard. Crown, 1968. 175p. $3.95. (Faber, 1968. 176p. £1.80.)

3–7 yrs.   A very satisfying collection, brimming with old favorites (versions selected by the compilers) and spiced with some selections not as well known; there are many familiar musical games and the accompaniments are as simple as they can be. The illustrations, chiefly black and white, have an antic charm. The selections are not grouped in any pattern but are in alphabetical order from "Aiken Drum" to "Where Are You Going To, My Pretty Maid?"

910   **Mitchell,** Donald, comp. *The Gambit Book of Children's Songs;* comp. by Donald Mitchell and Roderick Biss; illus. by Errol Le Cain. Gambit, 1970. 159p. $7.95. (Faber, 1970. £2.50.)

4–7   A traditional collection, and a good one. Donald Mitchell has chosen, as he states in the preface, to eschew the protest songs of today, and present "in a spirit of affectionate renewal" an anthology of old songs that have qualities that appeal to the young. The sources and the styles are varied, the piano accompaniments simple; the collection includes French and German songs, some classic rounds, songs gay and plaintive. Some of the selections have, in addition to the piano accompaniment, additional notation for percussion or for melody instruments. Separate title and first line indexes are appended.

911   **Mitchison,** Naomi. *African Heroes;* illus. by William Stobbs. Farrar, 1969. 205p. $3.95. (Bodley Head, 1968. 190p. £1.05.)

7—   Polished writing, the fluent and articulate prose of a storyteller whose historical and legendary material is based on an oral tradition, distinguishes eleven tales of great Africans. The settings are south of the Sahara, the time spans six centuries, 1300–1900. Facing maps show Africa today and the sites of the stories. Each account is followed by a brief explanatory note. There is much history in the book, particularly colonial exploitation from the African viewpoint, but the interest and importance of the historical material are put in shadow by the richness and dignity of the people and their intricate, deep-rooted traditions.

912   **Mizumura,** Kazue. *If I Built a Village . . .* T. Y. Crowell, 1971. 26p. illus. $4.50.

4–6
yrs.

Soft watercolors in patterned pictures complement the wistful, tender quality of the text, which envisions a world in which beauty is treasured and kindliness prevails. "If I built a village . . . if I built a town . . . if I built a city . . ." the animals would be free, fish would flash through the waters and the eagle soar in the sky, and, the book ends, "There would be people who would care and share with all living things the land they love." The conservation message is clear, although no mention is made of what it is that men are doing to destroy the beauty of wild things. Quiet, perhaps not for the child who insists on plot and action, but lovely.

913   **Molnar,** Joe, ed. *Graciela: A Mexican-American Child Tells Her Story.* Watts, 1972. 48p. illus. $4.50.

4–6

Graciela is twelve years old, one of ten children in a Chicano family, and she describes their yearly trip to Michigan to pick produce, their efforts to improve financial conditions and to get an education. She is candid about the prejudice against Mexican-Americans in their Texas town, but does not dwell on it, and she speaks with affection of her older sister, her father's going to school, a younger brother's illness. The text is based on taped interviews, the style matter-of-fact; the illustrations show a neat white house and a family of attractive children. The book does not negate the sorrier plight of most migrants and many Chicanos, but adds another dimension.

914   **Monjo,** Ferdinand N. *The Drinking Gourd;* illus. by Fred Brenner. Harper, 1970. 63p. (I Can Read Books) Trade ed. $2.50; Library ed. $2.92 net.

2–3

A story set in the years just prior to the Civil War, the simplicity of dialogue and exposition, the level of concepts, and the length of the story making it most suitable for the primary grades reader. The illustrations are deftly representational, the whole a fine addition to the needed body of historical books for the very young. Tommy Fuller, a New England boy (cheerfully mischievous in the Tom Sawyer tradition) shows that he can be responsible, and turns his imaginativeness to a great cause, when he helps save a slave family traveling north on the underground railway.

915   **Monjo,** Ferdinand N. *The One Bad Thing about Father;* illus. by

Rocco Negri. Harper, 1970. 63p. (I Can Read Books) Trade ed. $2.50; Library ed. $2.92 net.

2–3   Quentin Roosevelt never kept a childhood diary, but this invented one will do very nicely: it is consistently childlike, it gives a vivid impression of the vigorous Theodore Roosevelt and some of the flavor of the period, and it is above all a charming picture of family life. The one bad thing about father is, of course, that he is too busy to play with Quentin and his brother. The writing is ingenuous and candid, the illustrations attractive save for some rather blank children's faces.

916   **Monjo,** Ferdinand N. *The Vicksburg Veteran;* illus. by Douglas Gorsline. Simon and Schuster, 1971. 62p. Trade ed. $4.50; Library ed. $4.29 net.

2–5   Handsome pictures that have the flavor of old engravings add to the value of an excellent historical book for young readers. The story is told by the twelve-year-old son of Ulysses S. Grant, who served with his father in the Vicksburg campaign of 1863, when the North made a fifth attempt to capture the city that controlled the Mississippi. By running the shore battery and crossing below Vicksburg, Grant was able to circle through Confederate territory and achieve victory. The easy simplicity of style and the personal observation give the account an immediacy that makes it vivid; the book has none of the stiffness so often found in descriptions of military action.

917   **Moon,** Sheila. *Knee-Deep in Thunder;* drawings by Peter Parnall. Atheneum, 1967. 307p. Trade ed. $4.95; Library ed. $4.43 net.

6–9   This is one of Those Books, the much-discussed stories of fantasy that are written in high style, have allegorical or psychological depths for the perceptive, and present a real puzzle because so few of the readers who can appreciate the subtleties and cope with the language want to read (at length) about a little girl who goes on a long, hazardous journey with three vocal beetles and an ant of integrity. Maris, resting on a hillside, is transported to another world when she gazes into a strange stone; in this world the power of good is Them, and their opposites are the Beasts. Maris and her companions (they pick up a caterpillar, a spider, a boy, et cetera) learn that they have been chosen by Them to end the depredations of the Beasts; as they gain courage, they gain a small measure of success, and with increasing self-confidence and insight, Maris and her friends attain their goal. Although the story is brightened by amusing characterization and characterful dialogue, it is heavy with a relentless succession of exotic or dangerous episodes and with a self-conscious array of symbolism, mythological overtones, psychiatric interpretations,

and mystical experiences. The talking animals really are best
suited to younger readers, while the writing style (sometimes
beautiful, sometimes precious, often difficult) is best suited to
older readers.

918   **Moore,** Carman. *Somebody's Angel Child;* The Story of Bessie
Smith. T. Y. Crowell, 1970. 121p. illus. $4.50.

6–9   The author is a black musician, the subject the greatest blues
singer of them all, the story dramatic and sad—a blues story.
Unschooled, orphaned, a neglected slum child, Bessie was singing
and on the road before she was adolescent. She came up the
hard way, and when she hit the top, the Empress of the Blues
started down the hard way, too. Extravagant and generous,
Bessie slid into a hard-drinking penury that ended abruptly
with her accidental death before she was forty. The text
includes interpolated lyrics that read, as do most popular lyrics,
flatly, but they may appeal to the reader whose primary interest
is blues or jazz history. The writing is honest, the story
inherently dramatic. A bibliography, a selected discography, a
list of compositions and lyrics by Bessie Smith, and an index are
appended.

919   **Moore,** Clement Clarke. *A Visit from St. Nicholas;* a facsimile of
the 1848 edition; engravings by T. C. Boyd. Simon and Schuster,
1971. 22p. $2.95.

all
ages   A facsimile edition of the 1848 publication of the poem that
was to become a perennial favorite. The frontispiece is labelled,
"Santa Claus's Visit," but the illustrations show a figure that is,
save for his plump paunch, quite unlike the traditional Santa
Claus, but a portly, bearded gentleman clad in knee breeches and
buckled shoes. The book is small, the old-fashioned engravings
are interesting, and the poem loses nothing with the passage of
time.

920   **Moore,** Janet Gaylord. *The Many Ways of Seeing;* An Introduction
to the Pleasures of Art. World, 1968. 141p. illus. Trade ed. $10;
Library ed. $9.91 net.

8—   A stunning book, profusely illustrated, comprehensive in
coverage, and written in a style that has dignity and vitality.
It discusses the relationship between art and nature, and that
between the artist and his world, envisioning the perception of an
object in terms of light and color, of composition and line. The
author suggests ways in which the reader can try for himself
some of the ideas discussed and some of the ways in which he
can learn to see the elements of an art form. In describing the
work of individual artists, Miss Moore is at her best; she also
describes media, materials, and techniques. An excellent divided

bibliography, a list of the illustrations (alphabetically arranged by the artist's name but including page numbers) and an index are appended.

921   **Moore,** Lamont. *The Sculptured Image;* The Art of Sculpture as seen in Monuments to Gods, Men, and Ideas; illus. with photographs. Watts, 1967. 100p. $3.75.

4–9   A good first book about sculpture, with some three dozen works of art illustrated and described by an author experienced in museum education. The sculpture ranges from ancient to modern, with examples from the east, from Europe, and from the United States. The author discusses artistic effects and the ways in which they were achieved by the sculptor, and he explains the distinctive qualities of the examples, relating the art form to purpose, concept, and medium. A list of sculptors represented in the book and an index are appended.

922   **Moore,** Marian. *The United Kingdom;* A New Britain. Nelson, 1966. 224p. illus. Trade ed. $4.95; Library ed. $4.65 net.

7–9   A lively report on changing aspects of life in Britain is preceded by some historical and geographical information, with a good deal more interspersed throughout the book. Much of the writing has a rambling, conversational quality, but the author's interpretations of the British scene are astute and moderate. She discusses governmental structure, education, sports, industry, communication, law, Mods and Rockers, agriculture, the welfare state, the Royal Family, and so on: a bit of everything. A list of sovereigns, another of important dates, a reading list, and an index are appended. The many photographs are of good quality.

923   **Morey,** Walt. *Kävik the Wolf Dog;* illus. by Peter Parnall. Dutton, 1968. 192p. $4.50. (Collins, 1970. 160p. £0.17½.)

6–9   Kävik had been raised and trained as a sled dog by tough old Charlie One Eye, who never had a kind word or caress for his animals. The wolf dog was purchased by a wealthy American and injured in a plane crash when he was being shipped to Seattle; rescued by Andy, a boy of fifteen, the animal learned kindness for the first time in his life—and the kindness grew into affection. Sent on to Seattle, Kävik ran away and made his way north to Alaska and the boy to whom he belonged. The motivation is love, but there is no trace of sentimentality in the writing; the setting is vividly created, and the dangers of the long trek are described with pace and suspense. Kävik had lost his courage at the time of the accident, and Andy was teased by the other boys because his "champion" was afraid of other dogs; Kävik returns after his trip through the wilderness a hard-bitten fighter, and it is Morey's particular talent that he can make an animal character like this so powerfully real and so consistently animal.

924   **Morgan,** Edmund S. *So What about History?* Atheneum, 1969. 95p. Trade ed. $5.95; Library ed. $4.43 net.

4–6   Lively style and fresh perspective make this stimulating and unorthodox approach to history (it is not a history book) provocative, despite the fact that the text occasionally strays to tangential matters. The book stresses the significance of historical interpretation of material objects, from discarded junk to imposing government buildings, as evidence of living patterns and, in the United States, of adaptations from older societies to the new. History, the author points out, is the story of change: change in dress, in buildings, in ideas, and in institutions. To understand one's place in history is easier, he says, if one can "take the cover off the past and see what Americans have been."

925   **Morrison,** Lillian, comp. *Sprints and Distances;* Sports in Poetry and the Poetry in Sport; illus. by Clare and John Ross. T. Y. Crowell, 1965. 211p. $5.95.

6—   A very good poetry anthology: discriminating selection, good format, and—considering the limitations of the subtitle—a surprising range of moods and sources. The poems are grouped into sections entitled "The Games," "Races and Contests," "Pleasures of the Country," and so forth. Sources are cited; appended are indexes by author, by first line, by title, and by sport.

926   **Morton,** Miriam, ed. *A Harvest of Russian Children's Literature;* ed., with introduction and commentary, by Miriam Morton. University of California Press, 1967. 474p. illus. $13.50. (Univ. California P., 1967. 474p. £6.45.)

all
ages   A superb anthology for any collection, useful for a number of diverse purposes and, better still, a source of pleasure in its variety, scope, and quality. All of the material included is in print in Russia today; the selections range from classic writers like Tolstoy and Gorky to contemporary authors, some of whose work has already been published in English—Chukovsky and Sholokhov, for example. The book's contents are divided both by age groups and by genre or type of literature; the illustrations are also from Russian children's books. Many of the selections are preceded by notes about the author. The editor has provided a long, thoughtful, and informative introduction. Separate author and title indexes are appended. A treasure.

927   **Morton,** Miriam, comp. *Voices from France;* Ten Stories by French

Nobel Prize Winners; comp. and ed. by Miriam Morton. Doubleday, 1969. 212p. Trade ed. $3.95; Library ed. $4.70 net.

7—   A fine anthology of distinctive writing, each selection prefaced by an editorial comment. The translation is by the editor, save for one story translated by Lloyd Alexander. Eight of the twelve French authors who have been awarded the Nobel Prize for Literature are included: Camus, France, Gide, Martin du Gard, Mauriac, Mistral, Rolland, and Sartre.

928   **Mosel,** Arlene, ed. *Tikki Tikki Tembo;* retold by Arlene Mosel; illus. by Blair Lent. Holt, 1968. 43p. Trade ed. $4.50; Library ed. $3.97 net. (Bodley Head, 1969. 48p. £0.90.)

K–2   An amusing picture book to read aloud, since the crux of the story is the long, long name (for which the title is an abbreviation) with its rhythm, nonsense, and rhyme. When Tikki Tikki Tembo's brother falls into a well, it isn't too hard to summon help from the Old Man with the Ladder, who comes down from his hill in obliging fashion to rescue and dry out little Chang. When Tikki Tikki Tembo falls in—that's another story. The writing style has bounce and humor; the line and wash illustrations echo the humor of the folktale and have an appropriately Oriental beauty.

929   **Mother Goose.** *London Bridge Is Falling Down!* illus. by Peter Spier. Doubleday, 1967. 40p. $3.95.

K–2   A romping version of the singing game, each verse with its picture in a double-page spread, with most of the space devoted to illustrations filled with small—and often very funny—details. "How shall we build it up again?" is, for example, illustrated by a picture of an architect's office; one tiny detail is a portrait of a bewigged and rather pompous gentleman proudly holding his T-square. Many of the details have historical interest (a hogshead of tobacco labeled "Williamsburg Virginia Colony"). Some notes on the history of the bridge are appended, as are the words and music for the song.

930   **Mother Goose.** *Mother Goose Lost;* collected by Nicholas Tucker; illus. by Trevor Stubley. T. Y. Crowell, 1971. 30p. $4.50. (H. Hamilton, 1971. 30p. £1.25.)

2–5 yrs.   A university lecturer in experimental psychology, Nicholas Tucker was doing research on nursery rhymes for an article when he came across a number of unfamiliar rhymes that had not been included in the earliest anthologies. The rhymes chosen for this book range from a few that are a bit flat to others— the majority, by far—that have verve and rhythm and humor. The illustrations are colorful and gay, the whole a supplement to

more familiar collections. The book should interest adults
concerned with children's literature and delight the unconcerned
children for whom the literature exists.

931   **Mother Goose.** *Rimes de La Mere Oie;* Mother Goose Rhymes
rendered into French by Ormonde de Kay; designed and illus.
by Seymour Chwast, Milton Glaser, Barry Zaid. Little, 1971.
89p. $7.50.

3–6
yrs.   Sixty-eight Mother Goose verses in French are followed by the
same rhymes in English; there are no page references to the
French versions, but these are assigned page numbers at the
beginning of the book. The book, like *Mother Goose in French*
(translated by Hugh Latham and illustrated by Barbara Cooney)
is attractive but difficult to place for the child who is not
French-speaking, since the child who can read the verses as a
student of French will probably be too old for nursery rhymes,
and the preschool child who has no French will not appreciate
them. The book is probably best placed in a foreign language
collection. As in the Latham, the translations bend to accommodate
rhythm and idiom; of those rhymes found in both books, the
Latham falls more into the spirit of nursery rhymes, while this is
more polished as poetry; both will probably be wanted to round
out collections. Unlike Barbara Cooney's pictures, which have a
French flavor, those in this version are in varied styles and
techniques; those by Zaid are unimpressive; those by Chwast
intriguing, those by Glaser stunning.

932   **Mowat,** Farley. *The Curse of the Viking Grave;* illus. by Charles
Geer. Atlantic-Little, Brown, 1966. 243p. $4.50.

6–9   An adventure story set in the Canadian far north, where three
boys of disparate ethnic backgrounds live and hunt together.
Orphaned Jamie lives with his Uncle Angus Macnair; living with
them for a time are Peetyuk, the child of an Englishman and an
Eskimo, and the Cree boy, Awasin. When Angus is hospitalized
while away on a trip, the three strike out for a Viking grave in
the Barrenlands. Their experiences in the wilds, their encounters
with Indians and Eskimos, and their personal relationships are all
told in a lively and convincing story. The story line would seem
over-extended were it not for the exotic background and the
wonderful spirit of acceptance among peoples of different origins.

933   **Moyes,** Patricia. *Helter-Skelter.* Holt, 1968. 243p. Trade ed. $4.50;
Library ed. $3.97 net. (Macdonald, 1969. 165p. £0.90.)

7–10   Felicity ("Cat") Bell is eighteen, English, and mad for sailing;
she doesn't look forward, she tells us, to a visit with relatives—
but at least they live at a naval research base. Convinced that
she has seen something corpse-like in the water, and curious

about her uncle's reports of a security leak at the base, Cat snoops. Her snooping leads to some exciting adventure and even danger, in this better-than-average teenage mystery story, smoothly written (and convincingly Cat's own version) and artfully plotted.

934   **Murray,** Michele. *Nellie Cameron;* drawings by Leonora E. Prince. Seabury, 1971. 185p. $4.95.

4–6   Sometimes a child in a big family can feel she has no place. Nellie was nine, she felt lost in the shuffle, and she was miserably conscious of the fact that she couldn't learn to read. Sent to the school reading clinic, Nellie was both apprehensive and hopeful. Much of the story is devoted to Nellie's progress with a sympathetic teacher, but the book is balanced by family scenes and is perceptive in describing the relationships within the family.

935   **Myron,** Robert. *Modern Art in America;* by Robert Myron and Abner Sundell. Crowell-Collier, 1971. 219p. illus. $4.95.

7—   An excellent survey of American art in the twentieth century, chronologically organized, broad in scope, and including painting, sculpture, architecture, and such art forms as mobiles. The authors discuss both art movements and individual artists, architectural styles and the planning of model communities, techniques and criticism. The writing is direct and lucid, and the book is especially useful for the way in which it clarifies overlapping trends, conflicting theories, and the cause-and-effect relationships among individual artists, groups of artists, art critics, and cultural influences. A bibliography and an index are appended.

936   **Nathan,** Dorothy. *The Shy One;* illus. by Carolyn Cather. Random House, 1966. 179p. $3.50.

4–6   A pleasant story about a Russian Jewish family, set in a small Oregon town in 1921; the shy one is Dorothy, a fifth-grader, and she is timid about almost anything: meeting people, playing in a recital, barking dogs. She is shy about meeting her grandmother and her Uncle Max when they come over from the old country, and she yearns to be as confident and outgoing as her little sister. Spurred by a desire to help the school paper drive, she talks to some adults; spurred by a wish to have Max participate, she accompanies him on the piano for a class program. The book doesn't have a strong story line, but the episodes are tied together smoothly, and the period details are delightful.

937   **Nesbit,** Edith. *The Conscience Pudding;* illus. by Erik Blegvad. Coward-McCann, 1970. 46p. $3.29.

4–6   A Christmas story taken from *The New Treasure Seekers,* one of the books about the Bastable children that have become classics.

Here the children's father, in some financial difficulties, is going to
be away for Christmas and has told the maid to be thrifty and
prepare a plain pudding. Christmas is going to be bleak enough
as it is, the children decide, and they go into full production
on plans for an elaborate Christmas pudding. There are amusing
obstacles to gathering ingredients, cooking the pudding, and disposing of it, but it is the misinterpretation of recipe instructions
that will probably be most entertaining to readers; for example, the
pudding is to be served "ornamented with holly and brandy poured
over it." Instead of brandy, the Bastables decide to use water,
and they chop up the holly, mix it with water, and pour it
over the pudding. The period details are echoed with charm by
the illustrations, and there are enough of them to flavor the
story without robbing it of a timeless appeal.

938   **Nesbit,** Edith. *Long Ago When I Was Young;* illus. by Edward
Ardizzone. Watts, 1966. 127p. $5.95. (Whiting, 1966. 144p. £0.90.)

6—   First published in 1896 as a series of stories in a magazine
for girls, these twelve episodes from Edith Nesbit's childhood
are combined for the first time in book form. A long introduction
by Noel Streatfeild discusses the Nesbit books with discernment
and affection. Here the twelve episodes have the same vitality
and universality that distinguish the Bastable stories, so that
there is no sense of being old-fashioned despite the old-fashioned
setting. The author writes of the boarding school she disliked
and of the fellow pupil she detested; she describes a stay in
Paris, a frightening incident in Bordeaux, a happy summer on a
farm in Brittany, and an attempt to help an older brother stuff a
fox he'd shot by accident.

939   **Ness,** Evaline. *Sam, Bangs & Moonshine;* written and illus. by
Evaline Ness. Holt, 1966. 48p. Trade ed. $4.50; Library ed. $3.97
net. (Penguin, 1969. 36p. £0.17½.)

K–2   Sam (Samantha) is a small, mendacious girl and Bangs is her cat,
who talks to her; moonshine is the word for all of the fibs
Sam tells herself. When Sam's moonshine almost causes a
tragedy, she learns for herself the danger of lying. Thomas, a
very small, solemn child who firmly believes Sam's lies, is sent
off to a rock where he is exposed to tide and storm; patiently
waiting to see the mermaid there, he is rescued by Sam's father.
The three-color illustrations have a felicitous combination of
realistic approach and some stylized details.

940   **Neufeld,** John. *Edgar Allan.* Phillips, 1968. 95p. $4.50.

6–9   Twelve-year-old Michael tells the story of Edgar Allan, the Negro
baby who is adopted by his family. Michael's father is a minister
in a small California town, and he has told the adoption agency

that they wanted "someone who might need help more than other children." Michael and the two younger children accept Edgar Allan, but the oldest girl, fourteen, cannot—nor can the minister's congregation. For Michael, who has a high ethical sense, the prospect of giving the child up is a betrayal of all his parents have taught him. When criticism turns to persecution, Edgar Allan is sent away, and Michael finds it difficult to forgive his father. Unhappily, he accepts the fact that society is not ready to practice the love it preaches, and that even a good man may not be strong enough to resist the pressure of society. Despite the tinge of case history, this is an important and a touching book, especially adept in portraying the conflicts and relationships within the family.

941   **Neumann,** Rudolf. *The Bad Bear;* English text by Jack Prelutsky; pictures by Eva Johanna Rubin. Macmillan, 1967. 25p. $3.95. (Methuen, 1967. 26p. £0.67½.)

K–2   When first published in Germany in 1964, this was listed by the International Youth Library as one of the best books of the year. The illustrations are bold with color and busy with detail; the story is told in bouncy rhyme. "The nastiest bear that ever was born" is introduced as a voracious creature who spoils picnics and menaces the population in his search for food and more food. When the bear and the court fiddler fall into the same pit, the bear learns to sing and dance; this is the turning point in his life, and he becomes so amiable that he is the children's playmate and is pardoned by the governor at a feast in the palace garden. The plot is a bit thin, but the notes of nonsense and exaggeration are appealing.

942   **Neumeyer,** Peter F. *The Faithful Fish;* pictures by Arvis L. Stewart. Scott, 1971. 44p. $4.50.

K–3   Every time the Simpson children went fishing, they caught the same sculpin, an ugly fish and not good for eating, and threw it back. Disappointed at not having a fish dinner, the children were frustrated and also baffled by the sculpin's reappearance. Maybe he liked them, their mother suggested, and by the time the family left their vacation cottage, they certainly felt a surprising affection for the fish. On their heels came another family that had rented the cottage, and again there was a rush to go fishing, and again there was a quick tug on the line. Mackerel. One family is white, the other black, and the two episodes—although not balanced in treatment—augment each other, adding both to the impression of the delights of fishing (seldom touched on in children's stories) and of the summer vacationer's awareness of fleeting tenure. The illustrations are overly busy, the story told with brisk ease.

943

8–10

cont probs

Neville, Emily Cheney. *Fogarty*. Harper, 1969. 182p. Trade ed. $3.95; Library ed. $3.79 net.

There have been several books about high school dropouts, but few about the college student who abruptly leaves school as Fogarty did in his first year of graduate study. His mother put up with his loafing about, but was disturbed; Malone didn't mind Fog hanging around his garage, but couldn't understand why he didn't want a job; even fifteen-year-old Paul, who looked on Fog as his mentor, was baffled by such inertia. Fogarty, who has secretly been working on a play, goes to New York to watch rehearsals, lives through a disastrous performance at the Storefront Theatre, and goes off to think. He looks fruitlessly for work and suddenly is smitten by the realization that there is a place for people who love books and care deeply for children, that his whole relationship with young Paul has been that of pupil and teacher—and so he teaches. Very well written, economically cast, thoughtful, and timely.

944

5–7

Neville, Emily Cheney. *The Seventeenth-Street Gang*; pictures by Emily McCully. Harper, 1966. 148p. Trade ed. $3.50; Library ed. $3.27 net. (Harper & Row, 1967. 148p. £1.25.)

Although this story of a group of children in New York has a protagonist, it is the group itself that stands out; Minnow, the girl who is the catalyst, affects relationships within the group. Minnow has aggressive tendencies that are seldom repressed, and when a new boy moves into the neighborhood of the Seventeenth Street gang it is Minnow who keeps inciting hostility. The others really like Hollis. In the end, Minnow is forced to accept Hollis because of group pressure. Both as a group and as individuals, the children are drawn with devastating clarity; Minnow will remind many readers of the imperturbably mendacious Sarah of *Johnnie Tigerskin* (Duell, 1966). One of the most striking things the author does is to reflect, with percipient fidelity, the double behavior patterns children display as they move from the circle of their peers to the relationships with adults—particularly with parents.

945

5–7

Neville, Emily Cheney. *Traveler from a Small Kingdom*; pictures by George Mocniak. Harper, 1968. 197p. Trade ed. $3.50; Library ed. $3.27 net.

The small kingdom of Emily Cheney Neville's childhood was the Place, the small community of Cheney relations whose homes formed a self-sufficient oasis in the middle of South Manchester, Connecticut. In 1927 there was money for maids and governesses, there was leisure to play with assorted cousins of the small kingdom, and there was little to prepare a seven-year-old Emily for the world outside, for the death of a mother and the depression that made it necessary to learn to cook. The story flows like a gentle stream, clear and candid, gravely shadowed yet never sad; the Emily who is described in third person is seen with objectivity.

946   **Newlon,** Clarke. *Famous Mexican-Americans;* illus. with photographs. Dodd, 1972. 187p. $3.95.

6–9   Although the writing in this collective biography is often tinged with florid journalese, it is lively and informal, enthusiastic rather than adulatory. The foreword, by a Chicano psychiatrist and educator, gives good background for the biographies of twenty Chicanos who have become known for their achievements in many fields. Anglos can learn; Chicanos can be proud—that is the message. A list of source materials and an index are appended.

947   **Nickel,** Helmut. *Arms and Armor in Africa.* Atheneum, 1971. 58p. illus. $5.25.

5–9   The Curator of Arms and Armor for the Metropolitan Museum of Art describes and illustrates with his own drawings and with photographs both contemporary and ancient weapons and armor. The information in the text is related to facts about the cultures of the peoples discussed and the material is divided by region: West Africa, the Sudan, the Congo, East Africa, North Africa, and South Africa. A map precedes the text; an index is appended.

948   **Nickel,** Helmut. *Warriors and Worthies;* Arms and Armor through the Ages; color photographs by Bruce Pendleton; black and white photographs courtesy of the Metropolitan Museum of Art. Atheneum, 1969. 122p. Trade ed. $10; Library ed. $9.48 net.

6—   A superb history of arms and armor, the illustrations from the collection of the Metropolitan Museum of Art, of which the author is curator of arms and armor. The book begins with the arms of Egypt and Sumeria, includes Asian and Pre-Columbian military equipment, gives particularly detailed attention to developments in the 11th–16th centuries, and traces the development of swords and firearms, concluding with the weapons of the frontier in 19th century America. Although reference use is limited by the lack of table of contents or index, the book is useful as well as handsome, since historical background is given for many of the facts, and a glossary, labeled pictures of Gothic and Renaissance armor, and a listing of figures of speech derived from chivalric times or from ancient firearms are appended.

949   **Nic Leodhas,** Sorche. *Claymore and Kilt;* Tales of Scottish Kings and Castles; illus. by Leo and Diane Dillon. Holt, 1967. 157p. Trade ed. $3.95; Library ed. $3.59 net.

7–9   A collection of historical tales, some with folk tale overtones,

from the time of King Fingal in A.D. 211 to the reign of James
VI in the 17th century. Almost the first third of the book is
given to a long preface that gives background information for each
of the eleven tales. The writing style is heavier than that used
by the author in her previous books, and these tales have only a
hint of the humor that pervades the folk material. The historical
details are interesting, and the dialogue has the true cadence
of Scottish speech; the tales are varied, colorful, and dramatic.

950   **Nic Leodhas,** Sorche. *Sea-Spell and Moor-Magic;* Tales of the
Western Isles; illus. by Vera Bock. Holt, 1968. 207p. Trade ed.
$4.95; Library ed. $4.27 net.

4–6   A collection of folktales from the Hebrides, with one story about
the mythical island of eternal youth and the other nine each
representing one of the Western Isles of Scotland. The tales are
varied, rich with humor and sage lore, populated with giants,
fairies, and other fanciful creatures, but chiefly engrossing because
they are so well told, the colloquial flow of narrative tinged
with Gaelic.

951   **Nicole,** Christopher. *Operation Destruct.* Holt, 1969. 230p. Trade
ed. $4.50; Library ed. $3.97 net.

7–10   A fledgling spy comes through his first assignment: British vs.
Russian Intelligence, a new biological weapon at stake, and mortal
combat in, on, and under water. Jonathan enlists the help of a
pretty girl reporter in besting the too-omniscient-to-be-true
Nobel winner, Madame Anna Cantelna, on land and sea. And
train. The light-hearted style is a perfect channel for a blundering
youngster, the plot has the mad pace of "The Man from
U.N.C.L.E.," and nothing (save the triumph of one set of agents
over another) is according to formula—even the pretty girl, who
falls for a pop singer.

952   **Noble,** Iris. *Emmeline and Her Daughters;* The Pankhurst
Suffragettes. Messner, 1971. 190p. Trade ed. $3.95; Library ed.
$3.79 net.

6–10   A lively and informative biography of the woman who left the
seclusion of a Victorian home a half-century ago to crusade for
woman's suffrage. Emmeline Pankhurst and her three daughters
devoted the major part of their lives to leading Englishwomen of
all classes in the long struggle for equality. Imprisoned, scorned,
and at times beaten, the Pankhursts and their associates moved
from speeches and resolutions to mass demonstrations, hunger
strikes, and even destruction of property to gain publicity and
support for their cause. It took over thirty years—and there were
quarrels within the group bitter enough to cause permanent
rifts—but women got the vote. While there were other groups

working for women's suffrage, none achieved the stature of
Emmeline Pankurst's Women's Social and Political Union. The tone
of the book is admiring but far from adulatory, the author's
attitude that of enthusiasm for the cause and objectivity toward the
women. A bibliography and an index are appended.

953   **Nolen,** Barbara, ed. *Africa Is People;* Firsthand Accounts from
Contemporary Africa; illus. with photographs. Dutton, 1967. 270p.
$6.95.

8—   A most interesting anthology, each selection preceded by a brief
editorial note on the context of the excerpt and on the author.
Some of the contributors are well known (Jomo Kenyatta, Alan
Moorehead, Norman Cousins, Julius Nyerere) and some less so;
their backgrounds are as varied as their topics, which range from
old tribal patterns and the cultural conflict between old and new, to
the burgeoning growth and change in educational, industrial,
and cultural areas as well as in the political arena in Africa
today. A bibliography and an index are appended.

954   **North,** Joan. *The Cloud Forest.* Farrar, 1966. 180p. $3.95.

7–10   Although the protagonist in this fanciful suspense story is a boy
of twelve, the sophistication of the vocabulary and the nuances
of writing style indicate an appeal for a somewhat older audience.
First published in England, this is the tale of Andrew, who lives
with his adoptive mother, a teacher, at a girls' boarding
school although he attends a school in town. Andrew gets no
love from Miss Badger, and he cannot understand why she adopted
him. Andrew and his friend Ronnie find a ring that has magical
properties; from the ring the shy, quiet boy draws courage, and
dreams of the cloudy white forest where he comes into his own.
Few readers will be surprised to find that Andrew is the heir
to the local great estate, defrauded of his inheritance by a scheming
relative. Despite the melodrama and the element of evil
enchantment, the book has vitality because of the writing style,
which is good; the dialogue, which is very good; and the
characterization, which is masterful.

955   **North,** Joan. *The Light Maze.* Farrar, 1971, 186p. $4.50.

6–9   Kit Elton, recovering from illness and an unhappy love affair,
comes to stay with her godmother, Sally, and Sally's daughter
Harriet in a rambling old country house from which, two years
before, Sally's husband Tom had mysteriously disappeared.
Among his papers Kit finds references to the Lightstone and the
Light Maze; holding a milky, circular ornament in her hand, she
dreams she is in a corridor of light. This is the beginning of an
effort, by Kit and others, to penetrate the mystery of the
Lightstone, an adventure in which they leave the world and

enter the Maze. Woven through and into the fantasy is a sharply realistic and witty portrayal of village life that gives balance and validity to a story conceived with fresh, imaginative skill and written with grace.

956   **North,** Joan. *The Whirling Shapes.* Farrar, 1967. 183p. $3.95. (Hart-Davis, 1968. 176p. £1.05.)

7–10   A novel of adventure and fantasy that quickly establishes a mood of mystery and keeps its momentum while the mood deepens. The writing is skillful, with good dialogue and characterization, and the story line is tight save for a small diffusion at the close of the story. Liz, visiting her cousin Miranda's home in London, is baffled by the strange house that appears and disappears on the heath seen from her window. Steadily the whirling shapes that inhabit the heath trap one after another of the characters in the story . . . then they begin to consume the house itself. The five remaining people go back in time and are saved by Liz, chosen because she is the youngest, who makes a journey alone and closes the gap in time.

957   **Norton,** Mary. *Poor Stainless;* illus. by Beth and Joe Krush. Harcourt, 1971. 32p. Trade ed. $3.25; Library ed. $3.30 net. (Dent, 1971. £1.00.)

3–5   At long last, another story about the Borrowers, this one told as a reminiscence by Homily when Arrietty begs her mother for a tale about her girlhood. Homily obliges with an anecdote about the time one of her neighbors was lost. Hunting for Stainless, the Borrowers braved the dangers of unknown parts of the house, risking being seen by human beings. While the intrepid crew was searching, Stainless was having the time of his life. He had been trapped in a shoe that had been taken to town for repairs, and had been able to get back because he recognized the shopping basket and popped inside it—and meanwhile he had had a glorious week of living unseen in the rich resources of a store's candy counter. Brief and lively, delightfully illustrated, this has less substance than its predecessors, but it shares the charm of the miniature world of *The Borrowers.*

958   **O'Brien,** Robert C. *Mrs. Frisby and the Rats of NIMH;* illus. by Zena Bernstein. Atheneum, 1971. 233p. $5.95.

4–6   As a widowed mouse and mother, Mrs. Frisby needed help with her problem: how could she move without endangering the life of her sick son, who was not to be exposed to the inclement weather? Advised by a wise owl, she applied to the rats who lived under the rosebush and whose behavior was so mysterious. And so, within this fanciful framework, comes a second story, the saga of the rats of NIMH (a laboratory) who had been used in a series of experiments intended to raise their intelligence level. The rats were able to read and write, so they found a way to escape and were now able to create their own highly sophisticated and civilized community. Both the story and the tale within it are deftly told, fulfilling the first requisite of fantasy by making the impossible believable. The characters are credible, their adventures entertaining, and their conversation natural.

959   **O'Dell,** Scott. *The Black Pearl;* illus. by Milton Johnson. Houghton, 1967. 140p. $3.75. (Longman Young Bks., 1968. 144p. £ 0.80.)

7–12   It was legendary knowledge in Ramon's village that there was in the waters of Baja California a giant manta, the Manta Diablo, vicious and intelligent, large as the largest ship in La Paz harbor. This was the creature that Ramon angered when he found a giant black pearl in the watery cave that was the Manta Diablo's lair; his other enemy was the Sevillano, best pearl diver in Ramon's father's crew. Ominously circling its prey, the Manta pursues Ramon's small boat and, in killing the Sevillano, also dies; Ramon gives the black pearl to the Madonna-of-the-Seas, a gift of love. The stark simplicity of the story and the deeper significance it holds in the triumph of good over evil add importance to the book, but even without that the book would be enjoyable as a rousing adventure tale with supernatural overtones and beautifully maintained tempo and suspense.

960   **O'Dell,** Scott. *The King's Fifth;* decorations and maps by Samuel Bryant. Houghton, 1966. 264p. $3.95. (Longman Young Bks., 1967. 272p. £0.90.)

7–10   Fifteen-year-old Esteban sailed with Admiral Alarcon as a cartographer; carrying supplies for Coronado, the expedition went astray and a small group was put ashore to find Coronado's camp. Thus begins a harrowing story of the exciting and dangerous journey in search of the fabled gold of Cibola; the story is told, two years later, from the jail in which Esteban is awaiting trial. It is told in retrospect by Esteban, and it shifts periodically back to the prison and then to the trial. The transitions are smooth and functional; the story is vividly written. Accused of withholding the fifth share that is the due of the King of Spain, Esteban is given a three-year sentence, electing to stay in jail rather than to accept an offer of escape if he will go back to find the hidden treasure.

961   **O'Dell,** Scott. *Sing Down the Moon.* Houghton, 1970. 137p. $3.95.

6–9   Bright Morning is the young Navaho girl who tells the story of her people; like the heroine of *Island of the Blue Dolphins,* she has a quiet courage that prevails over circumstance. Her tribe is one of those forced out of their homes by white men and driven on the long march to Fort Sumner. It is Bright Morning who convinces her husband to escape; together they make their way to a small, hidden canyon where they can start anew and alone to live the peaceful Navaho way. The very simplicity of the writing, at times almost terse, makes more vivid the tragedy of the eviction and the danger and triumph of the return.

962

6–9

Women

Ogilvie, Elisabeth. *The Pigeon Pair.* McGraw-Hill, 1967. 182p. $4.50. (Angus & R., 1968. 176p. £0.90.)

It was Papa who called Ingrid and Greg his "pigeon twins," and it is Ingrid who looks back at eighteen to describe her childhood in a small Maine coastal town. Ingrid's family was poor, and the fact that Mama daydreamed and Papa boasted and talked about his family pride didn't help. The Snow family may have founded the town, but Ingrid Snow still wore hand-me-downs and was teased about them. The twins dreamed of the day when they could buy back the old Snow house, but as they grew older, Greg seemed to care less and less. Not until Greg committed an act of vandalism, desperate at hearing the house was going to be sold, did Ingrid realize that her twin still cared about their dream. The picture of the Snow's family life is given with an almost aching fidelity: the amiable, shiftless mother and the not quite honest father; Greg, defeated by his environment and withdrawing from people, and Ingrid grimly holding the family together after her mother's death. An honest and intelligent story.

963

2–5
yrs.

Ogle, Lucille. *I Spy;* A Picture Book of Objects in a Child's Home Environment; by Lucille Ogle and Tina Thoburn; illus. by Joe Kaufman. American Heritage, 1970. 189p. Trade ed. $3.95; Library ed. $3.79 net.

Two labelled pictures on each page afford small children the pleasure of recognizing familiar objects or learning new ones. Some of the illustrations may not be perfectly clear (is every bow a hair ribbon?), some of the pictures show objects that are not necessarily in the home environment (a rabbit, skis), and some of the objects are toys (rather than real machines or vehicles). On the whole, however, the book should be useful for extending vocabulary and for classifying objects. Several pages addressed to adults suggest various ways in which the book can be used to play games, the clues given by the adult (who says, "I spy. . .") stressing color, shape, size, function, etc.

964

Ojigbo, A. Okion, comp. *Young and Black in Africa.* Random House, 1971. 107p. illus. $3.95.

6–10   Seven excerpts from autobiographies, plus one reprinted article, each prefaced by the editor's introductory remarks, give a picture—collage in effect—of facets of African life. All but one of the selections are contemporary, and they include reminiscences of childhood, reactions to the United States, an example of the indignity and injustice of apartheid, and a country boy's experiences on a first visit to a city. The one older selection is from Olaudah Equiano's life story, the excerpt describing how he was kidnapped into slavery in 1756. The writing styles vary from flat narrative to a lively sense of the dramatic (Peter Abrahams) but the material is always interesting and often moving.

965   **Olsen,** Ib Spang. *Smoke;* written and illus. by Ib Spang Olsen; tr. by Virginia Allen Jensen. Coward, 1972. 40p. $4.95.

K–2   A new book from the winner of the Hans Christian Andersen Medal has Olsen's typical vigor and humor, and the combination of realism and fantasy he has used in the past. Here a family bent on a country outing discover that the air is everywhere polluted by smoke. They cap one set of chimneys in a factory with their personal belongings (with a hat grown ridiculously large covering one chimneytop, for example) and empty their pockets to pay for stopping the smoke in another factory. *What* they do is nonsensical, but it gets the message across: pollution is not somebody else's concern, but something each of us can work to abolish. The plot is servant to the message but the book is not overburdened, since the style is light and the pictures gay.

966   **Oppenheim,** Joanne. *Have You Seen Roads?* Scott, 1969. 35p. illus. $3.95.

K–2   An oversize book, handsomely designed, with fine photographs that complement and illustrate the text. The writing is poetic and vivid, so that it is jarring to have a frequent iteration of "Have you seen roads?" All kinds of roads are included: busy city streets, dreaming country lanes, tortuous mountain roads, placid riverways, locks and bridges, sky lanes and the unmapped roads of space.

967   **Orgel,** Doris. *The Good-Byes of Magnus Marmalade;* illus. by Erik Blegvad. Putnam, 1966. 32p. Trade ed. $2.75; Library ed. $2.68 net.

3–4   Illustrated with engaging black and white drawings, a charming book of light verse in which a small boy bids farewell to a school principal, a raincoat, a television announcer, poison ivy, et cetera. Sample: a farewell to his dentist. "You filled my tooth with gentle care, And yet I leave your dental chair With such great joy, it must be true: It's not your drill I hate, it's you!" The last few pages diverge: Magnus is described as going off somewhere, leaving his mother for the first time, then coming home. This seems to add little to the book, but doesn't detract much either. The poems are also nice to read aloud to smaller fry.

968   **Orgel,** Doris. *The Mulberry Music*; pictures by Dale Payson. Harper, 1971. 130p. Trade ed. $3.95; Library ed. $4.43 net.

4–6   A most moving story about a child's love for her grandmother and her adjustment to Grandma Liza's death. Grandma had always done whatever she pleased. If she wanted to wear a mulberry-colored sweatsuit ("Nobody wears that color," Mom said when her mother appeared in a home-dyed mulberry blouse and skirt) she did. Grandma Liza lived graciously, and Libby was terrified at the thought of losing her. The story is told in convincing fashion, bittersweet, with a home memorial service during which Libby realizes that the music played at her suggestion, Grandma's favorite—will stay with her always, just as will the memory of Grandma Liza.

969   **Orgel,** Doris. *Next Door to Xanadu*; illus. by Dale Payson. Harper, 1969. 160p. Trade ed. $3.95; Library ed. $4.43 net.

3–5   Patricia admits it: she's fat. The boys call her "fatsy Patsy," and she has no close friends. What she wants more than anything in the world is a bosom pal. And along comes Dorothy Rappaport, just her age, and right across the hall! The progress of their friendship is rapid, and Patricia is smitten with anguish when she learns that Dorothy is going to move away. But friendship has brought a measure of self-confidence: Patricia pulls herself together and makes their last days cheerful. There is no major action in the story, but the realistic and perceptive events and relationships are touched with humor and told in a style that is convincingly that of a girl of ten.

970   **Orgel,** Doris. *Phoebe and the Prince*; illus. by Erik Blegvad. Putnam, 1969. 31p. $3.64.

3–5   Sometimes Phoebe called her dog "Deardog" and sometimes she called him "Prince." A disappointed voice said one day, when Deardog had yipped with pain, "Oh. I thought you were speaking to me." Thus enters into Phoebe's life a flea with an exceptionally distinguished background. He admits it himself, as he describes (in verse) the past glories of his career at court, testily rebuking Phoebe when she interrupts. As suddenly as he hopped into her life, Phoebe's new friend departs with a blithe, "Auf wiederseh'n." Brisk, silly, and spiced with sense, this is a small portion of sophisticated writing that can be enjoyed by any reader but that has nuances that can be an additional attraction for the unusual reader. The illustrations are also sophisticated, small-scale and witty: Blegvad at his best.

971   **Ormondroyd,** Edward. *Broderick*; illus. by John Larrecq. Parnassus, 1969. 30p. Trade ed. $3.75; Library ed. $3.63 net.

K–2   A delightful story about an industrious mouse who sought, and found, a path to fame and fortune by his initiative and diligence. Broderick got the idea from a book on surfing (he was an avid reader) and made himself a surf board from a tongue depressor. Hundreds of wipe-outs later, he felt proficient enough to travel to the east coast for some rough surfing; a young man so admired him that he became Broderick's manager, and together they traveled the world giving performances to the plaudits of millions. This gay story is told with a straight face in polished style, the illustrations matching the deftness and humor of the writing. Appended is a brief list of other books about famous mice from other publishers—a courteous gesture.

972   **Ormondroyd,** Edward. *Theodore*; illus. by John M. Larrecq. Parnassus, 1966. 33p. Trade ed. $3.50; Library ed. $3.18 net.

3–6   A read-aloud story with realistic events and a subtle message
yrs.   in their interpretation. An aging toy bear, Theodore doesn't need to have a constant show of affection to know that his owner, Lucy, loves him. Accidentally caught in a laundromat load, Theodore emerges in unwonted cleanliness; he arranges a few small capers that will return him to his ordinary state of comfortable dirtiness. Retrieved by Lucy, Theodore is happy to hear her decline her mother's offer to wash the dirty toy; once again, Lucy has shown that she understands her bear and loves him just the way he is.

973   **Ormondroyd,** Edward. *Theodore's Rival*; illus. by John Larrecq. Parnassus, 1971. 31p. Trade ed. $3.50; Library ed. $3.63 net.

4–6   The sequel to *Theodore* is equally lighthearted. The scuffed
yrs.   toy bear who in that story was trapped in a washing machine is now more smudged than ever, and just as well loved. However, when Lucy gets a new animal for her birthday, Theodore is jealous of the other bear and not at all unhappy when it is lost during a shopping trip. When Lucy bemoans her panda, Theodore is surprised: a panda, and he had thought it another bear. He effects a rescue, and the two toys, no longer rivals, enjoy a tea party with Lucy. The plot is a variation on a familiar toy-story pattern, but it is told in fresh, humorous style, with Theodore as peppery a little character as before.

974   **Ottley,** Reginald. *Rain Comes to Yamboorah*; illus. by Robert Hales. Harcourt, 1968. 159p. $3.75. (Deutsch, 1967. 127p. £0.75.)

5–7   A sequel to *Boy Alone* and *The Roan Colt*, stories about a boy (never named) who works on a cattle station in the Australian Outback. Here the boy realizes for the first time his own importance in the tightly-knit and interdependent community of the station and begins to recognize the affection of all its members, from the two aborigine girls who are his companions to the motherly cook and the silent, self-sufficient old dogman, Kanga. Like the previous books, this has a compelling air of authenticity and wonderful evocation of mood and atmosphere.

975   **Oxenbury,** Helen. *Numbers of Things.* Watts, 1968. 29p. illus. $3.95. (Heinemann, 1967. 32p. £0.75.)

4–7
yrs.   A tall counting book from England, the shape used to great advantage for the contrasting facing pages. In heavy, clear type on one page, each on a separate line, "1, ONE, one, lion" and on the facing page, filling the long space, a mildly dolorous and quite amiable lion. The pictures are imaginative and intricately handsome, with humorous details that give an added fillip.

976   **Paine,** Roberta M. *Looking at Sculpture.* Lothrop, 1968. 128p. illus. Trade ed. $4.95; Library ed. $4.59 net.

4—   An introduction to an appreciation of sculpture, the text by a member of the staff of the Metropolitan Museum of Art, and most of the works of art (shown in photographs) being from the Metropolitan. The author discusses interpretation by the artist, the choice of material, and the role of material in design, and divides the book into sections on sculpture in the round, sculpture in relief, and constructions. The examples chosen range from ancient treasures of Greece and Egypt to mobiles and string compositions of today. An index to the illustrations, a glossary of terms, and a compilation of biographical notes are appended. Useful for art students in high school as well as elementary school.

977   **Panetta,** George. *Sea Beach Express.* Pictures by Emily McCully. Harper, 1966. 64p. Trade ed. $3.95; Library ed. $3.79 net.

4–6   An amusing story about an Italian-American family in New York City. Tony discovers that his mother wants desperately to get away from the hot city and visit Coney Island; Tony's father reluctantly agrees to go, and en route they gather a small neighbor. Giving his mother a receipt for him, of course. And so they go to eat, sun, swim, eat, swim, and eat: a dream-day come true. Were it not for the humor in the book it might be a bit cute, but it abounds in robust humor. It also has a feeling of family love that is conveyed with no sentimentality but with gay and simple zest.

978   **Panetta,** George. *The Shoeshine Boys;* illus. by Joe Servello. Grosset, 1971. 99p. Trade ed. $4.50; Library ed. $4.59 net.

3–5   Another story about the Italian-American family of *Sea Beach Express* reflects the plight of many families today: Papa loses his job. Maybe he could help a bit, Tony thinks, if he could shine shoes like the black boy he has seen in Central Park. So Tony accosts him, MacDougal Thompson, self-acclaimed champion shoeshiner. Tony has a rough time at first, but the advice he gets from MacDougal is encouraging, and the two boys finally decide to form a partnership and work together, each to a shoe. The Black and White Shoeshine Company is a great success. A pleasant tale, written with gentle humor and affection in an easy, natural style. The friendship of the boys and the relationships within the family are deftly handled, and the economic realities are treated in matter-of-fact fashion.

979   **Parker,** Arthur C. *Skunny Wundy;* Seneca Indian Tales; illus. by George Armstrong. Whitman, 1970. 224p. Trade ed. $3.95; Library ed. $2.96 net.

4–6   Written by the grandson of a Seneca chief, a collection of stories told by tribal storytellers, first published in 1926 and unavailable for many years. All of the tales are about animals, many of them "why" stories that explain animal habits or appearance, and many about tricksters. Skunny Wundy (a name used for brave boys, mighty hunters, or good storytellers) is the crafty character who tricks Fox into telling a tale every night for a moon, so that children may find stories about what animals used to do "in the dim long ago before people came to this world." Some of the tales, but very few, have seasons or plants as characters, or human beings, and almost all have a sly humor. The style retains the conversational quality of the oral tradition, and the collection should be useful for storytelling.

980   **Parker,** Elinor Milnor, comp. *Here and There;* 100 Poems about Places; illus. by Peter Spier. T. Y. Crowell, 1967. 170p. $4.50.

7—   A particularly nostalgic anthology, this compilation of poems about beloved places and place-names. Some of the selections are commemorative ("The Jewish Cemetery at Newport," "On the Extinction of the Venetian Republic") and some rollicking, but most of them are simply poems of affection for a familiar place. Author and title indexes are appended.

981   **Parker,** K. Langloh. *Australian Legendary Tales;* selected and ed. by H. Drake-Brockman; illus. by Elizabeth Durack. Viking, 1966. 255p. Trade ed. $4.50; Library ed. $4.13 net. (Angus & R., 1953. £1.37½.)

6–9   A selection of stories chosen from the several collections of aboriginal tales retold by Mrs. Parker and first published at the turn of the century. The tales are quite varied: some explain natural phenomena, some are fairy tales, some are tales of the cleverness of an animal, and some are ceremonial tales. There is much violence, a modicum of humor, and a great deal of

fascinating cultural detail. The illustrations are appropriately
stylized, some of the pictures composed in the manner of a
bark painting. A lengthy glossary, with a key to pronunciation,
is appended.

982   **Parker,** Richard. *The Old Powder Line.* Nelson, 1971. 144p.
$3.95. (Gollancz, 1971. 144p. £1.20.)

6–9   A deftly written fanciful story set on two time levels. Fifteen-
year-old Brian takes shelter from the rain on a railway platform
and is surprised when a steam train pulls in. Impulsively, he
jumps on and finds, at the end of his journey, that he is back
home—but in an earlier time. His mother doesn't know him,
but he understands when she points to a baby and says his
name is Brian, too. He is meeting himself. The story moves
back and forth, weaving a complicated mesh of déja vu events,
especially when other people learn what has happened and take
journeys with him. The fantasy is convincing, the characters
well drawn although not pictured in depth, and the intricacies
of the plot balanced by the quiet, matter-of-fact style.

983   **Parnall,** Peter. *The Mountain;* written and illus. by Peter Parnall.
Doubleday, 1971. 26p. $3.95.

K–3   An unusually good book on preserving ecological balance, lucid
enough in its message to be understood by preschool children,
sophisticated enough in its treatment to be appreciated by the
reader in primary grades. The illustrations are spare in composition
and beautifully detailed. The first pages show a mountain scene,
profuse with flowers, inhabited peacefully by animals. A few
people come who want to keep the mountain area just as it is.
Then Congress declares the mountain a National Park, a road is
built, more people come: tables, fountains, cars, lightpoles, and
litter everywhere. And at the end, one lonely flower struggling
up amidst a rubbish heap. The drawings have just a few touches
of sly humor, the case is not overstated and therefore all the
more effective.

984   **Parsons,** Ellen. *Rainy Day Together;* pictures by Lillian Hoban.
Harper, 1971. 29p. Trade ed. $3.50; Library ed. $3.79 net.

3–5   Gentle pictures echo the quiet affection of the text in a brief
yrs.   picture book that is tender without being sentimental. A small
girl describes a rainy day at home alone with her mother—
the things they do, wear, eat, and talk about. Daddy comes home
with a hug for his child, and his bearded face cold and wet
with rain. It's been a nice day. Simple and unaffected, this has
the double attraction of a loving family and of the pleasures
of everyday routine.

985   **Paterson,** A. B. *Waltzing Matilda;* illus. by Desmond Digby.

Holt, 1972. 32p. Trade ed. $5.95; Library ed. $5.59 net. (W. Collins, 1970.)

4–8 yrs.

The familiar words of the song, "Waltzing Matilda," were written years ago to the tune of an old English marching song; here they are illustrated with charming paintings in a picture book version first published in Australia in 1970 and designated there as the picture book of the year. Soft, vivid, and touched with humor, the pictures give a colorful impression of the old rascal who stuffed the jumbuck (sheep) in his bag and went off waltzing Matilda (carrying his swag, or pack), was pursued, jumped into the water-hole, and was drowned. A glossary is appended.

986   **Paul,** Aileen. *Kids Cooking;* The Aileen Paul Cooking School Cookbook; by Aileen Paul and Arthur Hawkins. Doubleday, 1970. illus. Trade ed. $4.95; Library ed. $4.70 net.

3–6

A really good cookbook for the young, the tone casual and gay, the instructions clear. There is a preface pointing out that simple recipes are for beginners of any age and giving general advice, including some on safety. The recipes are on double-page spreads: on the left-hand page, in large print, are a list of needed ingredients and a list of needed implements; on the right-hand page are the step-by-step instructions and the number of servings in the recipe. Section headings are: breakfast dishes, lunch dishes, dinner dishes, dessert dishes, party foods, snacks, and regional cooking. A relative index is appended.

987   **Pearce,** Philippa. *The Squirrel Wife;* illus. by Derek Collard. T. Y. Crowell, 1972. 61p. Trade ed. $4.50; Library ed. $5.25 net. (Longman Young Bks., 1971. 60p. £1.20.)

3–5

An original fairytale is printed in brown on pale beige, the pages framed by a delicate border design, the color illustrations dark and almost somber. The story incorporates many traditional elements of the genre: the cruel older brother and the kind younger brother who is the hero, the magical people who give the hero an object that can save him, the wife who is at one time human and at another assumes a beast-form, and the triumph of good over evil. Young Jack hears a call for help to which his brother's ears are shut, and goes into the forest to rescue one of the dread little green people. In gratitude he is given a ring that must be placed on a squirrel's paw; the squirrel grows up to become Jack's wife, sacrifices her human form to redeem him from the prison into which his jealous brother has had him cast, and becomes completely human when Jack, given a choice by the green people, chooses a human and beloved wife rather than a magic squirrel. The writing style is quiet and simple, with a smooth narrative flow.

988   **Pearlman,** Moshe. *The Zealots of Masada;* Story of a Dig. Scribner, 1967. 216p. illus. Trade ed. $5.95; Library ed. $5.09 net. (H. Hamilton, 1969. 184p. £1.05.)

8—   A fascinating account of the explorations and discoveries at Masada, the huge natural rock fortress which was the site of a dig in 1963–1965, when thousands of volunteers assisted the professional staff. Herod's palaces had been built here, and here the Zealot band of Jews, a hundred years after Herod, chose mass suicide rather than submit to the Romans. The book has great historical interest, great archeological interest, and a provocative sense of the excitement and adventure shared by the people who found the ornate buildings, the precious scrolls, the marvelous details of intricate engineering projects. An index is appended.

989   **Peck,** Richard, ed. *Mindscapes; Poems for the Real World.* Delacorte, 1971. 165p. $4.95.

7—   *Mindscapes,* the compiler states in his preface, is "designed to emphasize communication through a collection of poems, mostly modern, that deal in encounters with a real, hectic, unpretty, and recognizable world." And so it does, many of the selections speaking bluntly of the familiar and often unattractive scenes of every day, although some of the poems are lyric or lofty. Not quite as impressive an anthology as *Sounds and Silences,* also edited by Peck, but a good one. First line and author-title indexes are appended.

990   **Peck,** Richard, ed. *Sounds and Silences;* Poetry for Now. Delacorte, 1970. 178p. $4.50.

7—   An excellent selection of poems for young people, the topics of contemporary interest and grouped under such rubrics as realities or illusion, war or dissent. Some song lyrics are included; there is a representation of black poets and of some of the writers of the World War II generation; a few contributors are little-known, but the bulk of the anthology consists of accepted modern poets: Brooks, Updike, Levertov, Ferlinghetti, Shapiro, and others. An index of first lines and an author-title index are appended.

991   **Pellowski,** Anne, comp. *Have You Seen a Comet?* Children's Art and Writing from around the World; comp. by Anne Pellowski, Helen R. Sattley, and Joyce C. Arkhurst. Day, 1971. 121p. illus. $7.50.

4–12   Pictures chosen from the Information Center on Children's Cultures' international collection of children's art range from ingenuous, lively drawings by younger children to some stunning paintings by young adolescents. The techniques and styles are as varied as those of the writing, which is given in the original language and an English translation (with one exception: Turkish). Of the selections written in English, many were composed by children to whom it is a second language, the foreword reminds us. Some of the writing is humorous, some imaginative, some serious; the most noticeable quality of the collection is its universality— barring superficial cultural differences, the problems, pleasures, and aspirations of these representatives of seventy-five countries show very clearly how like each other are the young people of our world.

992   **Perovskaya,** Olga. *The Wolf in Olga's Kitchen;* tr. from the Russian by Fainna Glagoleva; illus. by Angie Culfogienis. Bobbs-Merrill, 1969. 229p. $5.50.

4–6   The childhood reminiscences of a writer of Russian children's books have the flavor of country life in the past, the appeal of a foreign setting, and the double attractions of animal stories and family life. Olga and her three sisters, whose father was a forester, shared a love of animals—especially wild animals. Each chapter of her story describes different creatures in the endless parade of pets: the two wolves brought home as new, staggering cubs, the ill-tempered donkey, a Siberian stag, a baby fox, a horse, a tiger cub. The descriptions of the animals are so affectionate yet unsentimental, the children so lively and natural, that the anecdotes have an appealing warmth and universality.

993   **Perrault,** Charles. *Perrault's Classic French Fairy Tales;* illus. by Janusz Grabianski. Meredith, 1967. 224p. $4.95. (Cape, 1967. 224p. £1.75.)

4–6   Thirteen tales are included in this collection, some lesser-known ones along with such durable favorites as "Cinderella" or "Puss in Boots." The print is rather small, but the spacious margins compensate (visually) for this; the illustrations are delightful in their vigor, charm, and melting colors.

994   **Perry,** Bill. *Our Threatened Wildlife;* An Ecological Study. Coward-McCann, 1970. 123p. illus. $4.29.

7–10   An excellent survey of wildlife resources, examining both those species that have become extinct (chiefly due to the carelessness or rapacity of mankind) and those that are rare and protected. The author discusses the many groups and agencies devoted to conservation, the kinds of refuges that have been set up, and some of the research into ecological problems that is changing conservation patterns. Throughout the book there is an explicit awareness of plant and animal relationships, with discussions of plant succession, the food chain, and predacity. An index is appended.

995   **Peterson,** Roger Tory. *The Birds;* by Roger Tory Peterson and the editors of Time-Life Books. Time, 1967. 128p. illus. $3.95. (Time-Life Internat., 1968. 128p. £1.05.)

6–10   This book is about the whole subject, the class Aves, rather than a compilation of descriptions of individual birds. There are few men better qualified than Mr. Peterson, and he has provided a book that is varied and stimulating as well as authentic. Its one weakness is the random arrangement of material, a weakness only partially mitigated by the index. The text includes discussions of migration, conservation, the language of birds, oddities and adaptations, habits and protective devices, breeding, and so on. A bit of everything, in lively prose. The appended reading list comprises recently published books on a broad range of topics within the subject field.

996   **Peyton,** K. M. *The Beethoven Medal;* illus. by the author. T. Y. Crowell, 1972. 185p. $4.50. (Oxf. U.P., 1971. 156p. £0.90.)

7–10   *adventure*   A sequel to *Pennington's Last Term* is as impressive as the first book. Here Patrick Pennington's story is told from the viewpoint of a girl who is in love with him. Ruth knows Pat only as the silent, strong boy who delivers bread; she is thrilled when he invites her out and irritated by her mother's disapproval. Pat is still a crusty and ambivalent character, devoted to his music and contemptuous of conformity. Ruth loves him no less when she learns he has been in jail for assault and she does not waver when he is again committed, having lost his temper and hit a policeman. Even her parents are impressed by Pat's musicianship when they hear him in concert, and they realize that they must accept him as he is. No less powerfully drawn here, Patrick Pennington is a striking and believable character, emerging in high relief from a story in which the other characters are solidly pictured and the plot is built with craftsmanship.

997   **Peyton,** K. M. *The Edge of the Cloud;* illus. by Victor G. Ambrus. World, 1970. 207p. Trade ed. $4.95; Library ed. $4.86 net. (Oxf. U.P., 1970. 160p. £0.30.)

7–10   A sequel to *Flambards,* in which the orphaned Christina goes against the wishes of the uncle with whom she lives, and runs off with his younger son Will rather than marrying Will's brother. Here the pair have just taken refuge with their aunt, Christina to stay until she comes into her fortune or Will's father dies, and Will to look for work. But Will's work is flying and the time is just prior to the first World War . . . so it is a long struggle for the engaged pair. The story ends in their marriage; the book, ostensibly a love story, has very little romance in it but is filled with fascinating details about the early days of flying, the experimental planes, the pioneer stunt men, the whole atmosphere of freedom and camaraderie. The style, the characters, the setting, and the plot are deftly interwoven.

998   **Peyton,** K. M. *Flambards;* illus. by Victor G. Ambrus. World, 1968. 206p. Trade ed. $4.95; Library ed. $4.90 net. (Oxf. U.P., 1970. 192p. £0.30.)

7–10   The vivid writing style and excellent characterization and dialogue lend depth and dignity to what is basically a well-worn plot. Orphaned girl comes to stay with relatives and discovers that she is going to inherit money and that her marriage to the handsome older son is planned. Older son turns out to be a bully, and the quiet, intelligent younger son is the true love. Here the characters of the older son and his father, two ignorant, cruel, and powerful men, are drawn with blistering realism, and there is added interest in the younger son because he is one of the first flyers (of an experimental plane) in England. The time is just before World War I, and the author raises several questions that reflect the changing times. The orphaned Christina, for example, cannot reconcile herself to the cruelty with which her uncle treats his servants, yet she cannot quite bring herself to admit that a groom is her equal as a human being.

999   **Peyton,** K. M. *Flambards in Summer;* illus. by Victor G. Ambrus. World, 1970. 189p. Trade ed. $4.95; Library ed. $4.91 net. (Oxf. U.P., 1970. 160p. £0.30.)

7–10   The third novel in a trilogy about the Russell family, a chronicle which received the 1969 GUARDIAN Award, set in England in 1916. Christina, young and widowed, decides to return to Flambards, the family estate, and when she finds that her brother-in-law has an illegitimate son, she brings young Tizzy (Thomas) to Flambards. Most of the story is concerned with Christina's problems in managing the estate and in coping with her complicated relationships with Tizzy's father and with a former employee with whom she has fallen in love. The plot is of less importance than the whole picture of country life in England, complete with period details and the niceties of social gradations; the characterization and dialogue are excellent.

1000   **Peyton,** K. M. *Pennington's Last Term;* illus. by the author. T. Y. Crowell, 1971. 216p. $4.50. (Oxf. U.P., 1970. 190p. £1.00.)

7–10   First published in England under the title *Pennington's Seventeenth Summer,* a perceptive study of a young man who is rebellious and, until he finds a channel for his emotions and a goal, hostile to authority. Regarded as a trouble-maker at school, drifting unhappily toward the end of the term, Penn is even reluctant to perform in a piano contest, although his musicianship is undeniable. Patrick Pennington is, with all his rancor and obduracy, a remarkably strong character, and is developed by the author with great skill in a story that has excellent dialogue and great pace in small incidents.

1001   **Phelan,** Mary Kay. *Four Days in Philadelphia—1776*; illus. by Charles Walker. T. Y. Crowell, 1967. 189p. $4.50.

5–7   An intensive examination of the crucial events of July first to July fourth in Philadelphia in 1776, with several chapters that describe the signing of the Declaration of Independence and the subsequent history of the document itself. The writing has a brisk urgency and a sense of immediacy as the tension mounts and the votes are weighed; and the historical characters are shown as very real and worried men since the delegates are divided, and the issue of whether or not to declare a dissolution of ties to the British Crown is pending. The book is exciting, authoritative, and more difficult to read than the format would indicate. The text of the Declaration, a bibliography, and an index are appended.

1002   **Phelan,** Mary Kay. *Midnight Alarm*; The Story of Paul Revere's Ride; illus. by Leonard Weisgard. T. Y. Crowell, 1968. 131p. $4.50.

4–6   As in *Four Days in Philadelphia—1776*, the author describes the details of four action-packed days that precede a historical event of the American Revolution. As Revere moves about the city, he mulls over the situation, giving the reader ample background (should he need it) for an understanding of the crucial nature of the immediate events. The book culminates, of course, with Revere's ride to Lexington and his capture (and mysterious release) by the British. The writing is brisk, the pace of action maintained, and the historical details smoothly incorporated; there is no feeling of suspense but the personal focus and moderate tone give a feeling of verisimilitude that makes familiar material have surprising interest.

1003   **Philipson,** Morris. *The Count Who Wished He Were a Peasant*; A Life of Leo Tolstoy; illus. with photographs. Pantheon Books, 1967. 170p. $3.95.

9—   A balanced, judicious, and colorful biography of the Russian writer who was in so many ways ahead of his time. Tolstoy's long life as an author of major importance, a distinguished philosopher, an impassioned reformer, and a controversial religious leader has drama and romantic appeal that is all the better set off by Mr. Philipson's measured prose. A selective bibliography is appended.

1004   **Phipson,** Joan. *Birkin*; illus. by Margaret Horder. Harcourt, 1966.

224p. $3.75. (Longman Young Bks., 1965. 192p. £0.80.)

5–7   An engaging story about children and their love for animals, set in a small Australian town. Birkin is a calf (named in error for an explorer, Birkin Wills, one of the children having misinterpreted a teacher's "Burke and Wills"). Several children share the work and trouble of caring for Birkin, and he indeed is more and more trouble as he grows big; he is struck by a car when he wanders off, hurt again when he strays, and then is almost drowned. However, two boys are saved by riding Birkin, since there have been flooding rains. The father of one of them, informed by the anguished children that Birkin is to be sold for slaughter, shows his gratitude by taking over the perpetual care of the animal. The setting has appeal, but the charm of the story is in the vivid characterization of the many children; there is plenty of action and humor in this vigorous but smoothly written story.

1005   **Phipson,** Joan. *Cross Currents;* illus. by Janet Duchesne. Harcourt, 1967. 192p. $3.75.

7–10   Another fine story set in Australia. Jim is seventeen and already at odds with his parents because he doesn't want to continue his education; when he is told that a thirteen-year-old cousin, Charlie, is going along on a family sailing trip, he bows out. His father becomes ill, and Jim is hastily telephoned to come sail the boat home; the circumstances are such that young Charlie is alone on the boat and Jim doesn't know it. Jim is annoyed by Charlie but as the days go by, Jim succumbs to the voice of common sense, to Charlie's admiration and his quiet courage, and to a feeling of responsibility. The sail itself is adventurous, and the tight-knit story line is sustained in pace and convincing in its development.

1006   **Place,** Marian (Templeton). *American Cattle Trails East and West;* illus. by Gil Walker. Holt, 1967. Trade ed. $3.95; Library ed. $3.59 net.

5–9   Well researched and smoothly written, a history of one aspect of pioneer America is enlivened by anecdotes and illustrated with bustling, busy drawings. The arrangement is primarily regional, but—insofar as possible—also chronological, the text beginning with Coronado's long trek up from Mexico to what is now Texas and concluding with the coming of the railroads. In addition to historical interest, the story of American trailblazing is full of drama and color: the "fever war" caused by the mysterious death of only northern cattle; the troubles of Saunders, who was arrested by his own side during the Civil War; the dangers of the wild country itself. A bibliography and an index are appended.

1007   **Place,** Marian (Templeton). *Gold Down Under;* The Story of the
         Australian Gold Rush. Crowell-Collier, 1969. 169p. $4.50. (Collier-
         Mac., 1969. 176p. £1.05.)

6–9   The Australian Gold Rush was started by a man who had, like
         many Australians, tried his luck in the gold fields of California;
         Edward Hargraves, remembering some rock formations like those
         of California, sailed home determined to become rich and
         important. Persistent in presenting his claims to Her Majesty's
         Government, Hargrave was finally successful . . . and that
         was a very small beginning, for there were rich deposits found
         by the gold-hungry prospectors. Although the writing is quite
         solid and serious, this is a dramatic book by the very nature of
         its material. Well-researched, the book includes accounts of the
         labor disputes, the anti-Chinese riots, the forays by outlaw bands,
         the importing of American stagecoaches, the effect on the
         Australian economy, but primarily of the wild surges of
         prospecting, the tedious labor of panning, the staking of claims,
         and the occasional fabulous strike that encouraged others to go
         on digging and sifting. A bibliography and an index are appended.

1008   **Place,** Marian (Templeton). *New York to Nome;* The First
         International Cross-Country Flight. Macmillan, 1972. 72p. $3.95.

4–7   In 1920, four single-engine wooden airplanes, each manned by
         two veterans of the fledgling air force of World War I, took off
         on a flight that was a landmark in aviation history. Four
         thousand, five hundred miles in open cockpits, with no landing
         fields, no radio for communication, no aerial maps—and the route
         lay over lakes and mountains. Brisk and direct, the writing is
         never overly dramatic, so that the very real drama and excitement
         of the hazards and triumphs of the flight are all the more
         effective. The trip, made in stages, is described in detail, so
         that the book should appeal especially to flight history buffs.
         An index is appended.

1009   **Platt,** Kin. *The Boy Who Could Make Himself Disappear.*
         Chilton, 1968. 216p. Trade ed. $4.95; Library ed. $4.70 net.

10—   Although it is a little difficult to believe in the sustained cruelty
         of Roger's mother, this is a story so moving and so well written
         that one must accept her as a person whose aberrant behavior,
         deeply sadistic and selfish, has gone without notice because most
         of it is directed, in private, toward her only child. Roger and
         his mother, newly divorced, have moved to New York, so that
         this disturbed child is making an adjustment to a new city, a
         new school, and to the divorce in addition to his burdens of rejection
         and a concomitant speech impediment. His efforts to improve, his
         sad musings on incidents of the past, his efforts to cope with

his mother's hostility, and his valiant efforts to cooperate with the speech therapist are brilliantly told.

1010   **Plotz,** Helen, comp. *The Earth Is the Lord's; Poems of the Spirit;* illus. with wood engravings by Clare Leighton. T. Y. Crowell, 1965. 223p. $5.

7—   An anthology of poetry about man and God, about man's searching, doubting, wondering, believing . . . a fine book that has been compiled with discrimination. The format is dignified and the range of poems wide, with emphasis on the work of contemporary poets. Author and title indexes are appended.

1011   **Plotz,** Helen, comp. *The Marvelous Light; Poets and Poetry.* T. Y. Crowell, 1970. 173p. $3.95.

7—   Like other Plotz anthologies, this has variety of style and mood, discrimination in selection, and a wide spectrum of forms and poet-oriented subjects. The poems range from ancient times to today, from romantic or somber reflections to the humor of Ogden Nash. Poets write of themselves, their work, and other poets— sometimes in tribute, sometimes in criticism or self-examination. First line, author, and title indexes are appended.

1012   **Plowman,** Stephanie. *My Kingdom for a Grave.* Houghton, 1971. 239p. $4.95. (Bodley Head, 1970. 286p. £1.50.)

8—   A sequel to *Three Lives for the Czar,* in which Andrei Hamilton, son of a French mother and a Russian father, has been brought up as a companion to the royal children and tells of the years that lead up to World War I. Here Andrei is an officer in an army that is disastrously organized and run, and his attempts to convince the childish, unstable Czar and the Czarina, under Rasputin's power, to take action, are as little use as the advice of others. It is through Andrei's eyes that we see the revolution, the banishment of the royal family, and their execution. The author's historical research is evident throughout the story, but is particularly impressive in the closing chapters in which Andrei tries to effect an escape plan for the family, fails, and later investigates the circumstance of their imprisonment, death, and burial. This is historical writing at its best: like Rosemary Sutcliff, Stephanie Plowman has both a sense of story and a familiarity with historical details, so that the fictional framework is unobtrusively permeated with authoritative minutiae.

1013   **Plowman,** Stephanie. *Three Lives for the Czar.* Houghton, 1970. 269p. $4.95. (Bodley Head, 1969. 280p. £1.40.)

8—   Historically based fiction that is set in a dramatic period and in a milieu that is vanished, that clearly is supported by intensive research, and that has an easy, flowing (and convincingly first-person) style and the unusual combination of romantic appeal and sociological value. Despite a tendency to iteration and the drawback of very small print, the story told by Andrei Hamilton, whose family had for many generations lived in Russia and whose childhood playmate had been the Grand Duchess Olga, is fascinating. It pictures harshly Nicholas II and his unhappy wife, assuming (not surprising in a young man who moved with familiarity among the nobility and royalty of several countries) that a more intelligent and beneficent ruler might have prevented the revolution.

1014   **Polland,** Madeleine. *To Tell My People;* illus. by Richard M. Powers. Holt, 1968. 209p. Trade ed. $4.50; Library ed. $3.97 net. (Hutchinson, 1968. 192p. £0.90.)

6–8   A story set in Britain at the time of the Roman invasion, its heroine a young girl who is taken captive by the soldiers and sent to Rome to be sold as a slave. Lumna has strayed from a small colony of lake-dwellers who live in poverty and ignorance, and she yearns to bring to her people all she has learned of a better way of life. When she escapes and returns to her home, Lumna is jeered at or ignored; sorrowing, she realizes that her tribe will learn nothing—they will only fight. The period is most convincingly drawn, the characterization deft, and the story line simple and strong.

1015   **Poole,** Josephine. *Catch as Catch Can;* illus. by Kiyo Komoda. Harper, 1970. 163p. Trade ed. $3.95; Library ed. $3.79 net. (Hutchinson, 1969. 136p. £0.80.)

5–7   A better-than-most mystery story set in the English countryside. Two cousins are witness to a man's jumping off a train and later find, in a pocket, a message in code. They realize that the prying woman who questioned them on the train has set her chauffeur on their trail, but can't understand why. Although the solution, when it emerges, is a bit of a letdown, the story itself is strong in pace and suspense, with one of the cousins taken prisoner by the chauffeur, escaping via chimney, and being chased up the stairs of a lighthouse. Tight in structure, deftly concocted, with good characterization and dialogue.

1016   **Poole,** Lynn. *Doctors Who Saved Lives;* by Lynn and Gray Poole. Dodd, 1966. 148p. illus. $3.50.

8—   A good collective biography, the subjects chronologically arranged from the fifteenth century to present times; the men whose lives are described briefly are all doctors who made important contributions to medical science, although that importance was not always recognized in the doctor's lifetime. Some of the subjects are men whose lives have been included in medical biographies fairly often, such as Paracelsus and Fleming. (Several of the greatest doctors of history were described by the Pooles in an earlier collective biography of scientists.) The particular value of this book is that it includes some men who are comparatively little-known; the writing style is serious and the medical material presented authoritatively. An index is appended.

1017   **Poole,** Lynn. *Men Who Dig Up History;* by Lynn and Gray Poole. Dodd, 1968. 175p. illus. $4.

7—   A most interesting compilation of brief accounts of the work of ten contemporary archeologists: Anderson, Bass, Broneer, Gejvall, Haury, Libby, Mallowan, Wheeler, Willy, and Yadin. There is some biographical information, but most of the book is devoted to the special fields or major projects of the scientists. Photographs of the ten men are included; an index is appended.

1018   **Portal,** Colette. *The Beauty of Birth;* ad. from the French by Guy Daniels. Knopf, 1971. 26p. $3.95.

3–6   Delicate and precise watercolor illustrations show the development of a baby in utero, from ovulation and conception through the embryonic and fetal stages to parturition. Especially interesting are the pages on which the author-artist shows the growth of individual anatomical features such as the hand, changing from a knobbly bud to the articulated perfection of an infant's hand. The text is accurate, straightforward, and lucid.

1019   **Potter,** Beatrix. *The Sly Old Cat;* written and illus. by Beatrix Potter. Warne, 1972. 35p. $2.50. (Warne, 1971. 36p. £0.60.)

3–5   First written and illustrated in 1906, this slight but engaging
yrs.   tale appears here for the first time in book form. Cat invites Mr. Rat to a tea party, and the visitor both resents getting only crumbs and fears he may be eaten. He outwits Cat by slipping the milk jug over her head, has his tea, and goes off to leave Cat to bang the jug off while he goes home and eats the last muffin, which he has prudently taken with him. Potter deftly establishes character, brief as the tale is, by referring to "Mr. Rat" but—more brusquely—to "Cat": no title for a miscreant. Yet Cat comes to no real harm, and if there is a lesson, it is a gentle one, the softness and humor of the illustrations robbing the story of any didacticism.

1020   **Potter,** Bronson. *Antonio;* woodcuts by Ann Grifalconi. Atheneum, 1968. 41p. Trade ed. $3.50; Library ed. $3.41 net.

4–5   A familiar theme, an unfamiliar setting, an adept variation. The theme is that of the left-out child who is inadequate and longs to gain status, and who does so in a crisis situation. The setting is Portugal, a small fishing village in which Antonio, because of a crippled hand, cannot hope to be a fisherman as do the other boys. He is an ox-boy, guiding the beasts who pull the fleet's small boats across the dunes. It is Antonio, using his familiarity with the beasts, who organizes a rescue operation when a wild storm threatens the fleet. The book has little dialogue, the writing spare and efficient yet successful in establishing mood and in sustaining pace.

1021   **Power,** Jules. *How Life Begins;* drawings by Barry Geller. Simon and Schuster, 1966. 95p. $4.95.

5–9   An excellent book on mating, reproduction, gestation, birth, hereditary characteristics, on those attributes that distinguish the non-living from the living, and on those that set man apart from other animals. The book is based on material used in a television program; the consultant for both was Dr. Milton Levine, consulting pediatrician to the Department of Health of New York City. The photographic illustrations and the diagrams are lucid, save for one in which it appears that the male genitalia are contained within the body; the corresponding text is quite clear. The writing is dignified, smooth, and straightforward; the material is well-organized, accurate, and logically presented. In fact, a fine job. The book is simple enough to be used by adults for younger children, and mature enough to be acceptable to older slow readers. An index is appended.

1022   **Powers,** David Guy. *The First Book of How to Run a Meeting;* illus. by Peter P. Plasencia. Watts, 1967. 62p. $3.75.

5–9   Although there is a note of heartiness in the first chapter ("Enjoy club meetings and enjoy getting things done") the text is crisply informative and logical throughout the rest of the book. The author explains very clearly the role of the chairman in conducting a meeting, the form and purpose of bylaws and constitution, the agenda, and—in particular—the different kinds of motions and amendments, the correct forms of address, and all of the major procedures for nominating, voting, and reporting at a meeting. A glossary, an index, and a simplified chart of motions (debatable, amendable, priority, purpose, required vote, and type of motion) are appended. A book that may be found useful by older readers also.

1023   **Prelutsky,** Jack. *A Gopher in the Garden;* And Other Animal Poems; pictures by Robert Leydenfrost. Macmillan, 1967. 26p. $3.95.

4–5   A collection that can be read aloud to younger children as well as read independently by the child old enough to enjoy the word-play. The rhythm, the repetition, the nonsense, and the satisfaction (whether realized or not) of internal rhyme have general appeal;

the illustrations have a benign inanity befitting the mood of the animal poems. "The Bengal Tiger likes to eat/ enormous quantities of meat. Now people have been heard to say/ that tigers hypnotize their prey. So please do not take foolish chances; avoid the Bengal tiger's glances."

1024   **Prelutsky,** Jack. *Toucans Two; And Other Poems*; illus. by Jose Aruego. Macmillan, 1970. 29p. $4.95.

K–2   Illustrated with pictures of engagingly silly animals, a collection of poems that are light, rhythmic, deft and humorous. The writer plays with words in nonsense fashion, but never deviates from facts about each creature. In its entirety: "Oysters/ are creatures/ without/ any features." The appeal of rhyme and rhythm is clear in such small gems as, "The ancient armadillo/is as simple as the rain/ he's an armor-plated pillow/ with a microscopic brain./ He's disinterested thoroughly/ in what the world has wrought/ but spends his time in contemplative/ armadyllic thought."

1025   **Preston,** Carol. *A Trilogy of Christmas Plays for Children*; music selected by John Langstaff; illus. with music, photographs, and diagrams. Harcourt, 1967. 135p. $3.95.

5–7   The three plays, used for many years at a school of which Miss Preston was headmistress, are variations on the Nativity theme. One is contemporary (with Nativity scenes in a play-within-the-play) and one adapted from Medieval folk and miracle plays; the third is based on English miracle plays and old carols. The dialogue is flavored with appropriate idiom and vocabulary without being too quaint; indeed, the plays are in the best of taste. Sources are discussed and quite complete instructions given for staging, lighting, simple choreography, et cetera. An appendix gives information about sources for obtaining appropriate music.

1026   **Price,** Christine. *Heirs of the Ancient Maya; A Portrait of the Lacandon Indians*; photographs by Gerturde Duby Blom. Scribner, 1972. 64p. $5.95.

6–9   Handsome photographs of Mayan ruins, of the green forest and the still blue waters of Lake Naha, and of the strong faces of the Lacandon Indians, so like the carvings on the ancient Mayan stelas, add visual appeal to a book that is beautiful in its sympathetic understanding of the Lacandons. Written in a poetic and musing style, the text describes the ruins that are still revered by this small band that withdrew from the conquerors and would not be conquered, a people who still follow the old ways and worship the old gods, who have only just begun to suffer from the encroachment of modern society into their lives, unpolluted by physical or emotional cankers.

1027   **Price,** Christine. *Made in Ancient Egypt.* Dutton, 1970. 153p. illus. Trade ed. $5.95; Library ed. $5.89 net. (Bodley Head, 1970. £1.60.)

6—   Informed and informative, written in a direct and dignified style, this is a fascinating study of the ancient Egyptians through their tombs and temples, their carving and pottery, and the many artifacts that have been recovered from royal burial chambers. The material is arranged chronologically and facts of historical and cultural significance are consistently related to the objects that reflect them. A dynastic table and map precede the text, which is profusely illustrated and which is followed by a list of illustrations (numbered and with source given) and a bibliography.

1028   **Price,** Christine. *Made in Ancient Greece;* illus. with photographs and drawings. Dutton, 1967. 160p. $5.95. (Bodley Head, 1968. 160p. £1.25.)

7–10   A book written with authority and enthusiasm, the illustrations profuse and the examples well chosen. The author focuses on the diversity of Greek art, some functional and some ornamental, and on the changes in technique as well as on the varieties of medium and form. The book is not a history of Greek art, but it may serve admirably as an introduction, since it discusses architecture, sculpture, pottery, coins, painting, jewelry, and ornamental objects for household use. Permeating the discussion is an attitude of appreciation, and inextricably a part of it is an awareness of the people of Greece: the artists, artisans, models, and consumers. A list of notes on illustrations and some books suggested for further reading are appended; a map of the world of the Greeks precedes the text.

1029   **Proddow,** Penelope, tr. *Demeter and Persephone;* Homeric Hymn Number Two; tr. and ad. by Penelope Proddow; illus. by Barbara Cooney. Doubleday, 1972. 39p. $5.95.

4–6   A retelling of the story of the goddess Demeter is illustrated by pictures that are bold and simple in composition and graceful in authentic detail. When her daughter Persephone is carried off by Hades and taken as his bride to the underworld, Demeter's grief and wrath cause the harvest's failure and the people's hunger. Zeus intervenes, and Persephone is free to visit her mother, whose joy brings beauty and abundance to earth once more. This imperishable legend of springtime is written in a stately, rolling style of translation that befits the poetic cadence of the hymn.

1030   **Proddow,** Penelope, tr. *Hermes, Lord of Robbers;* Homeric Hymn Number four; tr. and ad. by Penelope Proddow; illus. by Barbara Cooney. Doubleday, 1971. 43p. $4.95.

4–6   Handsome illustrations, strong in composition and delicate in detail, complement the simple but dignified retelling of the legend of the first days of clever Hermes, messenger of the gods. The infant son of Zeus steals from his cradle to fashion a lyre, then bounds off to steal the cattle of his brother Apollo. Caught, the sly Hermes soothes Apollo with the beauty of his music and wins him by giving him the lyre. Hermes promises never again to rob his brother but, the tale ends, ". . . down through the dark nights, he tricks the tribes of men." The text reads aloud smoothly, and the book gives a succinct version for storytellers.

1031   **Provensen,** Alice, comp. *The Provensen Book of Fairy Tales;* comp. and illus. by Alice and Martin Provensen. Random House, 1971. 140p. $4.95.

4–6   A choice selection of twelve modern fairy tales is illustrated by pictures that have the charm one might expect from the Provensens but with an added fillip of humor. The stories are by Andersen, Beston, Fillmore, MacManus, Manning-Sanders, Milne, Mordaunt, Picard, Howard Pyle, Katherine Pyle, Rackham, and Wilde. A choice selection, a handsome book.

1032   **Pugh,** Ellen. *Brave His Soul;* written by Ellen Pugh and with the assistance of David B. Pugh. Dodd, 1970. 144p. illus. $4.

7–10   For readers with a particular interest in history or in exploration, this should prove particularly interesting, since it both deals with an unusual theory in history and treats it with documented objectivity. The theory that there was a Welsh prince (Madog or Madoc) who, revolted by civil war and competiton for the throne within his family, exiled himself and came to the North American continent in 1170, is disputed—yet the author presents convincing evidence that such an event was probable, especially in some of the physical attributes and cultural traits of the Mandan Indians. Chapter notes give sources; a bibliography and an index are appended.

1033   **Pugh,** Ellen. *More Tales from the Welsh Hills;* illus. by Joan Sandin. Dodd, 1971. 124p. $4.25.

4–6   A member of the American Folklore Society, Ellen Pugh has told these tales, as she did those in *Tales from the Welsh Hills*, from memories of the stories as her Welsh grandparents told them. The patterns are typical of the genre: three pieces of advice that save a man from disaster, the princess who loves a poor lad, the driving out of the devil, etc. The style is good; there are occasional passages that are too formal for storytelling but that read well, but most of the writing is appropriate both for story-telling and for reading aloud.

1034   **Purdy,** Susan. *Festivals for You to Celebrate.* Lippincott, 1969.
192p. illus. Trade ed. $5.95; Library ed. $5.82 net.

4–7   An attractive and useful round-up of craft projects associated with
the holidays; those included are holidays most widely observed
in the United States (with the exclusion of patriotic holidays),
according to the preface, many of them of foreign origin. The
material is grouped by seasons, with suggestions for group
activities preceding the body of the text. Written with crisp
clarity, the directions for craft projects are easy to follow; the
information about each holiday is succinct, usually giving both the
origins of the holiday and a description of the way or ways in
which it is celebrated. A list of materials is included; a
bibliography, activities subject index, and an index are appended.

1035   **Randall,** Ruth Elaine (Painter). *I Elizabeth;* A Biography of the
Girl Who Married General George Armstrong Custer of "Custer's
Last Stand." Little, 1966. 260p. illus. $4.95.

7–9   A good biography, despite some weaknesses, not overly
fictionalized, and given color by authentic details for which the
source materials are listed. The life of Libbie Bacon is romantic
enough to be a Victorian novel, and the Civil War background
gives the book importance. One weakness is in the author's had-
he-but-known tendency: "She would never have dreamed that he
was the future war hero who would one day become the most
important person in all the world to her." Another is the fact
that there is a slightly patronizing note in the descriptions of
Negroes, especially in the description of a party the Custers
arrange for a servant. The book is not as impartial as is
Leighton's *Bride of Glory* (Ariel, 1962); both books are objective
in discussing the controversy over Custer's behavior. The
photographs are excellent; an index is appended.

1036   **Randall,** Ruth Elaine (Painter). *I Ruth:* Autobiography of a
Marriage. Little, 1968. 266p. illus. $5.95.

8—   Although the literary aspects of the lives of Ruth and James
Randall may be of paramount importance to readers of this
autobiography, it is above all the story of a happy marriage.
Mr. Randall's interests became his wife's, so that their work
together was the focus not only of their own lives but of a circle
of students and of other great Lincoln scholars. The author
writes with dignified candor of her husband's death and of her
own career.

1037   **Ransome,** Arthur, ad. *The Fool of the World and the Flying Ship;* A
Russian Tale; retold by Arthur Ransome; pictures by Uri
Shulevitz. Farrar, 1968. 45p. $4.95. (H. Hamilton, 1970. 48p.
£1.25.)

K–3   A retelling from *Old Peter's Russian Tales* is brought to life again with vigorous and colorful illustrations that effectively picture the sweep of the countryside, the ornate splendor of the palace and— above all—the vitality and humor of the peasant. The story is deservedly familiar in several folk variants: a company of men, each with one magical power, succeed together in achieving an impossible task; here the Fool's companions enable him to outwit the crafty Csar and win the hand of the lovely Princess.

1038   **Rappaport,** Eva. *"Banner, Forward!"* The Pictorial Biography of a Guide Dog; photographs by the author. Dutton, 1969. 127p. $6.95.

5—   Excellent photographs follow the progress of Banner, a Golden Retriever, from puppyhood through all the stages of her training as a guide dog for the blind. The text, written in an easy, straightforward style, is lucid in explanation of each step in the training process and is all the more effective for an absence of pity or sentimentality. Particularly interesting and dramatic are those scenes in which the grown dogs receive the last and most demanding lessons on crowded city streets and in which the dogs and their new owners meet and practice together.

1039   **Raskin,** Ellen. *Franklin Stein;* written and illus. by Ellen Raskin. Atheneum, 1972. 30p. $4.95.

K–2   Locked in an attic room, Franklin had been sawing and hammering away, making a complicated and ingenious construction (Rube Goldberg cartoon-type) which he called Fred. Franklin Stein's sister sneered at Fred, and when he (or it) was lowered from the attic window, other people saw him and agreed. "Evil . . . awful . . . Eek! . . . wicked," were some of the comments, and policeman Foster wrote in his book, "Atrocious, ferocious, ghastly giant monster . . ." But the judge of the pet show to which Franklin Stein and Fred were hurrying thought otherwise, and the fickle crowd was soon singing the praises of the ingenious piece of junk construction. The story is written with sparkling wit and in a sophisticated style, and the illustrations—which echo the humor of the text—are effective both in the use of color (bright, clear shades of red, blue, and green) and in the way in which they complement and supplement the story.

1040   **Raskin,** Ellen. *The Mysterious Disappearance of Leon (I Mean Noel);* written and illus. by Ellen Raskin. Dutton, 1971. 149p. $4.95.

4–7   To read this book, place tongue firmly in cheek. Mrs. Leon Carillon, married for reasons of business at the age of five, and separated from her giggling seven-year-old bridegroom immediately afterward, is now grown; in fact, a lady of some years as well as considerable means, and her whole life is dedicated to finding the lost Leon. For example, she wears nothing but purple because in the one brief meeting they've had, she wore purple and she thinks it will help Leon recognize her. The two children she has adopted plunge enthusiastically into the hunt, following clues, deciphering possible codes, soliciting the help of an elderly admirer of Mrs. Carillon's who is a puzzle expert. The problem is solved, and the whereabouts of the missing Leon discovered, but only after a series of incidents that have the lighthearted frenzy of a French farce. The story bubbles with fun, sly humor, and straight-faced nonsense like solemn footnotes and provocative clues.

1041   **Raskin,** Ellen. *Nothing Ever Happens on My Block*. Atheneum, 1966. 28p. illus. Trade ed. $2.95; Library ed. $3.75 net.

K–3   A small and entirely diverting book to read aloud or to be read by the beginning reader. Chester is a small and dour curb-sitter; glum and stony-faced, he voices his complaint. Nothing ever happens on his block. Other places, excitement—drama—ferocious lions—et cetera, et cetera, et cetera. But on his block? Nothing. Meanwhile, back of Chester, action on every page: children playing, a house on fire, cops and robbers, even a parachutist landing. The small details of the drawings are very, very funny and many of them carry over from one page to another to sustain momentum. Two small girls, for example, counting as they jump rope together: 36, 98, 307, 862 and past the thousand mark. Some pages on, one collapses; later, she is borne off on a stretcher; still later she reappears magnificently bandaged.

1042   **Raskin,** Ellen. *Spectacles*. Atheneum, 1968. 41p. illus. Trade ed. $3.50; Library ed. $4.14 net.

K–2   An amusing picture book about the trials and errors of a small girl who, unaware of her myopic misinterpretations, sees—fuzzily—strange creatures where only familiar objects exist. The distortion is cheerfully artificial; for example, the "ax" being held by an "Indian" is shown (all the pictures are in pairs, the real and the imagined) to be a lampshade that is sideways. Taken to a doctor, Iris puts up a stiff fight against spectacles, is won by the suggestion that she might look like a movie star, and is—as children so often are—enchanted by the new, clear world around her. The point is made with humor, the exaggeration enjoyable because it is deliberate.

1043   **Ravielli,** Anthony. *From Fins to Hands*; An Adventure in Evolution; written and illus. by Anthony Ravielli. Viking, 1968. 47p. Trade ed. $3; Library ed. $2.96 net. (Dent, 1970. 48p. £0.80.)

4–6   The beautifully drawn and meticulously realistic illustrations trace the slow development of the human hand from the skeletal structure of the first vertebrates. The author describes the adaptations of man's ancestors to living on land and to such adjustments as walking on two limbs and assuming an erect posture. Although the focus here is on the hand, there is mention of other anatomical changes (binocular vision, longer leg bones) and the book can be used by older readers because of the straightforward writing and the profuse and accurate pictures.

1044   **Reavin,** Sam. *Hurray for Captain Jane!* illus. by Emily Arnold McCully. Parents' Magazine, 1971. 30p. Trade ed. $3.95; Library ed. $3.78 net.

K–2   Coming back from a birthday party with three prizes, Jane refuses to share her black jelly beans or her sailor hat with her little brother and happily goes off to bathe with the soap he has disdained. Splashing about in the tub, Jane imagines a dream-of-glory in which she is the captain of a huge liner, always calm and in command, cheered and admired, intrepid . . . and, with a gurgling sound, the ocean disappears. The tub is empty, the sailor hat has changed shape. "Oh, maybe next time I'll be the captain of a jet plane," Jane says. Light, lively, and engagingly illustrated, the story is pleasant both for the imaginative qualities it displays and for the adventurous role Jane chooses.

1045   **Redford,** Polly. *The Christmas Bower;* drawings by Edward Gorey. Dutton, 1967. 192p. $3.95. (Cape, 1969. 192p. £1.05.)

5–7   Noah, as the only son and grandson of a department store family, had disappointed all his relatives because he shared the interests of the one queer member—Uncle Willie, a museum ornithologist. When the store's plan for a Christmas display that included live birds ended in disaster, it was Uncle Willie who came to the rescue. Several dozen tropical birds were rescued, but not before there had been a shopper's riot; later, it was again Uncle Willie who—with the help of Noah, some store employees, and a birdbanding association—caught the two really rare birds that had been left in the store. The department store setting is interesting, the information about birds not obtrusive; the characters are lively, only occasionally verging on stereotypes, and the plot and dialogue are brisk and breezy and bright.

1046   **Rees,** Ennis. *Brer Rabbit and His Tricks;* drawings by Edward Gorey. Scott, 1967. 42p. $3.95.

K–3   Three Brer Rabbit stories told in rhyming verse, illustrated with distinctive and humorous pictures by Gorey. The rhyme falters occasionally, but the rhythm and flavor of the verses are excellent; Mr. Rees has shed the burden of heavy dialect but kept intact the personalities of Brer Fox and Brer Rabbit and has even kept some of the language of the Harris dialogue. The three tales are "Brer Rabbit and the Tar Baby," "Winnianimus Grass," and "Hello, House!"

1047   **Rees,** Ennis. *More of Brer Rabbit's Tricks;* illus. by Edward Gorey. Scott, 1968. 42p. $3.95.

K–3   A companion volume to *Brer Rabbit and His Tricks* is also illustrated by Gorey's restrained and distinctive pictures, again giving three stories in simplified language. The stories are in rhyme; occasionally rhyme or meter falter a bit, but the telling is brisk, bouncy, and flavorful.

1048   **Reeves,** James, comp. *The Christmas Book;* illus. by Raymond Briggs. Dutton, 1968. 190p. $4.95. (Heinemann, 1968. 192p. £1.25.)

4–6   A welcome Christmas anthology of prose and poetry, varied in every way: genre, style, form, mood, and period. The black and white illustrations are very effective, the selections well chosen for the level of the reader, although much of the book is suitable for reading aloud to younger children. A good source for holiday storytelling, the book offers a range of authors from Ransome and Dickens to Dylan Thomas and Michael Bond.

1049   **Reeves,** James. *The Trojan Horse;* pictures by Krystyna Turska. Watts, 1969. 31p. Trade ed. $4.95; Library ed. $3.30 net. (H. Hamilton, 1968. 32p. £0.90.)

4–5   Looking back on a tragic experience of his childhood, a Trojan describes the invasion and sacking of his city as it appeared to a boy of ten. Ilias tells of the war and its causes, of the deaths of the sons of Priam, and of the huge horse that was built by the Greeks as an offering to the Gods—so the Trojans thought. The style is rolling and eloquent: "Great were the lamentations at the death of these heroes." The story is not obstructed by the personal narrative, and the large pages— although more appropriate in size to the picture book audience than to the middle-grades reader—are wonderfully used for the virile, exciting illustrations, not unlike the work of Keeping in their high sense of design.

1050   **Reggiani,** Renee. *The Sun Train;* tr. from the Italian by Patrick Creagh. Coward-McCann, 1966. 251p. $3.95. (Harrap, 1967. 194p. £0.90.)

7–10   A quite sophisticated novel that has social and political overtones. The protagonist, Agata La Rosa, is a Sicilian girl of thirteen who longs for a more civilized society than the oppressive feudalism of her own. The family moves to a mainland city where they find that there are problems as serious as those of rural Sicily.

Agata struggles with financial needs, social ostracism, paternal resistance to the new environment, and several brushes with petty criminals. She adjusts in a realistic fashion, and she is accepted by the family of a new boy friend. Probably the petty snobberies and suspicious prejudices between the Sicilians and the inhospitable Torino residents are the most effective aspect of the story, although the individual characterizations and the relationships are well drawn.

1051   **Reiss,** Johanna de Leeuw. *The Upstairs Room.* T. Y. Crowell, 1972. 196p. $4.50.

4–7   A remarkably effective record of the author's experiences as a child in Holland during the German occupation of World War II. Youngest child in a Jewish family, Annie, with her sister Sini, was hidden in a farmer's home for over two years, confined— with few exceptions—to a single room. The writing captures the ingenuousness and directness of a young girl, and the story candidly reveals the friction between the two girls and the abrasive bitterness in their parents' relationship. The characterization is excellent; particularly memorable are the three members of the sheltering family. The dialogue is excellent, the story gravid with dramatic suspense.

1052   **Reiss,** John J. *Colors.* Bradbury Press, 1969. 29p. $4.95.

2–5   Lovely to look at, an excellent first book for learning or
yrs.   practicing the names of colors. Several pages are devoted to each color: red, blue, yellow, orange, green, purple, brown, and black. On each page, handsomely designed and striking in the shades and values of each color, is a series of familiar objects; the whole text consists of the name of the color (yellow) and the names of the objects (baby chicks, lemons, squash, bumblebees, bananas, buttercups, daffodils, daisies). The artist takes occasional liberties—the daffodils are actually brown against the yellow page—but the overall impression is of glowing, sunny, cheery yellow.

1053   **Reiss,** John J. *Numbers.* Bradbury Press, 1971. 29p. illus. $4.95.

2–5   Like Reiss' *Colors*, *Numbers* is distinguished for its big, bold pic-
yrs.   tures and a lavish use of bright, rich colors. A stunning page, for example, has a large, scarlet 18, below which are the words "eighteen crayons" in white, with a bundle of varicolored crayons below—all against a black background. Each page has a colored background, a number almost four inches high, and a labelled picture, occasionally two. The numbers are one to twenty, moving by tens to one hundred, with a final page showing one thousand blue and green raindrops falling on the umbrella of a smiling

child. How nice to have such a useful book for learning to count be so lovely that it can also stimulate esthetic appreciation.

1054   **Rey,** Margret Elizabeth (Waldstein). *Curious George Goes to the Hospital;* by Margret and H. A. Rey. Houghton, 1966. 48p. illus. Trade ed. $3.25; Library ed. $3.07 net.

K–2   Written in collaboration with the Children's Medical Center of Boston, this read-aloud book has the same light humor as do the other books about George; in other words, the book fulfills its purpose without being painfully purposive. George swallows a piece of a jigsaw puzzle and is hospitalized after an X-ray reveals the cause of his discomfort. He has a short but lively period of recuperation, with a Georgian mishap as a last contribution to hospital life.

1055   **Rice,** Edward. *Mother India's Children;* Meeting Today's Generation in India. Pantheon Books, 1971. 176p. illus. Trade ed. $4.95; Library ed. $5.59 net.

7—   A series of interviews with young Indians, by a photographer and journalist, gives a varied and fascinating picture of India today: the immense riches and the immense poverty, the consciousness of caste, the minority groups, the young rebels of the city and the apathetic drudge of twelve who knows nothing and wants nothing. Sometimes the conflict is personal, sometimes it is that of the sophisticated daughter of a diplomat living in a different world from that of the elephant boy. Each interview is separate, and both the writing and the photography are first-rate.

1056   **Rich,** Louise Dickinson. *Three of a Kind;* illus. by William M. Hutchinson. Watts, 1970. 151p. $4.95.

4–6   Eleven-year-old Sally, a ward of the state of Maine, had never had a foster home in which she felt so happy as she did with Ben and Rhoda Cooper. She loved the freedom of the island, the simplicity and warmth of the Star Island community. When the Cooper's grandson came to stay, Sally felt a bit left out. Then she herself became so wrapt in the effort to help little Benjie that she forgot her own small problems, for four-year-old Benjie was totally withdrawn. He didn't move unless one moved him, he didn't speak or laugh. The way in which each of the characters reacts to Benjie, and the way in which the child begins to react, slowly at first and then in a rush, are logical; the characters are vibrantly real and the total picture of the island community balanced and sympathetic.

1057   **Richard,** Adrienne. *Pistol.* Little, 1969. 245p. $4.95.

7–10   Billy Catlett tells the story of his adolescence in the depression years in Montana, where the family had settled down after years of restless job-shifting on his father's part. Although the story carries through the bitter times after the family left town so that the two boys and their father could work at a dam site, most of the book is devoted to Billy—nicknamed Pistol—as a young wrangler on a ranch, learning to gentle a horse, to round up cattle, to take with equanimity the teasing of the hands. This is a wholly convincing picture of the quiet and thoughtful growth from boy to man; Billy saw the widening gulf between himself and his family and knew that with the painful feeling of responsibility for his mother, the clear realization of his father's weakness, and the lack of rapport between himself and his brother, he would have to strike out alone—and the story ends with Billy, slim savings in hand, leaving for the Chicago stockyards. An unusual setting for an unusual depression era story in a book that is distinguished by honesty, sensitivity, and some delightful scenes of cowboy humor.

1058   **Richardson,** Grace. *Douglas.* Harper, 1966. 230p. Trade ed. $3.50; Library ed. $3.27 net.

7—   It is probable that almost every reader of this book will know a Douglas—an intelligent, charming, undependable young person who lies with more fluency than cause, who fails repeatedly in all his efforts and who always has a plausible reason for the failure. A scholarship student, Douglas is expelled from a private high school, having caused trouble, told lies, and cut classes. When he comes to McGill University, some years later, Douglas hasn't changed; a series of people are at first charmed, then disenchanted. Then Douglas goes to London to make his mark; he comes home destitute, realizing for the first time that his friends have always thought of him as an odd character, and accepting for the first time their affection without their admiration. The writing style is smooth, the dialogue natural; although the scope of the story is small, it never becomes either dull or trivial; the incidents, the conversations, the reactions of Douglas' friends and his family all contribute to the sharp delineation of a type. And never, never does the author tell you what Douglas is, but lets Douglas and the other characters tell you.

1059   **Richardson,** Robert Shirley. *The Stars & Serendipity;* illus. with photographs and drawings. Pantheon Books, 1971. 129p. Trade ed. $5.95; Library ed. $5.99 net.

6–9   A fascinating introduction to some of the astronomical discoveries that have been made not through diligent pursuit of an accepted theory, but through the happy—if equally diligent—investigation of a deviant path: the serendipity of an unanticipated discovery. The text covers some of the exciting finds from ancient times to today, and includes the discovery of Uranus; the pinpointing, in

1862, of Sirius's companion star; the first accurate estimate of the velocity of light; the discovery of radio waves from outer space; and the reversal in polarity that is characteristic of the solar magnetic cycle. The writing has an informal zest. A glossary is appended.

1060   **Richoux,** Pat. *A Long Walk on a Short Dock;* decorations by George Porter. Morrow, 1969. 252p. $4.95.

6–9   A good first-person story about a pivotal summer in a girl's life. Terry, fifteen, is not yet ready for the dating game and is scornfully aware that an attractive new girl at the lake resort is merely pretending an interest in sailing. Vicki gets plenty of attention from Carl, the local boy who is an excellent sailor and who, Terry finally realizes, has been as convinced for years as she herself has, that they have nothing in common. The new rapport between the summer visitor, Terry, and the native, Carl, is reached in a completely believable way, and the story is free of the trademarks of the patterned summer-romance book: there is not really a triangle situation, and the dance Terry bribes a younger boy to take her to ends with Terry and her escort grimly dancing. The writing style has ease and flow, and there is just enough about sailing for the buff and not too much for the land-bound reader.

1061   **Richter,** Hans Peter. *Friedrich;* tr. from the German by Edite Kroll. Holt, 1970. 149p. $4.50.

6–9   The Schneiders, who lived upstairs, were a quiet, friendly couple whose only child, Friedrich, was just the same age as the writer. Together the boys started school, played outdoors, shared their toys. But this was Germany in the 1930's, and the Schneiders were Jews. As Friedrich's friend tells the story, it is clear that he and his family—loyal to Hitler—are aware of the injustice in the series of degrading and then frightening incidents in the Schneider's lives, but their protests are mild and they cannot see the broader implications of such persecution. All of them are small, unimportant people, and it is this modest milieu that makes the horror, told almost ingenuously by the member of the Jungvolk, even sharper. The writing is calm, the episodic story a stark condemnation. A chronology that cites the decrees and regulations of the Nazi regime is appended.

1062   **Riedman,** Sarah Regal. *Home Is the Sea:* For Whales; by Sarah R. Riedman and Elton T. Gustafson; illus. with photographs. Rand McNally, 1966. 264p. $4.50. (World's Work, 1968. 264p. £ 1.25.)

8—   A comprehensive, authoritative, and well researched book on whales: the different kinds of whales, dolphins, and porpoises;

their evolution, their anatomical structure, their habits, their life cycle. There are many anecdotes and a considerable amount of information about the training of these mammals and the research that has been and is being carried on. The style of writing is direct and serious, the material is well organized. The photographs and diagrams that illustrate and amplify the text are excellent. Tables of different species and their distinguishing characteristics are appended, as is a bibliography and a good relative index.

1063   **Rinkoff,** Barbara. *Member of the Gang;* illus. by Harold James. Crown, 1968. 127p. $3.50.

5–7   "Trouble—that spells trouble in my book," Woodie's father said, when he heard that Woodie had been hanging around with Leroy. But Leroy was a leader, an important guy, and Woodie wanted to be in his gang. Other kids played hookey and got away with it, so Woodie agreed to be the front man for a store robbery. When one of the gang was knifed in a fight, Woodie stayed with him and was picked up by the police, tried, and put on probation. Although the probation officer was black also, he was authority and Woodie resisted his arguments at first. Gradually Mr. Henry made Woodie see that there was no future in being tough, that his parents were right about getting an education, that being a member of the gang meant only trouble. An honest and sympathetic picture of an adolescent looking for the easy way to the only kind of prestige he thinks he can achieve, and an honest treatment of the modest success that authority has with such boys, since several of the gang members are only waiting for a chance to resume the pattern.

1064   **Rinkoff,** Barbara. *Name: Johnny Pierce.* Seabury Press, 1969. 124p. $3.95.

5–9   There are all sorts of reasons why a fifteen-year-old boy can stray into trouble. Johnny's were not very dramatic: his best friend seemed to be busy with other things, his parents seemed to prefer his younger brother and sister, and Mick and his gang seemed to be having fun and games. Johnny was only a passenger when the stolen car crashed, with Mick at the wheel, but his encounter with the police led him to take a sober look at the way he was drifting, and he concluded that there was no point in blaming other people: it was his life, and he was the one to change the pattern. Low-keyed and realistic, the story depends on natural development and perception rather than high drama, and it is the more convincing for that reason. Also important is the fact that other factors do not change: Johnny's friend is still busy with his own affairs, his siblings still avid attention-getters.

1065   **Rinkoff,** Barbara. *The Watchers.* Knopf, 1972. 130p. $4.99.

5–7   Sanford's head jerked. His fingers twitched. All the other boys
thought this new kid was a creep, but Chris felt sorry for him
and protected him, and Sanford clearly was beginning to worship
Chris and—just as clearly—beginning to be a nuisance. His
mother suggested that he play with normal kids, but to Chris
it was a challenge; unhappy in the home where his father's
gambling instigated violent quarrels, a friendless underachiever
at school, he needed someone to help. And Chris, who tells
the story, does help the other boy to become more active and
more confident. The achievement is realistic, the characters and
dialogue convincing, and the relationships, both between the boys
and the adults in their lives, perceptively drawn.

1066   **Ripley,** Elizabeth (Blake). *Copley;* A Biography. Lippincott,
1967. 72p. illus. $3.75.

6–9   As always, Elizabeth Ripley writes with quiet competence, in a
straightforward style and with a good balance of information
about the artist's personal affairs and the course of his career.
This is one of the few books about Americans in the author's
series of biographies of great artists. Copley, taught as a boy by
his stepfather, was able to earn his living as an engraver when
he was thirteen; marriage brought him money, and his talent
brought him an invitation to come to England. So, just avoiding
the Revolutionary War, Copley began anew in London, becoming
the most sought-after portrait painter there. The illustrations are
clear black-and-white reproductions of Copley's work; a
bibliography and an index are appended.

1067   **Ripley,** Elizabeth (Blake). *Hokusai;* A Biography. Lippincott, 1968.
71p. illus. Trade ed. $3.75; Library ed. $3.59 net.

6–9   One of the best in a good series of biographies of artists, partly
because of the setting and partly because of the character of the
artist: indomitable, ebullient, unconforming, and often amusing.
Dismissed by his master from a print design shop because of
his unorthodox approach to art, Hokusai (who had not then
adopted the name) led a hand-to-mouth existence until his work
became popular. Prodigiously productive, highly versatile,
bankrupt at the height of his career, Hokusai died at eighty-nine
having changed his name fifty times. One fact remained
unchanged, expressed by the tombstone inscription Hokusai
chose: "Old Man Mad about Painting." A bibliography and an
index are appended.

1068   **Ripley,** Elizabeth (Blake). *Rodin;* A Biography. Lippincott, 1966.
72p. illus. Trade ed. $3.75; Library ed. $3.39 net.

6–9   Another excellent book in Mrs. Ripley's series of biographies of
great artists; each page of text is faced by a photographic

reproduction, in black and white, of Rodin's work—almost all of it sculpture. Dissuaded from getting artistic education by his father, the young Rodin worked at several jobs while he yearned to become an artist; eventually he found tuition that did not depend on parental support and became a sculptor, although for many years his ability was unrecognized. The writing style is casual but dignified, with a good balance of information about the work of Rodin and about his personal life. A bibliography and an index are appended.

1069   **Ripley,** Elizabeth (Blake). *Velázquez; A Biography.* Lippincott, 1965. 72p. illus. Trade ed. $3.75; Library ed. $3.69 net.

7–10   Another good biography in the author's series of books about great artists; pages of text alternate with pages of reproductions (in black and white) of the artist's work. The text skims over Velázquez's childhood, focusing on his adult life and his work; the descriptions of paintings and information about court affairs and the Spanish royal family almost overshadow the biographical information. The text is written in a quiet, straightforward style; a list of illustrations precedes the text; a bibliography and an index follow it.

1070   **Robbins,** Ruth. *Taliesin and King Arthur;* written and illus. by Ruth Robbins. Parnassus, 1970. 30p. Trade ed. $3.75; Library ed. $3.87 net.

4–6   Ornately detailed and deftly composed illustrations show the small figures of a feudal court, stylized and romantic. The young poet Taliesin has come to Arthur's court at Caerlon, delighting the king and his retinue with strange tales and with his rare wisdom. At the Grand Contest of Poets on Christmas Eve, Taliesin tells the dramatic and magical story of his birth, King Arthur proclaims him the greatest bard of all, and the audience rejoices. The story mingles fact and legend, the style is poetic, and the tale within a tale should please readers addicted to folklore and legend.

1071   **Robertson,** Keith. *Henry Reed's Baby-Sitting Service;* illus. by Robert McCloskey. Viking, 1966. 204p. $3.50.

5–7   The indomitable Henry rides again; a third romp with Henry Reed and his friend, Midge Glass. This time Henry (as a result of a survey) discovers that one of the town's unmet needs is baby-sitting. In the course of this career, Henry meets some strong-minded babies, but he copes. The book has a plot line, but it is basically episodic; the appeals are in the humor of situation and dialogue, and in the bouncy, bright style of writing. Written in first person, the style is convincing as that of a sophisticated and inventive adolescent.

1072   **Robertson,** Keith. *Henry Reed's Big Show;* illus. by Robert
McCloskey. Viking, 1970. 206p. Trade ed. $4.50; Library ed. $4.13
net.

5–7   The indomitable Henry takes on another project and describes it in
the same ingenuous style that contrasts so amusingly with the
frenetic activity of the story. To the appeal of familiar characters
and believable adventures is added the contemporary attraction
of rock music, as Henry's ambitions to be a theatrical producer
crystallize first in a rock festival and then in a rodeo that
includes a knightly tournament. Would you believe that Henry
and his buddy, Midge, had planned an ordinary play?

1073   **Robinson,** Joan G. *Charley;* illus. by Prudence Seward. Coward-
McCann, 1970. 251p. $4.95. (Collins, 1969. 192p. £0.80.)

4–6   Aunt Emm, with whom Charley had been staying while her
parents were away, seemed to think everything Charley did was
wrong. When Aunt Emm was about to go off for a vacation,
she decided to send Charley to Aunt Louie's, a happy prospect
until she found a scrap of a letter that said "I don't want
Charley . . ." (It had read in full, "It's not that I don't want
Charley . . .") So Charley ran away, camping out in the open
and baffling the good people of the nearby village, who reported
that there were a lame child (Charley) and a simpleton (Charley)
at large. Taken in by a motherly woman after she has reached
the end of her resources, Charley is discovered and scolded by
Aunt Emm, but she realizes for the first time how constricted
a life her aunt leads and finds that she can pity the friendless,
lonely woman. The story has good characters, plenty of action
in small, believable adventures, and the perennial appeal of
making-it-on-your-own; the writing has vitality and pace.

1074   **Robinson,** Joan G. *Mary-Mary Stories;* written and illus. by Joan
G. Robinson. Coward-McCann, 1968. 96p. $3.49. (Harrap, 1965.
176p. £0.75.)

2–4   First published in England, seven short stories about Mary, the
youngest of five children and—in self-defense—so contrary that
she is called Mary-Mary. The light, brisk style has humor and the
plots of the several episodes are all believable. Mary-Mary
emerges triumphant from each encounter—the only one who
smiles at the photographer (after the older children have wailed
that she would ruin the group picture making faces) and the
proud donor of a surprise anniversary plant (having buried the
money for the bulb that should have been in the pot) when
her brothers and sisters all gave their mother perfectly ordinary
flowers. A good book for reading aloud to younger children, as
well as for girls who can read the book independently.

1075   **Robinson,** Lloyd. *The Stolen Election;* Hayes versus Tilden—1876.
Doubleday, 1968. 240p. Trade ed. $3.95; Library ed. $4.70 net.

7–10   A fascinating account of one of the shadier chapters in our
country's political history. In 1876, Samuel Tilden was expected
to win the presidential election . . . but some states had sent
in more than one set of electoral votes. Who could decide which
set to use? Tilden needed 185 votes; he had 184. For the election
to go to Hayes, the Republican candidate, every disputed vote
(Florida, Louisiana, Oregon, South Carolina) had to go to him,
and the managing editor of the New York *Times,* Reid, worked
with bitter determination and no scruples to see that that
happened. The bribery and corruption that ensued had an effect
on the future as well as on those concerned: "Everything was
duly agreed. The South would help make Hayes President, and
Hayes would give the South back to the white Democrats."
The tone of writing is dispassionate, the events dramatic; the
material is deftly handled, particularly in view of its complexity.
An index and a bibliography are appended.

1076   **Rocca,** Guido. *Gaetano the Pheasant;* A Hunting Fable; pictures
by Giulio Cingoli and Giancarlo Carloni. Harper, 1966. 60p.
Trade ed. $3.95; Library ed. $3.79 net.

4–5   First published in Italy in 1961, a fanciful story that is illustrated
by pictures that are varied in technique; there is no evidence
as to which pictures are the work of which of the two illustrators.
The oversize pages of the book are a fine vehicle for the most
lovely of the illustrations: soft, delicate yet vibrant paintings of
birds. The format is that of a picture book, but the vocabulary,
the concepts, and the plot seem more suitable for the reader
in the middle grades. Gaetano is more thoughtful than the rest
of the pheasants in a game preserve; having seen the carnage
of the hunting season, he determines to escape. Most of the other
pheasants either accept their lot, or they are dubious about
Gaetano's advice; in the end, only Gaetano and his mate reach
the shelter of an uninhabited island.

1077   **Rockwell,** Anne. *Filippo's Dome.* Atheneum, 1967. 82p. illus. Trade
ed. $3.50; Library ed. $3.41 net. (Macmillan, 1968. 88p. £1.05.)

6–9   The story of the construction of the dome of St. Mary of the
Flower, with a considerable amount of Florentine history as
background for the account of the long, slow building of the
church. Interrupted by plague and political turmoil, slowed by the
death of one architect and then another, the church was for a
long time completed save for the dome. Filippo Brunelleschi was
the inventive architect who, after twenty years of hoping and
planning, solved the problem of constructing the huge dome.
The architectural details are illuminating, and the dramatic history

has both historical and artistic interest; the writing style is a bit heavy.

1078   **Rockwell,** Anne. *Glass, Stones and Crown;* The Abbé Suger and the Building of St. Denis. Atheneum, 1968. 80p. illus. Trade ed. $3.75; Library ed. $3.59 net. (Macmillan, 1969. 80p. £1.05.)

6–10   This is a book as interesting for its historical material as for its architectural focus. With remarkable lucidity, the author traces the events in the life of the boyhood friend of Louis Capet, Suger; Louis became the King of France and Suger the Abbot of St. Denis. Fat and sometimes foolish, Louis was propped and sustained by Suger, whose life was dedicated to his king, his country, and his church. In the slow, patient years in which the old church of St. Denis was torn down, the new one was rebuilt with the innovatory features that became popular throughout Europe—the stained glass windows, the piers and buttresses, the ribbed vaulting and soaring pillars of Gothic architecture.

1079   **Rockwell,** Anne. *Temple on a Hill;* The Building of the Parthenon. Atheneum, 1969. 108p. illus. Trade ed. $3.95; Library ed. $4.95 net.

5–7   When the armies of Xerxes left Greece, the citizens of Athens returned to their city to find that it had been almost entirely destroyed. Under the leadership of Themistocles, then Cimon, then Pericles, the rebuilding of the city and its temples slowly proceeded. The author describes the planning and the building of the Parthenon, the work of Phidias, and the details of architectural construction as parts of the life of ancient Athens, so that the book has artistic and historical value. The maps, drawings, and diagrams are useful; the writing style is slow and serious, straightforward in architectural description and dramatically vivid in historical details.

1080   **Rockwell,** Anne. *The Toolbox;* illus. by Harlow Rockwell. Macmillan, 1971. 19p. $3.95.

1–2   "In my cellar there is a toolbox," the text begins, and goes on to describe each tool and—in a phrase or two—what it does. The pictures are clear, exact, and handsome; the print is large, and the ample white space sets off both, to add to visual appeal and ease of reading. Simple enough for the beginning reader, and also the sort of book over which a preschool child likes to pore. "It is my father's toolbox," the book ends, and in this picture a boy is watching his father hammering a nail.

1081   **Rodman,** Bella. *Lions in the Way.* Follett, 1966. 238p. Trade ed. $3.95; Library ed. $3.96 net.

7–10   A contemporary story of school integration in a Tennessee town, a town that had fought the Supreme Court decision for two years before capitulating. Eight students from a Negro high school had been selected to attend Fayette, a hitherto segregated school. All of the residual hostility in the community is stirred by an agitator who establishes a White Crusade. Robby, leader of the eight students, is particularly bitter at the attacks made by Joel, a white boy who had been his best friend when they were small. Two of the eight students drop out; order and cooperation are established after a white minister is severely injured and after the U. S. Army is called in. While the book is a fine documentary novel, it is slightly fragmented as a literary whole, since the emphasis seems to shift from the students to the adults in the story—in each case, portraying people on both sides of the issue. The minister who is injured, for example, moves almost into the role of the protagonist; for the most part, the protagonist is Robby. Despite the minor flaws, an important and an interesting book.

1082   **Roland,** Betty. *Jamie's Summer Visitor;* illus. by Prudence Seward. McGraw-Hill, 1967. 73p. $2.95. (Bodley Head, 1964. 76p. £0.55.)

4–5   Another story about the small Australian boy of *The Forbidden Bridge* who lives with his widowed mother on a farm in the bush country. Jamie is not enthralled at the prospect of a Christmas vacation visit from the daughter of an old friend of his mother's, and his forebodings are justified. Nola is disdainful about the farm and about Jamie's friends—when she isn't showing off; not until she breaks down in confessing a misdemeanor to Jamie's mother does it become apparent that Nola tries to be superior because she feels rejected. The plot is realistic, the characterization not deep but convincing, and the setting appealing; the Christmastime finale is jolly and warm.

1083   **Rollins,** Charlemae Hill. *Black Troubadour:* Langston Hughes. Rand McNally, 1970. 143p. illus. Trade ed. $4.95; Library ed. $4.79 net.

7–10   A good biography, written with warm affection, covering much of the same material that is in Hughes's autobiographical writing. Some of the incidents and relationships that are in the Meltzer biography are omitted, and Langston Hughes's patron, Mrs. Mason, is mentioned only as "an elderly woman." While this is not as analytical as the Meltzer book, it is competent. The divided bibliography includes dramatic works for which Hughes wrote the script or lyrics. Many photographs of the subject and other prominent Negroes are included; an index is appended.

1084   **Rose,** Karen. *A Single Trail.* Follett, 1969. 158p. Trade ed. $3.95; Library ed. $3.99 net.

5–6   Ricky wasn't nervous about starting in a new sixth-grade classroom; after nine moves he had cultivated an approach that made it easy to acquire new friends. He hadn't expected to deal with the sort of antagonism that Earl showed. As far as Earl was concerned, any white boy was an enemy. All Earl's affection went to his mother and small brother; in the classroom, he played the stupid clown. One brush with crime persuades Earl to stay away from an older delinquent, but his friendship with Ricky comes very slowly indeed and only after they are thrown together by coaching sessions with an invalid teacher. The situation is handled realistically, with major credit going to the teacher, understanding and persistent, and the young principal who patiently copes with Earl's hostility. The writing style is easy and natural; despite a few small plot contrivances, the story has a sturdy honesty. Both Ricky and Earl feel a conflict between their behavior and their self-images, and for each of them the new relationship is a step rather than a total solution.

1085   **Rose,** Karen. *There Is a Season.* Follett, 1967. 155p. Trade ed. $3.25; Library ed. $3.30 net.

7–10   A junior novel that explores one of the not infrequent (but infrequently written about) problems in the lives of adolescents, the problem of parental disapproval because of religious difference. Katie is fifteen, her religious conviction already wavering; she resents her mother's criticism of her friendship with Jamie, since he is a Catholic and Katie's family Jewish. She's also shaken by the fact that—despite her affection for Jamie—she finds Gary Berg attractive. Both problems are removed when Gary enlists in the Army and Jamie announces that he is entering the priesthood; in a final episode, in which Katie achieves a measure of adult sagacity, she describes the incidents of her brother's bar mitzvah ceremony. With a new realization of family solidarity and a new insight into human relationships, Katie is content to wait for whatever life will bring. The first-person approach gives an immediacy to Katie's problems, moods, and emotions; the characterizations are not deep but are convincing; the pace of the story is rather slow, but the universality of many of Katie's troubles should appeal to readers.

1086   **Rosen,** Sidney. *Wizard of the Dome*; R. Buckminster Fuller, Designer for the Future. Little, 1969. 189p. illus. $4.95.

7—   Buckminster Fuller had so many times been on the verge of success with his inventions, only to fail; it really seemed that he was at last going to see his dream realized when Beech Aircraft agreed to finance the manufacture of Dymaxion houses— but World War II ended and the company decided to make airplanes only. And there, again, was Bucky Fuller, a design pioneer whose work had been rejected. As he had so many times before, Fuller (now fifty) became fascinated with theoretical exploration, and out of his ideas about the tetrahedron in nature and the application of geodesic structure came his now-famous domes. The book has a good balance of personal life, career and professional information, and discussion of Fuller's theories; written in an informal but dignified style, it makes clear the importance and the innovatory quality of Fuller's work without being adulatory, and it is as candid about Fuller's days of despair as it is about the basic ebullience of his nature. A bibliography and an index are appended.

1087   **Rosenberg,** Nancy. *Vaccines and Viruses;* by Nancy Rosenberg and Louis Z. Cooper. Grosset, 1971. 157p. illus. Trade ed. $4.50; Library ed. $4.59 net.

7–9   An excellent review of the years of research on viruses and vaccines, arranged in chapters by diseases. These sections are preceded by a discussion of the nature of a virus and concluded by a chapter on the possibility of transduction, the genetic engineering process in which a virus is used to transfer hereditary traits and thereby repair defective cells. Written with informality and authority, the text covers much material that is familiar, but it includes recent findings and theories, is well organized, and is lucid in explanation of biological and chemical intricacies. An index is appended.

1088   **Ross,** Frank Xavier. *Transportation of Tomorrow;* illus. with drawings by the author and photographs. Lothrop, 1968. 160p. Trade ed. $4.50; Library ed. $4.14 net.

7–12   A survey of new developments in transportation methods and vehicles, with a preview of imaginable refinements. The book covers the same material, basically, as does Hellman's *Transportation in the World of the Future,* although there is here less concern with the community's problems. The book is capably written, comprehensive in coverage, and clear in its explanations of the designs and variations in air, land, and sea craft and the new systems that can accommodate their use. An index is appended.

1089   **Ross,** Laura. *Finger Puppets;* Easy to Make, Fun to Use; illus. by Laura and Frank Ross. Lothrop, 1971. 64p. Trade ed. $3.95; Library ed. $3.78 net.

3–4   Like many craft books, this can be used by adults to entertain children or by children themselves, and many of the puppets and puppet plays can be managed by very small children with assistance. There are several kinds of finger puppets: paint on the hand itself, bare fingers used in games, shadow figures made by fingers and hands, and fingers clad in various degrees of intricacy of costume. Several games and plays are given in full, as well as instructions for manipulating finger puppets and making costumes. A list of books and rhymes for finger puppets is appended.

1090   **Ross,** Laura. *Hand Puppets;* How to Make and Use Them; written and illus. by Laura Ross. Lothrop, 1969. 192p. Trade ed. $4.95; Library ed. $4.59 net. (World's Work, 1971. 192p. £1.60.)

4–7   A most useful book that gives instructions for making three kinds of puppets (paper bag, rod, and papier mâché), for building stages, for adapting a story for dramatic use, for writing an original puppet play, and for making costumes. Directions for construction are clear and simple, all materials—including those for sets and scenery—are comparatively inexpensive if not free, and the advice on procedures of production is succinct and sensible. Three complete puppet plays are included; a brief list of additional readings and an index are appended.

1091   **Ross,** Pat, comp. *Young and Female;* Turning Points in the Lives of Eight American Women; Personal accounts compiled with introductory notes by Pat Ross. Random House, 1972. 104p. $3.95.

7–10   Pat Ross, an articulate member of Feminists on Children's Media, has chosen selections from eight autobiographies of modern women, each showing a turning point in the author's life and each prefaced by an editorial note that gives some biographical information and facts about the author's career. Those careers are as varied as the authors' styles, so that the book has a lively contrast as well as subject interest. The women who write of being young and female are Margaret Bourke-White, Shirley Chisholm, Dorothy Day, Edna Ferber, Althea Gibson, Emily Hahn, Shirley MacLaine, and Margaret Sanger.

1092   **Roth,** Arnold. *Pick a Peck of Puzzles.* Norton, 1966. 76p. illus. Trade ed. $3.95; Library ed. $3.69 net.

3–5   A good book for the puzzle fan, liberally illustrated with humorous drawings in addition to the pictured puzzles. The selections are varied: riddles and rebuses, pictures with hidden clues, puzzles that play with words or numbers, and some odd bits and pieces such as lists of foreign words, tongue-twisters, and optical illusions. Some of the answers to puzzles are given at the back of the book; in some cases the answers are on the same page as the puzzles.

1093   **Rounds,** Glen. *The Snake Tree;* written and illus. by Glen Rounds. World, 1966. 95p. Trade ed. $3.95; Library ed. $4.21 net. (World Pub. Co., 1967. 95p. £1.40.)

5–7   In a series of brief essays, the author describes some of the events in the lives of the wild creatures who lived in and around an abandoned farmhouse. The butcher bird, for example, hung snakes he had killed on the thorns of a honey locust; a possum visited nightly; a colony of wasps was established on an old window shutter. Always a delight to the nature lover, Mr. Round's descriptions of the small affairs of the animal world are in an easy, conversational style; he does not attribute human characteristics to animals but does express, with grace and affection, animal idiosyncrasies in human terms. "The mockingbird who owned the abandoned farmhouse and the overgrown dooryard had the air of an old settler—tolerant of neighbors who knew their place, but a terror to those who crossed him."

1094   **Rublowsky,** John. *Music in America.* Crowell-Collier, 1967. 185p. illus. $3.50.

7—   A good history of music in our country from the time of the church-centered music of the first colonists to electronic music and the experimental work of Cage. The writing is detailed and quiet, but informal rather than stiff; a recurrent theme is the schism in American music, first that between sacred and secular music, and later between "popular" and "classical" music—a separation more rigid here than it was in Europe, where serious musicians were impressed by the vitality of American jazz. A large portion of the material in the book describes the contribution of Negroes to folk and modern music; one chaper is devoted to Indian music. A bibliography and an index are appended.

1095   **Ruskin,** Ariane, ad. *Art of the High Renaissance.* McGraw-Hill, 1970. 189p. illus. $9.95.

7—   A companion volume to that of Batterberry, reviewed above, with the same advantages of handsome illustrations, good coverage, and good index. Like the earlier volume, the book covers all of the arts; most of the work is Italian and the discussion of painters and painting is the major part of the text. The writing style here is rather more graceful, but both books are beautiful and informative, worthy additions to a fine series.

1096   **Ruskin,** Ariane, ad. *Nineteenth Century Art.* McGraw-Hill, 1968. 192p. illus. $9.95.

8—   Adapted from the text of a magazine series, a book as impressive as it is interesting, the vigorous prose and occasional poetic phrase accompanied by many reproductions of excellent quality. The author does not set art apart, but sees it as an evocation of its time, so that descriptions of paintings and discussions of individual artists are given within some matrix of contemporary events. There is material about architecture and a bit more about sculpture, but most of this history of art in the last century is devoted—brilliantly—to painting. Preceding the index is a numbered list of the illustrations, divided (as is the text) into their appropriate periods.

1097   Ruskin, Ariane, ad. *Prehistoric Art and Ancient Art of the Near East.* McGraw-Hill, 1971. 192p. illus. $9.95.

7—   Another impressive volume in a series distinguished for its beauty and for the high standard of writing, this book describes prehistoric art in Africa and Europe and the art of Egypt and Mesopotamia in ancient times. The reproductions of cave paintings, carvings, jewelry, architecture, and painting are excellent, with good placement and textual references. The writing is lucid and informed, giving the sort of information about cultural details that enriches the reader's understanding of the art forms that emerged from those cultures. A relative index is appended.

1098   Ruskin, Ariane, ad. *17th and 18th Century Art.* McGraw-Hill, 1969. 191p. illus. $9.95.

7—   Lucid and informative, a book that serves as an excellent introduction to the art history of two centuries, but is comprehensive and authoritative enough for the reader who is already acquainted with the subject. The text is divided by countries, chronological within the divisions, and profusely illustrated with full-color reproductions. An index and numbered list of illustrations are appended; the latter gives locations of art objects. Illustrations are, unfortunately, not indexed, so that there is no way to find quickly—for example—all of Canaletto's works represented, since they are not cited in the index, and the list of illustrations (in order) is by title.

1099   Russ, Lavinia. *Over the Hills and Far Away.* Harcourt, 1968. 160p. $3.75.

6–9   Peakie was almost twelve in 1917, and she found it hard to cope with her unpredictable mother and her all-too-predictable older sister, who in turn found Peakie a nuisance. Deeply attached to Jo March, her only confidante, Peakie found her ideal man to replace Jo. (She was still only twelve.) Then came convent school; two years later, a private school, then another. And then, for the first time, Peakie found a real friend. This would be merely a piece of nostalgia were it not so amusing; the writing is effervescent, and the characters highly individual without being exaggerated.

1100   Sachs, Marilyn. *Amy and Laura;* illus. by Tracy Sugarman. Doubleday, 1966. 189p. $3.95.

4–6   Here is the very good sequel to *Amy Moves In* and *Laura's Luck,* books about the two Stern sisters who live in the Bronx in the 1930's. Their mother, long hospitalized after being hit by a car, comes home; Amy joyously accepts Mama, wheelchair and all, but Laura finds that she feels a coldness to this invalid mother who has grown heavy and grey-haired. The denouement is Mama's declaration of independence; she wants to run her home and be a mother, not a liability—and Laura realizes that Mama is still Mama. The chapters alternately focus on one sister or the other, but the action is not separate; indeed, one of the appeals of the book is that (both in school and at home) there is a continuity of relationship within which there are shifts of motives and moods.

1101   **Sachs,** Marilyn. *The Bears' House;* illus. by Louis Glanzman. Doubleday, 1971. 81p. Trade ed. $3.95; Library ed. $4.70 net.

4–6   Fran Ellen sucks her thumb, she is dirty and unkempt, she is bullied by her classmates and despaired of by her teacher—who has no idea that this nine-year-old is one of four children whose mother has retreated into a psychotic state after desertion by her husband. There are two pleasures in Fran Ellen's life: the schoolroom doll house and its bear family, with whom she leads a fantasy life in which all her wishes come true, and the baby sister who is her special charge and dearest love. A suspicious teacher ferrets out the truth about Fran Ellen's family, and goes for help. There the story ends, with Fran Ellen, who has told it, talking to the bears in the doll house, given her by the teacher. Although the unrelieved pathos strikes a monotone note, the story is touching. The ending seems a bit inconclusive, but there are enough variety and action in the realistic incidents of home and school to give the story substance.

1102   **Sachs,** Marilyn. *Peter and Veronica;* illus. by Louis Glanzman. Doubleday, 1969. 174p. $3.95. (Macdonald, 1970. 168p. £1.00.)

4–7   A sequel to *Veronica Ganz,* in which Veronica, a perennial bully, met her match in the smallest boy in the class, Peter, who became her close friend. Here Peter and Veronica are beginning to be conscious of the fact that they are boy and girl, although they are still primarily just friends. Their relationship is tested and almost fails when Veronica fails to come to Peter's bar mitzvah—after Peter's long arguments with his mother, who can't see why a girl who isn't Jewish should be invited. Both the children are candid about it: their mothers are prejudiced. The problem and the dialogue concerning it are handled extremely well, as is the ensuing breach between the friends, a breach healed in a most natural way when Peter, who had been outraged by Veronica's absence on the great occasion, plans a small speech only to find that Veronica, far from feeling guilty, has seen that his battle was not really for her but for himself—and gets Peter to admit it.

1103 **Sachs,** Marilyn. *Veronica Ganz;* illus. by Louis Glanzman. Doubleday, 1968. 156p. Trade ed. $3.95; Library ed. $4.25 net. (Macdonald, 1968. 155p. £0.90.)

5–7 Veronica was thirteen and exceptionally tall for her age; used to being teased, she had always responded by bullying other children. How could a little shrimp who only came up to her shoulder bother her so much? But Peter did—until Veronica finally realized that he really admired her. Overwhelmed by the power of being a female, Veronica finally abandoned her former role and behaved like a girl. She didn't hit—she giggled. This breezy story is casually twined with another theme: Veronica and her younger sister adjust to the fact that their father (they live with mother and stepfather) is immersed in his own life, although he loves them. The people, the dialogue, and the relationships are realistic; the writing is lightly humorous, with only an occasional sequence that seems drawn-out.

1104 **Sackett,** Samuel J. *Cowboys & the Songs They Sang;* settings by Lionel Nowak; designed by Walter Einsel. Scott, 1967. 72p. $5.95.

5— More than a book of cowboy music, this collection of a dozen-plus songs (written in the simplest notation) gives a great deal of information about the cowboy and his way of life. Each selection is preceded by some background information and an old photograph or two, some of them fuzzy but all of them flavorful. The writing is simple, infrequently humorous, and pleasantly loquacious. A one-page bibliography and discography are appended.

1105 **Sacks,** Raymond. *Magnets;* illus. by Stefan Martin. Coward-McCann, 1967. 45p. $3.49.

2–4 An excellent first book on the subject. The writing is direct, simple, and clear; the text is nicely complemented by the illustrations, which are large, uncluttered, and carefully arranged in relation to the pertinent text. The author describes the attraction and repulsion of magnetic poles, the magnetic field, the way in which one can make a magnet, and the reason the new magnet can attract iron and steel.

1106 **Samachson,** Dorothy. *The First Artists;* by Dorothy and Joseph Samachson. Doubleday, 1970. 147p. illus. $4.95.

5–9 A competent survey of cave paintings and engravings, more extensive than the usual treatment of the subject. In addition to descriptions of such famous finds as Altamira and Lascaux, the authors discuss minor examples and they examine the work of cave artists of Australia, Africa and America as well as the more familiar European paintings, including styles, techniques, theories about significance, ethnographic parallels, and abstract or symbolic work. The photographs are good; a glossary and an index are appended; many pages are not numbered.

1107   **Samachson,** Dorothy. *The Russian Ballet;* And Three of Its Masterpieces; by Dorothy and Joseph Samachson. Lothrop, 1971. 159p. illus. Trade ed. $4.95; Library ed. $4.59 net.

6–10   A good history of the ballet in Russia, including the establishment of ballet schools and the roles of composer, director, and choreographer. The emphasis is on the past, although there is some discussion of contemporary ballet in Russia. The book concludes with detailed discussions (and plot synopses) of three Tchaikovsky ballets; only one (Swan Lake) is mentioned in the chapter devoted to the composer whose music gave the art form new depth. The book has less material about individual dancers than do most books on ballet, the emphasis being on training, the types of ballet that have become popular, and some of the characteristics of Russian ballet. The writing is dignified and direct, the drawings and photographs enticing for the balletomane. A glossary of terms, a list of great ballets of the past, a brief list of Soviet ballets (with literary origins and composer) and an index are appended.

1108   **Samachson,** Joseph. *The Armor within Us;* The Story of Bone; illus. with photographs. Rand McNally, 1966. 192p. $3.95.

8—   An interesting topic is discussed in an easy, smooth, and straightforward style, and discussed with authority; the text is detailed and serious, although none of the descriptions is incomprehensibly technical or difficult. Dr. Samachson discusses morphology, physiology, heredity, nutrition, endocrine secretions, surgery, et cetera, as all of these subjects are related to the animal—chiefly human—skeleton. He gives some medical history and describes, throughout the book, research and experimentation. A good glossary and an index are appended; a few advanced titles are cited for further reading.

1109   **Sammis,** Edward R. *Last Stand at Stalingrad;* The Battle that Saved the World. Macmillan, 1966. 96p. illus. Trade ed. $3.50; Library ed. $3.54 net. (Collier-Mac., 1966. 128p. £0.90.)

7–10   A vivid and moving documentary of the struggle for the city of Stalingrad; for months the fighting and bombing continued, the Russians holding out with grim tenacity until a counter-offensive could be mounted. The writing is crisp and straightforward, all the drama being in the harrowing facts. Illustrated with excellent battle maps and with many action photographs, the book gives a report on this major battle of World War II that is both informative and exciting. A detailed chronology, a brief bibliography, and an index are appended.

1110   **Sandburg,** Carl. *The Sandburg Treasury;* Prose and Poetry for Young People; illus. by Paul Bacon. Harcourt, 1970. 480p. $7.95. (Harcourt, Brace, 1971. 480p. £3.40.)

5–9   This includes five complete volumes by Sandburg: *Abe Lincoln Grows Up, Rootabaga Stories, Prairie-Town Boy,* and two books of poetry: *Early Moon* and *Wind Song.* The combination of poetry, humor, folk style, biography, and autobiography serves as a good introduction for the new reader of Sandburg or as a varied pleasure for those who are already his fans. The illustrations add little, and some of the pages are solid with print, but the book is useful as a sampling of Sandburg's work, as additonal material in a collection which does not have the single editions, and for home libraries.

1111   **Sanderlin,** George. *Across the Ocean Sea;* A Journal of Columbus's Voyage; illus. by Laszlo Kubinyi. Harper, 1966. 275p. Trade ed. $4.95; Library ed. $4.43 net.

8—   By combining excerpts from the journals of Columbus and of his son Ferdinand—and some others—with his own explanatory passages, Mr. Sanderlin has compiled a documentary record that is vivid and authentic. The book has also, thereby, those changes of pace and style that give depth and variety. The first part of the text gives a very good picture of the theories and fallacies held by men of ancient times about the nature of the world and the existence of lands other than those known; it continues throughout the book to describe investigations and voyages of others as well as that of Columbus, which is described, of course, in far greater detail. The result is that the reader learns the details of the voyage of Columbus and also gets a broad picture of the explorations of the mariners of the western world. A bibliography, an index, a "cast of characters," and a timetable of events are appended; many reproductions of old maps—fully captioned—are included.

1112   **Sasek,** Miroslav. *This Is Australia;* written and illus. by Miroslav Sasek. Macmillan, 1971. 60p. $4.95. (W. H. Allen, 1970. 64p. £1.25.)

4–7   The lively paintings of Sasek are combined with casually humorous captions that may be merely labels or can give considerable information. The book focuses on major cities, historical sites and new architecture, and on the plants and animals that are so intriguing to non-Australians, giving tangentially some impressions of the atmosphere and character of the country.

1113   **Sasek,** Miroslav. *This Is the United Nations.* Macmillan, 1968. 60p. illus. $4.95. (W. H. Allen, 1968. 60p. £1.25.)

4–7   This is as tidy a job as Sasek has done, the text striking a happy balance between informal comment and straight factual material, and the pictures doing fullest justice both to the United Nations buildings and to the artist's ability. The book describes both the functioning of the organization and the physical plant; especially striking are Sasek's presentations of the works of other artists. A useful double-page spread shows the flags of all participating nations.

1114   **Savage,** Katharine. *The Story of World Religions;* illus. with photographs and maps. Walck, 1967. 283p. $6.50.

8—   A discussion of the main religions of the world today: Judaism, Hinduism, Buddhism, Confucianism, Christianity, and Islam. The author makes no attempt at evaluating similarities or variations in belief or ritual, but describes each of the major faiths separately, giving good historical background. The writing lacks the color of the several books by Florence Mary Fitch, but it is equally objective and respectful in approach. The book is, indeed, a good companion volume to Baker's *World Faiths* (Abelard-Schuman, 1966) since each approaches the subject from a different viewpoint, Mrs. Baker's focus being on comparative religion. An index and a bibliography are appended.

1115   **Sawyer,** Ruth. *Joy to the World;* illus. by Trina Schart Hyman. Little, 1966. 102p. $3.95.

4–7   Six stories and six carols are included in this volume of Christmas legends, gathered for the first time in book form. The illustrations are decorative—often humorous, occasionally sentimental, bearably quaint. The stories are, as one might expect from one of the great storytellers, smoothly flowing in style, balanced and focused in construction, and colorful in phrasing. One story is from Serbia and one from Arabia; two are from Ireland, two from Spain.

1116   **Schaefer,** Jack. *Mavericks;* illus. by Lorence Bjorklund. Houghton, 1967. $3.50. (Corgi, 1970. 128p. £0.20.)

7–10   Old Jake Hanlon, living alone in a crumbling ranch house, remembers the past and the wonderful horses he'd known or had: the ones he's hunted, a particular one he was glad to see get away, a horse he'd rescued in Chicago and ridden back to New Mexico, and the mustangs he'd saved by sneaking out of jail to unlock a gate. The story moves back and forth from the old man's past to the present, closing with his death. This is a deeply romantic picture of the old West, written in a strong and flavorful prose that is occasionally reminiscent of O. Henry;

its strength is in the author's storytelling ability, his deliberate style, and his strong characterization. "Quiet and motionless, withdrawn into himself, he sits on the worn scuffed leather and his old mind moves, searching backward through the years. And now he is no longer an ancient cartoon figure . . . He is Young Jake Hanlon, point man of the Triple X trail crew . . ."

1117   **Scheffer,** Victor B. *Little Calf;* illus. by Leonard Everett Fisher. Scribner, 1970. 140p. $5.95.

7—   Little Calf is born in September, a sperm whale who shivers in the cold waters of the sea, not yet protected by the blubber that will grow. In the first year of his life, he is close to his mother except when she leaves him to feed; slowly he learns the sounds of danger and the joy of play. The book follows the whale harem through a year, sometimes describing Little Calf, often digressing to speak of other marine creatures or the men who hunt and study them, often pausing to discuss some aspect of cetology. The writing is almost poetry at times and never far from it at any time, beautifully imaginative in the use of language and always factual in giving information; the information is authoritative and fascinating.

1118   **Schell,** Orville. *Modern China: The Story of a Revolution;* by Orville Schell and Joseph Esherick. Knopf, 1972. 151p. illus. Trade ed. $4.95; Library ed. $5.49 net.

7—   Detailed and thoughtful, given impact by the quotation of source materials, this is an excellent analysis of the events that led up to the establishment of a communist regime and a description of what is happening in China today. A history section precedes the contemporary material, giving the reader a basis for understanding the dissatisfaction that led to revolt. The book is especially valuable for the clarity with which it treats the relationship between the communist faction and the Kuomintang. A descriptive bibliography and an index are appended.

1119   **Schick,** Eleanor. *City in the Winter;* written and illus. by Eleanor Schick. Macmillan, 1970. 28p. $4.95.

K–2   Jimmy wakes one cold morning to find that there is no school because of a blizzard. His mother goes off to work, and Jimmy spends the day with Grandma. He helps with chores, plays, feeds the birds, goes shopping only to find the stores closed, welcomes his mother, has dinner, and goes to bed. The precise, quiet pictures, clean-lined, are sedately attractive; the story is static but has the appeals of an unusual event and a familiar, everyday environment.

1120   **Schiller,** Barbara, ed. *Erec and Enid;* illus. by Ati Forberg. Dutton, 1970. 46p. Trade ed. $4.25; Library ed. $4.21 net.

4–6   Like the Hieatt book reviewed above, this is based on Arthurian legend; here the adaptation is restricted to the first part of the story. The knights of Arthur's court go to hunt the white stag and Erec, who is riding with Queen Guinevere, goes off to avenge the queen's attendant. The cruel knight and Erec fight, and Erec wins the hand of the lovely Enid. This differs from the Hieatt version in that Enid is the daughter of Erec's host rather than the captive of Sir Ider. The illustrations, dark burnt-orange, are dramatic against ample white space; the style of the retelling is fluid and courtly.

1121   **Schiller,** Barbara, ad. *The White Rat's Tale;* illus. by Adrienne Adams. Holt, 1967. 26p. Trade ed. $3.50; Library ed. $3.27 net.

1–3   A retelling of an old French folk tale, illustrated with charming pictures in delicate colors, graceful and subtly humorous in detail. A childless royal couple had a beloved pet, a white rat that could talk, sing, and dance; they asked the Fairy Queen to change their pet into a daughter—and so she did. "A little too pink of eye, a bit too white of hair, said the courtiers behind their hands." When it was time for the princess to marry, she requested the most powerful husband in the whole world. Not the sun, which could be obscured by a cloud, or the wind that blew the cloud, or the mountain that stood firm against the wind. All these she spurned, choosing the rat that could slowly nibble away a mountain. So the Fairy Queen obligingly changed the princess into a white rat again, and the happy pair were wed. The writing is graceful, with an occasional trace of tongue-in-cheek.

1122   **Schoen,** Barbara. *A Place and a Time.* T. Y. Crowell, 1967. 234p. $4.50.

7–10   Four cheers for Mrs. Schoen. She has written a convincing first-person novel for girls; her protagonist, Josie Frost, is candid but not vitriolic; the events of two mid-adolescent years are on such themes as are found in most teen-age novels, but they deviate firmly from pattern. Josie has a first crush and rebounds, spurned, to a nice, steady boy. At the close of the story it's the first crush, back again, not the reliable pal. She adjusts to a grandmother's death, to the fallibility of parents, and to the remarkable fact that some of her least bearable relatives turn out to have some good in them.

1123   **Schoenherr,** John. *The Barn;* written and illus. by John Schoenherr. Atlantic-Little, Brown, 1968. 40p. $3.95.

2–4   Strong pictures in black and white combine meticulously realistic drawings of animals with delicate background details. The drama of the illustrations is tempered by the quiet writing, which

describes the predatory excursions of a hungry skunk, himself
preyed upon by an owl who must feed three owlets. Low-keyed,
the text is less a story than a revealing vignette of the constant
struggle for survival in the animal world.

1124   **Schwartz,** Alvin. *The City and Its People;* The Story of One City's
Government; photographs by Sy Katzoff. Dutton, 1967. 64p.
Trade ed. $3.95; Library ed. $3.91 net.

4–7   Illustrated with good, clear photographs, this is an excellent
description of a metropolis of 300,000 people. Unlike Lavine's
The Mayor and the City (Random House, 1966) there is little
emphasis on the particular city; Trenton, New Jersey is used by
the author only to serve as an example. Mr. Schwartz describes
the administrative structure and municipal services and problems,
with some emphasis on urban renewal and the complicated
planning it demands.

1125   **Schwartz,** Alvin. *University;* The Students, Faculty, and Campus
Life at One University. Viking, 1969. 175p. illus. Trade ed. $5.95;
Library ed. $5.63 net.

7–10   A good overview of life on a campus; the school described here
is the University of Pennsylvania, but the author frequently
points out differences and variations. Among the areas discussed
are admissions—both from the point of view of the applicant
and the university, curriculum, extracurricular activities, social
life, student unrest, faculty, administration, etc. The book is candid
and objective in describing dissatisfaction with student-faculty
relationships, special privileges for athletes, discrimination, and
fraternities. Written in a straightforward style, a well-organized
and useful book. A list of publications on universities and colleges
and a relative index are appended.

1126   **Schwartz,** Alvin. *What Do You Think?* An Introduction to Public
Opinion: How It Forms, Functions, and Affects Our Lives.
Dutton, 1966. 189p. illus. Trade ed. $4.50; Library ed. $4.70 net.

9–12   A remarkably lucid and objective discussion of the factors that
contribute to the formation of opinion, of the uses to which
knowledge about this is put (such as market research), of the
pitfalls to avoid in forming an unbiased opinion, and of the
ways in which surveys and polls are conducted and questionnaires
compiled. The writing is brisk, the coverage broad, the tone
matter-of-fact, the examples and illustrations up-to-date. Charts,
tables, and photographs of propaganda and advertising techniques
are included; an index is appended.

1127   **Schwartz,** George I. *Life in a Drop of Water.* Natural History
Press, 1970. 174p. illus. $4.95.

6—   Detailed and comprehensive but not dry in style, a book that describes with a sense of wonder and scientific approach the minuscule marvels of water life: the delicate precision of diatoms, the efficient aimlessness of the amoeba, the grace of algae and radiolaria. The text describes structure, reproduction, locomotion, and other functions, and the superb magnified photographs illustrate them. A bibliography and an index are appended.

1128   **Scott,** Ann Herbert. *On Mother's Lap;* illus. by Glo Coalson. McGraw-Hill, 1972. 34p. Trade ed. $4.95; Library ed. $4.72 net.

3–5   Drawings based on the artist's stay in an Eskimo village
yrs.   illustrate a simple and tender story of the warmth and security of maternal cuddling, even when shared with a baby sister. Michael, happily rocking with Mother, hops off her lap again and again to garner beloved possessions; when his sister wakes and frets, he announces there is no room left for her. But there is, he finds, as they all snuggle together under the reindeer blanket. The large scale of the pictures makes the book easy to use with several children, the simplicity and familiarity of the situation are universal.

1129   **Scott,** Ann Herbert. *Sam;* drawings by Symeon Shimin. McGraw-Hill, 1967. 28p. $3.95.

3–6   Mother sent Sam out of the kitchen; his brother scolded him for
yrs.   touching a box and his sister for picking up her paper dolls; when Daddy barked at Sam to leave the typewriter alone, he just sat down and cried. A little rocking, a little attention from the others, a little job—and Sam was all smiles. The story is more an expanded situation than a plot, but it is adequate and it is certainly realistic. The illustrations are heart-melting in the fidelity of expression as Sam's small face is wistful or hopeful or delighted. Sam's family is attractive: Negro, middle class, ordinary; the only dubious aspect of the book lies in the fact that after the last picture of Sam (happily working away at his job) there is a double-page spread, not related to the text, showing Sam in a thoughtful, serious mood.

1130   **Scott,** Joseph. *Egyptian Hieroglyphs for Everyone;* An Introduction to the Writing of Ancient Egypt; by Joseph and Lenore Scott. Funk and Wagnalls, 1968. 95p. illus. $4.95.

7—   For a subject so complicated, involving so many diagrams, this is an outstanding accomplishment. The authors are lucid, organized, and thorough, their attitude toward the reader-learner firm but encouraging. They describe the hieroglyph, the Egyptian alphabet with its biliteral signs, determinatives and reading directions, and they provide a fairly long vocabulary. Pertinent subjects such as the deciphering of the Rosetta Stone, numbers, and what Egyptians wrote about add variety to an already interesting book. An Egyptian chronology, a map, and some identifying pictures of major deities are appended.

1131   **Seeger,** Elizabeth. *The Five Sons of King Pandu;* The Story of the Mahabhárata; ad. from the English tr. of Kisari Mohan Ganguli by Elizabeth Seeger; with illus. by Gordon Laite. Scott, 1967. 340p. $6.95. (Dent, 1970. 360p. £2.25.)

7—   A long and stately retelling of the great Indian epic; in a most useful and lengthy preface, Miss Seeger explains the kinds of deletions and changes she has made so that the story will read smoothly and will be retained in essence despite the omission of material—or simplification of names—that will make reading easier for the occidental reader. The five sons of King Pandu had been given him by the gods, and in the end, after all their adventures on earth, the five are reunited with their father and with their father-gods in heaven. The long passages of mannered prose and the small print combine to make heavy looking pages, but the hero tale style could not be simplified without sacrificing flavor. An important book as good source material but limited by its style in appeal to the general reader; for a study of comparative literature or of the genre, a valuable and interesting book.

1132   **Seeger,** Elizabeth, ad. *The Ramayana;* ad. from the English tr. of Hari Prasad Shastri; illus. by Gordon Laite. Scott, 1969. 244p. $6.95.

7—   From the legends preserved by storytellers the sage Valmiki, in 400 B.C., wrote the story of Rama, the avatar of God, the warrior-prince cast off by his father and condemned to wander for twice seven years. Rama and his wife are the incarnation of all that is good and beautiful, an embodiment of the religious devotion that is part of Indian art forms. The richly-colored illustrations are beautiful and appropriate, the rolling prose equally suited to the intricately sculptured story.

1133   **Segal,** Lore. *Tell Me a Mitzi;* illus. by Harriet Pincus. Farrar, 1970. 34p. $4.95.

K–2   Three hilarious tales ("Mitzi Takes a Taxi," "Mitzi Sneezes," and "Mitzi and the President") are set within the framework, brief but sturdy, of a small girl's pleas for a Mitzi story. The stories aren't all fantasy, but they border on it, the last one achieving the status of a tall tale. Mitzi decides to take her baby brother (a Character) for an early morning visit, so she gets in a taxi and asks to be taken to Grandma's; in the second story all the members of Mitzi's family enjoy illness, and in the third the President of the United States obligingly reverses a parade for the benefit of Mitzi's brother. The writing style is in grave contrast to the nonsense of the events, and the illustrations, while they do not boast attractive children, are full of vitality and humor, the busy urban neighborhood and homely people having a rueful charm.

1134   **Selden,** George. *Tucker's Countryside;* illus. by Garth Williams. Farrar, 1969. 167p. $3.95. (Dent, 1971. 168p. £1.10.)

4–6   A sequel to *The Cricket in Times Square* is just as charming in its humor, as pithy in dialogue, and as fortunate in its illustrations as the first book. Chester, the virtuoso cricket, appeals to his Times Square friends for help in preventing the tide of building that threatens the lovely meadow in which Chester and an assortment of distinguished animals live. This is at the same time a plea for conservation, an ebullient fantasy, a tender story of friendship, and a funny book. All that and the delectable, soft pictures make this an excellent book to read aloud to younger children as well as a delightful one for the independent reader.

1135   **Selsam,** Millicent (Ellis). *The Carrot and Other Root Vegetables;* photographs by Jerome Wexler. Morrow, 1971. 48p. Trade ed. $4.50; Library ed. $4.14 net.

2–4   Millicent Selsam's science writing is exemplary: clear, authoritative, and well organized, the writing style simple and direct without being choppy. The description of the life cycle of biennial root vegetables is made even more lucid by the sharp, enlarged photographs, and the book made more readable as well as attractive by the spacious page layout and the large print.

1136   **Selsam,** Millicent (Ellis). *How to Be a Nature Detective;* pictures by Ezra Jack Keats. Harper, 1966. 46p. Trade ed. $3.95; Library ed. $3.79 net.

2–4   Loud hurrahs! The nicest possible sort of book on animal tracks, written with no cuteness or patronizing and nicely gauged in reading difficulty, pace, and length of text for the primary audience. The format and illustrations are clear and attractive; both text and illustrations have a light note of humor. The book describes the tracks of some dozen creatures and it points out to the reader that one can use deduction to help in identification. Good beginning science, good nature study, good book.

1137   **Selsam,** Millicent (Ellis). *Is This a Baby Dinosaur?* and Other Science Picture-Puzzles; illus. with photographs. Harper, 1972. 32p. Trade ed. $3.95; Library ed. $3.79 net.

K–3   Handsome photographs, some magnified, and a lucid, informally written text make an enticing book for the very young naturalist.

Like Tana Hoban's *Look Again!* each picture of some detail of flora or fauna is provocatively deceptive, and each is followed by another picture (sometimes several) of the whole life-form. Unlike the Hoban book, which has no text, this gives a considerable amount of information about the plants and animals it pictures. A book to sharpen perception, to enjoy for its beauty.

1138   **Selsam,** Millicent (Ellis). *Milkweed;* photographs by Jerome Wexler. Morrow, 1967. 48p. Trade ed. $3.95; Library ed. $3.73 net.

2–4   A good first science book, illustrated with clear and attractive photographs. The author does not attempt to discuss every aspect of plant physiology (there is no mention of photosynthesis or of respiration) but describes in simple language the growth of a milkweed plant from a seed, the reproductive parts, pollenation, and distribution. The print is large, and the photographs often show parts in magnification; the role of insects is especially clarified by the illustrations, which are also used to compare the structure of the milkweed flower with a simpler flower.

1139   **Selsam,** Millicent (Ellis). *When an Animal Grows;* pictures by John Kaufmann. Harper, 1966. 64p. (I Can Read Books) Trade ed. $2.50; Library ed. $2.92 net.

1–3   An excellent first science book for the beginning independent reader, illustrated with soft, realistic pictures in black and white. The author compares the baby gorilla and the baby lamb, the first living in a close and dependent relationship with his mother for several months and the latter friskily independent soon after birth. Again, a helpless sparrow nestling and the duckling that walks just after birth are compared. Feeding and playing habits are described, too, in a simple text; format, print size, and length of text are appropriate for the intended audience.

1140   **Sendak,** Maurice. *Higglety Pigglety Pop!* or There Must Be More to Life; story and pictures by Maurice Sendak. Harper, 1967. 69p. $4.95. (Bodley Head, 1969. 80p. £0.90.)

3–5   "Once Jennie had everything . . . But Jennie didn't care. In the middle of the night she packed everything in a black leather bag with gold buckles and looked out of her favorite window for the last time." And so Jennie set off to find something else in life, whatever it was, that would make her happy; almost absent-mindedly, Jennie ate steadily as she acquired Experience, eventually becoming leading lady in the World Mother Goose Theatre. Having found more than everything, Jennie wrote her former master "As you probably noticed, I went away forever." The story has elements of tenderness and humor; it also has those typically macabre Sendak touches that were enjoyed by readers of *Where the Wild Things Are.* For example,

Jennie becomes, for a time, nurse to a fractious baby who is slated to be eaten by a ferocious lion; by saying the right words she saves the baby's life; later the baby appears, magically adult size, and selects Jennie as leading lady. The illustrations are beautiful, amusing, and distinctive; the story is freshly imaginative, subtly direct, wryly perceptive.

1141   **Sendak,** Maurice. *In the Night Kitchen;* written and illus. by Maurice Sendak. Harper, 1970. 35p. Trade ed. $3.95; Library ed. $4.11 net. (Bodley Head, 1971. 40p. £1.25.)

K–2   In the night kitchen, while a small child sleeps, wonderful things happen. Mickey, dreaming, falls into the kitchen, his clothes sliding away, and is put into the batter by the bakers (chanting as they stir, three Oliver Hardys like corpulent *Macbeth* witches) who think he is the milk. Mickey jumps out of the Mickey-cake, and goes flying off for milk through the night skies until he comes to the Milky Way, a huge bottle of milk into which he plunges, soaring up again to pour milk into the batter while the bakers carol rapturously at this deliverance. Then, cock-crow, and a sleepy Mickey tumbles through the air and into bed. A most engaging fantasy, the illustrations combining the meticulous draughtsmanship, the imaginative implementation, and the identification with a child's vision that are Sendak's happy forte.

1142   **Serraillier,** Ian. *The Challenge of the Green Knight;* illus. by Victor G. Ambrus. Walck, 1967. 56p. $5. (Oxf. U.P., 1966. 64p. £1.00.)

6–9   Based on a fourteenth-century poem of unknown authorship, this tale of romance and adventure is beautifully told and beautifully illustrated. Young Sir Gawain, answering the challenge of the mysterious Green Knight who appears to Camelot, promises a blow for a blow. He decapitates the knight, but the head reminds him of his promise; a year later, Gawain must present himself for the Green Knight's death blow. He tarries at a castle where the lord's beautiful wife tempts him three times; three times he resists, and when he meets the Green Knight he is spared, since this is the husband of the amorous lady; he appears as a Green Knight by the witchcraft of Morgan la Faye. The style is wonderfully right for the material: rich, rolling phrases, with stately cadence and completely natural use of language appropriate to the medieval setting and the subject.

1143   **Serraillier,** Ian. *Chaucer and His World.* Walck, 1968. 48p. illus. $5. (Lutt P., 1967. 48p. £0.80.)

8—   A good addition to an excellent series of broad examinations of historical periods in England, each volume focusing on a major literary figure. Here the biographical section is brief (unlike Halliday's *Chaucer and His World,* Viking, 1968) and there is little discussion of Chaucer's writing, although examples from *The Canterbury Tales* are used throughout the book to illuminate a discussion of a profession or a custom. The writing style is direct and vigorous, the illustrations profuse, the print small.

1144　　**Sewall,** Marcia, illus. *Master of All Masters;* An English Folktale. Little, 1972. 31p. $3.95.

3–5　　Cozy, comical drawings illustrate an old English folktale, brief and amusing, a story that can be told to a much wider audience than the middle-grade range that will read it. A servant is told by her new master that he has his own names for objects; being a clever girl, she learns them so quickly that when a fire threatens, she is able to tell him that "White-faced simminy has got a spot of hot cockalorum on her tail, and unless you get some pondalorum, high topper mountain will be all on hot cockalorum!"

1145　　**Shannon,** Terry. *Ride the Ice Down!* U.S. and Canadian Icebreakers in Arctic Seas; written by Terry Shannon and Charles Payzant. Golden Gate, 1970. 78p. illus. Trade ed. $4.95; Library ed. $4.79 net.

4–7　　The work of those men who clear the Arctic seas of dangerous floating ice is as exciting as the plot of any adventure tale, and in this description of the part played by the United States and Canadian Coast Guards there is, as well, a sense of the awesome and icy bleakness of the far North. The authors discuss the formation of icebergs, the organization of seventeen nations' services into the International Ice Patrol, and the work of the icebreakers. There is also a detailed account of the voyage of the tanker *S S Manhattan* through the Northwest Passage, a voyage that has already influenced (because of the knowledge it contributed) the design of ships, and may affect the pattern of world trade. A compendium of historical data about trips through the Northwest Passage and an index are appended.

1146　　**Shapiro,** Rebecca. *A Whole World of Cooking;* written and illus. by Rebecca Shapiro. Little, 1972. 70p. $4.95.

5–9　　Boys and girls who enjoy cooking should welcome this new cookbook, since none of the recipes is difficult and none of the ingredients hard to get. The cooking instructions are clear, but the book is not intended for a beginner, and gives no basic explanations of utensils or procedures and no glossary of cooking terms. The recipes are listed by country in the table of contents, and include one or two examples from most parts of the world. The author's relish for the delights of exotic dishes is limited to introductory remarks, but her enthusiasm permeates the book. Index entries are by type of dish—soups, meats, etc.

1147   **Sharmat,** Marjorie Weinman. *Getting Something on Maggie Marmelstein;* illus. by Ben Shecter. Harper, 1971. 101p. Trade ed. $3.50; Library ed. $3.79 net.

3–5   As Thad explains it, it is easy to see why he and Maggie are mortal enemies: they can't keep from taunting each other. Not only are they in the same class at school, but they live two doors apart. Thad's real problem comes when he goes to the Marmelstein's on an errand for his mother, gets involved in cooking, and is seen by his foe. That's it. She will tease him forever, so he *has* to get something on her in return. By dint of assiduous prying, he does—but when Maggie helps him out of a dilemma during the class play, Thad relents. Maggie thaws. Battle of the sexes ends in a draw. This amiable story is told and illustrated with humor, the characters come alive, and the classroom scenes are delightful.

1148   **Sharmat,** Marjorie Weinman. *Gladys Told Me to Meet Her Here;* illus. by Edward Frascino. Harper, 1970. 32p. Trade ed. $3.95; Library ed. $3.79 net.

K–2   Not for worlds would Irving have let Gladys know, when she finally showed up, what he had been going through. The style is gently doleful, as Irving's stream-of-consciousness envisions all the dire reasons why Gladys is late meeting him at the zoo and as he indulges himself alternately in daydreams of his best friend suffering and memories of her staunch loyalty. Amusingly illustrated, this is a story as enjoyable for the adult reader-aloud as it is for the young listener.

1149   **Sharmat,** Marjorie Weinman. *Goodnight Andrew Goodnight Craig;* illus. by Mary Chalmers. Harper, 1969. 32p. Trade ed. $2.95; Library ed. $2.92 net.

4–6
yrs.   "Craig." "What?" "I'm hungry." "Go tell Dad." "I'm not that hungry." "Craig." "What?" Two small boys have gone peacefully to bed; Andrew, the younger brother and occupant of the lower bunk, isn't sleepy. Craig tries to get to sleep but Andrew's insistence on conversation wakes him up; the boys get noisier and noisier, their father comes in with an ultimatum; eventually Craig and Andrew subside. The illustrations echo the engaging tone of the story, which is all in dialogue, and the boys sound like two small boys the world over.

1150   **Sharp,** Margery. *Miss Bianca in the Orient;* illus. by Erik Blegvad. Little, 1970. 144p. $4.95. (Heinemann, 1970. 128p. £1.25.)

6—   That ineffably ladylike mouse, Miss Bianca, Perpetual Madam President of the Mouse Prisoners' Aid Society, goes to India. Her heart has been touched by the plight of a small boy who is destined to be trampled to death (by elephants) for a very minor offense. As always, she is triumphant; as always, she is assisted by her ordinary but devoted admirer, Bernard. The plot is sheer marshmallow fluff, but the style and humor are gay, affectionate, and lightly sophisticated, and the illustrations are engaging.

1151   **Sharp,** Margery. *Miss Bianca in the Salt Mines;* illus. by Garth Williams. Little, 1967. 148p. $4.50. (Heinemann, 1966. 120p. £0.75.)

6—   You really have to write awfully well not to be cloying about a dainty little white mouse who writes poetry, chairs meetings, inspires love in every murine breast, and courageously leads an expedition to a salt mine to rescue an eight-year-old boy who is being held prisoner. Margery Sharp writes with charm, verve, just enough whimsy to be beguiling and just enough acerbity to be funny. Bianca and her three escorts effect the release of the prisoner through no miracles, but a series of determined or intelligent decisions. Our old friend Bernard is a stalwart, but the two elderly professors who have insisted on coming along have about the same function as stage comedians. They are fun, they give the author a chance to take pokes at academic life, and they double the opportunities for Garth Williams to be funny and enchanting at the same time.

1152   **Shaw,** Arnold. *The Rock Revolution.* Crowell-Collier, 1969. 215p. illus. $4.95. (Collier-Mac., 1969. 192p. £1.05.)

7—   A detailed and informed history of rock in all its manifestations, from the early rockabilly to the extended and diverse forms of psychedelic, protest, raga, and even religious rock of today. The author discusses the performers as well as the music, from the gyrating Presley to the catalysts like Dylan and the Beatles to the proliferating groups of famous or lesser-known combos. The contributions of Negro artists, the comments of critics, the relationship of rock to civil rights, and even the role of Tiny Tim are included in this excellent survey of what's happening in today's music. A glossary and an index are appended.

1153   **Shearer,** John. *I Wish I Had an Afro;* written and with photographs by John Shearer. Cowles, 1970. 45p. $3.95.

4–6   Books of running first-person commentary combined with photographs have become fairly common; here the quality of the photography and the candor and pathos of the text are uncommon. It is a verbal collage: Little John comments, his mother speaks, his father ponders. The parents are hard-working and conservative, the boy (age eleven) is swayed by what he sees around him: yearning for an Afro (". . . long hair don't make you any blacker . . ." says Big John) and impressed by the militancy of his sister's friends, horrified by drugs and what they have

done to the people around him, and imbued with his parents' high
ethical standards.

1154   **Shecter,** Ben. *Conrad's Castle*. Harper, 1967. 29p. illus. Trade ed.
$3.95; Library ed. $3.79 net. (Blackie, 1970. 32p. £0.90.)

K–2   An entirely diverting picture book in which a small boy's
castles-in-the-air are shown rising and growing, crenellated and
buttressed, pennants whipping in an imaginary wind. Meanwhile,
in real life, Conrad's chums are doing their best to distract
him with enticing offers of team captaincy, a peek at a dead
mouse, or attendance at a Public Spanking. The captions are
brief, the humorous illustrations carrying the burden of the story.

1155   **Shecter,** Ben. *Someplace Else*. Harper, 1971. 167p. Trade ed. $3.95;
Library ed. $4.43 net.

4–6   An amusing story about the trials and tribulations of Arnie, age
eleven, is told in an episodic book that closes on a serious
note with the death of Arnie's father. Although Arnie has his
ups and downs in school, suffers the nuisance of attention from a
girl he dislikes (his mother likes her), grieves for a lost dog, and
is worried when his mother has an operation, the recurrent motif
is the Rabbi. Preparing for his bar mitzvah, Arnie is hampered
by his intense dislike of old Rabbi Bleisch, a hostility so deep
that the boy feels guilty when Bleisch disappears. When he comes
back (from Miami) Arnie is so relieved that he is almost glad to
see the man. Perceptive and realistic, with good albeit not deep
characterization, and with lively, natural dialogue.

1156   **Sheehan,** Ethna, comp. *Folk and Fairy Tales from around the World;*
illus. by Mircea Vasiliu. Dodd, 1970. 151p. $4.50.

4–6   Seventeen stories, each from a different country, are followed by a
brief note to storytellers on using the material. Since each tale
has been chosen from a different collection (save for two, for
which no sources are cited) there is variation in style and in
the calibre of the tellings, but none are badly written, and several
have a fluent, conversational style that is pleasant to hear read
aloud. With few exceptions, most of the selections are in other
collections, but this anthology may provide additional sources for
the reader or the storyteller.

1157   **Sherburne,** Zoa. *Girl in the Mirror*. Morrow, 1966. 190p. $3.95.

7–10   The story of a girl of sixteen who is lonely and overweight;
Ruth Ann, motherless, clings to her father and is therefore
dismayed when he proposes to remarry Tracy Emery. Tracy refuses
to marry him until she is accepted by Ruth Ann, and it is some time
before the jealous girl can make that unselfish a gesture. When
her father is killed on his honeymoon trip, Ruth Ann realizes

her own deep need to be loved and needed, and she makes overtures to Tracy (herself crippled in the accident) that are spontaneous and genuine. The ending is dramatic in that the accident precipitates Ruth Ann's emotions, but it is realistic in not solving all the problems: Ruth Ann is still fat, still friendless.

1158   **Sherburne,** Zoa. *Too Bad about the Haines Girl.* Morrow, 1967. 191p. $3.50.

8–12   Melinda Haines is a nice girl, with a loving family and a steady, reliable boyfriend; it has been agreed that Jeff must continue with his education after they graduate from high school. When Melinda finds that she is pregnant, she tells Jeff that she is going to an abortionist; she changes her mind at the last moment and accepts the bitter fact that she must tell her parents and Jeff's mother that they must have a wedding immediately. The writing is honest, direct, and all the more touching because there is no note of pathos or of censure; Melinda's own agony is censure enough.

1159   **Shivkumar,** K., ad. *The King's Choice;* illus. by Yoko Mitsuhashi. Parents Magazine, 1971. 36p. Trade ed. $3.95; Library ed. $3.47 net.

K–3   A direct and simple retelling of an Indian folk tale, the illustrations in muted color and framed in stylized Eastern fashion. Told by his followers the fox, the leopard, and the vulture that camel meat is good, the lion king starts with them on a trek to the desert. Weary and footsore, they are grateful for a camel ride back to the cool forest. The three courtiers, anxious for a meal of camel, try to trick the beast into offering himself as food to the lion but are themselves tricked. They run off, and the wise lion comments that kindness is better than a crown, and that the camel will be his friend as long as they both live. A taut story, good for story-telling or for reading aloud.

1160   **Sholokhov,** Mikhail. *Fierce and Gentle Warriors;* tr. by Miriam Morton; illus. by Milton Glaser. Doubleday, 1967. 109p. $3.95. (Heinemann Educ., 1969. 86p. £0.35.)

9—   Three stories by the Russian author who was awarded the Nobel prize for literature in 1965. The title is well chosen, since each story reflects both the harshness and the tenderness of men in wartime. The first story is about a tough old soldier and his love for a newborn horse; the second describes a village child who is teased because his father is a Communist; the third is a most touching tale of two lost people who find each other after the war has taken both their families: a man who has lost a wife and three children, and a small orphan. The writing is strong in its directness, its universality, its compassion; the translation is sensitive and the illustrations attractive.

1161   **Shotwell,** Louisa R. *Adam Bookout;* illus. by W. T. Mars. Viking, 1967. 256p. $3.95.

4–6   Adam, eleven years old and recently orphaned, was unhappy living with two elderly aunts, so he decided (on the strength of an old Christmas card that had the note "Come see us!!!" on it) to go to relatives in New York. Surprised but hospitable, Cousin Kate welcomed Adam, and so he started school at P.S. 595 in Brooklyn—a far cry from Oklahoma. The friends Adam makes, and the problems they have—separately and together—are convincing: garrulous, inventive Saul Katz; and Willie Weggfall, just up from Alabama; and Cousin Kate, generous and patient when she isn't bemused in authorship. The characters ought to be stock figures, but they have life in them, and they are real; the author has, with a light touch and a perceptive eye made Saul, for example, much more than the stereotyped brainy little Jewish boy—he's a person.

1162   **Shotwell,** Louisa R. *Magdalena;* illus. by Lilian Obligado. Viking, 1971. 124p. Trade ed. $3.95; Library ed. $3.77 net.

5–7   In a story that has warmth, vitality, and humor, Louisa Shotwell describes the dilemma of a child who is balked by the fixed ideas of the grandmother with whom she lives, but who loves her Nani too much to rebel. Magdalena's hair seems to Nani a girl's crowning glory; to Magdalena it is simply something she is teased about. In Puerto Rico, Nani says, long braids give a girl character—but they aren't *in* Puerto Rico. Why, Magdalena wonders, is Nani so understanding about her friend's problems and so obdurate about hers? The problem is solved when Magdalena, influenced by an elderly, odd acquaintance, goes to a barber. A witch, Nani decides, and gets to work with preventive herbs. But Nani relents, accepting both the shorn child and her peculiar new friend. Spirited writing and solid characterization add to the attractions of a story that has good relationships and convincing changes in them, and has some lively and amusing school sequences.

1163   **Showers,** Paul. *Before You Were a Baby;* by Paul Showers and Kay Sperry Showers; illus. by Ingrid Fetz. T. Y. Crowell, 1968. 33p. $3.75.

2–3   Written very simply, with the format (short sentences, plenty of white space, a minimum of labeled diagrams, and large print) indicating independent use, although adults can use the book as a springboard for discussion of human reproduction. The illustrations show the stages of foetal growth, and (very tenderly) the infant child; the text is accurate, candid, and direct.

1164   **Showers,** Paul. *A Drop of Blood;* illus. by Don Madden. T. Y.

Crowell, 1967. 34p. (Let's-Read- and-Find-Out Books) $3.75.
(Black, 1964. 40p. £0.65.)

2–3   Crisp, straightforward writing and gay, cartoon-like illustrations
combine to make this introduction to the topic of human blood
clear, simple, and accurate. The author describes circulation and
the protective powers of the blood, the types of cells of which
blood is composed, and the reassuring fact that there is constant
replenishment of the blood supply—although the details of this
process are not given.

1165   **Shulevitz,** Uri. *One Monday Morning.* Scribner, 1967. 38p. illus.
Trade ed. $4.95; Library ed. $4.37 net.

K–2   One of the nicest read-aloud books about the imaginative play of
a small, solitary child to come along in a while. The setting is
urban, inner city, lower class; a small boy is seen alternately
engaged in such humdrum occupations as waiting at a laundromat
or riding on a subway, and such a fanciful, glamorous one as
being visited by a royal family whose party, cumulating through
the week, is a startling, glowing, visual contrast to the realistic
scenes. On Sunday the two worlds merge, and the boy sits
contentedly playing with a deck of cards.

1166   **Shulevitz,** Uri. *Rain Rain Rivers;* written and illus. by Uri
Shulevitz. Farrar, 1969. 28p. $4.50.

K–3   In her attic room a little girl hears the rain. Outside her window
the gutters are rain-swollen, the rain beats down on the city
streets and the few scurrying people, cold and wet. The rain
pours into country streams, the brooks feed the rivers, the
rain-lashed rivers pour into the frothing sea. Only at the end
is there a change of mood, as a pale, watery sun shines on
delightful puddles and the joyful children reappear. The little
girl feels the urgent freshening and sees her tiny potted plant
begin to grow. There is so much action and so sustained a mood
in the illustrations that the absence of a story line seems of little
importance.

1167   **Shull,** Margaret Wise. *Children of Appalachia;* written and
photographed by Margaret Wise Shull. Messner, 1969. 95p. Trade
ed. $3.95; Library ed. $3.64 net.

4–6   A good first book about the Appalachian region and its problems,
neither critically analytical nor sentimental. The fictionalization is
capable, enabling the full charm of mountain speech to emerge
but often forcing the speakers to bear the burden of giving
information contrivedly. The Napier family, farmers, have three
children whose activities include going to school (recitation about
Kentucky history) and to a hospital (community service) and to

town where their cousins, the Begleys, live. This permits a description of government programs; a visit by Bill Napier to a family back in the hills leads to a discussion about isolation and consequent deprivation for some of Appalachia, and a major factor in the area is, of course, the influence of mining—especially strip mining—on the way of life. An index is appended.

1168   **Shura,** Mary Francis. *Backwards for Luck;* illus. by Ted CoConis. Knopf, 1967. 133p. $3.95.

3–5   A very good story about relationships within a family, particularly the competitive relationship between brothers and the special bond between child and grandparent. Andy was a timid and superstitious nine-year-old who looked up to his older brother James, envying his courage even though he was irritated by the contemptuous teasing he got from James. A change in Andy came gradually, due largely to his forgetting himself to help a pet cat, and in part to Grandpa's moral support. Discovering that James, too, had his small fears was a big help to Andy, and to James it was rather a relief to drop his pretense. Perceptive in characterizations, tinged with humor, and written in an easy, competent style.

1169   **Shuttlesworth,** Dorothy Edwards. *Natural Partnerships;* The Story of Symbiosis; illus. by Su Zan Noguchi Swain. Doubleday, 1969. 62p. $3.95.

5–9   An oversize book, profusely illustrated with meticulous drawings of plant and animal life; some of the pictures are inadequately labeled and some are badly placed, but neither weakness prevails. The text is straightforward and rather dry in style, but lucid in explanation of mutualism, parasitism, and commensalism; it is divided by types of flora and fauna, chapter titles indicating "Plant and Animal Partners," "Birds and Beasts," "In the Insect World," or "When Two Plants Make One," for example. A brief final section discusses, very superficially, ecological balance. An index is appended.

1170   **Silverberg,** Robert. *The Calibrated Alligator;* And Other Science Fiction Stories. Holt, 1969. 224p. Trade ed. $4.95; Library ed. $4.59 net.

6–9   Nine science fiction stories are included in an original and varied collection, one of the best of which is the title story. In "The Calibrated Alligator" a prankster on a lunar base becomes involved in a biological experiment that succeeds in a totally unexpected way. One tale takes a poke at the fads in popularity of artifacts; another is the amusing account of a helpless man who gets shuttled from time belt to time belt when he calls the Friendly

Finance Corporation to ask for an extension on his loan. Several are serious, but it is the humorous short story at which the author excels.

1171   **Silverberg,** Robert. *The Morning of Mankind;* Prehistoric Man in Europe. New York Graphic Society, 1967. 240p. illus. $4.95. (World's Work, 1970. 240p.   1.50.)

8—   An engrossing description of early man (25,000 B.C. to the founding of the Roman Empire) and an equally interesting record of the early archeological and anthropological finds and theories that interpret the remains of his cultures. In discussing any tribe, culture, or a whole people, the author gives facts about the climate and the topography that may have influenced (or even produced) behavior patterns—a good scientific approach for the reader to learn along with facts about man's growing skills and knowledge, and the increasing complexity of human life. A divided bibliography and an index are appended.

1172   **Silverberg,** Robert. *Wonders of Ancient Chinese Science;* illus. by Marvin Besunder. Hawthorn Books, 1969. 126p. $3.95.

7—   Following a brief background history of China from 1994 B.C. this most informative book surveys the achievements of Chinese scientists, some of them familiar and many of them neglected for the hundreds of years in which the accomplishments were forgotten and the disciplines abandoned. Separate chapters describe the impressive astronomical observations, such scientific instruments as the magnetic compass and the seismograph, and such useful inventions as paper and printing, gunpowder and rockets, kites, wheelbarrows, umbrellas, and the fishing rod reel. A table of dynasties precedes the text; a bibliography and a relative index are appended.

1173   **Silverberg,** Robert. *The World of the Ocean Depths.* Meredith, 1968. 142p. illus. $5.95. (World's Work, 1970. 156p.   1.50.)

6—   An excellent survey of one of the great areas of scientific research today focuses (although it also discusses theories of formation and physical attributes of the oceans) on the discoveries that have been—and are being—made about marine life. The book is well written and is illustrated with interesting photographs and drawings; it gives information both about the men and machines used in exploration of the ocean depths and about the strange and wonderful creatures that have been found there. A bibliography and an index are appended.

1174   **Silverstein,** Alvin. *Germfree Life;* A New Field in Biological Research; by Alvin and Virginia Silverstein. Lothrop, 1970. 96p. illus. Trade ed. $4.50; Library ed. $4.14 net.

5–8   A good survey of the science of gnotobiology—the study of certain
         microorganisms on life forms that live in a sterile condition,
         germfree—written in a direct style, serious but not formal. The
         photographs are clear and informative, the material well organized.
         The authors discuss the early experiments that sprang from the
         conflicting theories of Pasteur and Nencki, give adequate
         background information on bacteria, and go on to discuss some
         of the experiments that are, through gnotobiology, making
         available new knowledge, pathological and surgical, that can
         improve treatment of tooth decay, cancer, and other diseases,
         and that can improve chances for survival (in some instances) in the
         operating theater. An index is appended.

1175   **Silverstein,** Alvin. *Metamorphosis: The Magic Change;* by Alvin
         and Virginia Silverstein. Atheneum, 1971. 74p. illus. $5.50.

4–7   Clear photographs add to the usefulness of a book that is written
         informally and crisply, is well organized, and emphasizes the
         process of metamorphosis as a change that gives young animal
         forms an advantage in the struggle for survival. The life forms
         discussed are butterflies, moths, honeybees, frogs, toads,
         salamanders, sea squirts, starfish, and eels. A pronouncing
         glossary is appended.

1176   **Simak,** Clifford D. *Prehistoric Man;* illus. by Murray Tinkelman.
         St. Martin's, 1971. 192p. $6.95.

7–10   This discussion of prehistoric man's progress from the cave
         and a nomadic existence to the technical and communication
         skills that marked the first civilizations is as concerned as was
         Hogben's *Beginnings and Blunders* with the domestication of
         animals, development of agricultural techniques, acquisition of
         crafts and skills. It includes, however, more discussion of theories
         of development and of the relationship between cultural and
         practical aspects of the lives of early men. The writing style is
         rather solid, but the book is well organized, thoughtful, and broad
         in viewpoint. An index is appended.

1177   **Simon,** Hilda. *Insect Masquerades.* Viking, 1968. 95p. Trade ed.
         $4.75; Library ed. $4.31 net. (Muller, 1969. 96p. £1.20.)

6–9   A very good book on imitative patterns or adaptations in the
         insect world, all operating to increase the survival potential
         whether the imitation serves to hide or to attract (and repel) or
         to entrap vicitims. The text is well organized and well written,
         save for an occasional remark that imputes purposiveness:
         "Instinct tells the monarch, the hornet, and the milkweed beetle
         that their best protection lies, not in trying to hide, but rather
         in showing their bright colors." or "The purpose of this
         masquerade is . . ." The illustrations are superb: clear and

informative, beautifully detailed. A brief reading list, morphological diagrams, a guide to finding masquerading insects in the garden, and a relative index are appended.

1178   **Simon,** Hilda. *Living Lanterns*; Luminescence in Animals; written and illus. by Hilda Simon. Viking. 1971. 128p. Trade ed. $4.95; Library ed. $4.53 net.

7—   Handsome illustrations in color, detailed and informative, add to the value of a text that is serious and straightforward but so clearly written that it is not dry. The author describes first the animal forms of land and air that possess self-luminescence, discussing both the morphology and physiology of each life form, then surveys the bioluminescent species of the sea. The book concludes with a chapter about research on the phenomenon itself, a brief bibliography, and an index.

1179   **Simon,** Norma. *How Do I Feel?* illus. by Joe Lasker. Whitman, 1970. 34p. Trade ed. $3.95; Library ed. $2.96 net.

4–6   Despite a staccato style, a book that explores lightly some of the emotions and reactions of a small boy. Carl, who speaks, is a twin; he is slow and rather timid while Eddie is brisk and confident. The boys and their older brother live with grandparents (no explanation given) and are affected by their relationship with each other, depressed when the adults quarrel and relieved when the quarrel is over. Carl is teased about a homemade sweater, is pleased at his own performance in school and helpful to Eddie, who can't write as well; he feels benificent when he helps Grandma, and he clearly looks up to his big brother. The illustrations have action and humor, and the book can be used nicely (as the author suggests in a preface for adult readers-aloud) as a base for discussion of a child's emotions.

1180   **Simon,** Norma. *What Do I Say?* pictures: Joe Lasker. Whitman, 1967. 36p. Trade ed. $3.95; Library ed. $2.96 net.

3–6   I say hooray for this book of basic etiquette for the very young,
yrs.   partly because of its simplicity, partly because the settings are a classroom and a home that will be familiar to the urban child in a poor neighborhood. Grandma, left to care for younger children while mother works, sits cheerily at the breakfast table in an old dress, apron, and slippers. The three children sleep in one bed, and any suggestion of squalor is eliminated by the scrubbed faces and the prevalence of affection and vivacity. Going through his day, the protagonist records his pattern (in large print) "Something's wrong. What do I say? Please help me." "I want to swing. What do I say? It's my turn." The children, assorted colors, are shown in all the various occupations of a

typical nursery or kindergarten class. The book is available in an English-Spanish edition.

1181   **Simon,** Seymour. *The Paper Airplane Book;* illus. by Byron Barton. Viking, 1971. 48p. Trade ed. $3.50; Library ed. $3.37 net.

3–6   Careful coordination of text and illustration make this an exemplary home demonstration book. The author uses the process approach, suggesting variations on the airplane and asking the reader to consider *why* a certain effect is obtained, or which change is most effective for a desired result. The book does, of course, show the reader how to make paper airplanes, but it is really used (and very deftly) to discuss what makes a real airplane fly, and how the various parts of a plane contribute to or affect its flight.

1182   **Singer,** Isaac Bashevis. *A Day of Pleasure;* Stories of a Boy Growing Up in Warsaw; with photographs by Roman Vishniac. Farrar, 1969. 227p. $4.50.

6—   A delightful compilation of nineteen stories, some of which were previously published in an adult book, *In My Father's Court.* The photographs are of members of the Singer family or of Warsaw scenes of the period. The crowded and busy slum ghetto provides some unforgettable characters, including the author's father, a rabbi with a great reputation for wisdom, and his indomitable wife, whose common sense sometimes put her husband's didactic pronouncements to shame. The book not only conveys, with gusto and humor, the Jewish community but also depicts with infinite charm the author as a child: questioning, eager, sensitive, and thoughtful.

1183   **Singer,** Isaac Bashevis. *The Fearsome Inn;* tr. by the author and Elizabeth Shub; illus. by Nonny Hogrogian. Scribner, 1967. 42p. Trade ed. $4.50; Library ed. $4.05 net. (Collins, 1970. 48p. £0.90.)

5–7   The inn belonged to Doboshova, the witch whose first husband had been a highwayman, whose second was half man, half devil: Lapitut. He and Doboshova had cast a spell on the road so that it led nowhere, and thus there was no escape for the three captive maidens Leitze, Neitze, and Reitze. Then there came to the lonely spot three young men, one of whom was a clever cabala student who outwitted the evil magicians and banished them to "the Mountains of Darkness where there is neither day nor night and dusk is eternal." Promptly the six young people paired off and proceeded to become affluent, respected, and surrounded by children and grandchildren. The style of writing is distinctive, mingling the Polish-Jewish humor and gusto with the fairy tale genre most deftly. The illustrations have a graceful vitality and a restrained use of color nicely complemented by a boldness of design.

1184   **Singer,** Isaac Bashevis. *Mazel and Shlimazel;* or the Milk of a Lioness; tr. from the Yiddish by the author and Elizabeth Shub; pictures by Margot Zemach. Farrar, 1967. 43p. $4.95.

3–5   A tale in the folk tradition, illustrated with lively, lovely illustrations and told with eloquent simplicity by a master-storyteller. In Jewish lore, Mazel is the spirit of good luck; Shlimazel is the embodiment of bad luck. The two engage in a power struggle, each engaging to bring to an appropriate conclusion the fortunes of a young peasant, Tam. Shlimazel almost ruins Tam's life, but Mazel comes to his rescue in the nick of time, leaving the lad betrothed (naturally) to a beautiful young princess. The author's triumph is that the story, really a moral tale, is more enjoyable as a good story than it is uplifting or minatory. It concludes, "Actually, Tam no longer needed Mazel, except once in a while. Tam had learned that good luck follows those who are diligent, honest, sincere and helpful to others. The man who has these qualities is indeed lucky forever."

1185   **Singer,** Isaac Bashevis. *When Shlemiel Went to Warsaw;* And Other Stories; tr. by the author and Elizabeth Shub; pictures by Margot Zemach. Farrar, 1968. 116p. $4.50.

5—   Eight stories, some of them based on traditional Jewish tales, are included in a new collection by one of the great storytellers of our time. One of the most amusing is "Shrewd Todie and Lyzer the Miser," in which the miser is outwitted as much by his greed as by Todie; another delightfully funny story is the saga of Shlemiel, so stupid that when he came back to his home town by mistake, he refused to believe it was his town and family. The writing has a cadence that is especially evident when the tales are read aloud; the length, the style, and the humor make them a happy source for storytelling; the individual reader will have the added pleasure of the Zemach illustrations, which are distinctive in their own right.

1186   **Singer,** Isaac Bashevis. *Zlateh the Goat;* tr. from the Yiddish by the author and Elizabeth Shub; pictures by Maurice Sendak. Harper, 1966. 90p. Trade ed. $5.95; Library ed. $4.99 net. (Longman Young Bks., 1970. 102p. £1.00.)

5–7   Although these seven tales were written for children, they will surely be enjoyed by adults. Based on middle-European Jewish folk material, the stories are told and illustrated with distinction. The Sendak illustrations are softly charming, with the humor and with just a bit of the grotesquerie of *Where the Wild Things Are*.

Mr. Singer achieves the ultimate in the genre—he never gets between the story and the audience.

1187   **Sitomer,** Mindel. *Circles;* by Mindel and Harry Sitomer; illus. by George Giusti. T. Y. Crowell, 1971. 33p. $3.75.

2–4   Attractive drawings, simple and large-scale, illustrate clearly the ideas presented in a good introduction to the manipulative charms of the "perfect" figure. The authors discuss the radius and diameter, the use of a compass, and the ways in which circle division points can be used to draw squares and triangles. The text is straightforward and lucid, an admirable example of science writing for the primary grades child.

1188   **Skrebitski,** G. A. *Forest Echo;* tr. from the Russian by Anne Terry White. Braziller, 1967. 71p. illus. Trade ed. $3.95; Library ed. $4.35 net.

5–8   Ten episodes about nature and animals, well written and smoothly translated; all of them are about incidents in the author's childhood: the story of a wild bird that became quite tame; another about a fox who brought food for her cub, captured by a hunter, and laid it on the threshold; a family fishing expedition to celebrate a birthday. There is, in addition to the appeal to nature lovers, a sympathetic and affectionate family situation.

1189   **Sleator,** William, ad. *The Angry Moon;* illus. by Blair Lent. Little, 1970. 48p. $4.95.

K–2   An adaptation of a legend of the Tlingit Indians of Alaska, the writing simple and staccato; the illustrations combine colorful, sometimes misty backgrounds and details of costumes or totems that are based on Tlingit designs. When Lapowinsa laughs at the moon, she disappears, leaving her friend Lupan desolate. He shoots arrows at the stars ("A strange idea came into his mind. 'Perhaps I can hit that star,' he said to himself.") and they form a ladder up which Lupan climbs. With the help of the grandmother of a tiny sky boy, he rescues Lapowinsa, using the four magic objects the grandmother had given him to foil the angry moon in pursuit of his escaped prisoner. An attractive book and an interesting legend useful for storytelling, but rather stilted when read aloud.

1190   **Slobodkin,** Florence. *Sarah Somebody;* illus. by Louis Slobodkin. Vanguard, 1970. 71p. $3.95.

3–5   Grandma had lived in Poland all of her ninety years, and she couldn't read or write. In 1893, few women were educated, so there didn't seem much chance that a nine-year-old girl in a Polish village would ever have a chance. But Miss Chesnov came from Warsaw and taught a small group of girls—so Sarah had her chance to become somebody. The story is simply told, the picture of a poor and loving Jewish family is warm and sympathetic, and the illustrations have Slobodkin's inimitable raffish economy of line.

1191   **Slobodkin,** Louis. *Round Trip Space Ship*. Macmillan, 1968. 168p. illus. $4.95. (Collier-Mac., 1969. 176p. £0.90.)

3–5   A sequel to *The Space Ship under the Apple Tree,* and just as light and amusing a story; Slobodkin's illustrations have their usual beguiling (and deceptive) simplicity of line. Eddie flies with his Martinean friend to Marty's home planet; they take along some forms of animal life (frozen for travel safety) and Eddie himself seems to be on exhibit. Later he learns that the Martinean sages have decided that they want to absorb some of the terrestrial manual know-how, having decided that life in Martinea was too sophisticated and automated. There is a hint of one-worldliness, a smattering of science with the fantasy, and great deal of cheerful humor.

1192   **Slote,** Alfred. *My Father, the Coach*. Lippincott, 1972. 157p. $4.50.

4–6   Many's the baseball book in which the rookie team beats the league champions, but few of them have as substantial a plot as does this. Ezell Corkins and his friends have been yearning to get into a league, but they are taken aback when Mr. Corkins announces he has arranged it—with himself as coach. He doesn't know anything about coaching, but one of the boys does; Obey is both a good athlete and a strong leader, and he's a take-charge boy. The team the boys most want to beat is the one sponsored by the bank and coached by its vice-president, Gardner. And Mr. Corkins hates Gardner, who patronizingly makes it clear each day that Willie Corkins is only a parking lot attendant. The characters and dialogue are convincing, the baseball sequences succinct and dramatic, and the ending a victory both for the team and for the little man whose courage is rewarded.

1193   **Smith,** Moyne Rice. *7 Plays & How to Produce Them;* illus. by Don Bolognese. Walck, 1968. 148p. $5.75.

5–8   The seven plays themselves vary from good to slightly awkward, but the book is valuable because it puts a premium on adaptation and production by young people. All of these plays adapted from stories by eminent children's authors have been put on by children, and each is followed by production notes. Some of the selections are delightfully funny, none puts a burden on an individual actor, and several are adaptable for large or small casts. A list of books about children's theater or on theatrical subjects is appended.

1194   **Smith,** Norman F. *Wings of Feathers, Wings of Flame;* The Science and Technology of Aviation; illus. with photographs and with drawings and diagrams by Bill Bradley. Little, 1972. 261p. $6.95.

7—   An aeronautical engineer gives an excellent survey of manned flight, including both the historical and technical aspects. The text discusses in detail the principles of flight and the problems of designing parts to overcome specific difficulties such as turbulence in laminar flow or overcoming shock waves in supersonic flight. Briskly and lucidly, the author describes the procedures in learning to fly, the instrument panel, navigation, and simulator training; he concludes with a chapter on the thermal barrier, on aircraft of the future, and on the effects of jet exhaust and shock waves on man's environment. A relative index is appended.

1195   **Smith,** Sarah Stafford. *The Ink-Bottle Club;* illus. by Anne Linton. Watts, 1967. 176p. $3.50. (Harrap, 1967. 176p. £0.80.)

4–6   A very pleasant story in itself, this is also used as a vehicle for half a dozen shorter tales told by some of the adult characters in the book. The important characters are the children who form the Ink-Bottle Club: two English children visiting in Dublin in 1913, their Irish cousins, and three neighboring children. The illustrations amplify the period flavor of the book; the plot is anecdotal, tied together by the unfolding of relationships and the emergence of distinctions of character. The dialogue occasionally has an old-fashioned stiffness, but the style on the whole is rather sprightly. A good family story.

1196   **Snyder,** Zilpha Keatley. *Black and Blue Magic;* drawings by Gene Holtan. Atheneum, 1966. 186p. $3.95.

5–7   An entirely diverting story that blends realism and fantasy in a most successful way; the illustrations add little. Harry Houdini Marco is an only child; his widowed mother runs a boarding house in San Francisco. Named (hopefully) by his father, a magician, the protagonist is clumsy, accident-prone, and all too often black and blue. One of his mother's boarders, grateful for Harry's kindness, confesses that he is a spirit and he gives Harry a magic potion. Result: wings. Painfully, Harry learns to fly, and he has some unusual adventures while the potion lasts. The book has a happy ending, made believable: Harry's mother marries the man that Harry has been scheming to get for a stepfather. Since the boarding house sequences are realistically concerned with chores, troublesome boarders, and trying to make ends meet, the element of fantasy is quite distinct and admirably set off. Harry, while flying, is seen by a few people and is assumed—to his disgust—to be an angel.

1197   **Snyder,** Zilpha Keatley. *The Changeling;* illus. by Alton Raible.
Atheneum, 1970. 220p. $5.25.

5–7   Everybody knew the Carsons. Disreputable and vagabond, they
were always in trouble, always moving away from town and back.
Ivy Carson was seven when she and Martha Abbott met, and
for mousy Martha it was a glorious beginning of long friendship
in which Ivy, wildly imaginative and firmly insisting she was a
changeling, led in fanciful play—interspersed with some mischief.
A natural dancer, Ivy was given the lead in a junior high play,
and a jealous competitor made it appear that Ivy was the
perpetrator of an act of vandalism. Although Martha's brother
confessed that he and two others had been the culprits, Ivy left
town. Only when she was a high school sophomore did Martha
learn that Ivy was dancing in New York, and she became sharply
aware that her own poise and popularity were due in large
measure to the salubrious influence of Ivy's personality. The
characterization is excellent, the writing style smooth and
vigorous; although the ending seems a bit pat for a book of
such vitality, the story as a whole has the same dramatic appeal
as did *The Egypt Game.*

1198   **Snyder,** Zilpha Keatley. *The Egypt Game;* drawings by Alton
Raible. Atheneum, 1967. 215p. Trade ed. $3.95; Library ed. $3.81
net.

4–7   Secretly, they met in the little yard back of the secondhand
shop, where nobody could see the Egypt Game; Melanie and
April even managed to convince Melanie's little brother Marshall
that it was fun pretending. When the neighborhood was
terrorized by the murder of a child, all outdoor play was forbidden,
but parents relaxed after awhile and April, who had left a book
in the yard, slipped out with Marshall one night and was found
by the murderer—and saved by Marshall. The murderer is a
minor character, the chief suspect having been a dour old man
who had secretly been watching and enjoying the Egypt Game.
Although the murder and the attack on April are blunt and
shocking, the total effect of the story is stunning in a literary
sense. The children are so real, their play so convincing and
dialogue so natural, that every one of them is a distinctive
character. They live in an urban university community, and the
variety of ethnic backgrounds is quite natural. The illustrations are
handsome, and they do a superb job of echoing both the mood
of the Egypt Game and of the personalities of the (eventually) six
children who participate in it.

1199   **Snyder,** Zilpha Keatley. *The Headless Cupid;* illus. by Alton Raible.
Atheneum, 1971. 203p. $4.95.

4–6   Having just acquired a very pleasant stepmother, David was
prepared to accept her daughter—but Amanda, resenting her
mother's remarriage, made no effort to become part of the family.
Her whole attention given to the occult, twelve-year-old Amanda
soon had her four stepbrothers and sisters going through a long
and complicated apprenticeship that would make them worthy to
share her absorption with the supernatural. It was when they
read about the fact that the house had once held a poltergeist
that a new stir of inexplicable activity began. David suspected
Amanda, but wasn't sure—because Amanda seemed, for the first
time, nervous. The solution is logical, the momentum deftly
sustained and knit into the theme of the unhappy Amanda's
angry resistance to her mother. The author portrays children with
acute understanding, evident both in her delineation of Amanda
and David and of the distinctively different younger children.
Good style, good characterization, good dialogue, good story.

1200   **Snyder,** Zilpha Keatley. *The Witches of Worm;* illus. by Alton
Raible. Atheneum, 1972. 183p. $5.25.

5–8   Blind, homely, and squirming, the newborn kitten looked like
a worm. She didn't even like Worm, Jessica thought, but she kept
him; she had little else in her life. She had long ago been dropped
by her few friends, and her mother was seldom home; the only
person she seemed to get along with was old Mrs. Fortune.
Rejected and hostile, Jessica became so emotionally disturbed that
she couldn't admit to herself that she had become cruel and
deceitful; she was bewitched and the cat possessed by a demon.
It was Worm that made her tell outrageous lies. When she learned
that her mother, who had already sent Jessica to a psychiatrist,
was thinking of a special school, Jessica decided she would try
exorcism. The evil is banished—logically—by an awakening of pity
for the cat, the therapy of tears, the understanding of Mrs.
Fortune, and a rapprochement with her dearest friend. The pace
and mood of the writing are compelling, the characterization
perceptive and convincing, the drama restrained. A book to
broaden a reader's understanding as well as a powerful story.

1201   **Sobol,** Donald J. *Encyclopedia Brown Saves the Day;* illus. by
Leonard Shortall. Nelson, 1970. 96p. Trade ed. $2.95; Library ed.
$2.90 net.

3–5   As in other books about the astute ten-year-old sleuth,
Encyclopedia Brown, this is a series of short mysteries, each of
them solved by the boy detective, each ending with a query as
to how he knew the solution. The answers, with full explanation,
are given at the back of the book. The writing style is lively
and humorous, and there is a challenge for the reader, but the

book is weakened by the fact that Encyclopedia will on occasion pursue an investigation when he already knows the answer: for example, in "The Case of the Kidnapped Pigs," one of the two children who report their prize pigs kidnapped gives his telephone number as "ZA 4-7575." Since the telephone dial has no "Z," he is immediately suspect—yet Encyclopedia rides six miles to talk to the four boys that the real culprit has said he suspected.

1202   **Sommerfelt,** Aimée. *My Name is Pablo;* tr. by Patricia Crampton; illus. by Hans Norman Dahl. Criterion Books, 1966. 143p. $4.25.

6–9   Set in Mexico City, an unusual and colorful story. A Norwegian boy, Fredrik, and a Mexican boy, Pablo, meet and become friends. Pablo cannot afford the license he should have in order to shine shoes; he is caught and sent to a reformatory. After he has gone back to living with Fredrik's family, Pablo is picked up by two of the tough older boys who had been in the reformatory and told that he must help them sell marijuana. Pablo's problems end when the two boys are in an accident and he need no longer fear reprisal or persecution of his family. A candid and moving picture of the plight of the poor and of the social pressures that operate in an urban environment.

1203   **Sonneborn,** Ruth A. *Friday Night Is Papa Night;* illus. by Emily A. McCully. Viking, 1970. 26p. Trade ed. $3.00; Library ed. $2.96 net.

K–2   Why, Pedro asked his mother, did Papa come home only on Friday night? Mama explained that Papa worked at two jobs to make enough money for his family, and that his work was far away. Satisfied, Pedro joined his older brothers and sister in the weekly preparation for Papa's coming. But Papa didn't arrive. Sadly they all went to bed, and then Pedro woke and looked out the window: Papa! The lights went on, and Papa—who had been with a sick friend—distributed small gifts. In the warmth and chatter and affection, Pedro decided again that Friday night was Papa night, the best time of the week. The structure is slight, but the story conveys a real feeling of family love, echoed in the illustrations of an attractive Puerto Rican family.

1204   **Sonneborn,** Ruth A. *Seven in a Bed;* illus. by Don Freeman. Viking, 1968. 27p. $2.95.

K–2   Mama and the baby and seven children got off the plane and were warmly greeted by Papa, who had come to America ahead of the family to make a home for them. Because the home wasn't quite ready, all the children had to sleep in one bed the first night, and the amusing pictures show the hazards of overcrowding. Papa put the boys on one side, girls on the other, but it was necessary to rearrange the belligerents several times before peace was declared. The last page shows the morning scene: two boys in a heap, one girl happily sleeping on the floor, and the other four distributed about the bed like so many jackstraws. Although the style is light and the situation here is temporary, the book should appeal to the children for whom a crowded bed is a way of life seldom reflected in children's books.

1205

6–8

Southall, Ivan. *Let the Balloon Go;* illus. by Ian Ribbons. St. Martin's, 1968. 142p. $3.95. (Methuen, 1968. 142p. £0.75.)

"A balloon is not a balloon until you cut the string and let it go." Fiercely, John Summer wanted to try a solo flight; for John this great adventure consisted of climbing a tree. A twelve-year-old spastic, the boy was protected and never left alone in the house—until the day his mother had to keep some appointments in town. Wild with delight and beset with a desire to do all of the things he was usually forbidden, John climbed a tree and was seen by neighbors, who called the police, afraid the boy would be killed. Furious, John insisted that he would come down by himself; a policeman began climbing to get him and had his shoe wedged in the crotch of a branch. Determined to make this one grand gesture, John came down, untied the man's shoe so that he could move, and then fell the short remaining distance. What John wants, he and his father decide, is a chance to say "no" to himself instead of hearing it from others. Although much of the intensity and suspense of the story are because of the fact that it is a spastic child who takes a risk to achieve independence, the importance of the book is in the fact that all young people reaching for maturity want John's chance to say "no" to themselves. The story starts slowly, but builds into a meaningful and dramatic construction, focused on a small, taut area like a pool of light on a dark stage.

1206

7–10

Spencer, Cornelia. *Sun Yat-sen;* Founder of the Chinese Republic. Day, 1967. 191p. illus. $4.95.

An objective and detailed biography, sedately written and competently organized; much of the material is inherently dramatic, and the usefulness and current interest of the book more than compensate for the static presentation. Sent to Hawaii at the age of twelve, Yat-sen was placed by his brother in an Anglican Church school, a milieu that has a far-reaching effect on the young patriot and intellectual who was later baptized a Christian, who became a doctor but was not interested in a medical career, and who was one of the leading spirits of the 1911 revolution. A bibliography, a chronology, a divided list of references, and an index are appended.

1207   **Spier,** Peter, illus. *The Erie Canal;* illus. by Peter Spier. Doubleday, 1970. 31p. $4.50.

4–6   The words of the rollicking song are the text; the illustrations follow a canal boat from Albany to Buffalo, the quiet stretches of water broken by passengers calling from other boats, by visitors on the tow line, by locks and towns and peddlers and the recurring danger of a low bridge. Like Spier's *London Bridge Is Falling Down,* the pages have spacious scenes and small, busy people. The details are fascinating, often amusing, and faithful to the time and locale. A page of information about canal business and the musical notation for the song are appended; endpapers show, enticingly, a vista with locks in the four seasons of the year.

1208   **Spier,** Peter, illus. *Hurrah, We're Outward Bound!* Doubleday, 1968. 36p. $3.95. (World's Work, 1969. 40p. £0.80.)

K–2   In the 16th and 17th centuries, the old French port of Honfleur was the embarkation point for many voyages, and in this engagingly illustrated book, one such voyage is pictured. The text does not describe the voyage, but consists of sea chanteys and rhymes; the historical information is provided in an appendage. The pictures follow the ship from Honfleur to New York to Dartmouth and back to the home port. The illustrations abound in liveliness and gaiety, and are very handsome indeed. Older children can best appreciate some of the illustrative details that have historical value or humorous appeal.

1209   **Spier,** Peter. *Of Dikes and Windmills;* written and illus. by Peter Spier. Doubleday, 1969. 187p. Trade ed. $5.95; Library ed. $6.70 net.

6—   A remarkably interesting book, profusely illustrated with maps, diagrams, and delightful drawings, and written with articulate ease. The author writes with competence of the long struggle of the Netherlands to claim and keep the land so battered by the invading seas, from the first signal victory of the water-pumping windmill to the complex hydraulic projects of today. The book is replete with anecdotes skillfully told, with colorful idiom, and with a vivid account of the 1953 flood. In addition to being a pleasure to read, the book contains a large amount of historical information. A relative index is appended.

1210   **Spykman,** E. C. *Edie on the Warpath.* Harcourt, 1966. 191p. $3.95. (Macmillan, 1967. 240p. £0.80.)

5–8   *Terrible, Horrible Edie* is with us again—in a fourth story about the Cares family, as entertaining as the other three. Edie, now eleven, is in a ferment of middle-child rebellion; her pre-adolescent moods, her role in the family constellation, and her inventive and lively mind are described with an amused sympathy. Edie is made completely believable, a combination of being lovable and being exasperating that every adult knows well.

1211 **Stambler,** Irwin. *Revolution in Light;* Lasers and Holography. Doubleday, 1972. 159p. illus. $4.95.

8— One of the fascinating frontiers of scientific investigation is explored in a book that describes the development of the first ruby laser by Theodore Maiman, and the subsequent research that has produced many variations (other kinds of lasers) and many practical applications since 1960. The descriptions of the operation of lasers, and of the intricate holographic techniques the laser made possible, are given in a direct style that uses no more technical terms than are necessary, but to understand the complexities of lasers requires some scientific background and vocabulary. No special knowledge is needed to understand the many ways in which lasers have already contributed to medicine, agriculture, industry, and communications. An index is appended.

1212 **Stanek,** Muriel. *Left, Right, Left, Right!* illus. by Lucy Hawkinson. Whitman, 1969. 29p. $3.50.

K–1 Of the several books that have appeared in the last year about the achievement of knowledge in the telling-right-from-left department, this the most effective. The reminder that grandmother gives Katie (a ring for the ring hand) is a sensible one, the information that her mother had the same problem is reassuring to Katie, and the discomforts she has suffered (walking down the wrong side of the school stairway) are familiar to readers and are adequate motivation for Katie's own desire to learn. Simply written, realistic, and useful, the book's modest but pleasant illustrations show a bespectacled heroine.

1213 **Starbird,** Kaye. *The Pheasant on Route Seven.* Lippincott, 1968. 74p. $3.50.

5–8 The title poem in this graceful collection is a lighthearted account of a pheasant who, bored with the monotonous life of the woods, ventured onto a public highway. "Well, *that* was darned surprising, Not to mention darned unpleasant." Most of the poems are about the inhabitants of Pleasantport: the priest, the town drunk, the gentle old aunt who collected friends, the incessantly questioning six-year-old neighbor. The reappearance of many of the characters knits the selections together, so that the book has a cohesion that adds to the charm of the deft character sketches, the humor, and the vitality of the writing.

1214 **Starbird,** Kaye. *A Snail's a Failure Socially;* And Other Poems, Mostly about People; illus. by Kit Dalton. Lippincott, 1966. 53p. $2.95.

4–6   A collection of light verse for the most part, with an occasional
poem that sounds a serious note; the small-scale black and white
illustrations have a good deal of humor and movement. The poems
are about animals, weather, human problems, friends, strangers,
and relationships—familiar topics, with an occasional odd twist.
The appeal of the book, nice to read independently or aloud,
is not in the beauty or the originality of the writing, but in
the swinging rhythm, the word play, the humorous concepts,
and the rhyme—the latter treated here and there with a cheerful
and clearly intentional disrespect.

1215   **Steig,** William. *Amos & Boris;* written and illus. by William
Steig. Farrar, 1971. 28p. $4.50.

K–2   Steig's engaging cartoon-style illustrations add to the fun of a
friendship between a huge mammal and a tiny one. Amos is a
mouse who falls off a ship he is sailing; Boris is the amicable
whale who rides him back to land. During their long journey,
the two become close friends and part with regret, knowing that
they will probably never see each other again. BUT fate intervenes.
During hurricane Yetta, Boris is stranded, gasping, on the shore,
and Amos is able to save his life (two elephants, hastily
summoned, roll Boris back to sea) and has the gratification of
having done for his friend what has been done by his friend
for him. No message here, just a pleasant tale, breezily told.

1216   **Steig,** William. *C D B!* Simon and Schuster, 1968. 44p. illus. $2.95.

4—   The cartoon characters of William Steig, familiar to *New Yorker*
magazine readers, here are used in combination with the game
of making words out of letter sounds and numbers. Deft and
highly entertaining, the book should appeal to those who enjoy
word play, have a detective instinct, or simply seek amusement.
Boy pointing to himself, and then to the dog he addresses,
"I M A U-M B-N. U R N N-M-L."

1217   **Steig,** William. *Dominic;* story and pictures by William Steig.
Farrar, 1972. 146p. $4.50.

4–6   In his first novel for children, William Steig has created an
engaging hero, a dog with heart of gold, nerves of steel, and
the varied talents of Renaissance Man. In a story with sophisticated
humor and picaresque plot, Dominic sallies forth to see the world
and to earn gratitude and acclaim for his generosity, his courage,
and his prowess at absolutely everything to which he turns
his paw—including the foiling of a dastardly troop of villains
who have been preying on the community. The animals of the
story are really people in disguise, but Steig's wit and his
insouciant illustrations make Dominic and his friends wholly
believable. A good story for reading aloud to third-grade children.

1218   **Steig,** William. *Sylvester and the Magic Pebble.* Windmill/Simon and Schuster, 1969. 29p. illus. $4.95.

K–2   An oversize book that affords the *New Yorker* cartoonist a splendid opportunity for illustrations that are both winsome and humorous, with a story that has the same qualities, plus an ingenuous, direct style of writing. Sylvester is a young donkey who finds a magic pebble; faced with a hungry lion, he desperately wishes he were a rock and the magic works. His parents search the neighborhood, call out the dogs, and resign themselves to their loss. The autumn leaves fall on Sylvester, a wolf sits on him to howl at the snowy sky, and spring comes at last. Trying to cheer themselves, Sylvester's parents picnic on the rock, and they just happen to pick up a pebble, and Sylvester just happens to wish he were alive again . . . and the magic works again. Joyful reunion, satisfying conclusion.

1219   **Steptoe,** John. *Stevie.* Harper. 1969. 22p. illus. Trade ed. $3.50; Library ed. $3.27 net. (Longman Young Bks., 1970. 12p. £0.80.)

5–7
yrs.   Robert is a small black boy, an only child who looks with no anticipation at the prospect of having Stevie, whose parents work, as a weekday boarder in his home. He has to take Stevie out to play, and his friends tease him. Stevie climbs all over Robert's bed. "And he was greedy too. Everything he sees he wants. 'Could I have somma that? Gimme this.' Man!" But when Stevie goes, Robert thinks about what fun it was to have a companion always there. He misses him. The story closes with Robert sitting, pensive, over a bowl of cereal grown soggy, admitting to himself that he is lonely. The illustrations are striking, in strong composition and rich colors, each full page capturing a familiar mood of childhood.

1220   **Sterling,** Dorothy. *The Making of an Afro-American;* Martin Robison Delany, 1812–1885. Doubleday, 1971. 352p. $4.95.

8—   A long and detailed biography, serious in tone, is as valuable for its contribution to the body of knowledge in black history as it is for the information given about an earlier fighter for black power. Son of a slave, Martin Delany was born free in 1812; when it was discovered that his family had learned how to read, the Delanys fled from Virginia to Pennsylvania to escape punishment for this breach of the contemporary code. Delany worked all his life, often leaving his family for years, for the cause of black independence. The education he fought for brought him a measure of recognition; doctor, explorer, author, public speaker, commissioned a major during the Civil War, official of the Freedman's Bureau during Reconstruction. An ardent worker for returning to Africa, Delany (who had originally opposed such

migration) was still planning to go there when he died. An
extensive divided bibliography and an index are appended.

1221   **Sterling,** Dorothy. *Tear Down the Walls!* A History of the American
Civil Rights Movement. Doubleday, 1968. 259p. illus. $6.95.

7—   A very good history of the Negro people, covering much of the
same material as does Goldston's *The Negro Revolution* (Macmillan,
1968) but written in a slightly less formal style. The author
describes the African beginnings of black Americans, the slave
trade, the abolitionists and the Civil War, such familiar figures
in Negro history as Carver, Douglass and DuBois, the Klan, the
black stereotype, and the accelerated pressures of recent years:
legislation, school integration, riots, voter-registration drives, and
new leaders. Like the Goldston book, this is comprehensive,
objective, and smoothly written. Emphases differ in treatment of
subjects; for example, there is no mention of the Communist
party in Sterling's account of the Scottsboro boys, whereas Goldston
uses the incident to illustrate Communist espousal of civil rights
causes. An index and a bibliography are appended.

1222   **Sterling,** Philip. *Sea and Earth;* The Life of Rachel Carson. T. Y.
Crowell, 1970. 213p. illus. $4.50.

7—   A beautifully balanced biography, written with skill and restraint.
Although her interest in biology did not emerge until college
(when she changed her major) there were indications throughout
the childhood of the quiet, studious Rachel that she found natural
phenomena fascinating. It was at Woods Hole that she decided
to specialize in marine biology, and her first job after getting a
higher degree at Johns Hopkins was writing radio scripts for
the Bureau of Fisheries. She knew that her writing in college
had been deemed excellent, and submitted an article to the
Atlantic Monthly, thus beginning another phase of a distinguished
career; it was her second book, *The Sea around Us,* that
made Rachel Carson famous. In 1958 she began work on *Silent
Spring.* A selected, extensive list of sources and an index are
appended.

1223   **Sterne,** Emma Gelders. *Benito Juarez;* Builder of a Nation; illus.
by Ray Cruz. Knopf, 1967. 195p. $3.95.

8–12   As much a history of the Mexican struggle for democratic
independence as it is a biography of Juarez, this serious book
has—although rather solidly written—a great deal of inherent
drama and color. It begins with the arrival of an orphaned
Zapotec Indian boy of twelve in Oaxaca; Benito Juarez had
come from his mountain village in search of work and education.
All his life he was to remember the discriminatory practices
in education under the rule of Spain, and all his life to work

for the people—all the people. In the turbulent years of
fighting for freedom, Juarez remained quietly devoted to his
cause; never flamboyant or hostile, he was dedicated to the law,
the common man, equality, education, and a united Mexico. A
list of books for suggested reading and an index are appended.

1224   **Stevens,** Carla. *The Birth of Sunset's Kittens;* photographs by
Leonard Stevens. Scott, 1969. 41p. $4.35. (World's Work, 1970.
44p. £0.90.)

K–3   A series of photographs show every detail of the always-wonderful
sight of tiny, blind-eyed kittens being born. The text explains
what is happening with matter-of-fact clarity: the muscles of the
cat's uterus are contracting, moving the kitten along the birth
canal; the kitten emerges, and the clinging amnion is eaten by
the cat. The mother cat gently licks and grooms her new family;
the kittens nurse. No cute posed pictures, no saccharine comment,
just the miraculous facts.

1225   **Stevens,** Leonard A. *The Town That Launders Its Water:* how a
California town learned to reclaim and reuse its water. Coward,
McCann and Geoghegan, 1971. 125p. illus. $4.49.

6—   When, in the 1950's, the regulations that determined the legal
purity standards for sewage effluent (the residue dumped into
natural streams) changed, the town of Santee, California was in
trouble. It could join a metropolitan system that would carry
sewage to the ocean, or could go it alone. The disposal and
purification system that the water district manager worked out is a
landmark in the story of water pollution and conservation. In
an area with only ten inches of rainfall in an average year,
Santee now has eight freshwater lakes for boating and swimming—
and all of the water comes from reclaimed sewage water! It took
years of trial and error, the solving of complex legal and financial
problems, and an educational campaign to make the concept
acceptable to the public, but the citizens of Santee now enjoy
the beauty and pleasure of water that is saved and safe. Diagrams
and photographs make the procedures clear, and the straightforward text has an unexpected element of suspense, since each
step of the venture was a calculated risk. An index is appended.

1226   **Stevenson,** Janet. *Women's Rights;* illus. with prints and
photographs. Watts, 1972. 96p. $3.75.

5–8   A history of the struggle for equal rights for women in America,
particularly the effort to gain the franchise. Short biographies
of pioneers in suffragism are followed by a chronological description of the fight for educational opportunities and the long years of
campaigning for the right to vote. The photographs are interesting,
the writing measured, objective, and clear, and the text particularly

valuable for its discussion of the nature of the forces marshalled against woman suffrage. A bibliography and an index are appended.

1227   **Stewart,** Mary. *The Little Broomstick;* illus. by Shirley Hughes. Morrow, 1972. 192p. Trade ed. $4.95; Library ed. $4.59 net. (Brockhampton, 1971. 128p. £0.95.)

4–6   First published in England, a fanciful story by a writer of popular adult novels. The writing style is excellent, the details inventive, the plot the weakest part of the story—full of action, much of which seems padded. Lonely on a visit to an elderly great-aunt, Mary is intrigued by the small black cat that appears and makes friendly overtures. He leads her to a strange flower— the flower's juice on her hands activates a broom—and off Mary goes, delivered to the door of a school for witches. She then discovers that the headmistress is conducting cruel animal experiments; with the help of a book of spells conveniently at hand she rescues the beasts, including her own cat; she flies home, pursued by the wicked witch, and is saved by the animals she has rescued.

1228   **Stiles,** Martha Bennett. *Darkness over the Land.* Dial, 1966. 269p. $3.95.

8—   An impressive novel about Germany under the Nazis, unusual in its presentation of an ordinary family. The Elends are neither cowards nor heroes; the adults are clearly in disagreement with the regime, but they neither protest nor fight. The youngest Elend, Mark, is ardently patriotic; he is all the more stunned, therefore, when he learns that he is a foster child and a despised Pole. All the family are dismayed to find that in the eyes of the American troops, they share the Nazi guilt. At the close of the story, Mark gives up a chance to go to America with his Polish uncle in order to stay and help rebuild Germany. Good characters, competent writing style, the excellent creation of locale, period, and atmosphere.

1229   **Stolz,** Mary Slattery. *By the Highway Home.* Harper, 1971. 194p. Trade ed. $4.95; Library ed. $4.43 net.

6–9   Mourning the brother who had died in Vietnam, resenting the fact that her parents don't want to talk about him, Catty Reed is also oppressed by sense that they are keeping something else to themselves. They are. Her father has lost his job, and the family has to sell its home and move to Vermont to stay with relatives who run an inn for elderly residents. Catty blossoms in the new environment, seeing more clearly the selfishness of her older sister, a charmer, enjoying the beauty of the countryside, adjusting to Beau's death, and falling in love with an older boy—a relationship handled with great tenderness. Although there are a few episodes that are weak, the book as a whole has an honesty and dignity that are impressive, the characters and dialogue deftly drawn and perceptively related.

1230   Stolz, Mary Slattery. *The Dragons of the Queen;* pictures by Edward Frascino. Harper, 1969. 49p. Trade ed. $3.50; Library ed. $3.27 net.

5–7   An unusual story in tempo and setting, with no child characters; were the writing style not so simple, this would be more a *New Yorker* short story than a children's book. A middle-aged American couple, unimaginative and pompous, have an experience that changes their lives in one enchanting Mexican night. Unable to find hotel accommodations, Mr. and Mrs. George Kenilworth of Boise, Idaho, accept the invitation of Dona Pascuala to stay the night in her crumbling but elegant casa. Aged one hundred two, surrounded by her dragons (seven dogs) and beloved by all the town, the old woman seems indeed a queen, and her dignity and charm captivate the visitors.

1231   Stolz, Mary Slattery. *Juan;* illus. by Louis S. Glanzman. Harper, 1970. 131p. Trade ed. $3.95; Library ed. $4.43 net.

4–6   Of all the children at Casa Maria, the orphanage of a small Mexican town, eight-year-old Juan was dearest to Concepción. She had been at Casa Maria all her sixteen years; she had no one and knew she would always be alone. Therefore, when an American couple gave a party for the children and singled out Juan for a present, Concepción's heart burned with jealousy. Nevertheless she was proud of her Juan, the rebellious child who so firmly maintained the delusion that his parents existed and would come for him. She wanted him to have the gift; Juan wanted to keep it but knew the other children would be resentful. Juan's decision is a meaningful one, since in giving up the present (the shining boots he had long craved) he also gives up his long-maintained insistence that he is different, he has parents. The plot is less impressive than the style, which is distinctive, and the setting, which is unusual and interesting; the characterization is excellent.

1232   Stolz, Mary Slattery. *Maximilian's World;* pictures by Uri Shulevitz. Harper, 1966. 60p. Trade ed. $2.95; Library ed. $2.92 net.

3–5   A sequel to *Belling the Tiger* and *The Great Rebellion,* in which the mice, Asa and Rambo, stay on their own side of the mousehole, where it is safe to be friends with the cat on the other side. Here the cat, Siri, is again a well-meaning, loquacious bore, and his victim is a tiny Chihuahua, Maximilian. Poor Maximilian, a captive audience, finally has An Adventure of his own; he happily pours it all out to Siri. In detail. In boring detail. Thus,

Siri learns what it means to be boring. As in the previous books, the writing is delightful, the plot simple, and the fun that is poked at the ways of mice and men is a bonus for the perceptive or the older reader.

1233   **Stolz,** Mary Slattery. *The Story of a Singular Hen and Her Peculiar Children;* illus. by Edward Frascino. Harper, 1969. 48p. Trade ed. $3.50; Library ed. $3.27 net.

K–3   The hen was surly, having wakened to the realization that she'd forgotten something again. She'd forgotten that she had no family. "Home, sweet barnyard," she muttered. Thus begins the silly endearing story of a vast adoption program: with no animal mothers in sight, the hen decided that all the barnyard young were hers. She had some difficulty getting the foal and the pigs to peep, and the kids didn't really work at their pecking, but one's children are one's children and the hen was determined to be proud of them. Chicks don't swim? HER chicks swam. In a wistful sunset scene, the hen is divested of her "chicks" when all their mothers appear, and she goes off to her lonely roost to dream about the family she will raise: fluffy, yellow babies who are destined for chickenhood. On the surface, a light-hearted story about animals, deftly told and amusingly illustrated; below the surface, sagacious perception, some of which will seep through to some children.

1234   **Stolz,** Mary Slattery. *A Wonderful, Terrible Time;* pictures by Louis S. Glanzman. Harper, 1967. 182p. Trade ed. $4.50; Library ed. $3.79 net.

4–6   Mady and Sue Ellen lived across the hall from each other and were best friends, different as they were: Sue Ellen never wanted to talk about anything serious, like freedom marches, and Mady did. Her father had been killed in a voter registration drive. Then another difference emerged when the girls had a chance to go to a summer camp: Sue Ellen was bitterly resistant, while Mady was thrilled. When they got to camp, same thing: Sue Ellen resistant, Mady thrilled. Realistically, despite the fact that Sue Ellen found herself enjoying some aspects of life at camp, she never wanted to go back, whereas Mady hated being back in the city but found that she enjoyed her wonderful time in retrospect by sharing her memories with her mother. A good book as a camp story or as a picture of friendship values, but the most striking aspect is the fact that both at home and at camp, the girls are in a racially mixed community where integration is not The Issue of the book. Mady and Sue Ellen are both Negro; while this is a fact that enters naturally into the dialogue, it is a minor fact compared to the importance of personalities and familial relationships.

1235   **Stone,** A. Harris. *Have a Ball;* by A. Harris Stone and Bertram
M. Siegel; illus. by Peter P. Plasencia. Prentice-Hall, 1969. 63p.
$3.95.

4–7   The process aproach to science is used most successfully here,
the suggestions for experimentation and demonstration clear and
simple, the explanations of theories (that underlie the principles
being demonstrated) only lightly suggested, so that it is incumbent
upon the reader to make the relationship. The materials used are
neither complicated nor expensive and the book is packed cover-
to-cover with intriguing questions. The material covers such
aspects as force, penetrability, rate of fall, spin, elasticity, and
momentum; the experiments test factors that affect performance
in these areas and they demonstrate some of the laws of physics.
A glossary is appended.

1236   **Stone,** A. Harris. *Rocks and Rills;* A Look at Geology; by A. Harris
Stone and Dale Ingmanson; illus. by Peter P. Plasencia. Prentice-
Hall, 1967. 70p. $4.50.

4–7   A book of home experiments for the beginning scientist interested
in geology; unlike most such books, this one suggests the
demonstration technique and leaves it to the reader to find out
what happens. The experiments illustrate some of the basic
processes in geologic change; for example, several simple ways of
checking solubility differences are suggested, and the relationship
between solubility and chemical weathering is pointed out. For
the youngest readers some adult help may be required to define
terms or explain techniques. What is NOT pointed out is the
answer to an experiment. A glossary is appended.

1237   **Storey,** Margaret. *Pauline;* illus. by Victor Ambrus. Doubleday,
1967. 210p. $3.95. (Faber, 1965. 176p. £0.75.)

6–9   One of the best junior novels for girls to come along in a long
time, this story of an orphaned English adolescent has memorable
characterization and dialogue, an interesting and wholly believable
situation of conflict, and a realistic solution. Pauline has come
to live with her uncle Harry's family, and she tries to love them
and to be grateful, but she is aware that Uncle Harry is a petty
tyrant and resents it. He is critical, rigid in his ideas, and—
perhaps worst of all—falsely hearty in his "little talks" to his
niece. Only when Pauline runs away to an aunt in London does
her uncle, aware that other adults disapprove of his strictures,
make concessions.

1238   **Storr,** Catherine. *Lucy Runs Away;* illus. by Victoria de Larrea.
Prentice-Hall, 1969. 69p. $4.25. (Bodley Head, 1962. £0.37½.)

3–5   First published in England, a sequel to *Lucy* in which the
dauntless heroine, playing detective, became involved with real

thieves. Here Lucy, bored by her sedentary summer, decides
that she will run away as soon as she turns ten. And she does,
at the age of ten years and three days, having chosen a coastal
town because she might find some interesting smuggling going
on. Consoling herself with the fact that nobody realizes that a
mysterious outlaw (herself) is on board, Lucy rides to the sea;
she falls asleep on the beach and calls for help when an old man,
having an early swim, flounders. Quite satisfied with her
adventure and the newspaper publicity, Lucy placidly accepts her
sisters' envious admiration, and announces that she will run
away again—farther—when she is twelve. Light style with just a
bit of a bite to it, good dialogue, and a satisfying plot.

1239   **Stoutenburg,** Adrien. *People in Twilight;* Vanishing and Changing
Cultures; illus. with photographs. Doubleday, 1971. 216p. Trade
ed. $4.95; Library ed. $5.70 net.

7–10   A survey of some of the groups that have existed as primitive
cultures, in the midst of an increasingly complex and mechanized
world, upon whom the impact of technological progress is making
changes. Among those discussed are the Eskimo, the North
American Indian, the Aborigines, the African Bushmen and
Pygmies, and various groups in South America and the South
Sea Islands. The tone of the writing is objective, but the author
ends with a gentle plea for understanding and for the wisdom
to assist where assistance is wanted and to desist where it is
not. A bibliography, an index, and endpaper maps are included.

1240   **Sullivan,** George. *Understanding Architecture.* Warne, 1971. 108p.
illus. $3.95.

5–9   Photographs and clear diagrams of architectural details supplement
the textual explanations of the styles and construction techniques
in building from the simplest post-and-lintel of ancient times to
the skyscrapers, prefabricated homes, and free design of today and
the ecologically oriented buildings that have been suggested for
the future. Although succinctly written, the book is comprehensive
in scope and lucid in style. A phonetic guide to pronunciation
of architectural terms and an index are appended.

1241   **Sully,** François, ed. *We the Vietnamese;* Voices from Vietnam; ed.
by François Sully and Marjorie Weiner Normand. Praeger, 1971.
270p. illus. $7.50.

8—   Writings about and by the Vietnamese, chiefly the latter, give a
collage of impressions of Vietnam. The voices come from both
north and south; they range from magazine articles on popular
subjects to official government correspondence. Much of the
material is historical, and a substantial portion of the book is
devoted to poetry, both traditional poetry and contemporary

protest. A brief, pithy editorial comment precedes each selection, and the book is, in balance, objective as well as informative. A short list of suggestions for further reading and an index are appended.

1242 **Surany,** Anico. *Monsieur Jolicoeur's Umbrella;* pictures by Leonard Everett Fisher. Putnam, 1967. 40p. $3.50.

3–5 Bold, startling blocks of color are used by Fisher, whose strong style is well-suited to the brisk humor of the story; the bright orange background for most of the pages is effective but a bit abrasive, and it is a relief when the cool blue of the night scenes appears. Oliva and 'Ti Mouche are two Haitian sisters who are not enchanted at the prospect of going back to school. They are also unhappy when the raps by Monsieur Jolicoeur's umbrella remind them sharply to stop daydreaming, once they are in school. So the two girls arrange a way to frighten their teacher to death—but he sees through them, is amused at the fact that they are pretending to be a ghost, and marches them home. The setting is delightful, the writing style has vitality and humor, and the illustrations capture the wry, affectionate tone of the story.

1243 **Susac,** Andrew. *Paracelsus; Monarch of Medicine.* Doubleday, 1969. 192p. Trade ed. $3.95; Library ed. $4.70 net.

7–10 A good biography of the sixteenth-century Swiss physician Theophrastus von Hohenheim—who either invented or was dubbed "Paracelsus"—above the authority of Celsus. Here, as in many other details, Susac's version differs from that of Rosen's *Doctor Paracelsus,* which does not include von Hohenheim's study with Trithemius, stressed here as a turning point in his career. Although both books tend to aggrandize not the man, but his contribution to medical history, they are not written in adulatory tone; here the author makes the book especially interesting by using his subject's life-long battles against entrenched ignorance to give a vivid picture of the state of medicine and, to some extent, all learning, in Europe at that time. The fictionalization is skilled, the writing competent. The brief epilogue mentions Paracelsus as the model for the Faust legend. A relative index is appended.

1244 **Sutcliff,** Rosemary. *Heather, Oak, and Olive;* illus. by Victor Ambrus. Dutton, 1972. 120p. $4.95.

5–8 Three tales of ancient times, each different in setting and all compelling, are told by a master storyteller who is also an excellent historian. The period details are vivid but do not overburden the stories, the structure is deft and sturdy, the characters strong. In "The Chief's Daughter," a boy who has been a captive since an unsuccessful assault by Irish raiders is set free by Nessan, the daughter of the clan chief, whose friendship for the Irish lad is stronger than her fear of being offered as a sacrifice to the Black Mother in his place. Britain during the Roman occupation is the setting for the second tale, in which an older man lets a young soldier take credit for his own valorous deed. A third tale of ancient times is set in Greece, where two lads forget their differences, Spartan versus Athenian, to become friends; the dramatic tale has a poignancy that is relevant to youth and war in any time. The black and white illustrations, handsome in themselves, echo the dignity and the romanticism of Rosemary Sutcliff's writing.

1245   **Sutcliff,** Rosemary. *Heroes and History;* illus. by Charles Keeping. Putnam, 1966. 152p. $4.50. (Batsford, 1965. 152p. £0.75.)

8—   Ten dramatic figures, ten vividly written descriptions of their exploits; these are not full or balanced biographies—they are not meant to be—but detailed accounts of the years and deeds of glory. There is more than enough historical background and there is, in some of the accounts, some discussion of truth versus legend and of verified sources versus gossip. The ten heroes described are Caratacus, Arthur, Alfred, Hereward, Lewellin, Owen Glyndwr, Robin Hood, William Wallace, Robert the Bruce, and Montrose. Exciting stuff. There are more names and place-names than the young reader in this country can easily absorb, but they lend color even if they remain unidentified. The illustrations are Keeping's usual bold style, but they prove quite distracting when they fill a page almost completely and face a page of solid (and small) print. An index is appended.

1246   **Sutcliff,** Rosemary. *Tristan and Iseult.* Dutton, 1971. 150p. $4.50. (Bodley Head, 1971. 134p. £1.20.)

6–8   To one of the great love stories of all time, Rosemary Sutcliff brings the felicity of historical detail and the lyric, flowing style of a master storyteller. Her version of the tale omits the love potion, ascribing the sudden admission of their passion to the fact that Tristan and Iseult touch for the first time when he carries her ashore while seeking harbor during the voyage to Cornwall. The quality that emerges most clearly from Sutcliff's retelling is the bittersweet urgency of the love between the Queen and Tristan.

1247   **Sutcliff,** Rosemary. *The Witch's Brat;* illus. by Richard Lebenson. Walck, 1970. 143p. $4.75. (Oxford U.P., 1970. 136p. £0.80.)

6–9   An evocative story of Norman England, based on the actual founding of St. Bartholomew's Hospital. Lovel, the witch's brat whose grandmother had been a healer, is a small crippled boy who, stoned by the villagers, takes refuge in a monastery where his knowledge of herbs is used and extended. When Rahere, the King's Jongleur (who founded the hospital) calls Lovel to join him, Lovel goes—and finds in his profession a satisfaction that makes it a joyful bondage. The story has strong, taut structure and good characterization, but is most distinguished by the colorful and consistent picture of a historical period.

1248   **Sutton,** Felix. *The Big Show;* A History of the Circus. Doubleday, 1971. 176p. illus. $4.95.

6–9   A history of the circus that emphasizes its development in this country, with detailed descriptions of such major impresarios as Barnum, Bailey, and the Ringling brothers, and of some of the great drawing-cards: Buffalo Bill, Tom Thumb, the Wallendas, Gargantua, and that "pioneer pachyderm," Old Bet. Separate chapters are devoted to each type of performer, and all of the text is enlivened by show biz anecdotes recounted in Modified Journalese. One chapter is devoted to some of the traditional tall tales of circus history, and an index is appended.

1249   **Swenson,** May. *More Poems to Solve.* Scribner, 1970. 64p. $3.50.

6—   A stimulating collection of new poems, of which some are riddle-poems, some shape-poems, some word-thing poems, and some that combine these excursions into structure or invitations to the reader to interpret. In these, and in the poems of space and flight, there is wit, perception, and an ebullient, imaginative use of language. The preface, "A Poem Is A Thing," is a small bonus.

1250   **Swortzell,** Lowell, ed. *All the World's a Stage;* Modern Plays for Young People; decorations by Howard Simon. Delacorte, 1972. 610p. $12.50.

7–10   "But as long as the young readers dare," says the compiler in an introduction that deplores the state of children's theatre, "there is hope for older ones." So, feeling that young people can produce and act in the best of adult plays that speak to or for them, he includes plays from this country and others, from a familiar Saroyan to two Brecht plays based on Japanese Noh, from a rock musical comedy based on *Twelfth Night* to Strindberg's fanciful *Swanwhite.* Each selection is prefaced by a brief introduction to the playwright and the play. A list of recommended readings is appended.

1251   **Syme,** Ronald. *Bolívar the Liberator;* illus. by William Stobbs. Morrow, 1968. 190p. $3.95.

4–7   There could be no more dramatic a story than Bolívar's—the gilded youth whose extravagant gambling shocked Paris, whose hauteur offended the Spanish Prince, whose Venezuelan fortune was lost forever when young Simón decided to put into practice the revolutionary ideas he had been acquiring. South America was under the Spanish thumb, and at first Simón Bolívar was just another hothead whose ragged army failed miserably. But he learned, he fought, and he won; born a multimillionaire and at one time president of five countries, he died a pauper, maligned by his enemies and exiled from his home. His biography is written succinctly and smoothly, with no trace of adulation but with an objective approach both to Bolívar's limitations and errors and to the political immaturity of his countrymen. A very brief bibliography is appended.

1252   **Syme,** Ronald. *William Penn;* Founder of Pennsylvania; illus. by William Stobbs. Morrow, 1966. 95p. Trade ed. $3.75; Library ed. 3.56 net.

5–7   A very good biography of William Penn, with illustrations that are rather stark and repetitive and with good, clear print. The author gives ample background about Penn's family in England, their position in the struggle between Roundheads and Cavaliers, and their reaction to the odd, new religion to which their William had become a convert. The text goes on to the more familiar material about the establishment of a colony in the New World and about the troubles Penn had, both financial and personal. The writing is matter-of-fact in tone and objective in mood.

1253   **Symons,** Geraldine. *Miss Rivers and Miss Bridges;* illus. by Alexy Pendle. Macmillan, 1972. 190p. $4.95. (Macmillan, 1971.)

6–8   The delightful heroines of *The Workhouse Child* are on the loose in London, where Pansy has come to visit Atalanta and is enthralled by the house, the glamor of Atalanta's actress mother, and the campaign being waged by the suffragettes of the pre– World War I period. Determined to participate in this good cause, the stalwart Atalanta and her friend disguise themselves in matronly garb and, as Miss Rivers and Miss Bridges, manage to create a considerable amount of disruption, with consequent newspaper publicity and a jail sentence. The setting and the period details are vivid, adeptly incorporated into the story, and the exploits of the protagonists are believable, funny, and exciting.

1254   **Taber,** Gladys (Bagg). *Especially Dogs . . . Especially at Still-meadow.* Lippincott, 1968. 191p. illus. $4.50.

6—   You don't even have to be a dog lover to enjoy the author's reminiscences about some of the dogs she has owned and loved. First of all, the writing style is trenchant, informal, and humorous; second, the facts about breeding and training dogs are interesting;

third, the affectionate (but not sentimental) tone that permeates the book has the same appeal as does seeing such affection in actuality.

1255   **Tabrah,** Ruth M. *Hawaii Nei;* illus. by Herbert Kawainui Kane. Follett, 1967. 320p. Trade ed. $4.95; Library ed. $4.99 net.

6–10   The people of Hawaii's eight islands speak of their state as "Hawaii nei," meaning "Hawaii, this place." Although there are other good books about Hawaii, this should be a welcome source of information, since it is well written, comprehensive, and well organized. The author is a Hawaiian resident, and her observations are acute and informed; the book covers history, geography, economy, holidays, folkways, ethnic groups, education, flora and fauna, natural phenomena, and a multiplicity of minor topics. A lengthy glossary and an extensive index are appended.

1256   **Talbot,** Charlene Joy. *Tomás Takes Charge;* illus. by Reisie Lonette. Lothrop, 1966. 191p. $3.95.

4–7   The story of two orphans in New York City. For days Tomás and Fernanda had been by themselves, the hope that their father would come dwindling each day; finally they hid. Rather than be taken by the dreaded Welfare people, they hid in an abandoned top-floor apartment in the market district and lived on what scraps Tomás could bring home; although Tomás was only eleven, he had to fend for both, since Fernanda had a neurotic fear of going outdoors. Tomás made friends with a young illustrator who used him as a model, and it was through Miss Barbara that changes for the better came: a doctor for Fernanda, a place for the two to live where they could have supervision with some measure of privacy, and a meeting with the Welfare people—who turned out to be helpful and sympathetic. The ending is realistic— their father has been killed in a traffic accident, so there is no last-minute reprieve. The children are to be supervised by a former landlady, a situation for which the reader is prepared by her previous kindness and concern. Very moving, quite believable. Wonderful neighborhood atmosphere, good writing style, and a sustained pace in the development of the plot.

1257   **Tamchina,** Jurgen. *Dominique and the Dragon;* trans. and ad. by Elizabeth D. Crawford; illus. by Heidrun Petrides. Harcourt, 1969. 37p. $4.25. (Longman Young Bks., 40p. £1.25.)

K–3   First published in German in 1968, this oversize book is used to good advantage for big, bold, imaginative pictures, some in color and all with humorous detail; page layout and marginal illustrations are good. The story is on a now-familiar theme, the much-feared dragon that turns out to be a very model of amicability. Here the fearful are the townspeople of

Avignon, who see a huge monster with fiery eyes and a saw-toothed back swimming down the Rhone. After several massive efforts at capture have failed, little Dominique bravely convinces the dragon to talk quietly. "*All* animals are nice," she says. "One simply must not anger them." So the dragon obligingly acts as a bridge across the river or as an entrancing playground for children. As for a time-saving device for trampling grapes, it proves the dragons are the last word.

1258   **Tanner,** Louise. *Reggie and Nilma.* Farrar, 1971. 184p. $4.50.

6–10   For Kim and her brother Tony, it was a joy to go to Nilma's Harlem apartment for weekends. Nilma and Reggie, her son, had lived with the family when there was a house; now that they were in an apartment, Reggie and Nilma each had keys. Because the relationships were so close, it was a particularly stunning blow to Reggie when he was suspected of a series of robberies in the apartment, a suspicion implanted by the insurance agent but entertained by Kim, who tells the story. Reggie is innocent and the culprit (a young neighbor) found, but the breach is irreparable: Reggie turns away completely from his white friends and from his grieving mother. Nilma is the strong character of the story, a conservative woman with delicacy and common sense, a victim both of the generation gap and of interracial tension. Despite the serious problems presented in the story, it is not somber: the style is light and sophisticated, the dialogue often amusing, and the characterization perceptive.

1259   **Tashjian,** Virginia A., comp. *Juba This and Juba That*; Story Hour Sketches for Large or Small Groups; illus. by Victoria de Larrea. Little, 1969. 116p. $4.95.

3–5   A compilation of riddles, songs, tongue twisters, stories, poems, et cetera, particularly useful for group play and for what the compiler refers to as her "story-hour stretch." Most of the games require a leader, most are very simple, and the book can be used with younger children as well as by the independent reader.

1260   **Tashjian,** Virginia A., ed. *Once There Was and Was Not*; Armenian Tales retold by Virginia A. Tashjian; based on stories by H. Toumanian; illus. by Nonny Hogrogian. Little, 1966. 85p. $4.50.

4–6   Seven folk tales selected from those told by folklorist Hovahnnes Toumanian and most beautifully illustrated by Nonny Hogrogian. There are familiar elements in many of the stories—the animal who puts up a façade of wealth for his master, the poor man who is saved by the animal he had befriended, the noodlehead who is easily hoaxed, the coward who is precipitated into the role of a hero. Mrs. Tashjian's style is delightfully right for the genre; the book is a pleasure to read aloud and a good source for storytelling.

1261   **Tashjian,** Virginia A., ad. *Three Apples Fell from Heaven;* illus.
by Nonny Hogrogian. Little, 1971. 77p. Trade ed. $4.50; Library
ed. $5.10 net.

4–6   "Once there was and was not in ancient Armenia," begins each of
the tales in this delightful collection, and each ends in the
traditional way: "Three apples fell from heaven: one for the teller,
one for the listener, and one for all the peoples of the world"—or a
variant of this. The style is excellent, the illustrations restrained,
delicate, and amusing. Some of the stories have elements of
magic or supernatural creatures, and some have animal characters,
but most of the tales are concerned with the foibles or feats
of people, and they are a happy addition to sources of materials
for storytellers.

1262   **Taves,** Isabella. *Not Bad for a Girl.* Evans/Lippincott, 1972. 95p.
$4.50.

4–6   Based on an actual event, this is the story of Sharon Lee, twelve
years old and a baseball player. When a Little League team
manager puts Sharon into the lineup to replace a boy on vacation,
she does well as a centerfielder in her first game. She doesn't
do well in her second game—and that's the end of her participation,
not because she is a poor player, but because of the abuse,
the caustic publicity, the illogical anger of the people in a small
town. While Sharon's humiliation and resentment are clear and
justified, it is the coach who is the most sympathetic character
in the story, a voice of reason and justice amid the sexist
hullabaloo. The writing style is not outstanding, but the issue is.

1263   **Taylor,** Elizabeth. *Mossy Trotter;* illus. by Laszlo Acs. Harcourt,
1967. 160p. $3.50. (Chatto, 1967. 160p. £0.80.)

4–5   A quiet, episodic story about a small boy's life in an English
village. Mossy is eight, his sister Emma four; between them is a
relationship compounded of competition and affection; between
Mossy and his mother there is a firm love punctuated with
moments of exasperation. The slim thread of the story is based
on Mossy's reluctant anticipation of being a page boy at a
wedding, his misery mitigated by the fact that the flower girl
turns out to be a compatible tomboy. Slow-moving, smoothly
written, and gently funny.

1264   **Taylor,** Mark. *Henry Explores the Jungle;* illus. by Graham Booth.
Atheneum, 1968. 40p. Trade ed. $5.95; Library ed. $6.50 net.
(Chatto, B. & O., 1969. 48p. £0.90.)

K–2   A sequel to *Henry the Explorer.* Henry sets off again with gun
(wooden stick) and provisions (lunch packed by mother) and his
trusty hound Laird Angus McAngus, who looks like an ambulatory
dustmop. Having airily told his mother, "We may find a tiger,"
it is a complete shock to Henry when he does meet one, an

amiable beast that has escaped from a circus wagon. In almost believable fashion, Henry traps the tiger in the wagon, earning a free seat at the circus and the surprised admiration of his mother. The bland style is a good contrast to the high drama of the jungle adventure, and the humor is the sort that enables small listeners to feel in on the joke—as when Henry routs his first "jungle" animals, a herd of innocuous cows.

1265   **Taylor,** Sydney. *A Papa Like Everyone Else;* illus. by George Porter. Follett, 1966. 159p. Trade ed. $3.95; Library ed. $3.63 net.

4–6   A story set in Czechoslovakia several years after the First World War; Papa had, a few years before, gone to America alone. Mama carried on the farm work with the help of the two girls, but she longed to join Papa; so did Szerena, but little Gisella—who didn't even remember him—thought they were just fine as they were. At the end of the story there is a description of the trip and of Gisella's happy realization, as soon as she sees Papa, that they are all a family. However, the plot here is, through most of the book, simply a vehicle used to describe the life in a small village, with some episodes about Czech or Hungarian folkways, but with most of the story revealing the pleasures or the rituals of the Jewish community.

1266   **Taylor,** Theodore. *Air Raid—Pearl Harbor!* The Story of December 7, 1941; illus. by W. T. Mars. T. Y. Crowell, 1971. 185p. $4.50.

6–10   Well documented and written with all the suspense of a mystery story, this is a detailed account of the events that led up to the disaster of Pearl Harbor. The story is told both from the American and the Japanese viewpoints, with all of the errors in planning, the gaps in communication, the secrecy of tactics and strategy; the text moves from the flurries of activity in Washington, the veiled manoeuvres of the fleet that had sailed from Japan in November, to the pre-Christmas relaxation of Pearl Harbor, the diplomatic backing and filling gaining impetus as December 7 approaches. A vivid documentary. A list of key figures, a bibliography, and an index are appended.

1267   **Taylor,** Theodore. *The Cay.* Doubleday, 1969. 137p. $3.95. (Bodley Head, 1970. 144p. £0.90.)

7–10   Torpedoed by a German submarine during World War II, an adolescent boy and an old man are shipwrecked on a tiny Caribbean island. Phillip, who has received a head injury, goes blind and is quite dependent on the old sailor, Timothy, who cares for him with infinite wisdom and compassion. By the time Timothy dies, Phillip—who at first disliked the man because he was black—realizes that he has been trained to be self-sufficient and that every act of Timothy's had been based on loving kindness.

The story is very well written, the bleak setting a foil for the dramatic situation. The two characters and their relationship are developed with skill; pace and suspense are artfully maintained.

1268   **Taylor,** Theodore. *The Children's War.* Doubleday, 1971. 166p. Trade ed. $3.95; Library ed. $4.70 net.

7–10   Dory Scofield loved the Alaskan wilderness where he could hunt and roam freely, and was far from delighted when a school opened in their small town. He resented the teacher, and she knew it. When World War II started, the community was apprehensive, because there was a naval station just off shore. The story flares into action when a paratrooper shows up to scout the station after it has been taken over by the Japanese. Dory, excited and patriotic, wants to help and does, but it is the quiet teacher, whose anti-war sentiments have annoyed him, that risks—and loses—her life to help the paratrooper. The setting is interesting, the characters well drawn, and the plot strong; it is, however, Dory's change from unthinking ardor to a sober realization of the horror of war that gives the book substance.

1269   **Taylor,** Theodore. *People Who Make Movies;* illus. with photographs. Doubleday, 1967. 158p. $3.95.

6—   A most interesting book, written by a motion picture press agent in a lively colloquial style with occasional errors ("slight of hand"?) and frequent witticisms. Each chapter is devoted to one job— either one so exalted as the producer or director, or one of lower rank, such as the stuntman or the publicist. The book contains a few anecdotes; they add appeal, but are hardly needed, since the industry has its own glamor which is fully exploited by the author. Mr. Taylor views his associates with wry sympathy, describing their duties, their problems, and the restrictions imposed upon them by time, money, weather, caprice, and their colleagues. A glossary and an index are appended.

1270   **Ter Haar,** Jaap. *Boris;* tr. from the Dutch by Martha Mearns; illus. by Rien Poortvliet. Delacorte, 1970. 152p. Trade ed. $4.50; Library ed. $4.17 net.

5–7   Translated from the Dutch, the 1966 Book of the Year, a World War II story with a message of brotherhood. Alone with his sick mother in besieged Leningrad, Boris goes into a danger zone to dig potatoes from the frozen earth. He and his friend Nadia are apprehended by Nazi soldiers and are not only kindly treated but escorted by them—at the risk of their lives—to the Russian lines. So Boris learns that the enemy can be both courageous and compassionate. The setting is dramatic, the writing vigorous, and the plot developed with pace and conviction.

1271   **Terry,** Walter. *Ballet: A Pictorial History.* Van Nostrand, 1970. 64p. illus. $5.95.

5–7   A good introduction to ballet, chronologically arranged, with background information in each section followed by brief notes on outstanding dancers of the period, giving a few biographical facts and the salient facts about each dancer's distinctive style or roles. The last section of the book, "Gallery of Modern Stars," while not comprehensive, has international scope. The writing style is informal, with an occasional phrase that seems written down. The photographs are intriguing, the print small; an index is appended.

1272   **Thompson,** Paul D. *The Virus Realm;* illus. by Mary Lybarger. Lippincott, 1968. 189p. $4.50.

7—   An interesting survey of a field that has both dramatic and pragmatic interest. Giving some historical background, the author goes on to discuss techniques of research in virus forms and the diseases they cause. Separate chapters describe the work done in plant viruses, viruses and cancer, the spread of disease, et cetera; the concluding chapter describes ways in which viruses can assume a useful function when controlled by man. Some comparatively simple home experiments are suggested; a bibliography and an index are appended.

1273   **Thompson,** Vivian Laubach. *Hawaiian Tales of Heroes and Champions;* illus. by Herbert Kawainui Kane. Holiday House, 1971. 128p. $4.95.

4–6   A dozen tales of ancient heroes, most of whom are either possessed of some extraordinary power or are in command of a creature or an object that can perform magic for them. The stories are well told and filled with color and action; although the plots differ, there is a similarity in the tales, each concerned with bold adventure and the besting of enemies. A useful source, as are the author's other retellings of Hawaiian tales and legends, for storytelling.

1274   **Thorarinsson,** Sigurdur. *Surtsey; The New Island in the North Atlantic;* tr. by Solvi Eysteinsson. Viking, 1967. 54p. illus. $6. (Cassell, 1969. 106p. £1.75.)

8—   An American edition of the fascinating account of the evolution of a volcanic island, written by the Icelandic geologist who observed the phenomena of eruption almost from the start. In November of 1963, the crew of a fishing vessel saw a fire at sea; this was the beginning of Surtsey. The text is quite comprehensible, but it makes no particular concession to the layman in the use of scientific terms; if details are not crystal clear the important facts are. The maps and diagrams are good;

the photographs in black and white and in color are stunning. They are bound separately at the back of the book, numbered, and a bit of a nuisance to handle; this is especially so because textual references are not in absolute sequence. The style is vivacious and the explanations of events lucid.

1275   **Thorvall,** Kerstin. *Gunnar Scores a Goal;* tr. from the Swedish by Anne Parker; illus. by Serge Hollerbach. Harcourt, 1968. 48p. Trade ed. $2.95; Library ed. $2.96 net.

3–5   First published in Sweden, a mild and realistic story about the youngest of three brothers, Gunnar, whose life consisted of hand-me-down clothes and (it seemed to him) all the disadvantages of being the underprivileged youngest. Gunnar turns out to have an aptitude for soccer, and he discovers when he hurts his ankle that his brothers can be very kind; even better, he finds that they are proud of his athletic prowess. Simply told, this should appeal to the growing body of small soccer fans for whom there are so few stories.

1276   **Tichenor,** Tom. *Tom Tichenor's Puppets;* text, drawings and photographs by Tom Tichenor. Abingdon, 1971. 223p. $5.95.

5—   A practical guide to puppetry includes chapters on hand puppets, and on marionettes, with several plays included for each kind. The photographs are useful, particularly in showing details of costume or of the manipulation of the puppets, and the book includes instructions on making puppets, costumes, and stages, and on mounting the plays. One chapter is devoted to using puppets in the story hour, another to use in the classroom, in movies, and in plays with people. The writing style is informal, with some material about the author's own puppets that seems extraneous, but this is compensated for by the many casual and useful bits of advice, drawn from his experience, on drawing faces, choosing materials, sewing, etc. A bibliography and an index are appended.

1277   **Tison,** Annette. *The Adventures of the Three Colors;* by Annette Tison and Talus Taylor. World, 1971. 17p. illus. Trade ed. $3.95; Library ed. $4.23 net. (Warne, 1971. 32p. £1.25.)

K–3   A slight plot about a boy experimenting with paint is used for a lesson in obtaining secondary colors from primary blue, yellow and pink. The book uses transparent overlays very cleverly, so that when a blue seal on the transparent page overlaps a pink flamingo, there is a purple turtle where there is overlap. The pages also show how all three colors make brown, and a final set of pages shows the variations that can be obtained with shades of the three primary colors. Attractive, and a very clear way of demonstrating color mix.

1278   **Titus,** Eve. *Anatole and the Piano;* pictures by Paul Galdone.
McGraw-Hill, 1966. 32p. $3.95. (Bodley Head, 1967. 32p. £0.53.)

K–3   Another captivating story about Anatole, cheese-taster
extraordinary, Parisian pianist, Mouse Magnifique. Only one
piano in Paris is worthy of Anatole's talents, and that one is a
museum-piece miniature; not only does Anatole receive the piano
as a gift (because he has done a noble deed that benefits
orphans and delights music lovers) but he has a concerto named
in his honor. Tongue firmly in cheek, Eve Titus has again produced
a blandly ridiculous, engaging tale.

1279   **Titus,** Eve. *Anatole and the Thirty Thieves;* illus. by Paul Galdone.
McGraw-Hill, 1969. 32p. $4.50. (Bodley Head, 1970. 32p. £0.75.)

K–2   By now Anatole has been firmly established as a mouse of
distinction, and here he proves again that he is worthy of his
reputation as a sleuth of uncanny shrewdness. While our hero is
on vacation there is a massive robbery at the cheese factory where
he works; by using deduction, induction, psychology, and who-
knows-what-mystic-acumen, Anatole finds the location of the
treasure (cheese) as well as the thieves. Great acclaim for the
"mouse magnifique." The usual potpourri of blandness, nonsense,
humor, and an ineffably Gallic atmosphere, all illustrated with
enormous brio.

1280   **Titus,** Eve. *Basil and the Pygmy Cats;* illus. by Paul Galdone.
McGraw-Hill, 1971. 96p. Trade ed. $4.50; Library ed. $4.33 net.

3–5   The great mouse detective sets off to find the home of the
pygmy cats, whose existence is substantiated by a design on an
ancient golden goblet from the British Mousmopolitan Museum.
With Basil, nothing is simple. Traveling with an archeological
party, he encounters his old enemy Ratigan, who has captured
a Maharajah and Relda, a concert artiste. (All mice, of course.)
Then there's a monster from Loch Ness—a volcano—the pygmy
cats—a lost civilization. All through this delightful nonsense, there
is word play and name reversal (Relda: Adler, Nagitar: Ratigan,
Elyod: Doyle) to add detective interest to the appeal of a tall
fanciful tale.

1281   **Titus,** Eve. *Why the Wind God Wept;* illus. by James Barkley.
Doubleday, 1972. 37p. $5.95.

4–6   Handsomely designed and illustrated, a story of ancient Mexico
is told in a dignified, rolling style that has the quality of folk
legendry. All of the gods of Mexico were content save one, the
Wind God, whose ceaseless wailing broke the people's peace.
A great warrior and a great hunter each tried to keep a vigil
through the night and learn why the Wind God wept—but
they had the hearts and minds of hunters and warriors, and they

heard no answer. Then a simple man, an unknown poet, volunteered; his heart and mind were open to the sounds of the air, and he heard the Wind God, and the people appeased him— and he was content, and still. The poet marries the Emperor's daughter (as is usually true, in folk literature, of the humble applicant) and his poetry is forever revered.

1282   **Todd,** Alden. *Finding Facts Fast;* How to Find Out What You Want to Know Immediately. Morrow, 1972. 108p. $5.95.

8—   The author, who teaches a course in research techniques at New York University, proceeds on the assumptions that the reader should master simple techniques in fact-finding before going on to those more complicated, and that it is necessary to practice— reading the book is not enough. The text includes information on library resources, bibliographies, and indexes, home reference collections and bookstores, the Government Printing Office and other sources such as the Congressional Record or alumni offices, specialized sources, guides to reference books, et cetera. It also discusses note-taking, interviewing, using inter-library loan, and other aspects of research, all of this divided into basic, intermediate, and advanced techniques. The writing is clear, direct, and well organized. A most useful book. An index is appended.

1283   **Todd,** Barbara K. *Juan Patricio;* illus. by Gloria Kamen. Putnam, 1972. 48p. (See and Read Storybooks) $3.29.

2–3   It seemed to Juan Patricio that everyone in Santa Fe had a job but him; everything he tried to do he wasn't quite adept enough to manage, whether it was helping Mamacita make the beds or helping their neighbor Mr. Garcia paint his house. The ending of the story is pleasant, undramatic but realistic—Juan Patricio offers to help take care of another neighbor's puppy. Not an exciting story, but a useful one for the primary grades reader for several reasons in addition to reading practice. For one thing, the author uses Spanish words in context without artificial translation into English, so that the Spanish-speaking child need not feel that his own language isn't quite good enough on its own. For another, all of the adults are encouraging albeit practical about Juan Patricio's help. Third, there is nothing in the book to say to the Anglo child that here is someone *different*— some phrases are Spanish, as are the names—but that here is a child with a problem that is universal.

1284   **Tolstoy,** Leo Nikolaevich. *Russian Stories and Legends;* illus. by Alexander Alexeieff. Pantheon Books, 1967. 224p. $3.95.

6–10   Of Tolstoy's tales in the folk genre, eight that are related to the theme of brotherhood are included in this volume. The stories reflect Tolstoy's deep concern with religion and morality; the plots are fresh, their patterns familiar. Perhaps due to the style of the translation, the stories have a ponderous quality that makes them a little difficult for the usual folk tale audience; they are particularly distinguished by compelling characterization and provocative themes.

1285   **Tomaino,** Sarah F., ad. *Persephone; Bringer of Spring;* illus. by Ati Forberg. T. Y. Crowell, 1971. 35p. $4.50.

3–5   A retelling of the Greek legend in which Persephone, stolen by Hades and taken to his underworld home, is brought back to earth and to her grieving mother, Demeter, for part of each year. The symbolism of the seasonal flourishing when Persephone returns to earth and to her mother, goddess of the harvest, is gracefully expressed in the retelling and illustrated with pictures that are both delicate and dramatic.

1286   **Townsend,** John Rowe. *Hell's Edge.* Lothrop, 1969. 223p. Trade ed. $4.25; Library ed. $3.78 net. (Hutchinson, 1970. 224p. £0.90.)

6–9   A runner-up for the Carnegie Medal when it was first published in England, this revised story of a Yorkshire town has a smooth blending of diverse elements. First, the theme of urban renewal; second, the mystery that surrounds the adamant refusal of a wealthy young woman to part with any land; third, the investigation of that mystery by a determined girl who has just moved to Hell's Edge (Hallersage) and finds herself more interested in the grimy place than she had ever thought she could be. There is pace and momentum in the plot, a setting that is realistic and contemporary, and a wonderful array of characters, their speech just enough tinged with local idiom to be flavorsome rather than quaint.

1287   **Townsend,** John Rowe. *The Intruder.* Lippincott, 1970. 220p. $4.50. (Oxf. U.P., 1970. 192p. £0.30.)

6–9   Set in a village in England, on the coast of the Irish Sea, a dramatic and compelling story with fine characterization, an imaginative plot, and a remarkable evocation of atmosphere and mood. Sixteen-year-old Arnold Haithwaite has never been told who he really is; he lives with his "dad" (he is the old man's illegitimate grandson but has not been told that) and he sees his dad fall more and more under the spell of the stranger, who claims his name is also Arnold Haithwaite, and who moves in and takes command of the household, his goal being to commercialize the town, once thriving and now moribund. The intruder is so plausible that none of the adults to whom Arnold turns for help take him seriously, although it is clear to the reader that the man is not only evil but criminal. The solution is unexpected but plausible, the exciting ending a fitting one to a tale pregnant with suspense.

1288   **Townsend,** John Rowe. *Pirate's Island.* Lippincott, 1968. 159p. $3.75. (Oxf. U.P., 1968. 146p. £0.75.)

5–7   Gordy was plump and pink-faced, with small eyes; his father was a pork-butcher. Little wonder that the bullies of his tough neighborhood teased him and called him "Porky," less wonder that his doting mother felt that her precious only child should stay safely at home and be comforted with food. But Gordon met a younger child who jolted him out of his isolation: Sheila, a bedraggled nine-year-old whose thirst for adventure and glamor led the two into a chase for treasure, achieving new status for both of them. The setting—an area known as the Jungle—has appeared in a previous Townsend book; here again the vitality and tenacity of the characters emerge in sturdy contrast against the seamy background.

1289   **Townsend,** John Rowe. *The Summer People.* Lippincott, 1972. 223p. $4.95.

6–9   Philip Martin, writing to his son and daughter-in-law, describes the summer when he was sixteen and vacationing with his family. Every day he and Sylvia Pilling, just his age and daughter of family friends, went off together while the adults approvingly beamed at this most suitable romance. What they didn't know was that the two separated each day, by agreement; Sylvia was in love with a local boy, a boatman and fisherman, who would certainly be disapproved of by her family, and Philip had met an odd, fragile girl in a deserted house: Ann. She is the only child of a woman who works at a resort hotel, and she brings Philip into her game of keeping house in the hideaway. The families' reactions, when the two are discovered, are swift and harsh, and the end of the summer brings unhappiness to both Sylvia and Philip. Realistically, the closing letter from Philip to his son divulges the fact that Sylvia and Philip did marry, but that the son married Ann's daughter seems contrived and coincidental and the epistolary framework weakens the story. The setting and the characters are well drawn, although Ann is a weak character and her relationship with Philip rather ponderously developed. The family scenes are very good indeed, and the writing is polished yet deceptively casual.

1290   **Townsend,** John Rowe. *Trouble in the Jungle;* illus. by W. T. Mars. Lippincott, 1969. 158p. Trade ed. $3.75; Library ed. $3.59 net. (Penguin, 1970. 144p. £0.20.)

5–7   First published in England under the title *Gumble's Yard,* the story of some slum children who show their mettle when they are temporarily deserted (although the children cannot know it is only temporarily) by adults. With the help of a friend, Kevin and Sandra pack up the two younger children and take refuge in the Yard, an empty warehouse, to avoid being taken to an institution. Kevin, who tells the story, describes his involvement with some criminals who also want to use the Yard, the dangerous confrontation, and the arrival of the police, just in time. Realistically, there is no pat ending; the delinquent, shiftless father and his mistress come back and a young curate advises Kevin to return to the fold: it may be the Jungle (the slum neighborhood) but at least it is a home where the family can stay together, and there may be slovenliness and neglect, but there is no cruelty. The milieu is deftly established, the characterization and dialogue are good, and the plot has pace and suspense.

1291   **Traven,** B., ad. *The Creation of the Sun and the Moon;* illus. by Alberto Beltrán. Hill and Wang, 1968. 65p. $3.95.

6–7   An ancient legend of Mexico is told with eloquence and dignity, unfortunately not matched by the illustrations, which give costume details of the Tzeltal Indians of southern Mexico but lack the distinction of the text. Once, long ago, the evil gods, jealous of the sun, extinguished it; only by human intervention could a new sun be made, and that human would have to give up forever his life on earth and wander in the heavens. The brave young Chicovaneg who offered to save the world was guided by the Quetzal to the Feathered Serpent whom he released from captivity (by dancing until "his magic rhythms freed the Feathered Serpent from the ropes and the rock.") and who, in gratitude, followed and aided Chicovaneg in his journey to the stars to gather light that would fashion a new sun. The shorter story of the creation of the moon again uses the concept of gathering light from the stars; it is the son of Chicovaneg who goes to make a little "Sun of the Night" that will give light but not heat and on which dwells forever the rabbit that was a faithful friend to the young hero.

1292   **Trease,** Geoffrey. *The Red Towers of Granada;* illus. by Charles Keeping. Vanguard, 1967. 186p. $3.95. (Macmillan, 1966. 192p. £1.25.)

6–9   An adventure story set in the time of Edward I. Young Robin of Westwood, cast out of his village as a leper, meets a Jewish doctor who assures the boy that he has only a minor skin disease. Although it is illegal for Jews to practice medicine, Solomon takes the boy into his home so that he can be treated. When Solomon's family goes to Spain, Robin goes also; in search of a rare medicine for Queen Eleanor, Robin has adventures, makes

Moslem and Jewish friends, and finds a bride. The background is exotic, characterization adequate, and the plot has pace and drama.

1293   **Trease,** Geoffrey. *This Is Your Century*. Harcourt, 1966. 343p. illus. $6.95.

8—   An impressive twentieth-century history—chiefly of the western world—written in an easy but quite dignified style, with good organization of material and a reasonable maintenance of objectivity. The author focuses on events in Great Britain and in the United States, yet gives full accounts of European or Asian political events of major importance or of concern to the west. The varied illustrative material is excellent; the most interesting quality of the book is a vivid and reiterated sense of the weaving together of men and events, at times affected by a relentless current, at times affected by dramatic accident. The author discusses men, wars, depression, suffragettes, strikes, flappers, bombs, apartheid, Wally Simpson; he is not sentimental enough to sound nostalgic to the young reader, which will probably make them enjoy the book all the more.

1294   **Treece,** Henry. *The Dream Time;* illus. by Charles Keeping. Meredith, 1968. 114p. $3.95. (Brockhampton P., 1967. 96p. £0.80.)

5–7   Although this has a theme that has been used before in stories about primitive times, it has a freshness that springs from the simplicity of the writing style and the consistency of the story: the bare plot, the elemental emotions, the stark speech patterns. The protagonist, Crookleg, is a dreaming boy who does not like to kill, who dreams of peace between the tribes and who wants only to fashion images that reflect the beauty he sees. He meets other tribes and learns that people only seem to differ, that basically they are the same. As Rosemary Sutcliff points out in her epilogue and tribute to Treece's last book, there are incongruities in the artifacts described, since they existed at different periods; this she attributes to the author's desire to stress that similarity among peoples.

1295   **Treece,** Henry. *The Last Viking;* illus. by Charles Keeping. Pantheon Books, 1966. 146p. Trade ed. $3.75; Library ed. $4.79 net. (Brockhampton P., 1970. 120p. £0.55.)

6–9   First published in Great Britain in 1964 under the title *The Last of the Vikings*. Harald Hardrada, last of the Vikings, just before he is killed in battle in England in 1066, remembers his youth; the story moves back to Harald's fifteenth year, when his brother is killed in battle and he escapes with the old Earl Rognvald. Harald travels to Iceland and to Novgorod, the narrative coming back to the scene of the prologue in England just as he is about to go to Miklagard; his last few moments before he is slain end the story. The background is colorful, the action fast-paced, and the characters, although not deeply drawn, are vividly believable.

1296   **Treece,** Henry. *Swords from the North;* illus. by Charles Keeping. Pantheon Books, 1967. 240p. $3.95. (Faber, 1967. 205p. £1.00.)

6–10   Based on a thirteenth-century Icelandic legend, this last volume of the Hardrada trilogy is filled with color, action, and vividly dramatic characters. The story is set in Byzantium between the years 1034 and 1044, where Harald enlists in the Varangian Guard and becomes a captain, thereby exposing himself to the jealousy and subsequent treachery of his Byzantine allies. Good as an adventure story or as a historical novel, this is endowed with depth by the style of writing: especially in the dialogue does the author capture the cadence and vigor of the language of the saga.

1297   **Trelease,** Allen W. *Reconstruction;* The Great Experiment. Harper, 1971. 224p. illus. Trade ed. $4.95; Library ed. $4.79 net.

7–10   An outstanding piece of historical writing, broad in scope and detailed in treatment, well written and authoritative, objective in tone and vividly communicating a sense of the rancor and the zeal, the idealism and the bitter discrimination of the Reconstruction years. The author is both careful and candid, achieving at once a sweep of narrative and fine-grid examination of the minutiae of events. A bibliography, reproductions of the important legislation of the period, and an excellent relative index are appended.

1298   **Tresselt,** Alvin R. *The Beaver Pond;* illus. by Roger Duvoisin. Lothrop, 1970. 32p. Trade ed. $4.50; Library ed. $4.14 net.

K–2   More than a description of the cycle of a beaver colony, this is a read-aloud book that introduces aspects of ecological balance in the very simplest terms. The style is forthright and unornamented, yet it has a poetic quality; the text and illustrations each can stand alone yet each complements the other; the illustrations are vivid with the woodland flora and fauna of the year's seasons. It was because of the beaver dam that the pond had come into being. Reeds grew on the shore, birds came to nest there, the animals of the forest came to drink. Each winter the pond slept under the ice, each spring the old beavers repaired their houses and the new litters of beaver young played. The hungry predators prowled and the beavers fled, the neglected dam broke, and the pond flowed away. But farther down the beavers had built a new dam, made a new pond, begun again. . . .

1299   **Tresselt,** Alvin R. *The Dead Tree;* illus. by Charles Robinson. Parents' Magazine, 1972. 28p. Trade ed. $4.50; Library ed. $4.19 net.

K–2   Illustrated with handsome pictures in soft-hued water colors, this gives much the same story that is in *Who Lives in This Log?* by Ross, but the text is far superior. Alvin Tresselt has the ability to give accurate information simply while using prose that has a poetic quality. The illustrations echo and amplify the mood of woodland stillness that is a background for the busy procession of creatures and plants that use a fallen tree for food and shelter. The text follows the tree's life from full maturity to its return to the rich humus of the forest floor.

1300   **Tresselt,** Alvin R. *The World in the Candy Egg;* illus. by Roger Duvoisin. Lothrop, 1967. 28p. Trade ed. $4.75; Library ed. $4.59 net.

3–7
yrs.   A delightful picture book for Easter, fanciful and gay. As the toys in a toyshop look through the window of a candy egg, they see a bright and busy farm scene filled with action and color. The egg is given to a small girl, who gently unwraps her treasure and looks with joy at the tiny world that is hers. The illustrations, a combination of collage and painting, are a riot of toys, flowers, ribbons, and decorations in the bright and vigorous colors of Spring.

1301   **Tripp,** Eleanor B. *To America.* Harcourt, 1969. 214p. illus. $3.95.

6–9   An unusual approach to the story of immigration, chronologically arranged and written in a solid, straightforward style. The author has chosen nine highly localized sources of American newcomers, each demonstrating a different reason for a journey to a new land. In the 1630's there was an exodus from Norwich, England of persecuted Puritans; in the years of the famine (1845–1848) there was an exodus from Skibereen, Ireland; in the first decade of the twentieth century, the Jews of Polotsk, Russia fled from oppression, and so on. The varieties of peoples and of their reasons for coming to America give a vivid picture of the diversity of our forebears. A section of reference notes is appended.

1302   **Tunis,** Edwin. *Chipmunks on the Doorstep;* written and illus. by Edwin Tunis. T. Y. Crowell, 1971. 69p. $4.95.

5—   Edwin Tunis, in his first book in the field of natural science, proves to be as adept in observation, as exact in beautiful drawings, and even more enjoyable as a writer than he has been in his earlier books. The informality and humor of the writing style add to the appeal of a book that gives a considerable amount of information on an appealing subject, and the illustrations in soft hues are both charming and informative.

1303   **Tunis,** Edwin. *Shaw's Fortune;* The Picture Story of a Colonial
Plantation; drawn and written by Edwin Tunis. World, 1966.
63p. Trade ed. $4.95; Library ed. $5.71 net.

4–7   If this book had no text, only captions to the illustrations, it
would be enjoyable and informative; the pencil drawings are
meticulous in detail, clearly based on authoritative familiarity with
plantation life. Shaw's Fortune is described as it evolved from a
cabin in a clearing to the almost self-sufficient establishment of
1752. Mr. Tunis discusses the clothing, education, recreation, and
family patterns of the Shaw family. Even more interesting are
the descriptions of the home industries and crafts of the plantation:
spinning and weaving, growing tobacco, gathering and packing
tobacco, hewing and sawing timber. The author mentions once,
briefly, the fact that slavery was taken for granted by the Shaws,
but not by the slaves, and lets it go at that; that was the way
plantation life was. The illustrations are useful for an older
audience as well.

1304   **Tunis,** Edwin. *The Young United States—1783 to 1830;* written and
illus. by Edwin Tunis. World, 1969. 145p. Trade ed. $7.95;
Library ed. $7.71 net.

5–9   As are previous Tunis books, this is oversize, handsome,
profusely illustrated with the author's fine, detailed drawings, and
written with a straightforward briskness. Topically organized, the
text describes the different kinds of communities of the period,
factories and inventions, schools and colleges, the growth of the
west, travel, the arts, et cetera. There is a minimal amount of
invention; the author explains in a prefatory note that occasionally
a family or a town is meant to serve as an amalgam and example
of the type. The index is extensive.

1305   **Tunis,** John Roberts. *His Enemy, His Friend.* Morrow, 1967. 196p.
Trade ed. $3.50; Library ed. $3.32 net.

7–10   A book that breaks sharply into two parts, a device that is
used here to stunning dramatic effect. The story is an indictment
of harsh and tragic imperatives of war. It took an unusual man
to become the friend of the villagers of Nogent-Plage, if you
were an occupying German soldier—and Hans von Kleinschrodt
was that unusual man: an athlete who coached local boys in
soccer, a friend to the priest, a companion to the schoolmaster.
Caught by official red tape, Hans was forced to permit the killing
of six hostages and to take the blame. Years later, he was playing
professional soccer on the German team in a world championship
game, and on the opposing French team the star was the son
of one of the hostages. The description of the game (excellent
sports writing) and of the pathetic and tragic events that follow

compose the second half of the book, and the contrast between the small Normandy village torn by grief and the frenzied enthusiasm of the stadium scene makes each the more vivid.

1306   **Turkle,** Brinton. *The Adventures of Obadiah.* Viking, 1972. 34p. illus. $4.50.

2–4   Act III. Obadiah, as appealing as ever, is the small Quaker boy of long-ago Nantucket whose vivid imagination acts as a catalyst for behavior that is, by Quaker standards, obstreperous. Here Obadiah's fanciful pronouncements (a wolf almost ate him, he caught a big lion on Chestnut Street) bring repeated, gentle rebukes. But the day that the family goes to the sheep-shearing, Obadiah exceeds himself: nonstop, he delivers the story of how he rode on a sheep and the sheep threw him into a tent and there were a clown and pig dressed alike and then in another tent a pretty lady asked him to dance . . . and so on. This time, however, Obadiah's adventure is real. Corroborated, after his family expresses disbelief, by an adult witness. Readers can share the complacent satisfaction that any child would feel in such a circumstance, and the whole book is gay and affectionate in tone. A lively tale, delightful pictures.

1307   **Turkle,** Brinton. *Obadiah the Bold;* story and pictures by Brinton Turkle. Viking, 1965. 32p. Trade ed. $3.95; Library ed. $3.77 net.

3–4   A short tale, appealing in content and attractively illustrated. The author uses both present and past tense in the beginning of the story, leaving to the details of illustration the setting of period. The family of Obadiah are Quakers of the early nineteenth century. Obadiah, a small boy who cherishes his spyglass, wants to be a pirate; when he plays pirates with his older brothers, they blindfold and frighten him. Obadiah (chunky, pert, and red-headed) decides he will be a sailor like his grandfather, instead.

1308   **Turkle,** Brinton. *Thy Friend, Obadiah;* written and illus. by Brinton Turkle. Viking, 1969. 32p. Trade ed. $3.95; Library ed. $3.77 net.

2–4   All those readers who delighted in the small Obadiah Starbuck, Nantucket Quaker of long ago, will welcome his reappearance. Here Obadiah is irritated by a sea gull that follows him—until the day he helps the bird when something is tangled in its beak; then his feeling changes. And that is how Obadiah discovers that one way to feel friendly is to do something for another. As his brothers and sisters tease Obadiah and his mother comforts him, the reader sees charming pictures of a large and loving family. The lovely illustrations are beautifully composed, with a skilful use of color and wonderful way with light.

1309   **Turner,** Philip. *Colonel Sheperton's Clock;* illus. by Philip Gough. World, 1966. 190p. Trade ed. $3.75; Library ed. $4.21 net. (Oxf. U.P., 1964. 200p. £0.75.)

6–9   First published in England in 1964, a delightful book about the small adventures of three friends who stumble on an interesting mystery while prowling about an old abbey in the north of England. Peter, David, and Arthur find a clue in an old newspaper clipping; they go on to unravel (believably) other clues that reveal the fact that a local resident, Colonel Sheperton, had been a secret agent and a hero in the First World War. The plot is admirably constructed, but the charm of the book lies chiefly in the deft humor of dialogue and the endearingly distinctive characterization.

1310   **Turner,** Philip. *The Grange at High Force;* illus. by W. T. Mars. World, 1967. 223p. Trade ed. $3.95; Library ed. $4.91 net. (Oxf. U.P., 1970. 222p. £0.50.)

6–9   Awarded the British Library Association's Carnegie Medal, this deftly written and amusing story is a sequel to *Colonel Sheperton's Clock.* Here the engaging Peter, David, and Arthur again solve a local puzzle that concerns community history; here, again, part of the charm of the book is in the distinctive local characters who are exaggerated just enough to be colorful but not quite enough to be ridiculous. Hunting for a lost statue that had been taken from a church niche centuries before, the boys are aided by a very indulgent, very salty, retired admiral.

1311   **Turner,** Philip. *Sea Peril;* illus. by W. T. Mars. World, 1968. 223p. Trade ed. $3.95; Library ed. $3.86 net. (Oxf. U.P., 1966. 212p. £0.90.)

6–8   A sequel to *Colonel Sheperton's Clock* and *The Grange at High Force,* those delightful books about England's substitute for Athos, Porthos, and Aramis. Peter, Arthur, and David are as inventive, articulate, and engaging a trio here as ever as they plan, construct, and operate a bicycle-powered punt and go exploring on the river. Their varied adventures are enjoyable, but it is the characters of the boys and their friends (plus a few eminently detestable enemies) that give the story its zest and color.

1312   **Turner,** Philip. *War on the Darnel;* illus. by W. T. Mars. World, 1969. 196p. Trade ed. $4.95; Library ed. $4.21 net. (Oxf. U.P., 1969. 168p. £0.90.)

5–9   A sequel to *Colonel Sheperton's Clock* and several other delightful books about three lively English boys whose ingenuity and curiosity afford them—and the reader—the pleasures of some fascinating capers. Here they engage in a mighty battle with another set of boys who have set up a river barricade and are asking a fee in the name of charity. The trio are all for the charity, but their spirits cannot resist the challenge, and they organize a counter-attack that is complicated, funny, clever, and successful. The characterization is good, the dialogue even better, and the setting firmly British.

1313   **Uchida,** Yoshiku. *In-Between Miya;* illus. by Susan Bennett. Scribner, 1967. 128p. Trade ed. $3.50; Library ed. $3.31 net. (Angus & R., 1968. 128p. £0.90.)

4–7   Miya Okamoto, twelve years old, felt that it was most unfortunate to be a middle child; the older ones had privileges and the youngest had no responsibilities. She, Miya, had only chores. And no appreciation. And no luxuries in her life, because her father (priest of a village near Kyoto) was so cautious and so lacking in ambition. When Miya went to visit relatives in Tokyo, she realized that they thought her father unsuccessful, and she resented this. Then, after she was home, a city friend came to visit, and Miya was overwhelmed by the realization that her friend had envied the warm simplicity of the Okamoto's family life. The book has the charm of the Japanese setting to enhance the basic appeal of an honestly told story about some of the most common problems of the pre-adolescent: her relationship to her family, conflicting goals, friendship values, and lack of self-esteem.

1314   **Uchida,** Yoshiko. *Journey to Topaz;* A Story of the Japanese-American Evacuation; illus. by Donald Carrick. Scribner, 1971. 149p. $4.50.

5–7   As soon as they heard the news of Pearl Harbor on the radio, the Sakanes were worried. How would it affect them? Yuki and her brother Ken were American citizens, but their parents had come from Japan and Dad worked for a Japanese firm. They learned soon enough: Dad was taken away by the F.B.I., they were all enemy aliens, and they would be evacuated from the coast along with all other Japanese-American residents. The story's central character is eleven-year-old Yuki, and it is through her reactions that the hurt bewilderment and resentment of these innocent victims is shown. Herded from her home to an Assembly Center and then to a Relocation Center at Topaz, Utah, Yuki adjusts to uprooting and even to the harsh life behind a barbed wire fence. The story, based on the author's personal experiences, is told with remarkable balance and objectivity.

1315   **Uchida,** Yoshiko, ad. *The Sea of Gold and Other Tales from Japan;* illus. by Marianne Yamaguchi. Scribner, 1965. 136p. Trade ed. $3.95; Library ed. $3.31 net.

4–6   Here are a dozen Japanese folk tales retold in a simple, quiet style. The tales have the folk appeal of universality, but they have a gentle, almost somber, quality that is distinctive. The illustrations are unusual; each story is illustrated by a page divided (horizontally) in three, each of the three panels showing separate parts of the story.

1316   **Uden,** Grant. *A Dictionary of Chivalry*; illus. by Pauline Baynes. T. Y. Crowell, 1968. 352p. $10. (Longman Young Bks., 1968. 360p. £3.25.)

6—   As useful as it is handsome, this profusely illustrated reference book is a mine of information about one of the most romantic periods of history. The dictionary arrangement is supplemented by cross-references and by a subject index; the entries are full and detailed; the illustrations form an attractive border to each page; the single column of type is easy to read; the writing style is lucid.

1317   **Uden,** Grant, ad. *Hero Tales from the Age of Chivalry*; retold from the Froissart Chronicles; illus. by Doreen Roberts. World, 1969. 160p. Trade ed. $3.75; Library ed. $3.61 net. (Longman Young Bks., 1968. 160p. £1.25.)

6–8   Based on the Berners translation, distinctively illustrated in black and white, twelve tales by the great poet-historian of the fourteenth century. Grant Uden explains, in a useful prefatory note, that any interpolation of his own is based on knowledge that Froissart would have had. Historically interesting, romantic in approach, the stories of chivalrous men and brave women are limited in appeal only by a rather heavy style of writing; the material is dramatic enough to compensate for this. A minutely detailed record of the events of a tournament, notes on the stories, and an index are appended.

1318   **Udry,** Janice May. *Mary Jo's Grandmother*; illus. by Eleanor Mill. Whitman, 1970. 26p. Trade ed. $3.75; Library ed. $2.81 net.

K–2   Like Benjie in *Benjie On His Own*, Mary Jo copes with grandmother's illness. Benjie turns to the neighbors in an urban environment; Mary Jo is hampered by the lack of a telephone and the rural isolation that is increased by a snowstorm. Mary Jo has stayed on with Grandmother after the family's Christmas celebration, and finds her on the pantry floor with an injured leg. She makes Grandmother comfortable with bedding, gives her coffee, and hikes off in the snow. A snowplow crew telephones Mary Jo's parents. Despite the crisis situation, this is a placid book, its emphasis on the relationships in a pleasant, middle class black family, the appeal of a visit to grandmother universal. Although the country setting is shown as attractive in both the text and the illustrations, the book does not condemn (as often happens) or unfavorably contrast city living.

1319   **Underwood,** Betty. *The Tamarack Tree;* illus. by Bea Holmes. Houghton, 1971. 230p. $4.95.

6–9   A story built on the case of Prudence Crandall's persecution by the townspeople who resented the inclusion of black students in her seminary. Canterbury, Connecticut was not ready, in 1833, to accept this, and its reaction precluded the attendance of a white girl who had come there and expected to attend. Bernadette had come to stay with the Fry family preparatory to attending Oberlin College, and her sympathy for Miss Crandall and her pupils was awakened by indignation when she learned that a sick girl had been refused medicine by a storekeeper. Bernadette's impulsive trip to the school to bring medicine leads to a friendship between her and one of the students. She brings Miriam home one day after she has been stoned by hostile boys, and finds that her foster mother, an abolitionist, is sympathetic and helpful. Her foster father is not, and Bernadette becomes even more aware of the subservient role of women as well as of the terrible injustice of prejudice against black people. The story moves with good pace, the characters are convincing, the historical material accurate and the fictional material realistic; the book gives, within its small frame of locale, a clear and vivid picture of the conflicting attitudes of the times.

1320   **Ungerer,** Tomi. *Orlando, the Brave Vulture.* Harper, 1966. 32p. illus. Trade ed. $3.95; Library ed. $4.11 net. (Methuen, 1967. 32p. £0.75.)

K–3   A picture book in which Ungerer's usual unlikely animal protagonist performs heroic deeds. The writing is blandly ingenuous and the plot blandly ridiculous. Brave Orlando, a sort of Mexican Batman, finds family pictures on the person of a stranded gold miner; he flies for help, the police trace the family, Orlando flies to Vermont, mother and son travel to Mexico, the boy is kidnapped and is rescued by Orlando. And so on. A felicitous mixture of grotesquerie, tongue-in-cheek tall tale, and fun.

1321   **Ungerer,** Tomi. *Zeralda's Ogre.* Harper, 1967. 28p. illus. Trade ed. $3.95; Library ed. $4.11 net. (Bodley Head, 1970. 32p. £1.25.)

K–2   An oversize book with entertaining illustrations and a tongue-in-cheek fairy tale. An ever-hungry ogre ravaged a village, preying on the children who were—naturally—his favorite food. In the forest lived the golden-haired Zeralda, a gourmet cook; when Zeralda met the hungry ogre, she cooked him so superb a meal that he hired her on the spot, gave up eating children, and settled down, a changed ogre. In fact, Zeralda grew up and

married him and they lived happily ever after. The illustrations
have a wry humor; the first picture of Zeralda, for example,
shows an idyllic clearing in the forest: a little cottage, a quaint
well, a host of madly amiable animals, fruit and flowers growing
prettily, and in the middle of it all, sweet Zeralda beaming at her
goat.

1322   **Unkelbach,** Kurt. *You're a Good Dog, Joe;* Knowing and Training
Your Puppy; illus. by Paul Frame. Prentice-Hall, 1971. 29p.
$3.95.

2–4   Like Unkelbach's book on this subject for older children, this is a
straightforward, comprehensive, and useful text on training; it also
may make a child feel more responsible than do parental
admonitions. It gives advice on diet, medication, housebreaking,
training by firm patience and praise for achievement, play, and the
puppy's comfort and safety. The illustrations extend the text, and
a list of "some things to know about your puppy," at the close
of the book, includes sensible precautionary measures about trips,
other animals, and such physical limitations as color blindness
and a poor sense of direction.

1323   **Ushinsky,** K. *How a Shirt Grew in the Field;* ad. from the
Russian of K. Ushinsky by Marguerita Rudolph; pictures by
Yaroslava. McGraw-Hill,1967. 32p. $3.25.

K–2   First published over a hundred years ago, this story of a Russian
child in the countryside is translated and adapted in a simple,
direct style that suits the guileless young protagonist, Vasya. The
illustrations have an echoing simplicity and some lovely, intricate
costume details. Vasya is told by his father that he is sowing
flax seeds, "so that shirts will grow for you and baby Anya."
Vasya is baffled: how can shirts grow? As the flax grows and
flowers, is cut and winnowed, beaten, combed, and spun; as
the cloth is bleached, cut, and sewn Vasya keeps doubting the
outcome. When the shirt appears, it becomes evident that the
industrious work of his older sisters has added to the product:
this is not just a shirt, it is a beautiful shirt with handsome
embroidery.

1324   **Van Iterson,** S. R. *Pulga;* tr. from the Dutch by Alexander and
Alison Gode. Morrow, 1971. 240p. Trade ed. $4.95; Library ed.
$4.59 net.

6–9   Chosen as the best children's book of 1967 in Holland, this is the
story of a Colombian waif, one of the floating children of the
urban poor. Pulga means "flea" and he was called that because
he looked years younger than fifteen; when he took a job as a
trucker's helper, Pulga had his first chance to see what life was

like outside Bogotá. The plot is anecdotal, the incidents tied together by the theme of Pulga's realization that he may be able to influence the direction of his life. His confidence is built up by some of the small adventures in which he takes part, and by the kindness of the trucker, Gilimon. In one incident, Pulga is responsible for saving the life of a kidnapped boy; the wealthy father wants to make a substantial show of gratitude— but Pulga has gone on his way by then, so there is no pat ending. The style is competent, with only an occasional indication that the story has been translated; the structure is tight, the characters not deeply drawn but wholly convincing.

1325   **Van Iterson,** S. R. *Village of Outcasts;* tr. from the Dutch by Patricia Pitzele and Joske Smedts. Morrow, 1972. 240p. Trade ed. $4.95; Library ed. $4.51 net.

7–9   Set in Colombia, this is the story of a leper colony, a village in which many of the stricken have a relative living with them. To the village comes old Don Pacho with his teen-age son Claudio, who has been selected by his older siblings to stay with his father. Claudio, who does not have the disease, gets work outside the village; he and his employer's daughter fall shyly in love. For Claudio there is a grave decision when he realizes that he knows the identity of a murderer in the leper colony: the suspect is a woman he has learned is the mother of the girl he loves, and the girl does not know her mother is in the colony. If he helps clear the mother, Claudio knows he will lose his love, for he had lied—knowing he would not be accepted if he admitted that he lived in the colony. This is both a dramatic story of adventure and a remarkable picture of complex relationships within an unusual setting. The characterization is deft and sharp, with convincing motivation and development, and the realistic ending of the story is neither heroic nor morbid.

1326   **Van Stockum,** Hilda. *Mogo's Flute;* drawings by Robin Jacques. Viking, 1966. 88p. Trade ed. $3.50; Library ed. $3.37 net.

4–6   A story of a Kikuyu child, with a rich background of cultural details and a deftly written, sympathetic picture of the protagonist that has a universal application. Mogo has always been a frail child; it is recognized that he is under a spell and his physical limitations are taken for granted. His younger sister, however, is sure that Mogo can do more—especially if he asks the help of the wise man of the tribe. The advice Mogo gets is quietly encouraging and psychologically sound. He must make more effort; for one thing, he must spend less time playing flute and more in physical exertion. Mogo, who has loved his flute partly as an escape device, really tries—and he succeeds in being accepted by his peers. There is no element of cultural conflict, Mogo accepting a ride in his uncle's truck with no less equanimity than he accepted the fact that he was under a spell.

1327   **Viereck,** Phillip, comp. *The New Land;* Discovery, Exploration, and Early Settlement of Northeastern United States, from Earliest Voyages to 1621, Told in the Words of the Explorers Themselves; comp. and ed. with preface and running commentary by Phillip Viereck; drawings by Ellen Viereck, with reproductions of original maps. Day, 1967. 244p. $15.

9—   A stunning book. The author has used excerpts from the writings of the explorers themselves, combining them topically, so that the reader has a series of comments on Indian dress or a compilation of descriptions of a region. The major part of the book is devoted to separate long accounts by explorers or colonists, and throughout the book Mr. Viereck's excellent commentaries are printed in italics to distinguish them from source material. The maps and drawings are good; a divided bibliography and an index are appended.

1328   **Vineberg,** Ethel. *Grandmother Came from Dworitz;* A Jewish Story; illus. by Rita Briansky. Tundra Books, 1969. 58p. $4.

4–7   In nineteenth century Russia, Jews were confined to the *shtetl*, the small cities of the Jewish pale, where life was centered on the synagogue. Sarah Mishkofsky's father was one of the few men in his shtetl who spoke Russian and was therefore delegated spokesman for his fellow Jews. Although her people's lives were circumscribed by discrimination and exclusion, Sarah was a happy child and later a contented wife and mother whose children all emigrated to America. One daughter, Nachama, who settled in New Brunswick, was the mother of the author. This is the first of a series of books on the origins of Canadians (a French edition of each will be published) and in each case the story will be based on the life of the author or illustrator of the book. The text here is sedate but the material is fascinating, giving a vivid picture of the restrictions upon Russian Jews, their rich communal life, and the heavy exodus to the United States and Canada. The illustrations, black and white, are rich in period detail and very attractive.

1329   **Viorst,** Judith *Alexander and the Terrible, Horrible, No Good, Very Bad Day;* illus. by Ray Cruz. Atheneum, 1972. 28p. $4.50.

K–3   The youngest of three boys, Alexander wakes to a series of mishaps. It is obviously going to be a horrible, no good, etc. His prognostication is entirely accurate, things go wrong before, during, and after school, and he periodically thinks of going to Australia. No sweetness-and-light ending here, as a cruel fate

pursues Alexander right up to bedtime; there is however, a
consoling note in mother's last, sympathetic remark. Some days are
like that—even in Australia. Small listeners can enjoy the litany
of disaster, and perhaps be stimulated to discuss the possibility
that one contributes by expectation. The illustrations capture the
grumpy dolor of the story, ruefully funny.

1330   **Vipont,** Elfrida. *The Elephant and the Bad Baby;* illus. by Raymond
Briggs. Coward-McCann, 1970. 30p. Trade ed. $4.50; Library ed.
$3.96 net. (H. Hamilton, 1969. 32p. £1.05.)

4–7
yrs.   When a book begins with the fact that once upon a time there
was an elephant, one doesn't usually see a placid modern scene:
factory buildings, carefully kept grounds, airplanes in the
background. The meeting of the elephant and the Bad Baby
(who doesn't do a thing from his perch on the elephant's back
except agree that he would like whatever the elephant suggests)
results in a series of petty thieveries, with a cumulating group of
shopkeepers irately chasing the two. Eventually the Bad Baby
is dethroned for not saying "Please," and everybody has supper
with the Bad Baby's mother. The illustrations are charming, the
prim details a foil for the vigor and humor of the trumpeting
cavalcade.

1331   **Vivier,** Colette. *The House of the Four Winds;* tr. and ed. by
Miriam Morton. Doubleday, 1969. 190p. $3.95.

6–9   A story of Paris during the occupation. In the House of the Four
Winds live the sort of people who are a cross-section of
middle-class Parisians. The Moscots are really named Moscowitz,
Polish Jews in hiding; the Selliers have a father who is in a
German prison camp. They and other people in the building
respond to privation with stamina and to danger with courage.
Michel Sellier, the protagonist, contributes by running a few
errands for the resistance; the one collaborationist family turn
informers and the Moscots are taken—and killed; the city brightens
as it becomes clear that the end of the war is near. Michel and
his friends seem too young for some of their activities, but the
strength of the book is, on the whole, the moderation and realism
of events. Michel does nothing heroic; the Moscots are not saved
in the nick of time; Michel's idol in the resistance is not found
alive after he has disappeared. It is the story of ordinary people
and that is drama enough.

1332   **Vlahos,** Olivia. *African Beginnings;* illus. by George Ford. Viking,
1967. 286p. Trade ed. $6.95; Library ed. $6.43 net.

9—   As impressive a piece of informational writing as it is a
literary one, this most interesting book describes the first
organized social life that emerged in folk and tribal patterns,

growing into kingdoms and societies rich in artistic acquirements, material wealth, and the complexities of sociological systems. Some of the peoples maintained a simple cultural pattern, others a rigid and intricate one; often there are diffusion and cultural feedback evident in legends and languages. The author writes with competence and vitality; the index is good and the long, divided bibliography is truly impressive.

1333   **Vlahos,** Olivia. *Human Beginnings;* illus. by Kyuzo Tsugami. Viking, 1966. 255p. Trade ed. $5.95; Library ed. $5.63 net.

5–10   Although this discussion of human evolution has an occasional note of flippancy, the information it gives is both accurate and well organized; the easy colloquialism of the style may add to the appeal of the book for the reader not already familiar with the subject. The author describes man by shinnying, she says, backward down the family tree, regarding him first as a primate, then a mammal, etc. She discusses theories and facts, differentiating between the two. The second half of the book covers the earliest social and cultural developments in man's history, from the first tools to the first cities. A list of suggestions for further reading, a list of sources for illustrations (very good ones) and an index are appended.

1334   **Vlahos,** Olivia. *New World Beginnings;* Indian Cultures in the Americas; illus. by George Ford. Viking, 1970. 320p. Trade ed. $6.50; Library ed. $5.96 net.

8–12   A lucid discussion of theories and findings of archeologists and anthropologists prefaces a text that is scholarly in its research background and approach but written with simple directness. Recently scientists have shown that men lived in the new world almost forty thousand years ago, that there were succeeding waves of migration from diverse points of origin, and that some peoples may have migrated during the interstadial (warm) periods that punctuated the fourth glacial stage. The text is divided into sections that describe the cultural patterns of various groups on the two continents: "Hunters," "Fishermen," "Gatherers," "Farmers," and "Empire Builders." The extensive bibliography, divided by chapters, cites adult material; an index is appended.

1335   **Waber,** Bernard. *A Firefly Named Torchy;* written and illus. by Bernard Waber. Houghton, 1970. 39p. Trade ed. $4.95; Library ed. $4.23 net.

K–2   Misfit-finds-niche stories are not rare, but to have a firefly's maladjustment solved by a factor inherent in urban environment is. Blithely told, the story has humor in style and concept, and the illustrations erupt with flashing color and vitality. Torchy's problem is that his light is too bright. He just can't produce a moderate, normal twinkle. "Nonsense," says his mother. "Any one can twinkle. All you must do is take your time about it." "Nobody is perfect," Owl says. "Look at it this way. There are many kinds of light in the world. You should be proud of yours. . ." But it is in the night lights of the city that Torchy finds his metier; exhilarated by the dazzling lights, he exceeds himself—and finds, homeward bound, that all he has energy left for is a modest, run-of-the-mill twinkle.

1336   **Wahl,** Jan. *Margaret's Birthday;* illus. by Mercer Mayer. Four Winds, 1971. 41p. Trade ed. $4.95; Library ed. $4.88 net.

K–2   Carrying some freshly-baked nutbread to his Aunt Cleopatra, James is accosted by a large and amiable giraffe, Margaret, who carries him off on a countryside ramble. With frequent hints about the nutbread. Next day she announces that it is her birthday. On birthdays one does something special, like eating nutbread. They share the nutbread. They then save a treed cat, participate in a community celebration, are discovered by Aunt Cleopatra and go home with her . . . for awhile. The story ends, "and then James and Margaret went out into the world." Merry and bland, the story is complemented by the amusing illustrations: for example, when James first points out to Margaret that this isn't the way to Aunt Cleopatra's, she hangs her head and says wistfully that she thought they might have some good times together and did he want to get off here? The picture shows the giraffe half-submerged in a stream, with James clinging to her downward-curved neck by hands and heels. "I'm not complaining," he answers hastily.

1337   **Walsh,** Gillian Paton. *The Dolphin Crossing.* St. Martin's, 1967. 134p. $3.75. (Penguin, 1970. £0.20.)

6–9   A story set in England in 1940, in which two adolescent boys participate in the evacuation from the beaches of Dunkirk. John and his mother live in a coastal village; their house has been taken over by the government and they live in a small cottage. Pat is a London lad, living in an abandoned railway carriage with his stepmother, who is about to have a child; both fathers are in the service. When the news of Dunkirk comes, John takes his father's boat and joins the rescue operation; Pat, who has never sailed before, shows both intelligence and courage as a mate. The contrast between these boys of such different backgrounds is sharply drawn, and the characterization and dialogue are good; the picture of wartime Britain is vivid. There is a slow building toward the drama of Dunkirk that makes the contribution of such boys believable, since it makes clear the quiet courage of British citizens.

1338   **Walsh,** Gillian Paton. *Fireweed.* Farrar, 1970. 133p. $3.95.
(Macmillan, 1969. 144p. £0.90.)

6–9   A story of London during the World War II blitz. Two adolescents,
each supposed to have been evacuated, have stayed in London.
Bill notices Julie hanging around a shelter and confronts her
with having run away; they decide to pool their resources—
his knowledge and protection, her money and companionship.
Innocently they set up housekeeping in an abandoned building
and take in a small waif. When the building is bombed Bill is
away; he returns to face Julie's death realizing he has come to
love her. But Julie isn't dead. Sent to a hospital, she recovers
and is reunited with her wealthy family. Bill realizes that he
will not be accepted, and is smitten with dismay when Julie
seems to be rejecting him also—a sad, believable, and sharply
etched ending to a convincing and dramatic story, beautifully
constructed and conceived.

1339   **Walton,** Richard J. *America and the Cold War.* Seabury, 1969.
197p. $4.95.

7—   An important book, this is a detailed and impassionate history of
the tangled international situation that has been threatening, since
the end of the Second World War, to erupt into conflict between
the world's leaders. Incident by incident, speech by speech,
decision by decision, the author examines the goals, ideals,
fears, reactions, evasions, and alliances of Russia and America
primarily, although he discusses China's role, the Cuban
revolution, the Dominican Republic, international treaties, and
the wars in Korea and Vietnam. He offers neither verdict nor
solution—just facts, and is careful to so state when comments are
conjectural. A section of notes, a list of important dates, a
bibliography, and an index are appended.

1340   **Walton,** Richard J. *Beyond Diplomacy;* A Background Book on
American Military Intervention. Parents' Magazine, 1970. 270p.
Trade ed. $4.50; Library ed. $4.12 net.

7–12   A fine history of aspects of American foreign policy, objective
in appraising the discrepancies between fact and popular belief.
Separate sections (some several chapters long) discuss the Mexican
War, the Spanish-American War, various episodes in the
relationships between the United States and Latin America, and
Lebanon. Eight pertinent documents are appended, as are an
index and a compilation of bibliographic and reference notes.

1341   **Watson,** Clyde. *Father Fox's Pennyrhymes;* illus. by Wendy Watson.
T. Y. Crowell, 1971. 56p. $4.50. (Macmillan, 1972. £1.50.)

3–6   Tidy little pictures in soft, bright colors, some in comic strip
yrs.   format, show the bustling activities of the fox world as Father

Fox and his friends celebrate Christmas, go to a fair, celebrate a wedding, have a picnic, etc. The rhymes are quite delightful in the best nursery tradition: bouncy, rhythmic, sometimes using nonsensical word sequence. There is variation of mood and pattern, but most of the rhymes beg for a game or a jump rope. For example, "Knickerbocker Knockabout/ Sausages & Sauerkraut/ Run! Run! Run! The hogs are out!/ Knickerbocker Knockabout."

1342   **Watson,** Sally. *Linnet*. Dutton, 1971. 256p. $5.95.

6–9   Set in London during the Elizabethan reign, a lively adventure story incorporates a perceptive picture of the schism between those Roman Catholics who were loyal to the Queen and those whose primary allegiance was to the church. It is loyalty to Elizabeth that effects a rescue for the heroine, Linnet, who has become embroiled with a polished knave who runs a training school for child thieves. When Linnet discovers that he has been lying to her about using her to help foil a plot against the Queen, she rallies the help of the children, who turn against their mentor. Full of action, period detail, nice bits of characterization, and a full measure of thieves' cant and Elizabethan language.

1343   **Watson,** Sally. *Other Sandals*. Holt, 1966. 223p. Trade ed. $3.50; Library ed. $3.27 net.

6–9   A story set in Israel today, some of the action taking place in Haifa and the rest in a kibbutz. The title refers to the fact that two families trade children for a summer; Devra is a cheerful, impulsive, loquacious twelve-year-old who has been brought up in the kibbutz and who trades places with Eytan, a self-pitying adolescent who makes no effort to improve the leg hurt in an accident, and who has absolutely no desire to spend a summer in the country. Each child has problems in adjusting; each benefits from the change, the improvement due in both cases to a combination of help from others and some self-discipline. The story moves back and forth between the two locations, a slightly awkward device because each locale has some amount of sub-plot. However, the story has so many positive aspects that the mechanics are of minor importance. Devra, for example, runs into the fact that the Arabs, whom she has always hated, consider themselves the chosen people. Brought up in the country, Devra has never had a chance to have an Arab friend or to realize that Arabs might feel that *they* were being splendidly tolerant. Eytan, bitter and suspicious, discovers that one can adjust to group living, that making an effort to be friendly can make one actually feel more friendly, and that the problems of others may often produce—as they have done with him—behavior symptoms that are misleading.

1344   **Wayne,** Kyra Petrovskaya. *The Awakening*. Grosset, 1972. 185p.
$4.95.

7–10   The author's background as a young actress and, during the
siege of Leningrad, a nurse, gives authenticity and color to the
story of a young Russian girl. Zina is a student at a school for
children who are musically gifted; enamoured of an older man,
she is accused by her tyrannical grandmother of having an affair
and fears that the man has been jailed after the matter is reported
by grandmother. Even when vindicated by a doctor, Zina is
harangued and carped at—no wonder she and her withdrawn
mother are relieved when grandmother is hospitalized. Through
the sympathetic Dr. Cohen, Zina meets his daughter, a student
at ballet school who becomes her best friend. Raissa disapproves
of Zina's new love affair with Victor, another dancer, knowing
that the boy has been the protégé of a prima ballerina and
that he is an opportunist. Victor's mistress takes pains to
let Zina see the situation, so that loss is added to the fact that
her mother has become mentally unstable and is hospitalized.
Desperately she turns to Raissa and is overjoyed when her
friend agrees to move, with her mother (just back from internment
as a political prisoner, widowed and broken) into Zina's apartment.
The story closes, "She had someone to love who needed her.
At last." Politically candid, psychologically sound, a story that is
dramatic in impact, perceptive in characterization, positive in its
assertion that youth can surmount what hardships it must.

1345   **Wayne,** Kyra Petrovskaya. *Shurik;* A Story of the Siege of
Leningrad. Grosset, 1970. 299p. illus. Trade ed. $5.95; Library ed.
$5.99 net.

7–10   A true story of World War II, the photographs showing the author
in uniform as a military nurse, and Shurik as a merry and
charming child. Kyra Petrovskaya had been an actress before
the war; serving in a hospital during the siege of Leningrad, she
had adopted the homeless orphan and had convinced the hospital
authorities to let Shurik work there. The author's experiences
while serving as part of a medical patrol unit at the front are
no more dramatic and chilling than are her descriptions of the
besieged city and its starving people. Most impressive is the
recurring evidence of indomitable courage and quick compassion.

1346   **Weik,** Mary Hays. *The Jazz Man;* woodcuts by Ann Grifalconi.
Atheneum, 1966. 42p. Trade ed. $3.50; Library ed. $3.41 net.

4–5   Set in Harlem, a strangely effective story with woodcut illustrations
that reflect the combination of harsh realism and brooding lyricism
of the story. Zeke is an only child, nine years old, almost a
recluse; his parents work and Zeke stays home alone. He doesn't

go to school; he hides when the school man comes around, because he doesn't want to be teased about his lame leg. Zeke's mother, exasperated by the fact that her husband can't keep a job, leaves; after that the boy is more and more often alone at night. All of his release and satisfaction have come to Zeke through listening to the jazz pianist across the way. At the end of the story, alone and hungry, the boy dreams of the lights and laughter, the rich foods and the smiling welcome that he finds in a visit to the jazz man. He wakes to find his reunited parents with him. It is a pity that the carefully detailed dream and the happy ending are so abruptly juxtaposed; a more gradual transition would have set off the dream sequence more effectively. However, the author has done an excellent job of showing with verisimilitude the grim facts of mores among the disadvantaged in the inner city and of creating a gentle, sensitive child, possibly neurotic, as the protagonist in this setting. Some aspects of the story almost demand, for some readers at this early level, adult explanation or discussion: the carefree attitude of Daddy, the decampment of Mama, and the fact that Zeke's failure to go to school is abetted by his parents.

1347   **Weiner,** Sandra. *It's Wings That Make Birds Fly;* The Story of a Boy. Pantheon, 1968. 55p. illus. $3.95.

5—   Based on taped conversations with Harlem children, primarily with one child, the author has given us a most moving picture of a young boy, a picture beautifully augmented by photographs. It is Otis himself who gives the book warmth and dignity, expressing in his candor all the need for love, the tender heart, and the stoic acceptance of his broken and shifting home life. His comments are sometimes poignant and sometimes funny and always genuine.

1348   **Weiss,** Harvey. *Collage and Construction.* Scott, 1970. 63p. illus. $3.95.

4–7   One of the best do-it-yourself books in art, simple enough for the younger reader, dignified enough for the older. A great variety of art forms are described, the text giving enough specific information to enable the amateur to design and construct simple projects but not so specific that his ingenuity will be hampered. The materials are easy to get, the projects range from simple collages to elaborate structures and include box pictures (some with lights), wire sculpture, string pictures, glass windows, etc. The author discusses not only the materials and techniques, but artistic conception: the focus on theme or shape, the interpretation of an idea or the composition of an abstract. Not rigid, but firm about design and quite liable to incite a burst of imaginative and original expression.

1349   **Westman,** Wesley C. *The Drug Epidemic;* What It Means and How to Combat It. Dial, 1970. 163p. $4.95.

7—   Drugs, says the author in a chapter on the legal aspects of the problem, "constitute the first epidemic in history which has been ignored for so long." He discusses the medical aspects; the psychological and sociological factors that predispose individuals to drug abuse or other behavior patterns that are a result of combined factors; therapeutic measures; social implications of the drug epidemic; and future prospects for solutions of the problems of drug abuse. A thoughtful and objective book, written for the mature reader, by a clinical psychologist now working with the Alcoholism and Drug Dependence Division of the Connecticut Department of Mental Health. An index, a glossary, and a list of addiction-referral services (by states) are appended.

1350   **White,** Elwyn Brooks. *The Trumpet of the Swan;* illus. by Edward Frascino. Harper, 1970. 210p. Trade ed. $4.50; Library ed. $4.11 net. (H. Hamilton, 1971. £1.25.)

4–6   A rare delight, the story of a trumpeter swan who overcomes the severe handicap of muteness. The book starts slowly with a long, realistic sequence in which a boy camping in the Canadian wilds observes the birth of five cygnets. With a flash of brilliance, the story erupts into fantasy as the level-headed mother and pompous father of the family discuss their nesting problems. One of the cygnets, Louis, cannot make a sound and it is for the sake of his disadvantaged child that the father steals a trumpet so that Louis will be able to woo a mate. The account of Louis's education, his practice sessions, his relationships with human beings in the course of a varied and distinguished musical career are hilarious, told with the distinctive blend of calm acceptance and the patently ridiculous that have made the author's *Stuart Little* and *Charlotte's Web* classics in their own time.

1351   **Wibberley,** Leonard. *Flint's Island.* Farrar, 1972. 166p. $4.50.

6–9   Although the jacket copy of *Flint's Island* states specifically that this is not a sequel to *Treasure Island,* it is, according to the author, an "attempt to supply the story of what happened to the remaining treasure." Set in 1760, the tale is told by Tom Whelan, one of the crew of the brig *Jane.* Landing on an uncharted island, they discover Long John Silver, who is prepared—he says—to share with them the buried treasure of the pirate Flint. Told in robust, rollicking style, the story that follows is one of treachery and greed, fighting for survival, and a felicitous mixture of treasure, villainy, and courage. Sequel or not, a rousing successor.

1352   **Wibberley,** Leonard. *Leopard's Prey.* Farrar, 1971. 184p. $4.50.

6–9   A sequel to the four books in the earlier "Treegate Series," set during the Revolutionary War. Here the nephew of Peter Treegate becomes involved in an incident that was one of the provocative causes of the War of 1812: the firing of the British frigate *Leopard* on the American frigate *Chesapeake,* and the impressment of several of its seamen. Young Manly Treegate is accused of helping a deserter and impressed as a powder boy, escapes and is picked up by a Haitian pirate and returned home when a large reward is offered. Although the pirate and his superstitious Mama Amelie seem almost comic opera characters, and the closing scene planned for a final curtain (Manly appears at the family's Christmas dinner just as Peter Treegate reads a letter from Washington saying that the boy is missing and presumed dead) the book has both dramatic and historical interest, is well written, and is strong enough to overcome such minor weaknesses.

1353   **Wier,** Ester. *The Barrel;* decorations by Carl Kidwell. McKay, 1966. 136p. $3.50.

5–7   Only twelve, Chance Reedy had already lived with seven foster families; his mother dead, deserted by his father, Chance was astounded when the Child Welfare people told him that he had relatives in Florida. Living alone in the swamp country were a grandmother and a brother; joyfully, Chance anticipated living with his kin. Gentle and quiet, Chance was intimidated by his boisterous, boastful—almost hostile—older brother Turpem. The barrel of the title is the testing ground insisted on by Turpem—a barrel in which Chance's small dog is shut in with a raccoon, the victor to stay alive—and it symbolizes the crucial situation for the brothers; there is a climax in which the timid Chance proves more brave than the braggart Turpem. The dialogue is richly idiomatic; the psychological basis of action rings true and the story line is tightly constructed.

1354   **Wilder,** Laura (Ingalls). *The First Four Years;* illus. by Garth Williams. Harper, 1971. 134p. Trade ed. $4.95; Library ed. $4.79 net.

5–9   Found among Mrs. Wilder's papers after her death, and published without revision, this is the story of her first years (1885–1889) as a farmer's wife on a South Dakota homestead. Laura had objected to farming, but promised her husband that she would try it with him for a few years. Although there were troubles: crop failures, storms, cyclones, and Indian trespassers, Laura took pleasure in her home and pride in her baby; when, in the fourth year, the house went up in flames, Laura was prepared to start afresh. Although this hasn't the lively antics of little girls to give it quite the same appeal as the Little House books, it has the same direct, ingenuous quality, the same satisfying observance of detail, and the same family-centered warmth.

1355   **Wildsmith,** Brian. *Brian Wildsmith's Birds*. Watts, 1967. 29p. $4.95. (Oxf. U.P., 1967. 32p. £0.90.)

4–6   Beautiful, beautiful. Brian Wildsmith has painted a series of pictures of birds—not single birds, but groups of birds. A wedge of swans, a siege of bitterns, a walk of snipe. The pages are sometimes crammed with jewel-tone colors, but some are even more effective in showing the birds as a frieze against an almost-monotone background. The humor will appeal to those readers who enjoyed Merriam's *A Gaggle of Geese* (Knopf, 1960) in which there are many more terms.

1356   **Wildsmith,** Brian. *Brian Wildsmith's Circus*; written and illus. by Brian Wildsmith. Watts, 1970. 29p. $4.95. (Oxf. U.P., 1970. 32p. £0.90.)

2–5 yrs.   Who needs words? The brilliant water color pictures leap from the page, the costumes glowing with color, the jugglers and acrobats tense with action, the big cats vibrant and snarling, the clowns and bareback riders splendidly poised. "The circus comes to town," it is announced at the start, and there is no further comment until, at the close, the last elephant shuffles off, and "the circus goes on to the next town."

1357   **Wildsmith,** Brian. *Brian Wildsmith's Wild Animals*. Watts, 1967. 29p. illus. $4.95. (Oxf. U.P., 1967. 32p. £0.80.)

3–5   It is the beautiful pictures that lend distinction to this book, glowing and vibrant with color. As in Wildsmith's book about birds, the text consists simply of identifying captions that use group names: a shrewdness of apes, a pride of lions, a skulk of foxes, et cetera. Although the format is more appropriate for younger children, it is to the middle group who are becoming interested in the curious fascination of words that the text and the foreword are directed.

1358   **Williams,** Ursula Moray. *The Cruise of the Happy-Go-Gay*; illus. by Gunvor Edwards. Meredith, 1968. 151p. $3.95. (H. Hamilton, 1967. £0.60.)

4–6   In Victorian times ladies stayed at home. Most ladies. Aunt Hegarty, that indomitable explorer, announced to her five small visiting nieces that she had to see a man about a boat, and that was the first step toward the wonderful voyage of the *Happy-Go-Gay*. Hopefully headed for desert island and buried treasure, the all-niece crew—augmented by small male stowaways—had a cruise replete with absolutely every adventure a girl could want, from ship's kittens to a native chieftain whose greatest treasure is a coronation mug with Queen Victoria's picture. The plot is delightfully nonsensical, the writing style sprightly, and the droll characters just enough overdrawn to be amusing.

1359   **Williams,** Ursula Moray., *The Moonball;* illus. by Jane Paton.
Meredith, 1967. 138p. $3.95. (H. Hamilton, 1969. 144p. £0.80.)

4–6   A charming fantasy written with flair and humor, the realistic
setting a nice foil for the establishment of the moonball as a quite
believable creature. Round and furry, the moonball is found by a
group of children who somehow realize it is a living thing; they
take turns caring for it and they unite in keeping it from would-be
scientific investigation. The fanciful element is original and deftly
handled; the characterization is perceptive, and the writing style
lively and often humorous.

1360   **Williamson,** Joanne S. *And Forever Free . . . ;* Knopf, 1966. 197p.
Trade ed. $3.95; Library ed. $4.99 net.

7–10   A story set in New York City in the years before and during
the Civil War. Fifteen-year-old Martin Herter, an orphan, comes
from Germany to live with his uncle. Martin works in Uncle
Werner's business, helps hide a fugitive slave, becomes interested
in city politics, and becomes even more interested in newspaper
work. As a reporter for the *Tribune*, Martin is on the scene of draft
riots, sees the fighting at Gettysburg, and meets Horace Greeley.
An informed, detailed, and colorful historical background gives
importance to a plot that serves only as a vehicle for some good
writing about the European immigrant, the rough politics of a
growing urban machine, and the varying reactions in the north to
the causes and conflicts of the Civil War.

1361   **Wilson,** Mitchell. *Seesaws to Cosmic Rays;* A First View of Physics;
illus. by Eva Cellini. Lothrop, 1967. 96p. Trade ed. $4.95;
Library ed. $4.59 net.

6–9   An introduction to the basic ideas and fields of physics, written
by a research physicist and illustrated with some ornamental
pictures and a greater number of useful diagrams. The chapters
are on such subjects as heat, light, the quantum theory, color,
electronics, et cetera; background information about theories and
scientists is given throughout the book. The text is printed in
double columns; it is jarring to find, after moving from left
column to right, an occasional page on which the text runs from
upper left to upper right, is broken by a mid-page drawing,
then moves to lower left and right.

1362   **Winn,** Marie, ed. *The Fireside Book of Children's Songs;* collected
and edited by Marie Winn; musical arrangements by Allan Miller;
illus. by John Alcorn. Simon and Schuster, 1966. 192p. $6.95.

all   A nice addition to the other Fireside collections, a nice book for
ages   adults and children to enjoy together or separately. There are
silly songs, singing games, quiet or lively songs, old favorites, and
less familiar songs. The book is divided into five sections:
"Good Morning and Good Night," "Birds and Beasts," "Nursery

Songs," "Silly Songs," and "Singing Games and Rounds."
The accompaniments are simple, the stylized Alcorn illustrations
most attractive in design but not in the repeated use of blatant
colors.

1363   **Winn,** Marie. *The Fisherman Who Needed A Knife;* A Story about
Why People Use Money; illus. by John E. Johnson. Simon and
Schuster, 1970. 36p. Trade ed. $3.50; Library ed. $3.39 net.

4–7   A companion book to *The Man Who Made Fine Tops,* which
yrs.   introduced the concept of division of labor, this is a good book
for the very young on the introduction of money as a common
medium of exchange. The two-color illustrations have the same
quality of sprightly amiability that the text uses to tell the story
of the fisherman who had trouble, in the days when everybody
traded what he had, getting the knife he wanted. The knifemaker
didn't need a fish, but wanted something else; the fisherman
trudged around making a series of trades before he got his
knife and the knifemaker the hat he wanted. They agreed that
it would be easier if everyone could use the same thing for
bartering—why not small, easy-to-carry pieces of metal? And so
the use of money began. To help adults explain and ramify the
idea of using money, several suggestions are appended.

1364   **Winn,** Marie. *The Man Who Made Fine Tops;* A Story about
Why People Do Different Kinds of Work; illus. by John E.
Johnson. Simon and Schuster, 1970. 35p. Trade ed. $2.95;
Library ed. $3.07 net.

K–2   A little book with a big message; the illustrations are pleasantly
effective in supplementing the explanation of division of labor. The
text does this with skill, the light fictional framework describing
the father who made his son a top, was importuned by other
men (who could not make tops) and who, in each case, traded a
product for another's product or labor or raw materials. These
terms are not used, but the ideas are perfectly clear and the
author discretely stopped when her point was made and elaborated
no more.

1365   **Winn,** Marie. *The Thief-Catcher;* A Story about Why People Pay
Taxes; illus. by Whitney Darrow, Jr. Simon and Schuster, 1972.
37p. $3.50.

K–2   Like Winn's other books in this series of "concept storybooks"
this is a simplified but quite adequate presentation for young
children of a single topic. Here the aspect of our society's
structure that is explained is taxation. The text describes a busy
community in which a series of thefts is perpetrated. Obviously,
the town needs a thief-catcher; clearly, the people of the town
are too busy with their own tasks to take on any added

responsibility. Finally one young man suggests that if each person contributed a little money, a thief-catcher could be hired just for that job. Taxes, the author says, are levied so that things can be done for the whole community: police protection, garbage collection, and other public services. Readers-aloud may wince at the phrase "this little bit of money" given by each citizen, but small listeners will understand the concept.

1366   **Winterfeld,** Henry. *Mystery of the Roman Ransom;* tr. from the German by Edith McCormick; illus. by Fritz Biermann. Harcourt, 1971. 186p. $4.50.

5–8   The lively boys of ancient Rome who unraveled a mystery in *Detectives in Togas* find another situation thrust upon them when a slave from Gaul divulges that he has a secret message: a senator is to be killed. Since the boys are all sons of senators, they and the slave, under the guidance of their teacher Xantippus (a wonderfully crusty character) become involved in a dramatic detective venture that has a good plot, suspense and good characterization, and an easy style that has vitality and humor.

1367   **Wohlrabe,** Raymond A. *Exploring Giant Molecules;* with drawings by Phil Jaget. World, 1969. 95p. Trade ed. $4.50; Library ed. $4.76 net. (World Pub. Co., 1969. 96p. £1.75.)

7—   An unusually lucid explication of a complex and multi-faceted subject, the organization of material and brisk writing style making the subject as comprehensible as it is fascinating. The author discusses monomers and polymers, explaining the structural difference between ordinary and giant molecules, and the use of structural formulas, chemical equations, and molecular models. All of these are used throughout the book in illustrating, in good diagrams, the giant molecules, natural or man-made, that have changed or served so many procedures for mankind. There is some historical background given, and much of the book is devoted to such aspects of polymer chemistry as plastics of various types, silicon-based polymers, and the ferment of biological research in the investigation of nucleic acids and proteins. Several experiments are suggested to the reader, with some dangerous substances or procedures carefully noted. An index is appended.

1368   **Wojciechowska,** Maia. *Tuned Out.* Harper, 1968. 125p. Trade ed. $4.50; Library ed. $3.79 net.

9–11   "One day I ought to find out how it is with other kids," Jim's journal begins on June 9, 1967, and it goes on to record a sixteen-year-old's love and respect for a brilliant older brother. The rest of the journal describes, in a story of intensity and bleak honesty, Jim's stunned disbelief when he finds that Kevin has been using marijuana and LSD, his efforts to dissuade Kevin, and his traumatic experience of being with his brother when Kevin has a trip so bad it results in hospitalization. At times the writing slows, but this seems curiously appropriate in a story in which the stunned protagonist is fighting against time. Candid, with no melodrama except the terrible melodrama of what is happening, and with a lack of didacticism that makes the message all the more effective.

1369   **Wood,** James Playsted. *The Snark Was a Boojum;* A Life of Lewis Carroll; with drawings by David Levine. Pantheon Books, 1966. 184p. $3.95.

8—   A biography of the eccentric and erudite man who was a member of the clergy, a brilliant mathematician, a Christ Church don, a gifted and passionate photographer, and an author for all time. Although this book has a heavy burden of comment, analysis, the opinion of Carroll's nonsense writing, it is a most eloquent portrait of an unhappy and talented man. The Reverend Dodgson had a penchant for little girls, and his pursuit of them as companions and as photographic models did not always meet with approval. His personality and his problems are discussed with a refreshing combination of candor and dignity, his writing is discussed with less objectivity. A bibliography is appended.

1370   **Wood,** Nancy. *Hollering Sun;* photographs by Myron Wood. Simon and Schuster, 1972. 96p. $4.95.

5—   Handsomely illustrated by excellent photographs, dignified in page layout, this is both a history of the Indians of the Taos Pueblo and a compilation of their poetic legends and beliefs. The first part of the book is a long introduction in which the author gives a history of the tribe, a history in which she identifies, with indignation, with the Taos viewpoint. The major portion of the volume comprises poems, sayings, and aphorisms collected over the period of a ten-year friendship with the Indians of the pueblo. The material is divided into "The Legends," "The Village," and "Nature," but there is an awareness of—and respect for—nature in all its forms that pervades all of the text.

1371   **Woodberry,** Joan. *Come Back, Peter;* illus. by George Tetlow. T. Y. Crowell, 1972. 152p. $3.95. (Longman Young Bks., 1970. 116p. £0.90.)

5–7   A story of the Australian outback by a former winner of the Australian Children's Book of the Year Award. The setting is vivid and evocative, the characters beautifully drawn, the story line dramatic, the style deliberate and direct. Ten-year-old Paul, lonely since the death of his brother, goes off for a night of camping, his jaunt prefaced by a full picture of life at the station and a perceptive picture of the relationships between settlers and aboriginals. There is less background given for the story of the other two boys: Johnnie is alone with a sick mother and two small children in a sun-baked shack. An aboriginal boy, Peter, shows up just in time to help the family, and when—at the mother's insistence—the two boys go off for help with the younger children in a pram, leading the goat (milk for the baby), it is the skill and courage of Peter that keeps them all alive in the long trek through the heat. They are ill and exhausted when they meet Paul, who takes over, mounting the other two boys on his horse and pushing the pram himself. The title reference is to the coincidence of names: Paul's dead brother had been Peter, and the aboriginal Peter is welcomed as a new brother who will live with Paul's family.

1372   **Wormser,** Richard. *The Black Mustanger;* illus. by Don Bolognese. Morrow, 1971. 190p. Trade ed. $4.95; Library ed. $4.59 net.

5–9   Dan Riker had come with his parents from Tennessee to Texas after the Civil War, learning along with his father how to catch and brand wild cattle. When his dad was injured, Dan learned that not many of the men in the big outfit nearby were anxious to help a Union man. One man was: the black mustanger, Will, who was part black, part Apache. He was also willing to let Dan act as his helper and earn a bit of cash. Out of this partnership came a real friendship, even Dan's mother coming to understand that having her son work for this black man meant that Dan was getting the best training he could for the life they had now. The setting is colorful, the construction of the story taut and economical, the plot well-paced and convincing.

1373   **Wrightson,** Patricia. *A Racecourse for Andy;* illus. by Margaret Horder. Harcourt, 1968. 156p. $3.75. (Hutchinson, 1968. 160p. £0.90.)

5–7   Once Andy had been like all the other boys, but now he was remote and detached, his mental processes too slow to keep up with the others. Convinced that an old tramp has sold him a racecourse for just a few dollars, Andy persists in acting the part of the owner. His friends try to reason with him and save him trouble, but Andy calmly goes his own way. The men working around the racecourse gently humor the retarded boy, and tactfully "buy" the property back. The compassion and understanding of the adults is heartwarming, but it is the protective allegiance of Andy's friends that is most impressive. The plot is unusual, characterization good, and style of writing distinctive.

1374   Wuorio, Eva-Lis. *Save Alice!* Holt, 1968. 165p. Trade ed. $3.95;
Library ed. $3.59 net.

5–7   A romping adventure story that begs to be translated to the
screen; it has a small, distinguished cast (British twins, an
American guest, an older cousin) a light love interest provided
for the older cousin, an exciting chase sequence (through Spain)
and a mystery (Why had an old woman pushed a caged bird
into the car?) with most villainous villains, determined to get
the bird for their undoubtedly nefarious reasons. All the action
is accompanied by merry dialogue, good characterization, and
a sustained pace.

1375   Wyler, Rose. *Magic Secrets;* by Rose Wyler and Gerald Ames;
pictures by Talivaldis Stubis. Harper, 1967. 64p. (I Can Read
Books) Trade ed. $1.95; Library ed. $2.19 net. (World's Work,
1968. 64p. £0.75.)

2–3   A first book about tricks that can be done by an amateur, very
simply written and very clearly illustrated for the beginning
independent reader who aspires to legerdemain. The text suggests
that an audience sees that to which its attention is directed,
and shows the small diversionary tactics that add to illusion.
The tricks are lucidly explained, and the whole book has a sort
of merry air.

1376   Wyndham, Lee, comp. *Tales the People Tell in Russia;* comp. by
Lee Wyndham; illus. by Andrew Antal. Messner, 1970. 95p.
Trade ed. $4.95; Library ed. $4.64 net. (J. Messner Inc., 1970.
95p. £2.50.)

3–5   Told with a gusto that is appropriate to the oral tradition of the
folktale, ten tales for which sources are cited in an appended
note. The book also contains three fables and a short list of
proverbs. The stylized illustrations are attractive in black and white,
the stories delightful to read or tell.

1377   Wyndham, Robert, comp. *Chinese Mother Goose Rhymes;* selected
and ed. by Robert Wyndham; pictures by Ed Young. World,
1968. 42p. Trade ed. $4.95; Library ed. $5.21 net. (World Pub.
Co., 1969. 48p. £1.87½.)

4–6   A most intriguing collection, the rhymes having both the universal
yrs.   attributes that appeal because of familiarity and the special charm
of an unfamiliar variant in the genre. Some of the poems, riddles,
and games have been translated for the book, and others have been
selected from *Pekinese Rhymes* (Pei-T'and Press, 1896) or from
Chinese Mother Goose Rhymes (Revell, 1900). The pages read
vertically and are handsomely bordered with columns of Chinese
letters; the illustrations are outstanding in the use of color and in
design, beautifully adapting modern technique to traditional style.

1378   **Wyndham,** Robert. *Tales the People Tell in China;* illus. by Jay
Yang. Messner, 1971. 92p. Trade ed. $4.95; Library ed. $4.79 net.

4–6   A selection of folk tales, legends, and pithy sayings is illustrated
in traditional Chinese style. The material is varied, selected
from many sources, and told in a fluid style that lends itself
to reading aloud or as a source for storytelling. Some of the
tales have historical bases ("The Borrowing of 1,000,000 Arrows"
is about a Chinese general, and "Gift of the Unicorn" is the
legendary story of Confucius's birth) but most are concerned
with magic and folk-wisdom.

1379   **Yaroslava.** *Tusya and the Pot of Gold;* retold and illus. by
Yaroslava. Atheneum, 1971. 27p. $4.75.

3–5   Illustrations in the style of old Ukrainian glass paintings are a
colorful accompaniment to a Ukrainian folktale, retold in direct
and unembellished style, pleasant to read aloud. Knowing that
the pot of gold he has found will be taken from him by the
authorities if they should hear about it, Tomas paves the way.
He tells his loquacious wife Tusya so many peculiar stories
that she repeats, that when the news of the pot of gold comes
along, it is assumed that it is simply another one of Tusya's
tales. Although the story ends with an affectionate scene between
husband and wife, it also has the moral that is so often found in
folk literature. A good story for telling.

1380   **Yolen,** Jane H., ed. *The Fireside Song Book of Birds and Beasts;*
arranged by Barbara Green; illus. by Peter Parnall. Simon and
Schuster, 1972. 223p. $9.95.

all   A delightful collection, with many old favorites, is delectably
ages   illustrated by the clean-lined drawings of Peter Parnall. They are
just right for the animal songs to be used by or with children,
and the piano accompaniments are not intricate. The songs are
grouped into sections: "Farmyard and House," "Field and Forest,"
and so on. An index of titles is appended.

1381   **Yolen,** Jane H. *Friend;* The Story of George Fox and the Quakers.
Seabury, 1972. 179p. $5.95.

7—   A strange man, George Fox. He believed that wars were wrong,
he wore his hair long, he spoke with passion for prison reform
and inveighed against slavery and the inequity of treatment of
women. He was, over three hundred years ago, a man whose
ideas speak to today's readers. Careful research and a forthright
style make this biography of the founder of Quakerism valuable
both as a biography and as a history of religion and religious
intolerance in England—and to some extent in America. George
Fox and his followers were persecuted, reviled, and repeatedly
jailed for their beliefs and often for their refusal to swear an

oath; although the tone of *Friend* is not effusive or laudatory, the book is a vigorous testament to Fox's religious dedication and his personal integrity. A bibliography and an index are appended.

1382   **Yolen,** Jane. *Greyling;* a picture story from the Islands of Shetland; illus. by William Stobbs. World, 1968. 29p. Trade ed. $3.95; Library ed. $3.86 net. (Bodley Head, 1969. 32p. £0.90.)

3–5   Based on the Scottish legend of the selchie, the seal that has turned into a boy, this tender story is illustrated with pictures that have a stark, poster-like quality that suits the rugged setting and a gracefulness in color and detail that suits the fantasy of the theme. A lonely, childless couple rescue a seal pup, and it becomes a selchie. None of the village folk know and not even the boy understands why the sea calls to him. When the father is near drowning, the townspeople are afraid to venture into the tossing waves, but the son dives in to save his father. The selchie becomes a seal once more, and each year a great grey seal comes to the shore and visits the man and his wife.

1383   **Yolen,** Jane. *The Seventh Mandarin;* illus. by Ed Young. Seabury, 1970. 30p. $4.95. (Macmillan, 1971. 32p. £1.25.)

2–4   Three-quarters of each double-page spread is given to the lovely illustrations for a tale in legend style, the text printed in the fourth column of space, framing the rich, lambent paintings. One of the tasks of the seven mandarins who guarded their king, long ago in an eastern land, was to fly the huge dragon kite while the monarch slept—for the king's soul was safe only when the royal kite flew. But the seventh and youngest mandarin learned, one night when a fierce wind blew the kite down, that there was no truth in the superstition. More, he learned of what went on in the city outside the palace walls; looking for the fallen kite, he had to leave the palace confines and so saw the misery of the people. So the good king discovered the harsh reality of life outside; the palace walls came down, and the land knew a peace and plenty it had never had. Good style, good storytelling despite a rather pallid ending, and great harmony between text and illustration.

1384   **York,** Carol Beach. *Nothing Ever Happens Here.* Hawthorn Books, 1970. 103p. $3.95.

6–9   Elizabeth lived with her aunt and widowed father in an ordinary house on a quiet street in a dull town. Bored, she daydreamed of living in New York or San Francisco. The only thing that happened that summer was that new tenants moved into the apartment on the second floor. Big deal. But Mrs. Hollis was pathetically friendly, and Elizabeth realized that she and Mr.

Hollis, old as they were, were deeply in love. Funny. Funny, too, that Ruby Hollis was so afraid of the two men who had appeared in town. When tragedy comes, Elizabeth shrinks with relief into the comfort of the dullness of her home. The author is most perceptive in her characterization of the women who build their lives on little things, of the triviality of their conversation, and of the careful façade that timid people build for their own solace. A truly touching book.

1385   **Yoshida,** Jim. *The Two Worlds of Jim Yoshida;* by Jim Yoshida with Bill Hosokawa. Morrow, 1972. 256p. $6.95.

8—   American-born, Jim Yoshida had gone with his mother to take his father's ashes to Japan and was caught by World War II. A dual citizen, he was conscripted by the Japanese Army and sent to China; after recuperating from severe illness, he discovered that he had lost his status as an American citizen. He served as an unpaid (and illegal) volunteer with the U.S. forces in the Korean War, hoping this would prove his loyalty. In 1954, he regained his citizenship. The book is interesting because of the information it gives about Japan's view of the war rather than because Yoshida himself is an interesting character; he's very much a typical soldier, an average guy. The fact that he's a judo expert adds color to the story, which is capably written—presumably by Bill Hosokawa, an experienced journalist.

1386   **Young,** Jean. *Woodstock Craftsman's Manual.* Praeger, 1972. 253p. Paper ed. $4.95; Cloth ed. $10.00.

8—   Whether the reader simply enjoys amateur craftsmanship or is looking for a remunerative skill, this offers a variety of crafts: beadwork, pottery, tie dye and batik, silkscreen, macrame, leatherwork, home recordings, candlemaking, embroidery. The instructions are clear, the illustrations (usually by the writer of each section) good size, and the suggestions for purchase of materials helpful. Best of all, the book is written with zest and informality.

1387   **Young,** Margaret B. *The Picture Life of Martin Luther King, Jr.;* illus. with photographs. Watts, 1968. 45p. $3.50.

2–3   A very good selection of photographs accompanies a very simple but quite adequate outline of Martin Luther King's life, the book having been published before his assassination. The vocabulary is simple, the print large, and the writing style straightforward, so that the book is eminently suitable for slow older readers as well as for the intended primary audience.

1388   **Yulya.** *Bears Are Sleeping;* words and music by Yulya; pictures by Nonny Hogrogian. Scribner, 1967. 18p. Trade ed. $3.95; Library ed. $3.89 net.

4–7
yrs.   In a simple, lovely setting of cool scenes of the quiet snowbound
forest, the musical phrases and the words of an old Russian
lullaby are given, a measure or two at a time. The whole melody
(a charming one) is repeated at the back of the book.

1389   **Yurchenco,** Henrietta, ed. *A Fiesta of Folk Songs from Spain and
Latin America;* illus. by Jules Maidoff. Putnam, 1967. 88p. $4.39.

4–6   A big book of songs, the level of the descriptive text limiting
use to the middle grades ("You can play these games, too . . .")
although the book can be used by adults working with younger
children. The book provides phonetic spelling as well as the
English translation of the Spanish lyrics; the musical notation
gives the melodic line and is coded for guitar chords. The songs
are gay and simple, many of them singing games. A book that
is entertaining as well as useful.

1390   **Zei,** Alki. *Petros' War;* tr. from the Greek by Edward Fenton.
Dutton, 1972. 236p. $5.95.

5–7   October 27, 1940—that was a day to remember! With high heart,
Petros watched the Greek troops march off to war with Italy,
gay and singing. But even that day, there was trouble—not enough
food in the stores, so quickly did the hoarders swoop. And six
months later, the Germans marched in. The story describes, in
vivid and beautifully translated style, the privation and ignominy
of living under occupation, the tenacious resistance of the
Athenians, and the dangers and small satisfactions that came to
Petros in his work with the Underground. The book ends with
the departure of the Germans and the liberation of Greece, an
ending in which Petros—young and resilient—looks forward to the
enjoyment of freedom, but it is clear that he will never forget
the time of death. The characters are sharply etched, the story
well paced and filled with action and drama.

1391   **Zei,** Alki. *Wildcat under Glass;* tr. from the Greek by Edward
Fenton. Holt, 1968. 177p. Trade ed. $4.50; Library ed. $3.97 net.
(Gollancz, 1969. 192p. £0.90.)

5–7   First published in Greece in 1963, a story of the struggle against
dictatorship as seen through the eyes of a child. Melia, who tells the
story, lives on an island and, with her older sister, is taught at
home. Both girls adore their adult cousin, Niko, who invents
marvelous stories about the stuffed wildcat that is a family
possession; the animal is used as a symbol when Niko becomes
involved in the struggle against the forces of the new regime.
The book is particularly effective in showing the reactions of the
very young and the very old to the abrasive imposition of a
Fascist Government. Although the story is set in the 1930's,
its local atmosphere is more important than the period. Well

written, deftly translated, and—despite the fact that the children in
the story seem quite young, while the subtler concepts and theories
are suitable for rather older children—an absorbing story.

1392   **Zemach,** Harve. *The Judge;* An Untrue Tale; illus. by Margot
Zemach. Farrar, 1969. 41p. $4.50. (Bodley Head, 1970. 48p. £1.05.)

K–2   An engaging and humorous nonsense story, told in rhyme and
illustrated with raffish deftness. Enthroned on his bench, a
curmudgeon of a judge hears a prisoner plead that he didn't know
that what he did was against the law, but that he had seen a
horrible beast. "This man has told an untrue tale. Throw him in
jail!" Each additional prisoner adds to the story; each infuriates the
judge. Dénouement: the horrible beast, exactly as described,
appears and swallows the judge, leaving five complacent prisoners
making no comment, but looking entirely satisfied.

1393   **Zemach,** Harve. *A Penny a Look;* illus. by Margot Zemach.
Farrar, 1971. 41p. $4.95.

K–3   Vaulting ambition takes a tumble in a sprightly version of an old
tale. Told with bland simplicity and illustrated with robust frenzy,
the story and pictures complement each other engagingly. An
insensitive and aggressive man has heard about the land of one-
eyed people, and he persuades his do-nothing but merciful
brother to come along on a trek to get there. Object: to capture
one man, bring him back, exhibit him, and get rich. The gentler
brother will be allowed to collect penny fees. But the tables are
turned: surrounded by one-eyed men, the malfeasant is captured
and exhibited, since he is a rarity, a man with two eyes. The
brother (even one-eyed men could see he'd never amount to
much) is no threat, so he is permitted to collect fees—a penny a
look. The humor robs the tale of didacticism, and the incidents
of the long journey are hilarious as they wade, climb, ride, and
fly to the accompaniment of one brother's worry about the fate
of the intended one-eyed captive and the other's brusque dismissal
of the plight that is about to be his.

1394   **Zemach,** Harve, ad. *The Speckled Hen;* a Russian nursery rhyme;
illus. by Margot Zemach. Holt, 1966. 33p. Trade ed. $3.50;
Library ed. $3.27 net. (Bodley Head, 1967. 48p. £0.63.)

4–6   A nonsensical Russian nursery rhyme, adapted and illustrated in a
yrs.   style that is bright and bouncy and just a bit daft. Grandmother
and Grandfather are delighted when their speckled hen lays a
speckled egg, and they are thrown into idiotic and fervent dismay
when the egg breaks. Panic spreads, member by member, through
the family; in a semicumulative text, catastrophes mount and the
story ends with Father standing on his head atop a haystack,
refusing to come down until another speckled egg has been laid.

Little substance, no message, just fun. The illustrations are lively, scratchy, full of vigor and humor; fortunately they are limited to red, brown, black, and white—full color would have been really distracting to the eye when combined with the scribbles of detail.

1395   **Zim,** Herbert Spencer. *Life and Death;* by Herbert Spencer Zim and Sonia Bleeker; illus. by Rene Martin. Morrow, 1970. 63p. Trade ed. $3.75; Library ed. $3.56 net.

4–7   A calm and quite comprehensive look at a subject usually handled either too gingerly or too sweetly. Some of the illustrations seem of little use but the text is very good: broad in scope, informative, and—in particular—invested with the attitude that the cessation of life is a part of life itself. The authors consider man's life span in relation to other living things, having discussed the nature of the latter; they describe the processes of aging and dying, the technicalities of burial and cremation, and some of the funeral practices of other times and other lands. The one significant piece of information that is not included is the fact that the services of a funeral director and the choice between cremation and earth burial are not absolute, but that it is possible to bequeath a body to an institution for medical research. An index is appended.

1396   **Zindel,** Paul. *The Pigman.* Harper, 1968. 182p. Trade ed. $3.95; Library ed. $3.79 net. (Bodley Head, 1969. 192p. £0.80.)

7–9   John and Lorraine, high school sophomores, have two great bonds: they are both in conflict with their parents and they both have capricious and inventive minds. Out of this comes their friendship with an elderly man they call the Pigman (his name is Pignati and he collects china pigs) whom they met when pretending to be collecting for a charity. They are not criminal, but John and Lorraine have the pliant amorality of the young. Mr. Pignati comes home from the hospital to find a wild party going on; shocked by his young friends' behavior, the trusting and loving Pigman succumbs to a stroke. For John and Lorraine, "there was no one to blame anymore . . . And there was no place to hide . . . Our life would be what we made of it—nothing more, nothing less." Although the writing (by John and Lorraine, alternately) has the casual flavor of adolescence, the plot has an elemental quality. Sophisticated in treatment, the story is effective because of its candor, its humor, and its skilful construction.

1397   **Zolotow,** Charlotte (Shapiro). *A Father Like That;* pictures by Ben Shecter. Harper, 1971. 29p. Trade ed. $3.50; Library ed. $3.27 net.

K–2   "I wish I had a father. But my father went away before I was born. I say to my mother, You know what he'd be like? 'What?' she says. . ." and the little boy tells her. He would come and talk when there were nightmares in the night, he'd never show off about what a good father he was at parent-teacher meetings, he'd make mother sit down and have a drink with him before dinner, and he'd never want to turn down the TV. The wistful catalog of perfection is lightened by humor, and the soliloquy catches both a child's way of thinking and his way of expressing his thoughts. Mother who is "sewing very fast," says in closing, "And in case he never comes, just remember when you grow up, you can be a father like that yourself!" The ending may not seem a solace to a child, and the phrase "in case he never comes" is rather ambiguous, since it isn't clear whether the real father may come back or a stepfather is being suggested, but the book in every other way has the same warmth and candor that has distinguished so many other small Zolotow gems.

1398   **Zolotow,** Charlotte (Shapiro). *If It Weren't for You*; pictures by Ben Shecter. Harper, 1966. 32p. Trade ed. $3.95; Library ed. $3.79 net. (Harper & Row, 1966. 32p. £1.85.)

3–6
yrs.   The loving X-ray Zolotow eye looks at dethronement; a child ruefully lists the joys of life with no small brother. "I could watch any program I wanted . . . and I could cry without anyone knowing . . . and my paintbrushes would never be mashed. . . ." The end isn't sugar-coated, but there is an admission that all is not gloom. The illustrations are engaging; the text needs no plot, since it will probably awaken Instant Recognition Reflexes on every page. A percipient and charming book.

1399   **Zolotow,** Charlotte (Shapiro). *When I Have a Son*; pictures by Hilary Knight. Harper, 1967. 29p. Trade ed. $2.50; Library ed. $2.57 net. (Harper & Row. £1.15.)

K–2   A small book, very funny and often touching; the innocent ferocity of the illustrations are (as they are in the author's companion piece, *When I Have a Little Girl*) an added pleasure. En route to his piano lesson, John resentfully tells the friend he is being forced to leave what a blissful life *his* son will lead. Certainly, no piano; just as certainly, triple malteds before dinner and no haircuts. A key of his own. Plain mustard sandwiches on rye, and so on. The whole thing is so engagingly absurd it might even make a small boy see what's funny in his own behavior.

1400   **Zolotow,** Charlotte (Shapiro). *William's Doll*; illus. by William Pene Du Bois. Harper, 1972. 32p. Trade ed. $3.95; Library ed. $3.79 net.

4–8
yrs.   The warmth and humor of the illustrations, the clean look of the pages, and the simplicity and restraint of the writing style are in perfect agreement in a book that is as endearing for its tenderness as

for the message it conveys: there is nothing, but nothing wrong with boys who play with dolls. William's father tries to discourage him by giving him a basketball and a train set; William enjoys both but it doesn't change his mind. When his grandmother comes to visit, he tells her dolefully that his friends and his brother taunt him, but grandmother is on William's side. "Nonsense," she says to William's protesting father when he says, "He's a boy!" She understands exactly why William wants a doll and should have one—so that when he grows up he will have had a chance to practice being a father, a chance to love and cuddle and care for the doll that represents the baby for whom he'll some day share a responsibility. So there, sexists.

Appendix

Addresses of American and British Publishers of Listed
Children's Books

AMERICAN PUBLISHERS

Abelard. Abelard-Schuman, Ltd., 257 Park Ave. S., New York, N.Y. 10010

Abingdon. Abingdon Pr., 201 Eighth Ave. S., Nashville, Tenn. 37202

Abrams. Harry N. Abrams, Inc., 110 E. 59th St., New York, N.Y. 10022

Addison. Addison-Wesley Pub. Co., Inc., Reading, Mass. 01867

American Heritage. American Heritage Pr., 330 W. 42nd St., New York,
    N.Y. 10036

Appleton. Appleton-Century-Crofts, 440 Park Ave. S., New York, N.Y. 10016

Ariel. Ariel Books. See Farrar

Assoc. for Childhood Education International. 3615 Wisconsin Ave., N.W.,
    Washington, D.C. 20016

Atheneum. Atheneum Pubs., 122 E. 42nd St., New York, N.Y. 10017

Atlantic. Atlantic Monthly Pr., 8 Arlington St., Boston, Mass. 02116

Atlantic/Little. Atlantic Monthly Pr. in association with Little, Brown & Co.

Basic. Basic Books, Inc., 404 Park Ave. S., New York, N.Y. 10016

Beacon. Beacon Pr., 25 Beacon St., Boston, Mass. 02108

Bobbs. Bobbs-Merrill Co., Inc., 3 W. 57th St., New York, N.Y. 10019

Bradbury. Bradbury Pr., Inc., 2 Overhill Rd., Scarsdale, N.Y. 10583

Chatham/Viking. 15 Wilmot Lane, Riverside, Conn. 06878. Distributed by
    Viking

Childrens Pr. Childrens Press, Inc., 1224 W. Van Buren, Chicago, Ill. 60607

Chilton. Chilton Book Co., 401 Walnut St., Philadelphia, Pa. 19106

Coward. Coward, McCann & Geoghegan Inc., 200 Madison Ave., New
    York, N.Y. 10016

Cowles. Cowles Book Co., Inc., 488 Madison Ave., New York, N.Y. 10022

Criterion. Criterion Books, Inc., 257 Park Ave. S., New York, N.Y. 10010

Crowell-Collier. Crowell Collier and Macmillan, Inc., 866 Third Ave.,
    New York, N.Y. 10022

T. Crowell. Thomas Y. Crowell Co., 666 Fifth Ave., New York, N.Y. 10019

Crown. Crown Pubs., Inc., 419 Park Ave. S., New York, N.Y. 10016

Day. The John Day Co., Inc., 257 Park Ave. S., New York, N.Y. 10010

Delacorte. Delacorte Pr. See Dell

Dell. Dell Pub. Co., 1 Dag Hammarskjöld Plaza, New York, N.Y. 10017

Dial. The Dial Pr., Inc. See Dell

Dodd. Dodd, Mead & Co., 79 Madison Ave., New York, N.Y. 10016

Doubleday. Doubleday & Co., Inc., 277 Park Ave., New York, N.Y.
    10017

For the address of any publisher not listed here consult the latest *Literary Market
Place* or Bowker's *Books in Print*.

Duell. Duell, Sloan & Pearce. See Meredith

Dufour. Dufour Editions, Inc., Chester Springs, Pa. 19425

Dutton. E. P. Dutton & Co., Inc., 201 Park Ave. S., New York, N.Y. 10003

Eriksson. Paul S. Eriksson, Inc., Pub., 119 W. 57th St., New York, N.Y. 10019

Evans. M. Evans & Co., Inc., 216 E. 49th St., New York, N.Y. 10017

Farrar. Farrar, Straus & Giroux, Inc., 19 Union Sq., W., New York, N.Y. 10003

Follett. Follett Pub. Co., 1010 W. Washington Blvd., Chicago, Ill. 60606

Four Winds. Four Winds Pr. See Scholastic

Funk. Funk & Wagnalls, Inc., 53 E. 77th St., New York, N.Y. 10021

Garden City. See Doubleday

Garrard. Garrard Pub. Co., 2 Overhill Rd., Scarsdale, N.Y. 10583

Golden Gate. Golden Gate Junior Books, 8344 Melrose Ave., Los Angeles, Calif. 90069

Golden Pr. Golden Pr., Inc. See Western

Grosset. Grosset & Dunlap, Inc., 51 Madison Ave., New York, N.Y. 10010

Hale. E. M. Hale & Co., Inc., 1201 S. Hastings Way, Eau Claire, Wis. 54701

Harcourt. Harcourt Brace Jovanovich, Inc., 757 Third Ave., New York, N.Y. 10017

Harper. Harper & Row, Pubs., 10 E. 53rd St., New York, N.Y. 10022

Harvey. Harvey House, Inc., 5 S. Buckhout St., Irvington-on-Hudson, N.Y. 10533

Hastings. Hastings House Pubs., 10 E. 40th St., New York, N.Y. 10016

Hawthorn. Hawthorn Books, Inc., 70 Fifth Ave., New York, N.Y. 10011

Hill. Hill & Wang, Inc., 72 Fifth Ave., New York, N.Y. 10011

Holiday. Holiday House, Inc., 18 E. 56th St., New York, N.Y. 10022

Holt. Holt, Rinehart & Winston, Inc., 383 Madison Ave., New York, N.Y. 10017

Houghton. Houghton Mifflin Co., 2 Park St., Boston, Mass. 02107

Knopf. Alfred A. Knopf, Inc., 201 E. 50th St., New York, N.Y. 10022

Lerner. Lerner Pubns. Co., 241 First Ave. N., Minneapolis, Minn. 55401

Lippincott. J. B. Lippincott Co., E. Washington Sq., Philadelphia, Pa. 19105

Little. Little, Brown & Co., 34 Beacon St., Boston, Mass. 02106

Longmans. Longmans, Green & Co. See McKay

Lothrop. Lothrop, Lee & Shepard Co., Inc., 105 Madison Ave., New York, N.Y. 10016

McCall. McCall Books, 230 Park Ave., New York, N.Y. 10017

McGraw. McGraw-Hill Book Co., 330 W. 42nd St., New York, N.Y. 10036

McKay. David McKay Co., Inc., 750 Third Ave., New York, N.Y. 10017

Macmillan. Macmillan Co., 866 Third Ave., New York, N.Y. 10022

Macrae. Macrae Smith Co., 225 S. 15th St., Philadelphia, Pa. 19102

Meredith. Meredith Pr., 250 Park Ave., New York, N.Y. 10017

Messner. Julian Messner, Inc. See Simon & Schuster

Morrow. William Morrow & Co., Inc., 105 Madison Ave., New York, N.Y. 10016

Natural History Pr. Am. Museum of Natural History, Central Park W. at
         79th St., New York, N.Y. 10024. Distributed by Doubleday
Nelson. Thomas Nelson, Inc., Copewood & Davis Sts., Camden, N.J.
         08103
Norton. W. W. Norton & Co., 55 Fifth Ave., New York, N.Y. 10003
Norton/Grosset. W. W. Norton in association with Grosset & Dunlap
Oxford. Oxford Univ. Pr., 200 Madison Ave., New York, N.Y. 10016
Pantheon. Pantheon Books, 201 E. 50th St., New York, N.Y. 10022
Parents' Magazine. Parents' Magazine Pr., 52 Vanderbilt Ave., New York,
         N.Y. 10017
Parnassus. Parnassus Pr., 2721 Parker St., Berkeley, Calif. 94704
Phillips. S. G. Phillips, Inc., 305 W. 86th St., New York, N.Y. 10024
Platt. Platt & Munk, Inc., 1055 Bronx River Ave., Bronx, N.Y. 10472
Plays. Plays, Inc., 8 Arlington St., Boston, Mass. 02116
Praeger. Praeger Pubs., Inc., 111 Fourth Ave., New York, N.Y. 10003
Prentice. Prentice-Hall, Inc., Englewood Cliffs, N.J. 07632
Putnam. G. P. Putnam's Sons, 200 Madison Ave., New York, N.Y. 10016
Rand. Rand McNally & Co., P.O. Box 7600, Chicago, Ill. 60680
Random. Random House, Inc., 201 E. 50th St., New York, N.Y. 10022
Reilly. Reilly & Lee Books, 114 W. Illinois St., Chicago, Ill. 60610
Ritchie. The Ward Ritchie Pr., 3044 Riverside Dr., Los Angeles, Calif.
         90039
Roy. Roy Pubs. Inc., 30 E. 74th St., New York, N.Y. 10021
St. Martin's. St. Martin's Pr., Inc., 175 Fifth Ave., New York, N.Y. 10010
Scarecrow. The Scarecrow Pr., 52 Liberty St., Metuchen, N.J. 08840
W. R. Scott. See Addison-Wesley
Scott/Addison. See Addison-Wesley
Scribner's. Charles Scribner's Sons, 597 Fifth Ave., New York, N.Y. 10017
Seabury. Seabury Pr., 815 Second Ave., New York, N.Y. 10017
Simon. Simon & Schuster, Inc., 630 Fifth Ave., New York, N.Y. 10020
Stein & Day. 7 E. 48th St., New York, N.Y. 10017
Sterling. Sterling Pub. Co., 419 Park Ave. S., New York, N.Y. 10016
Time-Life. Time-Life Books, Time-Life Bldg., Rockefeller Center, New York,
         N.Y. 10020
Tundra. Tundra Books, 465 St. Francois Xavier, Montreal 125, P.Q.
Tuttle. Charles E. Tuttle Co., Inc., 28 S. Main St., Rutland, Vt. 05701
Univ. of Calif. Pr. 2223 Fulton St., Berkeley, Calif. 94720
Univ. of Chicago Pr. 5801 Ellis Ave., Chicago, Ill. 60637
Vanguard. Vanguard Pr., Inc., 424 Madison Ave., New York, N.Y. 10017
Van Nostrand. Van Nostrand Reinhold Co., 450 W. 33rd St., New York, N.Y.
         10001
Viking. Viking Pr., Inc., 625 Madison Ave., New York, N.Y. 10022
Walck. Henry Z. Walck, Inc., 3 E. 54th St., New York, N.Y. 10022
Walker. Walker & Co., 720 Fifth Ave., New York, N.Y. 10019
Warne. Frederick Warne & Co., Inc., 101 Fifth Ave., New York, N.Y.
         10003

Washburn. Ives Washburn, Inc. See McKay

Watts. Franklin Watts, Inc., 845 Third Ave., New York, N.Y. 10022

Western. Western Pub. Co., 1220 Mound Ave., Racine, Wis. 53404

Westminster. The Westminster Pr., Witherspoon Bldg., Philadelphia, Pa. 19107

White. David White Co., 60 E. 55th St., New York, N.Y. 10022

Whitman. Albert Whitman & Co., 560 W. Lake St., Chicago, Ill. 60606

Whittlesey. Whittlesey House. See McGraw-Hill

Windmill. Windmill Books, 257 Park Ave. S., New York, N.Y. 10010

World. World Pub. Co., 110 E. 59th St., New York, N.Y. 10022

Young Scott. Young Scott Books. See Addison-Wesley

BRITISH PUBLISHERS

Abelard-Schuman. Abelard-Schuman, Ltd., Intertext Ho., Stewarts Rd., London, S.W.8.

W. H. Allen. W. H. Allen & Co., Ltd., 43 Essex St., London, WC2R 3JG.

Angus & R. Angus & Robertson, Ltd., 54–58 Bartholomew Close, London, EC1A 7EY.

Batsford. B. T. Batsford, Ltd., 4 Fitzhardinge St., London, W1H OAH.

G. Bell. G. Bell & Sons, Ltd., York Ho., 6 Portugal St., London, WC2A 2HL.

Benn. Ernest Benn, Ltd.—Benn Bros., Ltd., Bouverie Ho., 154 Fleet St., London, EC4A 2DL.

Black. Black & Co., Ltd., 2 Woodville Gdns., London, N.W.11.

Blackie. Blackie & Sons, Ltd., Bishopbriggs, Glasgow.

Blandford. Blandford Press, Ltd., 167 High Holborn, London, WC1V 6PN.

Bodley Head. The Bodley Head, Ltd., 9 Bow St., London, WC2 E7AL.

Brockhampton. Brockhampton Press, Ltd., Salisbury Rd., Leicester, LE1 7QS.

Cape. Jonathan Cape, Ltd., 30 Bedford Sq., London, WC1B 3EL.

Cassell. Cassell & Co., Ltd., 35 Red Lion Sq., London, WC1R 4SG.

Chatto. Chatto & Windus, Ltd., 40–42 William IV St., London, WC2N 4DF.

Chatto B & O. Chatto, Boyd & Oliver, 40–42 William IV St., London, WC2N 4DF.

Collier-Mac. Collier-MacMillan, 35 Red Lion Sq., London, WC1R 4SG.

Collins. William Collins, Sons & Co., Ltd., 14 St. James's Pl., London, S.W.1.

Corgi. Corgi Books, Ltd., Cavendish Ho., 57–59 Uxbridge Rd., Ealing, London, W.5.

Dent. J. M. Dent & Sons, Ltd., Aldine Ho., 10–13 Bedford St., London, W.C.2.

Deutsch. Andre Deutsch, Ltd., 105 Great Russell St., London, WC1B 3LJ.

Dobson. Dobson Books, Ltd., 80 Kensington Church St., London, W8 4BZ.

Evans. Evans Brothers, Ltd., Montague Ho., Russell Sq., London, WC1B 5BX.

Faber. Faber & Faber, Ltd., 3 Queen Sq., London, WC1N 3AU.

Gollancz. Victor Gollancz, Ltd., 14 Henrietta St., Covent Gdn., London, WC2E 8QJ.

H. Hamilton. Hamish Hamilton, Ltd., 90 Great Russell Sq., London, WC1B 3PT.

Harcourt, Brace. Harcourt, Brace & Jovanovich, Ltd. 24–28 Oval Rd., London, N.W.1.

Harper & Row. Harper & Row, Ltd., 28 Tavistock St., London, WC2E 7PN.

Harrap. George G. Harrap & Co., Ltd., 182–184 High Holborn, London, WC1V 7AX.

Hart-Davis. Rupert Hart-Davis, Ltd., 3 Upper James St., Golden Sq., London, W1R 4BP.

Heinemann. William Heinemann, Ltd., 15–16 Queen St., London, W1X 8BE.

Hutchinson. Hutchinson Publishing Group, Ltd., 178–202 Great Portland St., London, W.1.

A. Lane. Allen Lane, The Penguin Press, Vigo St., London, W1X 2HQ.

Longman. Longman Group, Ltd., Longman Ho., Burnt Mill, Harlow, Essex.

Longman Young Bks. Longman Young Books, Ltd., 74 Grosvenor St., London, W1X OAS.

Lutt P. Lutterworth Press, Albion Ho., Woking, Sy.

Macdonald. B. P. C. Publishing, Ltd., 49 Poland St., London, W1A 2LQ.

Macmillan. Macmillan International, Ltd., Little Essex St., London, W.C.2.

Mercier.The Mercier Press, Ltd., 4 Bridge St., Cork, Eire.

J. Messner. Bailey Bros. & Swinfen, Ltd., Warner Ho., Folkstone, Kent.

Methuen. Methuen & Co., Ltd., 11 New Fetter La. London, EC4P 4EE.

Muller. Frederick Muller, Ltd., Ludgate Ho., 110 Fleet St., London, EC4A 4AP.

Oak Tree P. Oak Tree Press, Ltd., 116 Baker St., London, W1M 2BB.

Oxf. U. P. Oxford University Press, Ely Ho., 37 Dover St., London, W1X 4AH.

Pan Bks. Pan Books, Ltd., 33 Tothill St., London, S.W.1.

Panther. Panther Books, Ltd., 3 Upper James St., Golden Sq., London, W1R 4BP.

Penguin. Penguin Books, Ltd., Harmondsworth, Mddx.

Rapp & W. Rapp & Whiting, Ltd., 105 Gt. Russell St., London, WC1B 3LJ.

Routledge. Routledge & Kegan Paul, Ltd., 68–74 Carter La. London, E.C.4.

Schlesinger. Roger Schlesinger, R. H. S. Publications, Ltd., 11 Kendall Pl., London, W.1.

Thames & H. Thames & Hudson, Ltd., 30 Bloomsbury St., London, W.C.1.

Time-Life Interna. Time-Life International, Ltd., Time & Life Bldg., 153 New Bond St., London, W.1.

Univ. Cal. Press. I.B.E.G., Ltd., 2–4 Upper Brook St., London, W1Y 1AA.

Van Nost Reinhold. Van Nostrand-Reinhold Co., Windsor Ho., 46 Victoria St., London, S.W.1.

Warne. Frederick Warne & Co., Ltd., 1–4 Bedford Court, London, WC2E 9JB.

F. Watts. Franklin Watts, Ltd., 18 Grosvenor St., London, W1X 9FD.

Whiting. Robert Maxwell, Ltd., Cowper Works, Olney, Bucks.

World Pub. Co. Barmerlea Book Sales, Ltd., "Annandale," North End. Rd., London, N.W.11.

World's Work. World's Work, Ltd., The Windmill Press, Kingswood, Tadworth, Sy.

Title Index

i

m

n

Developmental Values Index

461

Curricular Use Index

Music, 138 181 457 556 606 609 624 659 754 918 1094 1152 1389

Nature study, 225 258 325 351 394 397 428 461 490 552 557 563 663 664 735 829 833 839 872 906 907 994 995 1093 1123 1127 1137 1138 1166 1177 1188 1298 1299 1302

Physics, 153 290 356 521 584 667 738 1211 1235 1361
Psychology, 722 723 1126

Reading aloud, 7 25 31 40 42 69 73 76 85 88 117 125 126 139 159 167 176 203 213 214 257 264 265 266 271 303 307 309 311 312 318 337 345 354 355 358 383 395 405 406 407 454 466 477 491 492 494 504 507 509 522 531 532 533 548 558 573 586 588 591 612 616 640 641 668 670 679 680 681 684 693 696 763 764 776 785 790 791 792 794 804 819 828 835 836 837 840 844 845 848 852 868 869 870 871 899 908 926 928 950 967 979 980 981 990 993 1010 1023 1024 1029 1030 1031 1033 1037 1041 1046 1047 1048 1110 1115 1134 1144 1156 1159 1185 1186 1213 1214 1217 1249 1259 1260 1261 1285 1320 1376 1377 1378 1379
Reading, beginning, 128 143 144 225 657 721 798 821 914 915 1041 1080 1139 1375
Reading guidance, 543
Reading readiness, 502 503 876
Recreation, 368 415 416 457 724 761 824 875 910 1089 1259 1276 1348 1362 1380 1389
Religious education, 63 65 120 121 123 124 238 272 286 362 396 493 1078 1114 1132 1381
Russian, 547

Science, 4 39 44 53 61 64 100 109 110 118 153 154 160 163 220 225 290 291 308 324 325 335 351 356 365 427 428 490 513 515 521 562 563 568 584 623 630 663 667 672 673 715 730 760 767 795 872 877 878 900 907 995 1016 1043 1059 1086 1105 1108 1138 1139 1163 1164 1169 1173 1174 1175 1177 1181 1211 1224 1235 1236 1243 1272 1274 1298 1299 1333 1361 1367
Sex education, 110 315 403 515 1018 1021 1163
Social studies, 127 132 162 171 210 223 235 334 341 363 436 463 529 530 607 610 750 856 915 1118 1124 1167 1176 1239 1297 1304 1365
Spanish, 547 698
Storytelling, 1 3 27 69 70 85 203 214 271 302 303 309 311 312 358 439 454 466 477 507 508 509 510 517 528 532 533 548 549 550 558 571 572 573 586 640 668 679 680 681 774 785 804 840 848 868 869 870 871 926 928 950 979 981 987 993 1029 1030 1033 1037 1046 1047 1048 1115 1144 1156 1159 1185 1259 1261 1273 1291 1315 1376 1378 1379 1394

Transportation, 201 283 966

United Nations Day, 1113

Vocational guidance, 270 369

Zoology, 118 403 630 707 906 995 1062

Reading Level Index

Titles are arranged in order of increasing difficulty, with books for the preschool child and kindergartener first, followed by books for independent reading beginning with grade 1. The reading range is intended to be indicative rather than mandatory.

Subject Index

Type of Literature Index

Alphabet books, 189 514 876
Anthologies, 134 145 438 454 926 1048 1110
Anthologies, poetry, 7 8 31 88 103 126 159 264 265 345 354 355 494 504 531 553 693 790 792 794 818 819 828 840 844 852 925 980 989 990 1010 1011

Biography, 26 32 33 34 36 38 89 102 114 129 177 182 239 255 263 272 275 276 281 306 308 314 325 342 343 352 356 361 385 387 389 396 398 408 413 423 456 498 506 518 519 524 529 546 580 624 626 638 644 708 709 731 732 744 754 755 756 766 782 823 856 889 893 894 901 902 915 918 938 945 946 952 964 1003 1016 1032 1035 1036 1051 1066 1067 1068 1069 1083 1086 1091 1143 1182 1206 1220 1222 1223 1243 1245 1251 1252 1328 1345 1354 1369 1381 1385 1387

Counting books, 30 236 386 593 749 975 1053

Epics and hero tales, 35 173 178 570 571 572 573 671 911 1070 1120 1131 1132 1142 1245 1273 1317

Fables, 758 898 1076
Fanciful tales, modern, 13 14 18 19 20 21 22 23 40 41 42 82 106 125 139 152 164 166 168 190 206 222 243 286 289 300 305 307 327 346 347 349 350 373 381 382 383 405 406 407 451 452 455 477 486 487 539 540 541 542 561 568 588 589 590 591 592 617 619 628 649 653 654 656 657 658 675 683 684 725 745 762 765 769 770 771 772 800 808 842 849 850 880 881 908 917 954 955 956 957 958 965 970 971 972 973 987 1019 1039 1054 1134 1140 1141 1150 1151 1155 1165 1196 1215 1218 1227 1232 1233 1257 1278 1279 1280 1320 1321 1330 1335 1336 1350 1358 1359 1382 1392
Folk and fairy tales: African, 1 316 439 517 522 533 558 841; American Indian, 979 1189; Armenian, 612 1260 1261; Asian, 466 668 804 928 1315 1378; Australian, 981; Czechoslovakian, 548; Danish, 549; English, 302 303 1144; French, 3 46 993 1121; General, 868 869 870 871 1156 1393; German, 507 508 509 510; Greek, 27; Hungarian, 37 338; Indian, 1159; Irish, 309 679 680; Jewish, 1185 1186; Latvian, 358 640; Negro, 785; Nepalese, 586; Russian, 311 312 313 1037 1323 1376 1379; Scottish, 950; Swedish, 550; United States, 681 1046 1047; Welsh, 950 1033
Folklike tales, 203 271 1183 1184 1281 1383

Historical fiction, 55 77 78 79 80 101 107 111 141 187 191 192 193 194 195 226 237 278 279 393 409 410 411 412 431 440 441 444 448 476 598 600 648 650 652 759 788 857 914 916 949 960 961 997 998 999 1001 1002 1012 1013 1014 1061 1228 1244 1247 1253 1268 1270 1292 1295 1296 1305 1314 1319 1331 1337 1338 1342 1352 1360 1390 1391